Minute

Lord Lansdowne

I should like to speak
to you more fully about
this, at once after the
Cabinet on Wednesday.
At present it seems
to me full of risks, and
to carry with it no
compensating advantages,
Dec. 6, 1901.

S

Facsimile of Minute by the Marquess of Salisbury,
p. 80.

British Documents on the Origins of the War

1898–1914

Edited by G. P. GOOCH, D.Litt., F.B.A., and
HAROLD TEMPERLEY, Litt.D., F.B.A.

Vol. II

The Anglo-Japanese Alliance and the
Franco-British Entente

LONDON:

1927

59—2—2

(*Crown Copyright Reserved*)

Reprinted with the permission of
the Controller of Her Britannic Majesty's Stationery Office

JOHNSON REPRINT CORPORATION
111 Fifth Avenue, New York, N.Y. 10003

JOHNSON REPRINT COMPANY LTD.
Berkeley Square House, London, W.1

First reprinting, 1967, Johnson Reprint Corporation
Printed in the United States of America

VOLUMES I AND II

From the Occupation of Kiao-Chau
to the
Making of the Anglo-French Entente
December 1897–April 1904

VOL. II

The Anglo-Japanese Alliance and the
Franco-British Entente

Edited by
G. P. GOOCH and HAROLD TEMPERLEY
with the assistance of LILLIAN M. PENSON

TABLE OF CONTENTS.

Wt. 14075/961 2M 9/27 F.O.P. 15214

Foreword to Volumes I and II.

THE decision to publish a selection from the British Documents dealing with the origins of the War was taken by Mr. Ramsay MacDonald, Prime Minister and Secretary of State for Foreign Affairs, in the summer of 1924. It was confirmed and announced by Mr., now Sir, Austen Chamberlain in a letter of the 28th November, 1924 (published in "The Times" on the 3rd December), addressed to Dr. R. W. Seton-Watson. Some extracts from this letter were published by us in the Foreword to Volume XI, and it need only be said here that the Secretary of State for Foreign Affairs referred to "impartiality and accuracy" as being the necessary qualifications for any work which the Editors were to publish.

It was decided to begin with the year 1898 in view of the fact that certain influential members of the British Cabinet, alarmed by the hostility of France and Russia, then desired to substitute a policy of alliances for the traditional principle of "splendid isolation." It was felt, however, that the years covered in the first two volumes could be treated in a more summary fashion than would be desirable after 1904. The Editors cannot suppose that they have not omitted some important documents or despatches in a period so crowded with events; yet the most significant occurrences, such as the formation of the Anglo-Japanese Alliance and the Franco-British *Entente*, have been treated in great detail. Negotiations, on the other hand, which were adequately described in official publications at the time, such as those concerned with the troubles in Macedonia or in Crete, have been for the most part omitted.

The official records of Lord Salisbury's administrations were described by Sir Eyre Crowe in a memorandum of the 1st January, 1907, as being "sadly incomplete," all the most important business having been transacted under the cover of "private" correspondence. He also expressed a doubt as to whether "a methodical study of our relations with Germany during that interesting period" was possible from the official records alone. Lord Sanderson, however, questioned this view at the time, and considered that the story of the main transactions could be found in the official records. It would appear that the documents are fuller after the fall of Bismarck; but there is practically no evidence in our official records as to the first Anglo-German *rapprochement* which began in March, 1898, and which has been described at length from the German archives in Volume XIV of *Die Grosse Politik der Europäischen Kabinette*. The explanation is that this transaction was in the hands of Mr. Joseph Chamberlain, then Secretary of State for the Colonies, and was thus treated as a private matter. The Editors are, however, authorised to state that Mr. J. L. Garvin is preparing the official biography of Mr. Chamberlain, and that this publication is to be expected shortly. The *Life of Robert Marquess of Salisbury*, by Lady Gwendolen Cecil, will be completed in due course. The publication of the private papers of these two statesmen should therefore fill up the gaps. With regard to the Anglo-German negotiations of 1901 it is interesting to know that Sir Eyre Crowe minuted "that the most important of these [transactions] *were* recorded," and the Editors are in agreement with this conclusion. From 1901 onwards it would in fact appear that the archives are reasonably complete.

In accordance with the practice of the Foreign Office already observed in the case of Volume XI of this series, the documents in the present volumes containing information supplied or opinions expressed by certain Foreign Governments have been communicated to them for their agreement. The response has been generally satisfactory.

The Editors have inserted asterisks to indicate gaps or omissions in documents. As a rule these gaps are due to the unimportance of the matter omitted, in which case an indication of subject is usually given. In a few instances, they are due to a desire to consult the susceptibilities of the persons or of the Governments concerned; but the Editors have omitted nothing which they consider essential to the understanding of the history of the period. In addition to despatches and telegrams there are memoranda and minutes which are properly official documents. No objection has been raised by His Majesty's Secretary of State for Foreign Affairs to the publication in these volumes of any documents of the above kind, nor to the publication of certain similar papers or of private letters, which are not properly official documents, but which are preserved in the Foreign Office.

His Majesty the King has graciously consented to the publication of Minutes by King Edward. The Editors have also to acknowledge with thanks information or advice given by Lady Gwendolen Cecil with reference to the papers of the Marquess of Salisbury, by Sir Austen Chamberlain, the present Secretary of State for Foreign Affairs, with reference to the papers of the late Mr. Joseph Chamberlain, by the late Marquess of Lansdowne, by the Earl of Balfour, by Sir Ernest Satow, and by Sir Valentine Chirol. Such private papers as remain of Lord (Sir T. H.) Sanderson, (Permanent Under-Secretary of the Foreign Office during the years 1894 to 1906), have been at their disposal. Sir Ernest Satow has most kindly offered his private correspondence during the period, and a number of his private letters and of those of his correspondents are printed, which throw a most valuable light on British policy in the Far East. Permission was given by the late Marquess of Lansdowne to publication of two of his letters to Sir Ernest Satow. In conclusion the Editors desire to acknowledge the friendly assistance and advice of various officials at the Foreign Office, among whom they would like to mention the Librarian, Mr. Stephen Gaselee, C.B.E., Mr. J. W. Headlam-Morley, C.B.E., Historical Adviser, who arranged Volume XI for them, and Mr. J. W. Field; of the officials of the Public Record Office in London; and of Mr. W. S. Wright, who is in charge of the Diplomatic and Embassy Archives at Cambridge.

G. P. GOOCH.
HAROLD TEMPERLEY.

July 1927.

Note on Arrangement of Documents, &c.

The arrangement of the material in the present volumes differs in some particulars from that followed in Volume XI, since they cover a period of years, and the documents printed are a selection from the very large number in existence. The choice has been determined by the desire to provide as far as possible a full account of the principal incidents affecting the relations of the Great Powers, and the documents have been grouped in chapters and sub-sections accordingly. Within these chapters and sub-sections chronological order has been the rule followed. There are, however, a few exceptions. Some chapters include official memoranda or summaries reviewing events at a later date. These do not conform to the chronological rule, and have been printed in small type for purposes of differentiation. Similar methods have been used when extracts from documents have been grouped to illustrate a special point.

Chronological order as applied in these volumes is taken to be the date of despatch of the document, whether it is incoming or outgoing, since this method appears to the editors to be best calculated to secure a consecutive history of events.

Most of the documents are taken from the official series of Foreign Office papers in the Public Record Office. For the period 1898–1905 they are classified mainly by country (F.O. France, &c.) and within countries by years. For each year the diplomatic documents are separated from the commercial and other classes. Within the diplomatic class there are volumes of outgoing and incoming despatches, outgoing and incoming telegrams, communications with the Foreign Ambassador ("Domestic") and with other Government Departments ("Various"). Papers relating to certain subjects have been specially treated. Some have been placed together in a miscellaneous series (F.O. General), as in the case of The Hague Peace Conference. In other instances all papers relating to a certain geographical area have been placed together, as with African affairs (after 1899) and the affairs of Morocco. Correspondence with the British representative at Paris or elsewhere appears in these cases under F.O. Africa or F.O. Morocco. A third method was to separate the correspondence relating to a special aspect of affairs from the other papers of the country concerned, thus removing them from chronological sequence. This was the case with despatches on African affairs down to 1899, which appear in special series of F.O. France (Africa), F.O. Germany (Africa), &c.

Some papers which seemed to be missing from the Foreign Office archives have been supplied from the records of the Embassies. In such cases the reference is given to volumes of this series (e.g., F.O. 179/348). In a few other instances the only text found has been that printed either immediately or later for the confidential use of the Foreign Office (i.e., "Confidential Print"). These include some Foreign Office memoranda for which a reference number is given (e.g., 8883*). A few documents relating to the Anglo-German negotiations of 1901 were in a special file at the Foreign Office for which no reference number exists. The same is true of the text of the so-called "Windsor Treaty." The private papers of Lord Sanderson now in the Foreign Office are referred to as "Sanderson MSS."

The text printed is in every case verbally identical with that given in the source whose reference appears at the head of the document. The text of out-going despatches is therefore that of the draft retained by the Foreign Office, except where it is taken from the Embassy records. In the case of telegrams the original text is given wherever possible. In those cases where the original has not been found, the official paraphrase is reproduced, and is indicated by the letter "P" after the number of the telegram.

The spelling of proper names, capitalisation and punctuation will in future volumes be identical with that of the original document. In these volumes this has not been found possible. The text was printed in many cases from the "Confidential Print," and it was not discovered until after the documents were in type that the "Print" followed rules of its own in these respects. All verbal inaccuracies in the "Print" have been corrected, but it was not possible to alter the spelling, capitalisation and punctuation in all cases. It may be well to mention here that in the original records the spelling, and in particular that of proper names, is in no way consistent. For instance, Mouraviev is sometimes spelt in two different ways in successive despatches by the same writer; but it was thought undesirable to correct these and similar inconsistencies.

Plan of Volumes I and II.

Volume I.

Chapter I deals with Russia and the Far East from 1897 to 1899, beginning with the seizure of Kiao-Chau by Germany. It then describes the British overture to Russia between January and March 1898, a story which has never been told in detail and has hitherto been almost unknown. This approach was terminated by Russia's seizure of Port Arthur. The last part of the chapter illustrates the retort of Great Britain to the action of Russia—the British occupation of Wei-Hai-Wei—and the attitude of Japan. Some extracts from the private correspondence of Sir Ernest Satow, at that time British Minister at Tokio, are added.

The relations of Great Britain, Germany and Portugal during 1898 and 1899 are surveyed in *Chapter II*. The first part deals with the proposed loan to Portugal and the Anglo-German negotiations in this connexion. The text of the Secret Convention of the 30th August, 1898, first published in *Die Grosse Politik der Europäischen Kabinette* XIV. 347–55, is reproduced. The latter part of the chapter traces the negotiations with Portugal after this event and concludes with the Anglo-Portuguese secret declaration of the 14th October, 1899, often erroneously called the "Treaty of Windsor." The chapter ends with the visit of the British Channel Fleet to Lisbon in 1900 when British obligations to Portugal were indicated in official toasts.

Chapter III deals with Anglo-German friction in Samoa, and incidentally throws light on the Manila incident between Germany and the United States in 1898. The last part of the chapter describes the conclusion of the negotiations and the colonial concessions to Germany under the stress of the South African War at the end of 1899.

Anglo-French relations in 1898 form the subject of *Chapter IV*. The first part describes the disputed claims in the region of the Middle Niger, which were amicably settled by the Protocol of the 15th June, 1898. Several of the documents on the Fashoda crisis, which fills the second part of the chapter, were printed, in whole or in part, in Parliamentary Papers; but a full account from the British side is here given for the first time.

Chapter V opens with the delimitation of spheres of influence between Great Britain and France in North Africa, culminating in the agreement of the 21st March, 1899. The second part explains the refusal of Great Britain to accede to French wishes in regard to Muscat.

The first Hague Peace Conference of 1899 is described in *Chapter VI*. The instructions to the British delegates are printed for the first time; but only a few documents are needed, as nearly all the material was published on its conclusion.

Chapter VII, which covers the period of the South African War, reflects the views of Governments and Peoples on the long struggle and discusses the rumours of intervention or mediation.

Certain aspects of the relations of the Great Powers between 1898 and 1903 are illustrated in *Chapter VIII*. The chief reference is to Italy and the Triple Alliance. The numerous Blue Books dealing with Turkey in Europe and Asia during these years give nearly all the necessary information, but a few dispatches are printed at the end dealing with the Mürzsteg Programme of Turkish reforms, agreed upon between Russia and Austria-Hungary on the 1st October, 1903. This is followed by an important statement of Russian policy in relation to Afghanistan. There is also a comprehensive Memorandum on the Suez Canal between 1895 and 1898.

Volume II.

Chapter IX deals with the Far East (1900–1901). The first section relates to the Anglo-German Agreement of the 5th October, 1900, with reference to China. The interpretation placed on it by the British Government will be found at the end of this section. The circumstances attending Count Waldersee's appointment and conduct as Generalissimo of the Inter-Allied forces have not been touched upon, as the description in Parliamentary Papers is adequate. The affairs of Corea and Manchuria between 1900 and 1901 are next described. The chapter ends with some general comments from the private letters exchanged between Sir Ernest Satow, Sir Thomas Sanderson and the late Marquess of Lansdowne.

The proposals for an Anglo-German alliance in 1901 form the theme of *Chapter X.* There is no trace in the Foreign Office archives of the negotiations of 1898, which were conducted privately. In the correspondence presented in these pages special importance attaches to the Memoranda of Lord Lansdowne of the 24th May and the 11th November, 1901, and to the critical analysis of the negotiations by Lord Salisbury on the 29th May. While the German documents published in the *Grosse Politik* attribute the initiative to Great Britain, the British documents attribute it to Germany.

The negotiations leading to the conclusion of the Anglo-Japanese Alliance in January 1902 are traced in *Chapter XI.* Care has been taken to exhibit the various drafts of the Agreement in parallel columns. The labour expended on this task will, it is hoped, facilitate the work of students by revealing the ideas in the minds of the two Governments and the processes which led to their eventual agreement. Certain minutes indicate King Edward's warm approval of the Agreement.

Anglo-German relations during the years 1902–3 are illustrated in *Chapter XII.* The first section deals with the evacuation of Shanghai (July–December 1902) and restores many passages omitted in the Blue Book on that question; the second with the co-operation of the two Powers in the coercion of Venezuela; the third with the project of the Bagdad Railway, including a précis of despatches on the question from 1899–1903.

Russian policy in the Far East (1903–4) is the subject of *Chapter XIII.* It deals, in particular, with the retention of Manchuria, which led ultimately to the Russo-Japanese War. The despatch of Lord Lansdowne of the 8th February, 1904, is particularly important in this connection.

Chapter XIV contains the views of the British, French and Spanish Governments in regard to Morocco from 1898 to 1903 and reveals the growing interest of France in that country. It forms the prelude to the Anglo-French *rapprochement* which began in 1903.

The story of the making of the Anglo-French Agreements of April 8, 1904, is told at full length in *Chapter XV.* The important part played by Lord Cromer in the long and difficult negotiations is here first revealed. The letter of Lord Lansdowne of the 1st October, 1903, with M. Cambon's reply of the 26th October summarise preceding negotiations, and provide a starting point for the new arrangement. In this case, as in that of the Anglo-Japanese Alliance, care has been taken to print the original French and British drafts side by side with the final text. The chapter ends with some minutes and comments of King Edward on the *Entente.*

Abbreviations.

B.F.S.P	British and Foreign State Papers.
G.P.	Die Grosse Politik der Europäischen Kabinette.
Accounts and Papers	British Parliamentary Papers : Accounts and Papers.

Names of Writers of Minutes.

A. J. B. = Rt. Hon. A. J. Balfour (now Lord Balfour)	First Lord of the Treasury, 29 June, 1895–11 December, 1905; Prime Minister, 12 July, 1902–11 December, 1905.
F. B. = Mr. F. (later Sir F.) Bertie	Assistant Under-Secretary of State for Foreign Affairs, 1894–1905.
F. A. C. = Mr. F. A. (later Sir F. A.) Campbell ...	Senior Clerk, Foreign Office, 1896–1902; Assistant Under-Secretary of State, 1902–12.
J. C. = Rt. Hon. Joseph Chamberlain	Secretary of State for the Colonies, 1903.
L. = The Marquess of Lansdowne	Secretary of State for Foreign Affairs, 12 November, 1900–11 December, 1905.
P. = Earl Percy	Parliamentary Under-Secretary of State for Foreign Affairs, 1903–1905.
S. = The Marquess of Salisbury	Secretary of State for Foreign Affairs, 29 June, 1895–12 November, 1900; Prime Minister, 29 June, 1895–12 July, 1902.
T. H. S. = Sir T. H. Sanderson (later Lord Sanderson)	Permanent Under-Secretary of State for Foreign Affairs, 1894–1906.
F. H. V. = Mr. F. H. (later Sir F. H.) Villiers ...	Assistant Under-Secretary of State for Foreign Affairs, 1896–1906.

Minutes by King Edward.

(These are attached to the following despatches.)

The Marquess of Lansdowne to Sir F. Lascelles, No. 393A of December 19, 1901. No. 94, p. 83.

Sir F. Lascelles to the Marquess of Lansdowne, No. 1 of January 3, 1902. No. 95, p. 84.

The Marquess of Lansdowne to Mr. Whitehead, No. 91 of August 14, 1901. No. 103, p. 92.

The Marquess of Lansdowne to Sir C. MacDonald, No. 12 of January 31, 1902. No. 126, p. 121.

The Marquess of Lansdowne to Sir E. Monson, No. 113 of March 19, 1902. No. 145, p. 136.

The Marquess of Lansdowne to Sir C. Scott, No. 18 of January 15, 1904. No. 276, p. 235.

The Marquess of Lansdowne to Sir C. Scott, No. 47 of February 8, 1904. No. 295, p. 249.

The Earl of Cromer to the Marquess of Lansdowne, of July 17, 1903. No. 359, p. 301.

NOTES.—King Edward and the Anglo-Japanese Agreement, 1901-2, p. 122.

King Edward and the Formation of the Entente, pp. 400–1.

LIST OF DOCUMENTS.

CHAPTER IX.
THE FAR EAST, 1900–1901.

I.—The Anglo-German Agreement.

II.—Corea and Manchuria.

CHAPTER X.

THE ANGLO-GERMAN NEGOTIATIONS OF 1901.

CHAPTER XI.
THE ANGLO-JAPANESE AGREEMENT, 1901–2.

CHAPTER XII.
ANGLO-GERMAN RELATIONS, 1902–1903.
I.—The Evacuation of Shanghai.

II.—Venezuela.

III.—The Bagdad Railway.

CHAPTER XIII.

RUSSIAN POLICY IN THE FAR EAST, 1903-4.

CHAPTER XIV.

FRANCE, SPAIN AND MOROCCO.

CHAPTER XV.

THE ANGLO-FRENCH TREATIES OF APRIL 8, 1904.

CHAPTER IX.
THE FAR EAST, 1900-1901.

I.—THE ANGLO-GERMAN AGREEMENT.

No. 1.

Memorandum by Mr. J. A. C. Tilley.

Memorandum respecting the Relations between Russia and Great Britain. 1892–1904.(¹)

(No. 8338.)
(Extract.)   *Foreign Office, January 14, 1905.*

Towards the end of 1899 the "Boxer" disturbances began, which led to the armed intervention of the Powers. In July 1900 the disturbances spread to Manchuria, and the Chinese attacked the railway line. The Russians thereupon occupied the province with an army, and, on the pretext of an alleged attack on the foreign quarter at Newchwang, seized that town on the 4th August, and took possession of the custom-house, and began to collect revenue.

Count Lamsdorff assured Her Majesty's Minister at St. Petersburgh that the steps taken by the military authorities could only be of a temporary and provisional character. A little later the Russian Minister to London repeated the announcements, made at an earlier stage of the disturbances, of the principles on which Russia meant to act in China; these principles were :—

(1.) The maintenance of agreement between the Powers;
(2.) The maintenance of the existing system of government in China;
(3.) The exclusion of everything which might lead to a partition of the Empire; and
(4.) The establishment, by common effort, of a legitimate central authority, capable in itself of assuring order and security to the country.

They added that they would not fail to withdraw from Manchuria as soon as its pacification had been secured.

These principles did not prevent the Russians from making a speedy attempt to seize the whole of the line from Newchwang to Peking, or from claiming one section of that line "by right of conquest" or from contesting the claim of the British authorities to any share in the management of the line, and seizing 50 miles of railway material belonging to Messrs. Jardine, Matheson and Co. The interest of Her Majesty's Government in this matter was peculiar, inasmuch as the line from Peking to Shanhaikwan was mortgaged to British bondholders, whilst the rolling-stock and the profits of the other section, from Shanhaikwan to Newchwang formed the security of those bondholders. The remonstrances of Her Majesty's Government led the Russians to hand the *intra-mural* portion of this line to Count Waldersee, the Commander-in-Chief of the allied forces, for restitution to the British.

(¹) [*NOTE.*—The following extract from a Memorandum by Lord Sanderson dated 1907, is among his papers at the Foreign Office. It is a commentary upon Sir E. Crowe's *Memorandum on the Present Relations between Great Britain and Germany* (1907) :—

My recollection of the negotiations which led to the Anglo-German Agreement of October 1900 does not altogether tally with that given in the Memorandum.

The Emperor William having obtained from the Emperor of Russia a promise that he would not oppose the acquisition by Germany of a Chinese port, suddenly and much to the disgust of the Russian Gov[ernmen]t seized Kiao-Chou in November 1897, and there seems little doubt, notwithstanding the assurances which were given us on that occasion that she succeeded as part of the arrangement made with China in extracting from the Chinese Gov[ernmen]t certain preferential and possibly exclusive rights in the province of Shantung, the exact nature and extent of which however we have never to my knowledge precisely ascertained.

Within a few months the Russian Gov[ernmen]t demanded and obtained the lease of Port Arthur.

As a countermove, and more or less at the suggestion of the Chinese Gov[ernmen]t we obtained a similar lease of Wei-hai-Wei, and in order to disarm German opposition, which would have been very inconvenient when we had Russia with France at her back in antagonism to us, we gave Germany as assurance that we had no intention of interfering with her rights and interests in Shantung by this acquisition.

With these examples of Russian policy before them, Her Majesty's Government responded favourably to a proposal by the German Emperor for an Agreement in regard to the future action of the two Powers in China : the principles laid down in the Agreement, which was signed on the 16th October, 1900, were that the ports on the rivers and littoral of China should remain open to trade throughout China, so far as the two Powers could exercise influence; that they would not make use of the present complication to obtain any territorial advantages for themselves, and would direct their policy towards maintaining undiminished the territories of China; that in the case of another Power making use of the complications in China in order to obtain territorial advantages, they would come to an understanding as to the steps to be taken to protect their own interests.

Austria, Italy and Japan accepted all these principles; the United States the first two, without expressing an opinion on the third; Russia and France expressed general concurrence in the two first clauses, but the Agreement as a whole produced a very bad impression in Russia, and Her Majesty's Chargé d'Affaires, Mr. Hardinge, reported that the Russian Government only accepted the principles in so far as they coincided with their own interpretation of them.

Mr. Hardinge was told that if any complaint were made of Her Majesty's Government having concluded the Agreement without previous consultation with Russia, he was to dwell on the perplexity caused to Her Majesty's Government by the conduct and language of Russian officers in respect to the Newchwang–Peking Railway, and by their dealings with the property of British subjects on the railway.

Early in 1901 rumours began to spread as to an Agreement between Russia and China in regard to Southern Manchuria, which would establish a virtual Russian Protectorate over that province. The Russian Government were profuse in denials, but Great Britain, Germany, and Japan, at the suggestion of the latter, made declarations to China warning her against Treaties with any individual Power of a territorial or financial character.

From that time on the relations between Great Britain and Russia in China have consisted mainly in a series of endeavours on the part of His Majesty's Government to bring about the evacuation of Manchuria. The Convention under which that evacuation was to take place was signed by Russia and China on the 8th April, 1902, and the date fixed for the commencement

---

In 1899, the Russian Gov[ernmen]t having been seriously exercised by the grant to a British Company of a concession for a railway into Manchuria, we concluded an Agreement with Russia by which we precluded ourselves from obtaining for British subjects concessions for railways North of the Great Wale of China, and Russia renounced the right to obtain such concessions in the Yangtse Valley. We had in Feb. 1898 obtained from the Chinese Gov[ernmen]t a public engagement that no territory should be alienated in the provinces adjoining the Yangtsze and the language of the English press indicated a tendency to regard the valley of that river as the proper sphere of English influence in any partition of interests. The Germans were keen to prevent our acquiring exclusive rights or privileges in this enormous and important tract of country and when in 1900 the seizure by Russia of the railway between Tientsin and Ninchwang and other acts brought us into a somewhat acute controversy with the Russian Gov[ernmen]t, the German Emperor told Sir F. Lascelles that he was ready to give us his general support provided we would engage to observe the policy of the open door in the Yangtsze valley. At that time our relations with Germany were decidedly friendly and a considerable section of the Cabinet were in favour of an alliance or at least of an agreement for joint policy—an idea to which as I have already said Lord Salisbury was never very favourable.

Shortly after the Emperor's conversation Count Hatzfeldt proposed the Agreement to Lord Salisbury which was eventually signed in Oct. 1900. In its original wording it applied only to the region of the Yangtsze. Lord Salisbury did not welcome the idea of a fresh Agreement with any enthusiasm, but he accepted the discussion. He objected that the instrument was applicable only to one portion of the Chinese Empire in which Great Britain was specially interested, and Article I was worded so as to extend the principle of equal opportunities to ports on the littoral and in the rivers of China. Other Articles were added providing against the acquisition of territorial advantages in China by the Signatory or other Powers during the existing complications. The whole was regarded by Lord Salisbury as unnecessary but innocuous, and having a certain value in that it placed on record a community of policy between Great Britain and Germany and any Powers who adhered to it. The German Gov[ernmen]t no doubt valued it mainly on the ground that it kept the Yangtsze open to German industrial enterprise. When later on the tendencies of Russia to monopolise Manchuria became evident, the German Gov[ernmen]t declared that they had never considered the Agreement to apply to Manchuria, which was outside the sphere of German interests and influence, a contention of which no trace could be found in the negotiations, and Count Bülow rather indirectly revealed in a Parliamentary speech the original intention with which it had been proposed by calling it " the Yangtsze Agreement."

The whole proceeding was no doubt shifty and not over creditable, but I do not see that the Agreement, to the principle of which France, Italy, Austria, Japan and the United States agreed, and to which even Russia expressed a certain gratified assent, was in any way detrimental to our interests.]

of the evacuation was the 8th April, 1903; but when the latter date came, Russia had further conditions to be fulfilled by China, one of which, providing that no nationals other than Russian were to be employed in the north of China, the Russian Ambassador at Washington admitted to be aimed against England and the Englishmen in the Chinese Customs service. Other conditions virtually handed over Newchwang, a Treaty port, where the trade was almost exclusively British, American and Japanese, to Russian administration.

From the date of the Russian occupation the Customs revenues of Newchwang have been retained by Russia, and no account of them even has ever been rendered to China.

Further protests followed from Her Majesty's Government, but before another year was over the war between Russia and Japan brought all negotiations to an end.

No. 2.

Sir F. Lascelles to the Marquess of Salisbury.

F.O. Germany (Prussia) 1493.
(No. 155.)   Confidential.

Berlin, D. *June* 15, 1900.
R. *June* 18, 1900.

My Lord,

I called upon Count Bülow yesterday afternoon to take leave of him before my departure from Berlin on the 17th instant. . . . . [German public opinion.]

The conversation then turned to the state of affairs in China. Count Bülow said that although matters looked very serious, he was not without hope that the forces already sent by the different Powers would suffice to restore order. The Powers were apparently acting in perfect harmony, and he trusted would continue to do so. Germany had no selfish interests to seek in Peking. All that she wished was that order should be promptly restored, and that no impediments should be placed in the way of commerce. His Excellency hoped and believed that the integrity of the Chinese Empire would be maintained, and that the present disturbances would not lead to any serious complications. He added that the Germans engaged in commerce in China were convinced of the necessity of working together with the English. The interests of the two countries were identical. They both pursued the policy of the " open door," and, although there might be a certain amount of commercial rivalry, it was evident that the commerce of both countries would be increased by friendly understanding and co-operation.

I observed that this view had been strongly impressed upon me by conversations which I had had with persons connected with China, and I ventured to hope that a friendly understanding and co-operation between Germany and England might extend to other places besides China.

Count Bülow replied that he saw no reason why it should not exist everywhere (" partout ")

I have, &c.
FRANK C. LASCELLES.

(1) [*NOTE.*—The whole circumstances of the Boxer revolt (1900–1) are described with reasonable fulness in the *B.F.S.P.* XCIV. 1050–1299, XCV. 1136–1352, and XCVI. 864–1126, and no lengthy treatment of the subject is needed here.]

No. 3.

The Marquess of Salisbury to Sir C. Scott.

F.O. Russia 1603.
Tel.   (No. 107.)

Foreign Office, D 5 P.M., *July* 15, 1900.

Russian Chargé d'Affaires communicated on July 13th(1) a message from Count Lamsdorff, stating that on the 11th June Russian Minister at Tokyo had reported

(1) [This message is in *Accounts and Papers*, 1904 (*Cd.* 1936), CX, pp. 133–4.]

offer of Japanese Government to send troops to China conjointly with other Powers for preservation of Representatives at Pekin and of foreigners throughout China. This action on the part of Japan was quite natural, as her geographical position enabled her to send considerable reinforcements at once to Tien-tsin, and she has numerous subjects residing in China. The Russian Government at once informed the Cabinet of Tokyo that they saw no reason for interfering with Japan's liberty of action in this respect, the more so, as she had expressed the firm resolution of acting in complete accord with the other Powers. But the accomplishment of this task did not, according to the view of the Russian Government, imply any right to an independent settlement of affairs at Pekin, nor other privileges, except, perhaps, a larger pecuniary indemnity if eventually the Powers should consider it necessary to demand one.

Count Lamsdorff states that almost simultaneously he received from Her Majesty's Government a communication which already mentioned not a spontaneous decision of the Cabinet of Tokyo to participate in the collective action of the Powers, but a mission to be given by Europe to Japan to send to China considerable forces not merely to save the Legations and foreigners, but also with a view to the repression of the insurrectionary movement set on foot by the Boxers and the establishment of order at Peking and Tien-tsin. This manner of stating the question might, in the opinion of the Russian Government, infringe to a certain degree the fundamental principles which had already been accepted by the majority of the Powers as the basis of their policy, namely, the maintenance of union between the Powers, maintenance of the existing system of government in China, exclusion of anything which might lead to partition of the Empire, in fact, the re-establishment by joint efforts of a legitimate central Government capable of assuring order and security. The Russian Government consider that strict observance of these fundamental principles is indispensable for maintenance of durable peace in the Far East, and that it is essential to avoid all misunderstandings or omissions which might have dangerous consequences.

I have replied that Her Majesty's Government have never suggested that the action of Japan should confer on her any rights to an independent solution or any other privileges. They have never spoken to the Russian Government of a mission given by Europe to Japan. The fundamental principles of which Count Lamsdorff speaks have never been accepted by Her Majesty's Government, nor have we as yet discussed with other Powers the circumstances to which those principles might possibly apply. Her Majesty's Government have not expressed an opinion in favour of any steps except those which point to the relief of the Legations and of other foreigners.

No. 4.

Sir C. Scott to the Marquess of Salisbury.

St. Petersburgh, *July* 22, 1900.

F.O. Russia 1604.   D. 2 P.M.
Tel. (No. 73.)   R. 6·30 P.M.

Your telegram No. 107 of July 15: Japanese offer of troops.

Count Lamsdorff explained to me yesterday object of message communicated by Russian Chargé d'Affaires on 13th instant.

He said that it was to clear at once Russian Government from odium and entirely undeserved charge insinuated in the press and other quarters that they hesitated to accept assistance of Japan and thereby assumed the grave responsibility of hindering prompt relief of Legations.

He admitted that no mention of any European mandate to Japan for independent action had been made in the message which I communicated to him, and that arguments which I had used indicated co-operation. But he said that your Lordship's question had been understood at Berlin as implying an European mandate and that words ".... an expedition to restore order at Peking and Tien-tsin, if Japan is willing to undertake the task ...." might be so interpreted.

The misunderstanding was promptly cleared up, but the public press had drawn unjust deductions and instructions sent to Russian Minister at Tokyo ought to have made it quite clear that Russia would gladly welcome all available prompt assistance from Japan equally concerned with other Powers in meeting the common danger.

I said that I had no reason to believe that Her Majesty's Government had entertained any doubts on this point.

[The following documents supplement the information in the papers dealing with the Anglo-German Agreement, *B.F.S.P.*, XCIV, 897–906.]

No. 5.

Sir F. Lascelles to the Marquess of Salisbury.

F.O. Germany (Prussia) 1494.
(No. 203.) Very Confidential.
My Lord,

Berlin, D. *August* 1, 1900.
R. *August* 6, 1900.

On the morning of the 30th ultimo, I called upon Herr von Derenthall, who, during the absence of Baron von Richthofen, is acting as Under-Secretary of State for Foreign Affairs.

I told his Excellency that I had come to announce my return to Berlin, and my resumption of my duties as Her Majesty's Ambassador. I said that I had had the advantage of seeing your Lordship on the day before my departure from England, and was able to assure him of your desire to maintain the most friendly relations with Germany, and to co-operate with her in China.

I then alluded to a recent conversation I had had with Count Hatzfeldt, who had suggested that Her Majesty's Government should propose that a German officer should be placed in command of the allied forces in China. I said that your Lordship was not prepared to make such a proposal, and indeed I doubted whether you were prepared to make any proposals at all. Your experience during the Cretan question had not been very encouraging, as then any suggestions you made were at once refused, although they were subsequently accepted when put forward by others. The recent speech made by the Emperor, in which His Majesty spoke of no quarter being given, would make it very difficult for Her Majesty's Government to place English troops under a German Commander.

Herr von Derenthall replied that Count Hatzfeldt's suggestion was made a long time before His Majesty's speech was delivered. It was doubtful whether His Majesty would have consented to a German officer being placed in command of the allied forces, but a proposal to that effect would no doubt have pleased His Majesty.

I have heard from another source that the General Staff at Berlin are by no means in favour of the command being given to a German officer, on the ground that the Germans have no experience of Oriental warfare, and that the idea had been put forward with the view of giving satisfaction to the Emperor.

Herr von Derenthall then said that he gathered from what I had said that your Lordship's experience in the Cretan question had indisposed you to put forward proposals as regards China. I replied at once that it was certainly not merely the Cretan question, to which I had referred, and that the German reply with regard to the sending of Japanese troops had been a great disappointment to Her Majesty's Government, who had hoped that the German Government would have supported them in the communication which they had made to the Russian Government.

So far from this being the case, the German Government had waited for the reply of the Russian Government, before sending any answer at all themselves.

Herr von Derenthall having interrupted me to ask whether I wished Germany to quarrel "nous brouiller" with Russia, I replied that on the contrary, we hoped that Germany and Russia might remain the best of friends, but that it was a disappointment to the best friends of the former country to see her place herself in tow "à la remorque" of the latter, more especially at a moment when she had an opportunity of playing a leading part and exerting a decisive influence. But this was not the only disappointment which the friends of Germany in England had to support. All the public utterances of Count Bülow, though strictly correct, had been marked by great coldness towards England. To this Herr von Derenthall replied that Count Bülow had to consider public opinion in Germany, and that although his speeches had perhaps shown some coldness, the action of the German Government in preventing an intervention in the South African war had been decidedly friendly.

I replied that there was also a public opinion in England, which had to be consulted, and which could only form its judgment by the knowledge it possessed. It was impossible that Count Bülow's private conversations with me, and more especially the communications which the Emperor had frequently deigned to make to me, should be made public. I quite admitted that they had been of a most satisfactory character, but public opinion in England could only judge by public utterances, which I regretted to say had not been encouraging.

I propose to speak in the same sense to Count Bülow as soon as I shall have an opportunity of seeing his Excellency, who is expected to return to Berlin in a few days.

I have, &c.

FRANK C. LASCELLES.

No. 6.

Sir F. Lascelles to the Marquess of Salisbury.

F.O. Germany (Prussia) 1494.
(No. 210.) Confidential.   *Berlin*, D. *August* 9, 1900.
My Lord,   R. *August* 13, 1900.

Count Bülow returned to Berlin on the evening of the 5th instant, and left again for Norderney on the following night. He was good enough to ask me to call upon him on the afternoon of the 5th, and I had a long conversation with him, in which I held much the same language as I had used in my conversation with Herr von Derenthall, as reported in my despatch No. 203, Very Confidential, of the 1st instant.

I told his Excellency that I was enabled to assure him that your Lordship desired to maintain the most friendly relations with Germany, and would be glad of an opportunity of co-operating with her in China.

Count Bülow expressed his satisfaction at this assurance, and said that he had heard from Count Hatzfeldt that Her Majesty's Government had been annoyed ("froissé") by the answer which he had given to your Lordship's enquiry as to the employment of Japanese troops. I interrupted his Excellency to say that the term "froissé" did not appear to me to convey a correct impression, but rather that Her Majesty's Government had been disappointed at seeing Germany place herself in tow ("à la remorque") of Russia.

Count Bülow said that there was no question of Germany doing so, but his only object was to maintain complete harmony among the Powers, which might have been endangered by giving an European mandate to Japan. I at once replied that there had been no question of a mandate in your Lordship's proposal, which was that, as

Japan was the only Power which was able to send a sufficient force speedily to Peking, she should be allowed to do so.

Count Bülow regretted that there had been a misunderstanding on the subject of a mandate, and went on to speak of the condition of affairs in China. It was evident that the Europeans in Peking were still alive, but in a precarious position, and the question arose as to the best means of affording them assistance.

The difficulty of an immediate advance on Peking by the force now at Tien-tsin was evidently very great, and might lead to the massacre of the Europeans. Could I tell him what would be thought in England of an attempt to induce the Chinese, possibly by a financial offer, to convey the Europeans safely to Tien-tsin?

I replied that such an attempt would be regarded in England as most dangerous, as it was to be feared that the Chinese escort, if attacked after leaving Peking, would take to flight, and leave the Europeans to be massacred, even if they did not themselves join the attacking party.

I then alluded to the speeches which the Emperor had recently delivered, which breathed a very warlike spirit.

Count Bülow said I was so well acquainted with the Emperor that he need not explain His Majesty's character to me, and he could assure me that, whilst His Majesty was delivering these warlike utterances, he was at the same time giving commands to his Ministers to issue instructions in the most moderate and conciliatory spirit.

I have, &c.
FRANK C. LASCELLES

No. 7.

Sir E. Monson to the Marquess of Salisbury.

F.O. France 3496.
(No. 426.) Most Confidential.   *Paris,* D. *August* 17, 1900.
My Lord,   R. *August* 18, 1900.

. . . . His Excellency[1] is, in my opinion, a very different man from what he was two years ago, when I had to discuss with him the evacuation of Fashoda; and whatever may be the truth of the reported arrangement between France, Germany, and Russia—which, as far as united policy in the Far East is concerned, seems to me probable enough, however much the reverse in regard to European politics—I fear that he counts, with every chance of being right, upon the disinclination of those two Powers to recognise the validity of any arguments which may be put forward as to the predominant interests of Great Britain in the valley of the Yang-tsze Kiang, giving her legitimate ground for exclusive action in that region.

I have, &c.
EDMUND MONSON.

[1] [M. Delcassé. The earlier part of the despatch deals with French public opinion.]

No. 8.

Sir F. Lascelles to the Marquess of Salisbury.

F.O. Germany (Prussia) **1494.**
(No. 223.) Very Confidential.   *Homburg,* D. *August* 24, 1900.
My Lord,   R. *August* 27, 1900.

The Prince of Wales paid a visit to the German Emperor at Wilhelmshöhe on the 22nd instant,[1] and had the kindness to ask me to accompany him. I was thus

[1] [This interview is erroneously stated by Sir Sidney Lee (*Life of King Edward*, Vol. I (1925)), to have taken place on the 21st.]

enabled to have a long conversation with His Majesty, the principal points of which I had the honour to report to your Lordship by my telegram No. 29, and of which I will now attempt to give a detailed account.

In reply to my enquiry whether His Majesty considered that the Great Powers were at war with China, the Emperor said, "Most certainly," and expressed the hope that exemplary punishment would be inflicted on the Chinese, which would prevent the recurrence of the outrages that had led to our armed interference. His Majesty pointed out that, as far as he was aware, no official communication had been received from any of the Legations since the arrival of the international troops at Peking, the news of which apparently reached us through Japanese sources. He did not, however, doubt that the Legations had been relieved, and that the Imperial city had been bombarded. This, however, did not imply the termination of the war, which the Emperor thought might be prolonged for a considerable time. The capture of Pretoria had not put an end to the war in South Africa, nor would the capture of Peking put an end to the war in China.

His Majesty was most averse to the idea of entering into negotiations with Li Hung-chang, whose object he believed was to sow dissension among the Powers by playing off one against the other. The only Government with whom the Powers could treat consisted of the Emperor and Dowager-Empress if they were still alive; and His Majesty was convinced that Li Hung-chang, who left Peking more or less in disgrace, had not had any communication with their Imperial Majesties for some considerable time.

On my observing that the situation was one of extraordinary complication, and that I presumed that the Legations would now be withdrawn to Tien-tsin, a town in the occupation of the international troops, where they would find no Chinese authorities with whom they could negotiate, the Emperor said that the first thing to be done was to bring the war to an end. Count Waldersee had made his dispositions. He would treat each contingent as a separate force, and he intended to place the Russians on the extreme right, on account of their interests in Manchuria, and the English on the extreme left, taking care to place some other nationality between them and the French, with the view of avoiding any possible friction. His Majesty expressed some regret that Count Waldersee's appointment had been so long delayed, and insinuated that the delay had been due to your Lordship. I at once replied that Herr von Derenthal had warmly thanked me for the prompt and friendly manner in which your Lordship had agreed to Count Waldersee's appointment, and that I could not understand how your Lordship could be in any way responsible for the delay.

His Majesty replied that your Lordship's final answer had certainly been promptly given, but that Count Hatzfeldt had more than a month ago suggested to your Lordship the appointment of a German Commander-in-chief, and had failed to elicit a reply.

I observed that Count Hatzfeldt's suggestion was that your Lordship should propose a German Commander-in-chief, which was a very different matter, and the manner in which your Lordship's proposals were generally received was not encouraging. When your Lordship had proposed that Japanese troops should be allowed to go to Peking to relieve the Legations it was stated that your Lordship wished that an European mandate should be given to Japan, which was certainly not your Lordship's intention.

The Emperor replied that it would have been impossible for him to have returned a different answer to your Lordship's proposal. His object was to maintain a good understanding among the Powers. He was aware of the intense jealousy which existed between Russia and Japan, and was convinced that the former would never have consented to allow the latter to proceed alone to Peking. Even he himself could not have agreed to the murder of a German Minister being avenged by Japanese troops, and the very fact of those troops being sent to Peking with the consent of the Powers would have had the appearance of their having been intrusted with an European mandate.

I observed that, at the risk of being indiscreet, I could tell His Majesty that your

Lordship had been animated by the most friendly sentiments in consulting His Majesty with regard to the employment of Japanese troops, and that the disappointment caused by the unfavourable reply of the German Government had been proportionately great.

The Emperor repeated that it would have been impossible for his Government to have acted differently at the time. It was true that the Russians had subsequently said that they would not object to the employment of Japanese troops, but they had only done so after the possibility of such employment had passed away. One effect of the troubles in China had been to dispel the myth which the Russians had sedulously fostered that the Chinese were more friendly to the Russians than to other foreigners, whereas it was now proved that the disturbances, though anti-foreign in their nature, were directed quite as much, if not more, against Russia as against any other nation. The danger, no doubt, still existed that Russia, after attaining her own ends in Manchuria, might make a separate peace with China and leave the other Powers in the lurch.

I may mention that the statement of the Emperor's was elicited by a remark made by His Royal Highness the Prince of Wales, who was present during part of the conversation.

On my alluding to the objections which France had raised to the landing of British troops at Shanghae, the Emperor said that he was not at all surprised. There was a general suspicion that England was seeking special advantages for her commerce, to the detriment of other nations, and on my protesting against such an idea, and pointing out that our whole policy was based upon the principle of the open door, His Majesty said that, two years ago, Canada had granted preferential treatment to Great Britain, and it was not impossible that Australia might follow her example. If this were to be the case, England herself might find it to her interest to depart from the principle of the open door, and this, coupled with the fact that the United States, a protective Power, had possession of the Philippines, might cause serious detriment to the commerce of other nations in China. Now German commercial interests were second and not far inferior to those of England in the valley of the Yang-tsze, and if Her Majesty's Government could see their way to give assurances that they would maintain the policy of the open door, they would find the German Government on their side.

I ventured to observe that in view of the general suspicion with which England seemed to be regarded, it did not appear to me to be likely that any assurances she might give would be believed, but the Emperor replied that this suspicion would be dispelled by a formal undertaking on our part.

At the end of this conversation, which was marked throughout by His Majesty's usual gracious cordiality, I asked if His Majesty had any commands for me to transmit to your Lordship.

The Emperor replied in the negative, and asked me whether I had anything for him, to which I answered that I had nothing to add to what I had already said to Count Bülow and Herr von Derenthal, that your Lordship would be glad of any opportunity of co-operating with His Majesty's Government.

I have, &c.
FRANK C. LASCELLES.

[ED. NOTE.—The whole question of the appointment of Count Waldersee as international generalissimo is fully discussed in B.F.S.P. XCIV–V and also in G.P. XVI passim.]

No. 9.

Sir F. Lascelles to the Marquess of Salisbury.

F.O. Germany (Prussia) 1496.

Tel. (No. 30.)

Homburg, August 30, 1900.

D. 11·32 A.M.

R. 11·46 A.M.

I have received a telegram from Count Bülow stating that the Emperor was awaiting with great interest your Lordship's reply to His Majesty's overtures with regard to Chinese affairs. Count Bülow personally would consider it an auspicious precedent if England and Germany could arrive at a practical understanding on the question of the Yang-tsze. His Excellency adds that the Emperor would consider it very fortunate if I could find an opportunity of exerting my personal influence directly on your Lordship. I have replied to Count Bülow that I have at once telegraphed the substance of his telegram to your Lordship.

No. 10.

The Marquess of Salisbury to Mr. Whitehead.

F.O. Japan 525.

(No. 60.)

Sir,

Foreign Office, August 31, 1900.

The Japanese Minister called at this Office on the 27th instant and informed Mr. Bertie that the Japanese Government were alarmed at the speeches of the German Emperor and the intention which they heard was entertained by the German Government of sending large reinforcements to China, which might lead to the occupation of North China by a combination of Germany and Russia.

He enquired whether Her Majesty's Government knew of any understanding between Russia and Germany, and he asked confidentially, on behalf of his Government, what would be the attitude of Her Majesty's Government in such an eventuality.

Mr. Bertie informed Baron Hayashi that Her Majesty's Government knew nothing of such a combination.

I am, &c.
SALISBURY.

No. 11.

The Marquess of Salisbury to Sir F. Lascelles.

F.O. Germany (Prussia) 1496.

Tel. (No. 151.)

Foreign Office, August 31, 1900.

D. 3 P.M.

Your telegram No. 30 of 30th instant.

I am afraid that I have not rightly understood expressions which you have reported to me in your despatch, as having been used by the Emperor at recent interview. If M. de Bülow would kindly telegraph to you, or if he prefers it to me, the proposals which His Majesty desires to make with regard to Chinese affairs, I will of course give them my most respectful consideration. But I was not aware that Her Majesty's Government had proposed to us any course of conduct differing from that which we are pursuing now and have pursued for some time.

No. 12.

Memorandum by Mr. Bertie.([1])

September 13, 1900.

We may be able to arrange a *modus vivendi* with Germany to tide over the present crisis, but mere " open door " or " open port " and tariff declarations are not likely to satisfy her.

Her pretensions are large, for she starts from the theory that by her occupation of Kiao-chau and her agreement with China respecting Shantung she has acquired a special position there, and that it is not open unreservedly to British enterprise, but that the Yang-tsze region is open unreservedly to German enterprise.

What Germany will claim as her special field will probably be Shantung and the valley of the Yellow River. We shall have to undertake not to support any British application in that region.

Germany will further claim that between the Yellow River Valley and the north bank of the Yang-tsze River the division of good things between British and Germans must be absolutely equal, viz., that every concession granted to an Englishman must be counterpoised by one to a German. On these conditions the German Government may be willing to recognise to Great Britain the same rights in the Yang-tsze region *south* of that river as Germany claims in Shantung and the Yellow River Valley.

We should then have to fight out with the French and other Governments, who have not recognised our Yang-tsze sphere of interest, any claims which we desire to support in the special sphere conceded to us by Germany.

As to making use of Germany to come between the Russians and ourselves in China, we are not likely to have much success.

There cannot be a question at present of Germany undertaking the occupation or control of a sufficiently large tract of territory south of Peking for her to be a buffer between Russia and the Yang-tsze region. If ever she acquire such a position, and if Peking remain then the real capital of China, Russia and Germany will in combination control the Chinese Government to our detriment.

FRANCIS BERTIE.

([1]) [Original not traced. Text is taken from the Confidential Print.]

No. 13.

Sir F. Lascelles to the Marquess of Salisbury.

F.O. Germany (Prussia) 1494.
(No. 240.) Confidential.

Berlin, D. *September* 14, 1900.
R. *September* 17, 1900.

My Lord,

I returned to Berlin from Homburg on the 10th instant, and on the following morning called upon Baron von Richthofen, with whom I had some conversation on the state of affairs in China. He said that he was aquainted with the telegraphic correspondence which had passed between Count Bülow and me on the subject of the " overtures " which the Emperor had made to me at Wilhelmshöhe.

I replied that I had not understood His Majesty to make any definite proposals which could be considered as overtures, but he had no doubt seen from your Lordship's reply that you would be prepared to take into consideration any proposals that the Emperor might make. Baron von Richthofen replied that he had gathered that this was the case, and he hoped that the situation in China might lead to a satisfactory understanding between our two countries, which would enable them to act together. He had always desired that such an arrangement might be come to in the interests of both. I reciprocated this wish, and observed that, although public opinion in each country might not be friendly to the other, I believed that the true interests of both required common action on the part of their Governments.

With reference to the Russian proposal for the withdrawal of their forces from Peking, Baron von Richthofen said that it would seem that it emanated from the Emperor of Russia himself, who thought that it would be the means of settling the Chinese question. He had received a telegram from Count Hatzfeldt giving the substance of your Lordship's answer to the Russian proposal, which was to the effect that Her Majesty's Government did not consider that the time had yet come for the withdrawal either of Her Majesty's forces or of Her Majesty's Legation from Peking.

In the afternoon of the same day I called upon the Imperial Chancellor, who also alluded to the Russian Circular. Prince Hohenlohe did not disguise his disappointment at the proposal to withdraw the international troops from Peking, which he thought was perhaps partly due to the disinclination of the Russian Government to place their troops under the command of Count Waldersee. He trusted that this would not lead to a rupture between the two Governments, and it would seem now that the Russians recognised the necessity of keeping open the communications between Peking and Tien-tsin, which would require military force, and His Serene Highness thought it by no means improbable that they would reconsider their decision and arrive at the conclusion that circumstances did not allow of the immediate withdrawal of Russian troops from Peking.

My Italian colleague informs me that from various conversations he has had with Count Bülow, as well as from the language held by the Emperor, he is convinced that the German Government are sincerely desirous of coming to a good understanding with Her Majesty's Government.

I have, &c.
FRANK C. LASCELLES.

No. 14.

The Marquess of Salisbury to Sir F. Lascelles.

F.O. Germany (Prussia) 1491.
(No. 205.)
Sir, *Foreign Office, September 25, 1900.*

The German Ambassador called upon me on the 14th instant on my return to England from the continent, and again on the 18th instant, and discussed with me the position of affairs in China, and the principles on which the joint action of our two Governments in that country could be based.

It was agreed between us that the object to which our Agreement should be directed was that China should be kept open to the trade of all nations; that we should renounce for ourselves all attempts to take advantage of the present crisis for the purposes of further territorial acquisitions at the expense of China; and that we should oppose other Powers in making any similar attempt.

Count Hatzfeldt promised to bring me a draft of an Agreement between the two Governments embodying these views, to which the assent of other Powers might subsequently be invited.

I received from his Excellency yesterday the enclosed German draft, and discussed it with him this afternoon.

I told Count Hatzfeldt that I could not accept any special stipulations in favour of the principle of free trade in the Yang-tsze or in any other particular part of China, for its effect would be held to be, and, in fact, would be, to abandon free trade in the other parts of the Chinese dominions.

I proposed, therefore, the wording contained in the English draft, of which I also enclose copy.

Count Hatzfeldt took this proposal *ad referendum.*

I am, &c.
SALISBURY.

Enclosure 1 in No. 14.

German Draft of Agreement between Great Britain and Germany.

Die Kaiserlich Deutsche Regierung und die Königlich Grossbritannische Regierung sind einverstanden mit einander, für die beiderseitige Politik hinsichtlich Chinas nachstehende Grundsätze zu beobachten:—

1. Es entspricht einem gemeinsamen dauernden internationalen Interesse, dass der Yang-tsze, dessen Neben-flüsse und dessen Stromgebiet dem Handel und jeder sonstigen erlaubten wirthschaftlichen Thätig-keit für die Angehörigen aller Nationen ohne Unterschied frei und offen stehen. Dieses gemeinsame dauernde Interesse ist auch gemeinsam und dauernd zu schützen.

2. Die Kaiserlich Deutsche und die Königlich Grossbritannische Regie-rung wollen ihrerseits die gegenwärtige Verwickelung nicht benutzen, um für sich irgend welche territorialen Vortheile auf Chinesi-schem Gebiet zu erlangen.

3. Sollte eine andere Macht dergleichen territoriale Erwerbungen in irgend welcher Form vornehmen und die Kaiserlich Deutsche oder die Königlich Grossbritannische Regie-rung in Folge dessen für noth-wendig erachten, auch ihrerseits zu territorialen Erwerbungen zu schreiten, so werden beide Regie-rungen sich zuvor darüber verstän-digen.

Enclosure 2 in No. 14.

[English] Draft of Agreement between Great Britain and Germany.

The Imperial German Government and Her Britannic Majesty's Government have agreed to observe the following principles in regard to their mutual policy in China :—

1. It is a matter of joint and permanent international interest that the ports on the rivers and littoral of China should remain free and open to trade and to every other legitimate form of economic activity for the nationals of all countries without distinction.

2. The Imperial German Government and Her Britannic Majesty's Government will not, on their part, make use of the present complica-tion to obtain for themselves any territorial advantages in Chinese dominions, and will oppose, in such manner as may be agreed upon between the two Powers, any attempt on the part of any other Powers to obtain territorial advan-tages in a similar manner.

3. Should another Power endeavour, under any form, to obtain territorial acquisitions of this nature and should the Imperial German Government or Her Britannic Majesty's Government consequently consider it necessary themselves to proceed to territorial acquisitions, then the two Governments will come to a previous understanding on the subject.

No. 15.

The Marquess of Salisbury to Sir F. Lascelles.

F.O. Germany (Prussia) 1491.
(No. 214.) Very Confidential.
Sir,
          Foreign Office, October 2, 1900.
    Count Hatzfeldt continued to-day our conversation with respect to the question of the punishment of those responsible for the recent outrages in China. I informed his Excellency we were desirous to go as far with the German Emperor in that matter

as we reasonably could, especially as our sympathies were entirely with him in the desire to bring to justice the offenders by whom such great calamities had been caused. But there were two things to which I was afraid it was impossible I could consent. One was to the participation of British troops in any expedition to the west of the Province of Chih-li, to which at present the powers of Count Waldersee were restricted, and which might be rendered necessary if it was resolved that the offenders to whom he had alluded were at all costs to be arrested. The other reserve that I must make had reference to the consequences that would follow if China refused to deliver over for punishment the offenders in question. We readily admitted that until those offenders had been punished, China had no right to ask that she should be admitted to the benefit of any negotiations or Conventions on the part of the Powers; but I was not prepared to renounce the liberty of Her Majesty's Government to make any agreements in the future with the Chinese Government if it should seem to Her Majesty's Government to the interest of this country to conclude them.

His Excellency said that some slight modification in the views of the German Government on this question had taken place, and he explained to me, at all events provisionally, a much more limited proposal which the German Government had recently put forward. I enclose a copy of it to your Excellency. I promised him that I would consider it.

I am, &c.
SALISBURY.

No. 16.

Sir F. Lascelles to the Marquess of Salisbury.

F.O. Germany (Prussia) 1494.
(No. 249.) Confidential.   *Berlin, D. October 5, 1900.*
My Lord,   R. *October 8, 1900.*

Count Bülow received the Chiefs of Missions yesterday for the first time since his return to Berlin. The conversation which I had with him turned almost exclusively upon the Affairs of China. I began by alluding to the telegram which his Excellency had addressed to me to Homburg, from which I had gathered that the Emperor was under the impression that he had made overtures to me in the conversation with which he had honoured me on the 22nd August at Wilhelmshöhe. I had certainly not understood His Majesty to have made any definite proposals, but merely to have stated that, if Her Majesty's Government would undertake to maintain the principle of the open door in the Valley of the Yang-tsze, they could count upon the support of the German Government, and that I had replied to His Majesty that Her Majesty's Government had so frequently proclaimed the principle of the open door to be the basis of their policy in China, that I feared that no assurances they could give would be likely to dispel the suspicion with which they were regarded.

Count Bülow replied that the Emperor had given him a full account of the visit which the Prince of Wales had paid to His Majesty at Wilhelmshöhe and of the conversation which His Majesty had had with me, and with which His Majesty had expressed his complete satisfaction. His Majesty' as I knew, was apt to be impetuous, and, as he had mentioned the possibility of an understanding between our two countries with regard to the Valley of the Yang-tsze, had been impatient to learn that such an arrangement had been arrived at. . . . .(¹)

I have, &c.
FRANK C. LASCELLES.

(¹) [The latter part of this despatch deals with the punishment of Chinese criminals and is substantially reproduced in *B.F.S.P.*, XCV, 1148-9.]

No. 17.

The Marquess of Salisbury to Sir F. Lascelles.

F.O. Germany (Prussia) 1491.
(No. 224.) Very Confidential.

Sir,   *Foreign Office, October* 15, 1900.

Count Hatzfeldt and I continued on the 2nd, 5th, 9th, and 13th instants our discussions on the proposal of the German Government for an agreement as to the joint policy to be pursued by the two countries in China. I had stated on the 25th ultimo that I could not limit the declaration as to maintenance of commercial freedom to the basin of the Yang-tsze, as such a limitation might possibly seem to sanction the principle of restriction in other parts of China, and I had proposed that, in place of a limited reference to the Yang-tsze, a joint renunciation on our behalf of any special commercial restriction should be extended to all rivers and ports in China. To-day his Excellency pointed out to me that the German Government desired to live on good terms with that of Russia, and that they could hardly consent to an engagement which would pledge the German Government to press that of Russia for an extension of the principle of commercial freedom to portions of China in which that principle is not now secured by any Treaty. The words I suggested, he said, would include Port Arthur and the River Amoor, in regard to which Russia was under no obligation of the kind suggested.

Eventually, after considerable discussion, it was agreed that the declaration of the intention of the two Governments to uphold this principle should be made applicable to all Chinese territory so far as they could exercise influence.

I stipulated that, in order to prevent misconception, some expression should be introduced into the Agreement indicative of our intention to maintain all rights already enjoyed under existing Treaties, and a phrase to this effect was inserted in the preamble.

Some modifications were made in the language of Articles 2 and 3 of the draft in order to avoid any wording which could be interpreted as implying aggressive intentions on the part of the two Governments, and an Article was added providing for the communication of the Agreement to the other Powers principally interested for the purpose of inviting their adhesion to it.

I enclose herewith copy of the English draft as finally settled.

Count Hatzfeldt informed me that his Government wished that the Agreement when signed should be kept secret for ten days, in order that German public opinion might be prepared for its announcement, and that it should then be published simultaneously by the two Governments.

I am, &c.
SALISBURY.

Enclosure in No. 17.

English Draft Agreement, as finally Settled.

The Imperial German Government and Her Britannic Majesty's Government, being desirous to maintain their interests in China and their rights under existing Treaties, have agreed to observe the following principles in regard to their mutual policy in China :—

1. It is a matter of joint and permanent international interest that the ports on the rivers and littoral of China should remain free and open to trade and to every other legitimate form of economic activity for the nationals of all countries without distinction ; and the two Governments agree on their part to uphold the same for all Chinese territory as far as they can exercise influence.[1]

[1] [The German version of the last phrase was " wo sie einen Einfluss ausüben können,"
v. G.P. XVI, 250.]

2. The Imperial German Government and Her Britannic Majesty's Government will not, on their part, make use of the present complication to obtain for themselves any territorial advantages in Chinese dominions, and will direct their policy towards maintaining undiminished the territorial condition of the Chinese Empire.

3. In case of another Power making use of the complications in China in order to obtain under any form whatever such territorial advantages, the two Contracting Parties reserve to themselves to come to a preliminary understanding as to the eventual steps to be taken for the protection of their own interests in China.

4. The two Governments will communicate this Agreement to the other Powers interested, and especially to Austria-Hungary, France, Italy, Japan, Russia, and the United States of America, and will invite them to accept the principles recorded in it.

[Printed in *B.F.S.P.*, XCII, p. 31, reprinted here for convenience of reference.]

No. 18.

Lord Currie to the Marquess of Salisbury.

F.O. Italy 818.
Tel. (No. 39.)

Rome, October 25, 1900.
D. 11·50 A.M.
R. 12·42 A.M.

My despatch No. 167, October 23rd.

I have to-day received a Note from Minister for Foreign Affairs stating that the Italian Government, recognising in the Anglo-German Agreement the same principles which govern their policy in China, do not hesitate to give their adhesion thereto.

No. 19.

Mr. C. Hardinge to the Marquess of Salisbury.

F.O. Russia 1601.
(No. 356.) Confidential.
My Lord,

St. Petersburgh, D. October 26, 1900.
R. *November 5, 1900.*

The unexpected announcement of an Anglo-German Agreement respecting China has tended to intensify a feeling of irritation against Germany in political circles, which has undoubtedly been growing for some time past, since Germany has assumed such a prominent rôle in military and diplomatic action in China.

It is thought here that the conclusion by Germany of this Agreement with Great Britain may be the *contre-coup* to the somewhat brusque manner in which the German Emperor was corrected in his statement respecting the initiative taken in the appointment of Count Waldersee, that it may be a consequence of the order for the withdrawal of the Russian troops from Peking following immediately upon the appointment of the German Field-Marshal to the chief command of the allied forces, and an answer to the veiled condemnation of the German Emperor's words respecting no quarter for the Chinese, contained in the declaration made on the 15th August last of the policy of the Russian Government, with its reference to the humanitarian traditions of the Russian army, a reference which after the massacres by Russian troops in Manchuria, it would, perhaps, have now been better to have omitted.

It is also possible that this feeling of irritation may have been fostered by the conscious knowledge that Russian policy in dealing with the Chinese imbroglio has not met with that success which Russian patriotism may have expected, and that Russia, in adopting her own independent line of action of withdrawal of her troops and Legation from Peking, has failed to give the lead to any of the foreign Powers, even to her French ally, and has eventually found it necessary to modify her policy, owing to the refusal of the Powers to follow her example, to leave a considerable force in Peking, and to instruct her Minister to return to the Chinese capital. It is fully recognised at the same time, that the principal aim of Russian policy, in attempting to conciliate the Chinese, has been entirely frustrated by the needless cruelty and severity of the Russian troops. The appointment of Count Waldersee, the message of the German Emperor to the Emperor of China in which he takes his stand as the champion of Christendom, and the recent diplomatic activity of Germany, have been incidents which have tended to raise doubts in the minds of Russian patriots as to whether Russia has succeeded in assuming and maintaining that position of leadership amongst the allies which, from her vast interest and her powerful military situation in the Far East should, in their opinion, have been her due.

The conclusion of the Anglo-German Agreement, implying the defection of Germany to Great Britain, who has always been represented here as standing somewhat aloof from the other Powers with a view to securing her own selfish ends in China, has been a further shock to Russian feelings, and while dissipating all doubts, has brought home the conviction that Russia certainly does not hold amongst the allies that overwhelming position in China, which the policy of her Ministers and the reports of the proceedings of the Russian military and naval authorities have hitherto implied.

Whether such aspirations were legitimate may be a matter of opinion, but there can be little doubt that so far Russian policy in China has not met with any decided success, and the recognition of this fact, and of the prominence acquired by Germany in international affairs in the Far East has provoked here a feeling of smouldering irritation against Russia's Western neighbour. That this failure on the part of Russian diplomacy is, in one sense, to be regretted is undoubtedly the case, since the policy followed has, I believe, been directly inspired by the peaceful disposition of the Emperor, and initiated by His Majesty with the warm support of M. Witte and Count Lamsdorff, who have thus formed a potent party of peace, and whose policy the powerful military party has strongly but so far ineffectually opposed.

I have, &c.
CHARLES HARDINGE.

No. 20.

Mr. C. Hardinge to the Marquess of Salisbury.

St. Petersburgh, October 28, 1900.

F.O. Russia 1604.
Tel. (No. 120.)

D. 8·30 P.M.
R. 9·30 P.M.

Your telegram No. 210.

Following is translation from the French of a Memorandum which I have just received containing reply of Russian Government to the communication respecting Anglo-German Agreement :—

"The Arrangement concluded between Germany and England does not perceptibly modify, from our point of view, the situation in China.

"The first point of this Agreement, stipulating 'that the ports on the rivers and littoral of China, wherever the two Governments exercise their influence, should *remain* free and open to commerce,' can be favourably entertained by Russia, this stipulation not prejudicing in any way the *status quo* established in China by existing Treaties.

[15214]

c

" The second point corresponds all the more with the intentions of Russia, considering that, from the commencement of the present complications, she was the first to lay down the maintenance of the integrity of the Chinese Empire as a fundamental principle of her policy in China.

" As to the third point relating to the eventuality of an infringement of this fundamental principle, the Imperial Government, while referring to their Circular of the 25th of August, can only renew the declaration that such an infringement would oblige Russia to modify her attitude according to circumstances.

" The fourth point requires no remark."

Copy by post to-day.

No. 21.

The Marquess of Salisbury to Mr. C. Hardinge.

F.O. Russia 1597.
(No. 257 A.)
Sir,   *Foreign Office, October* 29, 1900.

I have received your telegram No. 120 of the 28th instant, informing me of the reply of the Russian Government to the communication which you were instructed to make to them on the subject of the Anglo-German Agreement relating to China.

I notice that in the 2nd paragraph of Count Lamsdorff's Memorandum the following words, viz., " that the ports on the rivers and littoral of China, wherever the two Governments exercise their influence, should *remain* free and open to commerce," are placed in inverted commas, as if purporting to be a textual translation from Article 1 of the Agreement.

This is, however, by no means the case. Article 1 reads as follows : " It is a matter of joint and permanent international interest that the ports on the rivers and littoral of China should remain free and open to trade, and to every other legitimate form of economic activity for the nationals of all countries without distinction ; and the two Governments agree, on their part, to uphold the same for all Chinese territory as far as they can exercise influence."

The wording of the Russian Memorandum is thus not merely an incorrect rendering of the Article in question, but also materially modifies the sense of it, for whereas the former would seem to imply that the action of Great Britain and Germany in favour of complete freedom for commerce and industry will be limited to those provinces in which they have special interests, the intention of the Article is that such action should extend to the whole of the Chinese Empire so far as the two Powers can exercise influence.

You should take an opportunity of pointing this out to Count Lamsdorff, whilst conveying to his Excellency the satisfaction with which Her Majesty's Government have learnt of the acceptance by the Russian Government of the principles recorded in Articles 1 and 2 of the Agreement.

I am, &c.
SALISBURY.

No. 22.

Sir F. Lascelles to the Marquess of Salisbury.

F.O. Germany (Prussia) 1496.
Tel. (No. 37.)

Berlin, October 30, 1900.
D. 1·40 P.M.
R. 2·15 P.M.

I had a long conversation this morning with the Emperor who had come with the Empress to the Embassy to pay a visit of condolence to Prince Christian. His Majesty deeply regretted the continuance of the war in South Africa, which he feared might be prolonged for a considerable time, and criticised somewhat severely the manner of conducting the war and especially the hospital arrangements.

With regard to China, he rejoiced at the conclusion of the Anglo-German arrangement to which he believed all the Powers would adhere,([1]) and would prove to the Chinese that Europe was united in not desiring the partition of China. This he hoped would speedily lead to a settlement of the Chinese question, which in addition to the punishment of the authors of the outrages, should in His Majesty's opinion contain a condition *sine quâ non* that all the fortifications of the rivers and ports of China should be demolished and the importation of arms into China should be strictly prohibited. He thoroughly approved the suggestion that terms of the settlement should be drawn up by the Foreign Ministers at Peking, who were the best judges of what was necessary.

On my mentioning Count Waldersee's action in handing over the railways to the Russians, the Emperor said that this had been done for purely military considerations. The Russians were in possession and moreover had a large number of military engineers. He had, however, instructed the Field-Marshal to hand over to the English the portions of the line from which the Russians withdrew.([2])

([1]) [By this date Italy and Austria-Hungary had already adhered, the United States had expressed full sympathy with Articles 1 and 2, regarding 3 as for the contracting parties. France had sent no answer, that of Russia is in Mr. Hardinge's telegram No. 120 of the 28th October (p. 17).]

([2]) [A longer account of this interview was given in Sir F. Lascelles' (Very Confidential) despatch No. 274 of the 31st October.]

No. 23.

Mr. C. Hardinge to the Marquess of Salisbury.

F.O. Russia 160½.
(No. 362.) Confidential.
My Lord,

St. Petersburgh, D. October 30, 1900.
R. *November* 5, 1900.

In the reply of the Russian Government to the communication of the text of the Anglo-German Agreement and to the invitation to accede to the principle recorded therein, handed to me in writing by M. Basily the day before yesterday, there are certain points to which I would wish to draw your Lordship's attention, upon which I abstained from making any remarks in my despatch No. 357, sent to your Lordship by post on the 28th instant. . . . . [Details follow.]

M. Basily, in a moment of expansion from his usual brilliant silence, told one of my colleagues that he considered the reply of the Russian Government as an acceptance of the principles recorded in the Anglo-German Agreement. This may be true as far as it goes, but the acceptance is not complete. The pith of the reply of the Russian

Government appears to me to be their acceptance of the principles recorded in the Agreement as far as they agree with Russian policy, and their determination to stand alone and to pursue their own policy in China unhampered by engagements to joint action with other foreign Powers.

I have, &c.
CHARLES HARDINGE.

No. 24.

Sir F. Lascelles to the Marquess of Salisbury.

F.O. Germany (Prussia) 1495.
(No. 274.) Very Confidential.   *Berlin,* D. *October* 31, 1900.
My Lord,   R. *November* 5, 1900.

In my telegram No. 37 of yesterday's date, I reported the principal points of a conversation which I had with the Emperor. . . . . [Domestic details.]

The Emperor went on to say that he regarded the conclusion of the Agreement as a most important matter, which he trusted would speedily lead to a settlement of the difficulties in China. There could be little doubt of the acceptance of all the Powers. Austria-Hungary and Italy had at once expressed their adhesion. Japan would certainly do so, as would also the United States after the Presidential election. Russia could not refuse, as she had herself proclaimed the necessity of maintaining the integrity of the Chinese Empire, and France would certainly follow the lead of Russia.

I observed that I understood that Russia had raised no objection to the first two Articles of the Agreement, but wanted explanations with regard to the third Article, which would, of course, fall to the ground if all the Powers adhered to the Agreement.

The Emperor replied that this no doubt was so, but Russia, in spite of her assurances to the contrary, was constantly annexing bits of China, and it was necessary to convince her that her action in this respect must cease. But the importance of the Agreement was not to be measured by the effect it might produce on the Powers of Europe, but by the effect it would produce on the Chinese. It would prove to them that all the Powers interested in China, including the United States and Japan, were united in their determination that a satisfactory settlement of the present state of things in China should be arrived at, and His Majesty believed that this result would shortly be attained. . . . . [Details follow.]

I have, &c.
FRANK C. LASCELLES.

No. 25.

Sir F. Lascelles to the Marquess of Lansdowne.

F.O. Germany (Prussia) 1520.
(No. 2.) Confidential.   *Berlin,* D. *January* 4, 1901.
My Lord,   R. *January* 7, 1901.

On the 1st instant I had a conversation with Baron von Richthofen on the affairs of China and was able to assure him of your Lordship's earnest desire to act in complete harmony with Germany. His Excellency said that the German Government were fully aware of your Lordship's views on the subject and entirely reciprocated your Lordship's wish. I went on to say that there were two points in particular to which your Lordship had drawn my attention on which you hoped that the German Government would share your views. First that the Representatives of the Powers who took no part in the expedition should not be on the same footing in the negotiations which would now be undertaken as the Representatives of the Powers more directly interested. It seemed indeed unjust that the votes of the Representatives of Spain, Belgium and Holland should have the same value as those of Great Britain and Germany.

Baron von Richthofen replied that it would be a matter of some difficulty to eliminate the Representatives of the three countries who had been admitted to the negotiations for drawing up the joint note, and indeed he thought there had been some advantage in the note being presented to the Chinese Plenipotentiaries by the Spanish Minister instead of by the Representative of one of the Powers who had larger interests in China.

The second point to which your Lordship had drawn my attention was the question of an indemnity. It was probable that a proposal would be made to augment the Customs and *Li-kin* duties so as to provide a fund to secure the loan which would be necessary to pay the indemnity. An increase of these duties would naturally affect those Powers who had a large commerce with China, and thus Great Britain and Germany have to bear a heavier burden than other countries.

Baron von Richthofen said that he did not share your Lordship's apprehensions on this point. An augmentation of the Customs duties would no doubt be the simplest method of raising whatever money might be necessary. Those duties were at present very low and could support a very considerable augmentation without in any way hampering trade. An increase of Customs duties moreover would have to be borne by the consumers and not by the producers and unless the increase were such as to render the duties prohibitive would not in the opinion of German experts reduce the volume of trade. Germany had considerable experience in dealing with countries which imposed a very high tariff, such as the United States and the South American Republics, and found that it was quite possible to carry on a large business in spite of such Tariffs. It would of course be necessary that the increase of Customs duties should be applied to all countries alike. The amount of indemnity to be claimed from China had not yet been determined, it would no doubt be large but his Excellency hoped not more than could be met by an increase of the Customs and *Li-kin* duties, and thus avoid anything in the shape of an international control of the Financial Administration of China which he presumed would be the alternative and which, he considered, was strongly to be deprecated.

Baron von Richthofen thoroughly approved of the suggestion that Sir Robert Hart should be consulted with regard to the increase of the Customs and *Li-kin* duties, and completely agreed with your Lordship that it would be advisable that the Ministers at Peking should dispose of as many points as possible on the spot and not refer them for discussion between the different Governments.

I have, &c.

FRANK C. LASCELLES.

No. 26.

Sir F. Lascelles to the Marquess of Lansdowne.

F.O. Germany (Prussia) 1520.
(No. 16.)   Confidential.   *Berlin, D. January* 18, 1901.
My Lord,   *R. January* 21, 1901.

On the evening of the 14th instant I called, by appointment, on Count Bülow, with whom I had not till then had an opportunity of conversing since my return to my post on the 30th ultimo. . . . .

I then told his Excellency that I had also had an interview with Lord Salisbury immediately after my arrival in London, and that his Lordship equally reciprocated the friendly sentiments which his Excellency had requested me to express to him and had assured me of the earnest desire of Her Majesty's Government to maintain the most friendly relations with Germany. His Lordship had, however, expressed some apprehension, which I had done my best to allay, with regard to the possible action of Germany in China, which might render it difficult for the two Governments to act together. It was possible that the Emperor might be tempted to make an expedition into the interior of China in order to capture the principal authors of the recent outrages, and it was also possible that His Majesty might demand some territorial acquisition as security for the indemnity which the Chinese Government might be called upon to pay, and Her Majesty's Government would be unable to agree to either of these two courses.

Count Bülow thanked me warmly for having mentioned Lord Salisbury's views on these two points, upon which he was happy to be able to reassure me completely. He was convinced that nothing would induce the Emperor to undertake an expedition into the interior of China, and that His Majesty was equally determined not to make any acquisition of territory which would, moreover, be in direct contradiction to the terms of our Agreement.

Count Bülow added that the Emperor's one wish with regard to China was that the question should be settled as soon as possible, and that the German troops might be brought back home.

I have, &c.
FRANK C. LASCELLES.

No. 27.

Sir F. Lascelles to the Marquess of Lansdowne.

F.O. Germany (Prussia) 1520.
(No. 20.) Very Confidential.
My Lord,

Berlin, D. January 21, 1901.
R. January 28, 1901.

During the banquet at the Palace on the 18th instant, the Emperor told me that he had been glad to hear that the Convention between Count Waldersee and the Russian authorities in China with regard to the Shan-hai-kwan Railway had at last been signed, and that the question might now be regarded as having been satisfactorily settled. His Majesty added that I could have no idea of the difficulties which had been encountered in coming to a satisfactory settlement.

On the morning of the 19th instant, when the Emperor called upon me to express his wishes and intentions in consequence of the alarming accounts of the Queen's health, His Majesty repeated what he had told me on the previous day, and said that he had taken the opportunity of the presence of the Grand Duke Wladimir to speak very seriously to His Imperial Highness with regard to the action of Russia in China. He had pointed out that the delay in the settlement of the Chinese question had been due to Russia. The Chinese had been on the point of agreeing to the demands of the Powers, when they were encouraged to further resistance by the insidious proposal of Russia that the troops should be withdrawn. His Majesty quite understood that Russia had interests to protect in Manchuria which might make it necessary for her to conclude separate arrangements with the Chinese. He had no desire to interfere with such arrangements, but the Russians must also understand that it was incumbent upon him to exact reparation for the murder of his Minister and the outrages which had been committed, and until this had been achieved his troops would remain in China, however much the Russians might dislike their presence there. Nobody could wish more earnestly than he did for a speedy termination of the Chinese difficulty and the return of his troops to Germany at the earliest possible moment, and he believed that Russia would best consult her own interests by using her influence with the Chinese to convince them that the Powers were in earnest, and would insist that the demands they had put forward should be complied with.

On my expressing the hope that this conversation would lead to satisfactory results, the Emperor said that he very much doubted whether the Grand Duke would report it to the Emperor of Russia, but that His Imperial Highness would certainly repeat it to Count Lamsdorff and other influential persons in St. Petersburgh, and that the Russian Government would thus be placed in possession of his views and intentions, which it was as well that they should know.

I have, &c.

FRANK C. LASCELLES.

No. 28.

The Marquess of Lansdowne to Sir F. Lascelles.

F.O. Germany (Prussia) 1518.
(No. 35.) Confidential.

Sir, *Foreign Office, January 22, 1901.*

Her Majesty's Minister at Peking has reported that on the 6th instant the Russian Consul at Tien-tsin issued a Circular to the Consular Body, stating that by an Agreement concluded between the Russian and Chinese Governments, Russia has acquired a Concession on the left bank of the Peiho within limits marked out by boundary stones. . . . . [Details follow.]

The Belgian Legation at Peking is reported to lay claim to a Settlement on the left bank of the river, opposite the German Concession, and about one kilometre in length, acquired by a notice given by the Belgian Consul at Tien-tsin on the 7th November; and the French Concession at Tien-tsin is said to have been extended by a Notification issued by the French Consul-General on November 20th; while similar action appears to have been taken by the Japanese Consul on December 28th.

By the Anglo-German Agreement of October 16th, 1900, England and Germany undertook not to take advantage of the present complications to obtain for themselves any territorial advantages in China, and this provision was accepted by the Russian Government, who stated that it corresponded all the more with their intentions, since Russia had been the first to lay down the maintenance of the integrity of the Chinese Empire as a fundamental principle of her policy in China. A Concession of the character of that said to have been made to the Russian Government at Tien-tsin: a Concession at first described as taken by right of conquest, and later on as obtained from the Chinese Government by negotiation, appears to greatly exceed the limits of an ordinary Settlement Concession and to amount to a territorial acquisition, and this at an important point on the water approach to Peking from the sea. Concessions, whether in that or any other part of the Chinese Empire, obtained during the disturbed state of the country are calculated to hamper the action of the Powers in endeavouring to arrive hereafter at a final settlement of affairs, and seem to be specially undesirable at the present moment.

I wish your Excellency to sound the German Minister for Foreign Affairs as to the view likely to be taken by the German Government of these transactions, and to ascertain, if possible, whether, in his opinion, it would be desirable that the Powers should arrive at a general understanding not to recognise, pending agreement amongst themselves, the validity of any Concessions or Settlements in China obtained since the outbreak of the Boxer disturbances and the siege of the Legations.

I am. &c.

LANSDOWNE.

No. 29.

The Marquess of Lansdowne to Viscount Gough.

F.O. Germany (Prussia) 1518.
(No. 49.)
My Lord,

Foreign Office, February 7, 1901.

I repeated to Baron Eckardstein to-day the substance of my conversation with Baron Hayashi in regard to the alleged agreement between Russia and China as to Manchuria. (See my despatch to Sir C. MacDonald, No. 17, Confidential, of the 5th February.)

I told Baron Eckardstein that it seemed to me advisable to give to the Chinese Government some such indication of our views as that suggested by Baron Hayashi. Such an expression of opinion would not commit us inconveniently; but it might have a useful effect in encouraging the Chinese to hold their own, while on the other hand I thought it desirable to meet the wishes of the Japanese Government who evidently attached much importance to the matter.

I said, however, that it would, in my opinion, be far better that if any advice of the kind were tendered, it should proceed not from His Majesty's Government alone, but from some of the other Powers also, and I asked him to ascertain how the German Government regarded the idea. . . . . [Details follow.]

I am, &c.
LANSDOWNE.

No. 30.

The Marquess of Lansdowne to Sir F. Lascelles.

F.O. Germany (Prussia) 1518.
(No. 54.)
Sir,

Foreign Office, February 12, 1901.

Baron Eckardstein informed me to-day, in reference to the conversation which I had with him on the 7th instant, and which was recorded in my despatch to your Excellency No. 49 of the 7th instant, that the German Government would instruct their Minister at Peking to make an intimation to the Chinese Government in the following terms :—

" In the opinion of the Imperial Government the Chinese Government should not conclude with any Power individual Treaties of a territorial or financial character before they can estimate their obligations towards all the Powers as a whole, and before the compliance with such obligations is accepted.''

The German Government would communicate this intimation to their Minister at Tokyo, and it would also be made at Berlin to the Chinese Minister there.

I expressed my satisfaction at learning that the German Government were prepared to adopt this course. Although the language used varied somewhat from that which we had suggested, it seemed to me that, in principle, the two announcements were in agreement, and I trusted that they would have a salutary effect.

I am, &c.
LANSDOWNE.

No. 31.

Sir F. Lascelles to the Marquess of Lansdowne.

F.O. Germany (Prussia) 1520.
(No. 46.)   Very Confidential.   *Cronberg*, D. *February* 26, 1901.
My Lord,   R. *March* 1, 1901.

On the 24th instant, shortly before my departure from Berlin to wait upon the King at Frankfort, I had a long conversation with the German Chancellor, whom I had not seen since my return to my post.

Count Bülow said that the Emperor had been much gratified by the reception he had met with in England, and that he rejoiced that the maintenance of the friendly relations between our two countries would be facilitated by the cordial friendship which existed between our two Sovereigns.   It would be a mistake to attach too much importance to the hostile tone of the press, which had been occasioned partly by the disapproval, which had been generally felt in Germany, of the war in South Africa, and partly by the discontent of certain parties with the internal condition of affairs, which had found expression in abuse of the Emperor for his prolonged absence from Berlin.   This feeling of discontent would subside on His Majesty's return to Berlin, and his Excellency was glad to think that there was no question of importance upon which any serious difference of opinion was likely to arise between our two Governments. In China we had been acting together, and had given similar, if not identical, advice as regards the inadvisability of the conclusion, by the Chinese Government, of separate arrangements with any particular Power, and he was glad to see that the Japanese Government had given advice in a similar sense.   The preparations which Count Waldersee had ordered for an expedition towards the interior had produced the desired effect, and an Edict had been issued by the Chinese Government, in conformity with the wishes of the Powers.

I interrupted his Excellency to say that I was sincerely glad to hear that this had been the case, and that Count Waldersee's threat had been successful.   It appeared to me to have been a dangerous-bit of bluff, which, if unsuccessful, would have entailed the necessity of an expedition into the interior, to which I knew that His Majesty's Government, and, I believe, the Governments of all the Powers, were strongly averse.

Count Bülow went on to say that he sincerely trusted that no difference would arise between our two Governments on the subject of the indemnities.   He understood that your Lordship objected to a very large indemnity being demanded, and whilst he agreed with your Lordship that the amount should not be excessive, he felt bound to demand adequate compensation for the murder of a German Minister, the losses which German subjects had sustained, and the expenses which the German Government had incurred. He need not tell me that the Chinese expedition was far from being popular in Germany, and he would certainly encounter great difficulties with the Reichstag unless he were able to show that some advantage had been obtained.

I replied that I understood that your Lordship objected to a very large indemnity being claimed, not so much on account of the amount as on account of the method of securing payment.   It would probably be necessary for the Chinese Government to raise a loan, the security for which would be an increase of customs duties, and if those duties should be raised beyond a certain point, the trade with China would be hampered and the chief sufferers would be England and Germany, whose commercial interests in China so far exceeded those of all other countries.

Count Bülow said that he would greatly regret any measure which would interfere with trade, but that he believed that the customs might be considerably increased without any evil effect, and he hoped that the total amount of indemnities claimed would not exceed the amount which China could pay.

His Excellency reminded me that he had always been in favour of a good understanding between our two countries, and he rejoiced to think that the friendly relations which existed between the two Government would be permanently maintained, and might, before long, be extended to the people of both nations.

I have, &c.

FRANK C. LASCELLES.

No. 32.

Extract from Speech by Count von Bülow in the Reichstag.

F.O. Germany (Prussia) 1520. *March* 15, 1901.

. . . . Divergencies of views doubtless existed among the Powers on the Chinese question. Some among them were pursuing commercial, others political, objects. Germany, in the speaker's opinion, belonged to the former category. The Anglo-German Agreement of the 16th October, 1900, had been concluded in that spirit. That Agreement was in no sense concerned with Manchuria; it contained no secret clauses, but had been communicated to the public *in extenso*. There were no German interests of importance in Manchuria, and the fate of that province was a matter of absolute indifference to Germany. On the other hand, it was of importance to her that at the present moment, while China's obligations towards the Powers were as yet unsettled, her estate should not be unduly reduced, and that she should not dispose of her assets *in fraudem creditorum* while the claims of the latter remained unsatisfied. Germany had consequently informed China that she would deprecate the conclusion at the present time of any Agreement by the latter, with no matter which Power, which would impair China's financial resources. Similar advice had been tendered to China by the United States, and the fact that several private Syndicates had recently taken advantage of China's plight to exact all manner of concessions from her had contributed towards determining the Imperial Government to adopt this view. . . . .

No. 33.

The Marquess of Lansdowne to Sir C. MacDonald.

F.O. Japan 538.

(No. 27.) Confidential.

Sir, *Foreign Office, March* 16, 1901.

Baron Hayashi left with me on the 9th instant the enclosed copies of telegrams received by him from the Japanese Minister at Berlin and from the Japanese Minister for Foreign Affairs.

I told him in reply to the questions which he had been instructed to ask me, that we had not been formally consulted by the German Government as to the various points which were discussed on the 6th of March at Berlin between the two Ministers.

But we had been given to understand that, in the event of hostilities between Japan and Russia, Germany would remain neutral.

" Benevolent neutrality " was an expression the precise import of which was not evident to me. An attitude which would keep the fleet of another Power in check could scarcely be described as neutral.

I said I had gathered from conversations with Baron Eckardstein that the German Government, while it would regard with disapproval the establishment of a Russian Protectorate over Manchuria, did not consider that German interests in that part of China were sufficiently marked to justify Germany in going to war in order to protect them.

So far as I was able to judge, the feelings ascribed to Germany in the preceding sentences were those which she really entertained, but I had of course no authority to make any intimation to him with regard to her policy.

The object of our diplomacy had been and was to discourage separate arrangements between China and individual Powers. We had, acting in concert with Japan and other Powers, intimated to China our disapproval of such arrangements. We had called the attention of the Russian Government to what appeared to be the striking inconsistency between Count Lamsdorff's language and the reputed provisions of the so-called Manchurian Agreement.

We should, I thought, be prepared to join with other Powers in a declaration that we refused to acknowledge the validity of any such agreements between China and individual Powers. We had also intimated to China our expectation that she would not commit herself further until she had received a reply to her request for mediation, and we had intimated to her that if she disregarded our warning, we should hold ourselves free to require compensation from her for any detriment which our interests may sustain.

I trusted that the result of our united efforts might be to prevent the execution of the Agreement. With regard to our attitude in the event of hostilities between Japan and Russia, which we should sincerely deplore, I could say nothing to him until I knew more as to the intentions ascribed to Germany, and I proposed to make enquiries upon this subject.

I communicated to the Japanese Minister to-day the substance of Sir F. Lascelles' telegram No. 17 in regard to the significance of the expression "benevolent neutrality," which occurred in the telegram which he had left with me on the 10th.

I said it seemed to me that the Japanese Minister at Berlin had formed a somewhat erroneous impression as to the import of the words as used by the German Government, and that it was evident that that Government held out no expectation that their conduct in the event of war between Russia and Japan would be of such a character as to hold the French fleet in check.

I told Baron Hayashi that it was probable that in the event of war between Japan and Russia His Majesty's Government, like that of Germany, would remain neutral, but that we were not likely to deprive ourselves of complete freedom of action as to the course which we might take, and which must necessarily be decided by circumstances which we could not at present foresee.

I am, &c.
LANSDOWNE.

No. 34.

The Marquess of Lansdowne to Sir F. Lascelles.

F.O. Germany (Prussia) 1523.
Tel. (No. 79.) P.   *Foreign Office, March* 16, 1901.

On Monday a question will be asked in Parliament as to whether the Anglo-German agreement applies to Manchuria. In extracts from Count Bülow's speech which are published to-day by the "Times" he is represented as saying that it has no reference to that province, and that this is made clear by the wording.

The opinion of H.M.G. is that clause (1), so far as ports in Manchuria are concerned, applies to that province, and that clause (2) applies to all parts of the Chinese Empire.

It would be unfortunate if any discrepancy should arise between the German interpretation of the agreement and ours, and everything possible must be done by us to avoid such an occurrence.

Are Count Bülow's views accurately represented by the "Times"?

No. 35.

Sir F. Lascelles to the Marquess of Lansdowne.

F.O. Germany (Prussia) 1524.

Tel. (No. 18.)

Berlin, March 17, 1901.

D. 2·44 P.M.

R. 6 P.M.

Your telegram No. 79.

The report in the "Times" is accurate. M. de Bülow distinctly stated in his speech that the Anglo-German agreement did not refer to Manchuria as is shown by the wording of the Agreement.

I am convinced that German Government always understood that the words " as far as they can exercise influence " were inserted for the purpose of excluding Manchuria from the agreement, and it seems to me that Count Hatzfeldt's objections to a previous draft on the ground that it would include Port Arthur and the River Amur as recorded in Lord Salisbury's despatch No. 224 of October 15th justify this interpretation.

No. 36.

Memorandum by Lord Lansdowne.

(Communicated to Baron Hayashi, March 25, 1901([1])).

F.O. Japan 545.

A doubt appears to have arisen as to the interpretation of certain passages in the Anglo-German Agreement.

Clause II, which pledges the two Governments to direct their policy towards maintaining unimpaired the territorial condition of the Chinese Empire, is, in the opinion of His Majesty's Government, applicable to the province of Manchuria.

But they cannot take upon themselves to say how that clause is interpreted by other Governments. . . . .

([1]) [In reply to an enquiry by Baron Hayashi on the 22nd March, 1901, as to whether the Agreement extended to Manchuria.]

No. 37.

The Marquess of Lansdowne to Sir F. Lascelles.

F.O. Germany (Prussia) 1518.

(No. 136.)

Sir,

Foreign Office, April 7, 1901.

Baron Eckardstein communicated to me to-day a despatch from Count Bülow in which reference was made to the following passage in a speech delivered by me in the House of Lords on the 28th ultimo :—

" I have made enquiries with regard to what took place when this Agreement was under negotiation, and I am told that the German Government did give us to understand that in their view Manchuria was not a place within which they consider that they had influence."

Baron Eckardstein was instructed to say that in the above passage I had correctly represented the position which the German Government had assumed, and that Count Bülow was obliged to me for the explanation thus afforded.

I am, &c.

LANSDOWNE.

No. 38.

Sir T. H. Sanderson to Sir F. Lascelles.([1])

F.O. Germany (Prussia) 1550.
Private.

My dear Lascelles,   *Foreign Office, March 5, 1902.*

I saw in some newspaper a day or two ago that a statement based apparently on official information had appeared in one of the German newspapers to the effect that Lord Salisbury had agreed during the negotiation of the Anglo-German Agreement of October 16th, 1900, that it should not apply to Manchuria, and had even at first proposed to insert a geographical limit in the Agreement for that purpose.

I send you therefore by Lord Lansdowne's desire copies of correspondence with Count Hatzfeldt during the negotiation of the Agreement and some minutes on them which show clearly—

1. That Lord Salisbury's proposed geographical limitation applied only to the latter portion of Article 1 of the Agreement, pledging the two Governments to "uphold" commercial freedom in the Ports on the rivers and littoral of China.

2. That he proposed to supplement this limitation by a stipulation reserving all existing Treaty rights. This stipulation would obviously have applied to Manchuria as well as to the rest of China.

3. That Count Bülow suggested an alteration in Article 2 (the Article providing against encroachments on the territorial condition of China) which Lord Salisbury accepted, though complaining that it weakened the Article, but that neither Count Bülow nor Lord Salisbury in any way proposed or suggested in this discussion that Manchuria was to be excepted from the scope of that Article, or that the geographical limitation which Lord Salisbury proposed to insert in Article 1 could apply to Article 2.

4. That the line proposed by Lord Salisbury (38° N. Lat.) was such that if it *had* applied to Article 2 of the Agreement, the two Governments would have solemnly bound themselves to direct their policy towards maintaining undiminished the territorial condition of the Chinese Empire, while leaving themselves and other Countries free to annex the Capital, the greater part of the province of Chih-li in which it is situated and the whole of Mongolia, all of which lie to the North of 38° N. Lat.

The only admission which we are prepared to make (and which Lord Lansdowne has in fact made) is that the German Government in the course of the negotiations intimated their unwillingness to come into controversy with Russia in regard to the observance of the principle of commercial freedom on the littoral and in the rivers of Manchuria, and that they are free to contend that they are not bound by Article 1 of the Agreement to enter into such controversy on the ground that they do not exercise influence in that part of the Chinese Empire.

[T. H. SANDERSON.]

Enclosure 1 in No. 38.

Count Hatzfeldt to the Marquess of Salisbury.

Mon cher Lord Salisbury,   *Londres, le 4 Octobre* 1900.

Je m'empresse de vous dire que mon Gouvernement, à qui j'ai rendu compte de notre dernière conversation sur les affaires de Chine, m'a autorisé à accepter les changements de rédactions proposés par vous à l'exception d'un point contre lequel, comme vous voudrez bien vous en souvenir, je me suis permis de suite d'élever quelques objections. Il s'agit de la dernière phrase de l'Article II qui commence par les mots "and will oppose." Le Comte de Bülow, qui est d'avis que notre arrangement doit

([1]) [The MS. draft of this letter is unsigned, but it appears to be from Sir T. H. Sanderson.]

poursuivre le but d'apaiser les soupçons relativement à des intentions secrètes de quelques Puissances en Chine, craint vivement que la rédaction proposée atteindrait le but opposé parce qu'elle serait considérée par l'opinion publique comme une menace contre d'autres Puissances. Par ces motifs le Comte de Bülow préférerait une autre rédaction de cette phrase, par exemple la suivante : "und werden auch ihre Politik daraufrichten den Territorial-Bestand des chinesischen Reichs unverkürzt zu erhalten." Si, comme je l'espère, vous n'avez pas d'objections contre cette rédaction, dont la portée pratique me semble exactement la même que celle de votre première rédaction, vous seriez bien aimable de me faire parvenir la traduction anglaise que vous comptez adopter pour cette phrase pour que je puisse la communiquer à Berlin.

Il va sans dire si vous désirez en causer avec moi d'abord demain ou après-demain, que je suis entièrement à votre disposition. Je vous serai obligé dans ce cas de vouloir bien me le faire savoir aussitôt que possible parce que, n'étant pas très bien portant, je tâcherais d'aller à Brighton demain dans l'après-midi si vous n'avez pas besoin de moi. . . . . [The rest refers to another matter—the Railway difficulty in Chih-li.]

En attendant, &c.
P. HATZFELDT.

Enclosure 2 in No. 38.

Count Hatzfeldt to Sir T. H. Sanderson.

German Embassy,
Dear Sir Thomas, *9, Carlton House Terrace, S.W., October* 4, 1900.
The proposed addition to Article I of the Draft Agreement which my father took away after his conversation with Lord Salisbury on Tuesday, is as follows :—
Add to paragraph after " distinction " :—

" And the two Governments agree on their part to uphold the same for all Chinese territory to the South of the 38th parallel of Latitude."

Believe me, &c.
H. HATZFELDT.

Enclosure 3 in No. 38.

Sir T. H. Sanderson to the Marquess of Salisbury.

Foreign Office, October 4, 1900.
Count H. Hatzfeldt says the proposed addition to Article I of the Draft Agreement was worded as written in the margin of annexed copy.

Will it not be desirable to have some saving clause that nothing in the Agreement shall be held to derogate from the intention of the two Governments to maintain the privileges already enjoyed by Treaty in ports of China to the North of the parallel mentioned?

Tientsin and Newchwang are very important to our trade.

T. H. S.

I agree that to prevent misunderstanding this will be a reasonable precaution.
S.

I enclose a note to Ct. H. Would you have it copied and forwarded?
S.

Enclosure 4 in No. 38.

The Marquess of Salisbury to Count Hatzfeldt.

My dear Count Hatzfeldt, *Foreign Office, October* 4, 1900.
Count Bülow's alteration will certainly deprive the clause of much of its force ; and will therefore diminish the protection we should obtain from it. Will you kindly

ascertain from your Government whether they would accept at the close of the Agreement a clause to this effect? :—

" It is understood that nothing in this instrument shall be held to diminish or affect in any degree any rights enjoyed by either of the two Governments in any part of China by virtue of Treaties at present in force."

This, I think, will be necessary to prevent misunderstanding.

Yours very truly,
SALISBURY.

Enclosure 5 in No. 38.

Count Hatzfeldt to the Marquess of Salisbury.

Particulière et confidentielle.
Mon cher Lord Salisbury,   *Londres, le 6 Octobre* 1900.
    Je me suis empressé de transmettre à Berlin la clause que vous désirez ajouter à la fin de notre arrangement. On me dit en réponse à ma question que, notre but n'étant nullement de mettre en question par cet arrangement les droits dont l'Angleterre jouit en Chine jusqu'à présent, nous n'avons pas d'objection en principe contre la clause que vous proposez, en supposant qu'elle se réfère aux traités publiés et connus qui ont été conclus jusqu'à présent par les deux Gouvernements avec la Chine. Mon Gouvernement est convaincu que cela est le sens et la portée que vous avez voulu attribuer à cette clause et qu'il serait seulement nécessaire d'en préciser un peu plus la rédaction, afin d'éviter que cette stipulation soit mal comprise par l'opinion publique des deux pays quand l'arrangement sera publié. Il suffirait pour cela, je crois, d'ajouter après le mot " treaties " un mot pour faire comprendre qu'il s'agit des traités connus et publiés conclus jusqu'à présent en Chine par l'Allemagne et l'Angleterre.
    Si nous sommes d'accord sur ce point, j'espère qu'il ne reste plus aucune difficulté relativement à la rédaction de l'arrangement. Je suppose, naturellement, en exprimant cet espoir, qu'il est bien entendu, si nous acceptons la clause finale en la précisant simplement un peu plus, vous accepterez également la phrase finale de d'article II proposée dans ma lettre du 4 courant, à savoir : " und werden auch ihre Politik daraufrichten, den Territorial-Bestand des chinesischen Reichs unverkürzt zu erhalten."
    Soyez assez bon pour me faire savoir quand vous désirez me voir pour causer de cette affaire et arriver à une solution définitive qui, j'en suis convaincu est également désirable dans l'intérêt des deux pays.

Veuillez, &c.
P. HATZFELDT.

Enclosure 6 in No. 38.

The Marquess of Salisbury to Count Hatzfeldt.

My dear Count Hatzfeldt,   *Foreign Office, October* 6, 1900.
    I can hardly accept your modification in the form in which you put it, for its effect would be that if there were any secret treaty between China and England (which there is not), our agreement would invalidate it. I confess that since you have altered it to make it agreeable to Russia, I am not very much in love with this agreement. It is liable to so much misunderstanding. I must certainly call a Cabinet to consider it as soon as my colleagues have all been elected.
    I shall be very happy to see you on Tuesday at five if you wish to see me.

Yours very truly,
SALISBURY.

II.—COREA AND MANCHURIA.

No. 39.

Sir E. Satow to the Marquess of Salisbury.

F.O. Japan 526.
(No. 39.)   *Tokyo,* D. *March* 31, 1900.
My Lord,   R. *May* 15, 1900.

With reference to my despatch No. 4 of January 12th, your Lordship will have received reports from Her Majesty's Chargé d'Affaires at Seoul regarding the demands now being pressed on the Corean Government by the Russian Chargé d'Affaires for a concession of land at Masampo.

As your Lordship is aware, Masampo is regarded by naval officers as one of the finest natural harbours in the Far East, conferring on any strong Power that holds it the command of the Tsuchima Strait.

Japan is accordingly very unwilling to see Russia establishing a naval station at that point, and public opinion has been much excited by the reports that have reached this country as to the tone and extent of the Russian demands.

I have on more than one occasion asked the Minister for Foreign Affairs whether he could give me any information, and he has recently confirmed to me the information as to Naipo, a small bay near Masampo, marked on the map enclosed* in Mr. Jordan's despatch to your Lordship, No. 30, Very Confidential, of March. 10th.

His Excellency added that he supposed the Corean Government would not be able to resist the pressure put on them. The Russian Government had intimated their desire to remove their naval hospital from Nagasaki to Masampo, and also to form a coal depôt there. In his Excellency's opinion this establishment, unimportant in the beginning, might later on assume a more formidable character, constituting a permanent menace to Japan. In that case Japan would be obliged to seek for an equivalent.

The language generally held in official circles is to the effect that Japan desires to remain on friendly terms with Russia, and to observe the stipulations of her written Agreements respecting Corea, but that there are limits beyond which she could not go in the direction of concession, with a due regard to her own safety. This language I believe to be perfectly sincere.

                I have, &c.
                ERNEST SATOW.

      * Not reproduced.

No. 40.

Mr. Jordan to the Marquess of Salisbury.

F.O. China 1454.
(No. 52.) Very Confidential.   *Seoul,* D. *May* 1, 1900.
My Lord,   R. *June* 12, 1900.

In continuation of my despatch No. 51 of yesterday's date, I have the honour to transmit herewith to your Lordship copies, in translation, of the Agreements signed on the 30th March last by the Russian Chargé d'Affaires and the Corean Minister of Foreign Affairs respecting the Russian Concession at Masampo and the guarantee for the non-alienation of Ko-je Do.

The papers have been furnished to me to-day in strict confidence by Mr. Hayashi, and their contents agree generally with the account of them given in my previous despatches.

The first prescribes the conditions under which a site for a coal depôt and a naval hospital is to be granted to the Russian Government within a distance of 10 *li* from the foreign Settlement at Masampo, and provides that the details of the arrangement shall be settled on the spot by a Commission composed of the Russian Consul at the port and a Delegate sent from the Corean Foreign Office here.

The second constitutes a reciprocal engagement, under which Russia undertakes never to apply for permission to rent or purchase, either for her own use or for the use of her subjects in the prosecution of commercial or industrial undertakings of any kind, any land on Ko-je Do, or on the opposite mainland extending as far as the harbour of Masampo, or on any of the surrounding islands, while Corea, on her part, agrees not to allow any other Government to rent or purchase land for similar purposes in any of the above-mentioned places.

The result of this would seem to be that Masampo and its approaches, which constitute by common consent far the finest harbour in the East, are virtually placed within the exclusive sphere of Russian influence, and are destined to become a Russian naval base, which will serve for the present to link together Vladivostock and Port Arthur, and which, considering its great natural advantages, may eventually take rank above either of these places in strategic importance.

Now that the matter is placed beyond doubt by the production of the papers, it will be interesting to see whether Japan will acquiesce in an arrangement which places her rival in a position that, notwithstanding the present pledges, will probably in time be converted into one of great strength almost within sight of her shores.

I have, &c.
J. N. JORDAN.

No. 41.

Sir C. Scott to the Marquess of Salisbury.

F.O. Russia 1599.
(No. 151.)   *St. Petersburgh*, D. *May* 30, 1900.
My Lord,   R. *June* 4, 1900.

I have the honour to enclose herewith translation of an article which appeared in the "Novoye Vremya" of the 23rd instant,([1]) in reply to an article in the London "Times," commenting in an alarmist tone on the Concession recently obtained by the Russian Government for the use of the Admiralty in the Corean port of Masampo.

It is, I think, regrettable that the "Times," on the unsupported authority of its Peking correspondent, should have given an interpretation to the character of this Concession which is at variance with that received from official sources, and thus given any occasion to the Russian press to insinuate that England was trying to raise a question between Japan and Russia in regard to a transaction which has apparently formed the subject of satisfactory explanations between those Governments.

On the appearance of this article, the Japanese Chargé d'Affaires came to the Embassy to ask me whether I had any official information to justify the alarm which the "Times" had expressed, as his information did not warrant such apprehensions.

He was relieved to learn that the interpretation which the "Times" had put on the Russian Agreement with Corea was not supported by any official reports which I had seen.

Count Mouravieff to-day referred to the "Times" article as a fresh instance of the mischievous influence of the press in encouraging international suspicion, and said that Mr. Brodrick had very correctly explained in the House of Commons the real nature of the engagements concluded by M. Pavloff which were in strict accordance with Treaty rights, and did not in any way impair the rights or interests of other countries in Corea.

I have, &c.
CHARLES S. SCOTT.

([1]) Not reproduced.

No. 42.

The Marquess of Lansdowne to Sir C. MacDonald.

F.O. Japan 538.
(No. 13.) Confidential.
Sir,   *Foreign Office, January* 29, 1901.

The Japanese Minister called on me to-day and left with me—

1. A Confidential note of the purport of a communication made by Count Lamsdorff to the Japanese Minister at St. Petersburgh in regard to the alleged Russo-Chinese Agreement as to Manchuria; and

2. A Memorandum containing the purport of the reply of the Japanese Government to a proposal made by the Russian Minister at Tokyo to neutralise Corea under the joint guarantee of the Powers.

I enclose copies of these communications.

Baron Hayashi dwelt with considerable earnestness on the risk of finding that Russia had permanently installed herself in Manchuria, and was evidently anxious to know what line His Majesty's Government intended to adopt.

I told the Minister that we had desired our Ambassador at St. Petersburgh to mention the matter to Count Lamsdorff as one which was attracting a good deal of attention in this country, but I said that it seemed to me extremely difficult for us to call in question the good faith of the plausible assurances and explanations which the Russian Government had offered, and would, no doubt, continue to offer upon this subject.

I am, &c.
LANSDOWNE.

Enclosure in No. 42.

Papers communicated to the Marquess of Lansdowne by the Japanese Minister,
January 29, 1901.

(1.)

Re *Manchuria*.

(Strictly Confidential.)

Count Lamsdorff answered that the question of Manchuria concerns Russia and China only;

That its occupation is the result of self-defence against Chinese aggression;

That Russia would be perfectly right even if she choose to make occupation permanent;

That she has, however, no intention of exercising her right of conquest;

That she will withdraw from Manchuria;

That she will, however, have to enter into some agreements with Chinese authorities to settle questions of railway, frontier, &c.;

That the reported Russo-Chinese Agreement is false.

(2.)

Re *Corea*.

On the 7th January Russian Minister at Tokyo, under instructions of his Government, proposed to neutralise Corea under the joint guarantee of Powers.

On the 18th January the Japanese Government directed the Japanese Minister at St. Petersburgh to reply to the Russian Government in the following sense :—

As the lease by Russia of a portion of Liaotung Peninsula was of a qualified and temporary nature, and as it did not extend to the Corean frontier, Japan did not object to it, and even agreed to the Protocol of 1898. But Russia's present position in Manchuria is totally different, and would naturally cause solicitude if Russia had not definitely announced her intention of withdrawing from there. The Japanese Government therefore consider it better to postpone negotiations until *status quo ante* shall have been restored. In the meantime, the Protocol of 1898 answers the purpose.

[*ED. NOTE.*—A despatch from Sir C. Scott of 6th February (received 11th February), giving Lamsdorff's views is published in *Accounts and Papers*, 1904 (*Cd.* 1936), CX, pp. 137–8.]

No. 43.

The Marquess of Lansdowne to Viscount Gough.

F.O. Germany (Prussia) 1518.
(No. 49.)

My Lord, *Foreign Office, February 7, 1901.*

I repeated to Baron Eckardstein to-day the substance of my conversation with Baron Hayashi in regard to the alleged agreement between Russia and China as to Manchuria. (See my despatch to Sir C. MacDonald, No. 17, Confidential, of the 5th February.)

I told Baron Eckardstein that it seemed to me advisable to give to the Chinese Government some such indication of our views as that suggested by Baron Hayashi. Such an expression of opinion would not commit us inconveniently; but it might have a useful effect in encouraging the Chinese to hold their own, while on the other hand I thought it desirable to meet the wishes of the Japanese Government, who evidently attached much importance to the matter.

I said, however, that it would, in my opinion, be far better that if any advice of the kind were tendered, it should proceed not from His Majesty's Government alone, but from some of the other Powers, and I asked him to ascertain how the German Government regarded the idea.

I handed to Baron Eckardstein a Memorandum, of which a copy is attached to this despatch, and he promised that he would let me know as soon as possible the decision of his Government.

I am, &c.
LANSDOWNE.

Enclosure in No. 43.

Memorandum given to Baron Eckardstein by the Marquess of Lansdowne, February 7, 1901.

His Majesty's Government understand that the Russian Government are pressing the Chinese Government to ratify the Agreement concluded between Admiral Alexeieff and the Chinese General Commanding in Manchuria in regard to that province.

They also understand that the Chinese Government would like, if encouraged by foreign Powers, to repudiate the Agreement, and punish the Tartar General who concluded it.

In these circumstances, the Japanese Government propose to inform the Chinese Minister at Tokyo that the conclusion of any such Agreement would be a source of danger to the Chinese Government, and that no arrangement affecting territorial rights in the Chinese Empire ought to be concluded between the Chinese Government and any one of the Powers.

[15214] D 2

His Majesty's Government are disposed to make a similar communication to the Chinese Minister in London.

Foreign Office, February 7, 1901.

[ED. NOTE.—As a result of this Baron Eckardstein informed Lord Lansdowne on the 12th that the German Government would intimate to the Chinese their opinion that it "should not conclude with any Power individual Treaties of a territorial or financial character before they can estimate their obligations towards all the Powers as a whole and before the compliance with such obligations is accepted." Lord Lansdowne regretted that the wording differed from that of our Memo. *v. Accounts and Papers,* 1904 (*Cd.* 1936) CX, p. 138.]

No. 44.

The Marquess of Lansdowne to Sir C. MacDonald.

F.O. Japan 542.　　　　　　　　　　　　　　　*Foreign Office, February* 18, 1901.
Tel.　(No. 13.)　Secret.　　　　　　　　　　　　　　　　D. 6·35 P.M.

Your telegram 4 secret of 15th.

Assurance to China suggested by Japanese Government appears to His Majesty's Government to be dangerously vague.

As the Japanese Government know from the Anglo-German Agreement to which they have given their adhesion, our policy is to maintain the integrity of China, and with that object we have joined them in warning China that any separate arrangements between her and any individual Power or Powers would, in our opinion, be a source of danger, &c.

Germany has made a somewhat similar intimation to China. We have therefore reason to expect that China will inform us and the German and Japanese Governments if pressure be put upon her to make such separate arrangements, and we should then be ready to consider with those Governments in full knowledge of the circumstances of the case which will have actually arisen what course should be taken.

Should China, on the other hand, make or have made separate arrangements of a territorial, financial, commercial or political character detrimental to our interests, we shall have to consider what steps are necessary in order to redress the balance.

I will inform Sir E. Satow of the Japanese suggestion, and I shall instruct him to make a representation in the above sense to the Chinese Plenipotentiaries, if the Japanese and German Governments are prepared to do the same.

On hearing from Japanese Government that they concur, I will communicate with the German Government.

No. 45.

The Marquess of Lansdowne to Sir C. Scott.[1]

F.O. Russia 1624.
Tel.　(No. 54.)　Confidential.　　　　　　　　　*Foreign Office, March* 4, 1901.

Your telegram No. 24 (of 27th February).

Express my thanks to Count Lamsdorff. We shall avail ourselves of his permission and present your despatch No. 41 of 6th February with the amendments suggested.

The presentation will somewhat allay, but will, I fear, not dispel, the apprehensions created by the publication of various versions of a Manchurian Agreement, which we are advised is now under discussion at St. Petersburgh.

[1] [Paraphrased in *Accounts and Papers*, 1904 (*Cd.* 1936) CX, p. 142.]

The terms of these certainly suggest the idea that much more is involved than a provisional and temporary arrangement for the purpose of preventing the recurrence of the recent disturbances and of protecting the railway.

No limit is assigned for the duration of the Agreement as a whole; and as to certain clauses, its termination is made to depend on fulfilment of conditions, compliance with which might be indefinitely delayed.

Other provisions again are, on the face of them, of an enduring character and in some cases inconsistent with the Treaty obligations of China to other Powers.

The Agreement is also described as providing for a separate arrangement with regard to the indemnity claimed by Russia for the destruction of the Trans-Manchurian Railway.

In our opinion, no arrangements calculated to affect permanently the territorial, political, financial or commercial status of China should be separately entered into by her with individual Powers.

We have expressed this opinion to her in reply to enquiries made as to our views, and we are glad to find that Russian Government disclaims the intention of making an arrangement of the kind.

But, in view of the persistent reports to which I have referred, His Majesty's Government trust that the actual text of the agreement or agreements may be communicated for their information.

[ED. NOTE.—B.F.S.P., XCIV, 1048-9, prints a despatch from Sir C. Scott to Lord Lansdowne of the 6th February (received the 11th February), describing Count Lamsdorff's views on the alleged Manchurian Agreement, and authorised by Count Lamsdorff on the 27th February. Also in *Accounts and Papers*, 1904 (*Cd.* 1936) CX, pp. 137-8.]

No. 46.

Sir E. Satow to the Marquess of Lansdowne.(¹)

Peking, March 6, 1901.

F.O. China. 1484.
Tel. (No. 66.)

D. 10 A.M.
R. 12·15 P.M.

Your telegram No. 55.
Following sent to Consul at Nanking March 2nd :—

" The Convention for the future Government of Manchuria proposed by Russia will have the effect of depriving China of her sovereignty over that region, and the prohibition to construct railways in Mongolia and Eastern Turkestan is equivalent to abandoning those regions also.

" You should urge Viceroy to memorialise the Emperor against this treaty, as it will form a bad precedent and probably lead to partition of China.

" Add that Li Hung Chang is about to sign if not prevented by orders from the throne."

Following from Nanking to-day :—

" Viceroy has already memorialised Emperor to refuse assent to Russian Convention. His Excellency earnestly begs British, Japanese and United States Governments to support China strongly in this refusal."

(¹) [Paraphrased in *Accounts and Papers*, 1904 (*Cd.* 1936) CX, pp. 143-4.]

No. 47.

Sir E. Satow to the Marquess of Lansdowne.

F.O. China 1484.
Tel. (No. 67.)

Peking, March 6, 1901.
D. 10 A.M.
R. 7 P.M.

Following is a translation of the Chinese text I have obtained which is evidently translated from the Russian :—

" The Emperor of Russia, being anxious to give evidence of his friendly feeling towards China, is willing to forget the hostile acts committed in Manchuria, and to hand back the whole of that country to China—its administration to be carried on as before.

" 2. Under Article 6 of the Manchurian Railway Agreement, the Administration is authorised to maintain troops for the protection of the line. The country, however, being at present in an unsettled condition, and such troops few in number, a body of soldiers must be retained until order is restored, and until China shall have carried out the provisions of the last four Articles of the present Convention.

" 3. In the event of grave disturbances the Russian garrisons will afford China every assistance in suppressing the same as far as lies in their power.

" 4. In the recent attacks against Russia, Chinese troops having taken a prominent part, China agrees, pending the completion of the line and its opening to traffic, not to establish an army (in those provinces). She will consult with Russia as to the number of troops she may subsequently wish to establish there.

" The importation of munitions of war into Manchuria is prohibited.

" 5. With a view to safeguarding the interests of the territory in question, China will, on representations being made by Russia, at once deprive of office any Military Governor or other high official, whose conduct of affairs proves antagonistic to Russia and maintenance of friendly relations.

" A police force, consisting of mounted and unmounted units, may be organised in the interior of Manchuria. Its numbers shall be determined after consultation with Russia, and from its armament artillery shall be excluded. The servants and subjects of any other Power shall not be employed in connection therewith.

" 6. In accordance with the undertaking given by China at an earlier date, she will not employ the subjects of any other Power in training soldiers or sailors in North China.

" 7. The neighbouring authorities will, in the interests of peace and order, draw up new special Regulations with reference to the neutral zone (see Agreement of March 27th, 1898) treated of in Article 5 of the Agreement relating to the lease (of part of the Liaotung Peninsula). China's autonomous rights in the City of Chinchon, secured to her by Article 4 of the Special Agreement (of May 7th, 1898) are hereby abrogated.

" 8. China shall not, without the consent of Russia, grant to any other Power, or the subjects thereof, privileges with regard to mines, railroads or other matters in conterminous (*i.e.*, with Russia) regions, such as Manchuria, Mongolia, and the sections of the new Dominion known as Tarbagati, Ili, Kashgar, Yarkand, and Khoten. Nor shall China, without Russia's consent, construct [rail]roads there herself.

" Except as far as Newchwang is concerned, no leases of land' shall be granted to the subjects of any other Powers.

" 9. China being under obligation to pay Russia's war expenses and the claims of other Powers, arising out of the recent troubles, the amount of the indemnity presented in the name of Russia, the period within which it will have to be paid, and the security therefore will all be arranged in concert with the other Powers.

"10. The compensation to be paid for the destruction of the railway lines, for the robbery of property, belonging to the Railway Administration and its employés, as well as claims for delay in carrying on the construction of the line, will form subject of arrangement between China and the Administration.

"11. The above-mentioned claims may, by agreement with the Administration, either in part or in whole, be commuted for other privileges. The grant of such privileges would involve a complete revision of the previous Agreement.

"12. In conformity with the undertaking previously given by China, it is agreed that a line may be constructed from either the trunk line or the branch line (of Manchurian Railway) in the direction of Peking up to the Great Wall, its administration to be governed by the Regulations at present in force."

In Article 5 and Article 6 prohibition to employ foreigners infringes on China's liberty of action.

Article 8 lays the foundation for future treatment of those districts in same way as Manchuria and is contrary to possible interests of other Powers.

Article 10 withdraws the railway indemnity from the purview of the Powers. (Germany has already arranged money indemnity for damage to Shantung railways with Governor of that Province.)

"Times" text is only a summary.

Sent to Tokio.

[Part paraphrased and end slightly shortened in *Accounts and Papers*, 1904 (*Cd.* 1936) CX, pp. 144–5. A revised version of August 1901 is printed in *ib.*, pp. 157–61.]

No. 48.

Sir C. Scott to the Marquess of Lansdowne.

St. Petersburg, March 7, 1901.

F.O. Russia 1625.   D. 8·30 P.M.
Tel.   (No. 27.)   R. 11 P.M.

Your telegram No. 54.

I read your message in French translation to Count Lamsdorff to-day, but did not leave him a copy.

He resented with considerable warmth the suggestion that the actual text of the conditions still under discussion with the Chinese Government for the evacuation of Manchuria by Russian troops should be communicated for the information of His Majesty's Government, in order to correct impressions raised by maliciously garbled and incorrect accounts in press of their nature and bearing.

He said that, even if terms had been definitely fixed and he had them in his portfolio before him, he would consider it incompatible with the character of an independent State in negotiation with another to communicate the details to a third party.

I pointed out to him that the words I had read contained neither protest nor demand for such a communication if the Russian Government did not desire to make it in order to dissipate misconceptions.

We were not dependent on the press for the version given us of the Articles under discussion, but he would perceive that China had asked for our views on them, and we had frankly given them, as we had a perfect right to do, and wished to make no secret of this to the Russian Government.

He said that Chinese had told him that the strong opposition of His Majesty's Government alone prevented them from accepting the Russian conditions, and the object in both cases was self-evident, and designed to sow dissension between the two Powers.

He maintained that question of Manchuria was quite apart from the questions which the Powers were negotiating in concert with China, and that Russia had a right to make what conditions she chose for its evacuation by her troops, and if China did not accept them, the occupation could continue. Russia was not pressing terms on China but China was pressing early evacuation on them.

He said that Germany had always understood that Russia would settle this question with China by a separate Agreement apart from the other negotiations, and that M. de Bülow had recently repeated that Germany was not concerned with any arrangements about Manchuria.

I said that I had no knowledge of Germany's interests, and that there was no question of Russia's rights to take what course she liked, but of China's right to free herself from Treaty obligations to other Powers—or to enter into separate Agreements permanently affecting her political, territorial, financial and commercial status, whilst in negotiation with other creditors.

Count Lamsdorff said that there was no intention of interfering with acquired rights of other Powers, or of injuriously affecting the other negotiations.

He could give me however, no more positive assurances than were to be found in the Emperor's declared intentions.

He regretted the violent suspicions and distrust of their loyalty displayed in Parliament and the English press, which was creating great irritation in the highest quarters in Russia, and he feared that the Emperor might finally lose patience.

I said that His Majesty's Government was not responsible for public feeling in England, but only anxious to allay unjust suspicions in the hope that [? a] frank and confidential communication to the Russian Government would assist them in doing so.

At the conclusion of a long interview Count Lamsdorff appeared to see matters in a calmer and more reasonable light, and I think that he will exert a moderating influence on his colleagues, the Ministers of War and Finance.

[*ED. NOTE.*—Telegram No. 59 of March 9 from Lord Lansdowne instructed Sir C. Scott to communicate Sir E. Satow's text of agreement and to point out to Count Lamsdorff that it was incompatible with the assurances of 6th February (*v.* note on p. 37). The telegram is paraphrased in *Accounts and Papers*, 1904 (*Cd.* 1936) CX, p. 145.]

No. 49.

The Marquess of Lansdowne to Sir E. Monson.

F.O. France 3539.   *Foreign Office, March 8*, 1901.
Tel. (No. 27.) Very Secret.   D. 11·30 P.M.

Relations between Japan and Russia seem to be getting strained.

Do you think that France is under any engagement to take part on the side of Russia in the event of war, or that without such obligation she would attempt to do so?

No. 50.

The Marquess of Lansdowne to Sir F. Lascelles.

F.O. Germany (Prussia) 1523. *Foreign Office, March 8, 1901.*
Tel. (No. 67.) Very Secret. D. 11·30 P.M.

Eckhardstein has repeated to me more than once that Hayashi tells him that the Japanese would probably go to war with Russia if she could be sure that this country and Germany would not allow France to help Russia, and that the spoils of victory would not be again snatched from her.

Have you heard anything of this, and have you any idea what Germany would say to such a proposal?

No. 51.

Communicated by Baron Hayashi.

F.O. Japan 545. *March 9, 1901.*

(a.)

Telegram from Japanese Minister at Berlin.

The German Vice-Minister for Foreign Affairs told me at my interview with him on March 6th that the German Government discountenance any action on the part of any single Power to turn the present situation for its own use, and that therefore they entirely disapprove Russian proceedings in regard to Manchuria. He strongly denied that there is any secret understanding with Russia on Far Eastern question and assured me that as German Government are well aware of the vital importance of Manchurian question to Japan, Germany will observe benevolent neutrality in case matters should come to a crisis. He added that this attitude of Germany will keep French fleet in check, while England will probably support Japan. I asked if he think [*sic*] that Russia will persist in her demands. He answered that as all Powers seem to disfavour Russian action she will not push matter to extremity.

(b.)

Telegram from Japanese Minister for Foreign Affairs.

You will ask Marquess of Lansdowne :—

1. Has British Government been consulted by Germany on the subject of remarks of German Vice-Minister for Foreign Affairs?
2. Does his Lordship think that the remarks represent *bona fide* attitude and final intention of Germany?
3. How far may Japan rely upon the support of Great Britain in case Japan finds it necessary to approach Russia?

MINUTES.

Lord Salisbury.—. . . . Baron Hayashi thought that the word " approach " Russia . . . . should probably be " resist " . . . .—*F. B.*

" Approach " seems to me all important. It only implies diplomatic support. " Resist " of course means fighting.—*S.*

No. 52.

Sir F. Lascelles to the Marquess of Lansdowne.

F.O. Germany (Prussia) 1524.
Tel. (No. 16.)

Berlin, March 10, 1901.
D. 5·47 P.M.
R. 6·30 P.M.

Your telegrams Nos. 67 and 70.

I gather from a long conversation which I have just had with the Japanese Minister that he is of opinion that German Government will not take any steps with regard to Manchurian Agreement which would bring them into conflict with Russia although they would be glad to see Russian aggressions stopped. Baron Richthofen's language to him was similar to that he held to me on the 7th instant as reported in my telegram No. 14.

Japanese Minister does not believe Russia will proceed to extremities if China should refuse ratification of agreement. It would certainly be to China's interest to hold out as long as possible, because if she yields she will have to meet similar demands on part of other Powers.

Japanese Minister does not believe in imminence of a war between Japan and Russia because the latter should invade Corea when Japan could not remain indifferent. Japan could certainly cope with the Russian forces on land but would be inferior at sea to the combined Russian and French fleets. It would therefore be most interesting to know what line France would take.

Japanese Minister is disinclined to believe a report that Germany is seeking to conclude a separate arrangement with China with regard to Shantung.

No. 53.

The Marquess of Lansdowne to Sir C. Scott.

F.O. Russia 1624.
Tel. (No. 60.) Secret.

Foreign Office, March 11, 1901.

Your telegram No. 30, Secret, of 9th.

Lord Cranbourne, in reply to a question in the House of Commons, said :—

"The despatch from His Majesty's Ambassador at St. Petersburgh reporting his conversation with the Russian Minister for Foreign Affairs on the subject of the Russian occupation of Manchuria, to which the Honourable Member refers, will be presented to Parliament at once. The text of this despatch was seen and approved by Count Lamsdorff at the end of last month."

Your despatch No. 41 of February 6th as amended at Count Lamsdorff's request was presented to Parliament on the 4th instant with the following footnote :—

"His Majesty's Ambassador in a telegram dated February 27th, 1901, states that Count Lamsdorff has no objection to the publication of this despatch as an accurate report of the language held by him in conversation with Sir C. Scott."

Without this footnote it would have appeared that the reassuring language quoted in your despatch had been used as long ago as February 6th.

It seems to us essential in order that the publication should have the desired effect to bring out the fact that your despatch had after an interval of three weeks been approved by Count Lamsdorff. We were careful not to go beyond terms authorised by him.

Explain this to Count Lamsdorff, and say that we do not quite understand the grounds of his complaint.

No. 54.

Memorandum by Mr. Bertie.

F.O. China 1501. *Foreign Office, March 11, 1901.*

Germany has assured Japan that there is no secret understanding between Germany and Russia respecting the Far East, and that, in the event of a crisis, Germany will observe a benevolent neutrality, the effect of which would be to keep the French fleet in check.

The Japanese Government ask whether His Majesty's Government have been consulted by Germany, and whether they believe the assurances given to Japan; and they further ask: "How far may Japan rely upon the support of Great Britain in case Japan finds it necessary to approach Russia?"

It is assumed by the Japanese Minister that "approach" in the context means "resist," which is war.

Unless Japan can make sure of neither Germany nor France taking an active part on the side of Russia, she will not fight Russia over the Manchurian Agreement. If the possession of Corea by Russia were at issue, Japan would fight, with or without support, and independently of whether France and Germany would remain neutral.

If Germany and England, in answer to the Japanese Government's inquiries, deprecated war, and said that if unfortunately war broke out between Japan and Russia, it would be the object of England and Germany to restrict as much as possible the theatre of it, and they would consequently remain neutral, so long as no third Power attempted to take part in it, then I think that such an assurance might be sufficient to satisfy Japan that France would not be allowed to join with Russia, and that Japan might fight Russia single-handed.

What Japan feels, or, rather, what is felt in that country, is that the Russian danger is advancing rapidly, and that it will not be long before Russia attempts to bring Corea within her sphere. Therefore, if Japan must fight for Corea, she had better do so over the Manchurian Agreement, before the Russian railway is completed.

If France were allowed to side with Russia, and they crushed Japan, the result might be a renewal of the triple understanding—viz., Russia, France, and Germany. Those three Powers would become supreme in China, and we should go to the wall.

If Russia alone, or in combination with France, defeated Japan, and we came to the rescue to prevent the obliteration of Japan, we should incur the lasting enmity of Russia and France, and a defeated, and probably ungrateful, Japan would not be of much use to us as against Russian encroachments.

It has been suggested that if Japan defeated Russia there would be grave danger to European interests in the Far East.

A great military and naval Power, with unbounded natural resources and an immense population such as Russia, is not likely to accept defeat permanently. She would reorganise for a further trial of strength, but such trial might be a long way off, and it would be greatly retarded by Japan being allowed to take as the spoils of war the Liaotung Peninsula. Its possession by Japan would be a guarantee that there would be no reconciliation between Russia and Japan. This would be an advantage to England and Europe. The yellow danger would be kept in check by Russia and the Russian danger by Japan.

If we do nothing to encourage Japan to look to us as a friend and possible ally against Russia and France, we may drive her to a policy of despair, in which she may come to some sort of terms with Russia. I do not say that it is probable, but it is possible, and our interests would greatly suffer if she did.

FRANCIS BERTIE.

No. 55.

The Marquess of Lansdowne to Sir F. Lascelles.

F.O. Germany (Prussia) 1523.   *Foreign Office, March* 13, 1901.
Tel. (No. 73.)   D. 6·15 P.M.
     Your telegram No. 14 of 7th.
     My telegram No. 70 of 9th.
     Japanese Government state to us that the German Government have informed their Minister at Berlin that they discountenance any action on the part of any single Power to turn the present situation to its own use, and that they therefore entirely disapprove Russian proceedings in regard to Manchuria; that as they are well aware of the vital importance of the Manchurian question to Japan, Germany will observe benevolent neutrality in case matters should come to a crisis, and that this attitude of Germany will keep the French fleet in check, while England will probably support Japan.
     The Japanese Government ask us how far Japan may rely upon the support of England. H.M. Government earnestly desire that there should be no misunderstanding between them and the German Government as to the attitude which they might respectfully adopt in certain eventualities and before they can reply to the Japanese Government, they wish to know whether the attitude of Germany is correctly described in the communication made to us by them, and, if so, in what will consist the benevolent neutrality of Germany and how it will keep the French fleet in check.
     Please enquire and telegraph at once.

No. 56.

Sir E. Monson to the Marquess of Lansdowne.

F.O. France 3533.
(No. 98.) Secret.   *Paris,* D. *March* 13, 1901.
My Lord,   R. *March* 14, 1901.
     I have not as yet succeeded in obtaining any information as to the existence of any fresh arrangement between France and Russia with regard to the obligations reciprocally contracted for military support outside of Europe. If any such fresh arrangement has been made, it has been done so quietly that the French Press at any rate has been led to ignore it.
     Pending my being successful in obtaining information on this point, I think it as well to advert briefly to the question put to me in your Lordship's telegram No. 27, Very Secret, of the 9th instant as to the probable disposition of France to give active support to Russia in the event of war between the latter and Japan. . . . . [Internal affairs.]
     It cannot be said that there is any enthusiasm over the China Expedition. Doubtless there was during the period of suspense as to the fate of the Foreign Legations at Peking as keen anxiety at Paris as in every other European capital. But once the safety of the besieged foreigners was known to be assured, interest in the general situation greatly diminished; and at this moment there seems to be more apprehension as to the extent to which German and Russian enterprise may drag the other Powers into further adventure, than satisfaction at the enforced participation of France in the complicated undertaking to which these Powers stand committed.
     Enthusiasm for the Russian Alliance has so cooled down in France that it appears to flame up only when the occasion serves to accentuate the animosity against England. That animosity is, I need not say, a large element in the stock-in-trade of the Nationalists; and it is the possibility of their employing it with success in stirring

up public opinion that constitutes, in my mind, the real danger to be considered in estimating the contingencies of French action in the Far East. . . . . [Details follow.]

I have, &c.
EDMUND MONSON.

No. 57.

Mr. Gubbins to the Marquess of Lansdowne.

F.O. China (Corea) 1513.
(No. 12.) Very Confidential.   *Seoul*, D. *March* 13, 1901.
My Lord,   R. *April* 29, 1901.

In the course of a visit which I paid to the Japanese Minister to-day, I took the opportunity to refer to the repeated rumours that in spite of the assurance given by M. Pavloff to the Emperor on the occasion of his audience on the 6th ultimo, which I had the honour to report to your Lordship in my despatch No. 7, Confidential, of the 13th ultimo, the Russian Government had expressed themselves in favour of Corea being placed under an International Protectorate.

Mr. Hayashi informed me that these rumours were true.(¹) The Russian Government had, he said, made a formal proposal for the neutralisation of Corea to the Japanese Government through the Russian Minister in Tokyo. The Japanese Government had replied through the Japanese Minister at St. Petersburgh declining the proposal, on the ground that the internal condition of Corea made it undesirable for the present at least to entertain any such proposition. Mr. Kato had at the same time communicated the substance of this reply to M. Iswolsky, who was thereupon instructed by his Government to explain that the proposal made through him was not intended to be a formal proposal, but merely a suggestion.

Mr. Hayashi said that he could not recollect the exact date of this proposal, but that it was made during his recent visit to Japan, and he added that your Lordship had been informed of what had passed through the Japanese Minister in London. He also gave as a reason for the refusal of his Government to entertain the Russian proposal, the probability of the neutralisation of Corea in the present backward condition of the country resulting in the creation of a second Egypt in the Far East.

I have, &c.
JOHN H. GUBBINS.

(¹) [*V.* memorandum of Baron Hayashi to Lord Lansdowne of the 29th January, 1901, No. 42, p. 34.]

[*ED. NOTE.*—A memo. by Mr. Tower on the Russian occupation of the Treaty Port of Newchang up to evacuation in September 1901 is printed in *Accounts and Papers*, 1904 (*Cd.* 1936) CX, pp. 161–5.]

No. 58.

Sir F. Plunkett to the Marquess of Lansdowne.

Vienna, March 15, 1901.
F.O. Austria 1313.   D. 6·50 P.M.
Tel. (No. 12.) Confidential.   R. *midnight.*

Your despatch No. 33.

As far as I can gather the view held by Austro-Hungarian Government is that France could not refuse the support of the French fleet to Russia in case Japanese should resist by force Russian pretensions in Manchuria, but they believe that French disapprove of Russian action and that support of French fleet would be very half-hearted.

Austro-Hungarian Government do not expect the proceedings of Russia will be pushed to the length of bringing on war, but Russia is breaking up the co-operation of all the Powers at Peking and has thus greatly increased the dangers and difficulties for Europeans in China.

Austria is disgusted but has no desire to take active action for interfering with what she cannot prevent.

No. 59.

Sir F. Lascelles to the Marquess of Lansdowne.

F.O. Germany (Prussia) 1520.
(No. 63.)   Secret.   *Berlin*, D. *March* 15, 1901.
My Lord,   R. *March* 18, 1901.

The Austro-Hungarian Ambassador called on me this afternoon having just left the Reichstag, where he had heard Count Bülow's speech on the situation in China which will form the subject of a further despatch.

M. de Szoegyenyi said that the speech contained nothing that we did not know before, and was, in fact, an amplification of a despatch recently sent to Count Hatzfeldt, which had been secretly communicated to him by Baron von Richthofen, and he considered that it was most satisfactory that the statement of the views of the German Government should, in the first instance, be addressed to the German Ambassador in London, as this showed their desire to act in harmony with His Majesty's Government.

I told M. de Szoegyenyi that I did not doubt that the German Government really desired to be on good terms with us, but that I had the impression that they would be by no means displeased if a conflict should break out between Russia on the one hand and Great Britain and Japan on the other. If such a conflict were to break out I believed that the sympathies of the German Government would be on the side of England and Japan, but I was convinced that Germany would remain a neutral spectator of the struggle. I quite understood that Germany, from her geographical position, could not afford to quarrel with Russia herself, but would be glad if the Russian aggressions in China were stopped by other Powers.

M. de Szoegyenyi replied that, in his opinion, the view I had taken of the situation was correct. Germany could not adopt a hostile attitude towards Russia, but would be glad if other Powers would, to use Prince Bismarck's expression, "pull the chestnuts out of the fire."

I observed that, in spite of the wishes of the German Government that "other Powers" should bear the brunt of the fighting, I trusted that a conflict would be avoided, as I was convinced that no Power had any inclination to go to war, and I was glad to see that the German Government inclined to the opinion that there was no immediate danger of war, and that Russia would not proceed to extremities at present.

I have, &c.

FRANK C. LASCELLES.

No. 60.

The Marquess of Lansdowne to Sir C. MacDonald.

F.O. Japan 538.
(No. 28.) Confidential.

Sir,
                                    Foreign Office, March 19, 1901.

The Japanese Minister called here to-day and stated that the following amendments to the Manchurian Agreement had been proposed by Count Lamsdorff to the Chinese Minister at St. Petersburgh :—

Article 4. In view of the fact that China attacked Russia, and for the purpose of ensuring the protection and construction of the Manchurian Railway, and to prevent a repetition of disturbances on the Russian frontier, China shall, after consultation with Russia, determine the number of troops and the places where they are to be stationed in Manchuria. The prohibition of importation into Manchuria of arms and ammunitions to be regulated in accordance with common agreement to be made with the Powers. In the meantime, China shall, of her own accord, prohibit such importation as a temporary measure.

Article 5. In order to secure peace in Manchuria, any Governor-General or high local official who has acted, or may act, improperly in regard to foreign relations shall at once be removed to another post upon a representation made by Russia. China may maintain infantry and cavalry for police purposes, the strength of which is to be determined in consultation with Russia until the complete pacification of Manchuria; but no artillery shall be permitted. and only Chinese shall be employed in those functions.

Article 7. The local authorities in the vicinity of the neutral zone, provided in Article V of the Convention for the lease of territory in Liao-tung, shall make special Regulations to maintain peace and order.

Article 8. China shall not, without previous consultation with Russia, grant to any other Power, or its subjects, railway and mining Concessions or any commercial advantages in the whole territory of Manchuria.

Article 10. The indemnities to be paid in compensation for the destruction of the railway and the property of the employés of the Railway Company, and also for the losses from the delay of work, shall be adjusted between China and the Railway Company, in accordance with the principles of assessment to be agreed upon between the foreign Representatives at Peking and to be approved by the Powers.

Article 12. The building of a railway into Manchuria from Shanhaikwan to Newchwang and Sin-min-ting with money borrowed from a private Company during September 1898 is in contravention of the previous Agreement between China and Russia. As compensation for this breach, and in order to speedily restore tranquillity in Manchuria, China shall concede to the Chinese Eastern Railway Company the right to build a railway from the main or branch line of its railway, extending it to the Great Wall on the boundary between Manchuria and the Province of Chihli.

Articles 1, 2, 3, 9, and 11 are maintained as originally drafted, while Article 6 has been entirely eliminated.

The Russian Minister for Foreign Affairs declared to the Chinese Minister that he would withdraw the draft if it were not signed within two weeks from the 13th March.

Baron Hayashi stated that a special Convention such as was being separately negotiated by Russia was held by the Japanese Government to be contrary to the principle of solidarity which at present united the Powers, and that such a separate Convention would materially lessen the capacity of China to meet her obligations towards the Powers. He was therefore instructed to state that the Japanese Government would be ready to join His Majesty's Government, should they hold the same view, in again advising the Chinese Government not to sign the amended draft of the Convention.

He added that his Government were of opinion that such advice renewed by the two Governments, and possibly also by the German Government, would be very effective.

I told Baron Hayashi that His Majesty's Government would repeat to the Chinese Government the warning already given in regard to separate Agreements with individual Powers, and that they would advise China not to sign the amended draft.

I am, &c.
LANSDOWNE.

[Already printed in *Accounts and Papers*, 1904 (*Cd.* 1936) CX, pp. 145–6.]

No. 61.

Sir C. MacDonald to the Marquess of Lansdowne.

Tokyo, March 22, 1901.

F.O. Japan 542.
Tel. (No. 10.) Secret.

D. 12·50 P.M.
R. 6 P.M.

Yesterday the Minister for Foreign Affairs informed me he had seen the Chinese Minister here and spoken to him in the strongest manner respecting the amended agreement which he said was aimed at sovereignty of China, and would certainly *lead to partition, for Japan would assuredly make similar demands to those* in amended agreement. Instructions to use similar language had been sent to Japanese Agents at Peking, Nanking and Hankow. Minister for Foreign Affairs is, however, not sanguine that our protests will have any effect, and is of opinion that China, through fear of Russia, will sign amended agreement.

He is distrustful of Germany, and thinks that she would like to see Japan involved in a war with Russia, basing his opinion on language held by German Government to Japanese Minister at Berlin respecting benevolent neutrality reported in your telegram No. 35.

Minister for Foreign Affairs said that if the French fleet could be kept in check matters might be different, but *unaided Japan had no intention to go to war over the Manchurian Question.* If Korea was touched he did not see how a war could be avoided.

Minister for Foreign Affairs begged I would treat his remarks as very confidential.

Sent to Peking.

No. 62.

Sir F. Plunkett to the Marquess of Lansdowne.

Vienna, March 25, 1901.

F O. Austria 1313.
Tel. (No. 17.)

D. 1·55 P.M.
R. 3 P.M.

Japanese Minister called again yesterday to try and find out how far His Majesty's Government intend going in regard to Manchuria. I expressed inability to give such information.

I gather from his language that Japan cares about Manchuria only in so far as Newchwang property concerned.

Any Russian encroachment on Corea would be resisted by Japan, and he feared in such a case that France would be obliged to support Russia with her fleet.

No. 63.

Sir C. Scott to the Marquess of Lansdowne.

St. Petersburg, March 26, 1901.

F.O. Russia 1625.

Tel. (No. 45.) Very Confidential.

D. 8·30 p.m.

R. 10 p.m.

Japanese Minister tells me that he had an interview with Count Lamsdorff yesterday, and under instructions told him the opinion of his Government as to the danger of separate agreements being concluded between China and any individual Power at this moment. He said that his Government, desirous as always to act in cordial relations with Russia, wished to tell him that Japanese as well as other Governments had been asked by China for their good offices with regard to the draft agreement respecting Manchuria which she was being pressed to sign within a specified time. Some articles appeared to Japan to affect the sovereignty and integrity of China and also certain treaty rights of other Powers. They wished, therefore, to make the friendly proposal that the draft before signature should be considered by the treaty Powers acting together in Peking. Count Lamsdorff politely but firmly declined to entertain any such proposal, as this agreement, which solely concerned two independent States, must be concluded without the intervention of any other Powers. He could, however, give the Japanese Minister the official assurance that the proposed agreement did not affect the sovereignty or integrity of China in Manchuria nor the treaty rights of any other Powers, and that it was of a provisional character and a necessary preliminary to the evacuation by the Russian troops, and he was anxious for its early signature in order to admit of its publication and thus remove all the unjust suspicions which had been aroused by fake reports with regard to it. As Count Lamsdorff begged Japanese Minister to submit his report of this conversation to him before sending it to his Government, the latter has requested me to consider the information as strictly confidential for the present.

[Paraphrased in *Accounts and Papers*, 1904 (*Cd.* 1936) CX, p. 148, last sentence omitted.]

No. 64.

Consul-General Fraser to the Marquess of Lansdowne.

F.O. China 1492.

Tel. (No. 9.)

Hankow, D. April 3, 1901.

At an interview the Viceroy asked me to submit to your Lordship by telegraph his Excellency's views on the subject of your Lordship's telegram No. 3, of 1 April, as follows :—

The Manchurian draft convention is not only so full of objectionable provisions that in the Viceroy's opinion its satisfactory amendment is out of the question, but it is "a separate agreement with an individual Power." To communicate the draft to the Foreign representatives at Peking would imply that it might possibly be accepted in some modified form. In addition to this objection the Court has been convinced by Li Hung-Chang that such publication of the text would be considered by Russia a *casus belli*. Seeing that, according to Li Hung-Chang, Russia announced that, failing the acceptance of her draft agreement within the time set by her, she would drop the question of restoring Manchuria to China, the Viceroy deems it preferable that the Chinese Plenipotentiaries be instructed officially to request the Ministers of the Powers at Peking to include in their deliberations the settlement of the situation in Manchuria.

E

It appears to his Excellency that by thus laying aside the proposed agreement China would leave Russia no pretext for exasperation with her and would likewise make it easier for Russia to back out of the overbearing attitude that she has at present taken up. The requisite Imperial orders could, his Excellency is sure, be obtained if your Lordship approves of this step.

No. 65.

The Marquess of Lansdowne to Sir C. Scott.

F.O. Russia 1618.
(No. 95.)

Sir,   *Foreign Office, April 5, 1901.*([1])

The Russian Minister called to-day and handed to Sir T. Sanderson a communication, copy of which is enclosed, announcing the intention of the Russian Government not to proceed further with the Manchurian Agreement, but to await the development of events, remaining faithful to the programme which they had followed from the beginning.

M. Lessar dwelt at some length on the exceptional position of Russia towards China, of her having been attacked by the latter and forced to occupy Manchuria, of her anxiety to bring the occupation to a speedy termination, and of the impossibility of submitting to the Ministers at Peking the special arrangements intended to effect that object.

He thought that the Chinese would suffer in the end by their opposition to the Agreement, and made some observations as to the immense expense to which Russia had been put.

I am, &c.
LANSDOWNE.

([1]) [A similar communication was made by Baron Eckardstein on this day to Lord Lansdowne.]

Enclosure in No. 65.

Memorandum communicated by Russian Embassy.

F.O. Russia 1634.   *April 5, 1901.*

Il y a quelque temps le Gouvernement Impérial est entré en pourparlers avec la Chine au sujet d'un Arrangement en vue de pouvoir procéder, dès que les circonstances le permettraient, à l'accomplissement graduel de l'intention exprimée par la Russie de restituer la Mandchourie à la Chine. Il est évident que dans ce but il était indispensable de savoir à une certaine date s'il était possible d'établir d'un commun accord avec le Gouvernement Chinois les conditions de l'évacuation de cette province.

Comme il appert des renseignements reçus, dans les circonstances actuelles un pareil accord, au lieu de servir de preuve manifeste des sentiments amicaux de la Russie envers la Chine, pourrait causer à cette dernière de graves difficultés. Aussi le Cabinet Impérial non seulement n'insiste pas auprès du Gouvernement Chinois sur la conclusion de l'Arrangement, mais se refuse même à tous pourparlers ultérieurs à ce sujet, et inébranlablement fidèle au programme qu'il a poursuivi depuis le commencement, attendra avec calme le développement des événements.

No. 66.

The Marquess of Lansdowne to Sir E. Satow.

F.O. China 1482.   *Foreign Office, April 5*, 1901.
Tel.   (No. 101.)   Confidential.   D. 5·35 P.M.

I learn from a confidential source that Russian Government does not intend to insist further on conclusion of Manchurian Agreement.

I understand that they say that they will await development of events and adhere to programme already announced.

No. 67.

The Marquess of Lansdowne to Sir E. Satow.

F.O. China 1482.
Tel.   (No. 103.)   *Foreign Office, April 5*, 1901.

The Chinese Minister has communicated telegrams from the Viceroy at Nanking and from Sheng Taotai.

The former states that he has communicated the draft agreement to the various Governments, and asks that His Majesty's Government will request the Russian Government to submit it to arbitration.

The latter states that the Russian Government are discussing the conversion of Manchuria into a Russian Province, and asks what steps China should take to prevent the execution of this threat.

I have informed the Chinese Minister that the strength of the Chinese Government is to sit still, and that His Majesty's Government would not help by interceding with Russia or suggesting arbitration.

That His Majesty's Government await the communication of the draft Agreement and that in the meanwhile, the fact of Russia remaining in Manchuria does not really alter the situation, that China has been wise in refusing to enter into separate agreements, and that, if she will invite the Powers to examine conjointly any Agreements of the sort, His Majesty's Government would instruct you to join in considering it and the action which China should take.

I repeated that the probable result of making one separate Agreement would be that other Powers would follow suit, and that each will have to take what it wants in order that it may not suffer relatively to the rest.

Instruct Mr. Brenan to inform Viceroy and Sheng Taotai, and repeat to Tokyo.

No. 68.

The Marquess of Lansdowne to Sir C. Scott.

F.O. Russia 1624.   *Foreign Office, April 5*, 1901.
Tel.   (No. 92.)   D. 7·5 P.M.

The Russian Minister has made following communication.

The Russian Government had entered into pourparlers with China for an arrangement under which the gradual restitution of Manchuria to China would have taken place.

It appeared, however, that such an arrangement instead of serving as a proof of Russia's friendliness to China might cause her great difficulties.

The Russian Government therefore not only does not insist on the conclusion of the arrangement but declines any future pourparlers on this subject.

Russia remains unalterably faithful to the programme pursued from the beginning and awaits the development of events.

No. 69.

The Marquess of Lansdowne to Consul-General Fraser.

F.O. China 1492.
Tel. (No. 5.) *Foreign Office, April* 5, 1901.
Your telegram of 3rd instant (Manchurian Agreement). We are in entire agreement with the Viceroy as to the object to be attained and he should advise the Court as he thinks best in regard to procedure to be followed.

The esential thing is that the Court should not sanction the draft agreement with Russia until it has been examined by the Foreign Representatives in Conference at Peking.

Inform the Viceroy and repeat your telegram and my answer to Peking and Tokyo.

No. 70.

The Marquess of Lansdowne to Sir F. Lascelles.

F.O. Germany (Prussia) 1518.
(No. 127.) Confidential.
Sir, *Foreign Office, April* 5, 1901.
Baron Eckardstein made the following communication to-day for the confidential information of His Majesty's Government :—

The Russian Ambassador at Berlin called at the German Foreign Office yesterday afternoon, and made, under instructions from his Government, a statement to the effect that the Russian Government had the intention, by the Agreement with China, to arrange for the gradual retrocession of Manchuria.

Meanwhile, however, the Russian Government had learnt that the Agreement had given rise to the spreading of false reports, and caused, therefore, some uneasiness. This Agreement, which was to have been a proof of the friendly sentiments of Russia towards the Celestial Empire, would, therefore, only have caused trouble to China. Having regard to this consideration, the Russian Government did not intend to insist any further on the conclusion of the Agreement, and would not continue the negotiations on the subject. Russia would await with calmness the development of matters, and adhere at the same time to her programme which she had already announced.

The Russian Ambassador gave Baron Richthofen to understand that an announcement of Russian policy in China would shortly be published in the " Official Messenger."

I am, &c.
LANSDOWNE.

No. 71.

Sir C. MacDonald to the Marquess of Lansdowne.

Tokyo, April 6, 1901.
F.O. Japan 542. D. 5·50 P.M.
Tel. (No. 16.) Secret. R. 10·30 P.M.
My telegram No. 14.
Minister for Foreign Affairs informed me of a conversation he had with Russian Minister on the 4th instant. Latter requested views of Japanese Government in detail respecting Count Lamsdorff's answer to their representations regarding

Manchurian Agreement. Foreign Minister said he could not give views of his Government, but if Russian Minister made a special request he would give him his own private views. Russian Minister assenting, M. Kato said these representations having been made at the request of China, one of the two independent States negotiating the agreement, Japan could not be accused of meddling, and for Russia to refuse even to consider suggestions made in a friendly spirit was a severe rebuff calculated to lead to a breach of diplomatic relations, and could, if Japan's intentions were not so pacific, be taken very seriously.

Secondly, when after the Chinese war, Japan was in possession of portion of South Manchuria, Russia stated that continued possession of such territory would interfere with the independence of Corea and was calculated to disturb the peace of the Far East. Russia now by this agreement proposed to enter into possession of the whole of Manchuria.

Thirdly, the conditions of the Manchurian agreement, which agreement was in possession of the Japanese Government would most certainly affect the sovereignty of China and her treaty rights with other Powers.

Russian Minister made no reply.

Though above are M. Kato's private views I think they are shared by rest of Cabinet.

No. 72.

Sir F. Lascelles to the Marquess of Lansdowne.

F.O. Germany (Prussia) 1520.
(No. 94.) Very Confidential.   *Berlin,* D. *April* 11, 1901.
My Lord,   R. *April* 15, 1901.

The Special Mission. under the Duke of Abercorn, to announce the King's accession, arrived in Berlin on the night of the 7th instant, and was received in a special audience by the Emperor at noon on the 9th instant and entertained by His Majesty at dinner on the evening of the same day.

I had later the honour of an Audience of His Majesty for the purpose of presenting the Letter by which the King accredited me as his Ambassador to His Majesty, when I ventured to express the hope that His Majesty would approve the passage in the Royal Letter in which the King had referred to my conduct heretofore as having met with His Majesty's approval.

The Emperor, who was personally most gracious and cordial, deigned to express his satisfaction at my reappointment because he was always able to speak to me perfectly freely and openly. This remark which was addressed quite as much to Baron von Richthofen, who was present at the Audience, as it was to me, was probably made intentionally to prepare me for what was coming.

I thanked His Majesty for his kindness in speaking openly and freely to me, and also for allowing me to answer in an equally open manner, and His Majesty then proceeded to act up to his words by indulging in a severe criticism of His Majesty's Government with whom he was sorely disappointed. They not only invariably rejected any suggestion he might make, but they would not even answer the questions he put to them with regard to their policy in the Far East. It was painful to him to see the diminution of England's prestige which was merely due to the fact that His Majesty's Government would not take advantage of the opportunities offered to them. They had displeased the Japanese who now felt that they could not count upon the support of England against Russia. Was it likely His Majesty asked that so favourable an opportunity for resisting the encroachments of Russia would occur again? At present the Japanese forces in the Far East were superior to those of Russia, but the latter would be continually increased and three years hence Russia would be supreme. It would then be too late, and His Majesty's Government would find that English prestige and influence was gone. This would certainly be the case unless His Majesty's Government bestirred themselves and ceased to believe the assurances which Count Lamsdorff gave to His Majesty's Ambassador at St. Petersburg, who received them with implicit faith. He had been deeply hurt to learn that one of His Majesty's Ministers, and one for whom he had hitherto entertained a kindly feeling, had recently expressed a suspicion that His Majesty might have entered into some secret arrangement with Russia, and considering all the efforts he had made to bring about friendly relations with England he could only regard this suspicion as an insult. It seemed, however, that he was to be distrusted whilst Count Lamsdorff was to be believed, and what would be the result? Russia was advancing all along the line, she had already secured a position of influence in Persia which formerly belonged to England, and very shortly she would make her appearance in the Persian Gulf, and then His Majesty expected to be told by his English friends that it was all his fault.

I did not attempt to stem His Majesty's torrent of eloquence or to enter into a discussion with His Majesty, and after some ineffectual attempts to ascertain the name of the Minister who had been unfortunate enough to incur His Majesty's displeasure—a point on which he declined to satisfy my curiosity—I said I should not fail to report His Majesty's language to your Lordship as faithfully as I could, even to the extent of repeating textually some of the expressions he had used and I turned the conversation by asking permission to deliver a personal message with which the King had charged me on my taking leave of His Majesty at Frankfurt at the conclusion of his recent visit to the Empress Frederick.

After presenting some recently arrived members of my staff to the Emperor and subsequently to the Empress who held a " cercle " in the adjoining room, I had the honour of being invited to join the Emperor and several of his guests in the smoking room. Here again His Majesty renewed the conversation with much animation. He reminded me of the assurances given by Russia with regard to Khiva and Merv, assurances which were accepted in England as a security against a further Russian advance towards India. Now Russia was on the Pamirs on the very frontier of India. She would continue advancing and England did nothing to stop her. This gave me the opportunity of asking His Majesty what he considered we ought to have done. He replied that if England did not understand her own business it was not for him to dictate her policy but it was painful to him to see the diminution of the influence and prestige of England which in his opinion was due to the neglect of His Majesty's Government to take advantage of their opportunities.

His Majesty told me that the Russian Ambassador in announcing the decision of his Government not to press for the signature of the Manchurian Agreement, had observed to Baron von Richthofen with rather a jaunty air that the policy of being friends with England did not seem to have brought much advantage to Germany but had been met with the very excellent reply that Germany's policy was dictated solely by German interests.

His Majesty also alluded to the Anglo-German Agreement which he called the Yangtse Agreement, and which I must know perfectly well was not intended to apply to Manchuria, and he referred to a conversation which he had had with your Lordship when he was in England in which he thought he had made it clear that, in the event of complications arising in the Far East, he intended to observe a benevolent but strict neutrality and he had certainly understood at the time that His Majesty's Government were prepared to do more than that.

During the whole of these two conversations His Majesty's manner was most friendly and cordial, and his language though strong did not betray any signs of anger. The impression left upon my mind is that His Majesty regrets that His Majesty's Government did not afford more active encouragement to the Japanese and that he is really distressed at being treated with suspicion.

I have, &c.

FRANK C. LASCELLES.

No. 73.

Sir T. H. Sanderson to Sir E. Satow.

Private.([1])   *April* 12, 1901.

You will be pleased to read that according to Lamsdorff there never was any draft of a Manchurian Agreement but only a programme of points to be discussed. Really the Russians are occasionally, to use their own term, colossal.

They are very friendly at this moment, notwithstanding their check. I fancy the Czar is all in favour of working on a good understanding with us, and has impressed this on his Ministers—and it would be much the best plan if it could be managed. But I am afraid the military party will take any opportunity to give us a nasty one.

([1]) From the private papers of Sir E. Satow.

No. 74.

Sir F. Lascelles to the Marquess of Lansdowne.

F.O. Germany (Prussia) 1520.
(No. 95.)   Very Confidential.   *Berlin, D. April* 12, 1901.
My Lord,   R. *April* 15, 1901.

I had a long conversation last night with Baron von Richthofen whom I met at an entertainment given by the Duke of Abercorn. He told me that the Emperor had given him an account of his conversation with me on the previous evening at a portion only of which he had been present, and I was gratified to find that His Majesty's account agreed entirely with my recollection of the conversation as reported in my preceding despatch.

Baron von Richthofen asked me what I thought of His Majesty's language. I replied that I was grateful for the gracious and friendly remarks which His Majesty had made to me personally. but that it was evident that His Majesty was very much displeased with the King's Government, as far as I could judge for not going to war with Russia.

Baron von Richthofen said that he did not understand that the Emperor had any idea of war between England and Russia but had probably thought that a firmer support of Japan by His Majesty's Government would have led to more satisfactory results. On my asking whether he really believed that Russia would have evacuated Manchuria without being forcibly compelled to do so, his Excellency shrugged his shoulders and observed that Japan had a stronger force in China than Russia. He thought however that what had most deeply impressed the Emperor and had led to such severe criticism was the report that an English Minister had expressed distrust of him. This was especially painful to His Majesty after the efforts he had made to establish friendly relations with us.

I observed that I had given prominence to this point in the telegram which I had addressed to your Lordship and would certainly bear it in mind in the detailed report of the conversation as I understood that it might have had considerable weight with the Emperor. I then alluded to the complimentary terms in which the Emperor had spoken of his Excellency's answer to the Russian Ambassador when he came to announce that the Russian Government had decided not to press for the signature of the Manchurian Agreement but to remain in the occupation of Manchuria.

Baron von Richthofen said that the announcement seemed to have been made in a different spirit in London and Berlin. In London an attempt had been made by the Russian Embassy to indicate that the action of the Russian Government was a friendly act towards England. Here on the other hand Count Osten Sacken had referred to the want of success which Germany had met with in her attempts to please England. Baron von Richthofen had thereupon pointed out that on three questions the action of Russia had been distinctly unfavourable to Germany, viz.: the withdrawal of the troops, the Tien-tsin concession which might interfere with German projects and the Manchurian Arrangement. Russia must therefore not be astonished if Germany followed the lead she had given her and shaped her policy solely in accordance with German interests.

I told Baron von Richthofen that I had been much struck during the Emperor's conversation by the similarity between the language he now held and that which he had used in a conversation with me towards the end of 1898 (see my despatch No. 338 of the 21st December, 1898, and subsequent despatches). Then the Emperor believed in the imminence of a war between England and France, and his language then might have been regarded as an incitement to us to go to war. Now although I did not suppose that His Majesty believed in the imminence of a war between England and Russia, his language might certainly bear the interpretation that in His Majesty's opinion we were wrong not to go to war. In both instances there was the same reproach that England did not take advantage of her opportunities.

Baron von Richthofen said that his attention had been called by one of his employees to the conversation to which I had alluded, and he had that very day read the account which the Emperor had given of it. He also had been struck by the similarity of the language which the Emperor had used on both occasions, but he would not admit that it amounted to an incitement to war, and I at all events was acquainted with the Emperor's habit of a certain exaggeration of expression. He believed that His Majesty's language might be explained partly by the non-acceptance by His Majesty's Government of the financial proposals which Dr. Stuebel had recently been charged to make with the view of bringing the Chinese question to an end, and partly, and perhaps more especially, by a report which had reached him, from what quarter Baron von Richthofen did not know, that one of the King's Ministers had cast a doubt on the sincerity of his friendship for England.

I have, &c.

FRANK C. LASCELLES.

No. 75.

The Marquess of Lansdowne to Sir E. Satow.

F.O. China 1483.
Tel. (No. 334.)   *Foreign Office, November* 13, 1901.
Your telegram No. 353 (of 9th November).
Reply to the Viceroys in the following sense :—

Their criticisms on the alleged Agreement have been attentively considered by His Majesty's Government. If the text is as reported some of these criticisms are certainly justified. Any monopoly of mining or commercial rights in Manchuria would be inconsistent with the Treaty rights enjoyed by Great Britain and other Powers, who would be unable to recognise the validity of such a grant and would probably have to reserve the right of compensating themselves at the expense of China for any detriment occasioned to them.

The payment of a further indemnity over and above the four hundred and fifty millions of taels on account of injury to the railways seemed to be inconsistent with Article 6 of the Protocol.

The provisions for the gradual evacuation of Manchuria and for arrangements pending the completion of that evacuation appear to be framed in such a manner as to restrict the sovereign rights of China.

On the other hand, Russia cannot be expected to withdraw at once and without precautions from territories which have been the scene of serious disturbances and which so closely adjoin her possessions, and the necessary provisional arrangements pending evacuation can scarcely fail to involve some derogation from the sovereign rights of China.

The policy of His Majesty's Government remains unaltered. It is well known that we desire to maintain the integrity and independence of the Chinese Empire, and other Powers are believed to favour a similar policy.

In these circumstances we shall be glad to consult with the Viceroys as to the best means of inducing the Chinese Government to bring these questions to the collective notice of the Powers.

You can ask the Viceroys how the terms now asked by Russia compare with those demanded last year.

Repeat to Tokyo.

No. 76.

Mr. C. Hardinge to the Marquess of Lansdowne.

F.O. Russia 1623.
(No. 331.) Very Confidential. *St. Petersburgh,* D. *November* 26, 1901.
My Lord, R. *December* 2, 1901.

I have the honour to report that I learned to-day indirectly from a Russian official source, which has hitherto proved trustworthy, that the negotiations which have for some time been in progress in Peking for the conclusion of a Convention for the evacuation of the Province of Manchuria by the Russians have come to a standstill, and that there is not much prospect of an agreement being arrived at.

The Russian Government were fully disposed to discuss the terms of the Agreement with Prince Ching, but it appears that the Chinese Government now refuse to accept the Russian terms. The attitude of the Chinese Government is said to be due to the opposition of the Japanese Government to the terms of the Convention, and in particular to that clause by which the use of Chinese artillery in the Province of Fengtien is prohibited. Count Lamsdorff is reported to be very much discouraged at receiving this second check in connection with the Manchurian Convention, and of the unwelcome necessity of maintaining the occupation of Manchuria, which I fully believe the Russian Government are very anxious to terminate as soon as possible on terms which shall ensure them a preponderating influence and position in that province.

The Marquis Ito arrived here yesterday, and was received at the railway station by the Japanese Legation and a Delegate of the Ministry for Foreign Affairs.

I hear from the same official source that the Marquis Ito failed in his Mission to raise a Japanese loan in Paris owing to the uncertainty which exists in the French capital as to the relations existing between Russia and Japan in connection with the Corean and Manchurian questions, and that he received encouragement from the French Government to come to St. Petersburgh in order to obtain assurances from the Russian Government which may satisfy French financiers and thereby facilitate the raising of a Japanese loan in Paris. I gather that it is hoped at the Ministry for Foreign Affairs that the presence of the Marquis Ito in St. Petersburgh may facilitate an arrangement between the Japanese and Russian Governments by which Japanese obstruction to Russian projects in Manchuria may be withdrawn in consideration for Concessions to Japan in Corea.

I have, &c.
CHARLES HARDINGE.

[*ED. NOTE.*—The developments in regard to Manchuria during 1902 and up to April 1903 are adequately given in *Accounts and Papers*, 1904 (*Cd.* 1936) CX, pp. 166–204.]

NOTE ON THE BOXER MOVEMENT.

[The private correspondence of Sir E. Satow here subjoined illustrates certain phases of the Boxer settlement, of which there is a reasonably full amount in the Parliamentary Papers.]

Sir T. H. Sanderson to Sir E. Satow.

March 1, 1901.

" I think you have got through it all remarkably well, although you made the blood freeze in the veins of some of us by the suggestion of turning the whole matter over to a European Conference. Those who have gone through that form of discussion look upon what you are enduring as preferable, particularly as the suffering in that case is vicarious. There are two points to be borne in mind (1) that a European Conference is useful for putting on record, or sometimes for bringing into shape, conclusions arrived at by a majority of the Powers—though the process may even then be very tedious—but that it is a very bad machinery for arriving at conclusions. (2) That a Conference in Europe in present circumstances would result in a secondary Conference sitting at Peking, and that each would constantly be referring to the other. Doomsday would find them both still sitting."

Sir E. Satow to the Marquess of Lansdowne.

March 23, 1901.

Tientsin. " In my opinion the action of the [British] Military Authorities in commencing to construct a siding across the disputed ground without a previous written understanding with the Russians was extremely imprudent."(¹)

Sir E. Satow to Sir F. Bertie.

April 11, 1901.

" Here we hoped that the Governments would have put their heads together and agreed to the principles on which war claims should be estimated. But that does not seem to have been done and the result is Germany including in her bill medals she is going to distribute and pensions to widows and orphans of soldiers, Japan asking for naval expenditure, Japan do [*i.e.*, pensions to widows and orphans of soldiers].

Sir T. H. Sanderson to Sir E. Satow.

April 12, 1901.

" The German Emperor who has I believe been very excitable since his accident is apparently furious with us for not having got into a quarrel with Russia over the business, and obviously that would have suited the Germans very well."

The Marquess of Lansdowne to Sir E. Satow.

May 31, 1901.

" I would humour the Japanese as much as possible. They are I am afraid a little sore, and perhaps not unnaturally. I wish I could help them financially, but it would be very difficult for us to guarantee their share of the bonds for them.

. . . . " I see that the German Emperor has with characteristic impetuosity assured the world that ' peace has been concluded.' "

(¹) [This refers to the Tien-tsin incident, when there was a conflict between British and Russian troops.]

Sir E. Satow to the Marquess of Lansdowne.

June 20, 1901.

" One may fairly say that, but for the British-Indian and Japanese contingents the inmates of the **Legations** would almost certainly have been starved out before the **arrival** of the relieving **columns."**

Sir E. Satow to the Marquess of Lansdowne.

July 6, 1901.

" If it is true that Lessar is to succeed him (de Giers) we may revive the idea of a general *modus vivendi* with Russia which, in my humble opinion, was so unfortunately frustrated by the New Chuang railway loan scheme, in which as it would seem from Li's remarks . . . . we were made a catspaw of by China and the political banker Mr. Hillier of Peking."

Sir E. Satow to the Marquess of Lansdowne.

August 29, 1901.

" There is every indication that once the present negotiations are over the policy of demanding concessions of China, all of which tend in the direction of disintegration, will be reverted to. It was this and not any missionary difficulties, that caused the anti-foreign outburst of last year."

The Marquess of Lansdowne to Sir E. Satow.

July 20, 1902.

" It is a nuisance to find that the weakness of the Chinese Government and the unscrupulous machinations of the Russians prevent us from clinching your agreements."

CHAPTER X.

THE ANGLO-GERMAN NEGOTIATIONS OF 1901.

[*EDITORIAL NOTE.*—Some of the documents printed in this chapter were preserved separately at the Foreign Office; others were in the ordinary files at the Record Office. No other material relating to an alliance during 1901 has been found. The Anglo-German discussions of this period are described in Eckardstein's *Erinnerungen*, 2nd edn., Vol. II, chapters 13–15, and *G.P. XVI*, chapter 106, and XVII, chapter 109. During a visit to Chatsworth, the 13th–17th January, 1901, Baron Eckardstein was assured by Mr. Chamberlain and the Duke of Devonshire that the time for "splendid isolation" was over; that England desired to settle all pending questions, especially Morocco and the Far East, in co-operation with the Triple or the Dual Alliance; that unlike some of their colleagues they would prefer the former; and that, failing agreement with the Triple Alliance, they would turn to France and Russia. The latter alternative was scouted by Baron Holstein and Count Bülow, who counselled the Emperor not to commit himself during his visit to England for the funeral of Queen Victoria. On the 7th February, Lord Lansdowne asked Baron Eckardstein whether Germany would join Great Britain and Japan in attempting to check Russia's aggressive action in China (see No. 43, p. 35), but the German Government was not disposed to antagonise Russia without substantial securities and compensations.

Lord Lansdowne's account of the conversation of the 18th March attributes the suggestion of an alliance to Baron Eckardstein, while the latter's report (*G.P. XVII*, 41–2) gives the initiative to the Foreign Minister. Baron Eckardstein, however, declares in his *Lebenserinnerungen* [2nd edn., 1920] II, 280–1, that on the 16th March, when he was Lord Lansdowne's guest at dinner, he gave his host a strong hint to come out with an offer of alliance, saying : " If there were a defensive alliance covering all eventualities, Germany would of course be in a position to localise a war between Russia and Japan by influencing France." This passage, he adds, was omitted from his telegram to Baron Holstein lest that eccentric should denounce him for going too far.

We have found no record of the interview with Count Hatzfeldt on the 22nd March (*G.P. XVII*, 46–48), when Lord Lansdowne asked the Ambassador whether he believed that his Government would be willing to make a defensive treaty with England. If so, would Germany prefer a simple defensive alliance or one merely covering an attack by two or more Powers? Should it be secret or submitted to Parliament, and should Japan be taken into consideration? On the 24th March, Count Bülow suggested that England should join the Triple Alliance, that the *casus fœderis* should be an attack by two Powers, that the Treaty should be made public, and that Japan might not care to join a purely defensive alliance. The German materials relating to the negotiations between 1898 and 1901 are summarised and discussed in Eugen Fischer's volume, *Holstein's Grosses Nein* [1925].]

No. 77.

The Marquess of Lansdowne to Sir F. Lascelles.

F.O. Germany (Prussia) 1518.

(No.   .)   Very Secret.

Sir, *Foreign Office, March* 18, 1901.

I had some conversation to-day with Baron Eckardstein on the subject of the correspondence which has recently taken place between the German and British Governments in regard to the action which the two Powers might take should Russia and Japan go to war.

I told Baron Eckardstein that your Excellency's telegram No. 17 of the 14th instant made it evident to us that the Japanese Minister at Berlin had misapprehended the purport of Herr von Mühlberg's statement to him, and that the German Government did not contemplate anything more than neutrality in the event supposed, and certainly not any action which would have the effect of keeping a third Power in check.

I added that Count Bülow's speech, which proclaimed the fact that in Germany's estimation the Anglo-German Agreement had no reference to Manchuria, seemed to me to emphasise what I had just said, and to put an end to any idea which might have been entertained as to the possibility of England and Germany combining for the purpose of "keeping a ring" for Russia and Japan.

Baron Eckardstein said that he did not differ from me, and that. speaking for himself only, he thought that no proposal of the above kind was likely to find favour at this moment.

On the other hand, he believed that the German Government, while averse from an agreement entered into solely with reference to the present situation in China, would entertain favourably the idea of an understanding of a more durable and extended character with this country.

The kind of arrangement which he contemplated might be described as a purely defensive alliance between the two Powers, directed solely against France and Russia.

So long as Germany or England were attacked by one only of the other two Powers the Alliance would not operate, but if either Germany or England had to defend itself against both France and Russia, Germany would have to help England, or England Germany, as the case might be.

He thought England, which had scattered and vulnerable possessions all over the world, was more likely to require help than Germany.

I told Baron Eckardstein that the proximity of Russia to Germany along so extensive a frontier made the situation of Germany quite as vulnerable as ours. His project was a novel and very far-reaching one, which would require careful examination, and which obviously I could not encourage without reference to my colleagues.

I said that, assuming the two Powers to be agreeable in principle to such a transaction, I saw at first sight no small difficulty in giving effect to it. Such a contract seemed to me to entail the adoption of an identic foreign policy by both Powers in all their external relations, because every complication in which one of the two might become involved might drag the other into the quarrel. It occurred to me, moreover, that it was far from easy to distinguish between the case in which a country was acting on the defensive and the case in which it was not. The first blow might be really struck in self-defence ; or, conversely, an attack might be brought on by political action of a deliberately provocative character. How were our mutual obligations to be defined so as to meet all such cases fairly?

Baron Eckardstein was careful to assure me that his suggestion was not made under instructions, but I feel no doubt that he has been desired to sound me.

[I am, &c.
LANSDOWNE.]

No. 78.

Sir F. Lascelles to the Marquess of Lansdowne.

Berlin, D. *March* 23, 1901.
(Tel.) Private.   R. *March* 23, 1901.

Your private telegram of yesterday. I cannot believe that Eckardstein would have suggested an alliance without authority. The idea is an old one dating back to August 1898 when I had a conversation with the Emperor to which he has more than once alluded as an " arrangement."(1)+ I will make enquiries and in the meantime I would suggest that Eckardstein should be reminded of a conversation I had with the Emperor in December 1898 in the course of which His Majesty endorsed Count Hatzfeldt's opinion that no formal alliance between England and Germany was necessary because if it became advisable for them to take common action the necessary arrangements could be made in a very short time. See my despatch No. 338 of 21st December, 1898.(2)

(1) [*V. supra* Vol. I, No. 122, pp. 100–1.]
(2) [*V. supra* Vol. I, No. 125, pp. 102–4.]

No. 79.

The Marquess of Lansdowne to Sir F. Lascelles.

F.O. Germany (Prussia) 1518.
(No. 110A.) Secret.
Sir,   *Foreign Office, March* 29, 1901.

I told Baron Eckardstein to-day that, owing to the Prime Minister's illness, I had been unable to make any further progress with the discussion of the subject which he had mentioned to me on the 18th March, as recorded in my despatch of that date, and on a subsequent occasion. I knew that Lord Salisbury's attitude towards the proposal was one of caution, and I therefore felt that without instructions from him I could not safely say much.

But I was aware, from conversation with my colleagues, that while on the one hand they cordially desired that there should be a good and well-assured understanding between England and Germany, directed towards the maintenance of peace and mutual protection against aggressive combinations on the part of other Powers, they regarded with a certain amount of apprehension the idea of an international arrangement of the somewhat indefinite but very far-reaching character which he had suggested to me. If the matter was to be advanced we ought to endeavour to form a more precise conception of the contingencies for which we desired to provide. There was one which he and I had already discussed, that of Japan going to war with Russia and being threatened by a combination of that Power with France. His proposal, as I had understood it, would not have provided for such a contingency, but only for cases in which either we or Germany were attacked by both Powers.

Baron Eckardstein said that in his view, if the proposed defensive alliance were to be entered into, it would virtually involve joint action in the case which I had supposed.

He told me, however, that he did not think the present moment propitious for pursuing the subject further. There was a certain amount of anti-British feeling at this moment in Berlin, and the temper of the Reichstag was irritable. Having regard to this and to Lord Salisbury's illness, he thought it wiser to leave matters alone for awhile. He was probably going to Berlin, and would speak to me again should the prospect become more favourable, perhaps after the Easter holidays.

I acquiesced, merely adding that I wished him and those with whom he was acting to know that his proposal had not been regarded with indifference or contemptuously put aside.

[I am, &c.
LANSDOWNE.]

No. 80.

The Marquess of Lansdowne to Sir F. Lascelles.

F.O. Germany (Prussia) 1518.
(No. 131A.)
Sir,   *Foreign Office, April* 9, 1901.

Baron Eckardstein told me to-day, with reference to our conversation on the 29th ultimo, recorded in my despatch of that date, that, from information received, he believed that the time had again become opportune for discussing the question of a defensive alliance between Great Britain and Germany.

I said that, until Lord Salisbury's return, I could not undertake to advance the consideration of this important subject.

I am, &c.
[LANSDOWNE.]

[Baron Eckardstein's telegram to Count Holstein on the 10th April, *Lebenserinnerungen* [2nd edn., 1920], II, 335, does not mention this exchange of opi_ion.]

No. 81.

The Marquess of Lansdowne to Sir F. Lascelles.

Private.

My dear Lascelles,   *Bowood, April 13, 1901.*

I thought it worth while to repeat to you by telegram the substance of Eckardstein's remarks as to your conversation with the Emperor. It is not always easy to determine how much of Eckardstein's communications are *de son propre cru.* On this occasion the impression left on my mind was that he had been told to say something of the sort to me, probably as a corrective of the Emperor's outburst. That performance was certainly difficult to justify. H.I.M. must have known that if we had wished to take a decided line as to Manchuria, Bülow's speech would have done more to discourage us than anything else which could have happened. But the " unmitigated noodles " must not be too quick to resent these singular ebullitions.

To come back to Eckardstein. That person, having seen the discomfiture of Stuebel, is now quite inclined to make the running again on his own account. He tells me that in his belief the time has once more become favourable for the discussion of the projects which he broached to me a few weeks ago for a defensive alliance between Great Britain and Germany, restricted to the contingency in which either Power might be threatened by a combination of other Powers. I told him that in Lord Salisbury's absence I could not take up so grave a question. He said that he understood this, and that all that had passed between us was quite unofficial, and that I must not suppose that the Emperor knew all about the communication which he was now making to me. I replied that I was perfectly aware that this conversation, like those which had preceded it, was unofficial, but that I was not sure whether I was to infer that his advances were made without any encouragement on the part of the Emperor. I had on the contrary formed an impression that H.M. Government had been sounded upon the subject of the proposed alliance with the unofficial concurrence of the Emperor. Eckardstein " hummed and ha'd " a good deal over this and finally replied that what had been done had been done with the knowledge of persons very near the Emperor, and who had means of judging H.I.M.'s ideas. He mentioned Holstein (have I spelt it right?) as one of these persons. This is perhaps worth passing on to you. I doubt whether much will come of the project. In principle the idea is good enough. But when each side comes, if it ever does, to formulate its terms, we shall break down; and I know Lord Salisbury regards the scheme with, to say the least, suspicion.

I shall be curious to see what Germany says to the American proposal. I fear they will have none of it. But unless the Powers will agree to a rough and ready compromise of the sort, I foresee an interminable wrangle, and an indefinite postponement of the withdrawal of the allied forces.

I should like to settle the indemnity question on moderate lines, without a *guaranteed* loan, and without touching the Maritime Customs save for the purpose of securing a real 5 per cent. instead of the lower rates now obtaining. Then withdraw all troops except those necessary to ensure the safety of the Legations—and then—as a new chapter in the story—take up the question of financial reform, regularisation of *li-kin*, abolition of Manchu pensions, &c., coupled with a substantial addition to the Tariff.

Stuebel was certainly not snubbed. I saw him twice—once for nearly an hour—and was most civil to him. I don't know whether Frank Bertie's logic was too unsparing for the Doctor's taste.(1) Things in Morocco look ugly. Do you hear anything?

Yours sincerely,

L.

(1) [Dr. Stuebel, Director of the Colonial Section of the German Foreign Office had visited London to discuss the raising of the Chinese maritime customs and German claims for compensation in South Africa.]

[ED. NOTE.—We have found no report of Lord Lansdowne's conversation on the 15th May, or of his reported suggestion that both parties should put on paper the draft of a Treaty. This assertion is made on the 17th May (G.P. XVII, 57–60), and signed by Count Hatzfeldt, but the conversation of the 15th must have been with Baron Eckardstein. For Count Hatzfeldt's report of the interview of the 23rd May, see G.P. XVII, 65–7.]

No. 82.

The Marquess of Lansdowne to the Marquess of Salisbury.

Dear Lord Salisbury,   *May 24, 1901.*

Please read the enclosed note of my conversation with the German Ambassador on the question of an Anglo-German Alliance.

If I remember right, you intended the project to be discussed by yourself, Balfour, Beach, Chamberlain, Devonshire and myself.

You will no doubt convene us or instruct me to do so.

And you may wish papers prepared.

Perhaps you will let the above members of the Cabinet see this last memo, when you have read it, or shall I print and distribute it? We printed my first paper.

Yours sincerely,

LANSDOWNE.

Enclosure in No. 82.

Memorandum by the Marquess of Lansdowne.

May 24, 1901.

At the time when the Prime Minister was about to leave England, and during his absence, Baron Eckardstein several times recurred to the subject of an Anglo-German Alliance or understanding, mentioned in the Very Secret paper which I submitted to some of my colleagues on the 20th March.

I told him that until Lord Salisbury's return it was impossible that the matter could be taken into consideration.

On the occasion of one of these interviews, Baron Eckardstein mentioned incidentally that Austria and Italy would have to be included in such an arrangement as he had proposed.

I said that this seemed to me a most important point. We had, I reminded him, until then, been discussing the possibility of a purely defensive alliance between England and Germany, against any other two Powers, and I had said to him that in my view the objection to such an arrangement was that this country might find itself dragged into a quarrel in which we had no concern, and which might have been in fact provoked by our ally, whose external policy might be quite beyond our control, although that ally was ostensibly defending itself from attack. These objections could, I thought, be urged with infinitely greater force if we were asked to enter into similar obligations to Austria and Italy as well as to Germany.

On the 23rd instant I had an interview with Count Hatzfeldt, whom (until the 20th instant) I had not seen for a long time, and who had expressed a desire to discuss this question with me. Baron Eckardstein had evidently repeated to him what I had said as to the extension of the Agreement to Austria and Italy. As to this, Count

Hatzfeldt said that, in his opinion, the foreign policy of Germany must always be based upon the closest intimacy with Austria. To his mind the idea of throwing Austria over was "néfaste." What it really came to was this. There would be two "unities"— one consisting of Great Britain and her numerous Colonies—the other of the members of the Triple Alliance, and the Agreement, if it was to be made at all, must be between the two groups.

Was I then, I said, to understand that the proposal was simply that we should join the Triple Alliance? Count Hatzfeldt answered in the affirmative.

We ought, he thought, to examine the bases of that alliance, and consider how far they suited our purpose.

I said that I was under the impression that the actual details of that alliance had not been communicated to us, and I was not sure that we were sufficiently informed as to its terms.

Count Hatzfeldt replied that there was nothing very mysterious about the Agreement in question. He had not got it by him, but it was perfectly natural that we should desire to consider the actual text.

During the conversation which followed, I dwelt upon the great difficulty of distinguishing clearly between the cases in which one of the allies might be attacked and those in which it might be defending itself. I also said that it seemed to me to follow from any such arrangements that each of the allies would have a right to claim a voice in guiding and controlling the external policy of the others.

I was afraid that in this country there would be a great reluctance to allow our liberty of action in regard to questions of foreign policy to be restricted in this manner.

Count Hatzfeldt did not deny that these inconveniences might result. We could not, however, expect to reap all the advantages of such an arrangement as he had proposed, without some corresponding disadvantages. Were we, he asked, prepared to continue our present "isolement"? We must be alive to the dangers which it invoked. If we recognised them, it was for our interest to join one of the two great groups into which the European Powers were divided. We might try Russia if we liked, "mais cela vous coûtera cher." As for Germany, if nothing should come of these overtures, she might find herself obliged to look elsewhere for alliances. He begged that I would not consider that when he said this he was using the language of menace, but the friction which existed between Germany and Russia was most inconvenient to his country, and it was a matter of notoriety that Russia could be easily "squared."

I promised Count Hatzfeldt that now that the Prime Minister had returned I would again lay the matter before him.

L.

No. 83.

The Marquess of Lansdowne to Sir F. Lascelles.

F.O. Germany (Prussia) 1519.
(No. 193A.) Secret.
Sir, *Foreign Office, May 24, 1901.*

In my despatches of the 18th and 29th March and 9th April I have recorded conversations with Baron Eckardstein in which the latter unofficially pressed on my attention the project of an Anglo-German Alliance.

In one of our interviews on this subject, which have recently been renewed by him, Baron Eckardstein mentioned incidentally that Austria and Italy would have to be included in such an arrangement as he proposed.

I said that this seemed to me an important point. . . . . [The rest is identical in wording with the preceding Memorandum.]

I am, &c.
[LANSDOWNE.]

No. 84.

The Marquess of Lansdowne to Baron Eckardstein.

My dear Eckardstein,   *May* 24, 1901.

I should have told you yesterday if there had not been persons present that my interesting and instructive conversation with the Ambassador in no ways diminished my desire to be favoured with the memorandum which you were good enough to promise me.

You may rely on my discretion in using it and on my undertaking to treat it as a private communication between yourself and myself.

Yours sincerely,
LANSDOWNE.

No. 85.

Memorandum by Sir T. H. Sanderson.

May 27, 1901.

I have sketched the outlines of a Convention of the kind which suggested itself at the end of our conversation on Thursday. It is, of course, open to many criticisms, but it may be useful for you to have something tangible to look at and to cut about.

I do not think you can really go far in questions of wording until you either have Eckardstein's memorandum or have seen the documents which Hatzfeldt proposes to show you.

The observations which occur to me at present are :—

There must be a certain amount of qualifying words to prevent either Party from being dragged into a quarrel of which it disapproves, and in which it would not have the necessary amount of popular support.

These qualifications are likely to be the cause of serious dispute—and the Germans will be much less scrupulous in making use of them to throw us over than we can be in leaving them in the lurch. Our public opinion would not allow it—theirs would.

However the Convention may be worded, it seems to me that it will practically amount to a guarantee to Germany of the provinces conquered from France, and that is the way in which the French will look at it. I do not see exactly what Germany will guarantee to us.

There should perhaps be some arrangement that neither Party should have the right to call upon the other to increase its armaments, but that would find its place more properly in some naval and military Agreement of a subsidiary kind.

T. H. S.

May 27, 1901.

Enclosure 1 in No. 85.

Draft Convention.

H.M. the King of the United Kingdom of Great Britain and Ireland, Emperor of India, and H.M. the German Emperor, disclaiming all aggressive intentions, and with the object of ensuring as far as possible the maintenance of the *status quo*, and of the general peace of Europe have resolved to conclude a defensive Alliance and have for that purpose appointed as their Plenipotentiaries :

Who, &c., have agreed upon the following Articles :—

Article I.

If, while pursuing the policy described in the Preamble of the present Convention, one of the High Contracting Parties should be involved in war with another Power for the defence of its legitimate interests, or in consequence of a defensive alliance contracted by it and made known to the other High Contracting Party, the said other High Contracting Party engages to maintain an attitude not less favourable than that of strict neutrality, and to take such pacific measures as may appear to it to be practicable for the purpose of preventing other Powers from attacking its Ally.

ARTICLE II.

Should, however, any other Power join unprovoked in hostile measures against the High Contracting Party so involved in war, the other High Contracting Party engages to come to the assistance of its Ally thus attacked, to support it so far as necessary and practicable with all its forces and not to make peace except with the concurrence of its Ally.

ARTICLE III.

This Convention shall remain in force for five years from the date of its signature at the expiration of which period it shall be open to renewal for a similar period. Notice of revision or of a desire to terminate the Agreement shall be given by either party a year before the expiration of this period.

ARTICLE IV.

It is agreed that this Convention shall not apply to any questions arising in the American Continent or involving war with the United States.

ARTICLE V.

Ratification clause.

Enclosure 2 in No. 85.

Amended Draft Convention.

H.M. the King of the U.K. of Great Britain and Ireland, Emperor of India, and H.M. the German Emperor, disclaiming all aggressive intentions,' and with the object of ensuring as far as possible the maintenance of the *status quo* and of the general peace of Europe, have resolved to conclude a defensive alliance, and have for that purpose appointed as their Plenipotentiaries :

Who, &c., have agreed upon the following Articles :—

ARTICLE I.

If one of the High Contracting Parties, in the defence of its legitimate interests, or in consequence of a defensive alliance contracted by it and previously communicated to the other High Contracting Party, should become involved in war with another Power, the other High Contracting Party engages to maintain an attitude not less favourable than that of strict neutrality, and to take such pacific measures as may be in its power to prevent other Powers from joining in hostilities against its Ally.

ARTICLE II.

Should any other Power join without provocation in hostilities against the High Contracting Party so involved in war, the other High Contracting Party engages to come to the assistance of its Ally, to conduct the war in common, and only to make peace in mutual agreement with it.

[15214] **F 2**

ARTICLE III.

It is agreed that this Convention shall not apply to questions on the American Continent, nor bind either High Contracting Party to join in hostilities against the United States of America.

ARTICLE IV.

This Convention shall remain in force for five years from the date of .its signature, at the expiration of which period it may be renewed for a similar term. Notice of a desire for its termination or revision shall be given by either Party a year before its expiration.

ARTICLE V.

Ratification clause.

No. 86.

Memorandum by the Marquess of Salisbury.

May 29, 1901.

This is a proposal for including England within the bounds of the Triple Alliance. I understand its practical effect to be :—

1. If England were attacked by two Powers—say France and Russia—Germany, Austria, and Italy would come to her assistance.
2. Conversely, if either Austria, Germany, or Italy were attacked by France and Russia, or, if Italy were attacked by France and Spain, England must come to the rescue.

Even assuming that the Powers concerned were all despotic, and could promise anything they pleased, with a full confidence that they would be able to perform the promise, I think it is open to much question whether the bargain would be for our advantage. The liability of having to defend the German and Austrian frontiers against Russia is heavier than that of *having to defend the British Isles against France.* Even, therefore, in its most naked aspect the bargain would be a bad one for this country. Count Hatzfeldt speaks of our "*isolation*" as constituting a serious danger for us. *Have we ever felt that danger practically?* If we had succumbed in the revolutionary war, our fall would not have been due to our isolation. We had many allies, but they would not have saved us if the French Emperor had been able to command the Channel. Except during his reign we have never even been in danger; and, therefore, it is impossible for us to judge whether the "isolation" under which we are supposed to suffer, does or does not contain in it any elements of peril. It would hardly be wise to incur novel and most onerous obligations, in order to guard against *a danger in whose existence we have no historical reason for believing.*

But though the proposed arrangement, even from this point of view, does not seem to me admissible, these are not by any means the weightiest objections that can be urged against it. The fatal circumstance is that *neither we nor the Germans are competent to make the suggested promises.* The British Government cannot undertake to declare war, for any purpose, unless it is a purpose of which the electors of this country would approve. If the Government promised to declare war for an object which did not commend itself to public opinion, the promise would be repudiated, and the Government would be turned out. I do not see how, in common honesty. we could invite other nations to rely upon our aids in a struggle, which must be formidable and probably supreme, when we have no means whatever of knowing what may be the humour of our people in circumstances which cannot be foreseen. We might, to some extent, divest ourselves of the full responsibility of such a step, *by laying our Agreement with the Triple Alliance before Parliament* as soon as it is concluded. But there are very grave objections to such a course, and I do not under-stand it to be recommended by the German Ambassador.

The impropriety of attempting to determine by a *secret contract* the future conduct of a Representative Assembly upon an issue of peace or war would apply to German policy as much as to English, only that the German Parliament would probably pay more deference to the opinion of their Executive than would be done by the English Parliament. But a *promise of defensive alliance with England would excite bitter murmurs in every rank of German society*—if we may trust the indications of German sentiment, which we have had an opportunity of witnessing during the last two years.

It would not be safe to stake any important national interest upon the fidelity with which, in case of national exigency, either country could be trusted to fulfil the obligations of the Alliance, if the Agreement had been concluded without the assent of its Parliament.

Several times during the last sixteen years Count Hatzfeldt has tried to elicit from me, in conversation, some opinion as to the probable conduct of England, if Germany or Italy were involved in war with France. I have always replied that no English Minister could venture on such a forecast. The course of the English Govern-ment in such a crisis must depend on the view taken by public opinion in this country, and public opinion would be largely, if not exclusively, governed by the nature of the *casus belli*.

No. 87.

Draft of Despatch from the Marquess of Lansdowne to Sir F. Lascelles.

F.O. Germany (Prussia) 1519.
(No.   .) Very Secret.
Sir,   *Foreign Office, May 30, 1901.*
    After the conversation with the German Ambassador, of which I have given an account in my despatch, Very Secret, of the 24th instant, relative to the project of an Anglo-German alliance which had originally been brought before me by Baron Eckardstein, I wrote to the latter gentleman asking if he could favour me with a written Memorandum which he had lately promised me containing his ideas as to the basis of such arrangement.

    I enclose copies of my letter, of one which I have received from Count Hatzfeldt requesting explanations on the subject and of my reply.

    I have heard nothing further from his Excellency on the subject, and I gather from a remark made to me by Baron Eckardstein, that the discussions are likely to be dropped for the moment.

                                                            I am, &c.
                                                            [LANSDOWNE.]

Enclosure 1.

The Marquess of Lansdowne to Baron Eckardstein.

Confidential.
My dear Eckardstein,   *Foreign Office, May 24, 1901.*
    I should have told you yesterday, if there had not been persons present, that my interesting and instructive conversation with the Ambassador in no ways diminished my desire to be favoured with the Memorandum which you were good enough to promise me.

    You may rely on my discretion in using it and on my undertaking to treat it as a private communication between yourself and myself.

                                                    Yours sincerely,
                                                    LANSDOWNE

Enclosure 2.

Count Hatzfeldt to the Marquess of Lansdowne.

Confidentielle.

Mon cher Lord Lansdowne,   *Londres, le 25 Mai 1901.*

Le Baron Eckardstein, qui se rend pour quelques jours à la campagne, vient de me communiquer une lettre Confidentielle que vous avez bien voulu lui adresser à la date d'hier.

Si, comme je l'espère, j'ai bien compris ce que vous avez bien voulu me dire dans notre conversation d'avant-hier, votre intention était de m'informer, après votre retour et après avoir consulté vos collègues, si nous sommes d'accord sur la base dont il était question. J'ai cru comprendre aussi que vous étiez d'avis, comme moi, qu'il serait temps alors de discuter entre nous et en toute confiance les questions de détail qui pourraient se présenter, en prenant pour point de départ les documents antérieurs qui se rapportent à la question.

Dans votre lettre au Baron Eckardstein il est question maintenant d'un Mémorandum tout à fait confidentiel que vous désireriez avoir et dont je ne savais rien jusqu'à présent. Le Baron Eckardstein ayant déjà quitté l'Ambassade pour aller à la campagne il m'est impossible de lui demander de quoi il s'agit. J'espère, par conséquent, qu'il n'y aura rien de perdu en attendant jusqu'à votre retour, et que vous voudrez alors me dire vous-même plus exactement de quoi il s'agit. Je n'ai pas besoin d'ajouter, je l'espère, que j'ai la confiance la plus absolue dans votre loyauté et votre discrétion, et que vous me trouverez tout disposé à vous témoigner cette confiance dans toute occasion où cela ne dépendra que de moi.

En attendant, veuillez m'écrire, mon cher Lord Lansdowne.

Votre bien sincèrement dévoué,

v. HATZFELDT.

Enclosure 3.

The Marquess of Lansdowne to Count Hatzfeldt.

Confidential.

My dear Count Hatzfeldt,   *Bowood, May 26, 1901.*

Many thanks for your letter of yesterday. I am sorry that you should have had the trouble of writing it.

Before our interesting conversation at the Embassy on the 23rd instant, I had, as you are aware, had several " academical " discussions upon the same subject with Baron Eckardstein. On the occasion of the last of these he was good enough to promise that he would let me have a Memorandum stating in general terms the basis of the arrangement which it might, in his opinion, be possible to make.

There was no question of details : these, as you point out, would have to be considered at a later stage.

I still think that it is of importance that I should be able to confirm my impression of what passed between yourself and myself, and between Baron Eckardstein and myself during your absence, by means of such a Memorandum. I hold this opinion the more decidedly because those " documents antérieurs " which might, you are good enough to suggest, form the point of departure, are not in the possession of the Foreign Office.

You will, I am sure, understand my desire that I should apprehend with absolute correctness the general principle upon which we might proceed.

I will not end this letter without thanking you cordially for the expressions of confidence and goodwill with which yours concludes, and assuring you that those feelings are cordially reciprocated by,

Dear Count Hatzfeldt,
Yours sincerely,
LANSDOWNE.

P.S.—I hope I have made it clear that I regarded the Memorandum as having the same personal and unofficial character as the conversations which had led me to ask for it.

L.

No. 88.

Count Hatzfeldt to the Marquess of Lansdowne.

Particulière et Confidentielle.

Mon cher Lord Lansdowne,   *Londres, le 30 mai* 1901.

J'avais espéré que j'aurais le plaisir de vous voir bientôt pour causer avec vous de l'affaire en question. Mais comme j'apprends à l'instant que vous ne reviendrez probablement pas en ville avant la semaine prochaine, je ne veux pas tarder plus longtemps à vous remercier de la lettre que vous avez bien voulu m'écrire à la date du 26 courant.

Je crains que je me suis mal exprimé dans notre dernière conversation si j'ai donné lieu par là à l'impression, dont vous voulez bien me parler, que j'ai suggéré comme point de départ un document antérieur dont le contenu comme vous voulez bien l'ajouter, n'est pas connu au Foreign Office. Telle n'a pas été ma pensée, veuillez en être persuadé, et ce que j'ai voulu dire était simplement que, si nous étions d'accord sur le principe général, tel que je me suis permis de l'indiquer, le document en question pourrait, dans mon opinion personnelle, servir ensuite comme base, non pas pour la discussion de ce principe, mais pour la discussion des questions de *détail* qui devraient nécessairement s'y rattacher.

J'espère que vous voudrez bien me faire savoir après votre retour quand je pourrai avoir le plaisir de vous voir et de vous expliquer mes idées à ce sujet. Si nous arrivons alors à la conclusion que l'affaire est assez avancée pour rendre utile une rédaction par écrit, je m'empresserai de soumettre la question à mon Gouvernement et de lui demander l'autorisation nécessaire pour participer à ce travail.

Veuillez agréer, mon cher Lord Lansdowne, l'assurance de tous mes meilleurs sentiments.

v. HATZFELDT.

[*ED. NOTE.*—The major part of this letter, printed in *G.P.* XVII, 72, had been submitted to Baron Holstein and approved by Baron Richthofen, the German Minister of Foreign Affairs.]

No. 89.

The Marquess of Lansdowne to Sir F. Lascelles.

Secret.   *Milburn, Esher,*

My dear Lascelles,   *June 9,* 1901.

I have not written to you for a long time, but there has not been much to tell you outside of what has been officially made known to you.

Just before the holidays, Hatzfeldt came to see me, and, after we had talked about China, &c., told me that he wished for a further conversation with me, indicating that it was to be with reference to the question which I had on several occasions discussed with Eckhardtein. I therefore went to see him at his house on the 23rd, and I enclose a note of what passed. I gather from what Eckhardtein tells me privately that Hatzfeldt's intervention has led to a good deal of misunderstanding, and that he must have represented my conversation with him as indicating much more alacrity on our part than we have actually exhibited.

Since then the poor man has become aware that he is to leave the Embassy, and, when I called upon him on the 7th, he did not recur to the suggested understanding which he probably felt he could not usefully discuss with me on the eve of his departure.

I am quite content to mark time for a while. I doubt whether it will be possible to make anything of what for convenience sake I would describe as the Eckhardtein proposal, and if we are to consider some alternative form of agreement, perhaps limited to particular eventualities—it could be more conveniently examined when Hatzfeldt has left.

He, poor man, is very unhappy, and told me that he had heard all sorts of stories of intrigues against him on this side. I said I was not aware of any, and that the F.O., I believed, had always regarded him with nothing but goodwill. I think it possible that there may have been some exchange of ideas between the King and the Emperor when the latter was here, altho' the King did not tell me so when I mentioned to him a few days ago that Hatzfeldt was probably going to be recalled.

As to China, I hope we have killed the proposal for a " hotch potch " loan. You will have been impressed by Rothschild's weighty condemnation of the project. I am trying to find some means of meeting the wish of the German Govt. that we should provide for a further improvement in the position of the Bondholders by giving them an interest in any surplus revenues of which China may hereafter be able to dispose. You will probably have received our views by telegram before you read this letter. I have no objection whatever to the principle of Bn. Richthofen's demand, and if it proves to be the case that, by the operation of existing sinking Funds or from other causes, China will certainly be richer by x in a given number of years, I do not see why we should not stipulate that a fixed sum equal to $\frac{1}{2}x$ shall be added to the sinking fund by which the new Bonds are to be extinguished.

But do if you can convince the German Govt. that they must not spring any more points of this sort on us. We have given way to them as to the amount of the Indemnities, as to the sinking Fund, and as to the increase of the customs to a full 5 per cent. If we can settle this further point, they ought to go in with us for all they are worth, and help us to close this chapter, and to deal with the great commercial problems which we must then tackle. I am inclined to think that *this* phase of the negotiations would be better conducted elsewhere than at Peking and certainly not by the same " crowd " of representatives. Satow, I think, suggested Shanghai. Will you find out if you can in what direction the German mind is moving upon this point? It may be better that the proposal if made should appear to be theirs.

Always my dear Lascelles,
Yours sincerely,
LANSDOWNE.

A propos of the first point of this letter : did you notice the close similarity of the Emperor's language to Waters, and Hatzfeldt's to me?

No. 90.

Sir F. Lascelles to the Marquess of Lansdowne.

F.O. Germany (Prussia) 1521.   *Homburg,* D. *August* 25, 1901.
(No. 206.)   Confidential.   Extract.   R. *August* 30, 1901.

. . . . The question of an alliance between England and Germany was also mentioned in the course of this conversation, and the Emperor seemed to be somewhat dissatisfied that the negotiations on the subject had not led to a definite result. The relations between the two countries could only be placed on the satisfactory footing which he most earnestly desired by the conclusion of a definite and binding Treaty. I ventured to reply that, at the risk of being indiscreet, I could assure His Majesty that your Lordship was in favour of such an alliance. It was not, however, quite easy for His Majesty's Government to depart from their traditional policy of avoiding alliances which would bind them for a long period, and a matter of so much importance required the greatest care and attention, which it would be difficult to bestow upon it at this season of the year. Count Bülow had, moreover, informed me that there was no necessity for haste. He had explained to me that the Triple Alliance was the pivot of the foreign policy of Germany, who desired at the same time to maintain friendly relations with England on the one hand and with Russia on the other, and he was prepared to continue this policy although he was personally of opinion that an alliance between our two Countries would provide a further guarantee for the maintenance of the peace of the world.

The Emperor replied that he quite understood that we could not conclude a Treaty of Alliance without giving up our policy of isolation, but that would be an advantage for us, for we ran the risk of finding a coalition of Powers against us. He would like to warn us against putting our faith in America, who was our most formidable commercial rival, and would certainly throw us over as soon as it suited her interest to do so. . . . .

[The Emperor's account of his conversation with King Edward and Sir Frank Lascelles at Wilhelmshöhe on the 23rd August is in *G.P.* XVII, 94–8.]

No. 91.

Memorandum by Mr. Bertie.([1])

November 9, 1901.

The German Emperor and Government have for sometime past urged His Majesty's Government to enter into a defensive alliance with Germany, and recently they have been more insistent in their advice that we should lose no more time in coming to terms with them, stating that otherwise we shall be too late as they have other offers.

The German Government lay stress on the danger to England of isolation, and enlarge on the advantages to her to be secured by an alliance with Germany. They have constantly and for some years past made use of these threats and blandishments.

There may be some danger but there are also advantages to us in isolation. On the other hand it would be a great relief to be able to feel that we had secured a powerful and *sure* ally for the contingency of an attack on the British Empire by two Powers such as Russia and France combined; but in considering offers of alliance from Germany it is necessary to remember the history of Prussia as regards alliances and the conduct of the Bismarck Government in making a treaty with Russia concerning and behind the back of Austria the ally of Germany, and also to bear in mind the

([1]) From the Sanderson *MSS.*

position of Germany in Europe as regards France and Russia, and her position in other parts of the world as regards the British Empire.

Germany is in a dangerous situation in Europe. She is surrounded by Governments who distrust her and peoples who dislike or at all events do not like her. She is constantly in a state of Tariff war with Russia. She has beaten and robbed Denmark, and for that purpose she took as partner Austria and then turned round on her confederate and drove her out of Germany, eventually making her a rather humble ally. She has beaten and taken money and territory from France. She covets the seaboard of Holland, and the Dutch know it; and, as the Belgians are well aware, she has designs on the Belgian Congo. The Pan-German agitation in the Austrian Empire and commercial questions may before very long bring about complications between Germany and Austria and the internal troubles of the Austro-Hungarian Empire detract from its value to Germany as an ally, while the state of Italy, politically, militarily and financially, is not such as to inspire the German Government with much trust in effective Italian support.

In these circumstances it is essential for the German Government to endeavour to obtain the certainty of armed support from England for the contingency of an attack on Germany by France and Russia combined, for if England be not bound to Germany and His Majesty's Government come to a general understanding with France and Russia, or either of them, the position of Germany in Europe will become critical. These considerations have made it incumbent on Germany to create and maintain distrust between the Powers not in alliance with her, and particularly between England and Russia and between England and France. She therefore does what she can to keep open sores between France and England. She is always ready with information for our consumption of Russian and French intrigues and probably she supplies the Russian and French Governments with particulars of our sinister designs.

Numerous instances might be given of the tortuous policy of the German Government, but for a good example of it we need go no further back than last Spring (March). They then informed the Japanese Government that they disapproved the Russian proceedings in regard to Manchuria, and being, they said, aware of the vital importance of the Manchurian question to Japan they would observe a benevolent neutrality in the event of matters coming to a crisis, and this attitude would keep the French fleet in check, while England would probably support Japan. On inquiry it turned out that "benevolent" neutrality meant "the strictest and most correct neutrality" towards all parties. The German Government could not answer for France, but they were strongly of opinion that France would follow the example of Germany. A month later (April) the German Emperor described His Majesty's Government as a "set of unmitigated noodles" for having missed the opportunity afforded by the Manchurian question of asserting the position of England in the Far East—and, as he did not say, of falling into the arrangement designed for them by His Majesty, viz: that they should ease the situation for Germany in Europe by joining with Japan in a war against Russia in the Far East. The Emperor further said that the Japanese were furious with England for not giving them active support, but of this we have not had any indication from Japan.

A formal understanding between England and Japan for the protection of their interests in the Far East by force of arms is of the utmost importance to both Countries, but at the time when the German Government were urging His Majesty's Government to resist Russia our military forces were fully occupied in South Africa and the Japanese Government though encouraged by Germany did not show much inclination to rely on her advice and go to war without being assured of the neutrality of France as well as of Germany.

Whatever hope may be held out to England and Japan of support from Germany no effective aid will be forthcoming from that quarter in opposition to Russia unless there be a general conflagration and Germany find herself obliged from European considerations to take part in the war. Her policy in the Far East—not a difficult one —is to foster ill-feeling between Russian on one side and England and Japan on the other and to encourage both sides to persist in their respective claims taking good care not to commit herself to either party.

Germany is for the open door in China in principle and relies on England Japan and the United States to keep it open; but she will never use force in support of it where it may bring her into collision with Russia. Of this her interpretation of the Anglo-German Agreement, which the German Government call the Yangtze Agreement, is good proof.

Germany would naturally be glad to see an Agreement made between England and Japan to resist Russian and French designs in the Far East and to maintain the *status quo* in China as her commercial interests would be protected without the necessity for her to offend Russia or France by being a party to the understanding, the existence of which the German Government would take good care should be known to Russia and France.

Friendship with Turkey is important to Germany as a counterpoise to Russian pressure on herself, the Austro-Hungarian Empire and the Balkans, and she derives commercial advantages from supporting the Sultan. In most questions in which His Majesty is concerned Germany sympathises with him and supports him to a certain extent, and only mildly deprecates Turkish proceedings when they are too flagrant to be supported, she does nothing to put a stop to them.

When lately it seemed probable that France would proceed to extremities with Morocco the German Government consulted to a certain extent with the other Powers interested in the independence and integrity of that Empire, and then drew back saying that she was not primarily interested, though in 1899 Count Hatzfeldt suggested to Lord Salisbury that it would be very desirable that there should be an exchange of views and ideas between the German and British Governments on the subject of Morocco.

If the recent proceedings of Germany with regard to Koweit, where she endeavoured to stir up not only Turkey, but Austria and Russia against us; and in regard to the Peking Conferences, where whilst pretending to fall in with our views, she voted and even moved resolutions against them, are to be looked upon as consistent with her assurances of friendship what would her attitude towards this country be if she held England bound by a defensive alliance?

The interests of England and Germany are not everywhere identical. In some parts of the world they are irreconciliable. For instance, Germany, whose intention it is to become a great naval power, requires coaling stations which she can fortify. Good ones on the highways of trade can only be got in the great seas by purchase from Spain; by force from Holland—for she would not sell—; by the spoliation of Portugal, which we should be bound to resist; from Siam, whose integrity within certain limits we have guaranteed; or from France as the outcome of a successful war.

If Germany seek a station in the Mediterranean it must be obtained from Morocco, Spain, Greece or Turkey, and to the detriment of our naval position.

I do not mention her ambitions in the American Seas. They may safely be left to be dealt with by the United States.

In the Indian and Pacific Oceans our Colonies of Australasia have interests which they sometimes consider to be gravely affected by the proceedings of Germany and France. In view of the effective assistance given to us by the British Colonies in the South African war they will all expect their desires to prevail in questions between His Majesty's Government and Foreign Powers whenever Colonial interests are concerned.

If we had a formal alliance with Germany we should either have to shape our conduct over a large extent of the globe in accordance with her views and subordinate our policy to hers as is the case with Austria and Italy, or, if we acted independently, whenever we took measures necessary for the protection of our interests in some distant part of the world we might be told by Germany that we were bringing about a situation which might lead to an attack on us by France and Russia, obliging

Germany without sufficient cause to take up arms in our defence, or Germany might find some moment opportune for herself, but inconvenient for us, for bringing on a war on a question on which we might not have a great interest. Discussions on these questions would cause bickerings and differences and might lead to estrangement and end in an open quarrel.

The best proof that isolation is not so dangerous as the German Government would have us believe is that during our two years of war, when we have had nearly a quarter of a million men locked up in South Africa, and we have had the opinion of the educated classes abroad as expressed in the Press, and the sentiment of the peoples of most countries against us, and when more than one Power would have been glad to put a humiliation on us, it has not been found possible to form a coalition to call upon to desist from war or to accept arbitration.

If we had an alliance making it incumbent on each ally to come to the aid of his partner when attacked by two Powers it might be difficult to decide whether in some particular case the *casus fœderis* had arisen for the attacking parties are not necessarily the real aggressors.

It would be much safer to have a Declaration of policy limited to Europe and the Mediterranean defining the interests which we shall jointly defend, as we have with Italy and Austria of which understanding I annex a summary. If once we bind ourselves by a formal defensive alliance and practically join the Triplice we shall never be on decent terms with France our neighbour in Europe and in many parts of the world, or with Russia whose frontiers are coterminous with ours or nearly so over a large portion of Asia.

In our present position we hold the balance of power between the Triple and Dual Alliances. There is but little chance of a combination between them against us. Our existence as a Great and strong State is necessary to all in order to preserve the balance of power, and most of all to Germany whose representations as to the disasters which await the British Empire if His Majesty's Government do not make an alliance with her have little or no real foundation. Treaty or no Treaty if ever there were danger of our destruction or even defeat by Russia and France Germany would be bound in order to avoid a like fate for herself to come to our assistance. She might ask a high price for such aid, but could it be higher than what we should lose by the sacrifice of our liberty to pursue a British world policy, which would be the result of a formal defensive alliance with the German Empire.

F. BERTIE.

No. 92.

Memorandum by the Marquess of Lansdowne.

Very Secret. *November* 11, 1901.

During the spring I was sounded by Baron Eckardstein, who then represented the Germany Embassy, as to the possibility of establishing a closer understanding between this country and Germany. An account of my conversation on this subject with Baron Eckardstein is contained in a draft despatch to Sir Frank Lascelles, dated the 18th March, a copy of which I attach to this Minute.

In the month of May Count Hatzfeldt, who had been unable to attend to business for some time, reappeared at the Embassy, and, at his instance, discussed the question with me at considerable length. An account of my conversation with him is contained in my Memorandum of the 24th May also annexed to this paper. It will be observed that Count Hatzfeldt's suggestions went much further than those made by Baron Eckardstein.

I submitted this Memorandum to the Prime Minister, who replied in a Minute, dated the 29th May, strongly deprecating an alliance with Germany. This Minute is also attached. About this time the state of Count Hatzfeldt's health again obliged him to leave the Embassy, and Baron Eckardstein, who once more replaced him, explained to me in confidence that, in the opinion of the German Government, Count Hatzfeldt had overshot the mark and had indeed muddled the case. Baron Eckardstein's suggestion was that in these circumstances it was better to leave matters alone, and to resume the discussion at some more opportune moment.

I had in the meantime made several ineffectual attempts to obtain, first from Baron Eckardstein and subsequently from Count Hatzfeldt, a description in writing of the kind of agreement into which we were invited to enter. The former had led me to expect that he would, after our informal exchange of ideas, be able to give me a written statement of the views of the German Government. Count Hatzfeldt, however, in an unofficial letter written just before his departure, threw cold water upon this idea, or at any rate refused to entertain it until matters had become further advanced.

Towards the end of the Session, Baron Eckardstein returned to the charge. He did not, however, produce any written proposal, and I told him that at such a time, when my colleagues were all busily engaged, it was useless for me to lay before them proposals upon so momentous a question. I think, however, we both understood that the discussion was to be renewed after the holidays.

Since the holidays, Count Metternich has conducted the business of the Embassy, but he has only just received his appointment as Ambassador. He has not reverted to the question, nor has Baron Eckardstein, whom I have frequently seen. The former may possibly have felt that so long as he was not fully appointed, he was scarcely in a position to take up so serious a negotiation. I have, however, received various indications which show that the question is still present to the mind of the German Government, and particularly to that of the German Emperor. Whatever, therefore, be the decision of His Majesty's Government, it seems to me that the time has come for frankly explaining our views to the German Ambassador. Unless some such explanation takes place we shall be accused of not knowing our own mind, and of breaking off negotiations in a discourteous and unfriendly manner.

The knowledge that we have been negotiating a Treaty with Japan, an incident of which the German Government is sure to hear, could scarcely fail to add to their irritation in such circumstances.

I may here be permitted to offer one or two observations on the Prime Minister's Memorandum. He suggests that the only liability which the German Government would assume under the proposed agreement would be that of having to defend the British islands against France, whereas we should be bound to defend the German and Austrian frontiers against Russia, a much heavier obligation. This statement does not, I think, quite correctly represent the proposal.

Count Hatzfeldt's idea evidently was that the liability of our allies would oblige them to range themselves on our side in any quarrel in which the British Empire might become involved, and we should not be more bound to defend the German and Austrian frontiers than they would be bound to defend Australasia and our African and American Colonies.

I fully admit the force of the Prime Minister's observation, that this country has until now fared well in spite of its international isolation. I think, however, that we may push too far the argument that, because we have in the past survived in spite of our isolation, we need have no misgivings as to the effect of that isolation in the future.

In approaching the Japanese we have, indeed, virtually admitted that we do not wish to continue to stand alone.

The Prime Minister contends that neither His Majesty's Government nor that of Germany are competent to enter into such an arrangement as that which was proposed.

I fully admit that it would be impossible for us to determine by a secret contract the future conduct of Parliament upon an issue of peace and war. It is, however, I think, quite clear that those who inspired these overtures contemplated an open alliance, which should be communicated to the Parliaments of both countries.

With regard to the effects which the Prime Minister anticipates for it upon German sentiment, and "in every rank of German society," would it not be true to say that the suspicion and dislike with which we are regarded in Germany are, to a great extent, the result of the "aloofness" of our policy, and that an openly declared change in that policy would not be without effect upon German sentiment?

I make these observations in order to guard against possible misunderstandings. I am, however, bound to admit, and I did not conceal this from Count Hatzfeldt or Baron Eckardstein, that I see great difficulties in the way of a full-blown defensive alliance with Germany such as that suggested by Count Hatzfeldt, difficulties which are, I should say at the present moment, virtually insuperable. I need only indicate some of them in the most general terms, *e.g.* :—

1. The impossibility of arriving at a definition of the *casus fœderis* which would not be either so rigid as to greatly hamper our freedom of action or so vague as to deprive the alliance of all practical value.
2. The certainty of alienating France and Russia.
3. Complications with the Colonies, which might not at all approve of the idea of hanging on to the skirts of the Triple Alliance.
4. The risk of entangling ourselves in a policy which might be hostile to America. With our knowledge of the German Emperor's views in regard to the United States, this is to my mind a formidable obstacle.
5. The difficulty of carrying Parliament with us at a moment when the Parliamentary situation is as little satisfactory as it is at present.

In these circumstances, and in the face of the decided views which the Prime Minister has expressed, I regard it as out of the question that we should entertain the German overture in the form in which it was presented by Count Hatzfeldt.

I would not, however, for these reasons refuse all further discussion of the question.

The objections to joining the Triple Alliance do not seem to me to apply to a much more limited understanding with Germany as to our policy in regard to certain matters of interest to both Powers.

We have already such an Agreement with her in regard to the Far East, and although her interpretation of that Agreement has not been by any means satisfactory to us, we might, I think, attempt to come to a similiar understanding in regard to other questions, *e.g.*, our policy in the Mediterranean and, perhaps, in the Persian Gulf. There are precedents for such an understanding. In February 1887 an exchange of notes took place between Lord Salisbury and the Italian Ambassador, recording the Agreement of the two Powers for the maintenance, so far as possible, of the *status quo* in the Mediterranean, the Adriatic, the Ægean and the Black Sea.(¹) No modification was to be allowed except after previous agreement between the two Powers which were to give one another mutual support in the Mediterranean. The character of this co-operation was to be decided when occasion arose. The Austrian Government gave its adherence to this understanding in March of the same year. Lord Rosebery, on coming into office, refused to recognise this Agreement, but I believe I am right in saying that in February 1896 Lord Salisbury expressed to the Austrian Ambassador his willingness to renew these declarations of common policy.

Some similar exchange of declarations as to the objects which Great Britain and Germany have in common and the interests in regard to which they are prepared to afford one another support might be offered to the German Government, the form which such support should take being reserved for consideration when the necessity should arise.

The arrangement would, no doubt, fall far short of what was suggested to us, but

(¹) [See A. F. Pribram, *Secret Treaties*, Harvard Press, U.S.A. [1921], I, 94–103.]

as a tentative and provisional step it might not be without value, and the offer would, at any rate, place it out of the power of the German Government to say that we had treated them inconsiderately or brusquely rejected their overtures.

L.

November 22, 1901.

No. 93.

Memorandum by the Marquess of Lansdowne.

Lord Salisbury, *December* 12, 1901.

You have asked me to state more precisely the heads of an Anglo-German under-standing of the kind contemplated in the concluding paragraphs of my minute of November 22nd.

I submit the following for your consideration :—

The Agreement would begin by reciting that the two High Contracting Parties have a common interest in :—

1. The maintenance of the general peace.
2. The maintenance of the territorial *status quo* on the shores of—

> The Mediterranean,
> The Adriatic,
> The Ægean, and
> The Black Seas.*

3. Freedom for the commerce and navigation of all nations in the Persian Gulf, and the prevention of any territorial acquisitions on its shores by other Powers which might interfere with that object.

4. The two High Contracting Parties would agree to co-operate in furtherance of the above policy, the nature of such co-operation to be determined whenever the occasion for it might arise.

5. The High Contracting Parties would agree to consult one another freely whenever events might seem to threaten the above-described interests, and also that in the event of changes affecting Art. II becoming inevitable they would consider in concert the measures to be taken in order to prevent such changes from operating to their detriment or to that of their allies.

An Agreement upon the above lines would amount to little more than a declaration of common policy and of a desire to maintain close diplomatic relations. Assuming, however, that both sides acted up to it in the fullest sense, it would be distinctly to the advantage of this country that peace should be maintained and that the *status quo* at Constantinople, in Albania, Macedonia and Bulgaria, in Tripoli and Morocco, and in Egypt, should not be disturbed. It would also be to our advantage to exclude Russia and Germany from establishing themselves strategically on the shores of the Persian Gulf.

My own impression is that the German Govt. (or the German Emperor) desire something much more precise and far-reaching than this, and that they would refuse an overture on the above lines. Should they do so, no great harm will have been done, and we shall have put it out of their power to accuse us of having " dropped " them.

L.

December 4, 1901.

---

* This would follow the Anglo-Italian agreement of 1887. [L.]

MINUTE.

Lord Lansdowne,

I should like to speak to you more fully about this, at or after the Cabinet on Wednesday At present it seems to me full of risks and to carry with it no compensating advantage.—*S.*

December 6, 1901.

No. 94.

Draft of Despatch from the Marquess of Lansdowne to Sir F. Lascelles.

F.O. Germany (Prussia) 1519.
(No. 393A.)   Secret.

Sir,   *Foreign Office, December* 19, 1901.

The German Ambassador called on me to-day on the eve of his departure for Germany.

After a brief conversation on various matters which had already formed the subject of communications between us, I referred to the discussions which had taken place between his Excellency's predecessor, Count Hatzfeldt, and Baron Eckardstein, on the part of the German Embassy, and myself during the spring and summer of this year in regard to the possibility of establishing closer political relations between Great Britain and Germany.

I reminded his Excellency briefly of the course of these discussions. They had begun as long ago as the month of March when I was sounded by Baron Eckardstein, who was then in charge of the Embassy, as to the possibility of an Agreement between this country and Germany. An account of my conversation is contained in my despatch to you of the 18th March. Baron Eckardstein had been at pains to explain to me throughout that his communications with me were of an unofficial character, but he had, at the same time, let me perceive clearly that he was not speaking without authority. These conversations had been renewed on several occasions, and I had thought it my duty to ask Baron Eckardstein, whose description of the proposed arrangement had been of a somewhat general character, to endeavour to obtain for me a more precise statement which I might submit to the Prime Minister, who was absent from England, on his return. On one occasion Baron Eckardstein had mentioned incidentally that Austria and Italy might have to be included in such an arrangement as he had proposed. I had replied that this seemed to me a most important point. I had observed to him that we had until then been discussing the possibility of a purely defensive alliance between England and Germany against any other two Powers, and I had said to him that in my view the objection to such an arrangement was that this country might find itself dragged into a quarrel in which we had no concern, and which might have been, in fact, provoked by our ally, whose external policy might be quite beyond our control, although that ally was ostensibly defending itself from attack. These objections could, I thought, be urged with infinitely greater force if we were asked to enter into similar obligations towards Austria and Italy as well as towards Germany.

Towards the end of the month of May, Count Hatzfeldt, whom I had not seen for a long time, had returned to England, and at his desire I had discussed the question at length with him. Count Hatzfeldt had said that the foreign policy of Germany must always be based upon the closest intimacy with Austria, and had explained that, under the arrangement which he suggested for our consideration, there would be two groups : one consisting of Great Britain and her Colonies, and the other of the members of the Triple Alliance, which we were invited to join, and that the Agreement was to be made between the two groups.

I had told Count Hatzfeldt that this proposal seemed to me to go further than anything which we had yet discussed, and I had said that we were, to the best of my belief, without information as to the terms by which the members of the Triple Alliance were bound, and that it was at least desirable that we should be placed fully in possession of the nature and conditions of the contract. Count Hatzfeldt had subsequently written me a private letter in which he explained that it was impossible for him to supply me with information upon this point until he had been told whether in principle we were disposed to accept such a proposal.

Almost immediately after this Count Hatzfeldt had fallen seriously ill, and it had become evident that it would be impossible for him to retain his post as Ambassador at this Court. The subject had therefore dropped, and I had, moreover, been told confidentially by Baron Eckardstein that Count Hatzfeldt was regarded by the German Government as having pushed matters rather too far and too fast, and that, for a time at all events, it was not thought advisable that the negotiations should be continued.

Towards the end of the Session Baron Eckardstein, who was once more in charge of the Embassy, had mentioned to me in confidence that he thought the time had come for renewing our discussions. I had, however, been obliged to tell him that at such a season, when the Members of His Majesty's Government were all busily engaged, it was useless for me to lay before them proposals upon so momentous a question.

Having thus recapitulated the history of the above discussions, of which records will be found in my despatches of 29th March, 9th April, the 24th and 30th May of this year, I told Count Metternich that I had waited to see whether he would mention the subject to me, as it seemed to be one to which, as soon as his position as Ambassador at this Court had been confirmed, he would be likely to refer. As, however, he had now held his appointment for some weeks, and as he had not mentioned the subject, I thought it desirable, in order that there might be no misconception, that I should approach it. I reminded his Excellency that I had not been successful in obtaining either from Count Hatzfeldt or from Baron Eckardstein anything beyond a most general indication of their views. From those indications I gathered that the proposal before us, if indeed it was still before us, was that the British Empire should join the Triple Alliance. We had considered this proposal very carefully. To my mind it certainly presented many attractive features. It was, I understood, to be a purely defensive Alliance. It would make for peace, which we desired. It would give us powerful allies, the value of whose assistance I certainly did not underrate. But we could not contemplate the possibility of entering into such a contract and withholding the knowledge of it from Parliament; and we had to consider whether, in present circumstances, it was possible for us to go to Parliament with such a proposal. His Excellency, who was so familiar with public life in this country, must be well aware of the suspicion with which any entanglement in foreign alliances was regarded by a large part of the British public. We should certainly be told that we ran the chance of involving ourselves and our great Colonies in disputes which did not concern us, and which might arise in almost any part of the world. This would be represented as a new and onerous obligation, and we should have considerable difficulty in defending ourselves for wishing to incur it. I was far from suggesting that all the arguments were on one side; but, looked at from a Parliamentary point of view, it was undoubtedly, if I might use the expression, a very stiff fence to ride at. We had to consider whether the conditions were favourable at this moment. His Majesty's Government had their hands full, owing to the South African war and for other reasons, and the temper of the two countries was not, it seemed to me, in a particularly favourable state. Germany had been suffering from a severe outbreak of Anglophobia, and I was afraid that this had provoked a corresponding feeling of irritation in this country. On the other hand, our relations with other Powers were not unfriendly, and our sudden adhesion to the German group might have unfortunate effects in other quarters. While, therefore, we certainly did not regard the German proposal with an unfriendly or indifferent eye, I did not think that for the moment we could afford to take it up.

Count Metternich replied that he was well aware of the history of the informal discussions which I had recapitulated; and I observed that he did not challenge the accuracy of the account which I had given of them. The German proposal was, he thought, perfectly distinct. He was not sure that I had correctly described it as merely implying the adhesion of Great Britain to the Triple Alliance. What was suggested was that there should be two great groups : the one consisting of the Triple Alliance, the other of Great Britain with her Colonies and dependencies. The Agreement between these two groups would be to the effect that, if either group were to find itself attacked by another Power, and that Power were to be joined by another Power or Powers, both groups should make common cause against the aggressors. Such an Agreement, his Excellency observed, would probably have ensured peace for half a century, and would have relieved us of many causes for anxiety. He had always thought that it was a magnificent opportunity for us, and he had wondered that we did not "jump at it." To his mind, our preference for isolation was unintelligible. He feared that that isolation was becoming more marked. Had we, he asked, noticed the approaches made quite recently by Italy to France? He regarded this as an indication that Italy had ceased to believe in us. The change was, he thought, due to the coldness with which we had treated Italy on several occasions. As instances of this he cited our arrangement with France in regard to the Hinterland of Tripoli, which, he said, had given much offence to the Italian Government. He also said that we had discouraged a visit which the King of Italy had desired to pay to the late Queen, and that we had shown a want of consideration for Italian interests in regard to questions connected with the Abyssinian frontier. It might be, his Excellency said, that it was our deliberate intention to pursue a less active policy in the Mediterranean. If so, we must not be surprised if those who had hitherto leaned towards us were to look in other directions for alliances. Italy, his Excellency thought, had most likely come to terms with France about other matters, not improbably as to the extent of French interests in Morocco.

I replied that there was no change whatever in our Mediterranean policy, and that our feelings of goodwill towards Italy were unchanged; and I mentioned the fact that within the last few weeks we had concluded a friendly arrangement with regard to the Erythræan boundary upon terms which the Italian Government admitted were extremely favourable to them; and I asked his Excellency whether the conduct of Italy might not be interpreted quite as much as an attempt to break away from the Triple Alliance as an attempt to shake herself clear of us.

Returning to the question of my discussions with Baron Eckardstein, Count Metternich proceeded to say that the German Government had certainly been under the impression that our failure to reopen them indicated a desire to drop the question altogether, and it was assumed that some event had happened which had led us to close the question. I interrupted his Excellency by saying that, if there was such an event, it was the arrival of the summer holidays, which had perforce for a time rendered further discussions impracticable. Count Metternich went on to say that he was glad I had given him these explanations, adding that he was bound to admit the justice of my observation to the effect that the present time was not a favourable one for further pursuing the question. He feared, however, that an opportunity so favourable as that which presented itself last summer might not again occur. In politics, his Excellency said, things never stood still, and his own opinion, which he expressed as one entirely personal, was that in the years which lay before us the tendency would be for Germany to move more and more towards Russia.

I replied that it would, to my mind, be most unfortunate if there should be any estrangement between our two countries, and I trusted that he would not consider that our inability to take so serious a step as that which had been proposed to us denoted any unfriendliness towards Germany. Speaking entirely for myself, I asked him whether, assuming that we could not accept the German proposal as it stood, it might not be possible for the two countries to arrive at an understanding with regard to the policy which they might pursue in reference to particular questions or in particular parts of the world in which they were alike interested?

His Excellency unhesitatingly replied that no such minor proposal was likely to find favour with the German Government. It was a case of "the whole or none."

At the close of the conversation, I expressed my hope that I had made it clear to his Excellency that if for the moment we regarded the object which the German Government had had in view as unattainable, we had come to this conclusion, not because we regarded the offer with indifference, but on account of practical difficulties the importance of which I had no doubt his Excellency would fully recognise.

I am, &c.

MINUTE BY KING EDWARD.

The King does not consider the language and arguments made use of by the German Ambassador to Lord Lansdowne as at all satisfactory.

E.R.

Marlborough House, S.W.,
  December 24, 1901.

[*ED. NOTE.*—Count Metternich's report of his interview with Lord Lansdowne on the 19th December, dated Berlin, the 28th December, 1901, is in *G.P.* XVII, 111–115.]

No. 95.

Sir F. Lascelles to the Marquess of Lansdowne.

F.O. Germany (Prussia) 1551.
(No. 1.) Confidential.   *Berlin,* D. *January* 3, 1902.
My Lord,   R. *January* 6, 1902.

On the 28th ultimo I had the honour of being invited to luncheon at the Neues Palais, and thus had an opportunity of conveying to the Emperor the friendly messages with which the King had charged me on my departure from London on the 22nd instant. Beyond reciprocating the King's friendly sentiments and His Majesty's desire for a cordial understanding between our two countries, the Emperor did not indulge in political conversation or give me the opportunity of doing so. His Majesty's manner and also that of the Empress was marked by their usual gracious cordiality.

I travelled to Potsdam in the same carriage as Count Buelow and had thus an opportunity of conversing with his Excellency, whom I had not seen since my return to Berlin. I said that, although I had not yet had an opportunity of seeing Baron von Richthofen, I had had a conversation on the previous day with Herr von Muehlberg, and had been somewhat surprised to learn that Count Metternich had not as yet reported an important conversation which he had had with your Lordship on the 19th ultimo, in which your Lordship had said that with every wish to meet the views of the German Government with regard to an alliance between the two countries, the excited state of public opinion on both sides made it inopportune to discuss the subject at present, and that it would be better to let it stand over for a time.

Count Buelow said that Count Metternich, who was now in Berlin, had not yet sent in a report of the conversation which he would probably make verbally, but he hoped that there was no misunderstanding on the subject, as Count Metternich had been instructed not to speak about an alliance unless the subject was broached to him by your Lordship.

I replied that that was exactly what had taken place. Your Lordship, in a recent conversation with me, had expressed the opinion that the time had now come when His Majesty's Government should give a reply to the proposals which had originally been made by Baron Eckardstein for an alliance between our two countries, which should take effect if either should be attacked by two Powers at the same time. The pourparlers had advanced to a certain point when Count Hatzfeldt, whose health had slightly improved, had a conversation with your Lordship, and explained that the proposed alliance must include both Austria and Italy as members of the Triple

Alliance. Shortly afterwards Baron Eckardstein had suggested that the question should be dropped for the time, but towards the end of the last Session of Parliament he had suggested a further discussion of the subject; your Lordship had pointed out that the matter was too important to be taken in hand at such a moment, but that you would be prepared to discuss it in the Autumn. Your Lordship was therefore of opinion that a further delay in replying to the German Government might be considered as a want of courtesy on the part of His Majesty's Government, and that you had therefore explained to Count Metternich the reasons which made it advisable not to pursue the subject at present.

Count Buelow thanked me for this explanation, which made the matter quite clear to him, and he agreed that the present was not an opportune moment for continuing the discussion. But he hoped that the question would not be dropped altogether, as he was convinced that an alliance such as had been proposed between the Triple Alliance on the one hand and Great Britain on the other would secure the peace of Europe for the next five and twenty years. He considered that such an alliance would be of the greatest advantage to both countries, and not more so to Germany than to England, who, he thought, had somewhat added to her difficulties by her neglect of Italy. The result had been that Italy had thrown herself into the arms of France and was no longer so friendly to England as formerly. . . . . [Possibility of friendly relations between Germany and England.]

I have, &c.
FRANK C. LASCELLES.

MINUTE BY KING EDWARD.

Quite satisfactory.

E.R.

No. 96.

Baron Holstein to Mr. Chirol.(¹)

(Strictly Confidential.)
Dear Mr. Chirol, *Berlin, January* 3, 1902.

In the first place I send you my best wishes for your health and your good humour in the coming year. Good humour is very essential, and we must not allow it to be impaired, even when discussing the war of words which is being waged by the organs of public opinion. This sort of warfare began in January '96. If the German Press, as you remark, is at present more outrageous than any other, it is only fair to say that no other country or sovereign has been treated in England as ours was six years ago, and you must not underrate the ingenuity which your countrymen showed at that time in " drawing their hostility home to us." A great part of to-day's harvest was sown then. A great part, not all of it. I remember your telling me one day, in '95 or '96, that you had noticed with surprise the amount of ill feeling prevalent here against England. The causes of this undeniable fact are various, some transient and some are more lasting. Among the latter the most prominent one is the conviction which has been inculcated into the minds of the last two German generations, not only that ever since 1864 England either sympathised with or materially assisted our enemies, but also that English policy, while keeping itself free from any sort of engagement, is leaving no stone unturned to bring about a great continental war.

The Pro-Boer feeling is merely a transient cause of exasperation, but I quite agree with you that while it remains effervescent, the time for an Anglo-German agreement has not come.

(¹) From the Sanderson MSS.

Are you aware that the idea of such an agreement originated in England? I am
not sure whether I told you, so I must do that now.

On the 21st of August 1898 Sir F. Lascelles informed the Emperor—who dictated
the substance of the conversation immediately afterwards—that after a luncheon of
Ministers at which Sir Frank was present—"it took the form of a Cabinet Council to
which I was invited being attached to Your Majesty's person." Mr. Chamberlain
brought forward the idea of a defensive alliance which was to become effective only
in case one of the contracting parties was attacked by at least two Powers. According
to Sir Frank Lascelles, Mr. Chamberlain thus supported his proposal: "Each one
of us is strong enough to fight any *one* Power that should attack him, but in case of
two Powers attacking, the issue is at least very doubtful. Therefore, should Germany
be assaulted by any *two* Powers *at once*, England is ready to assist with every armament
in her power to knock down one of her antagonists, whilst Germany is fighting the
other one; the same England would wish Germany to do, should the case be the
reverse."

The Emperor replied that he heard for the first time of an Anglo-German alliance
in this form, that the conditions deserved serious consideration.

Lord Salisbury had not been present when Mr. Chamberlain exposed his plan,
and serious doubts were entertained from the first in our official quarters, concerning
the Premier's acquiescence to it. As for myself I can show that I formally and
repeatedly expressed the conviction that no agreement of any kind would be come to
while Lord Salisbury had voice in the chapter. This view being held in higher
regions, instructions were sent to London to the effect that the German Representative
was not to broach the subject, but simply to receive and eventually discuss such
overtures as might be made to him. These directions have been so far acted upon,
except in one isolated case last summer, when poor Hatzfeldt in an access of nervous
over-excitement resulting from his fatal illness appears to have summoned Lord
Lansdowne to come to terms with Germany then and there. As soon as Eckhardstein,
who knew the purport of Hatzfeldt's instructions, was informed of what had occurred
in the interview, he hastened to Berlin to warn this Gov[ernmen]t. Thereupon
Hatzfeldt's official functions were immediately brought to an end, for even his best
friends were obliged to acknowledge that the steadiness of nerve, for which he had
always been famous, had deserted him. Cause and effect lay open before Lord
Lansdowne's eyes, and I therefore felt somewhat surprised to hear about a week ago
that your friend Lascelles referring to Hatzfeldt's last conversation with Lord
Lansdowne, had informed the Chancellor that the British Gov[ernmen]t considered
the present juncture as unfavourable for further discussion of an Anglo-German
Agreement.

Why not have let the matter rest, since nobody—to my knowledge at least—
had urged it? As it is, the British Gov[ernmen]t have taken advantage of the feverish
restlessness of an invalid—although he had been instantly disavowed in the most
conclusive manner—to send us the mittens in all form. This "Absage," which we
cannot help regarding as a gratuitous perhaps a premeditated snub, does not of course
improve the prospects for later on, and I even suspect that in Lord Salisbury's mind
this rebuff was intended to shelve for good the question of an Anglo-German agreement.
The Premier who is aware that the British fleet may be able to protect the British
Isles but not all the frontiers of the British Empire, who on the other hand is
decidedly hostile to any idea of a serious reform of your military system, has in all
probability determined to stick to isolation, and to await the great continental war,
which he thinks must come some day, and which perhaps would have come already, if
all parties concerned were not by this time aware that Lord Salisbury is waiting for it.
Should that hope fail and the worst come to the worst the old Byzantine expedient of
buying off Barbarians would still be practicable and might perhaps, in Lord Salisbury's
eyes, be preferable to a friendly agreement with the German Emperor.

I remember having predicted to you something of this kind in January 1896,
and I also remember to my regret that you were somewhat hurt then. You and I

ought not to take offence reciprocally, for we are both working in the same direction. If we cannot shape things according to our will, we must even look at and take them as they are.

To prove to you that I do not stand alone in my appreciation of England's military shortcomings, I am going to quote a recent remark of President Roosevelt's, for which I rely on your discretion. In a letter which he wrote in November last to a German in official position, the President discusses in a spirit of not unfriendly criticism the results of English military operations in South Africa, and finally says by way of summing up :

> "It seems to me that there will have to be fundamental reform in the British character if she (Great Britain) is to continue to stand in the front rank and to bear her burden of vast and widely extended Empire."

The "reform of character" can only apply to military matter. The President alluded evidently to the necessity that the individual Briton should take upon himself at least part of those onera to which all the great nations of the Continent have submitted in the course of the last century.

I have been told that Lord Rosebery said about a year ago, if the South African War lasted long enough, it might have the result of bringing about a military reform. Lord Salisbury does not appear to contemplate any much measure, nor does he seem to share Mr. Chamberlain's belief that Great Britain up-to-date is strong enough to tackle any single enemy. The Premier, therefore, still cherishes the hope of being able to keep the war epidemic out by strict isolation. What his chances are you know better than I, because you are better able to survey the general situation of Great Britain at home and abroad. I for one do not believe in the benefit of this kind of isolation, nor do I believe in a policy which is based upon the principles of doing one's fighting by proxy. I believe with Roosevelt in the necessity of reforming the "character" of your military system. My interest in those questions is based upon the belief that at some future time the two great Nations may yet get together, although in all human probability I shall not then be here to see it.

Hoping that during the holidays you achieved a mark at pingpong, which I understand to be the sensation of the hour,

I remain, &c.
HOLSTEIN.

No. 97.

Sir F. Lascelles to Mr. Chirol.

My dear Chirol, *Brunswick, January* 10, 1902.

I return with many thanks Holstein's most interesting letter which is satisfactory in so far as it shows that he wished to maintain a good understanding with us. I have a distinct recollection of my conversation with the Emperor at Friedrichshof on Aug. 26, 1898 and have refreshed my memory by reading over my official report and private letter to Balfour who was then in charge of the F[oreign] O[ffice]. In neither of these did I mention the names of the "influential persons" who were disposed to consider the desirability of an alliance with Germany, but it is true that I mentioned to the Emperor the fact that I had met several Ministers at a luncheon at Mr. Chamberlain's and the subject had been discussed. The Emperor's account therefore, as given by Holstein, making due allowance for H[is] M[ajesty's] usual exaggeration, is not an unfair account of our conversation. Subsequently the Emperor more than once alluded to the "arrangement" which had been come to, and twice at least I had been obliged to point out to him that there was no "arrangement" at all and that I had been speaking without instructions. So far then Holstein's account may be taken as correct, but his account of the subsequent proceedings is not quite accurate. It was Eckardstein who first broached the subject, possibly without instructions from the Wilhelmstrasse. Then Hatzfeldt recovered sufficiently to take the matter in hand, and it was Eckardstein's suggestion that the matter should drop for a time. Then, just before the end of the session he proposed that the conversations should again be renewed but Lord Lansdowne pointed out that so important a question could not be dealt with at a time when every one was leaving London, but that he would be prepared to discuss the matter in the Autumn. It was with the view of proving to Metternich that he had not lost sight of Eckardstein's suggestion that Lord Lansdowne made his communication to Metternich on Dec. 19 last. I naturally thought that Metternich would have at once reported this, and therefore I alluded to it in my conversations with Bülow and Richthofen. Metternich told me afterwards that he had intended to make a verbal report of his conversation with Lord Lansdowne but that I had anticipated him. It seems to me therefore either that Holstein has not been kept properly informed of what took place, or that he is deliberately seeking a grievance. In the latter case it would only be on a matter of form, as both Bülow and Richthofen quite agree that in view of the excited states of puplic opinion on both sides, the present would not be an opportune moment for continuing the discussions on a question which although dropped for the moment may be resumed later.

I am grateful to you for having sent me Holstein's letter before showing it to any one else, but I am sure it would interest Lord Lansdowne to whom you might also perhaps send this answer.

I am here for the purpose of presenting my credentials, and shall only get back to Berlin tomorrow evening so I shall have but little time before the Messenger goes, but I shall write to Lord Lansdowne that he may expect an interesting conversation with you.

Your ever,
F. LASCELLES.

No. 98.

Draft to Mr. Chirol.(1)

My dear Chirol, *January* 21, 1902.

I return with many thanks the interesting papers which you left with me yesterday.

Sir F. Lascelles has told you how far he is able to acquiesce in Baron Holstein's account of the statement which he made to the German Emperor in August 1898.

As regards the communications made here on the subject of a possible alliance between Great Britain and Germany I should not have thought it right to speak on such a subject if Baron Holstein had not first mentioned it to you. As he has done so I have obtained Lord Lansdowne's permission to correct some apparent misapprehensions.

The subject was first started by Baron Eckhardstein in conservation with Lord Lansdowne in March last, and was pressed by him on Lord Lansdowne's attention on several subsequent interviews. B[aro]n Eckhardstein stated that these conversations were unofficial but that he was speaking with authority. The discussions were deferred at Lord Lansdowne's request on account of Lord Salisbury's absence from England. In May Count Hatzfeldt, who had returned to the Embassy took up the subject in conversation with Lord Lansdowne, and stated that any agreement of the kind must be so framed as to include the members of the Triple Alliance. Upon C[oun]t Hatzfeldt's departure on leave B[aro]n Eckhardstein stated that His Exc[ellenc]y's intervention had complicated the matter, and suggested that for the time the discussions should be discontinued. Subsequently at the close of the Session

(1) From the Sanderson MSS.

Baron Eckardstein proposed that they should be renewed, but Lord Lansdowne pointed out that they could not be usefully pursued at a time when all the Ministers were dispersing for the holidays.

After C[oun]t Metternich's arrival here some indications led Lord Lansdowne to believe that the German Gov[ernmen]t might consider themselves slighted if the matter were allowed simply to drop *sub silencio* without some further explanation of our views. He therefore took an opportunity of discussing the subject frankly and fully with C[oun]t Metternich before the departure of the latter to Berlin for Christmas and explained to him the reasons for which we felt in present circumstances and especially in view of the present temper of the two Countries that we were unable to entertain the project.

Lord Lansdowne has been assured that his explanations have been accepted both by Count Bulow and by Baron Richthofen in the most friendly manner, and have been in no way regarded by them as indicating any want of cordiality or regard for the German Gov[ernmen]t.

The other portions of Baron Holstein's letter are largely expressions of personal opinion upon which I need scarcely comment. To anyone however who has worked, as I have, under Lord Salisbury for a succession of years the conception of him as waiting for and expecting to derive profit from a European war is, if I may be allowed the expression, grotesque. He has been perfectly outspoken to me on many occasions and the natural bent of his mind is certainly not optimistic but I have never heard him speak of a European war as impending in the near future, or as anything but a calamity which we should do out utmost to prevent.

It has happened not unfrequently in the last years that C[oun]t Hatzfeldt has come to me and complained "Voilà une [chose ?] que j'ai causé avec Lord Salisbury et que le diable me prenne si je comprends la politique de votre Gouvernement." To which I used to reply that he ought to know that we had not got a policy and worked from hand to mouth. I once repeated one of these outbursts to Lord Salisbury who laughed and said "I had no idea that our conversation had such far reaching objects yet you might tell Hatzfeldt that with a Parliamentary régime like ours, it is impossible to pledge the Gov[ernmen]t as to the course it will take in case of some future emergency."

What conclusions C[oun]t Hatzfeldt may have drawn or reported to Berlin after such interviews I of course have no means of conjecturing.

Endorsed " Cancelled."
I talked the matter over with Chirol—giving the general facts but in somewhat less detail.

T. H. S

Jan. 21.

CHAPTER XI.
THE ANGLO-JAPANESE AGREEMENT, 1901-2.

[*ED. NOTE.*—The first signs of *rapprochement* between England and Japan began in 1895. England then refused to join in the pressure put upon Japan by France, Germany and Russia to evacuate Port Arthur (the 23rd April, 1895, *G.P.* XV, 275–7) and abate the other demands on China after her victory over her. These steps are described in *G.P.* IX, 241–333 and more fully in Sir E. Satow's despatches to Lord Salisbury of the 26th March and the 4th April, 1898 (*v.* I, pp. 25–7 and 31–2), which should be carefully studied in this connection.]

No. 99.

The Marquess of Lansdowne to Sir C. MacDonald. (Tohyo)

F.O. Japan 538.
(No. 44.)   Confidential.

Sir,   *Foreign Office, April* 17, 1901.

The Japanese Minister spoke to me to-day with some anxiety about the position of his country in respect to Chinese affairs.

He told me that, in his opinion, Japanese interests were seriously threatened by the policy of Russia, and he added that it seemed to him highly necessary that the Japanese Government and that of His Majesty should endeavour to arrive at some permanent understanding for the protection of their interests in that part of the world.

Baron Hayashi was careful to explain that he was expressing his own views, and not those which he was authorised by the Japanese Government to convey to me.

I told the Minister that I would not fail to bear in mind what he had said, but that, without some substantive proposal for giving effect to such a policy as he had indicated, I could scarcely be expected to express an opinion in regard to its merits.

Baron Eckardstein mentioned two or three days ago that Baron Hayashi had used similar language to him, and had suggested, also as his own personal idea, that there might be an Agreement between Japan, Germany and Great Britain, based on the Anglo-German Agreement of last year, but going further, and pledging the three Governments to support the integrity of China and the maintenance of the open door at existing Treaty ports.

I am, &c.
LANSDOWNE.

No. 100.

The Marquess of Lansdowne to Mr. Whitehead.

F.O. Japan 538.
(No. 66.)   Secret.

Sir,   *Foreign Office, June* 21, 1901.

The Japanese Minister called on me to-day at my request, and I made to him a statement to the effect of the enclosed Memorandum,([1]) of which I handed him a copy.

Baron Hayashi expressed his thanks, and said that he would refer my proposal to the Japanese Government. He went on, however, to tell me that they were in hopes that they would be able to obtain out of the sum for which the Powers had already asked China an amount sufficient to compensate them for the loss which they would sustain in consequence of the difference between the rate of interest on the Chinese bonds and the rate at which their credit enabled them to borrow. He was under the impression that

([1]) [*ED. NOTE.*—Not reproduced. This refers to a Memo. by J. N. Jordan, dated London, 19 June, 1901, advising against a proposed loan to Corea.]

the total of 450,000,000 taels, at which the claims of the Powers had been fixed, provided for a considerable margin, and that out of this an addition might be made to the amount to be received by Japan, which, he said, he estimated at 25 per cent. of the original Japanese claim, or 10,000,000 yen. He told me that the Japanese Government had approached the German and United States Governments with a similar proposal.

I replied that, even assuming the existence of such a margin as he contemplated, the Powers were not very likely to allow the whole or the greater part of it to be absorbed for the benefit of Japan; other Powers would be sure to ask for similar assistance.

Baron Hayashi replied that in his belief the margin that had been allowed would prove to be sufficient to meet the Japanese requirements and still to leave a large surplus, which would be available for the purpose of meeting the unforeseen requirements of other Powers. He asked me how far we should be likely to go in assisting them in the manner described in my Memorandum. I said that I should be glad of further information as to the manner in which the extra amount now claimed by Japan had been computed, but that I thought we should probably be able to place bonds worth, at their face value, say, £500,000 at the disposal of the Japanese Government.

I am, &c.
LANSDOWNE.

No. 101.

The Marquess of Lansdowne to Mr. Whitehead.

F.O. Japan 538.
(No. 70.)   Secret.
Sir,   Foreign Office, June 26, 1901.

The Japanese Minister called here to-day and communicated to me the answer of the Japanese Government to the offer made to them by His Majesty's Government (see my despatch No. 66, Secret, of the 21st instant), with a view to facilitating the acceptance by Japan of the scheme for payment of the indemnities in Chinese bonds.

Baron Hayashi said that the Japanese Government, while appreciating the generous character of the offer, were not in a position to accept it, as it was not their intention to appeal for such assistance.

The Japanese Government had, by the declaration which they had made at Peking on the subject, desired to indicate that they must necessarily suffer loss if they were compelled to accept bonds in payment of their claim which had been calculated on the basis of immediate payment in cash, and that they considered, therefore, that they were entitled to some compensation.

The Japanese Government anticipated that this view, which they considered reasonable, would appeal to the sense of justice of the Powers, and would receive their support.

I am, &c.
LANSDOWNE.

No. 102.

The Marquess of Lansdowne to Mr. Whitehead.

F.O. Japan 563.
(No. 89.)   Secret.
Sir,   Foreign Office, July 31, 1901.

I had some conversation to-day with the Japanese Minister in regard to affairs in the Far East.

I said that I hoped that the question of the indemnities might now be regarded as disposed of, but that I could not conceal from myself that a number of other questions of the greatest difficulty were still waiting for solution.

I asked Baron Hayashi whether he was aware of the views of the Japanese Government as to the manner in which negotiations for a settlement of the questions arising under Article II of the Joint Note could most conveniently be conducted. It had seemed to me that the Peking Conference was a somewhat unwieldly piece of machinery, and it had occured to me that when we came to the question of commercial facilities and internal reforms some better agency might, even if only for the purpose of preliminary investigations, perhaps be adopted.

Baron Hayashi expressed agreement with what I had said, and added that he could not help thinking that it might be advisable that each of the Powers should conduct its own negotiations separately. But I did not gather that he had formed any very precise ideas upon the subject.

We then discussed the situation in regard to Manchuria.

Baron Hayashi told me that the Japanese had a strong sentimental dislike to the retention by Russia of that Province, from which they had, at one time, been themselves expelled.

But Japan's real concern was for Corea. Corea could not possibly stand alone, its people were far too unintelligent, and sooner or later it would have to be decided whether the Country was to fall to Russia or not. The Japanese Government could not possibly accept the former of these alternatives. They would certainly fight in order to prevent it, and it must be the object of their diplomacy to isolate Russia, with which Power, if it stood alone, they were prepared to deal.

I observed that in our view also it would be most unfortunate that Corea should pass into the hands of another Power. Corea was further off from us than from Japan, but, considering the importance of its geographical position, we could no more than the Japanese regard its fate with indifference.

I was speaking without authorisation from His Majesty's Government, but there was so much resemblance between the policy of our two Governments, neither of which harboured aggressive designs in the Far East, although both desired to maintain the *status quo*, that I thought it would be worth our while to consider what line of conduct we might follow, supposing the balance of power in the waters of the Far East to be threatened with serious disturbance. If the Japanese Government desired it, he (Baron Hayashi) would find me ready to discuss the matter with him with a view to the possible establishment of an understanding between our two countries.

Baron Hayashi received my suggestion attentively; such an understanding, he said, would, of course, have to be based on reciprocity of engagements, and that aspect of the case required careful examination; he asked my permission to refer to the matter again. There was, he said, many " unseen things " connected with it.

L.

No. 103.

The Marquess of Lansdowne to Mr. Whitehead.

F.O. Japan 563.
(No. 91.) Secret.
Sir,   *Foreign Office, August* 14, 1901.

The Japanese Minister reminded me to-day of the conversation recorded in my despatch No. 89, Secret, of the 31st ultimo, in which we had discussed the possibility of an understanding between the Japanese and British Governments with regard to affairs in the Far East.

Baron Hayashi told me that he felt no doubt that his Government would be glad to come to such an understanding, and asked me whether I was in a position to explain to him the conditions which we should require.

I replied that it seemed to me that as Japan was more immediately interested than we were, it was rather for the Japanese Government to formulate a statement of their requirements. We should then be able to say how far we could meet them, and upon what terms.

Baron Hayashi said that he did not for a moment suppose that there could be any question of an offensive or defensive alliance between us, and that, although he had not received instructions, he felt no doubt that the Japanese Government would desire, so far as China was concerned, to maintain the policy of the "open door" and the integrity of the Chinese Empire.

It was, however, with Corea that they were most closely concerned, and, as he had already told me, his country would go to war rather than see Corea fall into the hands of Russia, if they could be assured against the hostile intervention of a third Power.

I suggested to Baron Hayashi that it would be well that he should obtain from his Government definite instructions upon these points, and I undertook that I would in the meanwhile communicate what he had said to my colleagues and endeavour to be ready with a proposal on our side as soon as he was in a position to make a proposal on behalf of Japan.

[I am, &c.
LANSDOWNE.]

MINUTE BY KING EDWARD.

The King considers it most essential that we should give Japan our hearty support on all occasions when it is possible to do so.

E.R.

No. 104.

The Marquess of Lansdowne to Sir F. Lascelles.

F.O. Germany (Prussia) 1519.
(No. 304.)   Confidential.
Sir,   *Foreign Office, September* 11, 1901.

Count Metternich called at this Office on the 3rd instant and communicated a Memorandum which had been drawn up in answer to a paper handed to the German Emperor by the King at their recent meeting.

The paper in question was a series of notes on various questions which I had dictated under circumstances of considerable pressure by the King's desire for His Majesty's use and personal information in case the German Emperor should mention any of these topics to His Majesty in the course of conversation. It was not drawn up with any idea of its being communicated to the German Government as a written document, and I must request you to explain to the German Government that it must be regarded as a purely informal and unofficial document.

I enclose a copy of it and of the reply of the German Government for your confidential information.

I am, &c.
LANSDOWNE.

Enclosure 1 in No. 104.

*Memorandum on Questions which may be mentioned by the German Emperor
to the King.*

Chinese Negotiations.

His Majesty's Government have, in the course of the China negotiations, insisted upon the necessity of including in the arrangements with regard to the indemnities some provision which would preclude China from hereafter making separate arrangements with individual Powers for the repayment of her share of the debt. The object desired was of course to interpose difficulties in the way of "backstairs" transactions to which the Chinese Government might lend itself for corrupt reasons, or into which it might be coerced for the purpose of alienating territory or conferring exclusive privileges, in consideration of the remission of portions of the debt.

Our views upon this subject had been freely explained to the Representative of the German Embassy, and we had every reason to suppose that they were concurred in by the German Government.

On the other hand, it cannot be too clearly understood that we did not in the least desire to prevent China from paying off the whole or a part of the bonds before the expiration of the allotted time, provided this arrangement were made with the full knowledge and concurrence of the Powers, so as to prevent undue preferences being accorded to any of them.

It was therefore with some surprise that we learn that when the Protocol was believed to be nearly ready for communication to the Conference by the Committee the German Representative supported the Russian Minister in voting for the excision of the clause which had been framed with the above objects, though Sir E. Satow had informed us that the German Minister had instructions, and a satisfactory formula would probably be found.

We also noticed with regret that the German Representative did not support Sir E. Satow in voting against a most inconvenient arrangement, under which it was proposed that the conversion of the import duties from *ad valorem* to specific duties should be entrusted to an unwieldy Commission composed of Representatives of all the Powers, each of which was to be at liberty to have a vote.

Germany, the United States and Japan to act with Great Britain in further Negotiations.

We have expressed a hope that, in the important negotiations which will now have to be commenced under Article 11 of the joint note with regard to Commercial Treaties and commercial facilities, Germany, Japan and the United States, as the Powers most largely interested in the trade of the Far East, will associate themselves with us. It has been suggested that the new negotiations should take place at Shanghae, and they will obviously stand a better chance of success if the Representatives of the Powers less interested in Chinese trade are excluded. They can be given an opportunity of adhering at a later stage.

Claims of German Shareholders in Netherlands South African Railway Company.

Baron Eckardstein has intimated to me that Count von Bülow earnestly desires a settlement of the claims of the shareholders in the Netherlands South African Railway Company, and of the claims arising out of the deportations which took place from South Africa.

Attention has been given to both of these questions. I have communicated to Baron Eckardstein, confidentially, a proposal for an amicable settlement with the German shareholders, upon terms which he will no doubt report to the German Government.

Claims of Deported German Subjects.

The investigation of the claims of persons deported from South Africa is proceeding before Mr. Milvain's Commission, but up to yesterday no German claims had been submitted to the Commissioners. This is very unfortunate. There have been *pourparlers* with regard to the possibility of a settlement of all these claims out of Court for a lump sum, and in principle I am not averse to this idea, and to thereby avoiding the expense and trouble of a prolonged enquiry. It would, however, be very difficult for His Majesty's Government to consent to such a settlement until the Commission had had an opportunity of investigating some, at all events, of the German claims, and forming an opinion with regard to them.

Koweit.

It is possible that the question of Koweit may be mentioned to His Majesty.

His Majesty is aware that his Government have entered into special arrangements with the Sheikh, under which the latter is forbidden to alienate territory without their consent. The nature of this arrangement was fully explained in 1900 by Sir Nicholas O'Conor to Baron von Marschall at Constantinople. There are rumours that the Turkish Government intend to attack the Sheikh, and should these rumours prove to be well founded, it may be necessary to remind the Porte of the language held by Sir N. O'Conor in 1900 to the Turkish Minister for Foreign Affairs, when he said that Her Majesty's Government did not desire to interfere with the *status quo* or with the Sultan's authority in these parts, but that they could not, in view of their great interests in the Persian Gulf, view with indifference any action which would alter the existing condition of affairs or give another Power special rights or privileges over territory belonging to the Sheikh of Koweit, with whom Her Majesty's Government had certain agreements. He added that he trusted his Excellency would bear these remarks in mind in case any proposals were made conflicting with our interests, and he did so the more confidently as such proposals would probably also conflict with the interests of Turkey. Should anything be said to His Majesty with regard to German interests in the neighbourhood of Koweit, I suggest that an assurance might be given that we have no desire to refuse facilities to the German Government for coming to Koweit as the terminus of the Anatolian Railway, but that, in that case, a previous understanding with His Majesty's Government would be indispensable.

Morocco.

With regard to Morocco, the policy of the German and British Governments would appear to be identical. Both desire the maintenance of the *status quo*, and both would probably resent any indignity offered to the Moorish Envoy, who lately visited and was received with honour at the German and British Courts.

Enclosure 2 in No. 104.

Memorandum communicated by Count Metternich, September 3, 1901.

A "Memorandum on questions which may be mentioned by the German Emperor to the King" has been handed by His Majesty the King to His Majesty the Emperor. The Imperial German Government notes with satisfaction the manifest desire of His Britannic Majesty's Government to come to an understanding on the principal pending questions, and avails itself of this opportunity to explain the German point of view with regard to each one of the questions dealt with in the Memorandum.

1. *Chinese Negotiations.*

The instructions given to the German Minister in Peking have always been of a conciliatory nature. His Imperial Majesty's Government have been guided, throughout the Chinese troubles, by a desire to prevent a rupture between the Powers. Instructions of too technical or too special a nature have, as far as possible, not been given to Herr von Mumm.

According to the latest intelligence from Peking, an understanding has, in the meantime, been arrived at concerning the questions hitherto disputed, and the final Protocol has meanwhile been submitted to the Chinese Government for signature.

2. *Germany, the United States and Japan to act with Great Britain in future Negotiations.*

The proposal for a joint action of Germany, Great Britain, the United States and Japan in the negotiations which will now have to be commenced, with regard to Commercial Treaties and commercial facilities, deserves and will meet with the most serious consideration on the part of His Imperial Majesty's Government. At the same time, it appears indispensable to examine—with the co-operation of His Imperial Majesty's Minister in Peking—the question whether or to what extent the exclusion of those Powers which are supposed to have a lesser interest in Chinese matters might have the effect of drawing those Powers closer together, and thus forming a new and undesirable groupment of European States in the Far East.

Claims of German Shareholders in Netherlands South African Railway Company.

On first perusal of the British proposals, the following two conditions appear to be particularly onerous :—

1. That shareholders should receive a compensation of only £130. This amount would correspond to a quotation of about 156 per cent., whereas, according to the statutes of the Railway Company, the shareholders themselves have calculated the price at which the shares should be repurchased at $264\frac{1}{3}$ per cent., and whereas the shares before the war, and even as late as this last spring, have varied in value from 220 to 230 per cent. Even after the Report of the Transvaal Concessions Commission has considerably lowered the exchange value of the aforesaid shares, they still maintained at the time when the Memorandum was drawn up (*i.e.*, up to the 12th August) a rate of $173\frac{1}{2}$ per cent. Considering that the average dividend paid during the three years preceding the war, viz., 1897 to 1899, amounted to $12\frac{5}{12}$ per cent., the price now offered by the British Government falls considerably short of what the shareholders believe to be entitled to expect.

2. According to the British Government's proposals, all shareholders claiming repayment (under B) will be required to prove that their shares were private property previous to the outbreak of the war. With regard to this proposal, it must be remembered that—at least, up to the time when, in December last, the Committee for the Protection of German Interests ("Deutsche Schutzvereinigung") was formed—Transvaal Railway shares were considered by all capitalists as a good investment, and, there being no difficulty in disposing of them at all exchanges, must have gone from hand to hand very frequently. It will, therefore, be very difficult in many cases to prove the *bonâ fide* ownership for the period preceding December last.

Considering the possible far-reaching consequences of these proposals, the matter has been submitted to the "Deutsche Schutzvereinigung." This body, which represents the interests of the great majority of German shareholders, having been heard, the German answer on these two points, as well as on some others, will be explained in more detail to the British Government through the German Embassy in London.

Claims of German Subjects deported from South Africa.

As regards the claims of German subjects deported from South Africa, a list of all claims of this nature that have come to the notice of the Imperial German Government had been transmitted in April through the German Embassy in London to the " South African Deportation by the Military Authorities Compensation Commission." Dr. Sieveking, the barrister appointed to represent these German claims, has, however, in the outset, met with no opportunity of pleading these claims before the Commission owing to a decision of the latter that the claimants must appear before them in person. This decision was subsequently dropped as being unpracticable. At a later stage, Dr. Sieveking did not consider it opportune to bring any single claims before the Commission, because at that time *pourparlers* for the settlement of all these claims out of Court by a lump sum were taking place.

However, since in the Memorandum the desire is expressed that the Commission should investigate some of the German claims with a view to afford the British Government an opportunity of forming an opinion on them, Dr. Sieveking has been instructed to place those cases, which are now sufficiently prepared, before the Commission without delay.

3. *Kueit (Koweit).*

With regard to the third point, the German Government wish to state they have no desire to claim any sovereign or suzerain rights or privileges over territory belonging to the Sheikh of Koweit. This port has an importance for Germany merely as the proposed terminus of the Bagdad Railway. Germany has had no motive for enquiring into the questions of sovereignty or suzerainty with regard to this district; but wishes to point out that hitherto the Sultan in Constantinople has been regarded as the undisputed Sovereign of the Koweit territory. In so far as His Britannic Majesty's Government do not either " desire to interfere with the Sultan's authority in those parts," there appears to exist no difference of opinion between the German and the British Governments on this point. The exact nature of the arrangements existing between the British Government and the Sheikh of Koweit is not fully clear to the German Government, notwithstanding the explanations given in 1900 by Sir Nicholas O'Conor to Baron von Marschall at Constantinople. As, however, these arrangements appear to be limited to the sale of ground by the Sheikh, Herr Dr. von Siemens, the Chief Manager of the Bagdad Railway Company, will be instructed to come to a previous understanding with the British Government, when the time for purchasing land for a railway terminus and a landing-place at Koweit shall have come. In case this arrangement should not satisfy the British Government, the German Government will most likely express their desire to be given full cognisance of the arrangements entered into between the British Government and the Sheikh of Koweit.

4. *Morocco.*

In Morocco we follow a policy of reserve. The Morocco question by itself is not sufficiently important for us to justify a policy by which Germany might incur the risk of serious international complications.

No. 105.

The Marquess of Lansdowne to Mr. Whitehead.

F.O. Japan 563.
(No. 108A.)   Secret.
Sir,   *Foreign Office, October* 16, 1901.

Baron Hayashi informed me to-day, with reference to our conversation on the 14th of August—and my despatch No. 91, Secret, of that day—that he had now received authority from the Japanese Government to discuss with me the question of an understanding between the British and Japanese Governments.

He added that his instructions did not permit him to enter into details, as to which he could express his own opinion only.

At the outset of our conversation he asked me whether it would, in my opinion, be desirable that Germany should be a party to the understanding, which would, he thought, " look much more formidable " if it were to include Germany. I replied that our relations with Germany were of a very friendly and intimate description, but that it seemed to me that in the first instance, at all events, it would be desirable that Great Britain and Japan should endeavour to arrive at a clear idea of their requirements without reference to any other Power. German interests in the Far East were not as important as those of this Country or of Japan, but should Great Britain and Japan come to terms it would then be for them to consider, with reference to the scope and character of the Agreement, whether it was one to which we might invite Germany to become a party.

Baron Hayashi then proceeded to give me the following sketch of the arrangement which was contemplated by the Japanese Government. That Government was above all things interested in Corea, and it was a matter of life and death for them to keep Russia out of it. Their interest in Manchuria was only secondary, and due to the fact that encroachments in Manchuria might lead to encroachments in Corea. It was necessary for the Japanese Government not only to guard against the absorption of Corea by Russia, but to maintain the privileges conceded to their countrymen by the Russo-Japanese Agreement of 1898.

His Excellency evidently referred to Article III of the Protocol of April 13th of that year, which runs as follows :—

" Vu le large développement qu'ont pris les entreprises commerciales et indus-trielles du Japon en Corée, ainsi que le nombre considérable de sujets Japonais résidant dans ce pays, le Gouvernement Russe n'entravera point le développement des relations commerciales et industrielles entre le Japon et la Corée."

This agreement, Baron Hayashi said, conferred upon Japan rights of " industrial and commercial expansion " in Corea ; rights the exercise of which, he said very frankly, might lead to the establishment of political influence. It was therefore necessary for Japan to stifle in its inception any movement under which Russia might obtain preponderance in that Country.

As to China, the Minister said that the policy of Japan was identical with that of Great Britain. Both Powers desired to maintain the integrity and independence of China, and, in regard to Commercial matters, the policy of the " open door."

The object of the Japanese Government was to secure the support of Great Britain in giving effect to the above policy, and they therefore proposed that Great Britain should undertake to support Japan if Japan should find herself obliged to go to war in defence of it with more than one Foreign Power. If, on the other hand, Great Britain found herself at war with more than one Foreign Power in defence of her interests in any part of China, Japan would undertake to support us with her whole strength.

Baron Hayashi laid some stress upon the fact that the Japanese Government did not propose that the Alliance should take effect in case either England or Japan found themselves at war with a single Power. That, he thought, would be approaching too nearly to an offensive and defensive Alliance. If Japan were to be at war with Russia alone, it would be sufficient if Great Britain remained neutral ; the observance by her of a strict neutrality would of itself be of the greatest assistance to Japan, as it would deprive the Russian Fleet of the power of using British Coaling Stations.

He added that it was in his view possible that the understanding should be made to extend even to the action of the two Powers in regard to Siam.

I thanked Baron Hayashi for his statement, which I promised to refer to my Colleagues, and which I said appeared to me to form a useful basis for discussion. I added that I presumed that the two Powers would, in the event of such an under-

H

standing being arrived at, agree that neither of us should, without consulting the other, make separate arrangements, or come to separate understandings with another Power as to Chinese or Corean affairs, and that we should in all cases where there was a probability of the Agreement coming into force, undertake to communicate with one another in good time and with the utmost frankness. I also said that I thought that the two Navies might with great advantage work together even in time of peace, each Power affording the other facilities for the use of docks, harbours and coaling stations Baron Hayashi cordially agreed with this suggestion.

> [I am, &c.
> LANSDOWNE.]

No. 106.

Sir C. MacDonald to the Marquess of Lansdowne.

F.O. Japan 563.
(No. 137.) Secret.   *Tokyo, D. October* 24, 1901.
My Lord,   R. *December* 4, 1901.
.... As the matter had been submitted to your Lordship I did not discuss the points raised by Baron Hayashi—but I gathered from Mr. Komura that, although these points had been put forward by Baron Hayashi as his own personal ideas, they were in effect those of the Japanese Government.

Mr. Komura mentioned that the question as to whether the German Government should be asked to become a party to the agreement had been discussed between your Lordship and Baron Hayashi, and it had been decided that it would not be necessary to do so until the negotiations had reached a more advanced stage.

> I have, &c.
> CLAUDE M. MacDONALD.

No. 107.

The Marquess of Lansdowne to Sir C. MacDonald.

F.O. Japan 563.
(No. 113.) Secret.
Sir,   *Foreign Office, October* 29, 1901.
The Japanese Minister spoke to me to-day of the projected agreement between this country and Japan referred to in my despatch No. 108A of the 16th instant, and proposed that a clause to the following effect should be introduced into it :—

> "In view of the preponderating interests of Japan in Corea, His Britannic Majesty's Government shall acquiesce in the adoption by Japan of suitable measures for the maintenance of those interests."

I said that I did not altogether approve of the form in which the clause was drafted, but that I would endeavour to find some means of meeting the wishes of the Japanese Government in regard to Corea.

> L.

No. 108.

Sir C. MacDonald to the Marquess of Lansdowne.

Tokyo, November 1, 1901.

F.O. Japan 563.　　　　　　　　　　　　　　　　　　　D. 1·5 P.M.

Tel. (No. 54.) Secret.　　　　　　　　　　　　　　　R. 1·45 P.M.

With reference to the interview which your Lordship had with Baron Hayashi on October 16th respecting a possible understanding or arrangement between the Governments of Great Britain and Japan with regard to affairs in the Far East in case of certain eventualities, Mr. Komura informs me that Japanese Government are very anxious for an expression of opinion on the part of His Majesty's Government with regard to proposals put forward by Baron Hayashi at that interview. Mr. Komura is of opinion that if anything is to be done it should be done quickly.

No. 109.

The Marquess of Lansdowne to Sir C. MacDonald.

F.O. Japan 563.　　　　　　　　　　*Foreign Office, November* 1, 1901.

Tel. (No. 85.) Secret.　　　　　　　　　　　　　　D. 12 midnight.

You may assure Mr. Komura confidentially that no time will be lost. Cabinet had only just reassembled and question will come before it next week. I have explained situation to Baron Hayashi two days ago, and told him that I regarded it as extremely hopeful.

No. 110.

The Marquess of Lansdowne to Sir C. MacDonald.

F.O. Japan 563.

(No. 115.) Secret.

Sir,　　　　　　　　　　　　　　　　　*Foreign Office, November* 6, 1901.

I handed to-day to the Japanese Minister the accompanying draft of an Agreement between the Japanese and British Governments with regard to our policy in the Far East.(¹)

I told him that I had prepared the draft solely with reference to the possibility of either Power becoming involved in hostilities in consequence of events in China or Corea. This was in accordance with the understanding at which he and I had arrived, and I had therefore not felt that I was justified in extending the scope of the draft. On the other hand, I felt bound to tell him that an Agreement limited in this manner seemed to be in some respects an incomplete solution of the question. What after all was of importance to both Great Britain and Japan was that neither of them should be overwhelmed by a combination of foreign Powers. The disappearance of Great Britain as a sea Power in the Far East would be a calamity to Japan, and it would make no matter to her whether such a calamity were to be brought about by a quarrel originating in the Far East or by complications in some other part of the World.

Baron Hayashi replied that, speaking for himself, he felt the force of this observation, and that he would not fail to repeat it to the Japanese Government, to which he would at once refer the draft which I had placed in his hands. This he read through in my presence, and told me that the only criticism which occurred to him at the moment was that our mention of the absorption of Corea as a contingency against which we desired to provide did not quite sufficiently meet the requirements of Japan,

(¹) [*V. infra,* pp. 115–20.]

[15214]　　　　　　　　　　　　　　　　　　　　　　　　H 2

which desired to be protected not only against the complete absorption of Corea, but against any serious encroachments on the part of Russia in that country, or, indeed, any action on her part which might interfere with the preponderant influence exercised by Japan in many parts of Corea.

ambiguous.

L.

No. 111.

The Marquess of Lansdowne to Sir C. MacDonald.

F.O. Japan 563.
Tel. (No. 87.) Secret. *Foreign Office, November* 22, 1901.

From some remarks made to Bertie by Japanese Minister after his interview with me recorded in my telegram No. 86 of November 20th he seems to think that any agreement made with Japan would as a matter of course be published. I advocated conclusion of the negotiations before meeting of Parliament only because the Cabinet would, after commencement of the Session, be much occupied with other questions. If you find that Japanese Minister for Foreign Affairs is under any misapprehension as to this point you can explain that in our view question of publication would require very careful consideration, and that we should not think of publishing without previous consultation with Japanese Government.

L.

No. 112.

Sir C. MacDonald to the Marquess of Lansdowne.

Tokyo, November 25, 1901.
F.O. Japan 563.
D. 5·25 P.M.
Tel. (No. 57.) Confidential.
R. 11 P.M.

Mr. Yamaza, Acting Director of the Political Bureau of Foreign Office, called this morning with the following message from Mr. Komura, who is still confined to his bed and unable to receive visitors.

Mr. Komura begged me to convey to His Majesty's Government the assurance of the Japanese Government that the delay in coming to a conclusion in the alliance proposals was entirely due to his illness, and the absence of the Prime Minister and most of Ministers at autumn manœuvres, and was in no way connected with Marquis Ito's mission, which is of a private and unofficial nature; the Marquis is in no way authorised to discuss or make arrangements on behalf of Japanese Government.

Mr. Yamaza added as coming from Mr. Komura that the Japanese Government are very favourably disposed to the draft proposal, but as it was a new departure and one of great importance, they would like a little more time to consider it.

I begged Mr. Yamaza to thank Mr. Komura for his message, which I should lose not time in conveying to your Lordships. I pointed out that manœuvres had come to an end on 13th November, and that Mr. Komura had himself said on the 31st October that if anything was to be done it should be done quickly—my telegram No. 54. I reminded Mr. Yamaza that the original proposals for an understanding had come from the Japanese Government through Baron Hayashi. His Majesty's Government were therefore not unnaturally surprised at delay. It was also well known that no serious step was taken in Japan without Marquis Ito being consulted; his visits to Berlin and St. Petersburg at this juncture had doubtless given rise, and with much reason, to misgivings on part of His Majesty's Government. Mr. Yamaza promised to convey purport of my remarks to Mr. Komura.

No. 113.

Sir C. MacDonald to the Marquess of Lansdowne.

F.O. Japan 563.
(No. 149.)   Secret.   *Tokyo,* D. *November* 28, 1901.
My Lord,   R. *January* 3, 1902.

On the 21st instant I received your Lordship's telegram No. 86 (Secret), setting forth the terms of the draft Agreement relative to the maintenance of the *status quo* and general peace in the Far East, which draft Agreement your Lordship informed me you had handed to Mr. Hayashi, the Japanese Minister in London, on the 6th instant.

Some hours previously I had received your Lordship's private telegram referring to the above, asking whether I thought the delay in coming to a decision on the terms of the draft Agreement was in any way connected with Marquis Ito's visit to St. Petersburgh and Berlin.

It was not until the receipt of your Lordship's telegram No. 85 that I was aware that a draft Agreement had been presented; Mr. Komura had been laid up with an attack of pneumonia and was unable to see anybody; the Assistant Secretary of State had been appointed to Peking, and left for his post early in the month; I had therefore had no communication with the Foreign Office for some weeks. As secrecy is an important factor in these negotiations, and as Mr. Komura when I last saw him had pressed for an answer to Mr. Hayashi's proposals, this lack of communication with the Foreign Office was more an advantage than otherwise.

In my reply to your Lordship's private telegram I stated that Mr. Komura had been ill, and that his illness was sufficient to account for much of the delay, and pointed out that Mr. Hayashi would be in a position to know to what extent Marquis Ito was in touch with the alliance negotiations.

On the 25th instant I had a visit from a Mr. Yamaza, Acting Director of the Political Bureau, who called with a message from Mr. Komura on behalf of the Japanese Government, stating that the delay, which the Government very much regretted, was due to the absence of the Prime Minister and some other members of the Cabinet at the autumn manœuvres, also to the illness of Mr. Komura; the Japanese Government also begged that I would assure your Lordship that Marquis Ito's journey had nothing whatever to do with the alliance negotiations; that his tour had been sketched out some time previously; and that he was in no way authorised to conduct any negotiations. I replied that I would at once convey Mr. Komura's message to your Lordship, but pointed out that the autumn manœuvres were not of sufficient importance to interfere with so weighty a matter as the one in hand, and added that as it was well known that no serious step was taken without Marquis Ito being consulted, the visits of this statesman to St. Petersburgh and Berlin at this juncture would naturally cause uneasiness.

Mr. Yamaza did not reply to my remark about Marquis Ito being consulted, and I am of opinion that the Marquis is kept posted with what goes on here, though I do not think that he would enter into communication with any other Government except his own in the matter. As I have not yet seen Mr. Komura I cannot say what are his views with regard to the Draft Agreement. I think it not improbable that the Japanese Government are favourably inclined towards it, though they are somewhat alarmed at the magnitude of the step they have initiated and as to the effect it will have on other Powers.

I have, &c.
CLAUDE M. MacDONALD.

No. 114.

Sir C. Scott to the Marquess of Lansdowne.

F.O. Russia 1623.
(No. 343.)   Very Confidential.   *St. Petersburgh,* D. *December* 11, 1901.
My Lord,   R. *December* 16, 1901.

([1]). . . . Advantage was therefore taken here of the Marquis Ito's visit to convince him that there was no connection whatever between the questions of the evacuation of Manchuria and of Corea, and that Russia had no designs of any description against the independence of Corea or Japanese interests there; that the Russian Government intended to adhere faithfully to the understanding arrived at in 1896 and 1898 with Japan on this question, and that they were anxious to hasten on as much as possible the evacuation of Manchuria, although it would probably now be necessary to await the return of the Chinese Court to Pekin before proceeding further in the matter of the conclusion of the agreement, but that, in the opinion of the Russian Government, Japan was not advancing her own interests by offering any opposition to the conclusion of an agreement which did not affect any of her interests. . . . .([2])

I have, &c.
CHARLES S. SCOTT.

([1]) [Marquis Ito's visit to Paris.]
([2]) [Russo-Japanese relations.]

No. 115.

The Marquess of Lansdowne to Sir C. MacDonald.

F.O. Japan 563.
(No. 128.)   Secret.
Sir,   *Foreign Office, December* 12, 1901.

The Japanese Minister brought me to-day the enclosed copy of the draft Agreement which I had handed to him on the 6th ultimo, with the amendments suggested by the Japanese Government.([1])

Baron Hayashi told me that he had thought it his duty to inform me of these amendments at once, but that he would prefer not to discuss them in detail for the present. He had, he said, received from the Japanese Minister for Foreign Affairs a statement of the arguments by which the amendments were supported, and he desired to study this document at his leisure before endeavouring to explain to me in detail why each amendment was desired.

The Minister apologised for the delay which had taken place, adding that the Emperor had been obliged to take into his confidence some of the leading Japanese statesmen outside the Cabinet, without whose concurrence it was not likely that an Agreement of the kind would find favour.

In reply to a question from me, he mentioned the names of five gentlemen, who had, he said, been thus taken into the Imperial confidence. These were Count Inouyé, Marquis Yamagata, Marquis Ito, Viscount Oyama and Count Saiyo.

Baron Hayashi went on to say with reference to an observation which I had made to him on the occasion of our interview on the 6th ultimo (*v.* my despatch No. 115 of that date) that the Japanese Government would much prefer that the scope of the Agreement should not be extended beyond what was contemplated in the draft as it stood. If India, the Straits Settlements and Siam were to be brought within its scope, the liability would be one which the Japanese Government could not venture to assume.

He went on to say that the Japanese Government were decidedly in favour of publishing the Agreement down to the end of the new Article V, but that the remaining three Articles ought, in their opinion, to remain secret.

([1]) [*V. infra*, pp. 115–20.]

I told Baron Hayashi that I should be glad to take advantage of his proposal to postpone further discussion in order to examine the amended draft in consultation with my Colleagues. .I thought it right, however, to tell him, with reference to the new separate Article II, that we should be unlikely to agree to any contract which might interfere with our discretion in determining the strength of the naval force which we might maintain in any part of the world, a strength which would have to be determined by Imperial considerations, rather than with reference to purely local conditions.

I also said that the new separate Article III seemed to me to require explanation. The Agreement would, I thought, probably be criticised upon the ground that it might have the effect of entangling us in war with two great European Powers all over the world on account of some comparatively trivial quarrel between Russia and Japan over matters of purely local interest.

Baron Hayashi replied that under their Agreement with Russia entered into in the year 1898, Japan was given special rights in regard to Corea, and he pointed out that by an amendment in the preamble of the Agreement it was proposed that the two Powers should declare themselves specially interested in preventing the occupation of any part of the territory of Corea by any other Power.

L.

No. 116.

The Marquess of Lansdowne to Sir C. MacDonald.

F.O. Japan 563.
(No. 129.)   Secret.
Sir,   *Foreign Office, December 16, 1901.*
  The Japanese Minister left with me to-day the accompanying memorandum[1] explanatory of the amendments suggested by the Japanese Government in the Draft Anglo-Japanese Agreement.

I told Baron Hayashi that the amendments had not yet been considered by the Cabinet, and it was therefore impossible for me to intimate to him the decision at which His Majesty's Government were likely to arrive with regard to them.

I remained, however, of the opinion that the new separate Article II was likely to be objected to on the ground that it limited our discretion in determining the distribution of our naval forces.

Baron Hayashi observed that at this moment the strength of the Russian fleet in the Far East was equivalent to 120,000 tons, and that of France to 80,000 tons, the tonnage of Japan being, on the other hand, 200,000 and that of Great Britain 170,000 tons. As matters now stood it would therefore be open to Great Britain to diminish her naval strength by 50,000 tons. If, on the other hand, Russia were to increase her tonnage to, say, 200,000 tons, we should have to add proportionately to our naval strength.

Baron Hayashi informed me that the Japanese Government attached much importance to the new Separate Article III and to the amendment in the preamble which seemed to them necessary in order to prevent Russia from suddenly making herself mistress of important strategical points on the Corean coast.

I asked Baron Hayashi whether, in order to avoid the risk of one of the contracting parties being dragged into hostilities by the inconsiderate action of the other in regard to comparatively insignificant local disputes, it might not be possible to add words to the Agreement which would compel the contracting parties whenever their common interests were threatened, not only to communicate with one another, but to concert the actual measures to be taken by either or both of them before those measures were actually adopted.

Baron Hayashi replied that he feared that such previous consultation would be fatal to prompt action, and that, whilst the two Powers were deliberating, they might

[1] [*V. infra*, pp. 115-20]

find that the events which they had desired to anticipate had actually taken place. He added that in his opinion it was most unlikely that Japan, knowing as she must know what a war with Russia would mean, would light-heartedly involve herself in such a war for any but the most amply sufficient reasons.

I asked Baron Hayashi whether the Japanese Government remained of the opinion that it was desirable to communicate the Agreement to the German Government. He replied that the Japanese Government were still of opinion that we should endeavour to obtain the adherence of the German Government, and that he thought it was for us to decide when the moment had arrived for taking the German Government into our confidence.

L.

No. 117.

The Marquess of Lansdowne to Sir C. MacDonald.

F.O. Japan 563.
(No. 132.) Very Secret.
Sir,   *Foreign Office, December* 19, 1901.

The Japanese Minister a few minutes before the meeting of the Cabinet this afternoon sent me the enclosed memorandum on the subject of the draft Agreement referred to in my despatch No. 129 of the 16th instant.(¹) At his request I received him later in the evening, and discussed with him at some length the amendments proposed by the Japanese Government.

Before, however, referring to these in detail I again told him that there was a strong feeling amongst my colleagues that it would be desirable, if possible, to give a wider scope to the Agreement. It seemed, for instance, scarcely reasonable that, while we were to face the possibility of a war with two great European Powers in consequence of a dispute between Japan and Russia in regard to Corea, we were not to have any assistance from Japan should we find ourselves involved with the same two Powers in regard to a dispute as to India. We should, I thought, be less critical in our examination of the terms if we had reason to expect that we might depend upon the assistance of Japan in a war arising out of other than Chinese or Korean interests.

Baron Hayashi replied emphatically that his instructions from his Government left him in no doubt that it was useless to propose such an extension of the scope of the Agreement. He did not agree with us in considering the Agreement too one-sided. Japan had very little interest in the Valley of the Yangtse, and yet she would be compelled to support us should we find ourselves opposed by France and Russia in those regions.

I told Baron Hayashi that we were prepared to accept the new Article 5 proposed by Japan limiting the duration of the Alliance to five years, and that, in our opinion, that Article should form part of the main Agreement, and not be dealt with as a "separate Article."

Passing to the "Separate Articles," I told him that we desired, if possible, to dispense altogether with anything of the nature of a Secret or Separate Agreement. We should certainly be asked whether such an Agreement existed; we should not be able to deny its existence if there was one; and if we admitted its existence and refused to disclose its contents, we should find ourselves in an impossible position.

I therefore proposed that for Separate Article No. 1, providing for concerted action on the part of the Naval Forces of the two Powers, an exchange of notes should be substituted. This, I thought, would be quite sufficient for the purpose.

I had already informed Baron Hayashi of my anticipation that Separate Article No. 2, binding the High Contracting Parties to endeavour to maintain in the Far East at all time Naval Forces superior to those of the Powers having the largest Naval Force in those waters, would not be accepted by His Majesty's Government. Their objection

(¹) [*V. infra*, pp. 115–20.]

to any stipulation which might fetter their discretion in disposing of the distribution of their fleets was insurmountable, and I could hold out no hope that any proposal of the kind would be admitted. I pointed out to Baron Hayashi that the new Article 5, which we were ready to accept, provided a remedy for either Power in the event of its being dissatisfied with the manner in which the other Power had fulfilled its obligations under the Treaty.

Passing to Separate Article 3, I pointed out to Baron Hayashi the ambiguous and far-reaching character of the language employed. The Article, as it stood, would enable Japan to resort to any measures which she pleased, however reckless or provocative, in order to support her interests in Korea. We were quite prepared to take note of the Russo-Japanese Agreement of 1898, and to place it on record that we recognised the special rights secured to Japan by that agreement, and we might, if necessary, strengthen the language of the Preamble so as to make it clear that we desired to maintain the independence of Korea as well as of China. I suggested that the Japanese Government should dispense with Separate Article 3, and should endeavour to find words of the kind which I had suggested for insertion in the Preamble. Baron Hayashi replied that the Agreement of 1898 had reference only to the interest of Japan in the commercial and industrial development of Korea and in the Japanese population resident in that country. There was nothing in the agreement which touched upon '' military and political '' questions. I asked Baron Hayashi whether he would give me an illustration of his meaning. He replied that the kind of contingency against which the Japanese Government desired to guard was the appointment by Russia of military advisers to the Korean army, and more especially the acquisition by Russia of leases under which they would obtain control of important points, particularly upon the Corean Littoral facing Japan. The Russians had in fact lately made an attempt to obtain a lease at Masampho, a point of vital importance to Japan, and had been thwarted with the greatest difficulty. It might be necessary, in the event of an attempt of this kind being renewed, for Japan to act and to act promptly. She was free so to act at the present time, and she did not desire to part with that freedom or to feel that she would be left in the lurch by Great Britain should her action involve her in hostilities with France and Russia.

I said that I fully entered into the feelings of the Japanese Government, but that it was quite clear that we should have to scrutinise with very great care any contract entered into for a purpose such as that which he had described. I suggested that he should mention to his Government the criticisms which I had offered, and particularly that he should explain to them our desire to get rid altogether of the separate Articles.

Baron Hayashi told me that he would do this, and I promised that I would in the meantime carefully consider all that he had said to me.

As to the interpretation of the Agreement, I asked Baron Hayashi whether the Japanese Government would regard the interference of Russia with Manchuria as justifying them in going to war and possibly invoking our support.

He replied that if the safety of Korea were to be assured, the Japanese Government was not likely to go to war for the sake of Manchuria, or, indeed, of Mongolia, and other remoter portions of China. They were, of course, parts of the Chinese Empire, and we could if we liked, go to war for the sake of them. Japan would be obliged to come to our assistance if in that event France were to join Russia, but it was not likely that Japan would provoke hostilities for such a cause.

In conclusion, I told Baron Hayashi that I had taken note of the statement in the Memorandum which he had addressed to me this afternoon, to the effect that the Japanese Government thought it better to delay any overtures to Germany until terms had been definitely settled between us, and I said that we should act in accordance with this wish.

I am, &c.
[LANSDOWNE.]

No. 118.

Sir C. MacDonald to the Marquess of Lansdowne.

F.O. Japan 563.

(No. 154.)   Secret.   *Toyo,* D. *December* 23, 1901.

My Lord,   R. *January* 30, 1902.

In my telegram No. 65 of the 6th instant I had the honour to communicate to your Lordship the main points of my conversation with Viscount Katsura on the same day respecting the proposed Anglo-Japanese Agreement relative to affairs in the Far East.

I now have the honour to enclose a copy of a Memorandum recording the conversation in question, which has been drawn up by Mr. Whitehead, who was present on that occasion.

I have, &c.

CLAUDE M. MacDONALD.

Enclosure in No. 118.

Memorandum of an Interview with Viscount Katsura on December 6, 1901.

Secret.

Sir Claude MacDonald informed Viscount Katsura that he had understood from Mr. Komura, the Minister for Foreign Affairs, that the draft Agreement between Great Britain and Japan had been favourably received by the Japanese Cabinet, and that it had now been submitted to the Emperor, whose decision might be expected to-day or to-morrow.

Viscount Katsura replied that this was correct, and that he himself was very much in favour of the proposal. He pointed out, however, that the idea was so new and unprecedented that it required the most careful consideration, and that the Emperor had therefore instructed him to ascertain the opinion of the elder statesmen on the subject. He had accordingly sounded the elder statesmen singly, and had found them in general favourably disposed, so he had arranged to meet them privately in a body at Hayama (where he has a villa) to-morrow to decide upon the matter. He had no doubt that the result of this consultation would be satisfactory, but even if it were not so he was prepared to take the responsibility for the conclusion of the Agreement upon himself.

Sir Claude MacDonald then said that he learnt from Mr. Komura that the draft as communicated to Baron Hayashi by Lord Lansdowne had been amended in certain points (which Mr. Komura considered unimportant ones) before being submitted to the Emperor, and pointed out that, although these changes were considered by the Japanese Government not to alter the spirit of the Agreement in any way, His Majesty's Government might not be of the same opinion. He asked, therefore, whether his Excellency could tell him the purport of these amendments.

Viscount Katsura answered that the Amendments did not change any of the existing points in the draft, but consisted in three additional provisions, viz., a fifth Article in the body of the Agreement fixing the period for which it was to be in force at five years, with the option of prolonging it by mutual consent after that time; an additional clause to the Separate Article—providing that the Naval forces kept by the two Contracting Powers in Far Eastern waters should exceed those of certain other Powers, and a further additional clause by which Great Britain should recognise Japan's special sphere of influence in Korea. These proposed Amendments had been telegraphed by Mr. Komura to Baron Hayashi, for his information, but without direct instructions to communicate them to His Majesty's Government. Viscount Katsura thought, however, that Baron Hayashi would probably have done so on his own responsibility. His Excellency further said that after his meeting with the elder statesmen three or four days would probably elapse before the Minister for Foreign Affairs could communicate the final decision of the Japanese Government.

Sir Claude MacDonald pointed out that this delay was somewhat unfortunate, as, although the secret had hitherto been admirably kept (since the proposal was first made on the 6th November), the recent visit of Marquis Ito to St. Petersburg had given rise to various rumours in the press, and one paper had hazarded the guess that these proceedings pointed to a possible agreement between Japan or Russia or between Japan and Great Britain.

Viscount Katsura felt sure that the secret had in no way been divulged, and thought that Marquis Ito's reception at Petersburg was a fortunate circumstance, as it was calculated to divert the public from the true scent. What the newspapers chose to write could not be helped, but he was convinced that none of them had any real information. He thought these rumours were mainly due to the Dôbunkwai, a well meaning but not very intelligent Association of pronounced Russophobe tendencies, who had become alarmed as to what Marquis Ito might be doing and thought they would thwart him by spreading them.

His Excellency then asked whether Sir Claude MacDonald had heard of a suggestion made to Baron Hayashi by the German Chargé d'Affaires in London early in the year (while Marquis Ito was still Premier) to the effect that Germany, Great Britain and Japan should act together in the Far East. When Baron Hayashi had mentioned this suggestion to Lord Lansdowne the latter had replied that Germany's geographical position in Europe precluded her taking an independent line of action which was in any way directed against Russia.

Sir Claude MacDonald observed that it was perhaps fortunate that Parliament was not sitting either in England or Japan at the present moment, to which Viscount Katsura replied that this was no doubt the case in England, but that he did not much mind what the Japanese Diet might say or do.

Viscount Katsura then asked Sir Claude MacDonald what he thought the attitude of Germany would be if she were not asked to join in the Agreement, that is, whether she would range herself on the side of Russia.

Sir Claude MacDonald replied that, as the interests of Germany in the Far East were mainly commercial, she would have the maintenance of peace and of the *status quo* in China as much at heart as Great Britain and Japan, and that as the objects of the proposed Agreement were peaceful ones and such as she would herself endorse, she might be expected to preserve neutrality in case of a conflict.

His Excellency said that this was his view also, but that it would be well to be prepared for all eventualities, and that he thought therefore that in calculating the Naval forces to be maintained in the Far East by the two contracting parties the possibility of having to face a combination of three Powers should be kept in view.

J. B. WHITEHEAD.

No. 119.

The Marquess of Lansdowne to Sir C. MacDonald.

F.O. Japan 563.
(No. 133.) Secret.
Sir,
Foreign Office, December 31, 1901.

The Japanese Minister handed to me this morning the enclosed memorandum(¹) on the subject of the draft agreement referred to in my despatch No. 132 of the 19th instant.

Baron Hayashi explained to me that he was instructed to place these proposals before me informally, but that if they found favour with His Majesty's Government they would be communicated to us officially. Should we on the other hand have any

(¹) [*V. infra*, pp. 115–20.]

objections to the language used the Japanese Government would be obliged to us if we would favour them confidentially with our criticisms or indeed with a counter-proposal, should we desire to make one. He added that the Japanese Government were anxious that no time should be lost in concluding the Agreement.

I told Baron Hayashi that I much preferred to deal with the matters referred to in the Memorandum in the manner now proposed, rather than by separate or secret Articles of Agreement. It would, however, be necessary for me to examine with care the wording of the proposed note, and particularly of that paragraph which had reference to the strength of the Naval forces to be maintained by Japan and Great Britain respectively in the Far East.

I promised Baron Hayashi that I would make him aware as soon as possible of the views of His Majesty's Government.

[I am, &c.
LANSDOWNE.]

No. 120.

The Marquess of Lansdowne to Sir C. MacDonald.

F.O. Japan 563.
(No. 2.) Secret.

Sir, *Foreign Office, January 7, 1902.*

During the Marquis Ito's visit to me at Bowood on the 3rd instant, I had a conversation of some length with his Excellency as to the proposed Anglo-Japanese Agreement. He told me that he had been fully informed with regard to the progress of the negotiations, and that he was in entire sympathy with the proposal, and trusted that the Agreement would be concluded.

I explained to him that the Japanese Government had proposed important amendments in the original draft, and that these had yet to be disposed of by the Cabinet. I said that the Agreement would certainly be made public, and that I did not conceal from myself that it was likely to be severely criticised. It was an entirely new departure for us. Our policy of late, as he was aware, had been to avoid entangling ourselves in foreign alliances, and if that policy was to be abandoned and this country was to accept obligations such as those which we should incur under the Agreement, it would be necessary for us to satisfy Parliament that we obtained sufficiently valuable considerations in return.

I had, as he probably knew, explained to the Japanese Minister that the Agreement, even in its original shape, might be represented as more in favour of Japan than of Great Britain, and the amendments which the Japanese Government proposed to introduce rendered the draft still more open to such criticism. I quite understood that from the Japanese point of view it might be necessary for Japan to reserve to herself full liberty to take timely measures for the purpose of guarding against Russian encroachments in Corea. But it seemed to me that the terms of the notes which the two Governments were invited to exchange went too far in that direction, and that these stipulations were not balanced by any corresponding stipulations in favour of British interests. People would certainly notice for example that, whereas no foreign Power was to be allowed to occupy any portion, no matter how small, of Corean territory, the corresponding obligation in regard to China merely bound the Contracting Parties in a general way to maintain the integrity and independence of that Empire.

Marquis Ito admitted that Corea and China were not treated in the same way, but thought that it would be impossible for Japan to tolerate in the case of Corea the kind of encroachments which had been tolerated, and might be tolerated again, in the case of China. It was most important that there should be no misunderstanding between Japan and Great Britain as to the definition of their respective interests, and it was much better that such points as these should be frankly faced before the conclusion of an Agreement, and that there should be no " surprises " afterwards.

The Marquis then referred to Manchuria. Russia had, he said, obtained a strong hold upon that province. Did I think she was ever likely to relax her grip, and were we likely to go to war on this account?

I said that we had never concealed from ourselves that Russia had special interests in Manchuria, and was likely, whatever happened, to retain a predominant interest in that province, owing to her geographical position. We had to some extent admitted this by the Agreement of 1899, under which Russia had, in exchange for corresponding admissions with regard to our rights in other parts of China, obtained a preferential right to construct railways in Manchuria.

The Marquis here asked me whether this Agreement had ever been made public, and I replied that this was the case, and that it had been frequently referred to in Parliament.

As for the alleged Manchurian Agreement, to which he had referred, I told him that if its terms were in accordance with the versions which had reached us, it appeared to contain some stipulations which were inconsistent with the sovereign rights of China, and others which were apparently in conflict with her Treaty engagements. We had throughout recommended the Chinese Government to refuse its consent to covenants falling within these categories, and it gave me pleasure to know that our policy in this respect had been in entire agreement with that of the Japanese Government, with whose Representative our Representative had frequently co-operated. My impression was that Russia desired to extricate herself from military occupation of Manchuria, which was costly and inconvenient to her, but that she would arrive at an arrangement with the Chinese Government, some of the terms of which would very likely be withheld from our knowledge under which she would retain some kind of a lien upon the province. I did not, however, think it probable that the terms would be so objectionable as to force us into war with Russia. I might at any rate say that it seemed to me infinitely more probable that, if the Anglo-Japanese Agreement were concluded, we might be dragged into war by Japan with France and Russia over Corea, than that Japan would be dragged into war by us in consequence of the Russian treatment of the Manchurian question.

The Marquis then asked me whether, assuming that the Agreement was likely to be concluded, we should see any objection to the Japanese Government entering into an amicable arrangement with Russia for the protection of Japanese interests in Corea. He explained that he meant by this an Agreement in which the policy of the Russo-Japanese Agreement of 1898 would be carried a step further, by means of an understanding which would preclude Russia from political or strategical interference in Corea.

1 replied that much would depend on the character of the Agreement contemplated. It would, of course, be absolutely essential that it should be in no way inconsistent with the Agreement arrived at between Great Britain and Japan. It would obviously be improper that Japan should enter into a bargain with us affecting our common interests in the Far East, and should then enter into another bargain of a conflicting character with a third Power. If, however, the Marquis merely suggested that in the interests of peace Japan should do her best to obtain from Russia a recognition of the interests which we were ready to join her in protecting, a source of danger would be removed, and speaking for myself, I saw no reason why His Majesty's Government should disapprove.

The Marquis replied that nothing was further from his intention than to suggest that there should be a " double-handed " arrangement, but Japan desired peace, and such an understanding with Russia as he had sketched would certainly make for peace.

He then asked me what would be thought of the proposed Agreement between us by the United States and by Germany. He observed as to Germany that he was under the impression that she had at one time sought to throw Japan and Great Britain together. Was it likely that she should give her adherence to the Agreement, or was she likely to take any exception to it.

I replied that I felt confident that the United States would not disapprove. We had every reason to believe that she desired the maintenance of the *status quo* in the Far East. As to Germany, the Marquis, no doubt, referred to the occasion when Germany had promised Japan her " benevolent neutrality " in case of her going to war with Russia about Manchuria, and I reminded him of the circumstances under which we had elicited the fact that this " benevolent neutrality " was merely a strict neutrality, and not, as the Japanese Government had first been led to suppose, a neutrality which would have prevented the intervention of any other Power. It seemed to me, I said, impossible after what had happened that Germany should regard otherwise than favourably an Agreement between Great Britain and Japan. I did not, however, for a moment believe that she was likely herself to become a party to it.

We then had some conversation with regard to the Japanese proposal originally contained in separate Article No. 2, under which each of the Contracting Powers were to bind itself always to maintain in the Far East a naval strength at least equal to that of any other Power in those waters.

As to this, the Marquis said that the point being still under discussion between the two Governments, he would prefer not to say much about it. He read me, however, a lecture upon the necessity of a spirited naval policy in Chinese waters, dwelling upon the fact that at one time we had never tolerated any Russian usurpations in those regions (he instanced the Port Hamilton incident in 1885), whereas we had become much more tolerant of such usurpations of late.

At the close of our conversation, I expressed a hope that we should find the Japanese Government at one with us in continuing to support the Yang-tsze Viceroys by every means in our power. I told him that we proposed to press the Chinese Government to retain them in their posts, and to give them full opportunities of carrying out the reforms of which they were known to be in favour. I trusted that Japan also would give these distinguished men the support which they certainly deserved.

The Marquis replied that the views which I had expressed were certainly shared by him.

The Marquis called on me at the Foreign Office yesterday to take leave, and we had some further discussion upon the points dealt with above. I endeavoured to elicit from him whether he had, during his visit to St. Petersburgh, received any encouragement for the idea of an understanding with Russia as to Corean affairs such as he had hinted at in our first conversation.

He told me that the Corean question had been discussed by him during his visit to Russia in the most general terms only, but that he had gathered the impression that such an understanding was not impossible, and he had formed the same impression from information which had come to his knowledge before he left Japan.

He explained to me that Russia and Japan, as the immediate neighbours of Corea, were the two nations most immediately interested in that country. It was of the utmost importance to Japan that there should be no trouble in Corea, because any outbreak there was likely to spread and to lead to a conflagration in China as well. For this reason it was, in his opinion, which he was careful to explain to me must not be taken as committing the Japanese Government, most important to remove if possible all causes of difference between Russia and Japan as to Corean affairs. He added, however, that whilst Japan would probably be ready to come to reasonable terms with Russia, it was not unlikely that the latter Power might ask for an island in the neighbourhood of the Corean Strait as the price of such an arrangement, and Japan could not for an instant entertain such a proposal.

As to Manchuria, his Excellency told me that in his opinion it would, sooner or later, be necessary to impose a limit upon Russian encroachments in this direction, if not by the bayonet, then by some other means.

Recurring to the proposed Anglo-Japanese Agreement, I emphasised what I had previously said to him as to the necessity of depriving it of the one-sided appearance which I feared the Japanese amendments would give to it. He evidently realised the force of this criticism, and seemed to regard with favour my suggestion that if the Japanese stipulations as to Corea could not safely be weakened, we might correspondingly stiffen those parts of the Agreement which had reference to our interests in China.

He begged me, however, to bear in mind his unofficial position, and his désire that nothing which he might have said to me should be considered as forming part of the negotiations in progress between the two Governments.

At the close of our conversation, I mentioned briefly the discussions which had arisen with regard to the question of perpetual leases held by foreigners in Japan. I did not, however, attempt to enter into details or to elicit an expression of his own views as to the proper solution of the difficulty, but I dwelt upon the great importance of the matter to our commercial interests, and I expressed a hope that he would use his great influence for the purpose of bringing about an amicable settlement, perhaps by resort to arbitration. He promised to give the matter his best attention.

I am, &c.

[LANSDOWNE.]

No. 121.

The Marquess of Lansdowne to Sir C. MacDonald.

F.O. Japan 563.
(No. 6.)   Secret.
Sir,   *Foreign Office, January* 14, 1902.

I handed to the Japanese Minister to-day a copy of the enclosed draft Treaty between Great Britain and Japan.(¹)

I explained to Baron Hayashi that the draft had been very carefully considered by His Majesty's Government, and that I did not think it probable that any further modifications would be accepted by us. I further called his particular attention to the drafting of Article 1, which was designed to place the two Powers as far as possible under mutually equivalent obligations. This, as I had previously informed Baron Hayashi, was certainly not the case with the original draft as amended by the Japanese Government.

I further explained to him that, in our opinion, the Note, of which I had also handed him a draft, was not intended for publication, but merely as a confidential record of the views of the two Governments as to the matters dealt with therein.

Baron Hayashi promised to refer the drafts to his Government at the earliest possible moment.

L.

(¹) [*V. infra*, pp. 115–20.]

No. 122.

The Marquess of Lansdowne to Sir C. MacDonald.

F.O. Japan 563.
(No. 7.)   Most Secret.
Sir,   *Foreign Office, January* 18, 1902.

The Japanese Minister brought me to-day the enclosed Memorandum, with suggested amendments in the draft Agreement between Great Britain and Japan.(¹)

I told him that I should, of course, have to lay these proposals before the Cabinet, but that I was able to tell him without any hesitation that if the suggested amend-

(¹) [*V. infra*, pp. 115–20.]

ments in Article I were insisted upon the chance of concluding the Agreement would be seriously imperilled.

I pointed out to him—

1. That the proposed new drafting, which recited the special interests, "political as well as commercial and industrial," possessed by Japan in Corea, and then went on to refer to "the interests of Japan and Great Britain in China," was calculated to produce the very impression which, as he was aware, we had so much desired to avoid, namely, that while Japan was to be bound to Great Britain only in respect of interests which were common to both Powers, Great Britain was to be bound to Japan in respect of interests which were peculiar to the latter country. We had endeavoured, in our draft, to place both Powers on exactly the same plane.

2. That the omission from the new draft of the words enabling either Power to invoke the assistance of the other only in the event of their respective interests being threatened "by the aggressive action of another Power" had the effect of removing a safeguard to which we attached the greatest possible importance. There was a good deal of apprehension in our minds that Japan, in consequence of her close proximity to Corea, and her intense nervousness with regard to Russian intrusion in that country, might involve herself in a quarrel with Russia upon some insufficient pretext, and we desired to put it beyond all question that the *casus fœderis* could not arise except where the third Power was clearly the assailant. I would take upon myself to say that the Cabinet would not allow these words to be expunged.

As to the first point, Baron Hayashi told me that, while it was perfectly true that in China the interests of the two Powers were of a corresponding character, it could not be denied that in Corea Japan had special interests different from any possessed by us. The Japanese Government desired to see this admitted on the face of the Agreement.

As to 2, he said that it was his own impression that the words had been struck out without any intention of altering the meaning of the Article. The Japanese Government probably relied upon the declaration at the commencement of the Article, to the effect that both Governments were "entirely uninfluenced by any aggressive tendencies" in either country.

Baron Hayashi promised that he would telegraph my views at once to the Japanese Government.

The impression left upon me by our conversation was that we should be able to obtain the restoration of the words "by the aggressive action of any other Powers," but that we should have to discover some formula recognising the special interests of Japan in Corea.

I am, &c.
[LANSDOWNE.]

No. 123.

The Marquess of Lansdowne to Sir C. MacDonald.

F.O. Japan 563.

(No. 11.) Most Secret.

Sir, *Foreign Office, January* 24, 1902.

I handed to the Japanese Minister to-day the accompanying alternative draft of Article I of the proposed Anglo-Japanese Agreement, which had, I told him, been prepared in order to meet the desire of the Japanese Government that it should be made clear on the face of the Agreement that we did not dispute the right of Japan to take action in Corea in the event of her interests being seriously threatened by internal disturbances in that country.

We had, however, thought it desirable to add after the words "by the aggressive action of any other Power, or by disturbances arising in China or Corea" the phrase "and necessitating the intervention of either of the High Contracting Parties for the protection of the lives and property of its subjects." These words make it clear that the intervention of Japan would be regarded as admissible only if the "disturbances" were of a really serious character.

Baron Hayashi informed me that, in his opinion, there was no objection to the new draft, and that he would at once refer it to the Japanese Government.

L.

No. 124.

The Marquess of Lansdowne to Sir C. MacDonald.([1])

F.O. Japan 563.
(No. 11A.)
Sir, *Foreign Office, January* 30, 1902.

I have signed to-day, with the Japanese Minister, an Agreement between Great Britain and Japan, of which a copy is enclosed in this despatch.([2])

This Agreement may be regarded as the outcome of the events which have taken place during the last two years in the Far East, and of the part taken by Great Britain and Japan in dealing with them.

Throughout the troubles and complications which arose in China consequent upon the Boxer outbreak and the attack upon the Peking Legations, the two Powers have been in close and uninterrupted communication, and have been actuated by similar views.

We have each of us desired that the integrity and independence of the Chinese Empire should be preserved, that there should be no disturbance of the territorial *status quo* either in China or in the adjoining regions, that all nations should, within those regions, as well as within the limits of the Chinese Empire, be afforded equal opportunities for the development of their commerce and industry, and that peace should not only be restored, but should, for the future, be maintained.

From the frequent exchanges of views which have taken place between the two Governments, and from the discovery that their Far Eastern policy was identical, it has resulted that each side has expressed the desire that their common policy should find expression in an international contract of binding validity.

We have thought it desirable to record in the Preamble of that instrument the main objects of our common policy in the Far East to which I have already referred, and in the first Article we join in entirely disclaiming any aggressive tendencies either in China or Corea. We have, however, thought it necessary also to place on record the view entertained by both the High Contracting Parties, that should their interests as above described be endangered, it will be admissible for either of them to take such measures as may be indispensable in order to safeguard those interests, and words have been added which will render it clear that such precautionary measures might become necessary and might be legitimately taken, not only in the case of aggressive action or of an actual attack by some other Power, but in the event of disturbances arising of a character to necessitate the intervention of either of the High Contracting Parties for the protection of the lives and property of its subjects.

([1]) [Printed together with Agreement of same date in *B.F.S.P.*, Vol. XCV [1901–2], pp. 83–6, presented to Parliament, February 1902.]

([2]) [*V. infra*, pp. 115–20.]

The principal obligations undertaken mutually by the High Contracting Parties are those of maintaining a strict neutrality in the event of either of them becoming involved in war, and of coming to one another's assistance in the event of either of them being confronted by the opposition of more than one hostile Power. Under the remaining provisions of the Agreement, the High Contracting Parties undertake that neither of them will, without consultation with the other, enter into separate arrangements with another Power to the prejudice of the interests described in the Agreement, and that whenever those interests are in jeopardy they will communicate with one another fully and frankly.

The concluding Article has reference to the duration of the Agreement, which, after five years, is terminable by either of the High Contracting Parties at one year's notice.

His Majesty's Government have been largely influenced in their decision to enter into this important contract by the conviction that it contains no provisions which can be regarded as an indication of aggressive or self-seeking tendencies in the regions to which it applies. It has been concluded purely as a measure of precaution, to be invoked, should occasion arise, in the defence of important British interests. It in no way threatens the present position or the legitimate interests of other Powers. On the contrary, that part of it which renders either of the High Contracting Parties liable to be called upon by the other for assistance can operate only when one of the allies has found himself obliged to go to war in defence of interests which are common to both, when the circumstances in which he has taken this step are such as to establish that the quarrel has not been of his own seeking, and when, being engaged in his own defence, he finds himself threatened, not by a single Power, but by a hostile coalition.

His Majesty's Government trust that the Agreement may be found of mutual advantage to the two countries, that it will make for the preservation of peace, and that, should peace unfortunately be broken, it will have the effect of restricting the area of hostilities.

I am, &c.
LANSDOWNE.

No. 125.

Anglo-Japanese Agreement, January 30, 1902.

[The main stages in the drafting of the Agreement were as follows :—

1. On the 16th October, 1901, Baron Hayashi in a conversation with Lord Lansdowne sketched the main lines of the Japanese proposals, to which Lord Lansdowne added some further points.
     On the 29th October Baron Hayashi handed to Lord Lansdowne a draft clause, finally incorporated (with modifications in Article I).
2. On the 6th November Lord Lansdowne handed to Baron Hayashi a preliminary draft of the Agreement.
3. On the 12th December Baron Hayashi handed to Lord Lansdowne an amended draft.
     On the 31st December Baron Hayashi handed to Lord Lansdowne a draft of the Diplomatic Note to accompany the Agreement.
4. On the 14th January, 1902, Lord Lansdowne handed to Baron Hayashi an amended draft of the Agreement, together with an amended draft of the Diplomatic Note.
5. On the 18th January Baron Hayashi handed to Lord Lansdowne certain amendments to this Draft.
     On the 22nd and 24th January Lord Lansdowne handed to Baron Hayashi two amended drafts of Article I.
6. On the 30th January the Agreement with slight modifications was signed.

The table given below shows in Column I the successive proposals of the Japanese Government, in Column II the counter-proposals of the British Government, and in Column III the final form of the Agreement. The use of italics in the drafts indicates wording identical with that of the final text.]

JAPANESE DRAFTS.	BRITISH DRAFTS.	FINAL TEXT.
	November 6(¹). — The undersigned, duly authorized by their respective Governments, *actuated solely by a desire to maintain the* status quo *and general peace in* Far *East, being moreover specially interested in* preventing the absorption of Corea ͏ by any Foreign Power, and in *maintaining the independence and territorial integrity of* ͏ *China, and in securing equal opportunities* in that country *for the commerce and industry of all nations, hereby agree as follows :—*	The Governments of Great Britain and Japan, actuated solely by a desire to maintain the *status quo* and general peace in the extreme East, being moreover specially interested in maintaining the independence and territorial integrity of the Empire of China and the Empire of Corea, and in securing equal opportunities in those countries for the commerce and industry of all nations, hereby agree as follows :—

December 12.(²)
~~Far~~ Extreme

͏ or occupation of any part of its territory
~~Foreign~~ other

͏ *the Empire of*

~~country~~ Empire

Article I.

[*October* 16.—". . . That Government [the Japanese] was above all things interested in Corea. . . . It was necessary . . . not only to guard against the absorption of Corea by Russia, but to maintain the privileges conceded . . . by the Russo-Japanese Agreement of 1898 . . . "This Agreement . . . conferred upon Japan rights of 'industrial and commercial expansion' in Corea : rights the exercise of which . . . might lead to the establishment of political influence. . . . "As to China . . . the policy of Japan was . . . to maintain the integrity and independence of China and in regard to commercial matters, the policy of the 'open door.' . . ."]

October 29.—In view of the preponderant interests of Japan in Corea His Britannic Majesty's Government shall acquiesce in the adoption of suitable measures by Japan for the maintenance of those interests.(³)

December 12.—Great Britain recognises that Japan may take such suitable measures as she deems necessary to safeguard

November 6.—(No such clause.)

January 14.—Great Britain and Japan, *having mutually recognised the independence of China and of Corea, declare themselves to be entirely uninfluenced by any aggressive tendencies in either country.* The Japanese Government having, however, called the attention of His Majesty's Government to the special interests political as well as commercial, possessed by Japan in Corea, and His Majesty's Government having simi-

(¹) [For the earlier history of the preamble, see note 2.]
(²) [This draft is identical with that of the 6th November, except for the amendments indicated.]
(³) [Comment of Lord Lansdowne : "I said that I did not altogether approve of the form in which the clause was drafted, but that I would endeavour to find some means of meeting the wishes of the Japanese Government in regard to Corea." (16th October.)]

I 2

JAPANESE DRAFTS.	BRITISH DRAFTS.	FINAL TEXT.

December 12—(contd.).

and promote the preponderating interests which she actually possesses in Corea.([4])

December 31.([5])—Japan and Great Britain recognise the independence of Corea and declare themselves to be entirely uninfluenced by any aggressive tendencies in that region. But in view of Japan's preponderating interests in that country, Great Britain recognises the right of Japan to take such measures as she may find necessary to safeguard and promote those interests.

January 18.—Great Britain and Japan, *having mutually recognised the independence of China and of Corea, declare themselves to be entirely uninfluenced by any aggressive tendencies in either country. Having in view, however, the special interests* political as well as commercial and industrial, possessed by Japan in Corea, and the interests of Great Britain and of Japan in China,

the British and Japanese Governments recognise that if those interests should be threatened it would be admissible for each Power to take such measures as may be indispensable in order to safeguard its interests.([6])

January 14—(contd.).

larly called attention to the special interests of Great Britain in the Chinese Empire both Governments recognise that if those interests should be threatened *by the aggressive action of any other Power*, it would be permissible for either Power to take such measures as may be indispensable in the respective cases in order to safeguard them.

January 22.—Great Britain and Japan, *having mutually recognised the independence of China and Corea, declare themselves to be entirely uninfluenced by any aggressive tendencies in either country. Having in view, however, the special interests* of Great Britain and Japan, *of which those of Great Britain relate principally to China, while Japan, in addition to the interests which she possesses in China, is interested in a peculiar degree* both politically and commercially in Corea, the British and Japanese Governments recognise that if those interests are threatened *by the aggressive action of any other Power* it would be admissible for each Power to take such measures as may be indispensable in order to safeguard its interests.

January 24.—The High Contracting . . . .([7])

January 30.—The High Contracting Parties, having mutually recognised the independence of China and Corea, declare themselves to be entirely uninfluenced by any aggressive tendencies in either country. Having in view, however, their special interests, of which those of Great Britain relate principally to China, while Japan, in addition to the interests which she possesses in China, is interested in a peculiar degree politically as well as commercially and industrially in Corea, the High Contracting Parties recognise that it will be admissible for either of them to safeguard those interests if threatened either by the aggressive action of any other Power, or by disturbance arising in China or Corea, and necessitating the intervention of either of the High Contracting Parties for the protection of

([4]) [In the Japanese draft of this date, this was " Separate Article III." Lord Lansdowne commented on it as follows : " I pointed out . . . . the extremely ambiguous character of the language employed . . . . I suggested that the Japanese Government should dispense with separate Article 3, and should endeavour to find words of the kind which I had suggested for insertion in the Preamble . . . ." (12th December.)]

([5]) [This was part of the Draft Diplomatic note of this date. See below p. 120.]

([6]) [Comment of Lord Lansdowne : " I was able to tell him without any hesitation that if the suggested amendments in Article 3 were insisted upon the chance of concluding the Agreement would be seriously imperilled." (19th January.)]

([7]) [This draft is identical with the final text of the Agreement, except that the phrase " politically as well as commercially and industrially " ran " both politically and commercially." It was altered on the 28th January at the instance of Baron Hayashi. This draft was substituted for that of the 22nd January after consultation with Baron Hayashi and consideration by the Cabinet.]

JAPANESE DRAFTS.	BRITISH DRAFTS.	FINAL TEXT.
		the lives or property of its subjects.

Article II.

| [*October* 16.—" If Japan were to be at war with Russia alone it would be sufficient if Great Britain remained neutral."] | *November* 6.—*If either Great Britain or Japan,*(8) *in the defence* of the interests *above described,*(8) *should* . . .(9) | *January* 30.—If either Great Britain or Japan, in the defence of their respective interests as above described, should become involved in war with another Power, the other High Contracting Party will maintain a strict neutrality, and use its efforts to prevent other Powers from joining in hostilities against its Ally. |

Article III.

| [*October* 16.—" . . . they . . . proposed that Great Britain should undertake to support Japan if Japan should find herself obliged to go to war in defence of it with more than one Foreign Power. If . . . Great Britain found herself at war with more than one Foreign Power in defence of her interests in any part of China, Japan would undertake to support us with her whole strength."] | *November* 6.—Should any other Power *join in hostilities against* that . . .(10) | *January* 30.—If in the above event any other Power or Powers should join in hostilities against the Ally, the other High Contracting Party will come to its assistance and will conduct the war in common, and make peace in mutual agreement with it. |

Article IV.

	[*October* 16.—" I added that I presumed that the two Powers would, in the event of such an understanding being arrived at, agree that neither of us should without consulting the other make separate arrangements, or come to separate understandings with another Power as to Chinese or Corean affairs."]	
December 12.(11)—~~two~~	*November* 6.—*The* two *High Contracting Parties agree that neither of them will, without consulting the other, enter into separate arrangements with another Power* affecting *the interests* above described.	*January* 30 —The High Contracting Parties agree that neither of them will, without consulting the other, enter into separate arrangements with another Power to the prejudice of the interests above described.
to the prejudice of ~~affecting~~		

(8) [In Baron Hayashi's Draft of the 12th December the following annotations appear, the first in red ink and the second in pencil :—

" Japan or Great Britain "
" and as the result of measures adopted in pursuance of Art. IV of this Agrt."]

(9) [The rest of the draft is identical with the final text.]
(10) [The rest of the draft is identical with the final text. In this draft the opening sentence is amended in red ink to run as follows : " If in the above event any other Power should . . . ." In Baron Hayashi's draft of the 12th December the words " or Powers " are added in red ink. They are omitted in the British Draft of the 14th January.]
(11) [The draft is identical with that of the 6th November except for the amendments here shown. These appear on the draft in red ink.]

Japanese Drafts.	British Drafts.	Final Text.

<table>
<tr><td></td><td>**Article V.**</td><td></td></tr>
<tr><td></td><td>[*October* 16.—"I added that...
we should in all cases where
there was a probability of the
Agreement coming into force,
undertake to communicate with
one another in good time, and
with the utmost frankness."]</td><td></td></tr>
</table>

December 12.([12])

Japan   Great Britain

~~Great~~ ~~Britain~~ or ~~Japan~~

~~the~~

their

. . . as to measures to be taken by either or both of them for the protection of those interests.

November 6.— *Whenever, in* . . .([13])

January 30.—Whenever, in the opinion of either Great Britain or Japan, the above-mentioned interests are in jeopardy, the two Governments will communicate with one another fully and frankly.

December 12.—This alliance shall *remain in force for five years* from the date of the signing of the present agreement, and it may be renewed at the pleasure of the High Contracting Parties. *But if, when the date fixed for its expiration arrives, either Ally is actually engaged in war, the alliance shall,* ipso facto, *continue until peace is concluded.*([14])

Article VI.

January 14.([15])

January 30.—The present Agreement shall come into effect immediately after the date of its signature, and remain in force for five years from that date.

In case neither of the High Contracting Parties should have notified twelve months before the expiration of the said five years the intention of terminating it, it shall remain binding until the expiration of one year from the day on which either of the High Contracting Parties shall have denounced it. But if, when the date fixed for its expiration arrives, either ally is actually engaged in war, the alliance shall, *ipso facto,* continue until peace is concluded.

In faith whereof the undersigned, duly authorised by their respective Governments, have signed this agreement and have affixed thereto their seals.

Done in duplicate at London the 30th day of January, 1902.

(L.S.) LANSDOWNE.
(L.S.) HAYASHI.

([12]) [This draft is identical with the final text, except for the alterations or additions indicated. The first two are amendments in red ink; the last an addition in pencil.]

([13]) [This draft is identical with the final text.]

([14]) [This was numbered Article V in the text of this date. Lord Lansdowne commented "I told Baron Hayashi that we were prepared to accept the new Article V . . . . and that in our opinion that Article should form part of the Agreement and not be dealt with as a separate Article."]

([15]) [This draft is identical with the final text.]

Diplomatic Note accompanying the Agreement.

JAPANESE DRAFTS.	BRITISH DRAFTS.	FINAL TEXT.

[October 16.—" I also said that I thought that the two navies might with great advantage work together even in time of peace, each Power affording the other facilities for the use of docks, harbours and coaling-stations."]

December 12.—It is . . .([16])

Article I

and coaling

~~also for the use of coaling stations and~~

Article II. Each of the High Contracting Parties shall endeavour to maintain in the Far East at all times naval forces superior in efficacy to the naval strength of any other Power which has the largest naval forces in the Far East.

Article III. (Article I of main Agreement. See above pp. 115–6.)

November 6.—It is further agreed between the High Contracting Parties that *the naval forces* of the two Powers shall, *so far as is possible, act in concert* at all times([17]) and that *mutual facilities* will *be given for the docking* of the *vessels of war of one Power in the ports of the other,* and also for the use of coaling stations and *other advantages* conducive *to the welfare and efficiency of* their *respective navies.*

January 30.—In reference to the Agreement concluded by us to-day on behalf of our respective Governments, I have the honour to inform you that the $\frac{British}{Japanese}$ Government recognises that the naval forces of $\frac{Great\ Britain}{Japan}$ should, so far as is possible, act in concert with those of $\frac{Japan}{Great\ Britain}$ in time of peace, and agrees that mutual facilities shall be given for the docking and coaling of vessels of war of one country in the ports of the other, as well as other advantages conducing to the welfare and efficiency of the respective navies of the two Powers.

December 31.—([18]) . . .

1. The naval forces . . .([19])
2. Japan and Great Britain being convinced that a continuation of the rule which each of them has hitherto

January 14.—(?)([20]).

1. The naval forces . . .([19])
2. *At the present moment Japan and Great Britain are each of them maintaining* in the Far East *a naval*

At the present moment Japan and Great Britain are each of them maintaining in the Extreme East a naval force superior in

([16]) [The draft of the first part of Article I of the 12th December is identical with that of the 6th November, except for the amendments noted in the margin. (These are in red ink.) Separate Articles II and III appear for the first time in the draft of the 12th December.

In the draft of the 12th December these three Articles appear at the end of the Agreement as " Separate Articles." In the draft of the 6th November this article was first numbered " Article V " and appeared as part of the text of the Agreement itself : but the numbering was afterwards altered to " Separate Article " with a marginal query " Separate Article or Paper."]

([17]) [Amended in red ink to " in time of peace."]

([18]) [This is Baron Hayashi's Draft Diplomatic Note. This form was adopted by him to meet Lord Lansdowne's comments on the draft of the 12th December : " I proposed that for Separate Article No. I . . . . an exchange of Notes should be substituted.

I had already informed Baron Hayashi of my expectation that Separate Article No. 2 . . . . would not be accepted by His Majesty's Government." (19th December.)]

([19]) [This article is identical in wording with Article I of the 12th December, except that it ends " . . . . the respective navies of the two Powers."]

([20]) [This alternative draft was drawn up subsequent to Baron Hayashi's draft of the 31st December. It was probably this draft that was handed to Baron Hayashi on the 14th January.]

JAPANESE DRAFTS.	BRITISH DRAFTS.	FINAL TEXT.

pursued with advantage of maintaining in the Far East a naval force superior in efficacy to the naval strength of any third Power will tend to the consolidation of peace in that quarter, are each resolved to maintain as far as possible, the same naval superiority in future.

3. (Article I of main Agreement. See above p. 116.)

force superior in strength to that of any third Power. Neither Japan nor Great Britain has any intention of relaxing her efforts to maintain, so far as may be possible, available for concentration in the waters of the extreme East, a naval force superior to that of any third Power.

3. (Article I of main Agreement. See above p. 116.)

strength to that of any third Power. $\dfrac{\text{Great Britain}}{\text{Japan}}$ has no intention of relaxing her efforts to maintain, so far as may be possible, available for concentration in the waters of the Extreme East a naval force superior to that of any third Power.

[*ED. NOTE.*—The Final Text is printed in *B.F.S.P.*, Vol. XCV, [1901–2], pp. 33–4.]

No. 126.

The Marquess of Lansdowne to Sir C. MacDonald.

F.O. Japan 563.
(No. 12.) Secret.
Sir,

Foreign Office, January 31, 1902.

The Japanese Minister left with me yesterday the following memoranda with regard to the question of publishing the Anglo-Japanese Agreement and as to its communication to the German Government :—

"1. The Japanese Government favour early publication of the Agreement to prevent the exaggerated and mischievous reports concerning its object and scope. So far we have been successful to keep the negotiations secret, but after the signature it will become more difficult to prevent leakage. Then the publication should be simultaneous in both countries, and at least five days should be reserved after the arrangement."

"2. Regarding overtures to Germany, Japanese Government defer to views of British Government all that respects the time and manner of doing so. It would, however, be better that the invitation should be given without unnecessary delay. You will also discuss with Marquess of Lansdowne the nature of identical instructions which will be necessary to be given to the Japanese and British representatives in Berlin. But it may be better not to disclose the diplomatic note to Germany at first unless her attitude justifies doing so."

I told the Minister to-day that, in the opinion of His Majesty's Government, it would be desirable that the Agreement should be made public before long. We were strengthened in this view by the fact that in the first of the above memoranda the Japanese Government expressed its opinion that it might become more difficult to keep the matter secret now that the Agreement had actually been signed.

I asked Baron Hayashi whether he considered that the fact was likely to leak out at an early date, or whether it could, if necessary, be kept secret for a time. He informed me that it would be necessary for the Japanese Government to notify the Agreement to the State Council, which consisted of twenty-five members, and that when these gentlemen, as well as their secretaries became aware of the matter, the chances of maintaining secrecy would be much diminished. He did not, however, know whether this notification necessarily took place at once, and he promised me that he would enquire by telegraph as to this.

I told him that as soon as he was able to make me aware of the result of his enquiries, I would fix a day for the publication of the Agreement, and that I would take care that at least five days' notice was given to him.

As to the question of communicating the Agreement to the German Government, I told Baron Hayashi that I should probably see the German Ambassador on Monday and that I would then inform him confidentially of the purport of the Agreement.

I did not, however, contemplate that His Majesty's Government should make anything which could be described as an "overture" to the German Government. I did not myself think that it was likely that they would care to associate themselves with us in the matter and all that I proposed was to take them into our confidence. If any "invitation" was to be made to Germany, I thought it should come from the Japanese Government, supposing that they thought it desirable to offer such an invitation.

Baron Hayashi expressed agreement and told me that it would probably be arranged that the Minister for Foreign Affairs at Tokyo should make a similar communication to the German Minister at that place.

L.

MINUTE BY KING EDWARD.

I think that there should be no loss of time in informing German Government of the Anglo-Japanese Agreement—or else they will hear from some other source—secrecy being almost an impossibility. The Emperor will be much interested in hearing the news as he has strongly advocated a close alliance between Great Britain and Japan.

E.R.

No. 127.

Sir C. MacDonald to the Marquess of Lansdowne.

F.O. Japan 563.
(No. 6A.) Secret.   *Tokyo,* D. *January* 31, 1902.
My Lord,   R. *March* 29, 1902.

This morning, Mr. Komura, Minister for Foreign Affairs, called on me with a message from the Prime Minister to the effect that the Japanese Government had accepted the amendments proposed by His Majesty Government. He added that Mr. Hayashi has telegraphed also for "full powers," and for permission to sign the said agreement without delay; the permission to sign had been sent on the 29th instant, but it was not clear whether the full powers mentioned were required by telegraph or might be sent by post. Mr. Komura said that the agreement was one which came into force immediately after signature; ratification was not, therefore, necessary, and he did not see why special full powers should be required.

I asked M. Komura whether he had received any news of the signature of the agreement. On his replying in the negative, I showed him your Lordship's telegram which had reached me a few minutes before Mr. Komura arrived, stating that the agreement had been signed by Mr. Hayashi and your Lordship on the previous afternoon.

Mr. Komura did not conceal his satisfaction at the news I was enabled to give him, and expressed in warm terms his desire that the agreement would be the means of maintaining the *status quo*, and peace, throughout the Far East.

With regard to the publication of the terms of the agreement, Mr. Komura thought it would be desirable that these should be made public in London and Tokyo on the same day. He said that it was a subject of congratulation that the negotiations had been kept so secret both in England and Japan; he thought, however, that now signature had taken place, it would not be so easy to keep the existence of the agreement from becoming public, and he, therefore, proposed to instruct Mr. Hayashi to approach your Lordship with a view to a day being fixed for the official publication of the agreement.

Mr. Komura asked whether I thought His Majesty's Government would consider it necessary to inform the German Government of the signature of the agreement; personally he did not think it would be advisable to take the German Government into our confidence—and he believed this to be the opinion of the majority of the Cabinet—as he did not think they would consent to join us in the arrangement. I said that this was a point which would, doubtless, very seriously occupy the attention of His Majesty's Government. M. Komura thought that if the German Government were to be approached, it would be necessary to do so before the day for the publication of the agreement was fixed. This date Mr. Komura was evidently very anxious to make as early as possible.

After further expressions of extreme gratification at the satisfactory termination of long and délicate negotiations, Mr. Komura left.

I have, &c.

CLAUDE M. MacDONALD.

[NOTE.—*King Edward and the Anglo-Japanese Agreement*, 1901–02.

The despatch of the Marquess of Lansdowne to Mr. Whitehead of the 31st July, 1901, No. 89, which began the overture, is endorsed—

"*Appd. E.R.*"

So is the similar despatch No. 91 of the 14th August—and the King has added in pencil in his own hand :—

"*The King considers it most essential that we should give Japan our hearty support on all occasions when it is possible to do so.*"

No. 115 of the 6th November to Sir C. Macdonald is endorsed—

"*Appd. E.R.*"

Before the agreement was concluded King Edward urged its communication first of all to Germany (*v.* Minute on despatch No. 12 of the 31st January). This was done by Lord Lansdowne to Baron Eckardstein and embodied in a Memorandum of the 6th February, 1902 (F.O. Japan 560), by Sir F. Bertie. He records that the Baron thanked Lord Lansdowne " for the kind consideration shown by His Majesty's Government in communicating to the German Government the information about theAnglo-Japanese Agreement. The German Government regard such a communication as an indication of confidence in them. They regard the agreement as a general guarantee of peace in China and in the interest of commerce and trade. Count Metternich will call on Lord Lansdowne on his return to London."

The King wrote on this despatch—

"*This is most satisfactory. I always knew how pleased the Emperor and Count Bülow would be at being the* first *to be informed of the Anglo-Japanese Agreement.*

E.R."

No. 128.

Sir F. Lascelles to the Marquess of Lansdowne.

F.O. Germany (Prussia) 1551.
(No. 23.) Very Confidential.   *Berlin, D. February* 7, 1902.
My Lord,   R. *February* 10, 1902.

With reference to my telegrams Nos. 10 and 11 of the 5th and 6th instant, I have the honour to report that the Emperor gave me an opportunity of speaking to him privately after the annual dinner which His Majesty gives to the Ambassadors and which took place on the evening of the 5th instant.

I said that your Lordship had instructed me to endeavour to see His Majesty at once in order to communicate to him the substance of an agreement which I was aware had already been brought to His Majesty's notice. His Majesty thanked me and then made use of a phrase which I gathered was intended to convey His Majesty's satisfaction, and in order to make this point clear I asked whether he wished me to telegraph to your Lordship the very words which he had employed. His Majesty replied that I surely understood him well enough by this time to be able to translate his expressions into diplomatic language, and on my observing that I proposed to inform your Lordship that His Majesty approved of the agreement he authorised me to say that he had received the communication with interest and satisfaction. He would regard it as a strictly confidential communication for which he was grateful, but he expressed some surprise that the agreement had not been concluded earlier.

Yesterday afternoon I met Count Buelow, with whom I had a short conversation. He told me that the Emperor had given him an account of his conversation with me, in which His Majesty had expressed his thanks and satisfaction. His Excellency also said that he had instructed Count Metternich to convey to your Lordship the warm thanks of the German Government for the confidence which you had reposed in them, and to state to your Lordship that, although Germany was not a party to the agreement which had been concluded between England and Japan, she had no obligations as regarded any other Power, and was therefore not one of the Powers contemplated by the 3rd article of the agreement, whose participation in the hostilities, if they should break out, would entail the common action of the two contracting Parties.

I have, &c.

FRANK C. LASCELLES.

No. 129.

The Marquess of Lansdowne to Lord Currie.

F.O. Italy 852.
(No. 26.)   Confidential.

My Lord,   *Foreign Office, February 12, 1902.*

The Italian Ambassador informed me to-day that the Agreement concluded between Great Britain and Japan on the 30th January last, which was published in to-day's newspapers, seemed to him to be one upon which the Italian Government could not look otherwise than with favour.

In commercial matters they desired to maintain the policy of the "open door," and they felt that it was to their advantage that there should be no breach of the peace or violent disturbance of the *status quo* in the Far East or elsewhere.

The Agreement seemed to him calculated to produce this result, but he had of course not yet been instructed by the Italian Government to express any opinion on the subject.

I am, &c.

LANSDOWNE.

No. 130.

Sir C. Scott to the Marquess of Lansdowne.

                                       St. Petersburg, February 12, 1902.

F.O. Russia 1644.   D. 8·45 P.M.
Tel.   (No. 7.)   R. 11 P.M.

Your telegrams Nos. 7 and 8.

Count Lamsdorff at his weekly reception this afternoon informed me that the Japanese Minister had sought an interview with him this morning, and by orders from his Government had communicated full text of its agreement with H.M. Government.

He observed that he appreciated the courtesy of the Japanese Government in giving him the first intimation of this interesting document in so frank and friendly a manner.

As regarded the preamble and the articles defining the object of this agreement, their terms were in such complete accordance with intimated views and repeated declarations of the Russian Government that he was disposed to ask permission to associate Russia with the two Governments in their Agreement.

He was, however, at a loss to understand the precise bearing or necessity of the subsequent articles for the event of either ally being involved in hostilities with other Powers, and he was apprehensive of the effect on public opinion by the introduction of the word " war " into an Agreement for an essentially pacific and non-aggressive object.

He knew of no Powers having any intention to threaten the integrity, independence or interests specified in the Agreement, but the inference from the latter part of the Agreement that it contemplated such a possibility might suggest to other Powers to take similar measures of precaution.

I remarked that having only received the first intimation of this Agreement the previous day in a telegram giving its substance but not full text, H.M. Government was naturally unable to authorise me to make a similar communication at the same time as the Japanese Minister, but I pointed out its eminently pacific object and the fact that there had been no intention of keeping its existence a secret from other Powers.

Count Lamsdorff said he had at once sent the text of the Agreement to the Emperor with observations similar to those made to me.

No. 131.

The Marquess of Lansdowne to Sir E. Monson.

F.O. France 3574.
(No. 52.) **Confidential.**
Sir, *Foreign Office, February* 12, 1902.

The French Ambassador called upon me to-day and at once referred to the Agreement concluded on January 30th between Great Britain and Japan, and published in this morning's newspapers.

His Excellency expressed the opinion that there was too much " méfiance " in this country as to Russian designs in different parts of the world. He did not believe for a moment that Russia had any desire to annex territory in the Far East, and he quoted to me opinions which had been expressed to him by M. Lessar, who had said that in his view it would be most dangerous for Russia to add to her possessions on the confines of China until she had further consolidated herself in her Asiatic dominions.

I said that I had no desire to attribute sinister designs to the Russian Government, but that I thought they were often served in the remoter parts of the Empire by dangerous representatives whom they found it impossible to disavow.

M. Cambon said that he thought that this was to some extent due to the fact that the Asiatic Department, which was primarily responsible for such matters, went its own way, which was not always that of the rest of the Government; it was, however, a pity that there was so much distrust both on our side and on that of Russia.

I replied that I quite agreed as to this, and that I had always desired to see the establishment of more cordial relations between the two Governments. I had, indeed, myself made overtures with this object, and endeavoured to bring about a better understanding as to our interests both in China and in Persia, but I had not been successful.

His Excellency then observed that the Agreement seemed to him to recognise a situation which already existed, and that, Agreement or no Agreement, we should probably be unable to tolerate the partition of China or of Corea. That being so, he could not see what object we had in tieing ourselves by a hard and fast bargain to a yellow ally, who might involve us, in spite of ourselves, in troublesome quarrels.

I reminded his Excellency that the main object of the Agreement was to render it possible for one of the High Contracting Parties to involve the assistance of the other in cases in which the quarrel had been brought about by the aggressive action of another Power, and in which that Power had been joined by others.

Throughout our conversation his Excellency's tone was most friendly, and he did not let fall a single observation calculated to betray a consciousness that the Agreement was in any way directed against France.

I am, &c.
LANSDOWNE.

No. 132.

Question asked in the House of Commons, February 13, 1902 [*Parl. Deb.* 4th Ser. Vol. 102, p. 1247].

Mr. Lambert,—To ask the Under-Secretary of State for Foreign Affairs, if, in the Anglo-Japanese Agreement, the words '' Empire of China '' include without reservation the province of Manchuria.

Answer.

Lord Cranborne,—Manchuria is no more excluded from the scope of this Agreement than any other province of the Chinese Empire. The substance of the Agreement was communicated to the German Government. The Anglo-German Agreement is still in force. The hon. Gentleman is no doubt aware of the interpretation placed by the German Government on the application of the Agreement to Manchuria.([1])

No. 133.

Further question asked in the House of Commons, February 13, 1902 [*Parl. Deb.* 4th Ser. Vol. 102, p. 1247].

Mr. O'Mara,—Am I to understand that Manchuria is included in this Agreement?

Answer.

Lord Cranborne,—Yes.

No. 134.

Mr. Bertie to Sir C. MacDonald.

F.O. Japan 563.
Tel. (No. 13.)

Foreign Office, February 13, 1902.
D. 11 P.M.

My telegram No. 12 of 12th.

Count Lamsdorff, referring to Japanese Minister's communication of the Anglo-Japanese Agreement, told Sir C. Scott that the Preamble and Articles defining its object were in such complete accordance with repeated declarations of the Russian Government that he was disposed to ask for Russia to be associated with two Powers, but he did not understand precise bearing or necessity of subsequent articles, as he knew of no Power having any intention to threaten integrity, independence or interests

([1]) [*V. supra*, pp. 27–31.]

specified, but the inference from the agreement that such intentions existed might
suggest similar measures of precaution to other Powers.

F. B.

No. 135.

Sir E. Satow to the Marquess of Lansdowne.

Peking, February 13, 1902.

F.O. China 1530.   D. 6·50 P.M.
Tel. (No. 43.)   R. 6·10 P.M.

Prince Ching regards the Anglo-Japanese Agreement as another proof of the
friendship of England and Japan, and [? thinks] that it will considerably facilitate his
negotiations for the evacuation of Manchuria. He has given me his latest counter-draft
which I shall telegraph *in extenso* when translated. He has observed quite recently
signs of greater readiness to treat on the Russian side. I told him he had better not
hurry, and that I could not promise an opinion on his draft until I had submitted it
to your Lordship.

He said he had definitely given Russo-Chinese Bank agent to understand he would
not entertain proposed agreement (sent in my telegram No. 30).

Repeated to Tokyo.

[*NOTE.*—The following is an extract from a private letter from Sir E. Satow to Lord Lansdowne
of the 13th February, 1902 :—

" The news of the Anglo-Japanese agreement only got out here late yesterday afternoon,
and up to the present the only foreign opinion I have heard is that of my U.S. colleague
who thinks it the most important political event that has taken place for a long time.
He seems to think that the Japanese are burning to go to war to turn the Russians out
of Manchuria, and says they could easily put 100,000 men there in a month's time. But
I do not imagine events will move as swiftly as that."

It was stated in the House of Commons on the 13th February (*Parl. Deb.*, 4th ser., Vol. 102,
pp. 1246–7) that the Agreement had been communicated to the United States Government, but
that they had expressed no opinion on it.]

No. 136.

Sir E. Satow to the Marquess of Lansdowne.

Peking, February 14, 1902.(1)

F.O. China. 1530.   D. *February 14, 6·50 P.M.*
Tel. (No. 44.)   R. *February 15, 11 A.M.*

My telegram No. 43 (of February 13th).
Following is draft referred to :—

His Majesty the Emperor of Russia and His Majesty the Emperor of China, being
desirous of re-establishing the relations of amity which were injured by the disturbances
in China of the year 1900, have appointed Plenipotentiaries to negotiate on matters
relating to Manchuria.

Article 1. His Majesty the Emperor of Russia, desirous of manifesting anew to
His Majesty the Emperor of China proofs of amity and friendship, and of ignoring the
hostile attacks on peaceful Russian subjects which took place along the Russo-
Manchurian frontier, agrees that Chinese authority shall be restored in Manchuria,
and that the country shall return to Chinese dominion and administration such as
existed before its occupation by the Russian troops.

(1) [*V.* Sir C. Scott to the Marquess of Lansdowne, No. 34, Telegram of the 12th April, 1902.
The whole agreement was subsequently published on the 9th April in *Journal Officiel.*]

Art. 2. The Government of China declare that from the date of the return of Manchuria to Chinese administration, the terms of the Agreement of August 27th, 1896 Russian Calendar, with the Russo-Chinese Bank shall be faithfully observed *for ever*;([2]) and recognises the obligation to afford the fullest protection to the railway and railway employés in accordance with Article 5 of that Agreement, and to all Russian subjects and their affairs in Manchuria.

The Government of China, having recognised the above obligations, the Government of Russia, if no further disturbances arise and no obstacles are caused by the proceedings of other Powers, agrees to withdraw the Russian forces from Manchuria gradually.

The mode of withdrawal shall be as follows :—

Within four months from the signature of the Manchurian Agreement the Russian troops quartered in south-western part of Sheng-ching up to the Liao River shall be withdrawn, and the railways shall be restored to China.

Within further period of four months the Russian troops shall evacuate the remainder of Shen-ching and the Province of Kirin.

Within four months after the above mentioned period the Russian troops shall evacuate the Province of Hei-lung-chiang.

Art. 3. The disturbances of last year having been caused by Chinese Government troops stationed on Russian frontier, Governments of China and of Russia, in order to avoid a recurrence of those disturbances, agree as follows :—

Military Governors of Manchurian provinces shall be instructed to concert with the Russian military authorities in deciding on numbers of Chinese troops to garrison Manchuria and their stations until the Russian troops are withdrawn; and China agrees that over and above the arrangements concluded by the Military Governors with the Russian military authorities, which shall declare sufficient number of troops for the maintenance of order and the suppression of brigandage, there shall be no additions to garrison of trained soldiers. After the complete evacuation of Manchuria by the Russians, however, numbers of troops shall be arranged by Chinese Government, who will inform Russian Government of their movements. For if China maintains a large military force in Manchuria, Russia cannot but strengthen her frontier garrisons, and result will be increased expenditure in both countries, without advantage to either. With regard to organisation of a police force in Manchuria and the restoration of tranquillity, Military Governors of each province shall train Chinese foot and mounted men exclusively to fulfil police functions. Land assigned to Manchurian Railway alone shall be policed by other than Chinese police.

Art. 4. Government of Russia agrees to restore Shanhaikwan–Newchwang–Hsinminting Railways, which have been occupied and protected by Russian troops since the end of September 1900, to their owners; and the Government of China agrees :—

1. In case protective measures are required that the duty of protecting these railways shall be undertaken by China alone; that it will not be necessary to invite other Powers (or other Power) to protect, repair, or maintain them, and that no other Power shall be allowed to occupy territory from which Russian troops are withdrawn.

2. Completion and maintenance of the above-mentioned railways shall be conducted in strict accordance with terms of Anglo-Russian Agreement of April 16th, 1899, and Loan Agreement concluded with the British and Chinese Corporation on September 28th, 1898, for the construction of those railways.

([2]) [Omitted in published version.]

Corporation shall abide by all other engagements which have been entered into, and shall not take possession or on any pretext administer the Shanhaikwan-Newchwang–Hsinminting Railways.

3. Extensions of railways in South Manchuria, or branch lines, or the construction of a bridge, or the moving of terminus at Newchwang, or such like matters shall form subject of mutual discussion hereafter.

4. *If it appears on examination that*([3]) the expenses incurred by Government in the repair and maintenance of Shanhaikwan–Newchwang–Hsinminting Railway were not included in general indemnity, Chinese Government shall arrange necessary compensation with Russian Government.

Observations in a separate telegram.
Repeated to Tokio.

([3]) [In text of the 8th April : Read at beginning " As the expenses incurred."]

No. 137.

Sir E. Monson to the Marquess of Lansdowne.

F.O. France 3576.
(No. 55.) *Paris, D. February* 14, 1902.
My Lord, R. *February* 15, 1902.
M. Delcassé, who returned from Nice last night, held his adjourned diplomatic reception this afternoon.

Upon my entering his study he said that he had come back to find the Convention. I said that I presumed that M. Cambon had sent it to him. As for myself, I had not received the official text, but of course I knew of it from the newspapers, and I trusted that he liked it. He rejoined that we seemed to be taking a great deal of trouble about securing the integrity of China. A year and a half ago we concluded an Agreement with Germany for the same object. We did not seem to be satisfied with that, since we had now asked Japan to join us.

I replied that, for that matter, I hoped that we had only set an example which would commend itself to the majority of the Great Powers, who, I trusted, held the same views that we did as to the expediency of maintaining the status of the Chinese Empire unimpaired.

His Excellency answered that he could, at any rate, answer for France, and that it was not from her that any trouble would arise in regard to the integrity of China.

I assured him that I had always understood that such was his policy, and that I was firmly persuaded that he would pursue it, and upon this the subject dropped.

I have, &c.
EDMUND MONSON.

No. 138.

The Marquess of Lansdowne to Mr. Jordan.

F.O. China 1558.

Tel. (No. 3.) *Foreign Office, February* 15, 1902.

The Korean Minister informed me to-day that the Korean Government regarded with much satisfaction the agreement concluded on the 30th January between this country and Japan.

They were most anxious to show themselves worthy of the support which the agreement would give them, but they found it difficult to introduce Western ideas in Korea all at once, and the Emperor's officials were many of them incompetent and untrustworthy. The Korean Government placed great reliance on your advice.

I expressed the pleasure with which I had listened to the Minister's statement, and my hope that, strengthened by the existence of the new agreement, the Korean Government would have the courage to resist any insidious advances which might be made to them with the object of undermining their independence or obtaining concessions inconsistent with the interests of Korea and the just rights of other Powers.

No. 139.

Sir F. Plunkett to the Marquess of Lansdowne.

F.O. Austria 1322.

(No. 52.) Confidential. *Vienna,* D. *February* 16, 1902.

My Lord, R. *February* 18, 1902.

With reference to my despatch No. 45 of the 13th instant, I have the honour to report that the Vienna newspapers have almost unanimously approved of the Convention lately signed by your Lordship with Japan, and consider it as likely to contribute to the peace of the Far East in the same way as the Triple Alliance has secured the maintenance for so many years of peace in Europe. Count Goluchowski has so far not spoken to me on the subject although I have seen him twice since a copy of the Convention was communicated to him by the Japanese Minister.

My Russian colleague called on me this afternoon, and in the course of his visit spoke about the Convention. He said the Japanese Minister at St. Petersburg had communicated a copy to Count Lamsdorff with an accompanying Note explaining in friendly terms the peaceful objects of the Convention, and expressing the hope that the Russian Government would see with pleasure the new step thus taken for securing the peace of the Far East.

Count Kapnist said that, as Russia desired the maintenance of the *status quo* both in China and Corea she could not do otherwise than approve the principles laid down in Articles 1 and 2. The allusion in Article 3 to other Power or Powers was a trifle vague, but he hoped that time would show that it did not imply more than was said.

After some further remarks Count Kapnist said that Russia had no intention of settling down permanently in Manchuria but she might have to stay there for some time, as she must secure the safety of her railway communications, and that may take some time.

I said the Convention had been concluded with the view of securing peace and open trade to all in China and Corea, and that I thought it was in the interests of all parties, that it should have been concluded.

Count Kapnist said at all events the Convention has so far been well received everywhere; we must now wait and see how it will work in practice.

I have, &c.

F. R. PLUNKETT.

No. 140.

Sir C. Scott to the Marquess of Lansdowne.

F.O. Russia 1644.

Tel. (No. 11.)

St. Petersburgh, February 17, 1902.

D. 9.

R. 10·45.

Your telegram No. 11 of February 15th.

I had a conversation with Count Lamsdorff to-day in which I explained why we had not formally communicated, as Japanese had done, the Agreement to him, and I offered, if he would consider it a civility, to give him a copy, as soon as I received one, of your Lordship's explanatory despatch to Sir C. MacDonald. As yet I have only seen text in the "Times" newspaper.

He did not think it necessary and went on to amplify his remarks to me of last Wednesday.

He said that on himself and on all Russian Statesmen the impression made by the revelation of this Agreement was a completely calm one as its aims were in entire accordance with their own, but that it was impossible that it should not sound a somewhat disquieting note in the general public and throughout the world by its provisions for the eventuality of hostilities—each one asking what was the cause of these precautionary provisions and from whom is the danger apprehended by the Contracting Powers and who will decide that their interests are threatened.

These questions will suggest counter-precautions on the part of those who may consider themselves liable to the suspicion of attacking some interest of either Ally, demands will be made by those charged with national safety for increased armaments; movements of troops and other precautionary measures so distasteful to Foreign Ministers, so disturbing to foreign relations and so burdensome on populations.

From this point of view the publication of this Agreement, prepared in such secrecy and sprung at this precise moment when everything looked so peaceful, was a great discouragement to him.

I read to him the last part of your telegram, on which he observed that the realisation of the desire which he had always cordially shared for a frank and friendly understanding with us on all subjects in the Far East seemed incompatible with the wording of Article IV of the Agreement which limited the independence of each Ally, inasmuch as neither could conclude a separate Agreement with a third Power without consulting its Ally.

I pointed out that the article distinctly spoke of arrangements prejudicial to the interests described in the Agreement.

He said that the exact meaning and bearing of this Article required further explanation as it seemed to him to be in contradiction to what I had said that the Agreement did not diminish the hope H.M. Government had never ceased to entertain for a frank and friendly understanding with Russia.

He hinted that Japan also did not see that the article bore the interpretation he had given it.

He looked on the Agreement as retarding the realisation of this desire and regretted it on that account.

No. 141.

Sir C. Scott to the Marquess of Lansdowne.

F.O. Russia 1640.

(No. 61.) Confidential. Extract.

St. Petersburgh, D. February 20, 1902.

R. *February* 24, 1902.

. . . . I find, from conversation with my colleagues, that the impression which they have derived of the feelings with which Count Lamsdorff and other Russian

Ministers have learnt of our Agreement with Japan is, that while affecting calm, and even indifference, as to its consequences, they have been greatly discomforted by it, and acknowledge it as a diplomatic check, if not defeat. They profess surprise that Japan should have been induced to enter into an Arrangement with His Majesty's Government which secures to her protection of her commercial and industrial interests only in Corea and China, while she might easily have secured greater and more political advantages by an arrangement with Russia which was within her reach.

My Japanese colleague tells me that Count Lamsdorff's few remarks to him were very similar to those which he made to me in our first conversation, namely, surprise at the secrecy and suddenness of the step, without sufficient apparent cause, entire accordance with the professed aims and object of the Agreement, but inability to understand the motive for the alarming provisions against eventual hostilities. . . . .

No. 142.

Sir F. Plunkett to the Marquess of Lansdowne.

F.O. Austria 1322.
(No. 59.)   Confidential.   *Vienna, D. February* 26, 1902.
My Lord,   R. *March* 3, 1902.

Count Goluchowski is so absorbed by his constant attendance by the bedside of the Countess, who unfortunately remains still in great danger, that I have had no opportunity of speaking with him since I received your Lordship's despatch No. 23, Confidential, of the 12th instant, reporting the congratulations offered to your Lordship by the Austro-Hungarian Ambassador upon the Anglo-Japanese Convention of the 30th ultimo.

Count Lützow, whom I saw to-day, alluded in friendly terms to the Convention as a success for His Majesty's Government, and a further element of peace. He added that the Russians were not pleased, but seemed disposed to put the best face on what, for them, was a bad job.

This coincides with what my French and Italian colleagues have told me of the comments on the Convention made to them by our Russian colleague. They separately described Count Kapnist as having said to them that Russia understood very well that the Anglo-Japanese Convention was directed against her, but the Convention secured peace for five years, which suits Russia very well, as it gives her breathing time to complete her railways quietly, and consolidate her position.

Count Kapnist has not spoken to me on this subject since the conversation reported in my despatch No. 52, Confidential, of the 16th instant.

I have, &c.
F. R. PLUNKETT.

No. 143.

Sir C. Scott to the Marquess of Lansdowne.

                                                            St. Petersburg, March 5, 1902.
F.O. Russia 1644.   D. 8·40 P.M.
Tel.   (No. 23.)   Very Confidential.   R. 10 P.M.

Japanese Minister has had a conversation with M. de Witte who told him that there was no truth whatever in a current rumour that since the conclusion of the Anglo-Japanese Agreement he had withdrawn his opposition to strengthening Russian Military position in the Far East.

[15214]   K 2

On the contrary he was strongly supporting Count Lamsdorff in urging an early evacuation of Manchuria but he told Japanese Minister in confidence that the Minister of War and Military party were advocating retention of Manchuria and trying to discredit the policy which Count Lamsdorff and he were supporting, that the Emperor had been approached in this sense but M. de Witte was convinced that H.I.M.'s confidence in Count Lamsdorff was undiminished.

Count Lamsdorff told me in conversation a few days ago that he would place his resignation in the Emperor's hands if any departure was made from the policy clearly set forth in the authorised published declarations and assurances.

No. 144.

Sir E. Satow to the Marquess of Lansdowne.

F.O. China 1521.
(No. 61.)   Confidential.   *Peking, D. March* 11, 1902.
My Lord,   R. *April* 28, 1902.

With reference to my telegram of the 1st instant No. 53, and to previous correspondence upon the subject of the Russo-Chinese Convention regarding Manchuria, I have now the honour to transmit to your Lordship herewith translations of M. Lessar's original draft proposal, and of such parts of Prince Ch'ing's counter-proposals, the text of which formed the subject of my telegram No. 44 of the 14th ultimo, as differ from the Russian Minister's draft.

This document has been drawn up in such a manner as to facilitate as much as possible a comparison between the Russian demands and the Chinese counter-suggestions as contained in Prince Ch'ing's counter-draft.

I have, &c.
ERNEST SATOW.

Enclosure in No. 144.

M. Lessar's Draft of Russo-Chinese Convention.	*Prince Ch'ing's Counter-Draft.*
His Majesty the Emperor of Russia and His Majesty the Emperor of China, being desirous of re-establishing the relations of amity which were injured by the disturbances in China of the year 1900, have appointed Plenipotentiaries to negotiate on matters relating to Manchuria.	Same.

ARTICLE I.

His Majesty the Emperor of Russia, desirous of manifesting anew to His Majesty the Emperor of China proofs of amity and friendship, and of ignoring the hostile attacks on peaceful Russian subjects which took place along the Russo-Manchurian frontier, agrees that Chinese authority shall be restored in Manchuria, and that the country shall return to Chinese dominion and administration such as existed before its occupation by the Russian troops.	Same.

M. Lessar's Draft of Russo-Chinese Convention.

Prince Ch'ing's Counter-Draft.

ARTICLE II.

The Government of China declares that from the date of the return of Manchuria to Chinese Administration the terms of the Agreement of the 27th August, 1896 (Russian Calendar), with the Russo-Chinese Bank shall be faithfully observed for ever ; and recognizes the obligations to afford the fullest protection to the Railway and Railway employés in accordance with Article 5 of that Agreement, and to all Russian subjects and their affairs in Manchuria.

The Government of China, having recognized the above obligations, the Government of Russia, if no further disturbances arise and no obstacles are caused by the proceedings of other Powers, agrees to withdraw the Russian forces from Manchuria gradually. The mode of withdrawal shall be as follows :—

Same.

(*a.*) *In the year* 1901 (*Russian Calendar*) the Russian troops quartered in the southwest part of Sheng-ching Province up to the Liao River shall be withdrawn, and the railways shall be restored to China.

Within four months from the signature of the present Agreement the Russian troops, &c.

(*b.*) *In the following year, that is,* 1902 (*Russian Calendar*), the Russian troops shall evacuate the remainder of Shengching.

Within a further period of four months the Russian troops shall evacuate the remainder of Sheng-ching *and the Province of Kirin.*

(*c.*) *In the year* 1903 (*Russian Calendar*) *the possibility of withdrawing the remainder of the Russian forces quartered in the two provinces of Kirin and Heilung-chiang will be considered.*

Within four months after the above period the Russian troops shall evacuate the Province of Heilung-chiang.

ARTICLE III.

The disturbances of last year having been caused by Chinese Government troops stationed on the Russian frontier, the Government of China and Russia, in order to avoid a recurrence of those disturbances, agree as follows :—

Same.

The military Governors of the Manchurian provinces shall be instructed to concert with the Russian military authorities in deciding on the numbers of the Chinese troops to garrison Manchuria and their stations; and China agrees that, over and above the *numbers fixed by the military Governors in consultation with the Russian military authorities,* there shall be no additions to the garrison of trained soldiers, *and that no other troops shall be sent to*

The military Governors of the Manchurian provinces shall be instructed to act in concert with the Russian military authorities in deciding on the numbers of the Chinese troops to garrison Manchuria and their stations *until the Russian troops are withdrawn;* and China agrees that over and above *the arrangements concluded by the military Governors with the Russian military authorities which shall contemplate a sufficient number of troops for the main-*

M. Lessar's Draft of Russo-Chinese Convention.

Prince Ch'ing's Counter-Draft.

Manchuria. For if China maintains a large military force in Manchuria, Russia cannot but strengthen her frontier garrisons, and the result will be increased military expenditure in both countries without advantage to either.

tenance of order and the suppression of brigandage, there shall be no additions to the garrison of trained soldiers. *After the complete evacuation of Manchuria by the Russian forces, however, the numbers of the Chinese troops shall be arranged by the Chinese Government, who will inform the Russian Government of their movements.* For if China maintains, &c.

With regard to the organisation of a police force in Manchuria and the restoration of tranquillity, the military Governors of each province shall train Chinese foot and mounted men exclusively to fulfil police functions. The land assigned to the Manchurian Railway alone shall be policed by other than Chinese police. *In the armament of this police force cannon shall be forbidden.*

Same.

This last sentence is excluded.

ARTICLE IV.

The Government of Russia agrees to restore the Shanhaikuan-Newchwang–Hsinmingting Railways, which have been occupied and protected by Russian troops since the end of September 1900, to the owners; and the Government of China agrees:

Same.

1. That the troops of other Powers (or another Power) shall *not be allowed to* protect, repair, or maintain the railways so restored, or to occupy territory from which the Russian troops are withdrawn. In case protective measures are required, the duty of protecting these railways shall be undertaken by Chinese troops only.

1. In case protective measures are required, that the duty of protecting these railways shall be undertaken by China alone; that it will *not be necessary to invite other Powers* (or another Power) to protect, repair, or maintain them; and that no other Power shall be allowed to occupy territory from which Russian troops are withdrawn.

2. The completion and maintenance of the aforesaid railways shall be conducted in strict accordance with the terms of the Anglo-Russian Agreement of April 16th, 1899, and of the loan Agreement concluded with the (British and Chinese) Corporation on September 28th, 1898, for the construction of those railways. The Corporation shall abide by all other engagements which have been entered into, and shall not take possession of or on any pretext administer the Shanhaikuan–Newchwang–Hsinmingting Railways.

Same.

3. *Without the previous consent of the Russian Government, no* extension of railways or branch lines in South Manchuria

3. Extension of railways in South Manchuria, or branch lines, or the construction of a bridge, or the moving of the terminus

| M. Lessar's Draft of Russo-Chinese Convention. | Prince Ch'ing's Counter-Draft. |

M. Lessar's Draft of Russo-Chinese Convention.

shall be permitted, *no* bridge shall be built over the *Liuo River* at Newchwang and *no* terminus of the Chinese railways in this territory shall be moved.

4. The expenses incurred by the Russian Government in the repair and maintenance of the Shanhaikuan – Newchang – Hsinmingting Railways *thus restored shall be repaid.*

Prince Ch'ing's Counter-Draft.

at Newchwang, *or such like matters shall form the subject of mutual discussion hereafter.*

4. *If it appears on examination* that the expenses incurred by the Russian Government in the repair and maintenance of the Shanhaikuan – Newchwang – Hsinmingting Railways *were not included in the general indemnity,* the Chinese shall arrange the *necessary compensation with the Russian Government.*

[*ED. NOTE.*—A revised draft was transmitted by Sir E. Satow on 10th April, 1902 (R. May 26). Printed *Accounts and Papers,* 1904 (*Cd.* 1936) CXX, pp. 172–3.]

No. 145.

The Marquess of Lansdowne to Sir E. Monson.

F.O. France 3574.
(No. 113.)

Sir,   *Foreign Office, March 19, 1902.*

The French Ambassador handed to me to-day the enclosed note as to the manner in which the conclusion of the recent Agreement between Great Britain and Japan is regarded by France and Russia. He informed me that the Note would be published to-morrow in Paris and St. Petersburg.

I thanked M. Cambon for his communication adding that I had already received a similar communication from the Russian Chargé d'Affaires and that I hoped that the tendency of these events would be towards the preservation of peace in the Far East.

His Excellency replied that he entertained the same hope but speaking for himself he regretted the conclusion of our Agreement with Japan on the ground that it rendered more remote the prospect of a good understanding which he had at one time thought might be established between Great Britain and Russia.

I have, &c.
L.

Enclosure in No. 145.

Les Gouvernements Alliés de France et de Russie ayant reçu communication de la Convention Anglo-Japonaise du 30 Janvier 1902, conclue dans le but d'assurer le status quo et la paix générale en Extrême-Orient et de maintenir l'indépendance de la Chine et de la Corée qui doivent rester ouvertes au commerce et à l'industrie de toutes les nations, ont été pleinement satisfaits d'y trouver l'affirmation des principes essentiels qu'ils ont eux-mêmes, à plusieurs reprises, déclaré constituer et qui demeurent la base de leur politique.

Les deux Gouvernements estiment que le respect de ces principes est en même temps une garantie pour leurs intérêts spéciaux en Extrême-Orient. Toutefois, obligés d'envisager, eux aussi, le cas où soit l'action aggressive de tierces Puissances, soit de nouveaux troubles en Chine, mettant en question l'intégrité et le libre développement de cette Puissance, deviendraient une menace pour leurs propres intérêts, les deux Gouvernements Alliés se réservent d'aviser éventuellement aux moyens d'en assurer la sauvegarde.

Paris, le 3–16 Mars 1902.

MINUTE BY KING EDWARD.

The King regrets the French Ambassador's reply to Lord Lansdowne—but it shows more than ever the necessity of an agreement with Japan which naturally interferes with Russia's views and possible action.

E.R.

March 21, 1902.

No. 146.

Sir E. Satow to the Marquess of Lansdowne.

F.O. China 1521.
(No. 66.) Confidential.   *Peking, D. March 20, 1902.*
My Lord,   R. *May 12, 1902.*

The accompanying extract, in copy, from a despatch from His Majesty's Consul-General at Hankow contains a report of that portion of a recent interview which he has had with the Viceroy, which deals with the Anglo-Japanese Convention recently concluded, with special reference to the attitude of Germany in Chinese affairs.

Mr. Fraser states that the Viceroy expressed some anxiety lest the terms of the Convention might imply constant interference in Chinese affairs. His Excellency's information was based upon a Chinese translation which had reached him from Japanese sources, and he expressed much satisfaction when the real meaning of the clause he referred to, as shown by the English text, was explained to him.

I have, &c.
ERNEST SATOW.

Enclosure in No. 146.

Consul-General Fraser to Sir E. Satow.

(No. 12.) Extract.   *Hankow, March 3, 1902.*

His Excellency next suggested that, in view of a rumoured Franco-Russian Agreement as to the Far East, it was a pity that Germany had not also signed our compact. I replied that, according to the newspapers, Germany knew of, and approved, the Agreement. My own private opinion was that Germany, lying between France and Russia, and doubtful of the effective support of Italy and the perturbed Austria, was loth to rouse the hostility of Russia by such an overt act. She had certainly hastened to announce that Manchuria was beyond the purview of the Anglo-German Agreement of 1900.

The Viceroy assented with a chuckle, and enquired about the state of Austria and the new German Tariff, which I had mentioned as provoking the ill-will of her neighbours. He seemed much interested in the rival policies of protection and free trade, and announced himself in favour of duties as little burdensome as possible to the great body of the population. He recognised, however, that too great dependence on imported food-stuffs might prove a serious peril in time of war.

Reverting to the Anglo-Japanese Agreement, he remarked that the Chinese translation that had reached him from Japanese sources seemed to imply constant interference in Chinese affairs. I explained that the English text did not bear this interpretation. Both nations sought China's integrity and full independence. The clause he cited merely provided against the discussion and delay as to sending troops, which had given time for the Boxer madness to reach a disastrous height. In future, as I understood the text, the Signatory Powers would, in case of need, act without waiting to consult other nations; but neither Power would interfere unless their interests were so seriously affected that they could be safeguarded only by force of arms. With this explanation the Viceroy expressed himself highly pleased, and Mr. Liang undertook to make a careful translation of the English text for the Viceroy.

No. 147.

Sir F. Plunkett to the Marquess of Lansdowne.

F.O. Austria 1322.
(No. 86.)   Very Confidential.   *Vienna, D. March 26, 1902.*
My Lord,   R. *March 31, 1902.*

In the course of a visit which I paid yesterday to my French colleague, the conversation turned after a time on the publication of the Agreement recently come to between France and Russia in regard to the Far East.

Marquis de Reverseaux expressed satisfaction at the calm manner in which this Agreement had been accepted in London and elsewhere. I said that the Franco-Russian Agreement appeared to do little more than affirm the principles set forth in the Anglo-Japanese one, and I could not understand why it had been thought desirable to accentuate just in this manner the fact of the good understanding which everybody knows to exist between Paris and St. Petersburgh.

Marquis de Reverseaux replied that it was intended as a warning to Japan, who Russia believed was intoxicated by her alliance with a great Power like England, and would be tempted to seek any excuse for forcing on complications. I gathered from what my French colleague further said that the Russian Government harbour no doubt of the honesty of His Majesty's Government's intentions in the Far East, but they entertain strong suspicions that Japan proposes making the most of the opportunity she hopes to find in the Agreement lately come to with Great Britain.

I said such apprehensions seemed to me hardly well founded.

I have, &c.
F. R. PLUNKETT.

No. 148.

Sir T. H. Sanderson to Sir E. Satow.

(Private.)[1]   *May 9, 1902.*

As regards your reproach for not mentioning the signature of the Anglo-Japanese Agreement, I knew that the Agreement would become public property long before my letter reached you—and there really was nothing to communicate about it. There is nothing beyond the agreement itself except an interchange of notes promising one another docking facilities and expressing the intentions of later Governments to keep up their naval forces in the Far East.

I have always thought, and I still think, that the Agreement will have a steadying effect on Japan. There was a certain risk that she might at some emergency have a *coup de tête* and go for the Russians, which is certainly not desirable if pacific pressure would afford a solution, or lose heart and give way more than would be desirable either for herself or for us. As it is we hear stories somewhat similar to those which have reached you that, while Ito was at St. Petersburg, Witte and Lamsdorff dangled before him prospects of allowing Japan a free hand at Corea and on the mainland opposite Formosa if she would range herself on the side of Russia and France. Probably the offers were not very definite and anyhow the Japanese probably saw through them. If the stories are true it accounts for the considerable amount of irritation which we hear the Russians felt against the Japanese, when first the Agreement came out.

Some people have wondered why it was published when it was. The fact is that we were quite certain that it could not be kept secret for long, and that as we should certainly have it dragged out of us in Parliament it was much better to make a clean breast of it at once.

[1] From the private papers of Sir E. Satow.

CHAPTER XII.

ANGLO-GERMAN RELATIONS, 1902-3.

I.— THE EVACUATION OF SHANGHAI.

THE EVACUATION OF SHANGHAI (JULY TO DECEMBER, 1902).

[*ED. NOTE.*—In December 1902 the British Government laid a White-Book of 50 pieces before both Houses of Parliament as a command-paper. This is endorsed Cd. 1369, China No. 3 (1902). It was published in *P.P. Accounts and Papers*, 1902, CXXX, 353, but not in the *B.F.S.P.* series. Considerable omissions were made, partly owing to German representations, partly in order to conceal the serious friction that had taken place between the German and British Governments. As Sir Ernest Satow in a private letter to F. A. Campbell wrote later (the 2nd November, 1905) : " When the White Book was published, part of the correspondence had to be suppressed to avoid exciting public feeling." And at the time Count Bülow deprecated " putting oil on the fire."

The evacuation of Shanghai is treated in *G.P.* XVI, 449–91, but not very fully.

A suggestion was made as to evacuation by Baron Richthofen on the 10th April, 1901, in the telegram here printed.]

No. 149.

Sir F. Lascelles to the Marquess of Lansdowne.

Berlin, April 10, 1901.

F.O. Germany (Prussia) 1524.
Tel. (No. 25.)

D. 1·20 P.M.
R. 3·45 P.M.

Baron Richthofen who was present at my official audience of Emperor reported in my preceding telegram, told me later that the German Government had been disappointed at the want of success which Dr. Stuebel had met with in his recent mission to London. The German Government certainly did not desire to hamper trade with China. It was to their interest to encourage it, but the German merchants believed trade could support even a 15 per cent. customs duty, and the German Government were therefore disappointed that their proposal to raise the duty to 10 per cent. should have been met by a curt refusal without eliciting any counter-proposal.([1])

The question of expulsions from South Africa was less important, but might perhaps have met with more friendly consideration. But the danger of complications arising from presence of foreign contingents in China was so great that H.E. considered it was most important that a solution which would admit of the withdrawal of the European troops should be arrived at. The German Government in consequence of their Parliamentary situation could not withdraw their troops until satisfactory security for the indemnities had been obtained, and they were still of opinion that an increase of the customs duties would furnish the simplest solution. He believed amount of British claims had not yet been settled.

([1]) [The New Chinese Customs Agreement was signed at Shanghai the 29th August, 1902, fixing the customs duty at 5 per cent. by Great Britain, Austria-Hungary, Belgium, Germany, Japan, the Netherlands, Spain and China, *v. B.F.S.P.*, XCVII, 695–7.]

[*ED. NOTE.*—The first real idea of evacuation was mooted by Herr Mumm, the German representative at Peking, on the 15th June, 1901 (*G.P.*, XVI, 451). A number of German documents have been published between this date and the 30th July, 1902, when the British documents, as published in *Cd.* 1369, begin. On that date Sir Ernest Satow reported to Lord Lansdowne the Chinese desire for evacuation. *Accounts and Papers*, 1902 (*Cd.* 1369) CXXX, p. 357 (No. 1 of *Cd.* 1369). Nos. 2–10 give the story up to the 19th August, *ib.* pp. 357–9.]

No. 150.

The Marquess of Lansdowne to Sir F. Lascelles.

F.O. Germany (Prussia) **1550.**
(No. 75.)

Sir,   *Foreign Office, March* 18, 1902.

The German Ambassador, who is about to leave England for four weeks, called upon me to-day. I had previously warned him that there were two matters about which I should like to speak to him before his departure, as we should not improbably be questioned in Parliament in regard to them.

These were—

    1. The withdrawal of the international troops from China; and
    2. The German Concessions in Shantung.

As to the first, I told his Excellency that we were making large reductions, and that the French were following suit. Would it be possible for us to say that Germany would make corresponding reductions? We should, I said, find it very difficult to persist in our policy of largely diminishing our strength in China unless the same policy were followed by the other Powers.

Count Metternich informed me that the German Government were considering the question, and fully intended to reduce the number of their troops as soon as possible; they did not, however, yet possess sufficient data to be able to lay precise proposals before the Emperor. Germany had at present, in round numbers, 3,000 combatants in Chihli, and if they were to reduce those to 1,600, which was the number agreed upon by the Generals representing England, France, Japan, and Germany, Germany would have to withdraw 1,400 men. It seemed, however, doubtful to the German Government whether the reduced contingents would be able to hold all the places which had to be occupied by international agreement, and they thought it should be considered whether the officers in command should not first be instructed to work out a new plan for the distribution of the troops.

Besides this, his Excellency told me, that the "regulation" of the Pei-ho River, including the removal of the bar at its mouth, was a matter of the greatest importance, because, in the view of their military men, the situation of the Europeans at Peking would be precarious unless this work were carried out. The decision of the German Government in regard to the retention of the German troops would very likely be "essentially facilitated" if guarantees could be given for the prompt execution of the works in question.

His Excellency asked to be informed as to the opinion which His Majesty's Government held upon this point.

I told his Excellency that, as I understood the matter, the proposal that each of the four Powers should retain 1,600 men in Northern China, and that certain places between Peking and the sea should be occupied, had originated with Field-Marshal Count Waldersee, and that I presumed that the question of the sufficiency of this force and its distribution had been considered by him at the time. Our idea was to reduce our force at once to 2,000 men, which would leave a margin for employment at any places which might require special protection. I had, however, no objection to asking Sir E. Satow, by telegram, whether he and his colleagues had satisfied themselves that the distribution of the troops which might be left in North China had been sufficiently considered, and I presumed that I might take it that if it should prove to be the case that this question had been properly examined on the spot, the German Government would reduce their force to a number of about 1,600 men.

Count Metternich expressed concurrence, adding that he assumed that whatever reduction agreed to would be carried out, *pari passu*, by the Powers concerned. . . . .([1])

                                       [I am, &c.
                                         LANSDOWNE.]

([1]) [Details as to German concession in Shantung.]

No. 151.

[This document (No. 11 in *Cd.* 1369, *Accounts and Papers*, 1902, CXXX, pp. 359–60) was somewhat altered, the part in square brackets being omitted from the published version.]

Foreign Office to India Office.

F.O. China 1552.
Secret.
Sir,   *Foreign Office, August* 20, 1902.

His Majesty's Minister at Peking telegraphed on the 30th ultimo that the Viceroy at Nanking had requested the Acting British Consul-General at Shanghae to urge His Majesty's Government to withdraw the British troops from Shanghae, in conjunction with the French, German, and Japanese troops.

Sir E. Satow was informed, in reply, that His Majesty's Government would have no objection to this course, provided that other Powers took similar action.

An enquiry was, at the same time, addressed to the Governments concerned, and replies having been received to the effect that they were ready to agree to a joint withdrawal, His Majesty's Government intimated to the Chinese Government their willingness to propose a date on which evacuation should begin, [so soon as they learned that the Commercial Treaty, which Sir J. Mackay had negotiated with the Chinese Commissioner had been signed.

There appears to be every prospect of the Chinese Government accepting the Treaty, and] I am directed by the Marquess of Lansdowne to enquire what is the earliest date by which arrangements could be made for the withdrawal of the British force. He desires to have this information, in order that he may be in a position to make a definite proposal to the other Powers who have garrisons at Shanghae for the simultaneous evacuation of the port.

[It is advisable that the intention of His Majesty's Government to propose a date for withdrawal should be kept secret, in order that this action may not be forestalled by other Powers.]

No. 152

[This document was, by German request, omitted from *Cd.* 1369 altogether.]

The Marquess of Lansdowne to Sir F. Lascelles.

F.O. Germany (Prussia) 1550.
(No. 212.)
Sir,   *Foreign Office, August* 26, 1902.

With reference to my despatch No. 207 of the 19th instant, I have to inform your Excellency that Baron von Oppell, of the German Embassy, had called at the Foreign Office on the 16th instant and made the same communication to Sir T. Sanderson as Count Metternich made to me on the 19th instant, but he also told him that the German Government understood that the French Government wished that there should be an Agreement between the four Powers on the subject of the withdrawal of their forces from Shanghae, and that that Government had made the reservation that if any Powers again sent troops to Shanghae they would do the same.

Baron von Oppell further stated that the German Government had not thought it necessary to make such a reservation, because they thought it was sufficiently implied in what had occurred, and that it appeared to them that all that was necessary was to arrange appropriate conditions ("Modalität") for the withdrawal.

I am, &c.
LANSDOWNE.

No. 153.

[ED. NOTE.—A note of Sir Frank Lascelles of the 22nd September to Baron Richthofen, German Foreign Secretary, is printed in G.P., XVI, 465.

The Eckardstein Note of the 7th October, received the 8th October, is printed correctly in No. 22 of Cd. 1369, Accounts and Papers, 1902, CXXX, pp. 362–3.

The Marquess of Lansdowne to Sir E. Satow of the 10th October is paraphrased in No. 27 of Cd. 1369 (ib. p. 364) and the last sentence omitted. The whole text is therefore given here.]

The Marquess of Lansdowne to Sir E. Satow.

F.O. China 1529.
Tel. (No. 252.)   *Foreign Office, October* 10, 1902.

Your telegram No. 295 (of October 10th) and Sir C. MacDonald's No. 57 (of October 9th.

Withdrawal from Shanghai.

Following is third condition proposed by German Government :—

"The Peking Government and Yangtze Viceroys shall engage not to grant to any Power special advantages of a political, military, maritime or economic nature, nor to allow the occupation of any other points commanding the river either below or above Shanghai."

It is explained that "economic advantages" is not intended to apply to individual concessions, but only to grants excluding free competition.

I have told Japanese Minister that I see no objection to undertaking that evacuation should be simultaneous and uniform, nor any reason against each of the Powers making reservation as to re-occupation, and that I thought we might fall in with suggestion contained in passage of German Note, which runs :—

"The Imperial Government are chiefly anxious to see that no State obtains from China directly or indirectly such compensation for the evacuation of Shanghai as shall benefit that State alone."

German Chargé d'Affaires here says that the Chinese Government have accepted the conditions which the German Government have suggested.

Ascertain whether Chinese Government have accepted the third condition above described, and urge them strongly not to commit themselves until they have heard further from us.

Please repeat to Tokyo.

No. 154.

[ED. NOTE.—Lord Lansdowne's note to Baron Eckardstein of the 11th October is printed as No. 28 of Cd. 1369, Accounts and Papers, 1902, CXXX, p. 365.

Sir E. Satow's telegram No. 304 of the 15th October is mutilated in No. 31 of Cd. 1369 (ib. p. 366). The whole is reproduced here. The rebuke sent by Lord Lansdowne to Prince Ching and Prince Ching's reply are not published here, as the paraphrases in Cd. 1369 (Nos. 33 and 39,34 ib. pp. 366 and 368) are substantially correct. But a Memo. to the Japanese Minister (Baron Hayashi) the 28th October, summarising these, and other, circumstances is printed, together with the documents showing impression produced on the Japanese Government.]

Sir E. Satow to the Marquess of Lansdowne.

           Peking, October 15, 1902.
F.O. China 1531.   D. 4·15 P.M.
Tel. (No. 304.)   R. 10·30 P.M.

Your telegrams Nos. 252 and 255.

Prince Ching on 13th October denied to me that the German Chargé d'Affaires had said anything to him about conditions, and declared that he had merely stated the willingness of the German Government to evacuate simultanously with the other Powers. In face of his denial, it seemed useless to urge him not to consent. The Wai-wu-pu repeated this denial on 14th October.

German Chargé d'Affaires tells me that all the conditions mentioned in German Chargé d'Affaires' note to your Lordship of 7th October were embodied in the note addressed by him to Prince on 7th October. That he had made the communication verbally beforehand, and obtained their consent. That he has also received telegraphic replies from Acting Viceroy of Nanking, and from Viceroy of Hankow, so that Chargé d'Affaires in London was correct in stating to your Lordship that Chinese Government had accepted. The written reply of Prince Ching was received by German Legation the day before yesterday, and must have been actually signed at the moment Prince Ching was making denial.

I would suggest that any communication which His Majesty's Government may instruct me to make to him should contain the criticism of German proposal given in the last paragraph of your Lordship's reply to German Chargé d'Affaires, with a special reference to Shantung, Kwangtung and Yunnan. An alternative would be to inform the Chinese Government that [? in view of] way they have behaved on present occasion, His Majesty's Government will not withdraw their troops.

I should also take an opportunity of reproaching the Prince for deceiving me in a matter in which His Majesty's Government had sought to benefit China, especially after the friendly support they have given to this Government on so many occasions.

Prince had evidently been persuaded to keep the matter secret by German Chargé d'Affaires, who also admits now that he was instructed not to communicate to me the third condition.

Under the circumstances, I think that it would be desirable to be unyielding as to the Chenchow murders.

(Repeated to Tokyo.)

No. 155.

Memorandum for Communication to Viscount Hayashi.

F.O. Japan 558.
Secret.   *Foreign Office, October* 16, 1902.

His Majesty's Minister at Peking has received secret intelligence that about two months ago the French Government were informed by the German Government that Sir James Mackay had tried to obtain the consent of the Nanking Viceroy to the eventual occupation of Chingkiang and Kiang-Yin forts by Great Britain.

It is represented that the information was conveyed to the French Government in such a manner as to convince them of its truth.

Sir E. Satow has been asked whether the intelligence as to this misrepresentation of Sir J. Mackay's commercial negotiations with the Yangtze Viceroys is quite certain.

Prince Ching on the 13th instant denied to Sir E. Satow that the German Chargé d'Affaires had said anything to him about conditions, when speaking of the evacuation of Shanghai, and declared that he had merely stated that the German Government were willing to evacuate simultaneously with the other Powers.

This denial was repeated by the Wai-wu-pu next day.

Sir E. Satow has, however, learnt from the German Chargé d'Affaires that all the conditions which were communicated to H.M. Government on the 7th instant were embodied in the Note addressed to Prince Ching on the same day.

The conditions had, moreover, been communicated to the Chinese Government verbally beforehand, and their consent obtained by telegraphic replies had also been received from the Acting Viceroy of Nanking and from the Viceroy of Hankow.

The written reply of Prince Ching was, Sir E. Satow was informed, received by the German Legation on the 13th instant. and must have been actually signed at the time when Prince Ching, who had evidently been persuaded by the German Chargé to keep the matter secret, made his denial.

H.M. Minister at Peking has been instructed to inform Prince Ching that H.M. Government deeply resent his treatment of them. Sir E. Satow is to remind Prince Ching that in the face of much opposition from Foreign Powers H.M. Government have constantly upheld Chinese interests, and that it was due to their initiative that France and Germany, the two Powers with whose Representatives the Chinese Government have been communicating secretly with regard to the terms on which evacuation should take place, consented to the withdrawal of their forces.

Sir E. Satow is to state that H.M. Government are compelled by Prince Ching's duplicity to reconsider their attitude, and that if, in consequence, the withdrawal of the troops does not take place the responsibility will rest with Prince Ching.

Sir E. Satow has been instructed to communicate to Prince Ching the substance of the reply made by H.M. Government to the proposals communicated by Baron v. Eckardstein, and to inform him that no regard will be paid by H.M. Government to any pledges given by the Chinese Government or by the Viceroys limiting their freedom of action or that of H.M. Government in the future as regards the maintenance of order and the protection of the interests of England in the Yangtze region.

No. 156.

Memorandum for communication to Japanese Minister.(¹)

Foreign Office, October 28, 1902.

On the 20th October, His Majesty's Minister at Peking delivered a note to Prince Ching in the terms of the instructions sent to him on the 16th October (to which reference is made in the Memorandum communicated to Viscount Hayashi on the 16th October).

A similar warning was given to the Viceroy of Wuchang by His Majesty's Consul-General on the 19th instant.

In regard to the warning to the Chinese Government that His Majesty's Government would not pay any regard to pledges given by the Chinese Government or Viceroys limiting their own freedom of action or that of His Majesty's Government in the Yang-tsze region, Prince Ching volunteered the assurance that nothing written by him would be allowed to affect the rights of Great Britain on the Yang-tsze.

No formal reply has been received from the Chinese Government to Sir E. Satow's note.

His Excellency, on hearing what were the objections of His Majesty's Government, undertook that he would sign no Agreement on the subject that had not been submitted to the Powers. He trusted, however, that His Majesy's Government would support him in demanding that Shanghae should be evacuated without any special conditions and in contending that the conditions proposed should, in the interests of justice, be altered so as to embrace all Chinese possessions, and should be guaranteed by all the Powers in a joint Agreement with the Chinese Government.

On the 22nd October, His Majesty's Consul at Nanking made the same communication to the Acting Viceroy as had been made to the Viceroy of Wuchang.

His Excellency replied that he knew nothing of the conditions proposed by Germany in connection with the evacuation of Shanghae; but he gave an assurance that he would not enter into the engagements referred to, which, by limiting China's freedom of action, would be derogatory to her status as an independent country.

(¹) [Original not traced. The text is taken from the *Confidential Print.*]

On the 25th October the Viceroy of Wuchang made the following communication to His Majesty's Consul-General at Hankow :—

" The German Consul-General at Shanghae had the previous day handed him a note embodying the conditions on which the German Government agreed to evacuation. His Excellency had declined to sign a Secret Agreement on the subject, whereupon the German Consul-General had replied that he had no desire for secrecy or objection to the proposal being known; he had added that the German Government only wanted an exchange of notes and not a formal Agreement."

His Majesty's Minister at Peking is in direct communication with His Majesty's Minister at Tokyo, who has been instructed to keep the Japanese Government informed of what passes in regard to the question of the evacuation of Shanghae.

His Majesty's Consul-General at Hankow has been instructed to remind the Viceroys at Wuchang of the warning given to the Chinese, referred to at the beginning of this Memorandum, and to add that His Majesty's Government will consult with the Japanese Government as to the best mode of supporting the Viceroy in his resistance to the German proposal.

No. 157.

The Marquess of Lansdowne to Sir C. MacDonald.

F.O. Japan 550.
(No. 112.)
Sir,   *Foreign Office, October* 28, 1902.

I mentioned to the Japanese Minister to-day that I had not yet received any reply to the letter which I had addressed on the 11th instant to the German Chargé d'Affaires on the subject of the evacuation of Shanghae.

In the meantime, however, we had learned that the Representatives of the German Government were putting pressure upon the Viceroy of Hankow, with the object of inducing him to give his consent to the German proposal, which the Peking Government had promised, though not in writing, to entertain favourably.

I gave to Viscount Hayashi the accompanying Memorandum, in which the situation is described, and I told him that His Majesty's Government desired to encourage the Viceroy in his resistance to the German scheme, and that we should be glad if the Japanese Government would join us in supporting him in his refusal to give his consent to it.

Viscount Hayashi undertook that he would at once communicate what I had said to the Japanese Government, and inform me as soon as possible of the result.

I am, &c.
LANSDOWNE.

No. 158.

Sir C. MacDonald to the Marquess of Lansdowne.

                                                     Tokyo, October 31, 1902.
F.O. Japan 554.   D. 5·50 P.M.
Tel. (No. 68.) Confidential.   R. 10 P.M.

Your telegram (No. 55) of 28th October (evacuation of Shanghae).

Japanese Minister for Foreign Affairs has just informed me that instructions in following sense were telegraphed to Japanese Minister in London to-day : Japanese Government recognising fully the principle of the " open door " in China, are fully prepared to join with His Majesty's Government in supporting Wuchang Viceroy in insisting that German condition should apply to entire Empire of China. They think, however, that it would be inadvisable to press that this condition should be agreed to by all the Powers, as this would entail great loss of time and the evacuation of Shanghae would be indefinitely postponed.

Minister for Foreign Affairs further informed me that German Minister had called yesterday, and stated that, acting under instructions from his Government, he begged to inform Japanese Government that, as German conditions had been accepted by the Central Government at Peking and by the Wuchang Viceroy, the German troops would evacuate Shanghae as soon as necessary preparations could be made.

No. 159.

Sir C. MacDonald to the Marquess of Lansdowne.

Tokyo, October 31, 1902.
D. 6·10 P.M.
R. 8 P.M.

F.O. Japan 554.
Tel. (No. 69.) Very Confidential.

My immediately preceding telegram.

Japanese Minister for Foreign Affairs, to whom I had already read Sir E. Satow's telegram to your Lordship, No. 328, and Mr. Fraser's telegram of 25th October from Hankow, was at a loss to know how German Government could reconcile statement that their condition had been accepted by Central Government and Viceroy of Wuchang with information contained in said telegrams.

I suggested that perhaps German Government considered acceptance, qualified with the condition that it should apply to whole Empire was sufficient. I (? added that) Viceroy had undoubtedly not signed acceptance. Minister for Foreign Affairs was of opinion that Germans were now in a hurry to evacuate to prevent possibility of their being formally asked to join other Powers in extending their own condition over the whole of Chinese Empire including Shantung.

I said I thought this was not improbable.

No. 160.

[*ED. NOTE.*—Count Metternich's note of the 1st November (received the 3rd November) is printed intact in No. 43 of *Cd.* 1369, *Accounts and Papers*, 1902, CXXX, p. 369.([1]) The account of the conversation given in No. 44 of *Cd.* 1369 (*ib.* pp. 369–70) should have the following passage added.]

The Marquess of Lansdowne to Mr. Buchanan.

F.O. Germany (Prussia) 1550.
(No. 278.) Extract.
Foreign Office, November 3, 1902.

At the close of our conversation, I told Count Metternich that I could not help regretting that the German Government should have disposed of this question by direct arrangement with the Chinese Government, and without our concurrence.

His Excellency replied that the German Government had made us the proposal contained in Baron Eckardstein's note of the 7th October, but that we had refused to accept it. It was therefore natural that they should come to terms with China.

I said that my study of the documents had certainly led me to suppose that the German Government had approached the Peking Government before anything had been said to us.

([1]) [Based on Instruction of Count Bülow of the 26th October, *G.P.*, XVI, 474–5.]

L

His Excellency replied that he was not sure, but that he "hardly" thought this was the case. The German Government was, he added, anxious to act with us in China, and if we desired to make any observations upon the note which he had given me they would be gladly considered.

No. 161.

Sir F. Lascelles to the Marquess of Lansdowne.

F.O. Germany (Prussia) 1552.
(No. 222.) Confidential.
My Lord,   London, November 4, 1902.

In the course of our conversation on the 1st instant, Count Bülow referred to the negotiations which were going on with regard to the evacuation of Shanghai by the foreign contingents. He said that the interests of Germany and England in China were identical and that the German merchants who traded with China had impressed upon him the necessity of the authorities of the two countries acting together. All that the German Government had done in asking for certain assurances from the Chinese Authorities was for the purpose of securing the principle of the Open Door. Count Bülow did not explain the nature of the assurances for which the German Government had asked, and as I was aware that the question was being discussed by your Lordship and Count Metternich, I thought it best to avoid arguing the question with his Excellency. I therefore confined myself to expressing the hope that some means might be found for making arrangements for the evacuation, which I understood both our Governments desired to effect as soon as possible.

I have, &c.
FRANK C. LASCELLES.

No. 162.

Mr. Buchanan to the Marquess of Lansdowne.

F.O. Germany (Prussia) 1552.
(No. 224.) Confidential.   Berlin, D. November 4, 1902.
My Lord,   R. November 10, 1902.

Baron Richthofen, on whom I called this afternoon referred in the course of our conversation to the question of the evacuation of Shanghai, and said that he hoped that the interview which Count Metternich was to have with your Lordship to-day would lead to a satisfactory solution of the question.

I reciprocated this wish, but added that I would not conceal from his Excellency the fact that the proposal which had been put forward by the German Government had caused a very unpleasant impression in England.

On his Excellency remarking that, in advocating the principle of the "open door," the Imperial Government had but exercised the right common to all Governments of proposing what they thought best from their own point of view, I replied that this principle had always received the adherence of His Majesty's Government and was, in their opinion, already sufficiently safeguarded by existing agreements. We had, however, been rather painfully surprised to find that the Imperial Government had with the help of the French Government and without calling us into their confidence, induced the Government of China to promise their assent to a proposal that could only be directed against ourselves.

Baron Richthofen here interrupted me by saying that the German proposal had been communicated simultaneously to all the Powers concerned.

I replied that his Excellency was no doubt correct in saying this of the official communication but that, unless I was mistaken, assurances had been obtained from the Chinese Government before the Government of His Majesty had been approached on the subject. The chief centre of British interests in China was, I said, on the Yangtse, just as Russian, French and German interests had their centres in other parts of that Empire; and yet it was only on the Yangtse that China was asked to give a pledge never to grant any special privilege to any one Power. What wou'd have been said in Germany had His Majesty's Government told the Chinese that they would not evacuate Shanghai until they had received assurances that no special privileges should ever be given to any Power in Shantung?

Shantung, Baron Richthofen interposed, was altogether outside the question, whereas it was but natural to refer to the Yangtse in dealing with the conditions on which Shanghai was to be evacuated.

I did not, I replied, see how the geographical position of Shanghai accounted for the fact that the operation of the clause in question should have been restricted to the Yangtse and I feared that the action of the Imperial Government had been prompted rather by a distrust of England. . . . .[1]

I have, &c.
GEORGE W. BUCHANAN.

[1] [Refers to English distrust of Germany.]

No. 163.

[The following passage should be added to No. 47 of *Cd.* 1369, *Accounts and Papers*, 1902, CXXX, p. 371.]

The Marquess of Lansdowne to Count Metternich.

F.O. Germany (Prussia) 1562.
Extract.   *November 6, 1902.*

I venture, in conclusion, to refer to a point which was mentioned towards the close of our conversation. I expressed my regret that the German Government should have disposed of one of the conditions which they desired to attach to the evacuation of Shanghae, by direct arrangement with the Chinese Government and without the concurrence of His Majesty's Government. Your Excellency thereupon remarked that the German Government had made to His Majesty's Government the proposal in Baron Eckardstein's note of the 7th October, but that His Majesty's Government had refused to accept it, and that it was therefore natural that the German Government should come to terms with China.

On referring to the information in possession of this Department I find that, whereas Baron Eckardstein's note was dated the 7th October, the note to the Chinese Government from the German Chargé d'Affaires at Peking, requiring the assurances suggested by Baron Eckardstein, bore the date of the 5th October, and that the German Chargé d'Affaires had, before addressing this note to the Chinese Government, obtained from them verbal assurances of their consent to his demands.

My reply to Baron Eckardstein's note was dated, as your Excellency may remember, the 11th October, which was only three days after I had received the note, and was the earliest date on which I had an opportunity of consulting my colleagues on the German proposals.

No. 164.

The Marquess of Lansdowne to Mr. Buchanan.(¹)

(No. 301.) Very Confidential.

(Extract.) *Sandringham, November* 14, 1902.

The Emperor then referred briefly to the evacuation of Shanghae.(²) He regarded the incident as now virtually closed, and was ready to withdraw his troops at once if we would do the same.

I said that we had already given our instructions, and that the precise date of the departure of the international forces would, I supposed, depend upon the date at which sea transport could be procured for the different contingents. We should take our troops away as soon as the ships were ready.

I added that the fact that Germany had thought it desirable to make a special arrangement with China as to the conditions of evacuation did not affect us. The Emperor did not take up my observation, but said that he had always been ready to withdraw his troops, and that there had been a mistaken impression to the contrary. All that he desired was that the conditions of withdrawal should be such as to render it unnecessary for them to return.

I said that I felt sure His Majesty would understand that we should regard with a jealous eye any arrangements affecting our position in the Yang-tsze region. Our people saw that other Powers had got what they wanted in different parts of China, Russia in Manchuria, Germany in Shantung, and France elsewhere, whereas in the region where we had the largest interests we had obtained no corresponding privileges. The Emperor said that it was quite true that Russia had got what she wanted in Manchuria, but that in Shantung Germany had got nothing except what was secured to her in the promontory of Kiao-chow itself.

I observed that to the best of my belief we had never been actually informed of the nature of the arrangement entered into between Germany and China in regard to Shantung.

The Emperor here remarked that he had asked Lord Salisbury many years ago to assist him in obtaining a coaling station in China, but that he had received a snub for his pains. He had, therefore, been obliged to help himself. It was absolutely necessary for the development of Germany that she should have coaling stations.

At this point His Imperial Majesty was summoned to take his place at the end of one of the Sandringham coverts, and our conversation came to an end.(³)

(¹) [No original has been found of this despatch. The text is taken from the *Confidential Print.*]

(²) [The despatch details a conversation with the German Emperor at Sandringham.]

(³) [For the Kaiser's report to Count Bülow (the 12th November) *v. G.P.*, XVII, 117.]

No. 165.

[*ED. NOTE.*—The four documents that follow were not published in Cd. 1369. The correspondence was ended by a note of Count Metternich of the 20th November, replied to on the 28th by Lord Lansdowne. The accounts by the latter of his conversations with Count Metternich on the question of the publication of the documents are given under the respective dates of the 26th and 30th November, 1902. The actual evacuation of troops from Shanghai began on the 20th December with a German contingent, the British beginning to leave on the 22nd and the French on the 26th–27th (*v. G.P.*, XVI, 491, confirmed by telegram 391, Townley to Lord Lansdowne, Peking, December 20, 1902).]

Count Metternich to the Marquess of Lansdowne.

F.O. Germany (Prussia) 1562.

(Translation.) *German Embassy, London,* D. *November* 20, 1902.

My Lord, R. *November* 21, 1902.

The Imperial Government observe, from your Excellency's note of the 6th instant, that the British Government regret the Agreements come to between Germany and

China regarding the evacuation of Shanghae. The Imperial Government do not think that they should understand this regret to mean that the British Government advance the claim that negotiations and discussions between foreign Governments and China should not take place except with the knowledge and sanction of England. The Imperial Government hold this view the less, inasmuch as England, acting for herself alone, and without the participation of the other directly-interested Powers, proceeded to the conclusion of a Treaty, which, in the most incisive manner, regulated commercial relations and intercourse with China.

The Imperial Government in due course informed the British Government of the conditions which they considered indispensable for the evacuation of Shanghae, and simultaneously also brought them to the knowledge of the directly-interested Government of China. The latter then replied that they had no objection to offer to these conditions, and accepted them. If the Chinese Government subsequently declared that they extended to the whole of China their acceptance of the demand made by my Government in the case only of the Yang-tsze territory, that no preferential rights should be granted in that region, the Imperial Government had no occasion to raise objection if the lesser demand was included in the larger concession made by China. The Imperial Government had, therefore, no hesitation in declaring as fulfilled the condition affecting the Yang-tsze, which they consequently neither withdrew nor modified.

By this declaration, the Imperial Government thought that they were meeting the wishes of the British Government, whose objection to this condition meanwhile became known to them. The Imperial Government are, however, unable to see anything in the whole matter whereby British rights or legitimate interests are prejudiced. France has also made a communication at Peking of an essentially similar nature to that made by the Imperial Government, and has also received a like reply from China.

From the foregoing, it will appear that no great importance should be attached to the dates of the communications made by my Government to your Excellency and to the Chinese Government, to which reference is made in your Excellency's note.

The Imperial Government, on the other hand, entirely share your Excellency's view, that the declaration made to them by China that she would grant no preferential rights does not affect the already existing stipulations of universally known older Treaties.

In conclusion, I would inform your Excellency, in obedience to my instructions, that His Majesty the Emperor, my gracious Sovereign, has issued the necessary orders for the evacuation of Shanghae by the German troops. This further proves that, as regards the question of the evacuation, practically no difference at all exists between the views of the Imperial and British Governments.

With, &c.
P. METTERNICH.

No. 166.

The Marquess of Lansdowne to Mr. Buchanan.[1]

(No. 321.)   Confidential.

Sir, *Foreign Office, November* 26, 1902.

I had some further discussion to-day with the German Ambassador with regard to the papers to be included in the Blue Book to be presented to Parliament on the subject of the evacuation of Shanghae.

His Excellency again expressed his hope that we should avoid the publication of any papers likely to create ill-feeling between our two countries. I told him that I was ready to fall in with his views, and that I had revised the proofs with this object.

[1] [No original has been found of this despatch. The text is taken from the *Confidential Print.*]

I mentioned in particular that I proposed to omit the concluding paragraphs of my letter to him of the 6th instant, in which I called attention to the fact that the German Government had addressed themselves to the Chinese authorities while they were engaged in a friendly discussion with us as to the conditions of evacuation, his Excellency's reply to me of the 20th instant, and also my rejoinder, which I had drafted, but which had not yet reached him. I added, however, that if we suppressed these documents it must be on the distinct understanding that none of them were made public in Germany, either through official or unofficial channels. Count Metternich unhesitatingly accepted this condition.

I am, &c.
LANSDOWNE.

No. 167.

The Marquess of Lansdowne to Count Metternich.

F.O. Germany (Prussia) 1562.

Your Excellency, *Foreign Office, November* 28, 1902.

I have had the honour of receiving your Excellency's note of the 20th instant upon the subject of the arrangements come to between Germany and China regarding the evacuation of Shanghae.

I should not think it necessary to prolong the correspondence were it not for the fact that the German Government appear to have, at certain points, misapprehended the views of His Majesty's Government.

His Majesty's Government have by no means advanced a claim that no negotiations and discussions between foreign Governments and China should take place except with the knowledge and sanction of England. In this particular case, however, they did not conceal their regret that the German Government, at a moment when the two Governments were in friendly and confidential communication in regard to the withdrawal of the international force at Shanghae, should have made a private arrangement with the Peking Government as to the conditions upon which the German portion of the force was to be withdrawn.

His Majesty's Government had looked upon Baron von Eckardstein's note of the 7th October as embodying a condition which we were invited by the German Government to examine and discuss with them, and not as the announcement of a decision already arrived at by the German Government, and by them communicated to the Chinese authorities.

The information in our possession leaves, however, no room for doubt that the terms of this private arrangement were not revealed to us until after the assent of the Chinese Government had been demanded and promised.

It is for this reason that His Majesty's Government are unable to share the opinion which you have expressed to the effect that no great importance should be attached to the dates of the communication made by the German Government to myself and to the Chinese Government respectively.

You cite as an analogous case the conduct of the British Government in negotiating at Shanghae a Treaty regulating the commercial relations of Great Britain and China "alone, and without the participation of the other directly interested Powers."

On this point I would remind you of a conversation which I had with Baron von Eckardstein on the 7th August, 1901, which you will, no doubt, find recorded in the archives of your Embassy. On that occasion I called his attention to a suggestion, thrown out in a speech which I had made in the House of Lords, as to the possibility of transferring to Shanghae the negotiations under Article 11 of the Peking Protocol. I said that it had occurred to me that the four Powers most interested in the trade of the Far East, of which Germany is one, might appoint representatives for the purpose of such negotiations, and that, if they arrived at a satisfactory arrangement, they might endeavour to obtain the adherence of the other Powers. Baron von Eckardstein undertook to address an enquiry on the subject to the German Government, and inform me of the result. On the 16th of the same month your Excellency informed me that the question was under the consideration of the German Government, but the result was never communicated to His Majesty's Government. The negotiations undertaken by them were carried on without mystery, and in accordance with the policy enunciated in the Protocol of Peking, to which all the Powers were parties, and they will all under most-favoured-nation treatment equally benefit by the provisions of the Treaty which this country has concluded with China, while the Tariff and surtax stipulations will not become effective unless and until they receive the adherence of the other Powers interested in the China trade.

I am therefore at a loss to understand how the two cases can be regarded as in any way analogous.

I have, &c.
LANSDOWNE.

No. 168.

The Marquess of Lansdowne to Mr. Buchanan.([1])

(No. 331.)
Sir, Bowood, November 30, 1902.

I asked the German Ambassador to-day whether he had yet received any instructions from the German Government with regard to the publication of certain documents which we proposed to include in the Blue Book on the evacuation of Shanghae. His Excellency told me that he had just received by telegram instructions on the subject. The German Government were of opinion that in my despatch No. 212 of the 26th August to Sir F. Lascelles, Baron Oppell's statement to Sir T. Sanderson had not been quite adequately reproduced. The despatch was worded in such a way as to suggest that Baron Oppell's intimation as to the attitude of the French Government, which he had made incidentally, was intended to be the principal subject of his communication. This was not the case. It seemed to the German Government that the account of my conversation, contained in my despatch No. 207 of the 19th August to Sir F. Lascelles, sufficiently covered the ground dealt with by Baron Oppell, and they therefore suggested for my consideration that No. 212 might be omitted from the Blue Book. If, however, we were not prepared to admit it, the German Government would like to make some alterations in the text.

In the next place, his Excellency said that the German Government would be glad to omit from my despatch No. 278 of the 3rd November to Mr. Buchanan my statement that the British Government did not consider themselves bound by the German arrangement with China. Count Metternich explained to me that Count Bülow believed that if this statement were to be published it would attract a good deal of attention in Germany, and that "public opinion there would take the matter up and demand further elucidation." I told Count Metternich that I did not see how we could agree to the omission of this passage, which embodied an important declaration as to the manner in which we regarded the German arrangement about China. I reminded his Excellency that the only documents with regard to the publication of which we were bound to consult the German Government were those purporting to contain an account of statements made on their behalf. I promised his Excellency,

([1]) [No original has been found of this despatch. The text is taken from the *Confidential Print*.]

however, that, on my return to London, I would at once refer to the Blue Book, and furnish him with a reply upon the points to which he had called my attention.

I am, &c.
LANSDOWNE.

No. 169.

[The following despatch from the British Acting Consul-General at Shanghai of the 3rd December, 1902, gives the German despatch of the 24th October to the Viceroy of Nanking.]

Acting Consul-General Mansfield to the Marquess of Lansdowne.(¹)

Confidential.   *Shanghae, D. December 3, 1902.*
My Lord,   R. *January 13, 1903.*
    I have the honour to enclose translation of copies of despatches (obtained from an indirect source) exchanged between the German Consul-General at Shanghae and his Excellency Viceroy Chang Chih-tung, relative to the evacuation of Shanghae by the German troops. I have sent similar translations to His Majesty's Minister at Peking.

I have, &c.
R. W. MANSFIELD.

    (¹) [No original has been found of this despatch. The text is taken from the *Confidential Print.*]

Enclosure 1 in No. 169.

German Consul-General to the Viceroy of Nanking.

Translation.   *October 24, 1902.*
    The German Government is willing to withdraw the German troops stationed at Shanghae, but only simultaneously with the other Powers.
    If in the future the other Powers again land troops at Shanghae, Germany claims the right to do likewise. Moreover, the Chinese Government, with the Yang-tsze Viceroys, must enter into an undertaking not to grant special privileges in the Yang-tsze Valley to any one of the Powers : such as administrative powers, military or naval influence, engineering privileges, trading monopolies, or other kinds of rights, as such would be to act against the spirit of the most-favoured-nation clause.
    With regard to the approaches to Shanghae, and points in the Yang-tsze Valley strategically important, such must not be conceded to any other Power. This clause is to prevent subsequent misunderstandings. I have the honour to request your Excellency to look into these clauses and also to agree to them.

I have, &c.

Enclosure 2 not reproduced.

No. 170.

Memorandum by Sir Eyre Crowe.

Memorandum on the Present State of British Relations with France and Germany.

(8886)
(Extract.)   *Foreign Office, January 1, 1907.*
    As if none of these things had happened, fresh German demands in another field, accompanied by all the same manifestations of hostility, were again met, though with perhaps increasing reluctance, by the old willingness to oblige. The action of Germany in China has long been distinctly unfriendly to England. In 1895 she tried to obtain from the Chinese Government

a coaling station in the Chusan Islands, at the mouth of the Yang-tsze, without any previous communication with the British Government, whose preferential rights over the group, as established by Treaty, were of course well known. The manner in which Kiao-chau was obtained, however unjustifiable it may be considered by any recognized standard of political conduct, did not concern England more than the other Powers who professed in their Treaties to respect China's integrity and independence. But Germany was not content with the seizure of the harbour, she also planned the absorption of the whole of the large and fertile province of Shantung. The concession of the privileged rights which she wrung from the Chinese Government was obtained owing in no small degree to her official assurance that her claims had the support of England who, needless to say, had never been informed or consulted, and who was, of course, known to be absolutely opposed to stipulations by which, contrary to solemn British treaty rights, it was intended to close a valuable province to British trade and enterprise.

About this time Germany secretly approached Russia with a view to the conclusion of an Agreement, by which Germany would have also obtained the much desired foothold on the Yang-tsze, then considered to be practically a British preserve. These overtures being rejected, Germany wished at least to prevent England from obtaining what she herself had failed to secure. She proposed to the British Cabinet a self-denying Agreement stipulating that neither Power should endeavour to obtain any territorial advantages in Chinese dominions, and that if any third Power attempted to do so both should take common action.

The British Government did not conceal their great reluctance to this arrangement, rightly foreseeing that Germany would tacitly exempt from its operation her own designs on Shantung, and also any Russian aggression in Manchuria, whilst England would solemnly give up any chances she might have of establishing on a firm basis her well-won position on the Yang-tsze. That is, of course, exactly what subsequently did happen. There was no obvious reason why England should lend herself to this gratuitous tying of her own hands. No counter-advantage was offered or even suggested, and the British taste for these one-sided transactions had not been stimulated by past experience. Nevertheless, the policy of conciliating Germany by meeting her expressed wishes once more triumphed, and the Agreement was signed—with the foreseen consequences : Russian agression in Manchuria was declared to be altogether outside the scope of the stipulations of what the German Chancellor took care to style the " Yang-tsze " Agreement, as if its terms had referred specially to that restricted area of China, and the German designs on Shangtung continue to this day to be tenaciously pursued.

But Germany was not content with the British renunciation of any territorial claims. The underhand and disloyal manœuvres by which, on the strength of purely fictitious stories of British plans for the seizure of various Chinese places of strategical importance (stories also sedulously communicated to the French Government), Germany wrung out of the Peking Court further separate and secret guarantees against alleged British designs, on the occasion of the termination of the joint Anglo-Franco-German occupation of Shanghae, betrayed such an obliquity of mind in dealing with her ostensible friends that Lord Lansdowne characterised it in the most severe terms, which did not prevent him from presenting the incident to Parliament in the form of papers from which almost every trace of the offensive attitude of Germany had been carefully removed, so as not to embitter our German relations. And this was after the reports from our officers had shown that the proceedings of the German troops in Northern China, and the extraordinary treatment meted out by the German General Staff to the British and Indian contingents serving, with a loyalty not approached by any of the other international forces, under the supreme command of Count Waldersee, had created the deepest possible resentment among all ranks, from the British General Commanding to the lowest Indian follower.

II.—VENEZUELA.

[*ED. NOTE.—G.P.*, XVII, Chapter 112, shows the German side and suggests that very early in 1902 the German Government wished to be associated with Great Britain in the Venezuelan affair.]

No. 171.

The Marquess of Lansdowne to Mr. Buchanan.([1])

F.O. Germany (Prussia) 1550.
(No. 185.)

Sir, *Foreign Office, July* 23, 1902.

The German Ambassador told me to-day that in the opinion of the German Government the time was approaching when it would be necessary for the Powers interested in Venezuela to put pressure on the Venezuelan Government.

([1]) [*Cf.* despatch of same date printed *P.P. Accounts and Papers*, 1903, LXXXVII (*Cd.* 1399) p. 845.]

He observed that a new Ministry was about to be formed and he thought the opportunity might be a good one for making it clear to them that some form of coercion would if necessary be applied. What did I think of a pacific blockade of the Venezuelan Ports during the export season?

I told his Excellency that we should be quite ready to confer with the German Government with a view to joint action, but that I should like to consider his proposal further before expressing an opinion as to its opportuneness in present circumstances.

I am, &c.

LANSDOWNE

No. 172.

The Marquess of Lansdowne to Sir F. Lascelles.

F.O. Venezuela 445.
(No. 269.) Confidential.
Sir,   *Foreign Office, October* 22, 1902.

I had some conversation to-day with the German Ambassador in regard to the measures which might be taken for the protection of British and German interests in Venezuela, and I handed to his Excellency a copy of the accompanying Memorandum.([1])

Count Metternich informed me that he was in daily expectation of instructions from his Government upon the subject.

I mentioned to him in the strictest confidence that should we be driven to resort to coercive measures, His Majesty's Government were disposed to think that the most convenient form of coercion would be the seizure of the Venezuelan gun-boats.

I thought it, however, most important that our intentions should not be allowed to leak out, for fear the Venezuelan Government should move the gun-boats to some inaccessible place up the Orinoco or another river.

Count Metternich observed that he did not see why we should not resort to a blockade as well as to the seizure of the gun-boats.

I explained that a so-called pacific blockade seemed to us useless for the purpose which we had in view, whilst a belligerent blockade might involve us in troublesome questions with other Powers.

I am, &c.

LANSDOWNE

([1]) See No. 173.

No. 173.

Memorandum for communication to the German Ambassador.

F.O. Venezuela 445.   *Foreign Office, October* 22, 1902.

His Majesty's Government have within the last two years had grave cause to complain of unjustifiable interference on the part of the Venezuelan Government with the liberty and property of British subjects.

In three instances the objects of this interference were British trading vessels from the Colony of Trinidad, which were pursued by Venezuelan guardacostas on a suspicion of smuggling or trading in arms, and this plea was made the excuse for a violation of British territorial waters, the seizure of the property of British subjects, and in one instance the wilful destruction of the vessel.

In two further cases a similar unsupported charge was made the excuse for the seizure, and confiscation or destruction of British vessels in Venezuelan waters; while incidents of this nature reached their culminating point, when, on the 30th June last, the British ship "Queen," while on her voyage from Grenada to Trinidad, was overhauled by a Venezuelan gun-boat on the high seas off Carupano, stripped of her sails and papers, and finally confiscated on a bare suspicion of having carried a cargo of arms to Venezuela, the crew being put on shore and left destitute.

No efforts had been spared by His Majesty's Minister at Carácas in each of the earlier cases to obtain an amicable settlement, but in none of them had satisfactory explanations been forthcoming. On the occurrence of the still more flagrant interference with the "Queen," it was felt that a continuance of such conduct could not be tolerated, and His Majesty's Minister at Carácas was instructed on the 29th July to record a formal protest against the action of the Venezuelan Government, and to intimate clearly to the President and Minister for Foreign Affairs, that unless explicit assurances were received that such incidents should not recur, and unless full compensation were promptly paid to the injured parties wherever shown to the satisfaction of His Majesty's Government to be justly due, His Majesty's Government would take such steps as might be necessary to exact the reparation which they were entitled to demand in these cases, as well as on account of the claims of the British Railway Companies, and for any loss arising out of the conduct of the Venezuelan Consul at Trinidad.

With reference to the two later points, it may be mentioned that there are several British Railway Companies in Venezuela which have large claims against the Government in respect of services rendered, damage to property from Government troops, and in some instances for default of guarantee or loss by depreciation of Government Bonds; while with regard to M. Figueredo, the Venezuelan Consul at Trinidad, it may be stated that his conduct has given rise to the gravest complaints on the part of the Trinidad Government, both on account of the irregularity in the discharge of his Consular functions, and his assumption of unwarranted authority by the collection of customs duties for Venezuela within the British Colony of Trinidad.

The reply of the Venezuelan Government to the formal protest of His Majesty's Minister practically ignores the remonstrances of His Majesty's Government, while it makes no allusion whatever to the threat that they may be compelled to take steps to obtain reparation for the wrongs complained of.

The reply is based on the decision come to by the Venezuelan Government to postpone any reply to all representations on the part of His Majesty's Government from the time of the injuries caused by the "Ban Righ," so long as the situation created by the despatch of that vessel from this country continued.

In connection with the already well-known case of the "Ban Righ," it may be explained that the vessel was detained for some time under surveillance in British waters, and was only allowed to leave the Port of London in January last after examination of her papers and cargo, on receipt of an assurance from the Colombian Representative at this Court that the vessel was intended for the service of his Government, and that no state of war existed between Colombia and any other Power.

His Majesty's Government had in these circumstances no further ground for detaining the vessel, and the fullest explanations were afforded to the Venezuelan Government on the subject.

In view of the unsatisfactory nature of the Venezuelan reply, His Majesty's Government are compelled to consider what steps may be necessary to enforce their demands, but before proceeding to ulterior measures they propose to intimate their regret at the manner in which their representations have been received, and to state that they are unable to admit that the serious causes of complaint put forward can be disposed of by a refusal to discuss them, and that if such a refusal is persisted in, it will become their duty to consider what steps they should take in view of such refusal for the protection of British interests. His Majesty's Government are, however, unwilling to exclude at once all possibility of proceeding with negotiations, and they are therefore ready to consider any further communication which the Venezuelan Government may be prepared to make.

As the German Government have expressed their willingness to unite with His Majesty's Government in putting pressure upon Venezuela, they may perhaps think it expedient to associate themselves with His Majesty's Government in this preliminary step, and in such case they may be disposed to instruct their Representative at Carácas to inform the Venezuelan Government that the Imperial Government are aware of the communications which have passed between this country and Venezuela, and that the British and German Governments have determined to act together in pressing the claims of their subjects upon the attention of Venezuela.

No. 174.

The Marquess of Lansdowne to Mr. Buchanan.(¹)

F.O. Venezuela 445.
(No. 306.)
Sir,
                                                              Foreign Office, November 11, 1902.

The German Ambassador informed me this evening that the German Government were prepared to join with us in addressing a final warning to the Venezuelan Government, and I communicated to him the substance of my telegram to Mr. Haggard of this day's date. I explained that as I had received no reply to the communication which I had made to His Excellency on the 22nd October, I had thought it better not to delay making this intimation, which was, as he would observe, couched in general terms, but I undertook to telegraph at once to Mr. Haggard, desiring him to put himself in communication with his German colleague.

Count Metternich went on to acquaint me that, in the opinion of the German Government, there were four points which required examination in connection with the joint action which the British and German Governments contemplated.

1. We ought, in the first place, to formulate both the British and the German claims. The latter consisted of (*a*) claims for damage sustained during the civil war in the years 1898–1900, amounting to 1,700,000 bolivares. These would be placed in the first line, but if Germany were driven to resort to measures of coercion, she would also claim (*b*) 3,000,000 bolivares for losses during the present civil war, and (*c*) a guarantee for interest on the capital (amounting to 41,000,000 bolivares) held by German creditors in Venezuela, and notably for that invested in the "German" Railway in that country.

Count Metternich presumed that the British claims would be capable of classification on analogous lines, our "first line" claims being, no doubt, those for injury to British shipping.

2. As to diplomatic proceedings, the German Government were prepared at any moment to deliver an ultimatum in regard to the claims falling under class (*a*), and he presumed that we were ready to do the same in regard to our shipping claims. In these circumstances, the German Government thought it would be desirable that each Power should, in presenting its ultimatum, call attention to the claims put in by the other.

3. With regard to measures of coercion, the German Government were prepared to accede to our suggestion that the first step should be the seizure of the Venezuelan gun-boats, and they proposed that we should instruct our naval authorities in those waters to concert a plan for carrying out this project.

It was, however, conceivable that the seizure of the gun-boats might fail to bring about the submission of the Venezuelan Government, and we should be prepared for this eventuality, and for the further measures which it might necessitate. Should such further measures become inevitable, the German Government consider that a " pacific blockade " should be resorted to. They realised, however, that a blockade directed against Venezuelan shipping only would be unavailing, because the greater part of the commerce of Venezuela was carried in foreign bottoms. The blockade

(¹) [Part printed *Accounts and Papers*, 1903 (*Cd.* 1399), LXXXVII, p. 862.]

should, therefore, extend to neutral vessels to this extent, that should such vessels attempt to run the blockade they would be turned back or "sequestrated." Count Metternich was instructed to point out to me that blockades of this kind had been resorted to by England in 1837 against New Granada, and in 1842 and 1844 against St. Juan and the Nicaraguan ports; by England and France in 1845 and 1847 against the Argentine ports, by England in 1882 against Rio, and by France in 1884 against Formosa.

Count Metternich was also able to tell me that at the beginning of the present year, when the question of coercing the Venezuelan Government first came up for consideration, the possibility of resorting to a blockade of the kind described had been mentioned by the German Government to the Government of the United States, who had intimated that no difficulties need be anticipated.

Such a blockade could not fail to be efficacious, because it would destroy the customs revenue of Venezuela, and also cut off her foreign food supplies, upon which she was largely dependent.

4. As to the joint execution of measures of coercion, the German Government recognised that there was a sharp distinction between the character of the British and German "first-line" claims; nevertheless, the two claims ought to stand or fall together, and we ought to exclude the possibility of a settlement between Venezuela and one of the two Powers without an equally satisfactory settlement in the case of the other. Each Government ought, therefore, to come to an understanding before it embarked upon a project of coercion that neither Government should be at liberty to recede except by mutual agreement; and before common action was initiated, we ought to come to a clear understanding to this effect.

I told Count Metternich that it seemed to me only reasonable that if we agreed to act together in applying coercion, we should also agree that each should support the other's demands, and should not desist from doing so except by agreement. I should, however, like to examine his proposals carefully before committing His Majesty's Government to accept them. The question of pacific blockades was full of difficulty, and I was aware that some of our highest authorities had great doubts as to the possibility of such a measure. At any rate, as the German Government evidently desired that once embarked we should travel with them to the end of the voyage, it was only reasonable that we should spare no pains to find out whether there were likely to be any obstacles in our course.

His Excellency made some suggestions as to the possible co-operation of the British Council of Foreign Bondholders with the Disconto Gesellschaft in regard to the Loans of 1881 and 1896, which I asked him to be good enough to let me have in writing.

I am, &c.
LANSDOWNE.

No. 175.

The Marquess of Lansdowne to Mr. Buchanan.([1])

F.O. Venezuela 446.

(No. 318.) Extract.   *Foreign Office, November* 26, 1902.

([2]) . . . . Count Metternich handed to me a draft of the German ultimatum, of which I enclose translation.

3. As regards the coercive measures to be adopted, the Imperial Government are prepared, first, in conjunction with Great Britain, to proceed to the seizure of the Venezuelan ships of war. For this purpose the following German men-of-war are at

([1]) [The first part of this despatch is printed in *Accounts and Papers*, 1903 (*Cd.* 1399), LXXXVII, pp. 872–3.]

([2]) [Details as to German claims.]

once available: the larger cruiser "Vineta," the small cruisers "Falke" and "Gazelle," and the gun-boat "Panther."

With regard to a blockade of Venezuelan ports, I repeated that we entertained strong objections to such a blockade as had been proposed by the German Government, and that we had committed ourselves decidedly to the view that it was from an international point of view a measure which ought not to be adopted. I said that I fully realised that in the event of the seizure of the gun-boats not producing the desired effect we should have to adopt ulterior measures, and I asked whether the German Government would not in such an event be ready to resort to a belligerent blockade.

Count Metternich then proceeded to discuss the whole question. His Excellency said that the objection of His Majesty's Government that they had themselves protested against the treatment of their merchant-vessels at the time of the French blockade of Formosa Island in 1884 was, in the opinion of the Imperial Government, met by the contention that the British Government in their correspondence with the French Government at the time expressly declared that they regarded that blockade not as a pacific, but as a belligerent blockade, and therefore had no reason then to enter into a discussion as to the real grounds for a pacific blockade. On that occasion the British Government entirely recognised the French measures of blockade after the French Government had explained that they would abstain from searching or capturing British ships on the high seas.

But the search or capture on the high seas of neutral vessels would not be required in a blockade of Venezuelan ports as proposed by the German Admiralty. These proposals were specifically explained in drafts for the declaration of blockade and for an agreement to be made respecting that blockade, which were handed to me by Count Metternich, and of which translations are enclosed. According to this Agreement, the ports of Maracaybo and Puerto-Cabello were to be blockaded by the German naval forces, and the port of La Guayra as well as any further ports on the east coast of Venezuela by the British naval forces. The German Admiralty requested that the British West Indian ports, especially Port of Spain, Castries and Kingston, with their stores of coal, provisions, &c., should always be open without formalities to the German vessels for their supplies, repairs, landing of sick, as well as for bringing in captured ships.

In the view of the German Government no previous declaration of war would be necessary, and, therefore, no breaking off of diplomatic relations. They did not accordingly propose to recall their Chargé d'Affaires, but would, if necessary, send him to La Guayra, where he would probably be safer.

His Excellency asked me whether I thought any further communication to the United States Government should now be made. I replied that we had made a communication of our intentions within the last few days, and that it seemed to me that no further announcement was necessary.

With regard to the further proposal of the British Government for the seizure of Venezuelan Custom-houses, the Imperial German Government considered that the strength of the forces on board the German ships of war now in Venezuelan waters would only suffice to hold the port of Puerto-Cabello for any protracted period. Moreover, the seizure of the Custom-houses would fail in its object, as the Venezuelan Government would presumably remove their Customs barriers behind the port towns.

Lastly, it appeared possible that the United States of America might raise difficulties if portions of Venezuelan territory remained occupied for some time. For the reasons above stated, the Imperial German Government preferred a pacific blockade as being, in their opinion, the most effective means of coercion.

Some misapprehension must have arisen on this point, and I told Count Metternich that I had never regarded the seizure of the Custom-houses as an advisable form of coercion.

I am, &c.
LANSDOWNE.

No. 176.

The Marquess of Lansdowne to Mr. Buchanan.

F.O. Venezuela 446.
(No. 329 A.)
Sir,   *Bowood, November* 29, 1902.

The German Ambassador told me to-day that he had received further instructions from his Government in regard to the Venezuelan question. They were to the following effect :—

1. The German Government were prepared to accept our views with regard to the three points mentioned in my despatch No. 318 A of the 26th instant. It was understood that the two Powers were to act together until the claims of both had been satisfied. The German Government also thought that the ultimata should be sent to the President of the Republic, and not delivered by the Representatives themselves.

2. The German Government were of opinion that the ultimata should be delivered as soon as possible, and that we should proceed, with the least possible delay, to the seizure of the Venezuelan gun-boats.

3. The German Government agreed to the sequence of steps proposed, as explained in the Memorandum enclosed in my despatch above referred to; the moment for presenting the ultimata to be arranged between the Representatives of the two Powers in Venezuela in consultation with the two Senior Naval Officers. An interval of twenty-four hours to be allowed to elapse after the presentation of the ultimata, and the Representatives to remain at La Guayra for a further period of twenty-four hours to await developments.

4. His Excellency informed me that instructions had been sent to Herr von Pilgrim by the German Government yesterday. The German Ambassador at Washington would be instructed to ask the United States Government to take over the protection of German interests after Herr von Pilgrim's departure.

5. His Excellency informed me that the German Commodore was at Curaçao on board the "Vineta." The Commodore had been instructed yesterday to come to an understanding with the British Admiral as to joint action so soon as he received a communication from the Admiral intimating his readiness to confer with him.

His Excellency informed me that the "Vineta," "Gazelle," and "Panther" were at Curaçao, and the "Falke" at Puerto Cabello, all ready for action.

His Excellency expressed a hope that I should be able to inform him at an early date of our ideas in regard to the further measures of coercion which might be resorted to in the event of the seizure of the gun-boats not having the desired effect. The German Government did not, however, consider that the uncertainty which existed as to the nature of these further measures need prevent us from proceeding with the steps as to which we were already in agreement.

Count Metternich enquired at the close of our conversation whether I was able to give him any information as to the French claims upon the Venezuelan Maritime Customs, and I told his Excellency that I was making enquiries as to the extent of these.

I am, &c.
LANSDOWNE.

No. 177.

The Marquess of Lansdowne to Count Metternich.

F.O. Venezuela 447.

Dear Count Metternich,   *Foreign Office, December 2, 1902.*

I enclose, in accordance with my promise, a short Memorandum, in which I have recapitulated the substance of my observations on the subject of the ulterior measures of coercion which might be applied to Venezuela.

Yours sincerely,
LANSDOWNE.

Enclosure in No. 177.

Memorandum.

His Majesty's Government recognise that it is absolutely necessary that the two Governments should decide upon ulterior measures of coercion to be resorted to in the event of the seizure of the gun-boats failing to produce the submission of the Venezuelan Government.

These ulterior measures might be of two kinds : (*a*) seizure of custom houses or other important points on Venezuelan territory; or (*b*) a blockade.

His Majesty's Government are advised that alternative (*a*) should be avoided. In order to provide against the possibility of a reverse it would be necessary to employ a considerable force. The town of La Guayra is commanded by high land in the close vicinity, and it might be necessary to occupy these heights in order to prevent the force from finding itself exposed to rifle fire. A preliminary bombardment might even be necessary.

La Guayra is described as exceedingly hot and unhealthy, and any force landed there would certainly suffer in health. Puerto Cabello is also most unhealthy.

His Majesty's Government would dislike locking up a number of troops at any of these ports; moreover, if the occupation were prolonged, troublesome international questions might arise between the Powers concerned and the United States Government.

For these reasons His Majesty's Government prefer alternative (*b*).

They hold, however, strongly, for reasons which have been explained to Count Metternich in the Foreign Office Memorandum handed to his Excellency on the 29th ultimo, that a so-called pacific blockade of the kind recommended by the German Government is a measure unjustifiable in international law, and one which they are precluded from resorting to by explicit declarations made from time to time on behalf of former British Governments. In their view, the measures suggested by the German Government in the note handed by the German Ambassador to Lord Lansdowne on the 21st of November could not be taken except as acts of war.

On the other hand, His Majesty's Government hold that a blockade, having once been proclaimed, it is open to the Powers enforcing it to mitigate its severity by means of any Regulations which they may think fit to make for that purpose, and, this being so, they see no reason why, in the event of a blockade of the Venezuelan ports by Great Britain and Germany, such measures as those contemplated by the German Government, and described in the Memorandum already referred to, might not be adopted.

It would, in their view, be necessary to give timely warning to neutral Powers that such Regulations were about to be enforced.

Foreign Office, December 2, 1902.

No. 178.

Note by the Marquess of Lansdowne.(¹)

F.O. Venezuela 448.   *Foreign Office, December 8,(?) 1902.*

I have spoken to the Lord Chancellor about this. He holds decidedly that it is not desirable that we should endeavour to come to an agreement with the German Government as to the explanations which each of us might offer of the measures taken to enforce the blockade by the two Powers. We have laid it down clearly that we regard those measures as implying a condition of war, and we have left the German Government in no doubt as to this. Should they resort to the same measures and endeavour to convince the persons to whom they are applied that they are consistent with a condition of peace, that will be their affair.

It is of course most important that we should not put it in the power of the German Government to assert that we have misled them, or slurred over the difficulty. They cannot, however, pretend that we have done so. If Count Metternich speaks to me again I will remind him of our views as expressed in my memorandum of the [2]th instant.

If having those views before them the German Government find themselves in trouble either with their own Bundesrath or with the owners of neutral vessels, they will have no one to thank but themselves.

L.

(¹) [The note is attached to a memorandum on joint action by the Legal Adviser to the Foreign Office.]

No. 179.

The Marquess of Lansdowne to Mr. Buchanan.

F.O. Venezuela 448.
(No. 353 A.)
Sir,   *Foreign Office, December 18, 1902.*

I received this evening a communication from Count Metternich to the effect that the German Government, being specially desirous to remove all points of difference in dealing with the Venezuelan question, had decided to establish a blockade *jure gentium.* They intended to ask on Monday for the sanction of the Bundesrath; this need not delay the commencement of operations, and the German Commodore had been instructed to make all the necessary arrangements with Admiral Douglas. The German Government did not press for an identic notification of blockade, but desired that the announcement should be simultaneous.

Count Metternich mentioned a proposal that the Italian ships should blockade two ports to the westward of La Guayra. With regard to the exact nature of Italian co-operation, I have told M. Pansa that this seemed to be a matter for settlement between the naval officers on the spot.

I am, &c.
LANSDOWNE.

[15214]   M

No. 180.

Sir Michael Herbert to the Marquess of Lansdowne.

Washington, December 16, 1902.

F.O. Venezuela 448.
Tel. (No. 60.) Confidential.

D. 11 A.M.
R. *December* 17, 1902.

Although I have, so far, no reason to believe the United States Government will change their attitude, there is a growing feeling of irritation in Congress, especially in the House of Representatives against the action of the two Powers, chiefly owing to the bombardment and the sinking of Venezuelan ships. The administration is not suspicious of us, but it is undoubtedly apprehensive as to German designs. The impression prevails in Washington that Germany is using us, and our friends here regret, from the point of view of American good feeling towards us, that we are acting with her.

No. 181.

The Marquess of Lansdowne to Sir F. Lascelles.

F.O. Venezuela 448.
(No. 362.)
Sir,

Foreign Office, December 18, 1902.

The German Ambassador informed me to-day that the German Government were in entire agreement with us as to the manner in which the Venezuelan proposal for arbitration should be treated.

He was, in the first place, instructed to tell me that it would be the leading principle for the German Government, in the further treatment of the Venezuelan question, not to do anything which might provide "ammunition" for use against the British Government by those who had so strongly condemned British and German co-operation. The German Government fully recognised the difficulty in which this opposition had placed us, and would spare no efforts in order to dispel the false impressions which had been created, and to disprove the calumnies which had been circulated. They recognised that resort to arbitration would be likely to produce a salutary effect, and they considered that action should be taken upon the Venezuelan proposal at once, without waiting until Washington "exchanged the rôle of post-office for one of a more active character."

The German Government were accordingly prepared to accept at every point the suggestions which we had made to them. . . . .([1])

[I am, &c.
LANSDOWNE.]

([1]) [Rest of despatch printed *Accounts and Papers*, 1903 (*Cd.* 1399), LXXXVII, pp. 893–4.]

No. 182.

The Marquess of Lansdowne to Sir F. Lascelles.

F.O. Venezuela 449.
(No. 369.)
Sir,

Foreign Office, December 22, 1902.

I spent some time to-day with the German Ambassador comparing the drafts of the communications which the British and German Governments are to make to the United States Government in reply to the Venezuelan proposal for arbitration (*vide* papers marked (A) and (B)).([1])

([1]) [Not reproduced. The communication drawn up by Great Britain is printed in *Accounts and Papers*, 1903 (*Cd.* 1399), LXXXVII, pp. 899–900.]

I again pointed out to Count Metternich that it was, in my opinion, most important that, except so far as the main principles were concerned, neither Government should take upon themselves to speak on behalf of the other. We were agreed (1) that there was to be arbitration; (2) that a part of our claims were to be excluded; (3) that the President of the United States should be invited to arbitrate.

In the British draft we had given an account of the reservations which we desired to make, but we referred to them as reservations made only " so far as the British claims are concerned." The German draft, on the other hand, described the two Powers as desiring to make " the following reservations," and there were several passages in them in which the British as well as the German claims were coupled with those of Germany.

After some discussion we agreed that Count Metternich should telegraph to the German Government proposing that in paper (B) the two Powers should be referred to as making " certain reservations " instead of the " following reservations "; that No. 1, which now begins: " Among the German and English claims are some which, in their present stage, are not suited for submission to arbitration," should begin: " Among their claims are some which are not suited for submission to arbitration." We further agreed that in Nos. (2) and (3) the words " German and English " might be omitted, and we also decided to add to both drafts a paragraph intimating that should the President of the United States be unable to undertake the duty of arbitration we contemplated recourse to the Hague Tribunal.

I am, &c.
LANSDOWNE.

No. 183.

Memorandum communicated by German Embassy, December 25, 1902.

F.O. Venezuela 449.
Translation.

The Imperial Government have accepted the proposal relative to a reference of their claims against Venezuela to arbitration, under certain reserves which have just been communicated to the American Ambassador, and in doing so, they have expressed a hope that the President of the United States will undertake the task of Arbitrator.

In concert with the British Government, the Imperial Government believe to have found in such a reference to arbitration every guarantee for a satisfactory settlement of the matter, so that this course deserves preference to the alternative recently proposed by the Venezuelan Government, of negotiating with the two Powers through the intermediary of the American Minister at Carácas.

No. 184.

Sir M. Herbert to the Marquess of Lansdowne.

F.O. Venezuela 449.
(No. 355.) Confidential.   *Washington,* D. *December* 29, 1902.
My Lord,   R. *January* 8, 1903.

With reference to my telegram No. 60 of the 16th instant relative to the feeling in political circles in Washington on the subject of the joint action taken by Great Britain and Germany against Venezuela, it is perhaps satisfactory to note the absence of apprehension in regard to the course pursued by Great Britain and the confidence universally expressed that she has no intention of questioning the Monroe doctrine, as laid down by the President of the United States. The fact that she was acting with Germany and the sinking of the Venezuelan ships created a good deal of irritation at first, especially in the House of Representatives; but Lord Cranborne's statement in the House of Commons that no British men-of-war took part in the latter apparently unnecessary act of destruction, the Prime Minister's remarks in support of the Monroe doctrine, and the outcry in the English press against joint action with Germany have produced a revulsion of feeling in favour of Great Britain, and, during the last few days, I have even heard relief expressed at the presence of the British fleet alongside that of Germany in Venezuelan waters, which is looked upon as a guarantee that Germany will be restrained from taking any action which might bring her into collision with the United States.

The Administration has been most friendly throughout, and, if the dispute be referred without delay to arbitration, which at the moment of writing seems probable, it will be almost safe to affirm that the friendly relations between Great Britain and the United States, instead of being impaired, have, if anything, been strengthened by the Venezuelan incident. As one of the leading New York newspapers points out this morning, "the American people in general have come to place a higher value than they ever placed before on the mutual goodwill and the co-operation in common causes of the two great branches of the English-speaking race, the great Empire, and the great Republic."

On the other hand, the outburst in this country against Germany has been truly remarkable, and suspicion of the German Emperor's designs in the Caribbean Sea is shared by the Administration, the press, and the public alike. Nor is this feeling likely to abate in the near future, for, although it is, to a great extent, spontaneous at the present moment, it will continue to be fostered by the naval authorities, who have never forgotten Admiral Diedrichs, and who wish to increase the navy, and by the powerful ship-building firms of Cramp in the East and Scott in the West, who want more orders for ships.

When I think of the flattery lavished upon this country during the past year by the German Emperor, and the persistent attempts made by German diplomacy to discredit my predecessor, and sow dissension between Great Britain and the United States, I confess to regarding the present attacks on Germany with a certain feeling of complacency, if not of satisfaction.

The New York "Staats Zeitung," the reputed organ of the German Embassy, has been loud in its lamentations, during the past week, at the unfortunate result of all its efforts, and, somewhat in the *tu quoque* vein, ascribes the present anti-German feeling in this country to malicious stories invented in England.

I have, &c.

MICHAEL M. HERBERT.

No. 185.

The Marquess of Lansdowne to Sir F. Lascelles.

F.O. Venezuela 480.
(No. 35A.)

Sir, *Foreign Office, January 22, 1903.*

Count Bernstorff called at this Office to-day on behalf of the German Ambassador, and communicated a copy of telegraphic instructions sent yesterday to Count Quaadt, the German Chargé d'Affaires at Washington, on the subject of the German claims against Venezuela.

From the copy enclosed for your Excellency's information, you will observe that the only point on which these instructions differ from those sent to His Majesty's Ambassador at Washington is contained in the following passage : "We have, moreover, come to an understanding with England, who is similarly claiming the immediate payment of £5,500, to the effect that the two Representatives are not to enter into further negotiations with Mr. Bowen until the first set of demands both on the German and on the British side have been complied with."

Count Bernstorff stated that Baron Sternburg, who is proceeding to Washington to take charge of the Imperial Embassy, and will arrive in about a week's time, has been furnished with more detailed verbal instructions exactly in accordance with those sent to Sir M. Herbert.

Count Quaadt had reported to the Imperial Government that Mr. Bowen had not as yet offered any satisfactory guarantee for the payment of the claims, and they did not therefore consider it necessary at present to accede to the application for raising the blockade.

The German Government, Count Bernstorff said, were most desirous of acting on every point in agreement with His Majesty's Government.

They had again raised the question of obtaining satisfaction for the attack on the German Legation at Carácas and the imprisonment of Germans, but would not press the point if I still held the opinion which I had expressed to Count Metternich on the 30th December last.

Count Bernstorff was informed that I had not altered my views on this matter.

He further stated that the German Government had had under consideration the question of meeting the cost of the blockade and also the expenses of the Mixed Commission or the Arbitral Tribunal. They did not desire to make any claim if an immediate settlement were effected, but were disposed, if the matter were to be referred to the Tribunal at the Hague, to make a separate claim in each case. They were, however, quite ready to adopt the same course as His Majesty's Government.

Having regard to the present position of the negotiations, it would not, in my opinion, which I have communicated to Count Metternich, be advisable to make any further demands upon Venezuela at this moment. The expenses incurred by His Majesty's Government on account of the Commission or Arbitration Tribunal could probably be defrayed by the deduction of a small percentage, which should in no case exceed 5 per cent., on the Award pronounced.

With regard to the mode of procedure, the German Government concur in the view of His Majesty's Government that each country should have its own Tribunal or Commission. In the case of a Mixed Commission, they propose that the Umpire should be named by a member of the Corps Diplomatique at Carácas; if, on the other hand, the case is referred to the Hague, they suggest that the Umpire should be chosen by the President of the Swiss Confederation.

I have told Count Metternich that, in my opinion, the best arrangement would be for a British and a Venezuelan Commissioner to meet in the first place, and that any points upon which they cannot come to a decision should be referred to an Umpire who might be chosen by them.

I am, &c.
LANSDOWNE.

No. 186.

Communication from Admiralty, January 23, 1903.

Commander-in-Chief, North America and West Indies, to Admiralty.

F.O. Venezuela 480.
Tel. (No. 14.)   *January 23, 1903.*

German Commodore, acting quite independently and without consulting either Montgomerie or myself, appears to have commenced bombarding at Maracaybo. I entirely disagree with his action. I saw him last week and no mention was made of his intention. Pending further instructions I propose to take no steps to support him.

MINUTE.

. . . . Should we, in order to make quite safe, ask the Admiralty to telegraph confidentially approving the Admiral's intention not to take part in these German proceedings?—*F. H. V.*

Say that unless their Lordships have already done so we suggest that it should be well to express approval and hope that he will be careful to avoid associating himself with any such severe measures.—*L.*

No. 187.

Admiralty to Commander-in-Chief, North America and West Indies.

F.O. Venezuela 480. *Admiralty, January* 24, 1903.

It is very satisfactory to see from your telegram No. 14 of the 23rd January how fully you comprehend the meaning of their Lordships' instructions as conveyed in their telegram No. 176(¹) of the 16th December, and the policy of His Majesty's Government. It is of the utmost importance that His Majesty's ships should not be implicated in any indiscreet or violent action, and that matters should be kept as quiet as possible pending negotiations.

(¹) [The text of this was as follows :—

Instruction to be given to all ships concerned in operations off Coast of Venezuela not to land men, nor bombard forts nor sink any ships without the authority of the Admiralty.]

No. 188.

Sir M. Herbert to the Marquess of Lansdowne.

F.O. Venezuela 480. *Washington,* D. *January* 24, 1903.
Tel. (No. 16.) R. *January* 25, 10 A.M.
Venezuela.

German Chargé d'Affaires informed me to-day that in his instructions it is stated that one Power cannot raise the blockade without the consent of the other.

I replied that Germany was not mentioned in my instructions relative to the raising of the blockade.

No. 189.

Sir M. Herbert to the Marquess of Lansdowne.

F.O. Venezuela 480. *Washington, January* 26, 1903.
Tel. (No. 21.) Secret. P. D. 1·45 A.M.

With reference to my immediately preceding telegram there is a feeling of intense irritation in the United States against Germany, and in default of an early settlement there may be an outburst of feeling which may produce a strained situation and place the President in a position of serious embarrassment. . . . .

[Rest deals with claims.]

No. 100.

The Marquess of Lansdowne to Sir F. Lascelles.

F.O. Venezuela 480.
(No. 37A.)
Sir,   *Foreign Office, January* 27, 1903.

The German Ambassador called upon me to-day, and we further discussed the position of the Venezuelan negotiations. I communicated to his Excellency the substance of my telegram to Sir M. Herbert No. 14 of the 26th instant. He told me that the German Government were making enquiries similar to those which we had made. It did not seem to them that the assignment of 30 per cent. of the revenue of the two ports was a sufficient provision, if it was to be made use of, not only for the purpose of compensating the three blockading Powers, but also for that of satisfying the claims of the other Powers, as well as the requirements of the whole of the external debt of Venezuela.

Count Metternich told me that he thought it essential that in any case a special arrangement should be made for the settlement of the first rank claims. As to these, Germany would expect to be paid in cash, if our first rank claims were to be met by cash payment. If we accepted a security they would accept a security also, which might take the shape of a first call upon the assigned customs revenues.

His Excellency mentioned to me that the German Government was under the impression that under the Venezuelan Constitution, it was not within the power of the President to hypothecate the revenues or to contract international obligations of any kind without the sanction of the Venezuelan Congress. His Excellency referred me to Article 4 of the Constitution, § § 2A, 9A, 10, and 16, published in the Official Gazette of the April 19th, 1901. He thought it might be necessary that in these circumstances we should discover some means of obtaining a hold over President Castro until such time as his action had received the necessary sanction of Congress. The President was quite capable of repudiating the bargain upon the ground that the consent of Congress was not forthcoming. His Excellency asked me whether I did not think that we might obtain permission to hold the Customs-houses of the two ports until Congress had been convened and the necessary sanction obtained.

I said I thought this mode of procedure would be most objectionable. It would be a pity at the last moment to take a step which we had from the first deprecated, for reasons which were familiar to his Excellency. We might, however, I thought, obtain a distinct undertaking from Mr. Bowen that the consent of Congress would be procured, and I thought that would probably be sufficient. I added that I would at once call Sir M. Herbert's attention to the point, and tell him that we should require to be satisfied with regard to it.

I told his Excellency that I was far from desiring to hurry over what were, I hoped, the final stages of this troublesome negotiation. He must, however, I thought, be aware that a great deal of irritation had been created both in this country and in the United States by the German bombardment of San Carlos. His Excellency said that he proposed to supply us with a full account of this incident, which had arisen in consequence of an attack upon the " Panther " while she was attempting to maintain the blockade in Lake Maracaibo, across which large quantities of provisions were being conveyed. Count Metternich was convinced that if a British ship had been attacked under these circumstances, it would have returned the fire and probably have continued it until the fort was silenced. I told his Excellency that I should be grateful for any information as to what had occurred, but that there was undoubtedly an impression that the reprisals had been excessive.

I am, &c.
LANSDOWNE.

No. 191.

The Marquess of Lansdowne to Sir F. Lascelles.

F.O. Venezuela 480.
(No. 39.)

Sir,   *Foreign Office, January 30, 1903.*

I read to the German Ambassador to-day the draft of my telegram No. 21 to Sir M. Herbert. His Excellency explained to me that he regarded with some apprehension the proposal to invite the President of the United States to decide whether the three blockading Powers were to be compensated for their claims, other than first rank claims, from a fund which was also to be used for compensating the Powers who had not taken any part in the blockade operations. His Excellency begged that Sir M. Herbert should, for the present, be instructed only to discuss this proposal with his German and Italian colleagues, but not to put it forward officially in his negotiations with Mr. Bowen, until an opportunity had been given to the German Government for further considering the matter. His Excellency told me that he felt no doubt that the President's decision would be adverse to us.

I am, &c.
LANSDOWNE.

No. 192.

Sir M. Herbert to the Marquess of Lansdowne.

F.O. Venezuela 480.   *Washington, D. January 31, 1903.*
Tel. (No. 39.)   R. *February 1, 1903,* 8 A.M.

I have seen the German Minister who informs me that the President told him this morning that he earnestly hoped that a prompt settlement of the Venezuelan dispute would be arrived at as public opinion in this country was growing more and more irritated.

No. 193.

The Marquess of Lansdowne to Sir F. Lascelles.

F.O. Venezuela 481.
(No. 42.)

Sir,   *Foreign Office, February 2, 1903.*

The German Ambassador told me to-day that the German Government had been informed of a proposal said to be favoured by our Ambassador at Washington, to the effect that the three Powers should demand from the Venezuelan Government compensation for the expense to which they had been put in connection with the blockade of the Venezuelan ports. The proposal was, Count Metternich told me, one which did not much commend itself to the German Government, and they doubted extremely whether any figure which the Powers were likely to mention would be acceptable to President Castro. The German Government remained of the opinion that the best plan was that the three Powers should insist upon obtaining priority for their claims, although they might, if necessary, be content with less than 30 per cent. of the customs revenues of the two ports as security. If this arrangement were impracticable, the German Government thought that we should have recourse to arbitration.

I told Count Metternich that the idea of claiming compensation for the cost of the blockade seemed to us worthy of being entertained only in the event of the three

Powers being unable to obtain special recognition for their claims in some other form. I said that we had no desire to exhaust the resources of Venezuela and that if our first-rank claims were settled at once and arrangements made for settling our other claims within a reasonable time, we did not care what terms were accorded to the other Powers.

I preferred to speak of a "separate settlement" rather than of "priority" . . . .([1])

I am, &c.
LANSDOWNE.

([1]) [Details follow.]

No. 194.

Sir M. Herbert to the Marquess of Lansdowne.

F.O. Venezuela 481.   *Washington, February 4, 1903.*
Tel. (No. 49.)   R. 9 P.M.

Statements appear in the papers this morning, inspired by Mr. Bowen, that the German Minister is taking a different line from his colleagues who are placing obstacles in way of a settlement.

At the request of German Minister, who is new to this kind of thing, I hasten to assure your Lordship that we are all three acting in perfect harmony.

No. 195.

The Marquess of Lansdowne to Sir F. Lascelles.

F.O. Venezuela 481.
(No. 45 A.)
Sir,   *Foreign Office, February 4, 1903.*

The German Ambassador called upon me this afternoon, and I read to him the substance of Sir M. Herbert's telegram No. 45.

Count Metternich told me that he had received a telegram from Count Bülow, from which he learned that Mr. Bowen was apparently attempting to detach Germany from us by holding out separate inducements to her Representative at Washington. The German Government had no intention of allowing themselves to be influenced by these machinations, and would co-operate loyally with us, feeling no doubt that we should do the same by them. Baron Speck von Sternburg had been instructed to act in concert with Sir M. Herbert, and would certainly do so.

I thanked his Excellency for this communication, and expressed the satisfaction which it gave me to know that our Representatives were in such close touch with one another. I said that, in our opinion, Mr. Bowen's conduct seemed to have rendered a complete settlement at Washington unattainable, and that the best course would now be to embody in Protocols, to be signed by our Representatives at Washington and by Mr. Bowen, the terms which President Castro had already undertaken to accept, the question of a separate settlement for the three Powers being reserved for adjudication either by the President or by the Tribunal at the Hague.

I am, &c.
LANSDOWNE.

No. 196.

The Marquess of Lansdowne to Sir F. Lascelles.

F.O. Venezuela 481.
(No. 46 A.)
Sir,

Foreign Office, February 5, 1903.

The German Ambassador informed me to-day that the German Government were prepared to modify the draft of the Protocol to be signed by Mr. Bowen and the German Representative at Washington in such a manner as to make the text accord as closely as possible with the text of our draft, which had been shown to the German Embassy. They trusted that Sir M. Herbert would be instructed not to enter into negotiations with Mr. Bowen with regard to the Protocol until the German Minister at Washington had received his instructions, and had had an opportunity of comparing notes with Sir Michael.

I told Count Metternich that Sir M. Herbert, who was, I knew, in constant communication with Baron Speck von Sternburg, would be specially instructed to confer with him in regard to the question of the Protocols.

I then mentioned to his Excellency the proposal of which His Majesty's Government had been made aware on the previous day, that the three Powers should receive 30 per cent. of the customs revenue of the two ports for three months.

Count Metternich told me that, in his opinion, the offer was altogether inadmissible, although he had not yet received instructions with regard to it.

I told his Excellency that if the sum offered to us had been in addition to an arrangement for the satisfaction of our first-rank claims we might possibly have entertained it, but that as the first-rank claims amounted to 73,000l., and the sum offered would, according to our calculations, probably not exceed 53,000l., I did not see how we could accept it. It seemed to me, therefore, that we should have to adhere to the position which we had agreed to take up on the occasion of my last conversation with him.

Count Metternich expressed his entire concurrence. He further informed me that he was instructed to say that it was, in the opinion of the German Government, indispensable that they should receive 5,500l. in cash on account of their first claims, and that arrangements should be made for securing, presumably by an assignation of the customs revenues, the prompt payment of the balance of those claims. This was with the German Government a point of honour, and they trusted that we should act with them in insisting on the satisfaction of the first-rank claims as a whole. He told me that before the issue of the ultimatum the Venezuelan Government had offered the German Government a complete settlement of their claims, in order, if possible, to detach them from us.

I told his Excellency that, in our opinion, President Castro had entered into an agreement to settle the first-rank claims (which were expressly withheld from arbitration), as a preliminary to the commencement of the negotiations with Mr. Bowen at Washington.

His Excellency called my attention to·the wording of Article V in the draft Protocol, which he thought did not make it sufficiently clear that we were not prepared to agree, except as the result of an adverse decision by the Tribunal at the Hague, to an arrangement under which our claims would be settled conjointly, and out of the same fund as those of the whole of the Powers having claims against the Venezuelan Government. In his opinion the engagement to refer to arbitration the three points mentioned in my telegram No. 29 of February 2nd, should either be recorded in the Protocol, or should be made the subject of a separate, but simultaneous, arrangement with the Venezuelan Government. We should not leave it in the power of the Venezuelan Government to elude their obligation in this respect.

I told his Excellency that we certainly contemplated that the reservation of the three points should form the subject of a simultaneous arrangement, and I subsequently instructed Sir M. Herbert to amend the concluding paragraph of Article V of the Protocol so as to make it clear that the distribution therein referred to should be subject to the decision which might be arrived at by the Tribunal at the Hague upon the three reserved points.

I am, &c.
LANSDOWNE.

No. 197.

The Marquess of Lansdowne to Sir F. Lascelles.(¹)

F.O. Venezuela 481.
(No. 48A.)   Confidential.
Sir,   *Foreign Office, February* 6, 1903.

Count Metternich being indisposed, Count Bernstorff called at this Office on behalf of his Excellency, and made the following communications :—

1. The German Government desired to express their thanks for the statement which I had made yesterday, to the effect that His Majesty's Government fully intend to maintain united action in regard to Venezuela.
2. Mr. Bowen had told the Italian Ambassador at Washington that the main principle of his diplomacy was to create discord between Baron Speck von Sternburg and Sir M. Herbert. This information had been telegraphed to Berlin by Baron Sternburg, and was communicated very confidentially by Count Bernstorff.
3. The German Government considered quite inadmissible the proposal put forward by Mr. Bowen, that the three Powers should accept the total of 30 per cent. of the Venezuelan customs for three months in satisfaction of their first-rank claims, and had instructed Baron Sternburg to join Sir M. Herbert in refusing it.

I am, &c.
LANSDOWNE.

(¹) [Part printed *Accounts and Papers*, 1903 (*Cd.* 1399), LXXXVII, pp. 943–4. Paragraphs marked 1 and 2 were omitted.]

No. 198.

The Marquess of Lansdowne to Sir M. Herbert.

F.O. Venezuela 481.   *Foreign Office, February* 7, 1903.
Tel. (No. 41A.)   Secret and Private.   D. 8·30 A.M.

It may be convenient to you to know our views with regard to possible developments of the Venezuelan situation. Bowen's object appears to be not to facilitate an equitable settlement but to create dissensions between the Powers. We should therefore not be sorry to break off negotiations with him.

It is, moreover, absolutely necessary for parliamentary and other reasons that a settlement should be effected without further delay. If, therefore, Bowen shows a disposition to create difficulties over the Protocol, which are likely to cause delay, it would, in our opinion, be better to abandon the attempt to effect a direct settlement with him, and you should propose to revert to the alternative of referring the questions in dispute to the Tribunal at The Hague.

The President intimated to us on the 27th December last that the Governments of Great Britain, Germany, Italy and Venezuela had all of them accepted in principle the proposition of such a reference, and that if he could be of any service in arranging the preliminaries of such an understanding he would gladly hold himself at the disposition of the Powers concerned.

In compliance with a suggestion from the United States Chargé d'Affaires the conditions embodied in my Memorandum of December 23rd were communicated by the U[nited] S[tates] Gov[ernmen]t to the Venezuelan Government. Those conditions were subsequently accepted unreservedly by the Venezuelan Government, and it was upon this understanding that we authorised you to commence the discussions which have been proceeding at Washington. We should therefore certainly stipulate that the reference to The Hague Tribunal be made subject to these conditions, which would leave it open to the Tribunal to examine the claims of other Powers as well as those of the three blockading Powers and to determine without any restrictions the amount of compensation payable by Venezuela as well as the security to be given and the means to be resorted to for guaranteeing punctual payment.

We should, of course, be ready to raise the blockade as soon as the preliminaries of reference had been satisfactorily arranged.

No. 199.

Sir M. Herbert to the Marquess of Lansdowne.

F.O. Venezuela 481.
Tel. (No. 58A.) Secret. P.   *Washington, February 7, 1903.*
Venezuela. I have received your Lordship's telegram No. 41A of to-day.

Mr. Bowen would be perfectly willing, if he saw our Protocol, to sign it at once, and a settlement could be reached to-day if we were alone. The stumbling-block is the German and Italian conditions in 2nd Article of their Protocol, and for this my colleagues are to blame, inasmuch as they did not, as we did, make their conditions clear to Mr. Bowen at the outset. Throughout the negotiations we have been consistent, and, except preferential treatment, which is to be referred to The Hague Tribunal, have obtained all that we originally asked for. Consequently, in view of public opinion here, it would be folly on our part to take the lead in breaking off the negotiations with Mr. Bowen. If we are bound to support the German and Italian demands, which are, in my opinion, unfair, for the reasons above stated, let Germany propose to break off negotiations, but do not let the proposal come from Great Britain. Application by His Majesty's Government of pressure to Germany and Italy to modify 2nd Article of their Protocols is what I would advise. I feel myself bound to warn your Lordship that a great change has taken place in the feeling of this country towards us since I wrote my despatch No. 355 of December 27th last, and that our good relations with this country will be seriously impaired if this Alliance with Germany continues much longer. The time has almost come, in American opinion, for us to make the choice between the friendship of the United States and that of Germany.

No. 200.

The Marquess of Lansdowne to Sir M. Herbert.

F.O. Venezuela 481.   *Foreign Office, February 9, 1903.*
Tel. (No. 47.) Confidential.   D. 10 P.M.
I have explained to the German Ambassador with the utmost frankness the gravity of the situation and importance of immediate settlement. I impressed upon him that our position would be almost intolerable if, having obtained Bowen's compliance with our own demands, we were to break off on account of refusal by

Venezuela to accede to extreme German demands in respect of claims differing materially from our own.

I did not think position of Germany would be enviable if negotiations fell through under such circumstances.

I said that we had no intention of deserting Germany, but that it was absolutely necessary that we should endeavour to find some way out of the difficulty. I thought Germany required the fulfilment of two conditions in regard to balance of her first-rank claims :—

1. That she should have a safe guarantee for prompt payment, *vide* German note of December 22nd ; and
2. That those claims should not be subject to revision.

In order to facilitate (1) we were ready to agree that in any settlement which might be arrived at balance of German first-rank claims should have priority over British claims other than those covered by payment of £5,500.

I said that I thought Venezuelan Government could not object to (2), and that we were of opinion that it might reasonably be demanded.

Count Metternich promised to telegraph this suggestion to the German Government.

I told him confidentially that you were under the impression that there had been some misunderstanding between German Chargé d'Affaires and Bowen.

Do what you can to bring about an agreement on the above lines.

No. 201.

The Marquess of Lansdowne to Sir F. Lascelles.

F.O. Venezuela 482.
(No. 59.)

Sir, *Foreign Office, February* 12, 1903.

The German Ambassador informed me to-day that Baron Sternburg had telegraphed on the 11th instant to the German Government announcing that Mr. Bowen had asked him to "arbitrate" as to the amount which Germany might receive on account of her first-rank claims and as to the period within which they were to be paid. Mr. Bowen had undertaken to submit to Baron Sternburg's decision.

Baron Sternburg had proposed to the German Government that he should name five months as the period within which the whole of the German first-rank claims were to be paid, and that he should designate certain sources of revenue not yet defined which might be given as security. Count Metternich went on to say that the German Government had agreed to accept payment of their first-rank claims (excluding those to be settled by a cash payment of £5,500) in five months, and had instructed Baron Sternburg to stipulate that the revenues assigned were to be regarded as sufficient by Baron Pilgrim, lately German Chargé d'Affaires at Carácas. They desired, moreover, that payment should be made by monthly instalments to begin on April 1st next. Baron Sternburg had been authorised to modify points of detail both as to the amount of the instalments and as to the commencement of the payments.

Count Metternich went on to say that he had received a despatch from the German Government, in which he was informed that they did not anticipate any further difficulty with regard to the settlement of their claims, and also that they accepted the first part of the wording of Article V of the draft British Protocol.

With regard to the concluding portion of Article V, he was instructed to say that the German Government presumed that it was our intention that the proposed arbitration should be between the three blockading Powers on the one side, and the other Powers having claims against Venezuela on the other, and that Venezuela should be excluded.

I told Count Metternich that that was not our intention. In our view, as the Protocols which were to be signed by Venezuela on the one side, and the three Powers on the other, reserved the question of a separate settlement for arbitration, it could scarcely be contended that Venezuela would not have a *locus standi* before the Tribunal. Our idea was that the arbitration should be between Venezuela and the three Powers, and that it should be open to the other Powers to take part in it.

Count Metternich said that he thought Venezuela might perhaps be allowed a hearing as a witness, but not as a party to the arbitration.

I said that I could not see that the difference was one of any practical importance, and I reminded his Excellency that the German Government had, in fact (see Sir M. Herbert's telegram No. 60), already consented to refer to The Hague Tribunal a number of questions as to the resources of Venezuela and her liabilities, which could not possibly be disposed of without evidence from the Venezuelan Government.

I earnestly trusted that this point would not be pressed at the last moment, or allowed to stand in the way of a satisfactory settlement, which at last seemed to be within reach.

I am, &c.
LANSDOWNE.

[*NOTE.*—The Protocol was signed on the 13th February. The text is printed in *Accounts and Papers*, 1903 (*Cd.* 1538), LXXXVII, pp. 945–52.]

III.—THE BAGDAD RAILWAY.

[*EDITORIAL NOTE.*—In October, 1888, when Constantinople had been at last connected by railway with Central Europe, the Turkish Government gave a concession to a group of financiers, headed by the Deutsche Bank, to purchase the line from Haidar Pasha (opposite the capital) to Ismid, and to continue it to Angora. The Anatolian Railway Company was formed in 1889 to work the concession, and in 1890 one million was invested by British capitalists. Angora was reached in 1892, and in 1893 a new concession was granted for a line from Eski-Shehr (midway between Haidar Pasha and Angora) to Konia, which was completed in 1896. The right to build to Bagdad and Basra was secured in principle by the Convention of the 23rd December, 1899, which left details to be settled later. An Imperial Iradé of the 18th March, 1902, definitely awarding the Bagdad railway concession to the Anatolian Railway Company, was succeeded by the definitive Convention of the 5th March, 1903, which granted a concession for 99 years to a new corporation, the Bagdad Railway Company (in which the Anatolian Railway Company was to take shares), for a line from Konia to Basra, via Adana, Mosul and Bagdad, including branch lines to Aleppo, Urfa, Khanikin (on the Russian frontier), and a point on the Persian Gulf to be settled at a future date. The new concession included not only a large kilometric guarantee, but mining rights, harbour facilities, and privileges of inland navigation. An authoritative record of British policy may be found in an article entitled " The Bagdad Railway Negotiations " in the *Quarterly Review*, October, 1917, by Alwyn Parker, formerly Librarian of the Foreign Office. The best account of the whole problem is by Professor E. M. Earle, in his work, *Turkey, the Great Powers and the Bagdad Railway*, New York [1923].]

No. 202.

[*NOTE.*—The following précis of despatches was sent by Sir N. O'Conor to Sir T. Sanderson on the 29th April, 1903 :—

Précis of Despatches.

F.O. Turkey 5322.

There is no serious British competitor in the field, and I doubt whether there is any financial group in London anxious to obtain the Concession or who would accept it if offered on the terms probably acceptable to the Germans. Mr. Rechnitser cannot be considered such. The main feature of his proposal is the absence of any kilometric guarantee, and this brands it as counterfeit, for no one would undertake the work without a solid security of some sort, and I have not thought it advisable to support him. But his action may have shown the Germans that it is important that we should assist, or at least abstain from competing. The Sultan's idea of building the railway himself is absurd. Sooner or later the Germans will, if they persist, obtain the Concession on fairly reasonable terms, but at the present, the difficulties in their way are so great that the German Emperor would probably appreciate any support that would turn the scale in their favour. It is, therefore, a matter for consideration whether this support should not be given by Her Majesty's Government. For my part, I would like it to be accorded, as the result of a request from the German Government, and combined with some understanding securing to British capitalists a right to co-operate on fair terms in the prolongation of the existing railways to Bagdad and Basra. Some scheme by which the Smyrna–Aïdin Railway would at the same time be amalgamated with the larger enterprise would not, I think, be unacceptable to the owners of the English line, and would in the long run be to the advantage of British trade and influence.(1)

An Iradé has been communicated to Baron von Marschall, granting the Concession in principle. The details will be determined after the return of the Technical Committee. The difficulty is the kilometric guarantee; and eventually long and difficult negotiations will ensue, leading, quite possibly, to a demand for British financial co-operation.(2)

Russia will possibly be obliged to seek a counterpoise, and is rumoured to be trying to get an important Railway Concession in the Erzeroum region.

Dr. von Siemens still hoped to come to an understanding with the Aïdin Railway. It would be far better to make the line an international one.(3)

Sir E. Law might remark, in a private letter to Dr. von Siemens, that he has heard that the Railway Co[mmission] is proposing to acquire a port at Koweit, and that he hopes it will not be unduly pressed, as Dr. von Siemens is probably aware that intimate relations exist between Her Majesty's Government and the Sheikh. Sir E. Law thinks that Dr. von Siemens would grasp the situation, and avoid discouraging British capitalists by any action which would have an unfavourable effect on the London market. A similar hint might be given to the German Ambassador.(4)

It is proposed to apply the increased customs duties as guarantee for a loan of some £T. 20,000,000 for the construction of the Bagdad Railway. This loan may entice foreign—and especially British—capitalists. A fixed part has already been reserved for the French investor, and a similar arrangement may be made for the British, both France and England obtaining likewise a share in the work of construction.

This arrangement might have an effect on the Koweit question.(5)

Transmits Report of Co[mmission]. The discouraging accounts which it contains of the state of the country and the small estimate of receipts would hardly tempt the investor, unless accompanied by exceptionally satisfactory arrangement for kilometric guarantees.(6)

Transmits copy of letter to Dr. von Siemens. We have shown good-will without engaging to do what he want, viz., to agree to the increase of customs duties arising from the specific Tariff to be handed over to the Anatolian Railway Company. The debt and many others will want a share.(7)

Have written to Dr. von Siemens expressing satisfaction that he has opened the door to British capitalists, but, as he can understand, I cannot venture an opinion on the financial side of the question, though I shall be very pleased to see British capitalists co-operating with Germans in this great enterprise . . . . I think it would be a pity to stop here and not do what we can in other ways to bring about an international arrangement. The Russian Ambassador has stated that he would not oppose the Railway if confined to French and Germans, but that if England joined he would do all he could to frustrate its realisation.(8)

One of the results of M. Delcassé's visit to St. Petersburgh was that M. de Witte undertook not to oppose the Bagdad Railway.

Without some impulsion from official quarters, British capitalists may not be disposed to move in the matter. It is not my object to lead British investors to put their money blindly into the work, but merely to urge, as strongly as I can, that a British Syndicate should be formed to enter into negotiations with the German and French groups, and to enquire for themselves into the merits and details of the scheme, so as to be in a position to obtain for the British public, as well as for British trade, such advantages as may be reaped by those who participate in the original Concession.

I believe that the Ottoman Government is pledged, in principle, to a kilometric guarantee. I also believe that without such guarantee it will not be possible to raise a loan calculated roughly

(1) To Foreign Office, No. 526 (Vol.), the 9th November, 1899.
(2) To Foreign Office, No. 554, the 30th November, 1899.
(3) To Foreign Office, No. 602 (Vol.), the 27th December, 1899.
(4) To Foreign Office, No. 24 (Vol.), the 22nd January, 1900.
(5) To Foreign Office, No. 175, the 19th May, 1900.
(6) To Foreign Office, No. 231 (Vol.), the 3rd July, 1900.
(7) To Sir T. Sanderson, the 26th January, 1901.
(8) To Sir T. Sanderson, the 23rd February, 1901.

at £20,000,000 for the construction of the Railway, and that with such guarantee investors run very little chance of losing their money.

A kilometric guarantee is essential, and this must be raised by an increase of the customs dues. This will fall on British imports, which exceed those of other countries; but we would find it difficult standing alone, as we probably should, to oppose or question the right of Turkey to apply this revenue to such purposes as it thinks wisest for the country. It is unpleasant to contemplate the construction of a railway traversing the whole of Asia Minor and terminating in the Persian Gulf in which Great Britain takes no part or share.(⁹)

The Convention omits all mention of the specific guarantee to be given to the Bagdad Railway. The revenues of the vilayets will evidently not suffice, and the Company must look to other sources as the increase of customs dues.

In this letter they doubtless apprehend Russian opposition, which I have always expected. M. Zinoview's remarks lend colour to this : he threatens to increase the war indemnity. The French susceptibilities are such that they will find it difficult to work harmoniously with the Germans. If our object, like Russia's, was the impoverishment of Turkey, we should be able to show good reason for objecting to an increase of customs duties for the benefit of a foreign railway. My belief is that our commerce will increase with the development of the country, and that the burden of the new duties will fall chiefly on the consumer. I am convinced it is to our interest, politically and commercially, to assist in the development of this country, and there is no more effective means than by constructing railways. The Aïdin Railway prospects at first were very gloomy, but it has turned out a highly profitable undertaking, and it is quite probable that the Bagdad Railway may prove equally so. I hope that the English Syndicate will spare no pains to come in on a footing of equality with the French and Germans.

There is also the question of credit and prestige, and the Germans cannot put so large a capital into this country without being prepared to support the stability of an Empire in which they have staked so much. From the date of the signature, the German Government is directly interested in the highest degree in the maintenance of the Ottoman Empire.(¹⁰)

We have the opportunity now of exercising considerable pressure by making equal participation in the Railway one of the essential conditions of our consent to the increase of customs duties, and intimating that without our good-will the London market will not subscribe.(¹¹)

Has told Baron von Marschall that our attitude towards the proposed increase of customs must depend on our having an equal participation.(¹²)

Has told Mr. Gwinner that the support of the city could best be attracted by letting it be understood that British capitalists could have the construction of the eastern end.(¹³)

The Administrative Council is to consist of eleven members, and the Germans and Turks together will have a permanent majority on the Board.(¹⁴)

(⁹) To Foreign Office, No. 239 A, the 1st July, 1901.
(¹⁰) To Foreign Office, No. 31, the 27th January, 1902.
(¹¹) To Sir T. Sanderson, Telegraphic, the 18th March, 1902.
(¹²) To Foreign Office, No. 173, the 10th April, 1902.
(¹³) To Lord Lansdowne, the 23rd October, 1902.
(¹⁴) To Foreign Office, No. 124, the 10th March, 1903.

No. 203.

Sir N. O'Conor to the Marquess of Lansdowne.

F.O. Turkey 5249.
(No. 239 A.)   Confidential.   *Therapia, D. June 25, 1901.*
My Lord,   R. *July 8, 1901.*

I have the honour to report to your Lordship that I was informed some time ago that one of the results of M. Delcassé's late visit to St. Petersburg was that M. Witte undertook not to oppose the Bagdad Railway scheme, in which a French Syndicate is interested to the extent of 40 per cent., provided the loan which he desired to raise in Paris received the support of the French Government.

This report is confirmed by the French Ambassador, M. Constans, who informs me that the German and French Syndicates have respectively agreed to give Russian capitalists 10 per cent. of the holdings in case they wish to take part in the enterprise.

I am further informed that at a meeting of the 23rd April at Berlin the terms of the draft Convention to be submitted to the Imperial Ottoman Government were discussed, and I hope at an early date to be able to send to your Lordship, confidentially, the *procès-verbal* of this meeting.

Your Lordship is aware that by an additional clause or annex to the Berlin Convention of May 1899, Dr. Von Siemens stipulated that a share should be preserved for British investors, and that the only reason why the exact amount was not fixed was due to their wishes not being known.

Since then no action, so far as I can learn, has been taken in London, and I am afraid that without some impulsion from official quarters British capitalists may not be disposed to move in the matter. Mr. Babington Smith has, at my suggestion, again written to Mr. Clinton Dawkins on the subject, but I have not heard with what result.

In venturing to allude to this question it is not my object to say anything, even if I could properly do so, to lead the large class of British investors to put their money blindly into this work, be its future prospects what they may, but merely to urge as strongly as I can, that a British Syndicate should be formed to enter into negotiations with the German and French groups and to enquire for themselves into the merits and details of the scheme, so as to be in a position to obtain for the British public, as well as for British trade and commerce, such advantages as may be reaped by those who participate in the original Concession.

I believe the Ottoman Government to be pledged in principle to a kilometrical guarantee. I also believe that without such guarantee it will not be possible to raise a loan, calculated, roughly, at £20,000,000 for the construction of the railway, and that with such guarantee investors run very little risk of losing their money. It is intended both by the Ottoman Government and the Anatolian Railway Company, that a part at least of this guarantee shall be derived from the increased customs duties consequent on the new Treaties of Commerce.

This fact alone and apart from the broader political and commercial considerations involved in the question, seems a reason for British co-operation. The burthen of the new customs duties falls on British imports inasmuch as they exceed those of other countries; and although we may not like to see a large portion of these duties appropriated to a railway guarantee, I believe it would be very difficult, standing alone as we probably should, to oppose or to question the rights of the Turkish Government to apply this revenue to such purpose as it thinks most conducive to the economic development of the country.

There was a time when we might, perhaps, have done so, had we come to an understanding with Russia to oppose any increase of the present customs duties, but we would have started from different points of view, the one antagonistic to any improvement in the economic condition of the country; the other interested in its development and material prosperity, and probably disagreed in the end.

It is unpleasant to contemplate the construction of a railway traversing the whole of Asia Minor and terminating in the Persian Gulf, in which Great Britain takes no part or share.

I have, &c.
N. R. O'CONOR.

No. 204.

The Marquess of Lansdowne to Sir F. Lascelles.

F.O. Turkey 5249.
(No. 71.)
Sir, *Foreign Office, March* 18, 1902.

I told the German Ambassador to-day that the question of the attitude of H[is] M[ajesty's] Government towards the Bagdad Railway had been a good deal discussed of late, and it might be as well that I should inform him of the purport of the answers which I had given when questioned upon the subject.

We did not regard the project with unfriendly eyes; but if it was to be carried into effect with our support and good will, we should expect that a share, at least equal to that given to any other Power, should be given to this country in respect of the capital employed for construction of the line, of its management when completed, and of its orders for materials.

Count Metternich observed that, so far as he was aware, "the door was open," and there was no reason why any amount of British capital should not be invested in the line. On the other hand, if it were once constructed with capital from other countries, we could not expect to be allowed to come in afterwards.

In reply to a question from him, I said that I understood the proposal to be that the Turkish Tariff should be increased in order to provide the necessary funds for a kilometric guarantee. It would no doubt be for us to consider, when the time came, whether we were justified in such an increase, and that would depend to a great extent on the adequacy of the share assigned to us in the enterprise.

I am, &c.
LANSDOWNE.

No. 205.

Sir N. O'Conor to the Marquess of Lansdowne.

F.O. Turkey 5249.
(No. 173.)   *Constantinople*, D. *April* 10, 1902.
My Lord,   R. *April* 21, 1902.

I asked the German Ambassador yesterday whether he could tell me the result of the negotiations which I understood had taken place between British capitalists and the Deutsche Bank in regard to the former's participation in the Bagdad Railway.

Baron von Marschall replied that Dr. Zander, President of the Anatolian Railway, had only just returned, and that, as soon as he saw him, he would find out if any arrangement had been come to and let me know.

I reminded his Excellency of the efforts made by Dr. von Siemens to enlist British capital, and I said I was somewhat surprised at learning recently that we had been kept so long in the dark as to the real terms and conditions upon which the French Syndicate had eventually agreed to share in the cost of the construction of the line. In any case, it was now evident that British capitalists could only count upon the support of His Majesty's Government, or take part in the enterprise upon the conditions that they obtained the same terms as others in regard to the direction, materials, plant, &c.

I went on to say that, inasmuch as the kilometric guarantee was to be mainly provided by the increased customs duties, which would fall heavily upon British imports, we naturally desired to know beforehand how far it was to our interest to consent to this increase, particularly as it was to be appropriated to a specific purpose. Our attitude in regard to the Commercial Treaty, as well as in respect to other matters, must necessarily depend upon this consideration,, but I was sure that, if this point was settled satisfactorily, there would be no difficulty in connection with the terminus of the railway in the Persian Gulf.

Beyond signifying his general concurrence in these views, Baron von Marschall made no remark.

I have, &c.
N. R. O'CONOR.

MINUTE BY LORD LANSDOWNE.

It would, to my mind be a great misfortune if this railway were to be constructed without British participation. The line will be a most important highway to the East with a *débouché* on the Persian Gulf. It is clearly for our interest that the enterprise should be given an international character and that we should have our full share in the control of the line as well as of any advantages to be derived from its construction and maintenance. What has been said above shows that, if the project is to be successfully financed, our consent to (1) increase of customs duties, and possibly also to (2) creation of monopolies, is indispensable.*

I have discussed the matter informally with the French and German Ambassadors, and I have told them that our attitude would depend upon our being given a share at least equal to that of any other Power in the enterprise.

But if we are to insist upon having such a share some one must be prepared to receive it. I have been endeavouring to ascertain whether there is any prospect of the scheme being supported in the City. The result of my enquiries has been to show that unless the British Government gives practical proof of its confidence in the undertaking by giving it material support in one shape or another British financiers are not likely to come forward.

Lord Rothschild and Lord Revelstoke suggest that His Majesty's Government should take a part of the ordinary shares. None of the other Governments are, so far as I am aware, doing anything of the kind. In order to secure the international character of the railway we might propose to France and Germany that we should each of us take a certain amount of shares. It is, however, not unlikely that we shall be told that German and French " groups " are ready to come forward without any such inducements.

It would, no doubt, be most unusual for a British Government to invest public money in such a project. On the other hand, the acquisition and retention by the British Government of a certain number of shares seems to be the only mode of securing for this country a permanent share in the control of the railway. If we were merely to guarantee a certain number of shares we should have no security that those shares would not find their way into the hands of foreign holders.

Unless we are able to secure a footing from the outset, it will not be easy for us to come in at a later stage except on the most onerous terms. As matters stand, however, we are confronted with a twofold difficulty : (a) the resistance of the city to come forward except upon terms to which we may find it impossible to agree; and (b) the doubt as to our ability to veto the project by refusing to accept the new Tariff.—L.

---

* It must, however, be borne in mind that if France, Germany, Austria, and Italy were all to give their assent to the increased Tariff, we might have some difficulty in holding out. Our position would be awkward if the Porte were to proceed to impose the Tariff without our consent on the ground of urgent necessity, and the fact that we should be able to look only to Russia for support or co-operation would increase the difficulty. [L.]

No. 206.

The Marquess of Lansdowne to Sir E. Cassel.

F.O. Turkey 5322.

Dear Sir E. Cassel, *Foreign Office, February 4, 1903.*

It may be convenient that I should summarise in a few words the substance of what I said to you and Sir C. Dawkins this afternoon with regard to the probable attitude of H[is] M[ajesty's] Government in reference to the Bagdad Railway.

We are favourably disposed towards the project, and we should regard it as most undesirable that it should be carried out without our concurrence and without a sufficient participation on the part of this country in the construction, administration, and control of the line.

I gathered from our conversation that, in your opinion, our good-will might be evinced in several ways—

1. By the grant of a subsidy for the carriage of mails to India;
2. By facilitating the introduction of the new Turkish Customs Tariff; and
3. By aiding the promoters to obtain a terminus, probably at or near Koweit, in the Persian Gulf.

I see no reason why proposals of this kind should not be entertained by us.

I venture to say that, in my opinion, it would be desirable that, politically, the line should, so far as possible, be placed upon an international basis, so that no part of it would be controlled or guarded by a single Power. I said that such a course seemed to me best calculated to remove the international rivalries to which the construction of such a line was sure to give rise.

[15214] N 2

These few observations will probably give you a sufficient idea of the manner in which the question is likely to be regarded by His Majesty's Government. They are, however, of a very general character, and you will no doubt find it convenient, when you have had time to consider them, to describe to us in your own language the nature of the assurances which you would like to receive before identifying yourselves with the scheme.

I understand from you that, although you and Sir C. Dawkins were at present in possession of the field, your idea was that the support of the other great houses should be obtained, and you were good enough to add that, if for any reason we preferred it, some firm other than those with which you are connected should take the leading part in bringing out the scheme, and in any transactions which might be necessary with His Majesty's Government, you added that you would be ready to consider favourably any suggestions which we might desire to make to this end.

Yours, &c.
LANSDOWNE.

No. 207.

Memorandum by Sir T. Sanderson on a Conversation with Mr. Barry.

F.O. Turkey 5322.
Confidential. *February 23, 1908.*

Mr. Barry, of the Imperial Ottoman Bank, called in consequence of an enquiry, which I had made by Lord Lansdowne's instructions, as to the nature of an Agreement said to have been signed by Sir Hamilton Laing at Berlin with the Deutsche Bank in regard to the Bagdad Railway scheme.

He said that nothing had been signed by Sir H. Laing, who had merely gone from Paris to Berlin at the request of the French branch of the Ottoman Bank to confer with Dr. Gwinner. But the result of the conference had been that an Agreement had been signed later, of the contents of which he had only received information on Friday last.

The Agreement corresponded with the terms of which Lord Hillingdon had given Lord Lansdowne a summary in March 1902; but there was a fresh arrangement as to the distribution of shares, which was as follows :—

25 per cent. to		Germany;
25	,,	France;
25	,,	England;
10	,,	The Anatolian Railway Company;
15	,,	Various (" divers ").

The Board of Directors was to be as follows :—

8 German;
8 French;
8 English, 1 to be nominated by Ottoman Bank;
1 Austrian, nominated by Deutsche Bank;
2 Swiss, of whom 1 nominated by Deutsche Bank and one by Ottoman Bank;
3 to be nominated by Anatolian Railway.

The Agreement had, however, been signed subject to two reservations. The French group had made their acceptance conditional on the approval of the French Government, which was dependent on Russian participation; while the Germans had reserved the question of Switzerland being chosen as the domicile of the new Company.

The former of these reservations went very far, in Mr. Barry's opinion, towards nullifying the Agreement.

T. H. S.

No. 208.

Foreign Office to Messrs. Baring Brothers and Co., Ltd.

F.O. Turkey 5322.

Gentlemen, *Foreign Office, February 24, 1903.*

As you are no doubt aware, negotiations have been going on for some time past with regard to the possible participation of British financiers in the scheme for the construction of a railway from Konieh to Bagdad and the Persian Gulf for which a concession has been granted by the Turkish Government to the Anatolian Railway Company.

The Deutsche Bank of Berlin, the establishment in charge of the financial arrangements in connection with the concession, has offered a share in the project to Messrs. J. S. Morgan and Company and Sir E. Cassel, and Lord Lansdowne has been in communication with Sir C. Dawkins, representing Messrs. Morgan, and with Sir E. Cassel in regard to the probable attitude of His Majesty's Government towards the participation of a British group in the undertaking.

At an interview which they recently had with his Lordship, he informed them that His Majesty's Government view the project with favour, and that they would regard it as most undesirable that it should be carried out without their concurrence and without a sufficient participation on the part of this country in the construction, administration, and control of the line.

Sir C. Dawkins and Sir E. Cassel suggested that the goodwill of His Majesty's Government might be shown in the following ways: by the grant of a subsidy for the carriage of mails to India; by facilitating the introduction of the new Turkish Customs Tariff; and by aiding the promoters to obtain a terminus at or near Koweit, on the Persian Gulf.

Lord Lansdowne said he saw no reason why proposals of this kind should not be entertained by His Majesty's Government, and he expressed the opinion that it would be desirable that, politically, the line should be placed so far as possible on an international basis, so that no part of it would be controlled or guarded by a single Power. Such an arrangement, Lord Lansdowne thought, seemed that best calculated to remove the international rivalries to which the construction of such a line was sure to give rise.

In the course of the interview Sir C. Dawkins and Sir E. Cassel explained that they proposed to endeavour to obtain the support of the other great financial houses of this country in the matter.

They added that if, for any reason, His Majesty's Government preferred that some house other than those with which they were connected should take the leading part in bringing out the scheme, and in any transactions which might be necessary with His Majesty's Government, they would be ready to consider favourably the suggestions which Lord Lansdowne might desire to make to this end.

Lord Lansdowne has carefully considered this point, and I am directed by his Lordship to inform you that it would give great satisfaction to His Majesty's Government if the management of the British participation in the scheme were to be placed in the hands of your house.

I am, &c.

T. H. SANDERSON.

No. 209.

Sir N. O'Conor to the Marquess of Lansdowne.

F.O. Turkey 5322.
(No. 125.) Confidential.　　　　　　　　　*Constantinople*, D. *March* 8, 1903.
My Lord,　　　　　　　　　　　　　　　　　R. *March* 16, 1903.

I think it may be worth while to report to your Lordship, in connection with the subject of the Bagdad Railway, a conversation which I had a few days ago with M. Testa, now the German Delegate on the Council of the Ottoman Foreign Debt, but who has been for upwards of twenty years the confidential and highly esteemed first Dragoman of the Embassy.

In reply to some tentative remarks as to the possibly critical position of the Bagdad Railway in the event of Russian advance or aggression upon Turkey, M. Testa said that the German Government had never entertained any anxiety upon this score, nor did he think there was reason to do so. In his opinion Germany would never take up the cudgels or quarrel with Russia on account of Turkey. Their interest in keeping on good terms with their Eastern neighbour far outweighed any possible advantage to be gained by taking Turkey's side. If at any time hostilities unfortunately broke out between the two countries, their policy would be to give Turkey the best advice they could and to assist her in every legitimate way consonant with neutrality, but they would not run the risk of complications with Russia to save her from defeat, however crushing. They would remain passive spectators. If Turkey were successful, they would be quickly reinstated in their present favourable position, and if she were unsuccessful, he felt confident the first thing Russia would do would be to promise to respect their interests in regard to the Bagdad Railway, the Haidar Pasha Port, &c. Supposing even that the war resulted in Russian acquisition of territory traversed by the railway, it was possible, no doubt, that she might object to leave the line in foreign hands, but in this case she would be forced to buy it almost at a fancy price. Germany had, in this respect, created a valuable precedent in Alsace-Lorraine, where they had bought up the French railways at the full market value, and probably the same course would be followed in regard to the Bagdad line. The last thing Russia would desire would be to risk fresh complications by disregarding the vested commercial interests of other countries, and the more so if the railway became, as he thought was now not improbable, an international concern.

I have, &c.
N. R. O'CONOR.

No. 210.

Sir N. O'Conor to the Marquess of Lansdowne.

F.O. Turkey 5322.
(No. 126.) Confidential.　　　　　　　　　*Constantinople*, D. *March* 10, 1903.
My Lord,　　　　　　　　　　　　　　　　　R. *March* 16, 1903.

In my despatch No. 103 of the 25th ultimo, I had the honour to enclose to your Lordship a copy of the Contract signed in Paris on the 18th ultimo between the Deutsche and Imperial Ottoman Banks with regard to the Bagdad Railway, and in my despatch No. 124 of the 10th instant to enclose a copy of the Statutes of the loan which is to be issued in this connection.

I asked M. Constans on the 6th instant whether he had heard anything of an intention to set aside 10 per cent. of the capital for the Ottoman Government, to which he answered in the negative. He seemed, I thought, rather inclined to doubt the accuracy of the report, and he reminded me that the French group had only consented to the Anatolian Railway being allotted 10 per cent. on condition that they themselves were given an equal sum out of the Swiss participation to be placed under the control of a French bank.

He then read to me, confidentially, a despatch forwarding the Contract of the 18th February, in which M. Delcassé stated that, in acknowledging its receipt, he had reminded the senders that he still adhered to the declaration he had made in the Chamber of Deputies on the 24th March, 1902, which was to the effect that the approval of the French Government would only be given to the project provided there was absolute and entire equality between the French and German participation in every respect.

This statement of M. Delcassé was, M. Constans said, clear and explicit. If, therefore, the Germans attempted to outwit them by allotting 10 per cent. to the Turkish Government, which would naturally be under their control, they would certainly defeat their own ends.

He noticed, he added, in the Contract between the banks, that an equal share was reserved for England in case a British group decided to participate. He hoped the railway would be an international concern, and he would much sooner see the Company finally established with, than without, British participation.

I have, &c.
N. R. O'CONOR.

No. 211.

Memorandum by the Marquess of Lansdowne.

F.O. Turkey 5322. *Foreign Office, March 12, 1903.*
Sir E. Cassel told me to-day that there had been further negotiations with regard to the Baghdad Railway, and that they were still in progress. He was insisting upon two points :—

(1.) That the Anatolian Railway should be brought into the arrangement, and (2) that whatever arrangement might be made with regard to the representation of the Powers concerned upon the Board of Management, that arrangement should in the future be upheld, even if a part of the share capital now held in one country should be transferred to another. The original basis of control would remain undisturbed, and vacancies which might arise would be filled upon in accordance with the original constitution of the Board.

Sir Ernest thought that some such arrangement was in force with regard to the management of the Suez Canal, and it did not seem to him to matter whether vacancies were filled up by the Governments concerned or by the national groups.

No. 212.

Messrs. Baring Bros. and Co. to the Marquess of Lansdowne.

F.O. Turkey 5322.
Private.
My Lord, 8, *Bishopsgate Within, London, March* 20, 1903.
We have the honour to enclose you copy of a letter received this morning from Mr. Gwinner, of the Deutsche Bank.

Lord Revelstoke returns to town on Sunday evening, and proposes to leave London for Paris by the 2 o'clock train on Monday, to attend the meeting referred to, and should there be any point on which you desire to see him previously, he would have pleasure in calling on you at any hour and place you suggest.

We have, &c.
For Baring Bros. and Co. (Limited),
G. FARRER, Director.

Enclosure 1 in No. 212.

Mr. Gwinner to Lord Revelstoke.

Dear Lord Revelstoke,   *Berlin, March* 18, 1903.

I have been much pleased to hear from Sir Clinton Dawkins that you will undertake to officially represent the British group which is about to take an interest in the Bagdad Railway.

A meeting has been arranged with Sir Clinton Dawkins, in Paris, on Tuesday morning next, when I hope to see you. We will then have an opportunity of discussing and settling details. Meanwhile, and in reply to an enquiry from Sir Clinton Dawkins, who tells me to place myself in communication with you, I beg to say that the several participations in the capital of the Bagdad Railway Company are to be as follows :—

	Per cent.
The Anatolian Railway Company	10
,, French group	25
,, German ,, ...	25
,, British ,, ...	25
The other countries : Austria, Switzerland, &c. ...	15

I further enclose draft of a letter which I am ready to give you if we come to terms, and in order to comply with the desire of His Majesty's Government. . . . .

A. GWINNER.

Enclosure 2 in No. 212.

Draft of Letter.

In conformity with your desire, I beg to state that myself and my friends will use their best endeavours to bring about the control and working of the Anatolian Railway Company's line from Haida Pasha to Konia as part of an internationally-controlled railway line from sea to sea. This undertaking is given on condition that the British group you represent, which is about to join in the Bagdad Railway, shall continue to use their best endeavours towards the realisation of this scheme, and particularly favouring such measures as will enable the Turkish Government to give and fulfil the guarantees promised in aid of building the railway.

It is further understood that you shall give us a satisfactory assurance to the effect that if and when we shall have been able to bring about the international control of the Anatolian line, upon a similar basis as the control of the Bagdad Railway in which your group is joining, then His Majesty's Government will aid to achieve the following subjects :—

1st. To allow Turkey to increase her customs revenue and pledge the increase for the Bagdad Railway guarantees;

2nd. To secure for the Bagdad Railway line as large a share as possible of the Indian mail and passenger service, as soon as a route shall be established viâ the Persian Gulf shorter than viâ Suez;

3rd. To provide at Koweit all terminal facilities required, including an Ottoman custom-house.

Regarding this latter point, I wish to add that it is purely a desideratum from the economical point of view. Indeed, it would be most prejudicial to traffic on the Bagdad Railway if the Turkish custom-house should not be established at Koweit, but somewhere in the desert, say at Zobeir, which is the junction for Basra. Goods must pass the custom-house, where they are unloaded from ship to rail; to oblige merchants to unload once more, where no agents, officers, and facilities can be kept, would seriously hamper trade and largely reduce the practical value of the railway to the public and to its owners.

I beg to kindly confirm your agreeing to the above, and am, &c.

Chairman of the Ottoman Railway of Anatolia.

Berlin,   , 1903.

No. 213.

Memorandum given to Lord Revelstoke, March 23.

Formula for the Assurances to be given by His Majesty's Government.

F.O. Turkey 5322.

1. To agree to a reasonable increase of the Turkish Customs Tariff in connection with the pending negotiations for a new Commercial Treaty, and to offer no opposition to the inclusion of a portion of the increased customs revenue among the guarantees for the Bagdad Railway.

2. Should the new route offer substantial advantages over existing routes for the carriage of mails and passengers to India, to make use of it for the purpose upon terms to be agreed upon between His Majesty's Government and the Company.

3. To give assistance, not, of course, pecuniary, towards the provision of a terminus with proper facilities at or near Koweit, and co-operate in procuring convenient customs arrangements.

No. 214.

Memorandum by the Marquess of Lansdowne.

F.O. Turkey 5322.   *Foreign Office, April* 7, 1903.

I had an interview with Lord Revelstoke this morning and with Lord Revelstoke and Sir E. Cassel this afternoon upon the subject of the Bagdad Railway. Lord Revelstoke left with me the Memorandum marked "A," giving an account of the meeting which took place at Paris on March 24th. He also gave me copies of his correspondence with Mr. Gwinner marked "B," and we had some conversation as to the amendments which Lord Revelstoke proposed to insert in the assurances asked for by Mr. Gwinner.

I told Lord Revelstoke and Sir E. Cassel that a serious attempt[1] was apparently being made to discredit the enterprise, and to render it impossible for H[is] M[ajesty's] Government to associate themselves in any way with it, upon the ground that it was closely connected with the German Government and detrimental to British interests. We felt that, until we were better able to judge of the proportions which this hostile movement might assume, it would be desirable that we should avoid giving it any further encouragement. The matter would come before Parliament before the House

---

[1] [*V.* articles in *National Review* (of April) and *Spectator* (of 4, 11, 18 and 25 April), 1903.]

adjourned, and we should, therefore, be better able in a few days to decide as to our future action. My own view was that the attack was founded upon misapprehensions, and I strongly deprecated any modification of the attitude which we had hitherto assumed. I was assured by Sir E. Cassel and Lord Revelstoke that they had up to the present in no way committed H[is] M[ajesty's] Government. The formula given to Lord Revelstoke on March 23rd had been used only for the purpose of sketching " suggestions " which might be made *to* H[is] M[ajesty's] Government on the part of the British group, should the British and foreign groups be able to come to terms. It was in these circumstances entirely for us to decide whether we desired to proceed further, and if the negotiations were continued, nothing could be concluded either as to the constitution of the Board of Directors or as to other matters of detail until we had been thoroughly satisfied. They explained to me that, in their view, the participation was to take place upon a " basis of absolute equality as between English, French, and German interests," and that " no one group was to be given any superiority or control." They also explained that the Anatolian Railway would be amalgamated with the main project, and that the three members of the Board who had been described as to be nominated by the Anatolian Railway would be nominated by the whole Board. France, Germany, and England would have eight members each, and no one Power would, therefore, be able to override the wishes of the other two, which would command 16 votes out of a total of 30.

LANSDOWNE.

No. 215.

Question asked in the House of Commons, April 7, 1903 [Parl. Deb., 4th ser.,
Vol. 120, pp. 1247–8].

Mr. Gibson Bowles.—To ask the First Lord of the Treasury what communications have passed between His Majesty's Government and Foreign Governments relating to the German Anatolian or Baghdad Railway, or to its extension to Koweit on the Persian Gulf; with what Governments have such communications passed, and what is their effect, and has been their result; have His Majesty's Government been approached with any proposal for giving encouragement to the building of that railway either by guaranteeing to it a postal subsidy or in any other manner; if so, what policy do they propose to pursue in the matter; and will he lay on the Table any correspondence that has taken place.

Answer by Mr. A. J. Balfour.

There have been no formal communications between His Majesty's Government and any foreign Government on the subject of the Baghdad Railway.

The proposed railway is not, as suggested in the Question, to be a German railway.

The subject was referred to in two brief conversations, one with the French and one with the German Ambassador, about thirteen months ago. Lord Lansdowne then stated that we should not regard the undertaking with unfriendly eyes provided that British capital and British interests were placed at least on terms of equality with those of any other Power.

I am not aware that these conversations have (in the language of the Question) had any " results," or have exercised any influence on subsequent events.

Communications have been and are still going on with British capitalists on the subject. No final arrangements have been arrived at. The proposals under consideration involve no guarantee of a postal or any other subsidy. The suggestions to be made to us are, we understand (1) that British capital and British control are to be on an absolute equality with the capital and control of any other Power; (2) that, in respect to the negotiations which are now going on with the Turkish Government for a new

Commercial Treaty (and which, quite apart from the Bagdad Railway, raise the question of increasing the Turkish Customs), His Majesty's Government should not object to a reasonable increase in these duties, although a part of the increase is to be used in guaranteeing a railway so important for the commercial interests of Turkey; (3) that, if the railway should prove to be a substantially better route for conveying the mails to India, it may be used for conveying those mails, on terms to be agreed upon hereafter; (4) that His Majesty's Government should assist, not by money or the promise of money, but by their good offices in providing a proper terminus at or near Koweit.

These suggestions will be carefully considered.[1]

[1] [V. further discussion, *Parl. Deb.*, 4th ser., Vol. 120, pp. 1358–78, of 8th April.]

No. 216.

Memorandum by the Marquess of Lansdowne.

The Bagdad Railway.

F.O. Turkey 5322.   *Foreign Office, April 14, 1903.*

. . . . Subject to the satisfactory adjustment of these points,[1] which might be examined in detail by a small Committee not necessarily composed of Members of the Cabinet, I hope the Cabinet will authorise the British group to proceed with the negotiation.

Although our abstention may have the effect of retarding the completion of the line, I feel little doubt that it will eventually be made. That it should be made without British participation would, to my mind, be a national misfortune. It will be a most important highway to the East. It will shorten the journey to India by about three days. It will open up new regions, some of which will certainly prove rich and productive. It will have a terminus in the Persian Gulf, in which our interests are supreme. I submit that we ought not to let such a line be made over our heads; and that we should insist upon having our full share in its control, as well as in any advantages to be derived from its construction.

But for the anti-German fever from which the country is suffering, I am convinced that we should be unanimously supported in holding and acting upon these views, nor, so far as I am able to judge, has the attempt to discredit us for having consented to examine the project with an open mind produced much effect on the public.

The alternative policy appears to me to be attended with serious difficulties. It is, I understand, suggested that we might oppose the increase of the Turkish Tariff, a part of which increase will be appropriated for the purpose of providing the indispensable Turkish guarantee. We have, however (in July, 1900), already informed the Turkish Government that we are prepared to accept the proposed increase (from 8 to 11 per cent.) on certain conditions, and I am told that, in the opinion of the Board of Trade, such an increase would not, if fairly levied, materially hamper the more important branches of British trade. We should at any rate, I conceive, find ourselves in a very false and embarrassing position were we—perhaps in concert with Russia—to oppose the revision of the Tariff solely for the purpose of obstructing a great and useful enterprise, warmly supported by other Powers.

An attempt to block the line at the Persian Gulf end might be equally difficult. Koweit is not the only spot at which a terminus can be found, and if the Sultan pleases to grant a débouché, say at Umkasr, a few miles to the north of the Sheikh's territory, it might not be easy for us to resist. We are, I take it, not prepared to sterilise the Persian Gulf so far as the flow of commerce is concerned, and I do not believe that

[1] [V. Draft letter received from Messrs. Baring on the 20th March, p. 184. The earlier part of the despatch refers to a memorandum by Sir T. Sanderson, not reproduced.]

we should be allowed to veto a commercial port at the terminus of the new line. But if we abstain from participation, or if the line is made in spite of us, that port would be a foreign port at the end of a foreign line, and we should not find it easy to regulate its management; we should be told that those who had paid the piper were entitled to call the tune.

There remains the policy of neutrality. "Why," it is said, " need we declare ourselves? The line may not be built, or may, at all events, not be finished for many a long day. Do not let us announce at this stage that we will on certain conditions agree to the appropriation of a part of the yield of the increased Customs Tariff, or that we will give facilities at Koweit. It will be time enough for us to show our hand as to the former point when the Company actually approaches the Turkish Government, and as to the latter point, when the line is nearing the Gulf. As to the mails, we shall always send them by the shortest route."

A policy of this kind is, no doubt, open to us, but its adoption means, unless I am entirely mistaken, that the British group, which is now ready to interest itself in the enterprise, will refuse to do so. The three conditions described in this paper represent, I believe, the minimum which the British houses are prepared to accept in the way of inducement. If that minimum is refused, they will withdraw. Could we in that event look forward with safety to reconquering hereafter the position which we are at this moment free to assume in regard to the line? I doubt it.

My strong conviction is that in all cases such as this, the best policy is to treat the question as one of common and international interest—an international free port, open to all, and unfortified, at Koweit would not be a source of danger to us, while its existence would be an answer to those who accuse us of desiring to treat the Persian Gulf as a British lake. If Russia desires access to the Persian Gulf, let her build a line from Erivan to Bagdad, and obtain running powers over the "Anatolian" Railway between Bagdad and Koweit. Russia would in that case build a costly and probably not very profitable Railway; we should not be any the worse, and Persia would regain her freedom of constructing Railways in other parts of her territory.

I may add that at a Conference of Representatives of the Admiralty, Foreign Office, India Office, and War Office, held in November last to consider various questions relating to Persia, the Director of Military Intelligence expressed the opinion, in which the other Members of the Conference agreed, "that it would be a great mistake to oppose the project, which we ought, on the contrary, to encourage to the best of our power, provided we can acquire a proper share in the control of the railway and of its outlet on the Persian Gulf."

L.

No. 217.

The Marquess of Lansdowne to Sir C. Scott.

F.O. Turkey 5322.
(No. 86.)   *Foreign Office, April* 14, 1903.

. . . . I took the opportunity of asking H[is] E[xcellency] the Russian Ambassador whether he had noticed the attention which our newspapers had lately been paying to the Bagdad Railway question. I explained that I was not in a position to discuss that question officially, and, as he had no doubt observed, we were as yet uncommitted. It would, however, be most interesting to me to know how he regarded the matter. My own personal feeling, I said, had always been in favour of giving an international character to these great enterprises. His Excellency said that the Russian Government had never liked the scheme, which they regarded as intended to give Germany a dangerous preponderance in Asia Minor.

I replied that I understood this feeling if the railway was indeed to be a German railway. My information was, however, to the effect that the scheme had undergone considerable modifications, and that the British financiers who were interesting themselves in the matter were to be approached on quite a different basis. France, Germany, and Great Britain were, I believed, to be offered an absolutely equal participation; and each of the three groups was to have to same number of Directors. Out of a total of thirty, eight would be assigned to Great Britain and the same number to France and Germany, the remaining six being given to the other parties interested. This arrangement would obviously put it out of the power of any one group to dominate the rest. His Excellency seemed impressed by my statement, and asked me whether I had any objection to his repeating it to the Russian Government. I said that he might do so, but I begged him to make it clear that any opinions which I had expressed were my own only, and given to him without prejudice. I did not, moreover, pretend to any knowledge of Company promotion, and I felt that I was at a disadvantage in endeavouring to explain the situation to him.

No. 218.

Memorandum communicated by Lord Revelstoke, April 21, 1903.([1])

The following Memorandum has been communicated to me by Lord Revelstoke.

L.

April 21, 1903.

In view of the public criticism which has been directed against the Bagdad Railway, it may be desirable to give a short statement of the financial aspect of the scheme from the point of view of the English group.

The Anatolian Railway from the Bosphorus to Konia, of which the Bagdad line is a continuation, has been constructed and is being worked and controlled by German interests. It has so effectually developed the districts through which it passes that the imports of grain into Constantinople, which formerly came from the Russian Black Sea ports, are now mainly carried over the Anatolian Railway.

The whole of the money for the construction of the railway (about £7,000,000) was raised by shares and bonds issued by the Railway Company, under a kilometric guarantee on the part of the Imperial Ottoman Government. The *modus operandi* with regard to the Bagdad Railway is different. The share capital for the railway is £600,000, and it is not contemplated that the Railway Company shall issue bonds. The Imperial Ottoman Government undertake to provide the means for constructing the railway by issuing their own bonds at the rate of about £10,700 per kilometre in respect of each section of 200 kilom. These bonds will bear 4 per cent. interest, with a sinking fund providing for redemption during the term of the concession (99 years), and are to be secured by the section of the line for which they are issued, and, in addition, by such other special security as shall be agreed upon between the Government and the Railway Company.

In respect of the first section of 200 kilom., an Agreement as to this special security has been arrived at with the Imperial Ottoman Government, which will pledge—

				Per Annum. £ T.
From the dimes of Konia	...	...	...	36,000
From the dimes of Ourfa and Aleppo	...	...	70,000
Total	...	...	...	...	106,000

([1]) [Original not traced. The text is taken from the *Confidential Print*.]

These dimes are being encashed by the Commission of the Imperial Ottoman Public Debt.

The British group are satisfied that the securities provided for the first section of 200 kilom. are sufficient.

Turkish Government Bonds of a similar kind have recently been successfully placed both in France and Germany, and there is every reason to suppose that the issue in respect of the first section will be readily taken by French and German investors. The English group, in the course of their negotiations, have distinctly stated their view that, at any rate for a considerable time to come, these bonds would not command a ready market in England until the earning power of the sections by which they are secured had been demonstrated.

At the end of the concession the line of railway reverts to the Imperial Ottoman Government.

The British group made it a condition that the Anatolian Railway should not remain under German control, but should be brought under the same control as that which was to be adopted in the case of the Bagdad Railway, so that the whole line from sea to sea should be under international management. Should it be found impracticable, before completion of the first section of 200 kilom., to fulfil this condition in regard to the Anatolian Railway, the British group would be free from responsibility to provide further capital.

The control was to be as follows :—

The Board to consist of 30 members—
    8 to be appointed by the English group;
    8 ,,   ,,   ,, German group;
    8 ,,   ,,   ,, French group;
    3 ,,   .,   ,, Anatolian Railway;

and the remaining three members by the Austrian and Swiss groups.

A construction Company was to be formed, in which a similar principle of control was to be adopted, provision being made for the representation of an English, German, and French firm of contractors on the Board. It was thus provided that British contractors should have an equal opportunity of participating with Continental firms in the construction of the line.

The amounts to be realised by the securities available are considered ample for carrying out the construction.

April 20, 1903.

No. 219.

Question asked in the House of Commons, April 23, 1903 [*Parl. Deb.* 4th ser. Vol. 121, p. 222].

Mr. Gibson Bowles.—I beg to ask the First Lord of the Treasury have His Majesty's Government received a copy of the Turkish Convention relating to the Anatolian Railway Company (Baghdad line), quoted by Mr. Vice-Consul Waugh in his Report dated the 9th March, 1903, as showing that the entire management of the line from Konia to the Persian Gulf is secured in German hands, independent of the nationality of the capital which might be raised to build the line, and, if so, when was it proposed to lay it upon the table of the House.

Mr. Balfour.—A copy of the convention between the Turkish Government and the Anatolian Railway Company to which my honourable friend refers is in our possession. The convention, a summary of which was published in the "Times" of yesterday, leaves the whole scheme of railway development through Asia Minor to the Persian Gulf entirely in the hands of a Company under German control. To such a Convention we have never been asked to assent, and we could not in any case be a party to it.   The alternative arrangements which have lately been under our consideration were, on the contrary, designed to place the railway, including the existing Anatolian Railway, throughout its whole length from sea to sea, under international control, and to prevent the possibility of preferential treatment for the goods or subjects of any one country.   In these arrangements it was suggested, *inter alia*, that equal powers of control, construction, and management should be given to German, French, and English interests.   After careful consideration of these proposals, His Majesty's Government have come to the conclusion that they do not give to this country sufficient security for the application of the principles above referred to; and they have therefore intimated that they are unable to give the suggested assurances with regard to the policy which they might hereafter adopt as to the conveyance of the Indian mails by the projected route, as to facilities at Koweit, or as to the appropriation of a part of the Turkish customs revenue in aid of the contemplated guarantee.

No. 220.

Sir N. O'Conor to the Marquess of Lansdowne.

Pera, April 24, 1903.

F.O. Turkey 5322.
Tel.   (No. 77.)

D. 7·10 P.M.
R. 7·30 P.M.

Director-General of Ottoman Bank informs me that Paris group hears from Berlin that British syndicate has withdrawn from Bagdad Railway.   Deplores their decision all the more as he considers participation of British and French groups would have insured the international character of railway.

No. 221.

Sir N. O'Conor to the Marquess of Lansdowne.

F.O. Turkey 5322.
(No. 217.)
My Lord,

Constantinople, D. April 28, 1903.
R. *May* 4, 1903.

I am not yet aware whether the refusal of British capitalists to participate in the Bagdad Railway enterprise is definite and final or whether the door is left open for the reconsideration of the question after the completion of the first section from Konia to Eregli.

In any case, I think it my duty to lay before your Lordship such remarks as I have to offer after a careful consideration of the various objections raised in the press and in Parliament against British participation in this enterprise.

With regard to the anti-German feeling, which has to a large extent influenced the attitude of the press and of public opinion in this matter, it is sufficient to point out that the questions involved in the construction of the Bagdad Railway affect our material interests in the regions to be traversed, and that the effect of the solution given to these questions will be felt over a long series of years.   It is, therefore, to be regretted if too much influence is exercised by movements of opinion due to causes which are probably less permanent in their character. . . . . [Details as to constitution of Company.]

. . . . It has been pointed out in the course of the discussions in the press and elsewhere that, so long as the Anatolian Railway from Haidar Pasha to Konia remains in German hands, the international character of the line from Konia onwards will not be a sufficient guarantee for impartial treatment; that the German Company will, in fact, hold the key of the door by which the through traffic must pass. This is a point of the first importance, deserving careful consideration; but an examination of the whole position will go far, at any rate, to dispel any anxiety on this account. In the first place the representatives of the Anatolian Railway Company have formally announced their readiness to vest the control of their line in the International Company at some future period; and there are sufficient guarantees for the carrying out of this undertaking in the fact that it would be open to the British Government, in the event of failure to carry it out, to refuse the promised facilities for a port in the Persian Gulf, and to withdraw their assurance as to the conveyance of the Indian mails; and also in the fact that, when the Bagdad line has been completed throughout the greater part of its length, it would be so indispensable to the prosperity of the Anatolian line that the latter could not afford to take up a hostile or exclusive attitude. This is the more certain since Haidar Pasha does not afford the only point of access. It is evident that the Bagdad line must have an exit somewhere on the Gulf of Alexandretta, and it is also clear that, by combination with the French line from Smyrna to Afioun Kerahissar or the English line from Smyrna to Dineir, a competing outlet could be secured at Smyrna.

While insisting upon the extreme importance of the eventual internationalisation of the whole line from sea to sea, I would point out that the drawbacks resulting for British commerce from the existing ownership of the Anatolian line and of the harbour at Haidar Pasha are frequently exaggerated. It has often been stated, and gains colour from the remarks in Mr. Vice-Consul Waugh's Report, that goods arriving by train at Constantinople and ferried to Haidar Pasha without breaking bulk would be specially exempted from quay dues, to which goods arriving by sea are subject. If such a provision existed, it would act unfavourably to German commerce as well as to British, since it is inconceivable that heavy goods coming from Germany should abandon cheap sea transport for the far more costly land transport. Besides, it may be assumed from the statement made in the "Times" of the 24th instant by Herr Gwinner, or some other high official of the Bagdad Railway, that no such provision does, as a matter of fact, exist.

If the Railway be regarded merely in the light of an industrial speculation, it is necessary to bear in mind that without a sufficient kilometric guarantee the construction is more than problematical, and that, supported by a kilometric guarantee, the shareholders will probably be as well or better protected from loss of their capital than in the average of such undertakings in semi-civilised countries.

No one supposes that the whole Railway will pay at once. Whatever may be the final development, many years must pass before the entire line will pay, though certain sections may be remunerative from the start.

Fears have been expressed that at one moment or another either Germany or France, or possibly both countries, may, for political reasons, come to terms with Russia and find it in their interest to make over their share, or else to buy off her hostility by supporting her claims for Russian access to the shores of the Persian Gulf. These are contingencies, however, which might arise in any case, whether England participates or not in the construction of the Railway. Indeed, an arrangement with Russia would be more urgently required, and at the same time more easy of accomplishment, if England stands out than if she participates.

As regards the probability of incurring Russian hostility, it must be remembered that French financiers have certainly not engaged themselves in the scheme without the approval of their Government, and I have reason to believe that this approval was given with the knowledge and consent of their ally. Although, therefore, it cannot be expected that Russia will view with indifference any extension of foreign, and specially perhaps, of British, influence in the region of the Gulf, it does not seem likely that this enterprise is of a nature to arouse her ill-will towards England in a specially marked degree.

For the reasons given above I can hardly anticipate that it will be the policy of His Majesty's Government to oppose by all such means as are available the construction of this Railway. Such a policy would be, in fact, the exact opposite of that which has been almost invariably pursued by Great Britain, namely, the policy of supporting the extension in all parts of the world of the means of communication and commercial intercourse. Our attitude will, I presume, be one of neutrality; and I anticipate that, in that case, the Railway will be built, perhaps with some delay and increased difficulty, but still, that it will eventually be completed. The German side of the dual partnership will certainly be the stronger, and there will be an increasing tendency for the whole of this great Railway, and eventually of the other railways in Asiatic Turkey, to be drawn into the German orbit.

Nor must it be forgotten that the Railway Concession carries with it many valuable privileges and advantages. Apart from the large orders for materials for railway construction, &c., it secures extensive mining rights on each side of the line, the right of navigation of the Tigris and Euphrates during the construction of the railway, a Concession which will probably be unlimitedly extended, a commercial outlet either at Koweit or elsewhere in the Persian Gulf, an exceptionally favourable position in the future for all enterprise connected with the irrigation of Mesopotamia, &c. Moreover, it can hardly be supposed that no effort will be made to supplant British navigation in its privileged position in the Persian Gulf, and to take advantage of the opportunity to compete with British shipping in those waters.

It is also to be feared that the preponderance of foreign Powers in the valley of the Tigris will react upon British influence in Western Persia in the same way as England's exclusion from a public enterprise so intimately connected with the progress and development of the country will affect her prestige and position throughout Asia Minor.

I have, &c.
N. R. O'CONOR.

No. 222.

Sir F. Lascelles to the Marquess of Lansdowne.

F.O. Turkey 5322.
(No. 110.)   *Berlin,* D. *May* 8, 1903.
My Lord,   R. *May* 11, 1903.

· Your Lordship's speech delivered in the House of Lords on the 5th instant has attracted considerable attention in the German press, and I have the honour to bring to your notice in particular an article in the "National Zeitung" entitled "England and the Persian Gulf."

This article begins by quoting your Lordship's declaration that Great Britain would "regard the establishment of a naval base or a fortified port in the Persian Gulf by any other Power as a very grave menace to British interests." This warning cannot be directed against Germany, who has no territorial ambitions on the Persian Gulf, and the statement that British "policy should be directed to protect and promote British trade in Persian waters" without excluding the legitimate trade of other Powers is not only in accordance with British tradition, but from a German point of view satisfactory.

Note is then taken of the formulation of the axiom, as it is called, that political supremacy in the Persian Gulf is a vital interest of Great Britain. This the "National Zeitung" reviews in connection with the growth and strength of Russian influence in Persia. It regards your Lordship's language as a proof that a change is in process, and that the commercial negotiations at present taking place at Tehran will result in a manner favourable to our position in Persia.

In North Persia it is too late for us to try to weaken Russian supremacy. In the South it is otherwise. The question of South Persia is bound up with that of the railways in future to be built there. Whatever, from an objective point of view, may be the legality of the British claim on Persia to build such railways, one thing, the article considers, is certain in fact. Your Lordship has declared to the world our intention to build them. For this reason the question of the Bagdad Railway is all important for Great Britain. It will certainly be built, and it is for us to see that below Bagdad it shall be under British control. This has already been remarked in England. Hence the proposal which appeared in the "Times," to agree to the project on condition that the building of the line is begun at both ends at once. Further, the needs not only of Indian defence but of Indian expansion, as recent utterances of Lord Curzon have hinted, make the English lay particular value on the lands about the Persian Gulf. And in the same connection engineers of repute have lately made an appeal to British enterprise representing the irrigation of Mesopotamia as a proper field for the outlay of capital. Everything in fine points to the preponderance of British interests in the Persian Gulf, and your Lordship's speech laying emphasis on these will be well received.

I have, &c.
FRANK C. LASCELLES.

No. 223.

Sir N. O'Conor to the Marquess of Lansdowne.

F.O. Turkey 5322.
(No. 380.) Confidential.   *Therapia*, D. *July* 4, 1903.
My Lord,   R. *July* 13, 1903.

With reference to my telegram No. 106 of the 30th ultimo, I have the honour to report to your Lordship that I learnt from M. Constans two days ago that, after careful examination of the Memorandum presented to him by M. Auboyneau, acting on behalf of the Ottoman Bank, M. Delcassé refused his consent to the Agreement made between them and the Deutsche Bank in regard to the Bagdad Railway, and at the same time asked M. Constans for his opinion.

The French Ambassador, in replying, stated that the conditions did not seem to him to secure equal participation for his countrymen.

Forty per cent. of the capital was allotted to each financial group, but as the remaining 20 per cent. was distributed as to 10 per cent. to the Austrians, 5 per cent. to the Swiss, 2 per cent. to a Milan group of bankers, and 3 per cent. to a Constantinople group, all of whom were, he believed, more or less directly under the influence of the Deutsche Bank, the assurance of equal participation was illusory. Besides this, I understood M. Constans to say that a German should represent the Board of Directors on the Administrative Council. This Council was apparently to be composed of twenty-six members, ten each to the French and Germans, and the others to represent the smaller units who were affiliated to the Deutsche Bank, while the Ottoman Government were to have two Delegates.

M. Constans went on to tell me that at first M. Delcassé was inclined simply to notify his non-acceptance of the proposals and his refusal to allow a quotation on the Paris Bourse, but eventually it was decided, after laying the matter before the Council of Ministers, to state formally the demands of the French Government, and to leave the Germans to accept or refuse them as they pleased.

He had not yet heard the answer from Berlin, but he believed the German Embassy here gave it out that the French proposals were unacceptable, and that they would probably come to terms eventually with the English.

His Excellency added that he was a strong advocate of the scheme, provided that a British Syndicate also participated, and he was even desirous to come to an arrangement with the Germans alone, though not so strongly as with the participation of England. But he was now afraid that if such serious differences showed themselves even before the Company got to work, there would be little chance of the two groups working harmoniously later on, and he thought it likely, on the whole, that his Government would refuse their sanction and approval.

He was told that the German Embassy wished him to report to his Government that if his Government refused to participate it would have a baneful effect upon the good relations between the two countries which the German Government were so anxious to bring about, but he did not attach any importance to this report, which was, moreover, one that concerned his Government rather than the Embassy.

Whatever was the end of the negotiations, he thought the Germans would construct the Konia–Eregli section by themselves; but whether in this case the Turkish Unified Bonds would be given a quotation on the Paris Bourse, or his Government would agree to a modification of the customs dues, was another matter.

In connection with the general question of the Bagdad Railway, I beg to report to your Lordship that I have been indirectly informed by a gentleman who is in close touch with the German Embassy, and gives me to understand that he speaks with authority, that it is considered at Berlin and in Government circles that M. Gwinner was too exacting in the terms and conditions which he sought to get accepted by the British Syndicate; that the Germans are now inclined to allow them to construct the Persian Gulf end of the line, provided they are allowed to retain the Haidar Pasha–Konia sections; and that it is hoped an understanding on this basis may be eventually brought about.

It is possible that some such views may be entertained by certain financiers at Berlin. If so, they are probably indicative of the swing of public opinion, and possibly due in part to the vexation and disappointment felt at the breakdown of the French negotiations.

While it is, perhaps, right that I should mention the matter to your Lordship more as gossip than otherwise, I do not think the proposal is by any means a definite one, inspired by any responsible authority.

There are, perhaps, political wire-pullers who would be only too glad to launch in the press some story of fresh negotiations between British and German financiers which would considerately appear about the time of President Loubet's visit to England.

I have, &c.
N. R. O'CONOR.

No. 224.

Sir N. O'Conor to the Marquess of Lansdowne.

F.O. Turkey 5322.
(No. 831.) Confidential.   *Constantinople*, D. *December* 15, 1903.
My Lord,   R. *December* 21, 1903.

Dr. Gwinner, President of the Deutsche Bank, called upon me two days ago, shortly after his arrival here, to preside at to-day's meeting of the Bagdad Railway Company.

After expressing his regret that his negotiations with the British Syndicate last spring had not resulted in their participation in the Bagdad Railway, he said that he attributed the breakdown entirely to the sudden ebullition of public opinion, which had deterred His Majesty's Government as well as the Syndicate from proceeding with the business. The anti-German feeling prevalent in England at that moment no doubt contributed to this result; but he believed that if the question had been fully explained to the British public, and they had been made aware of the conditions offered by the Deutsche Bank, their views would have been considerably altered, and the way left open for a resumption of negotiations at a future and not very distant date. The members of the British Syndicate did not wish to expose themselves to the ill-feeling consequent upon proceeding with negotiations, which were viewed so unfavourably both in political circles and in the city. Sir Clinton Dawkins was already tainted by his connection with the Morgan group, who were at the moment unpopular on account of the shipping combine, and Sir E. Cassel, who, though now a naturalised British subject, was at one time a German, was also in a delicate position. Lord Revelstoke was the only representative of English finance who had not some reason to proceed with extreme caution; but even he did not care to face the outcry which was set going by the "National Review" and other papers, who were clamouring for an understanding with Russia.

Mr. Gwinner proceeded to say that he had practically accepted the terms and conditions laid down in Sir E. Cassel's letter, and had agreed to amalgamate the Anatolian section in the Bagdad Railway. He had done so with the consent of his Government, and he had only altered a single word in Sir E. Cassel's proposals by substituting "Ottoman" before customs with reference to the Koweit terminus; and he was quite prepared, had he been pressed, to give up even this amendment. The Railway Company did not care in the least whether Koweit was a British Protectorate occupied by British troops, but they were anxious to avoid goods and passengers being subjected to two Customs inspections as might be the case were they to have a Customs at Koweit and another somewhere in the desert outside the Koweit area.

I said that in face of the strong exhibition of public feeling which had no doubt, in great measure, prevented an understanding between the Syndicates, it seemed to me that there was still a way in which an arrangement could have been brought about to our mutual advantage, namely, by the Deutsche Bank consenting to give the construction of the Persian Gulf end to the British.

Mr. Gwinner replied that for his part he would have been quite willing to agree to this, but if he did so, he could not have been expected to give up the Anatolian section while leaving the Persian Gulf end to England. Apart from this, there was a political side to the question; and he was unable to say with certitude whether his Government would have been willing to agree to an arrangement which would be viewed with great displeasure by Russia, and possibly place them in a delicate position towards that Power.

Mr. Gwinner added that the French Government had declined to sanction the participation of the French group, and had refused a quotation on the Paris Bourse for their shares. The first meeting of the Bagdad Railway Company would be held on the 15th instant, when the Board of Directors and the Administrative Council would be chosen.

Dr. Gwinner evidently did not consider that the unofficial character of the participation of the French group affected materially the German position, or need cause them any anxiety.

I have, &c.
N. R. O'CONOR.

MINUTE.

It is to be observed that he admits frankly that the insensate outcry which arose against the scheme had the effect of choking off the British financiers quite as much as the British Government. If it had not been for the "scuttle" of the financiers, I should have been in favour of sticking to our position.

I have never believed that we could have come to terms on the basis of securing the Gulf end of the line for ourselves. We should have had all the other Powers on our backs at once. As Dr. Gwinner points out, we could not have expected to attain the "internationalisation" of the Anatolian Railway, if we had insisted upon such a condition.—L.

[ED. NOTE.—The sharp controversy during 1903 arising out of the grant of a preference to Great Britain by the Canadian Government is sufficiently described in *Correspondence with the Governments of Belgium and Germany*, 1903. *Accounts and Papers.* 1903 (*Cd.* 1630), LXXV, p. 31.]

CHAPTER XIII.
RUSSIAN POLICY IN THE FAR EAST (1903-4).

No. 225.

Memorandum by Mr. Langley.

Engagements of Russia as to respecting the Independence and Integrity of the Chinese Empire.

F.O. China 1621.   *October 26, 1903.*

On the 28th of August, 1900, the Russian Chargé d'Affaires made a communication as to the intentions of the Russian Government in North-East China.([1])

After referring to the fundamental principles which Russia had proposed as a basis of common action when it had been decided to send troops to China, and which included—

1. The maintenance of the existing system of Government in China;
2. The exclusion of everything which might lead to the partition of the Empire;

M. Lessar stated that, with regard to these principles, an agreement has been come to between nearly all the Powers. The Imperial Government, having no other object in view, remained faithful to these principles, and intended in the future to adhere strictly to the programme laid down therein.

He said that directly the pacification of Manchuria was attained, and the necessary measures had been taken to ensure the security of the railroad, Russia would not fail to withdraw her troops from Chinese territory, provided that such action did not meet with obstacles caused by the proceedings of other Powers.

On the 6th of February, 1901, Sir C. Scott reported that Count Lamsdorff had denied the allegations in the press that Russia was engaged in concluding a Convention with China which would give Russia new rights and a virtual Protectorate in Southern Manchuria, or that the Emperor had any intention of departing in any way from the assurances which he had publicly given that Manchuria would be entirely restored to its former condition in the Chinese Empire as soon as circumstances admitted of it.([2])

When it came to the final and complete evacuation of Manchuria the Russian Government would be obliged to obtain from the Central Government of China an effective guarantee against the recurrence of the recent attack on her frontier and the destruction of her railway, but had no intention of seeking this guarantee in any acquisition of territory, or of an actual or virtual Protectorate over Manchuria.

At the close of the abortive negotiations for a Manchurian Convention with China, the Russian Government, in April 1901, published an official communiqué on the subject of Russian policy in China.([3])

They gave a history of events since the outbreak of the Boxer disturbances, and concluded by stating that, as obstacles had been placed in the way of China concluding an arrangement with Russia, it was impossible to at once take the measures which had been in view for the gradual evacuation of Manchuria.

While remaining, therefore, faithful to the programme which had been so often

---

([1]) [To Sir C. Scott, No. 190A, of the 28th August.]
([2]) [Sir C. Scott, No. 41, of the 6th February, 1901.]
([3]) [Sir C. Scott, No. 100, of the 6th April, 1901.]

formulated, the Imperial Government would await with calmness the further progress of events.

On the 19th of March, 1902, the Russian Chargé d'Affaires communicated a Memorandum stating that the Governments of France and Russia having received communication of the Anglo-Japanese Convention, concluded for the purpose (among other things) of maintaining the independence of China and Corea, had been fully satisfied at finding in it the affirmation of the essential principles which they had themselves repeatedly declared to constitute, and which remained the basis of their policy.[4]

On the 8th of April, 1902, Russia signed with China an Agreement respecting Manchuria. One Article of this Convention provided for the evacuation of Manchuria in three sections, the last of which was to be evacuated on the 8th October, 1903.

Sir C. Scott reported on the 27th April, 1903, that Count Lamsdorff had informed the United States Ambassador at St. Petersburgh, who had made enquiries about the new demands upon China which Russia was making as conditions of evacuation, that he might telegraph to the United States Government the most positive assurance that the Russian Government would faithfully keep to its pledges in regard to Manchuria, as given in the official announcement made by the Emperor's authority, and to the rights of other Powers.[5]

Treaty Rights of other Powers in Manchuria.

Other Powers have most-favoured-nation treatment in Manchuria, which in our case is enjoyed under Article LIV of the Treaty of Tien-tsin, which runs :—

> "The British Government and its subjects are hereby confirmed in all privileges, immunities, and advantages conferred on them by previous Treaties; and it is hereby expressly stipulated that the British Government and its subjects will be allowed free and equal participation in all privileges, immunities, and advantages that may have been, or may be hereafter, granted by His Majesty the Emperor of China to the Government or subjects of any other nation."

[4] [Memorandum communicated the 19th March, 1903, by Russian Chargé d'Affaires.]
[5] [Sir C. Scott, No. 119, of the 27th April, 1903.]

No. 226.

Sir C. MacDonald to the Marquess of Lansdowne.

F.O. Japan 565.
(No. 50.)   Very Confidential.   *Tokyo,* D. *April* 27, 1903.
My Lord,   R. *June* 2, 1903.

On the 7th instant I had a visit from Major-General Tamura, who came acting under instructions from Marshal Baron Oyama, Chief of the General Staff, to inform me of the movements of Russian troops on the Corean frontier and the neighbourhood of Newchwang. No great importance was attached to these movements which Marshal Oyama thought were connected with telegraph operations on the Corean frontier; on the following day I received a repetition of Mr. Townley's telegram, No. 79, to your Lordship containing similar information as to movements of Russian troops, and stating that the Russian Chargé d'Affaires in Peking had told Prince Ching that this movement was intended to counteract a threatened Japanese movement on the frontier. On enquiry at the General Staff I was informed that there was absolutely no foundation for this statement. The above information I at once telegraphed to your Lordship. For several days following there were many rumours in the press as to movements of Russian troops in Manchuria, and the question as to whether the Russians would carry out their assurances respecting the evacuation was generally discussed.

On the 23rd instant Mr. Townley's telegram to your Lordship informed me that the Russians had demanded seven conditions from China before carrying out any further evacuation of Manchuria. The Japanese Foreign Office informed me that they had received similar news, but that the conditions were six in number; further enquiries were being made in Peking.

This morning Baron Komura handed me a full text of Russian demands which had been received the previous evening, and which he said has been very confidentially communicated to Mr. Uchida (Japanese Representative in Peking) by Mr. Lien Feng of the Wai-wu Pu; these conditions had been telegraphed to Mr. Hayashi in London, with instructions to show them to your Lordship. Mr. Uchida had been instructed to protest in general terms against the Russian demands which the Japanese Government considered highly objectionable, as being derogatory to the sovereignty of China and detrimental to the interests of the Powers; but Baron Komura informed me that specific protests respecting each particular Article of the demands were being prepared by him. The Japanese Government had also approached the American Government, and Mr. Hay had stated to the Japanese Representative in Washington that the points which the American Government objected to were Article III as to the non-opening of new Treaty ports in Manchuria, and Article IV relative to the engagement of foreigners. The American Representative in St. Petersburgh had been instructed to ask the Russian Government for explanations respecting the above two points. I said that it would be important if the American Government could be induced to stand in line on this question with the Japanese and British Governments, for Russia seemed anxious not to alienate the sympathy of the American people, and the Russian Government appeared more inclined to listen to representations made by America than those made by any other Power. Baron Komura said this was undoubtedly the case.

His own opinion was that the Civil part of the Government in Russia—in other words, the peace party—who had arranged the Convention entailing the evacuation of Manchuria, "had been compelled by the military party in Russia to put forward these demands to 'save their face.'"

His Excellency did not think that the demands were seriously put forward, and he thought that China would in all probability, fortified by the protests of Japan, England, and perhaps America, refuse the Russian demands, in which case, Russia would in all probability remain in occupation of Manchuria.

This would, of course, mean an absolute breach of their Convention with China, and a disregard of all assurances given to the various Powers. A permanent occupation of Manchuria by Russia would, in due course, mean a permanent occupation of Corea by the same Power, which would threaten the very existence of Japan. Consequently, said his Excellency, it behoved Japan to consider whether the time had not come to speak, for if she remained silent now and allowed Russia to remain in possession, the occasion for speaking might never occur again, and Japan's silence at this juncture would certainly impair her rights to assert herself later.

His Excellency spoke with unwonted seriousness, and said, as I was taking my leave, that he considered the situation exceedingly grave. He added that of course the views he had expressed were his personal ones, and no decision had yet been come to in the matter by the Cabinet. I said that I hoped that the earliest information would be given to His Majesty's Government, should the Japanese Government contemplate taking a decision, and his Excellency assured me that this would be done.

Though Baron Komura was careful to state that the views he had expressed were his personal ones, there is no doubt whatever that they are shared by the Government and the Japanese people, and, judging from all the information at my command, it is certain that, should Russia not carry out her promises with regard to evacuation, the very gravest consequences may ensue.([1])

I have, &c.

CLAUDE M. MACDONALD.

([1]) [In the despatch No. 73 of the 10th June, 1903, Lord Lansdowne approved the language held to Baron Komura as reported here.]

No. 227.

The Marquess of Lansdowne to Sir M. Herbert.

F.O. America 2525.   *Foreign Office, April* 28, 1903.
Tel. (No. 127.)   D. 7·20 P.M.

Your telegram No. 138 of April 27th : Evacuation of Manchuria.

British Ambassador at St. Petersburg reports that United States Ambassador has been instructed to ascertain whether reported demands are accurate, and if so, to point out clearly and formally that especially the first two are diametrically opposed to interests, intentions and rights of United States, as officially explained to Russian Government and incompatible with assurances given by them. This version of instructions received by United States Ambassador at St. Petersburg seems to go considerably further than that given in your telegram. But in any case you may assure United States Government that it is the desire and intention of His Majesty's Government to act in accordance with what we conceive to be the policy of the United States, viz., to open China impartially to the commerce of all the world, to maintain her integrity and independence, and to insist upon the fulfilment by the Chinese Government of Treaty and other obligations contracted towards us.

We fully appreciate reasons for which United States Government prefer to act independently, but in pursuit of the above policy we are prepared to follow the United States step by step up to any point that may be necessary for the protection of our common interests in China. We hope United States Government will keep us fully informed of any action which they may take. You should explain to the Secretary of State that statement of Russian Ambassador that second condition is necessitated by Sir R. Hart's desire to flood the country with his employees is absurd. United States Government is no doubt aware that for some time past Sir R. Hart has been admitting foreigners in large numbers to the Chinese service, and he has quite recently appointed a Russian as commissioner at Newchwang.

We understand that out of thirty-five members of the service engaged since June 1899, only four have been British.

[Paraphrased with omissions, *Accounts and Papers,* 1904 (*Cd.* 1936), CX, p. 190.]

No. 228.

The Marquess of Lansdowne to Sir C. MacDonald.

F.O. Japan 564.
(No. 47.) Confidential.
Sir,   *Foreign Office, April* 29, 1903.

The Japanese Minister communicated to this Office on the 27th instant a Memorandum, a copy of which is enclosed, containing an account of the demands made by the Russian Government on China as the conditions of the evacuation of the second portion of Manchuria.

Viscount Hayashi called upon me to-day, and I repeated to him the substance of my conversation with the Russian Ambassador, who had visited me earlier in the afternoon. I also read to him my telegram to you of the 28th instant No. 12.

The Minister told me that the information upon which the above-mentioned Memorandum has been based was derived from Prince Ching, and he did not see what object the Prince could have had in inventing such statements. Viscount Hayashi told me that in his belief the Russian proposals had been inspired by General Alexeieff, Russian Governor at Port Arthur. M. Plançon was an extremely able man, who had been Head of the Asiatic Department in the Foreign Office at St. Petersburg, but he did not consider that it was likely that he had initiated these proceedings.

Viscount Hayashi promised to keep me fully informed as to the intentions of the Japanese Government.

I am, &c.
LANSDOWNE.

[Last three paragraphs omitted in *Accounts and Papers*, 1904 (*Cd.* 1936), CX, p. 192. Memo. following reproduced intact.]

Enclosure in No. 228.

Memorandum communicated by Viscount Hayashi, April 27, 1903.([1])

Russian Demands on China.

1. No portion of territory restored to China by Russia, especially at Newchwang and in the Valley of Liao-ho, shall be leased or sold to any other Power under any circumstances; if such sale or lease to other Power be concluded, Russia will take decisive steps in order to safeguard her own interests, as she considers such sale or lease to be a menace to her.

2. The system of Government actually existing throughout Mongolia shall not be altered, as such alteration will tend to produce regrettable state of affairs as the uprising of the people and the disturbances along the Russian frontier; the utmost precaution shall be taken in that direction.

3. China shall engage herself not to open, of her own accord, new ports or towns in Manchuria, without giving previous notice to the Russian Government, nor shall she permit foreign Consuls to reside in those towns or ports.

4. The authority of foreigners who may be engaged by China for the administration of any affairs whatever, shall not be permitted to extend over any affairs in Northern Provinces (including Chile), where Russia has the predominant interests.

In case China desires to engage foreigners for the administration of affairs in Northern Provinces, special offices shall be established for the control of Russians; for instance, no authority over the mining affairs of Mongolia and Manchuria shall be given to foreigners who may be engaged by China for the administration of mining affairs; such authority shall be left entirely in the hands of Russian experts.

5. As long as there exists telegraph line at Newchwang and Port Arthur, the Newchwang–Peking line shall be maintained, as the telegraph line at Newchwang and Port Arthur and throughout Shangkieng Province is under Russian control, and its connection with her line on the Chinese telegraph poles at Newchwang, Port Arthur, and Peking is of the utmost importance.

6. After restoring Newchwang to the Chinese local authorities, the Customs receipt there shall, as at present, be deposited with the Russo-Chinese Bank.

7. After the evacuation of Manchuria, the rights which have been acquired in Manchuria by Russian subjects and foreign Companies during Russian occupation shall remain unaffected; moreover, as Russia is duty-bound to ensure the life of the

([1]) [A longer and different statement in Telegrams 98–9, Very Confidential, Townley to Lansdowne of the 23rd April, 1903.]

people residing at all the regions traversed by the Railway, it is necessary, in order to provide against the spread of epidemic diseases in the Northern Provinces by the transportation of passengers and goods by railway train, to establish at Newchwang a quarantine office after the restoration of the place to China; the Russian Civil Administrators will consider the best means to attain that end. Russians only shall be employed at the posts of Commissioner of Customs and Customs Physician, and they shall be placed under the control of the Inspector-General of the Imperial Maritime Customs. These officials shall perform their duties conscientiously, shall protect the interests of the Imperial Maritime Customs, and shall exhaust their efforts in preventing the spread of those diseases into the Russian territories. Permanent Sanitary Board, presided by Customs Taotai, shall be established. The foreign Consuls, Commissioner of Customs, Customs Physician, and Agent of Chinese Eastern Railway Company, shall be Councillors of the Board. As regards the establishment of the Board and the management of its affairs the Customs Taotai shall consult with the Russian Consul, and the Customs Taotai shall devise the best means to obtain funds necessary for the purpose.

April 27, 1903.

No. 229.

The Marquess of Lansdowne to Sir C. Scott.

F.O. Russia 1663.
Tel. (No. 55.) *Foreign Office, May 2, 1903.*
My telegram No. 45 [of April 29th : Evacuation of Manchuria].
Russian Ambassador has informed me that the information which has reached His Majesty's Government as to the alleged Russian demands it not at all correct.
The discussions proceeding at Peking concern Manchuria alone, and have reference to certain guarantees indispensable to secure the most important Russian interests in the Province, after the withdrawal of the troops.
Measures which might tend to exclude foreign Consuls or obstruct foreign commerce are far from entering into the intentions of the Russian Government, who consider the development of foreign commerce one of the main objects for which they have constructed lines of Railway in these parts.

No. 230.

Communication from Viscount Hayashi..

Japanese Minister for Foreign Affairs to Viscount Hayashi.

F.O. Japan 572. *May 4, 1903.*
On the 29th April last the Russian Chargé d'Affaires at Peking produced to Prince Ch'ing, who expressed to him China's refusal of the new Russian demands in regard to Manchuria, a note requesting three assurances of the Chinese Government, that the Valley of the Liao-Ho shall not be alienated to any other country, that no new ports or towns in Manchuria shall be opened to foreign commerce and the residence of foreign Consuls, and that the Governmental system in Mongolia shall not be changed.
The Chargé d'Affaires at the same time added that, should these assurances be given, Russian military party would be appeased, and the Manchurian evacuation executed without any delay as the necessary preparations had been already made.
The Prince at once refused to comply with the request for the reason that such assurances concern China's sovereignty.

The Chargé d'Affaires then asked for a written reply to that effect as he would like to communicate with the Russian military authorities in Manchuria.

This was given to him by the Prince on the following day.

It is learnt also from the Prince that the Chinese Minister at St. Petersburgh has telegraphed to his Government that the Russian Foreign Office stated that it was quite unaware of the new Russian demands on China, and that the question should be settled at Peking.

You are hereby instructed to express to the British Government that under these circumstances it is highly desirable that the Representatives in China of the Powers who have warned her not to consent to the Russian demands should be constantly on the watch in regard to Russian action at Peking.

No. 231.

Sir C. Scott to the Marquess of Lansdowne.

F.O. Russia 1660.
(No. 136.)   St. Petersburgh, D. May 14, 1903.
My Lord,   R. May 18, 1903.

(¹) . . . . Reference having been made to the influence of public opinion and the press, Count Lamsdorff said that he had been thoroughly astounded and perplexed by the exaggerated reports and the campaign of accusations of Russia which had been appearing in the English and American press lately.

He said that M. Witte had burst into his room a few days ago in a state of complete bewilderment, and asked him if he could in any way account for the reports of military movements to the Yalu River and reoccupation and fortification of Newchwang, which had created something like a panic on the Exchange of St. Petersburgh.

Count Lamsdorff had been utterly unable to account for them, as he knew of a certainty that no military movements were likely to take place except in preparation for embarking those troops which were to be withdrawn from Manchuria by sea. He was not aware of Newchwang having been yet evacuated, and there was certainly no intention to send any more troops there.

Count Lamsdorff went on to say that he had ascertained that all these false reports had been telegraphed in the same form to different parts of the world, and, he believed, originated from some Agency at Yokohama, possibly in order to carry out some *coup* on foreign Exchanges, but the attempt was a most mischievous and dangerous one; equally unaccountable were the reports which had been disseminated from Peking of Russian designs, and of the conclusion of a new Convention with China containing further detailed conditions for the evacuation of Manchuria.

Nothing of the kind was, he said, taking place; the Russian Chargé d'Affaires had simply been in negotiation with the Chinese Government in order to obtain certain indispensable guarantees in accordance with the engagements which China had undertaken under the Manchurian Convention, for the adequate protection of Russia's important interests in that province, the protection of her frontier, and of the costly railway which Russia had constructed to Port Arthur, and of the commercial interests of that important artery of trade.

There was no intention of departing from the published declarations and assurances which had been given with regard to the evacuation of Manchuria, or infringing on the Treaty rights of other Powers, and far from desiring to place any obstacle whatever in the way of foreign trade with Manchuria, the Russian Government in the interest of their own railway were only too anxious to forward its development by every possible means.

(¹) [Refers to conversation with Count Benckendorff.]

I said that I had certainly read all the sensational reports to which his Excellency had been referring, some of them of a very confused and contradictory nature, but that I had had no occasion or authority to mention them to him, still less to imply the slightest doubt of the Emperor's intentions to strictly carry out the engagements with China and the public assurances and declarations which had been repeatedly given in connection with them.

It was true, however, that these reports had created great sensation in England, and I saw that your Lordship had been grateful to his Excellency for authorising Count Benckendorff to give him the reassuring explanations which had been communicated to Parliament.

Count Lamsdorff said that he had been glad to be able to do so, and he seemed to thoroughly appreciate the manner in which this delicate incident had been treated by His Majesty's Government.

He said, however, that as regarded public opinion and the press in England, he thought that the exercise of a little common sense should have satisfied any one that if it had even been considered in the interest of Russia to take permanent possession of Manchuria or annex it to the Empire she could easily have done so on the outbreak of the disturbances, on the just ground that China had attacked and practically made war on Russian territory.

I said that, had she done so, I was afraid no true friend of Russia would have been able to compliment her on the wisdom or value of such an embarrassing addition to her responsibilites.

Count Lamsdorff smiled, and said that they would be quite right, and that it was for that very reason that he had resolutely refused ever to countenance such an idea, as the acquisition of Manchuria would be a hindrance rather than a gain, and it would not secure more protection for their frontier or railway than they hoped to secure by the arrangements which they were making with China in view of the withdrawal of the temporary occupation.

Count Lamsdorff complained especially of the London "Times," which, he said, seemed to be inspired by irreconcileable hatred and suspicion of Russia.

I said that it was certainly very disagreeable to be constantly the subject of odious and unjust charges in the public press, and we could sympathise with him, as during the late war in South Africa there appeared to be no charge or suspicion too monstrous to be credited against our Government and troops by the foreign press, and the only thing to be done was to remain calm and hope that time would do justice.

I did not think the "Times" was the only offender in this instance, but that journal had recently displayed a feverish anxiety to be credited with having foreign correspondents, particularly in the Far East, much earlier and better informed as to what was going on than the official Representatives of the Foreign Office, and, indeed, to be itself more capable of directing the foreign relations of the country than the Crowns responsible advisers.

The United States' Ambassador, to whom I related some of Count Lamsdorff's observations, saw his Excellency immediately afterwards in order to take leave of him before going on a short holiday to the United States. Mr. McCormick told me afterwards that Count Lamsdorff begged him when he saw Mr. Hay to repeat to him the explanations which he had already given of Russia's real intentions in regard to Manchuria, and to contradict emphatically all reports of designs hostile to the interests and trade of other countries in that part of China.

I have, &c.
CHARLES S. SCOTT.

[Reproduced as an extract with some alterations in *Accounts and Papers*, 1904 (*Cd.* 1936), CX, pp. 201–2.]

No. 232.

Mr. Townley to the Marquess of Lansdowne.

Peking, June 20, 1903.

F.O. China 1603.   D. 6 P.M.
Tel. (No. 158.)   R. 4 P.M.

Manchuria.

I saw Prince Ching yesterday. He told me that arrangement would shortly be concluded which would preserve Manchuria to China without losing any of her sovereign rights. He could not give me details. I warned him that the Treaty rights of other Powers must be respected and that any concessions to Russia calculated to threaten British possessions in Asia would be strongly opposed. He gave me assurances on both points. Japanese Minister will press for the terms of the arrangement as to the opening of treaty ports. China, he said, will open them if she sees fit after the Russian evacuation. Prince said that Newchwang Customs duties will be paid into the Customs Bank as before as soon as Russian occupation ceases.

(Sent to Tokyo.)

[Paraphrased in *Accounts and Papers*, 1904 (*Cd.* 1936), CX, p. 208.]

No. 233.

Mr. Townley to the Marquess of Lansdowne.

Peking, June 23, 1903.

F.O. China 1603.   D. 7·55 P.M.
Tel. (No. 165.) Confidential.   R. 11 P.M.

My telegram No. 158.

Prince Ching yesterday assured Japanese Minister that he would not conclude secret arrangement with Russia. He said he had seen a Memorandum explaining China's reasons for refusing conditions, and did not speak in the same confident tone as to me of early settlement.

He said he had told Russian Minister that he was ready to take into consideration proposals respecting the customs revenues and Sanitary Board at Newchwang, former on the basis of portion continuing to be paid into Russo-Chinese Bank, and the remainder into the Customs Bank (direct contradiction of what he told me), latter on the basis of Sanitary Boards at Shanghae and Chefu. Japanese Minister seems inclined to doubt Prince's sincerity.

(Sent to Tokyo.)

No. 234.

Mr. Townley to the Marquess of Lansdowne.

Peking, June 29, 1903.

F.O. China 1603.   D. 4·30 P.M.
Tel. (No. 169.)   R. 3·15 P.M.

Japanese Minister hears from authoritative source that the Russian Minister has returned Memorandum mentioned in my telegram No. 165 (of 23rd June) on the ground that it does not offer possible basis for negotiation. If the information is correct it would seem to show Chinese Government is maintaining a firm attitude.

Russian Minister goes to Port Arthur 1st July to meet Russian Minister of War.
(Sent to Tokyo.)

No. 235.

Sir C. MacDonald to the Marquess of Lansdowne.

F.O. Japan 568.
Tel. (No. 45.)

Tokyo, July 1, 1903.
D. 2·30 P.M.
R. 12·15 P.M.

My telegram No. 42 (of June 25th) and Mr. Townley's telegram No. 169 (of 29th June).

If information about return of Memorandum is correct it would also seem to show that Russian Minister is still pressing demands which according to Count Lamsdorff do not exist and that there is no such arrangement as asserted by Prince Ching—see Mr. Townley—telegram No. 158 (of June 20th).

(Sent to Peking.)

No. 236.

Sir C. MacDonald to the Marquess of Lansdowne.

F.O. Japan 568.
Tel. (No. 48.) Secret.

Tokyo, July 2, 1903.
D. 7·25 P.M.
R. 5·45 P.M.

My telegram No. 47 of today.

From a private conversation I have had with Marquis Ito this afternoon, I think it is not improbable that the nature of the arrangement with Russia would be a free hand for Japan in Corea with equal facilities for Russia in Manchuria on the part of Japan.

No. 237.

The Marquess of Lansdowne to Sir C. MacDonald.

F.O. Japan 564.
(No. 88.) Secret.
Sir,

Foreign Office, July 3, 1903.

The Japanese Minister informed me to-day that he had been instructed by the Japanese Government to make the following communication to His Majesty's Government in strict confidence.

The Imperial Government had been observing with close attention the development of affairs in Manchuria, and they now viewed with great concern the present situation there.

So long as there were some grounds for the hope that Russia would in good faith fulfil her engagements with China and carry out her assurances to other Powers in regard to the question of the evacuation of Manchuria, the Imperial Government maintained an attitude of watchful reserve; but the recent action of Russia in demanding from China new conditions in connection with the evacuation and in consolidating rather than relaxing her hold upon Manchuria compelled them to believe that she had abandoned the intention, if she ever seriously entertained it, of retiring from that province.[1]

Unrestrained permanent occupation of Manchuria by Russia would create a condition of things very prejudicial to those interests, the defence of which was the object of the conclusion of the Anglo-Japanese alliance. Such occupation would be

---

[1] [An explanation was made by the Russian Ambassador on the 11th July, *v.* Lansdowne to Scott, printed in *Accounts and Papers*, 1904 (*Cd.* 1936), CX, pp. 211–2.]

destructive of the principle of equal opportunity. It would also manifestly impair the territorial integrity of China. Moreover, it would be a continual menace to the independence of Corea, which Japan was bound to maintain at all hazards for the sake of her own tranquillity and safety.

The Imperial Government believed that the policy of forbearance which they had hitherto pursued was a wise one, but they could not but come to the conclusion that the time had arrived for a change in that policy.

In these circumstances, they found it absolutely necessary to ask themselves what course they should now take in order to safeguard their imperilled interests. In studying this question, the Imperial Government had not failed to keep constantly in mind their special relations with the British Government.

That Russia had certain legally-acquired and well-established special interests in Manchuria was a fact which it would be as unwise to ignore as it was impossible to deny. Starting from that point of view, the Imperial Government, for their part, were disposed in the first place to offer to Russia a solution of the present situation based on the clear definition of those interests, as well as of Japan's interests in Corea, mutual recognition of the right of the two Powers to take certain defined measures for the protection of those interests, when and so long as they were menaced, and a mutual engagement to respect the independence and the territorial integrity of China and Corea, and to maintain the principle of equal opportunity for the commerce and industry of all nations in those two countries. A settlement embodying these principles would, it was believed, be entirely fair to all parties.

It was not necessary at this time to attempt to say what the result of Russia's rejection of such proposals would be, but the responsibility for whatever consequences might ensue would lie solely upon her.

Referring to Article 4 and Article 5 of the Anglo-Japanese Agreement, Viscount Hayashi was instructed to invite the British Government to a full and frank exchange of views concerning the common interests of the two Powers, which had been placed in jeopardy by the action of Russia. Viscount Hayashi was to add that the Imperial Government would be glad to know what steps the British Government proposed to take in defence of their threatened interests, and at the same time to express the hope entertained by the Imperial Government that the British Government would agree with them as to the wisdom of the course of action which the Imperial Government propose to take as above indicated.

I thanked Viscount Hayashi for making me aware of the views of the Japanese Government upon a subject in which we took so great an interest. I asked him whether he had any idea of the steps which they would be likely to take in the event of the Russian Government paying no attention to their representations.

Viscount Hayashi said that he had no information upon this subject.

I told him that I felt bound to lay his statement before my colleagues, and that I would do so as soon as possible, although I might not have an opportunity during the next few days, owing to the visit of the French President.

I said that I thought it most important that we should endeavour to arrive at an understanding with the United States in regard to the action which they would be likely to adopt in dealing with these questions.

I am, &c.
LANSDOWNE.

No. 238.

The Marquess of Lansdowne to Sir C. MacDonald.

F.O. Japan 564.
(No. 95.)
Sir,   *Foreign Office, July 13, 1903.*
The Japanese Minister made to me to-day the following statement :—

" 1. All the details of the proposals to be made to Russia have not yet been worked out, and they will be necessarily left for future development during the negotiation. But, broadly speaking, the Imperial Government intend to ask from Russia recognition of Japan's special interests in Corea, as alluded to in the Anglo-Japanese Alliance, and, on their part, they propose to offer their recognition of Russia's special interests in railway enterprises in Manchuria.

" 2. Such reciprocal recognition of the respective special interests logically requires mutual recognition of right to adopt appropriate measures to protect those interests. Accordingly the Imperial Government intend to propose reciprocal recognition of right of each Power to despatch troops to its sphere of interests in order to protect its recognised interests there, when those interests are mènaced by internal disturbances, but upon the condition that all troops so despatched should be immediately withdrawn when their mission is accomplished.

" 3. These, with the remaining items of the proposals as already communicated to the British Government, represent the chief points of the Imperial Government's scheme, and, subject to necessary modifications in the course of negotiation, the Imperial Government intend to adhere to those points.

" 4. The Imperial Government desire an amicable adjustment of outstanding questions between Japan and Russia regarding their special interests respectively in Manchuria and Corea, and with that view they intend to alone approach Russian Government with certain friendly proposals, as the project does not, in their opinion, lend itself to joint or parallel action. As common action thus forms no part of the scheme of the Imperial Government, and as its strict secrecy is of the utmost importance at this juncture, they can see no advantage in communicating with United States' Government on the subject.

" However, if the British Government intend to propose, in regard to the Manchurian question, combined action on the part of the interested Powers in order to bring a strong pressure on China and Russia, Imperial Government hope to be informed so before they approach Russia with the proposals now in question."

I told Viscount Hayashi that I would lay the matter before my colleagues to-morrow. I asked him whether the stipulation in clause 2, under which each Power was required to withdraw its troops from Manchuria and Corea respectively " when their mission is accomplished," would be held to apply to troops which the Russians might find it necessary to employ for the protection of their railway. He said that this was not intended, and that the case contemplated was *e.g.*, that of the despatch of a force to quell a Boxer outbreak in Manchuria. He told me that the " remaining items " mentioned in clause 3 were those referred to in the following passage which occurs in the Memorandum which he left with me on the 3rd instant :—

" Mutual engagement to respect independence and territorial integrity of. China and Corea, and to maintain principle of equal opportunity for the commerce and industry of all nations in those countries."

With reference to the concluding sentence of clause 4, he told me that it was inserted because in the view of the Japanese Government combined action by the Powers interested would be incompatible with such a friendly negotiation as was contemplated by the Japanese Government. In reply to a question of mine, he observed that the Japanese Government regarded such a friendly negotiation as much more hopeful than combined pressure by the Powers.

I took the opportunity of informing Viscount Hayashi of the substance of the communication made to me on the 11th by the Russian Ambassador. (See my despatch to Sir C. Scott, No. 184, of July 11.)

I am, &c.
LANSDOWNE.

No. 239.

Memorandum communicated to Viscount Hayashi.

F.O. Japan 572.
Confidential.   *July* 16, 1903.

His Majesty's Government have had under their consideration the Memoranda communicated on the 3rd and 13th instant([1]) by Viscount Hayashi to the Marquess of Lansdowne.

It has been the constant desire of His Majesty's Government to co-operate with other Powers, and particularly with Japan, in bringing about the prompt evacuation of Manchuria. A separate Arrangement between Russia and Japan for this purpose might be held to denote a weakening in the good understanding which has hitherto prevailed between Japan and Great Britain, an understanding which found expression in the Anglo-Japanese Agreement of 1901 [1902]. Such an Arrangement should, therefore, in the opinion of His Majesty's Government, be approached with caution on the part of the Japanese Government. His Majesty's Government have, however, never concealed from themselves that the interests of Japan in Corea are of a special kind, and it does not surprise them to find that she should desire to provide a prompt and efficacious means of safeguarding those interests. They further understand that, in the opinion of the Japanese Government, this object can be best attained by a direct Arrangement between Russia and Japan of the kind indicated in the two Memoranda.

His Majesty's Government would, in these circumstances, certainly not criticise in an unfriendly spirit an Arrangement desired by their ally, and consistent with the interests and Treaty obligations of Great Britain as well as Japan.

The proposal is, they understand, to the following effect :—

1. Russia would recognise the special interests of Japan in Corea.
2. Japan would in like manner recognise Russia's special interests in railway enterprises in Manchuria.
3. Should those interests be menaced by internal disturbances, Russia and Japan would respectively recognise each other's right to send troops into Manchuria and Corea, but upon the condition that all troops so despatched would be withdrawn so soon as their mission had been accomplished.
4. Russia and Japan would mutually undertake to respect the independence and territorial integrity of China and Corea, and to maintain the principle of equal opportunity for the commerce and industry of all nations in those countries.

As to 1. His Majesty's Government would welcome a recognition by Russia of the special interests of Japan in Corea.

They have themselves, in the Anglo-Japanese Agreement, already admitted that Japan has such interests, and they consider that it would be to their advantage that the position of Japan in that country should be strengthened.

2. They have themselves already recognised, in the Anglo-Russian Agreement of 1899, Russia's special interest in railway enterprises to the north of the Great Wall

([1]) [*V.* Nos. 237 and 238 *supra.*]

[15214]   P

of China. Russia has by the same Agreement acknowledged that this country has corresponding interests in other parts of China. So long as Russian action in Manchuria is confined to what is legitimately required for the protection of her railways, His Majesty's Government see no reason why Japan should object.

3. Seems to require further explanation. Every nation has the right to send troops into the territory of another for an adequate national object, committing thereby what may be taken as an act of war, with the full knowledge of the consequences. His Majesty's Government assume that what is intended in the present instance is that Japan should be content to leave to Russia the duty of restoring order in Manchuria, and would not take umbrage at such a proceeding on the understanding that Russia would not take umbrage at similar proceedings on the part of Japan in Corea.

4. The proposed mutual engagement of Russia and Japan to respect the independence and territorial integrity of China and Corea, and to maintain the principle of the open door, involves the reaffirmation by these two Powers of a principle to which His Majesty's Government have repeatedly given their adhesion, and it is satisfactory to them to be assured that the Japanese Government still intends to support that policy.

If the interpretation which His Majesty's Government have placed upon the proposed Agreement is correct, they see no reason for dissuading the Japanese Government from entering into it. It is, however, obvious that His Majesty's Government must reserve to themselves the fullest liberty of reviewing their position when the Agreement (the details of which are understood to be under discussion) has been completed. It will then be their duty to consider whether it is necessary for them to take any special measures for the protection of British interests, or whether it might not rather be desirable for them to become parties to the Agreement, provided that analogous arrangements could be made in regard to those portions of China in which Great Britain is specially concerned.

They regard it, moreover, of the utmost importance that the negotiation with Russia should not be conducted in a manner which might suggest that the Anglo-Japanese Agreement had been in any way impaired, and they will be glad if the Japanese Government will continue to keep His Majesty's Government fully informed of the progress of their communications with the Russian Government.([1])

Foreign Office, July 16, 1903.

([1]) [Sir C. MacDonald to Lord Lansdowne, Telegram No. 57 of the 20th July (received the 20th July), states Japanese Government had shown him this memorandum and communicated their " grateful thanks " and " their high appreciation of [its] terms."]

No. 240.

Sir C. MacDonald to the Marquess of Lansdowne.

Tokyo, July 17, 1903.

F.O. Japan 568.   D. 5·45 P.M.
Tel. (No. 56.) Secret.   R. 7·30 P.M.

Japanese Minister for Foreign Affairs this morning told me the replies sent to your Lordship's recent queries respecting advisability of communicating to United States Government intention of Japanese Government respecting direct arrangement with Russia, and secondly, to request for details of said arrangement.

Japanese Minister for Foreign Affairs begged me to say that Japanese Government are earnestly anxious for peace, but they think the best and only means of obtaining it is by negotiating direct with Russia, and that any delay in doing so will be provoking war.

He said further that the Japanese Government had arrived at determination to address Russian Government after very careful consideration and he earnestly hoped that His Majesty's Government would see no grave objection to this course.

As stated in my telegram No. 53 I do not think any objection we may make will deter them.

They also wish to act alone in this matter, and, considering that their interests are more vital than ours, and that they are prepared to go further, I venture to think that they are right.

No. 241.

Communication from War Office, July 29, 1903.

Note on Russian Position in Manchuria, by Lieutenant-Colonel Wingate, D.A.Q.M.G. for Intelligence, China.

F.O. China 1619.

. . . . It is easy, in my opinion, to say that Russian ascendency as the chief political and future governing power, in the three Eastern provinces, is assured —for at least so long as no Power shall drive her out at the point of the bayonet— a by no means easy task.

The Japanese place reliance on the assistance which might be afforded them by the Chinese in Manchuria. This I consider a very doubtful factor. The wealthier Chinese merchants in Mukden and other important towns would gladly welcome any Government so long as it might be powerful, and show a chance of permanency. The number of Chinese of all classes who speak and are learning the Russian language is quite remarkable; they show great facility in acquiring the language. The Russians, on the contrary, make no attempt at acquiring Chinese; indeed, they openly express their intention to force the Russian language on all who reside or travel in Manchuria.

Port Arthur is fast becoming a Far Eastern "Kronstadt." Some 60,000 Chinese labourers are at work on the new town, harbour, dockyard, fortifications, and military roads and buildings. The place will soon be an enormous fortress without a weak spot in it. It is intended next year to turn all business persons out of the old town, which will be burned, and the ground, after being allowed to lie fallow for awhile, will be utilised for military and naval purposes. The merchants and others will either have to go to the new town now in course of construction or remove to Dalny. . . . . [Details.]

My visit to Manchuria has confirmed me in the belief—

1. That the Russians have obtained a stronger hold over the country than is generally supposed.
2. That they are perfectly in earnest in their intention to gradually obtain the mastery over the country until it shall have, by force of circumstances, become a Russian province.
3. That nothing will cause them to withdraw in any way except force.
4. That they are very anxious to avoid a conflict, but that they will accept a challenge sooner than give way.
5. That the results of a conflict with Japan alone might be disastrous to Japan, while, even were she to get the best of the war, Russia would not suffer greatly.
6. Russia will not be content to remain on the left bank of the Liao River, which is, in any case, a bad and unnatural boundary. . . . . [Distribution of troops.]

No. 242.

The Marquess of Lansdowne to Sir C. Scott.

F.O. Russia 1658.
(No. 213.)

Sir,   *Foreign Office, July* 29, 1903.

The Russian Ambassador told me to-day that M. Delcassé had repeated to the Russian Ambassador at Paris the substance of a conversation which had taken place between himself and Mr. Chamberlain during M. Delcassé's visit to London.

M. Delcassé had been struck by a remark which he understood Mr. Chamberlain to have made, to the effect that this country was not opposed to the idea of arriving at an understanding with the Russian Government, but that such an understanding was rendered difficult owing to the manner in which Russia was opposing us " in the Yang-tsze Valley."

Prince Ourousoff had reported this conversation to Count Lamsdorff, who was puzzled by Mr. Chamberlain's reference to Russian opposition in the Yang-tsze Valley. Count Lamsdorff did not know what was referred to. The Russian Government had no desire to oppose us in the Yang-tsze Valley, and they were by no means averse from the idea of coming to an understanding with us if such an understanding could be arrived at.

I replied that I doubted whether Mr. Chamberlain could have referred to our difficulties with Russia as being peculiar to the Yang-tsze Valley. My impression, at any rate, was that, by the Anglo-Russian Agreement of 1899, we had already arrived at a partial understanding with regard to that part of China. On the other hand, there were certainly other points at which we had, unfortunately, failed to come to an understanding.

I referred particularly to Manchuria and to the position of the two Powers in Newchwang. I said that I had myself always been in favour of an amicable arrangement with Russia, and I had more than once suggested, but without success, the possibility of making one.

His Majesty's Government would, I felt sure, not repel any overture which might be made to us, but in such a case it would be necessary for Russia to show us more confidence than she had hitherto vouchsafed, and to let us know, particularly in reference to Manchuria, what terms she was endeavouring to obtain from the Chinese Government. At present we were to a great extent in the dark, and obliged to rely upon reports of Chinese origin, which were no doubt not always of a trustworthy character. If Russia would put us in full possession of her ideas, and if she would bear in mind that for any concessions which she obtained from us we should expect corresponding concessions from her, I believe that we might put an end to the unfortunate rivalry which had so long prevailed between us in China and in other parts of Asia. We had, I said, always recognised that Russia had special interests in that part of China which adjoined her possessions, and we should be ready to consider in the most friendly spirit an arrangement based, on the one hand, upon the recognition of those interests by this country, and, on the other, upon the recognition by Russia of the analagous interests of Great Britain in other parts of the Chinese Empire.

I am, &c.

LANSDOWNE.

[Reproduced as an extract with some omissions, *Accounts and Papers*, 1904 (*Cd.* 1936), CX, pp. 214–5.]

No. 243.

The Marquess of Lansdowne to Sir C. Scott.

F.O. Russia 1658.
(No. 226.)
Sir,   *Foreign Office, August* 12, 1903.

The Russian Ambassador referred to-day to my conversation with him, reported in my despatch No. 194 of the 15th ultimo, and said that since it had taken place he had heard from Count Lamsdorff, who had again assured him that the evacuation of Manchuria was to take place at an early date, although that date could not exactly be fixed.

Count Benckendorff again spoke of the possibility of a general understanding between the two Governments, and I repeated that we should be glad to arrive at one but that it must, of course, include the Manchurian question. We could, however, of course not come to terms unless we were fully informed as to the intentions of the Russian Government.

Count Benckendorff again asked me whether, if we were satisfied upon this point, we should be likely to assist in bringing about an arrangement between the Russian and Chinese Governments. I said that we should certainly make no secret of our concurrence if we were thoroughly satisfied. Meanwhile, however, I was afraid that our attitude must remain observant and critical.

I am, &c.
LANSDOWNE.

[Reproduced in *Accounts and Papers*, 1904 *(Cd.* 1936), CX, pp. 215–6.]

No. 244.

Sir C. Scott to the Marquess of Lansdowne.

F.O. Russia 1661.   *St. Petersburgh, D. August* 27, 1903.
(No. 258.)   Secret.   R. *August* 31, 1903.
Russian Viceroy.

I saw Count Lamsdorff yesterday. His conferences with the Emperor seem to have quite satisfied him [that] Emperor's real intention is not to curtail Foreign Minister's responsibility for foreign policy in Far East, but to simplify matters by creating one agent for carrying it out there, eliminating intervention of other departments. Emperor's words, according to Count Lamsdorff, were much to this effect : " The supreme authority rests with me, and in regard to foreign policy you and I are inseparable."

I trust Count Lamsdorff is justified in feeling this confidence. I cannot help having misgivings.

[*ED. NOTE.*—On the 13th August, 1903, Vice-Admiral Alexeieff was appointed by the Czar Viceroy of the Far Eastern Provinces.]

No. 245.

Sir C. MacDonald to the Marquess of Lansdowne.

F.O. Japan 566.
(No. 130.)   Very Confidential.   *Tokyo, D. September* 4, 1903.
My Lord,   R. *November* 3, 1903.

I have this morning seen Baron Komura, and his Excellency has confirmed the information received yesterday with regard to Count Lamsdorff's suggestion that the negotiations respecting an understanding between Russia and Japan concerning Manchuria and Corea should take place at Tokyo and not at St. Petersburgh.

The Japanese Government at once telegraphed and asked whether the transfer of negotiations implied an acceptance of the bases, which the Japanese Government had proposed, and Count Lamsdorff replied that this was not necessarily the case; instructions had therefore been sent to Mr. Kurino to state that the Japanese Government could not consider the question of transfer until the bases of the negotiations had been accepted and agreed to by both Governments.

In the course of conversation with me, Baron Komura pointed out that it would be uselss to negotiate unless the bases were agreed upon, and the Japanese Government were now pressing the Russian Government on this point; but he was bound to confess that absolutely no progress had been made. He added that, supposing the Russian Government ultimately accepted the proposed bases, he personally did not see how the Japanese Government could refuse the Russian proposal to hold the negotiations in Tokyo. He was well aware of the gravity of the question of transfer, which doubtless meant that the Russians would try to place the negotiations into the hands of Admiral Alexieff, still the Japanese Government were so anxious for peace that they were determined to meet the Russians in every possible way. But it was essential that a basis of negotiation should be agreed upon before any progress could be made.

I have, &c.
CLAUDE M. MacDONALD.

No. 246.

Sir C. MacDonald to the Marquess of Lansdowne.

F.O. Japan 566.
(No. 131.)   Secret.   *Tokyo, D. September 4, 1903.*
My Lord,   R. *November 3, 1903.*

At the interview I have mentioned in my immediately preceding despatch, Baron Komura volunteered the information that he personally did not think that the Russians meant to negotiate, and the question of transfer of negotiations to Tokyo had only been made to gain time. Beyond agreeing with him in general terms, I did not discuss the point, though I think it not impossible that this is what the Russian Government are aiming at.

In all my conversations with the Foreign Minister I have been most careful to abstain from any suggestion that might, in the least degree, have the appearance of encouraging precipitate or hasty action.

For this reason, though I personally think that firmness in dealing with the Russian Government would probably be more conducive to a peaceful settlement than a policy of over-much conciliation, I have carefully abstained from saying so.

As I have stated in a previous despatch, Marquis Ito is strongly in favour of an arrangement with Russia at almost any price, and I have been informed that he has stated that the present perplexities of the Japanese Government, and the action of Russia in Manchuria and on the frontiers of Corea is the direct outcome of the Anglo-Japanese alliance.

This, I need hardly say, is not the opinion of the Government or of the nation at large. The former made the alliance because they foresaw that Russia would behave much as she has done, and that, alliance or no alliance, her advance towards Corea would continue and menace the peace of the Far East.

The Japanese Government trusted to the alliance to help in keeping the peace; should they be disappointed in this hope, they doubtless thought that it would be useful to have a powerful friend upon whom they might rely in time of trouble to exercise a very benevolent neutrality.

I have, &c.
CLAUDE M. MacDONALD.

No. 247.

Sir C. MacDonald to the Marquess of Lansdowne.

F.O. Japan 566.   *Tokyo,* D. *September* 15, 1903.
(No. 132.)   Extract.   R. *November* 3, 1903.

    . . . . At an interview I had yesterday with Baron Komura we discussed the Russian proposals, which, he thought, were not so drastic as ones which had previously been put forward by the Russian Government and their Agents in Peking. He considered, however, that the first proposal, which stated that China should " give assurance that the three Manchurian provinces should never be ceded to any foreign Power, and that no piece of land in those provinces, whether large or small, should be leased, or pledged, or disposed of in any manner whatever," was altogether contrary to the principle of the open door and of equal opportunity, and would be an impairment of the territorial integrity of China. . . . .

No. 248.

Sir C. MacDonald to the Marquess of Lansdowne.

F.O. Japan 567.
(No. 145.)   *Tokyo,* D. *October* 1, 1903.
My Lord,   R. *November* 3, 1903.

    In a despatch dated the 5th August, addressed to your Lordship by His Majesty's Representative at St. Petersburgh, his Excellency concurs in an opinion put forward by Baron d'Aerenthal to the effect that " the Russian Government would be glad to see its way to arrive at a peaceful arrangement with Japan, if that country seriously desired it, and made practical proposals."

    As your Lordship is aware, the Government of Japan, so long ago as the first week in July, determined to put an end to a situation which was becoming dangerous by " making alone to Russia certain friendly proposals for an amicable adjustment of the questions between Japan and Russia, concerning their respective special interests in Corea and Manchuria."

    Before arriving at this decision, the Emperor called in Council, besides the Cabinet Ministers and high Ministers of State and those of his personal household, the members of the " Genro," or elder statesmen, such as Marquis Ito, Count Inouyé, Count Yamagata, and other veteran statesmen who may be termed the makers of new Japan, showing that the resolution to address Russia direct, and to make to her practical proposals with a view to coming to an arrangement for the preservation of peace, was evidently the earnest wish, not only of the Emperor and his Government, but of the representatives of all who have a stake in this country.

    By the end of the month, this proposal had taken form, and in the early days of August had been presented to Count Lamsdorff by Mr. Kurino, Japanese Representative in St. Petersburgh, who on the 13th August reported that Count Lamsdorff had stated that the Emperor had no objection to an exchange of views between the two Governments, and that he, Count Lamsdorff, was in favour of an understanding. Count Lamsdorff also had read the proposal made by the Japanese Government, and had not expressed disapproval.

    On the 26th August Sir Charles Scott telegraphed to your Lordship and stated that Mr. Kurino had seen Count Lamsdorff, who said that the Japanese proposals were under consideration, and that the Japanese Representative judged from Count Lamsdorff's tone that Russia would be prepared to negotiate. The Japanese Government continued to press for an answer to their proposal, and were particularly anxious to ascertain whether the Russian Government would accept the said proposal as a basis of negotiation.

On the 9th of September Sir Ernest Satow reported that he had been informed by Prince Ching that the Russian Minister had made fresh proposals respecting the evacuation of Manchuria; some of these proposals were so objectionable as to call forth protests from Sir Ernest Satow and Mr. Uchida, the Japanese Representative at Peking.

On the 15th of September the Russian Government informed the Japanese Government that they would like to present counter-proposals, and suggested that a basis for negotiation might be arrived at, formed on the Japanese proposals and these counter-proposals.

No mention was made of the objectionable demands made in Peking by the Russian Representative on the 9th.

Notwithstanding this, the Japanese Government have accepted the suggestion, and are now patiently awaiting the Russian counter-proposals; they have also expressed their willingness to transfer the negotiations to Tokyo, which will mean that, should the negotiations ever take place, they will take place between the Japanese Government and Admiral Alexeieff, the newly-appointed Viceroy at Port Arthur.

During this time, as your Lordship is aware, the Russians have not been inactive in the valley of the Yalu, the Corean frontier, and in Seoul. It will thus be seen that while the Japanese Government have been patiently endeavouring to arrive at a peaceful arrangement with Russia, the Russian Government cannot be said, even by their most friendly critics, to have been similarly engaged.

In a despatch dated St. Petersburgh the 22nd June, Sir Charles Scott enclosed the translation of a newspaper extract from the "St. Petersburgh Zeitung," which contains a "candid statement of the apparent inconsistencies of Russian policy in the Far East, due to a diversity of interests in the Government," with the result, as his Excellency states, that the Russian Government "incurs with an apparent show of reason the imputation of intentional bad faith." This diversity of interests is well known to the Japanese Government, and they never fail whenever possible to make allowances for the same. In the course of conversation yesterday Baron Komura referred to a leading article in one of the important newspapers which pointed out the very apparent inconsistency between Russia's being willing to negotiate with Japan at St. Petersburgh while she was pressing demands at Peking which were contrary to the basis of negotiation which Japan had proposed at the former place. In explanation of this inconsistency the Foreign Minister stated to me that he was quite sure that M. Lessar had been pressing these demands some weeks before the 9th of September, on which day they first became public; consequently they were anterior to the St. Petersburgh *pourparlers.* I am unaware whether Baron Komura really believed this, but it at any rate showed a desire on his part to "make the best of things."

Again, as reported in my telegram of the 1st of May last, Baron Komura put down to "serious diversity of opinion in the counsels of Russia" the facts that the Russian Chargé d'Affaires presented certain demands at Peking, that Count Lamsdorff solemnly denied that any demands had been made, that the Russian Ambassador at Washington said that the demands had been made, but that they were directed against His Majesty's Government, and, lastly, that Admiral Alexeieff had published an official notification that the Province of Shinking, having been completely evacuated, was free to foreigners. This province, like the others in Manchuria is still in Russian occupation.

I have dwelt upon this diversity of interest because it is a very serious stumbling-block in the earnest endeavour the Japanese Government are making to arrive at a peaceful arrangement with Russia.

In conclusion, I would beg to state as my firm conviction that it is the sincere and earnest wish of the Japanese Government and people that peace should be maintained, but the latter can only judge from plain facts and cannot make allowances for diversity of interests in the same manner and to the same extent as the former can.

In my humble opinion, it would therefore be well if the Russian Government were to endeavour to unite their interests and treat Japan more seriously, otherwise the temper of the people may prove too much for the undoubted pacific intentions of their rulers.

I have, &c.

CLAUDE M. MacDONALD.

No. 249.

Sir C. MacDonald to the Marquess of Lansdowne.

Tokyo, October 22, 1903.

F.O. Japan 568.

D. 8·5 P.M.

Tel. (No. 107.) Secret.

R. *October* 23, 7·30 A.M.

MY telegram No. 99.

Negotiations between the Japanese Minister for Foreign Affairs and the Russian Minister still continue.

For Article IV of Russian counter-proposals Minister for Foreign Affairs suggests the following :—

"Recognition of right of Japan to send troops to Corea for the purpose mentioned in Article II or for purpose of suppressing insurrection or disorder calculated to create international complications."

Minister for Foreign Affairs hopes to carry his point.

For Article VI Baron Komura proposes " mutual engagement to establish a neutral zone on the Corea–Manchurian frontier extending 10 kilom. on each side into which, etc. . . . ."

Russian Minister accepts subject to approval of his Government.

Baron Komura proposes that Article VII of Russian proposals be struck out and following three Articles substituted : Article VII. Engagement on the part of Russia to respect China's sovereignty and territorial integrity in Manchuria, and not to interfere with Japan's commercial freedom in Manchuria.

Article VIII. Recognition by Japan of Russia's special interests in Manchuria and of right of Russia to take such measures as may be necessary for the protection of those interests so long as those measures do not infringe stipulations of preceding Article.

Article IX. Mutual engagement not to impede connection of the Corean railway and the East China railway when those " shall have been eventually extended to the Yalu."

Russian Minister has so far refused to entertain the suppression of Article VII of Russian proposals or substitution of the Japanese Articles VII and VIII. He agrees to IX subject to his Government's approval.

Baron Komura says that Japanese Government would be very grateful for confidential expression of opinion by H.M. Government on the Russian counter-proposals and Japanese amendments to same, as above stated.

No. 250.

The Marquess of Lansdowne to Sir E. Monson.

F.O. France 3617.

(No. 541.) Most Secret.

Sir,

Foreign Office, October 26, 1903.

At the close of my conversation with the French Ambassador to-day I asked him whether it was true that Count Lamsdorff was expected at Paris.

2. M. Cambon said that he believed Count Lamsdorff was expected, but that he was without precise information as to the date of the visit.

3. I said, explaining that I was expressing merely my personal sentiments in the most unofficial manner possible, that I could not help hoping that Count Lamsdorff's discussions with M. Delcassé might indirectly have an effect upon the attitude of the Russian Government towards that of this country. The exchange of ideas which had recently taken place between the French and British Governments had been, I rejoiced to think, characterised by the utmost frankness on both sides. It seemed to me most unfortunate that we had hitherto entirely failed in establishing the same kind of diplomatic relations with the Russian Government. I did not think the fault lay on our side, for I had more than once made proposals in that direction, but without success. On the other hand, it certainly seemed to me that the Russian Government had been far from open in their dealings with us. Their conduct placed us in a very embarrassing position. We had more than once received from them specific pledges; for example, with reference to the evacuation of Manchuria, which we had loyally accepted and upon which we had relied when we were questioned in Parliament.

4. Those pledges remained unfulfilled, and I was afraid that a feeling of impatience and mistrust had obtained possession of the public mind in this country. We were no doubt told that the obstructiveness of the Chinese was to blame. There might be some truth in this, but it was impossible to test the truth of the assertion unless the Russian Government would really tell us what they wanted. As it was we had to trust to versions of their demands obtained from various sources some of which were probably untrustworthy. The result was that when we were appealed to for advice, we had to give it upon a statement of the facts which was one-sided and which we could not test. I was not sure whether Count Lamsdorff fully realised these considerations.

5. M. Cambon listened with evident sympathy to what I had said. He observed that we probably did not know the extreme difficulty of Count Lamsdorff's position, which had been considerably impaired by the creation of the new Far Eastern Viceroyalty. Not only did General Alexeieff's appointment encroach upon his functions as Minister for Foreign Affairs, but besides this the Emperor had gone the length of appointing M. Bezobrazoff, who enjoyed His Imperial Majesty's special confidence, to be a kind of special Foreign Minister to the new Viceroy with direct access to His Imperial Majesty.

6. Some of the difficulties were therefore, M. Cambon thought, inherent in the situation. He agreed with me nevertheless in principle, and he would repeat, quite informally, to M. Delcassé the substance of what I had said.

I have, &c.
LANSDOWNE.

No. 251.

The Marquess of Lansdowne to Sir C. MacDonald.

F.O. Japan 568.   *Foreign Office, October* 26, 1903.
Tel. (No. 53.)   D. 6·45 P.M.

Your telegram, Secret, of 22nd October, No. 107.

Our views on the Russian counter-proposals and Japanese amendments are as follows :—

Arts. I, II and III of the counter-proposals seem to us unobjectionable. They reaffirm but go somewhat further than provisions to be found in existing Treaties between Japan and Russia.

Article IV. We concur in amended version proposed by M.F.A.

It would probably be desirable to retain stipulation that Russia should be informed and troops recalled when mission accomplished.

Article V seems unobjectionable if Japan is satisfied that it does not preclude her from taking part in improvement of roads, railways and telegraphs. It may, however, be more prudent not to raise the point.

Article VI. Japanese amendment seems reasonable. Russian clause neutralises an unnecessarily large area.

Article VII. Russian clause involves abandonment by Japan of rights already secured to her by Treaty and formally recorded in the Anglo-Japanese Agreement; on the other hand, it seems to us superfluous, in view of pledge already given by Russia, to require her to reaffirm her intention to respect integrity of China and commercial freedom of Japan in Manchuria. We suggest as best mode of dealing with this point that Japanese Article VII should be omitted and that after the words "those interests" in Japanese Article VIII, which would become Article VII, the following should be substituted : *Begins :—*

"So long as such measures do not infringe her existing engagements to respect the independence and territorial integrity of the Chinese Empire and the Treaty rights of other Powers in regard to freedom of commercial intercourse."

We see no objection to new Japanese Article IX. You are authorised to make a communication in this sense to the Japanese M.F.A.

No. 252.

Sir C. MacDonald to the Marquess of Lansdowne.

Tokyo, October 27, 1903.

F.O. Japan 568.
Tel. (No. 108.) Secret.

D. 9·55 P.M.
R. 10·20 P.M.

Your telegram No. 53.

Russian Minister has agreed, *ad referendum*, to Article IV as altered by the Minister for Foreign Affairs (see my telegram No. 107). With regard to your Lordship's suggested alteration of Japanese Article VIII, Minister for Foreign Affairs thinks that Russian Government would not agree, because Russian Minister has several times stated during negotiations that his Government would never enter into any engagement with any Power or with all the Powers to maintain integrity of China, or to respect Treaty rights or commercal interests of such Powers in China. She would make a declaration to the above effect, but would enter into no engagement.

Baron Komura, on the other hand, has informed Russian Minister that the Japanese Government would never consent to Article VII of Russian counter-proposals.

From the above there does not seem much hope of favourable issue of negotiations.

No. 253.

The Marquess of Lansdowne to Sir C. MacDonald.

F.O. Japan 568.
Tel. (No. 54.) Secret.

Foreign Office, October 28, 1903.
D. 4·20 P.M.

Your telegram No. 108 of 27th October. Russo-Japanese negotiations.

Communicate following suggestion to Japanese Government for their consideration :—

1. Omission of Russian Article VII.
2. Following modification of Japanese Article VIII in place of that suggested in my telegram No. 53 of 26th October : "So long as such measures do not interfere with Japan's Treaty Rights or Commercial freedom in Manchuria."

No. 254.

Sir C. MacDonald to the Marquess of Lansdowne.

F.O. Japan 567.
(No. 164.) Secret. Extract. *Tokyo,* D. *October* 29, 1903.
My Lord, R. *December* 1, 1903.

(¹) .... As a result of my queries, I elicited from him(²) the following information, which he asked me—for the time being at any rate—to keep absolutely secret :—

The Japanese Government do not think there will be any war because they think the Russians are not prepared and will not fight; they think that the Russian Government will ultimately give a pledge to respect China's sovereignty and territorial integrity in Manchuria which will, at any rate, prevent the annexation of that province, though it will not loosen the hold that Russia now has there. (Baron Komura admitted that he thought Russia would fight sooner than be turned out of Manchuria.) He thought the Russians would continue to consolidate their position in Manchuria. This the Japanese could not prevent, but the negotiations, if brought to a successful conclusion (and of this Baron Komura seemed to entertain very little doubt), would permit the Japanese to consolidate their position in Corea, which they would strain every nerve to do.

I cannot, of course, say whether the Russians will withdraw in so marked a degree from the position they have taken up, as set forth in their own counter-proposals, but if they do a collision will have been postponed, at any rate for some time to come.

I have, &c.
CLAUDE M. MacDONALD.

(¹) [Detailed amendments to Article 8.]
(²) [Baron Komura, Japanese Foreign Minister.]

No. 255.

Sir C. MacDonald to the Marquess of Lansdowne.

F.O. Japan 568. *Tokyo,* D. *November* 2, 1903.
Tel. (No. 113.) Secret. R. *November* 2, 1903, 7·30 P.M.

Following amendments to the Russian counter-proposals have been officially handed to Russian Minister for Foreign Affairs :—

Article I. Mutual Engagement to respect the independence and territorial integrity of Corean and Chinese Empires.

Articles II, III, IV, and VI, remain as proposed by Minister: see my telegrams Nos. 99 and 107 of 7th and 22nd October.

Article V. Engagement on the part of Japan not to undertake on the coast of Corea any military works capable of menacing the freedom of navigation in the Straits of Corea.

Article VII. Russian counter-proposal altered to the following : "Recognition by Japan that Manchuria is outside her sphere of special interest, and recognition by Russia that Corea is outside her sphere of special interest."

Article VIII. Recognition by Japan of Russia's special interests in Manchuria, and of right of Russia to take such measures as may be necessary for the protection of those interests.

Article IX. Engagement on the part of Japan not to interfere with the commercial and residential rights and immunities belonging to Russia in virtue of her treaty engagements with Corea, and engagement on the part of Russia not to interfere with the commercial and residential rights and immunities belonging to Japan in virtue of her treaty engagements with China.

Articles I and IX are the most important, and the Minister for Foreign Affairs expects most opposition in connection with them.

Minister for Foreign Affairs informed me that above articles, were of course, subject to discussion and alteration.

The old Article IX regarding railways becomes Article 10.

Suggestion in your telegram No. 53 (of 26th October) respecting Article V (has been) adopted.

No. 256.

The Marquess of Lansdowne to Sir C. MacDonald.

F.O. Japan 568.   *Foreign Office, November 2, 1903.*
Tel. (No. 56.)   D. 6·5 P.M.

Your telegram No. 112 of November 1st. Russo-Japanese negotiations.

The suggestion in my telegram No. 54 of October 28th was prompted by the consideration that Russia was already so distinctly pledged to the maintenance of the *status quo* in Manchuria that it seemed doubtful whether the Japanese Government would be well advised to insist on a further assurance to the same effect, particularly if this point alone stands in the way of a satisfactory settlement.

No. 257.

The Marquess of Lansdowne to Sir E. Monson.

F.O. France 3617.
(No. 554.) Secret.
Sir,   *Foreign Office, November 4, 1903.*

The French Ambassador, who has just returned from Paris, told me this morning that he had reported to M. Delcassé the substance of the conversation recorded in my despatch No. 544, Secret, of the 28th ultimo explaining that the observations which I had made were personal and of a wholly unofficial character.

Count Lamsdorff, on his arrival at Paris, had spoken to M. Delcassé as to the situation in the Far East, and had said that the Russian demands upon Japan were of a very moderate character, but that he was extremely anxious with regard to the attitude of the Japanese Government and particularly as to the manner in which their policy might be affected by the hope of English support. This observation had given M. Delcassé the opportunity of observing that he had good reason to know that the British Government was far from desiring to follow a provocative policy, but that our great difficulty was that both as regards China and Japan we had been left persistently in the dark as to the policy and intentions of Russia. M. Delcassé had suggested that a little more frankness was desirable and would be calculated to smooth difficulties. Count Lamsdorff had recognised the fairness of this contention, and had said that he would give Count Benckendorff instructions the effect of which would, he hoped, be to deprive us of cause for such complaints in the future,

M. Cambon added that M. Delcassé had gone out of his way to express the opinion that the position taken up by the Japanese Government was reasonable. He understood that they insisted that the *status quo* should be maintained in Corea, whilst they were prepared to recognise the special interest of Russia in Manchuria.

Count Lamsdorff had replied that he did not differ.

I gathered from M. Cambon that the impression produced by Count Lamsdorff's visit was that he was still able to exercise a useful influence over the Emperor's councils.

LANSDOWNE.

No. 258.

The Marquess of Lansdowne to Mr. Spring-Rice.

F.O. Russia 1658.
(No. 307.)
Sir, *Foreign Office, November 7, 1903.*

The Russian Ambassador, whom I had not seen since the 12th August, called on me this morning.

He told me that during his absence from this country he had had conversations with Count Lamsdorff as to Anglo-Russian relations at St. Petersburgh, earlier in the autumn, and again within the last few days at Paris. On the first occasion he had found Count Lamsdorff well disposed towards this country, and on the second his language was of an even more friendly character. Count Lamsdorff had instructed his Excellency to express his appreciation of our considerate and straightforward policy, particularly in so far as Macedonian affairs were concerned, and he admitted that although we had maintained our right to be critical our criticism had been neither unfair nor unfriendly. Count Lamsdorff felt strongly that it was of importance that an endeavour should be made to remove all sources of misunderstanding between the two Governments, and that there should be "a change for the better" in our relations. Count Benckendorff was therefore instructed to discuss frankly with me the various questions outstanding between Great Britain and Russia, with the object of arriving at an agreement as to the manner in which they should be dealt with. In the meantime, the Russian Government would be careful to avoid any action bearing the appearance of hostility to this country. Count Benckendorff had been told that he was to go back to St. Petersburgh early in the new year for the purpose of reporting the result of his discussions with His Majesty's Government.

I expressed the pleasure which it gave me to learn Count Lamsdorff's views, and my readiness to contribute, so far as I was able, to such an understanding as has been suggested.

I was the more pleased at the prospect which was thus opened for us, because I had been seriously concerned at the position into which the two Powers were apparently drifting. I should be wanting in frankness if I did not tell his Excellency that the attitude of the Russian Government in regard to the question of our relations with Afghanistan had created a most unpleasant impression in our minds.

I pointed out to his Excellency that the Russian demand, which had originally been merely that Afghan and Russian officials should be allowed to communicate with one another in regard to purely local questions of a non-political character, had undergone a remarkable development, the latest Russian demand being apparently for a right of direct intercourse with Afghanistan upon questions of all kinds, whether political or not, and for the right to send Russian Agents into Afghanistan.

Count Benckendorff here interrupted me by observing that the demand to send Agents into Afghanistan had been dropped, and that the proposal, thus limited, might form the subject of discussion between the two Governments. I said that I was glad to hear that the proposal to send Agents had been given up, but I reminded his Excellency that the last communication (that dated 6th October) which we had received from the Russian Government had closed the discussion in almost peremptory terms, so much so that I should have considered it inconsistent with my duty to reopen it. The action of the Russian Government, in refusing to allow a Russian officer to meet the British officer deputed to re-erect the boundary pillars on the Afghan frontier, seemed to me entirely inconsistent with the alleged desire to maintain amicable relations with this country. The pillars had originally been set up by British and Russian officers acting together, and it was surely natural that their restoration should be effected in a similar manner. I could not understand how the Russian Government should have declined a friendly overture made in the circumstances which I had described.

Count Benckendorff replied that the case was not one in which a new boundary was to be demarcated. All that was necessary was that certain posts which had fallen down should be set up again, and for this purpose it had not seemed necessary to resort to combined action.

I said that I was unconvinced by this argument, and that the incident would certainly produce a very· bad effect on public opinion in this country. Count Benckendorff made no real attempt to defend the Russian note, and said something to the effect that Count Lamsdorff was away at the time when it was written, and that some official of the Russian Foreign Office was the author of it.

The conversation then turned to the Far East.

I again told his Excellency that we were constantly placed in an embarrassing position owing to the ignorance in which we were kept as to the actual demands put forward by Russia in her negotiations with Japan and China. Count Benckendorff expressed the opinion that no serious difficulty was to be anticipated in coming to terms with the Japanese Government, but they must not fortify the south sea-board of Corea. As to China, he was without information as to the causes which led to the reoccupation of Mukden. I said that he must not be surprised if uncharitable comments were made upon the conduct of Russia in this matter. She had announced that the whole province was to be evacuated by the 8th April, and now, six months later, we found her troops going back to the city of Mukden, from which they had been withdrawn not long ago.

Count Benckendorff dwelt upon the peculiar situation which had been created by the establishment of the new Far Eastern Vice-Royalty. The result had been that the foreign policy of Russia at this point was no longer one and undivided. He evidently wished me to understand˝ that many things happened for which Count Lamsdorff could not be held responsible.

I said that I thought his statement disclosed a grave and most alarming condition of things. How was it possible for us to come to satisfactory understandings with a Foreign Office within which two separate, and, perhaps, conflicting influences were at work? Count Benckendorff agreed with me that the arrangement was most inconvenient, but said significantly that he thought this phase was passing off.

Coming back to Macedonia, Count Benckendorff said that Count Lamsdorff was anxious to have it understood that the policy of the Russian Government did not differ in principle from ours. They had preferred to retain Hilmi Pasha with European assessors rather than appoint a Christian Governor, because they thought the former course the most promising under present conditions. It was a question of opportunity, and Count Lamsdorff admitted that a still further development of the scheme might eventually be inevitable.

I took the opportunity of mentioning to Count Benckendorff that, owing to the outrageous conduct of the Thibetans, who had broken off negotiations with our Representative, seized British subjects, and carried off the transport animals of a friendly State, it had been decided to send our Commission, with a suitable escort, further into Thibetan territory, but that this step must not be taken as indicating any intention of annexing or even of permanently occupying Thibetan territory.

I am, &c.

LANSDOWNE.

No. 259.

The Marquess of Lansdowne to Sir E. Monson.

F.O. France 3617.
(No. 627.)

Sir,   *Foreign Office, December* 11, 1903.

I asked the French Ambassador to-day whether he had any information as to the alleged arrival of a Russian squadron at Chemulpo.

His Excellency replied in the negative.

I told him that we too had no confirmation of the rumour. It was, however, one which had caused serious apprehension in our minds. H.E. was no doubt aware that, under our Agreement with Japan, our intervention could only be demanded in case that Power were assailed by two others. On the other hand, public opinion here might render it extremely difficult for us to remain inactive if Russia were to find some pretext for attacking Japan and were to endeavour to crush her out of existence.

It seemed to me in these circumstances that it was the duty of our two Governments, which were, I rejoiced to think, at this moment in such friendly relations, to do all in their power to keep the peace.

His Excellency said he entirely agreed with me and that we ought, both of us, to " pour as much cold water as possible " on the embers. He expressed his conviction that Russia did not really desire to bring on a quarrel with Japan. The matter had been fully discussed during Count Lamsdorff's visit to Paris. The Japanese Minister had then sought an interview with M. Delcassé, and had assured him that all that Japan wanted was firstly, the maintenance of the *status quo* in Corea, and, secondly, the recognition of her Treaty rights in Manchuria. Count Lamsdorff had told M. Delcassé that these demands seemed to him perfectly reasonable, and that he saw no reason why an arrangement should not be come to on that basis.

His Excellency said he would repeat what I had said in confidence to M. Delcassé, and we agreed that it was desirable for the British and French Governments to watch the course of events in the Far East with attention, and should occasion arise, to do our best to exercise a moderating influence upon the disputants.

LANSDOWNE.

No. 260.

Sir C. MacDonald to the Marquess of Lansdowne.

Tokyo, December 14, 1903.

F.O. Japan 568.   D. 7·45 P.M.
Tel. (No. 126.)   R. *December* 15, 8 A.M.

Following are Russian counter-proposals to Japanese amendments, they were handed to M.F.A. on December 12th. (I have changed order in order to preserve secrecy of cypher) :—

No. 2. Recognition by Russia of Japan's preponderating interests in Corea, and of the right of Japan to assist Corea with advice tending to improve the civil administration.

No. 1. Mutual engagement to respect the independence and territorial integrity of Corean Empire.

No. 8. Abrogation of all previous agreements between Russia and Japan respecting Corea.

No. 7. Mutual engagement not to impede the connection of the Corean and East China railways, when those railways shall have been extended to the Yalu.

No. 3. Engagement on the part of Russia not to oppose the development of the industrial and commercial activities of Japan in Corea nor the adoption of measures for the protection of those interests.

No. 4. Recognition by Russia of the right of Japan to send troops to Corea for the purpose mentioned in preceding article, or for the purpose of suppressing insurrections or disorders capable of creating international complications.

No. 6. Mutual engagement to consider the territory of Corea to the north of the 39th parallel as a neutral zone within the limits of which neither of the contracting parties shall introduce troops.

No. 5. Mutual engagement not to make use of any part of the Corean territory for strategical purposes, and not to undertake on the Corean coast any military works capable of menacing the free navigation in the Straits of Corea.

M.F.A. informs me with regard to above that he still hopes that negotiations may not be broken off. He bases these hopes on the fact that Article VII of the original Russian counter-proposals relative to Manchuria, being outside Japan's sphere, has been abandoned, and that Articles IV and VII are as suggested by Japan.

On the other hand, no mention whatever is made of Manchuria in the reply, and as the basis of negotiations from the Japanese point of view was a settlement of questions between Russia and Japan in which their special interests were concerned in Manchuria and Corea, and the most important point a recognition by Russia of Japan's treaty rights with China in Manchuria, M.F.A. thinks the reply " most unsatisfactory."

It is to be noted that Article No. 6 retains the neutral zone, which means that Russia can send her troops as far as Corean frontier, but Japan must stop 200 miles short of it.

Above is most secret.

Gist of above telegraphed to Peking.

No. 261.

The Marquess of Lansdowne to Sir C. MacDonald.

F.O. Japan 568. *Foreign Office, December* 18, 1903.
Tel. (No. 68.) D. 7·20 P.M.

Your telegram No. 132 of December 17th. Russo-Japanese negotiations.

It seems to us that Japanese Government will be fully justified in asking Russian Government to amend its proposals for reasons which M.F.A. indicates.

It might be possible to meet difficulty as to Manchuria by addition of a clause in which Japan would recognise special interests of Russia in that Province subject to formal recognition by Russia of Treaty rights of Japan and other Powers.

See my telegram No. 54 of October 28th.([1])

([1]) [*V. supra*, No. 253, p. 219.]

No. 262.

Sir C. Scott to the Marquess of Lansdowne.

F.O. Russia 1662.
(No. 441.)   *St. Petersburgh,* D. *December* 22, 1903.
My Lord,   R. *December* 28, 1903.

I have the honour to report that, at the first interview which I had on the 11th instant with Count Lamsdorff, on my return to my post, his Excellency, referring to the message which he had begged Count Benckendorff, whom he had met in Paris, to convey to your Lordship, said that Count Benckendorff had sent him very full reports of several conversations which he had had with you on the subject of various questions pending between Great Britain and Russia, with regard to which he had instructed the Ambassador to invite a frank exchange of views, as he considered the present moment a very opportune one for endeavouring to arrive at a friendly understanding.

Count Benckendorff, he added, had also sent him a full report of the conversation in connection with the same questions with which His Majesty the King had honoured him at Windsor.

Count Lamsdorff expressed much satisfaction with the ready response which you had made to his suggestion by enabling Count Benckendorff to furnish him with so frank an expression of your views on the different points which had been under discussion.

I informed Count Lamsdorff that your Lordship had been good enough to furnish me, on my departure from London, with full records of your conversations with Count Benckendorff to which he had been alluding, and that I was anxious to impress upon him the importance which I knew you attached to receiving in exchange an early and equally frank expression of the views of the Russian Government, and I said that you had expressed an earnest hope that it might be such as to lead to a satisfactory understanding.

I trusted that Count Benckendorff would be enabled to do so at an early date, and I ventured to remind him that Parliament would reassemble on February 2nd.

Count Lamsdorff promised me to bear this in mind and do his best to meet your Lordship's wishes in this respect.

No reference was made in the course of this conversation to any of the particular questions or points which formed the subject of your Lordship's conversations with the Russian Ambassador, and Count Lamsdorff apparently quite agreed in the view that their independent discussion at the two capitals might only entail risk of confusion and misunderstanding.

The subject was not again alluded to at the second interview which I had later with his Excellency.

I have, &c.
CHARLES S. SCOTT.

No. 263.

Sir C. Scott to the Marquess of Lansdowne.

                          St. Petersburgh, December 22, 1903.
F.O. Russia 1663.   D. 8·25 P.M.
Tel. (No. 159.) *Very Confidential.*   R. 9·40 P.M.

Far East: Sir C. MacDonald's telegram No. 134.

Nature of present stage of negotiations is being kept secret here, but Count Lamsdorff is conferring with Emperor to-day, and it is reported that Japanese answer arrived yesterday. It is expected that negotiations will be continued.

I do not share the view referred to by Sir C. MacDonald that the policy of Russian Government is deliberately inspired by any hostile intentions. A war in the Far East would, it is openly admitted here, be most unpopular with the mass of the Russian nation, as the interests at stake there do not appeal to general public with the same force as interests nearer home, which would be handicapped by it.

The difficulty in consenting to negotiations about Manchuria has, I suspect, not been raised by Russian Foreign Office, but by Viceroy, who is probably insisting that no negotiation about Manchuria shall take place until he has settled pending question of conditions with China, while China is, on her side, waiting result of Russo-Japanese negotiations.

Alarming reports in press of probable rupture of negotiations created something like a panic on Exchange here yesterday.

No. 264.

Sir C. Scott to the Marquess of Lansdowne.

St. Petersburgh, December 28, 1903.

F.O. Russia 1663.
Tel. (No. 162.) Secret.

D. 9·48 P.M.
R. 10·45 P.M.

Far East. From a hint given in a very well-informed quarter, I gather that it is the Emperor himself who is offering most determined objection to proposal to contract any formal Treaty engagement regarding Manchuria with Japan or any other Government than that of China. If this be so the position requires very careful handling, and nothing should be done to prejudice the earnest efforts which, I am told, are being made by powerful influences here to prevail on His Majesty to satisfy Japan in some form or other that Russia has no designs against her Treaty rights or those of other Powers in Manchuria or in any other province of China. . . . .

No. 265.

The Marquess of Lansdowne to Sir C. MacDonald.

F.O. Japan 568.
Tel. (No. 78.)

Foreign Office, December 30, 1903.

D. 11 P.M.

The Japanese Minister, acting under instructions, made a statement to me on the 29th instant to the effect that Japan's latest proposals were the irreducible minimum she could accept.

If Russian Government should refuse to reconsider their latest counter-proposals Japanese Government would no doubt resort to energetic measures, and wished to know whether they might look to us for support and in what direction.

I assured him that obligations of His Majesty's Government under Anglo-Japanese Agreement would be fulfilled according to the spirit as well as the letter, but as I understood that indication was desired as to our action in circumstances where *casus fœderis* had not arisen I enquired what the "energetic measures" would be and what kind of support Japanese Government would desire.

Viscount Hayashi was without instructions on these points, but suggested that we might assist a good deal by observing a "benevolent neutrality." He hoped we would give Japanese fleet facilities for coaling. We might also permit use of Colonies for transmission of communications, and he had reason to know that the Japanese Government thought that we might perhaps lend them money. I said that

Q 2

Sir M. Samuel had already sounded me, but there were serious difficulties in the way of such a transaction, and it would be necessary to consult my colleagues.

In reply to enquiry whether Japanese Government had in their mind possibility of diplomatic support or mediation by this country, he said they were now entirely occupied with warlike preparations.

He also said, in answer to further enquiry, that nothing would be done before the receipt of the Russian reply, but I gathered that if it were unsatisfactory Japan would probably seize Masampo.

No. 266.

The Marquess of Lansdowne to Sir M. Durand.

F.O. America 2521.
(No. 232.) Confidential.
Sir,   Foreign Office, December 31, 1903.

The American Ambassador called upon me to-day and said that he had received a telegram from the United States Government, informing him that the President desired to be supplied promptly with the fullest information available as to the situation in the Far East, and as to the manner in which it was regarded in Europe. Mr. Choate was under the impression that a similar telegram had probably been addressed to the other American Embassies.

I told his Excellency that I presumed that the American Government was well informed as to the progress of the negotiations between Russia and Japan, and that I did not know that I had any particular information to place at his disposal.

Mr. Choate observed that the American Government no doubt obtained, either through their Minister at Tokyo, or from the Japanese Minister at Washington, the same information as that with which His Majesty's Government were supplied. I said that if there were any points in regard to which we were better informed than the United States Government, I would gladly place any knowledge which I possessed at his Excellency's disposal. My general impression was that the Japanese Government would not consent to the Russian counter-proposals, and that if the Russian Government remained obdurate and refused absolutely to make concessions either in respect to Manchuria or Corea, the Japanese Government would take measures to vindicate their rights.

Mr. Choate asked me whether the reply lately returned by the Japanese Government had been accompanied by a time-limit. I said that I had no reason to suppose that such a limit had been fixed, but that I felt convinced that if the Russian Government were to keep the Japanese Government waiting too long for an answer, they would resort to active measures of one kind or another.

I expressed the satisfaction with which I learnt that the United States Government were taking so keen an interest in the Far Eastern question.

I am, &c.
LANSDOWNE.

No. 267.

[NOTE.—These private letters of Sir Ernest Satow are given as illustrating the general situation to the end of 1903.

Sir Ernest Satow to Lord Lansdowne.

August 27, 1903.

I found him [Admiral Sir C. Bridge] a good deal disturbed by the fact that the Russian Squadron is superior to ours in number of battleships and large cruisers. Such a thing as our squadron at a foreign station being outnumbered by that of any other Power, he says, has never occurred within the memory of man.

. . . . The news that the Japanese have officially addressed the Russian Government on the Manchurian question seems of great importance. If the Russians refuse to discuss it, will not the Japanese Government find themselves compelled to declare war? For if they sit down quietly under a rebuff Russia will take the whole of Manchuria and ultimately Corea, to which she is already stretching out her hand at Yongampho.

I think Admiral Bridge would agree with me that the result of a war in which Japan fights Russia singlehanded would be her defeat and the loss of Corea. Then Russia becomes the dominant Power in this part of the world, and will swallow up at least all northern China.

You were good enough to tell me that you thought Japan had some reason for considering that we had not afforded her sufficient support since the conclusion of the alliance, and I find Sir Cyprian [Bridge] deeply impressed with the same view. He had just heard of the detention of the "Argonaut" at the China Station and I told him I thought it was for the purpose of putting heart into the Japanese.

May I venture to say that to let Japan be ousted by Russia would be a disaster to us also? With our assistance she would have nothing to fear even if the Russians were determined to provoke her to declare war as many Russian officers declare is what will be done. But if Russia is victorious over Japan, then though we shall not have lost a ship or a man, we shall be powerless in the Far East.

Sir E. Satow to Mr. W. E. Davidson (Legal Adviser to the Foreign Office).

November 18, 1903.

China seems in a bad way and a première partition of this Far Eastern Poland seems to be imminent. If Japan goes to war, it will give the Germans the opportunity they have long desired of extending their sway over Shantung. I trust England will be faithful to her compact with Japan.

Sir E. Satow to Lord Lansdowne.

December 29, 1903.

The Japanese mean business—and the Russians are making a mistake if they think they can intimidate them.]

No. 268.

The Marquess of Lansdowne to Sir C. MacDonald.

F.O. Japan 576.
(No. 6.) Secret.
Sir, *Foreign Office, January* 5, 1904.

Viscount Hayashi called at this Office to-day, and made a statement to the following effect :—

> In view of the possibility of mediation being proposed by any Power or Powers in connection with the present Russo-Japanese relations, it was necessary to prevent any misunderstandings about the attitude of the Japanese Government in the matter.

Mediation at this juncture would not be agreeable to the Imperial Government, for the following reasons :—

1. Should Russia seek or accept mediation, she would do so simply for the purpose of gaining time in order to strengthen and consolidate her position in the Far East without any desire to come to a complete and permanent understanding on the present question.
2. Japan had put forward extremely moderate and conciliatory proposals, in the belief that, as the result of friendly negotiations with Russia, a satisfactory arrangement would be brought about. If, however, the settlement of the present question was to be effected by recourse to mediation instead of by direct and friendly negotiations, as at first intended, the Imperial Government would be compelled to modify their proposals, and to seek such further guarantees as would more effectually prevent future complications in addition to those she had originally contemplated.

[15214] Q 3

3. In view of the above considerations, any attempt to bring about mediation at this juncture would, in the opinion of the Imperial Government, prove ineffective, and consequently result in advantage to Russia.

Viscount Hayashi stated that his Government still hoped that it might be found possible for this country to come to the assistance of Japan financially by means of some private arrangement between the two Governments, but he admitted that the reasons given to him against such action were very strong.

He stated that the reason why Japan was so anxious to obtain financial assistance was that it was believed that the war, should hostilities ensue, might last two or three years; that Japan by drawing upon her reserves would be able to fight for a year; and that, by increasing taxation and by the issue of paper money, she could continue the struggle for six months more, but that she would then have exhausted her resources.

I am, &c.

LANSDOWNE.

No. 269.

The Marquess of Lansdowne to Sir C. MacDonald.

F.O. Japan 576.
(No. 7.) Secret.

Sir,   *Foreign Office, January 6, 1904.*

I had some conversation to-day with the Japanese Minister upon the subject of the communications which he had recently made to this Office. He told me that he regarded the statement made by General Bezobrazoff to the Japanese Legation at St. Petersburgh as of extreme importance, and as correctly representing the policy by which the Russian Government was actuated at the present time. He seemed to regard it as most improbable that the Russian answer, however conciliatory in tone, would be of a kind which the Japanese Government could accept. In his view it was essential that the valley of the Yalu River should not remain in Russian hands. The area covered by the timber Concession, in which General Bezobrazoff himself was interested, was very extensive, and if Russia were allowed to remain in occupation of it she would be in a position to strike with fatal effect at Japan whenever she pleased. A few years hence she would be able to strike with greater certainty than at present, and the Japanese Government were therefore determined to accept nothing less than a settlement which would have the effect of interposing a substantial barrier to Russian aggression at this point.

Viscount Hayashi referred again to the question of financial assistance from this country, and told me that although he quite understood that it might be most inconvenient to us to increase our borrowings, or add to our liabilities at the present moment, he did not think it desirable to dwell too much upon this consideration when explaining to the Japanese Government the reasons for our refusal. It would be difficult to convince them that we could not get the money if we really wished to do so. He asked me, therefore, whether I had any objection to his dwelling more particularly upon the political objections to such an operation on the very eve of a possible outbreak of war.

I said that he was quite correct in assuming that we were actuated by political as well as financial considerations. There could be no doubt that if a Japanese loan were guaranteed by His Majesty's Government, or a large sum lent by them to Japan at the present moment, the impression would be created that we were departing from our neutrality, and, in effect, giving active encouragement to Japan. The result would certainly be to create serious and widespread apprehensions. The transaction would moreover, have to be defended in Parliament, and might not be justified without difficulty. We had observed with satisfaction his statement that Japan had resources sufficient to carry her through the first year of a war, or, perhaps, an even longer time; so that the denial of immediate assistance would not in any way prejudice her during the initial, and probably most important, stages of the campaign.

I am, &c.
LANSDOWNE.

No. 270.

The Marquess of Lansdowne to Sir C. Scott.

F.O. Russia 1683.   *Foreign Office, January 8, 1904.*
Tel. (No. 11.)   D. 10·20 P.M.

Russian Ambassador to-day made a formal statement to me that Russia had no intention of preventing foreign Powers from continuing to enjoy in Manchuria their Treaty rights.

I expressed satisfaction, but stated that public here were looking for concrete evidence of Russia's intention to fulfil her promises.

Why, for example, I asked, could she not evacuate Newchwang at once?

I understood from him that this communication had probably been made to all the Powers in order to meet the Japanese demand for an assurance of this nature.

[This telegram was expanded into a despatch, which, with the formal statement of the Russian Ambassador, is printed in *Accounts and Papers*, 1904 (*Cd.* 1936), CX, pp. 229–30.]

No. 271.

The Marquess of Lansdowne to Sir C. MacDonald.

F.O. Japan 580.   *Foreign Office, January 8, 1904.*
Tel. (No. 8.) Secret.   D. 10 P.M.

Your telegram No. 9 of 7th January: Russo-Japanese negotiations.

Japanese Minister informed me to-day that it seemed to him almost out of the question that Japanese Government should accept last Russian proposals. They would certainly object to Article VI in its present shape and to placing on record that Manchuria and its littoral were outside their sphere of interest. Proviso as to treaty rights was, he thought, illusory, and would confine Japanese to Newchwang. Russian Government would certainly prevent ratification of Japanese Treaty under which fresh ports were to be opened.

Proviso excluding settlements would render it impossible for Japanese to remain in Manchuria except on sufferance.

(Repeat to Peking.)

No. 272.

Sir F. Lascelles to the Marquess of Lansdowne.

F.O. Germany (Prussia) 1593.   *Berlin, D. January 8, 1904.*
(No. 5.) Confidential. Extract.   R. *January 11, 1904.*

. . . . I then asked whether there was any truth in a report which had reached me, that the Russians had stated that they would not regard the occupation of Masampo by Japan as a *casus belli*, and Count Bülow said that he believed that the Japanese had been told that their occupation of the southern coast of Corea for police purposes would not be considered as an act of war. There could be no doubt, Count Bülow said, of the pacific intentions of the Emperor of Russia and of the Russian Government, and he believed that the Japanese Government were sincerely desirous of avoiding war. Public opinion in Japan was, no doubt, excited to a dangerous extent, and there was, perhaps, a feeling in Japan that it would be more to her advantage to begin hostilities before the Russians had increased their forces in the Pacific, but he was in hopes, more especially after receiving Count Osten Sacken's declaration, that means would be found for maintaining peace . . . .

I have, &c.
FRANK C. LASCELLES.

No. 273.

Sir F. Lascelles to the Marquess of Lansdowne.

F.O. Germany (Prussia) 1593.   *Berlin, D. January 8, 1904.*
(No. 6.)   Very Confidential.   Extract.   R. *January 11, 1904.*

     . . . . Count Bülow said he did not believe that the Far Eastern question had been discussed between the two Emperors. He had not been present, so could not say positively what had taken place, but the German Emperor had given him an account of what had been said, and there was not a word about his having promised the support of Germany to Russia in case of a war with Japan. Count Bülow did not believe there could have been the slightest foundation for the story.

On my observing that even if the story had been true I should not have been inclined to attribute too much importance to it, as I was aware from personal experience that the Emperor was sometimes in the habit, more especially in private conversation, of indulging in exaggerated expressions, Count Bülow said that even if the story had been true, His Majesty would have been unable to fulfil his promise. Germany was a constitutional country; the consent of the Reichstag would be necessary to enable German forces to be employed in warlike operations; and I might take it from him as perfectly certain that, in the event of a war between Russia and Japan, nothing would induce Germany to depart from an attitude of perfect neutrality.

No. 274.

The Marquess of Lansdowne to Sir C. MacDonald.

F.O. Japan 576.
(No. 12.)   Secret.
Sir,   *Foreign Office, January 11, 1904.*

     The Japanese Minister asked me for an interview to-day. He told me that the Japanese Government had instructed their Minister at Peking to advise Prince Ch'ing that if war should break out between Russia and Japan China would do well to maintain neutrality. This for three reasons : first, because it seemed to the Japanese Government desirable that the theatre of war should be as restricted as possible; secondly, because they did not wish the number of belligerents to be increased; and, thirdly, because they were of opinion that if China were involved in war disorders would break out in that country, and would lead to the intervention of interested Powers.

     Viscount Hayashi said that the Japanese Government would be glad to be favoured with an expression of the views of His Majesty's Government upon this subject. I replied that I thought I could take upon myself to say that the advice given to Prince Ch'ing was sound.

Viscount Hayashi then told me that the Japanese Government had observed a rumour that the Russian Black Sea Fleet was likely to pass through the Straits in order to repair to the Far East. The Japanese Government hoped that, if there were any question of such an occurrence, they might count upon the "good offices" of His Majesty's Government. I said that I could not undertake to say what action we might think it necessary to take in consequence of an incident of this kind, but that we should undoubtedly regard it as a grave violation of the Treaty engagements entered into with us and other Powers by Russia.

Viscount Hayashi further informed me that the German Government had officially intimated at Tokyo that they had no interests in Manchuria or Corea, and that, in the event of hostilities breaking out, it was their intention to observe a strict neutrality.

We then had a short conversation upon the subject of the communication made to me by the Russian Ambassador on the 8th instant, the substance of which I had made known to the Minister. He told me that its language seemed to him dangerously vague and quite unsatisfactory from the Japanese point of view. The Russian declaration that foreign Powers would be allowed to enjoy in Manchuria the rights acquired by them under existing Treaties was accompanied by the reservation that this assurance was given without prejudice to the conditions which might in the future finally determine the relations of Russia with Manchuria. It was, moreover, to be observed that in the communication made at Tokyo to the Japanese by the Russian Government, it was expressly stated that Japan was to be secured in the enjoyment of existing Treaty rights, "exclusive of the establishment of Settlements." The latter words implied a most dangerous limitation. Except in Newchwang, the Japanese had at present no extra-territorial rights in any part of Manchuria, and the Russian clause was evidently intended to condemn them for all time to live in other parts of that province on sufferance under a virtually Russian Government.

I am, &c.
LANSDOWNE.

No. 275.

The Marquess of Lansdowne to Sir C. MacDonald.

F.O. Japan 576.
(No. 14.) Secret.

Sir,   *Foreign Office, January 14, 1904.*

The Japanese Minister left with me to-day the enclosed copy of the instructions given to the Japanese Minister at St. Petersburgh.

Viscount Hayashi told me that the demands embodied in these instructions were to be regarded as final, and that if an answer was not received within a reasonable time, or if the answer were unsatisfactory, the Japanese Government would have to take steps for the protection of their interests.

I asked him whether he could tell me what the Japanese Government would consider a reasonable time.

He replied that he was unable to give me information upon this point, but that upon the last occasion about a fortnight had been allowed to elapse.

I am, &c.
LANSDOWNE.

Enclosure in No. 275.

Instructions to the Japanese Minister at St. Petersburgh.

You are hereby instructed to deliver to Count Lamsdorff a verbal note to the following effect, which you will say, is intended to confirm to him the views of the Imperial Government communicated to Baron Rosen on the 13th instant:—

The Imperial Government, in order to arrive at a pacific solution of the pending question, and to firmly establish the basis of a good relation between Japan and Russia, and, in addition, with a view to protect the rights and interests of Japan, have given most careful and serious consideration to the reply of the Imperial Russian Government which was delivered by Baron Rosen on the 6th instant. They have finally come to the conclusion that the following modifications are necessary—

1st. Suppression of the first clause of Article V of the Russian counter-proposal (presented to the Japanese Government through Baron Rosen on the 11th December last), that is to say, "not to use any part of Corean territory for strategic purposes."

2nd. Suppression of the whole article concerning the establishment of a neutral zone.

3rd. The Russian proposal concerning Manchuria to be agreed to, with the following modifications :—

(a.) Recognition by Japan of Manchuria and its littoral as being outside her sphere of interest, and an engagement on the part of Russia to respect the territorial integrity of China in Manchuria.

(b.) Russia, within the limits of Manchuria, will not impede Japan or other Powers in the enjoyment of rights and privileges acquired by them under existing Treaties with China.

(c.) Recognition by Russia of Corea and its littoral as being outside her sphere of interest.

4th. Addition of an Article to the following effect :—

Recognition by Japan of Russia's special interests in Manchuria, and of the right of Russia to take measures necessary for the protection of those interests.

The grounds for these amendments having been frequently and fully explained on previous occasions, the Imperial Government do not think it necessary to repeat explanations. It is sufficient here to express their earnest hope for reconsideration by the Russian Government. It should be further remarked that the suppression of the clause excluding the establishment of settlements in Manchuria is because of its conflict with stipulations of the new commercial Treaty between Japan and China. In this respect, however, Japan will be satisfied if she receives equal treatment with another Power which has already acquired similar right in regard to settlements in Manchuria.

The statement in the Russian reply that the Japanese Government have agreed to the original wording of Article V of the Russian counter-proposal is erroneous, such agreement having never been expressed by the Imperial Government.

The above-mentioned amendments being proposed by the Imperial Government entirely in a spirit of conciliation, it is expected that they will be received with the same spirit at the hand of the Russian Government, and the Imperial Government further hope for an early reply from the Russian Government, since further delay in the solution of the question would be extremely disadvantageous to the two countries.

No. 276.

The Marquess of Lansdowne to Sir C. Scott.

F.O. Russia 1677.
(No. 18.)
Sir, *Foreign Office, January 15, 1904.*

During the course of a conversation with the Russian Ambassador to-day, I recurred to the communication which he had made to me on the 8th instant (see my despatch No. 6, Confidential, of the 8th January). I said that we had found some difficulty in placing an interpretation upon the sentence in which it was said that "*without prejudice to the conditions which would determine in the future the nature of her relations with Manchuria,* Russia considered it indispensable to declare at once that she had no intention of preventing foreign Powers from continuing to enjoy the rights acquired by them by virtue of the Treaties in force." I confessed that I had interpreted those words as an intimation that in the event of the relations of Russia and Manchuria being modified, perhaps by the establishment of a Russian Protectorate over that province, or even by its annexation, Russia would regard the assurance that foreign Powers should continue to enjoy their Treaty rights in that province as no longer binding upon her. It had, however, been suggested to me that the phrase which had been translated from the original Russian into French, and from French into English, was susceptible of a different interpretation, and might mean that the Powers were to enjoy their rights whatever change might hereafter take place in the position of Manchuria. I thought it most important that there should be no misunderstanding as to the meaning of this most important passage.

His Excellency evidently felt considerable difficulty in answering my question. He said that neither the English nor the French version quite adequately represented the Russian text, and he gave me several alternative formulas, which, however, did not seem to me to remove the ambiguity. I finally wrote down and handed to his Excellency the following question :—

" Do the words ' without prejudice to the conditions which would determine in the future the nature of her relations with Manchuria ' mean that the foreign Powers will continue to enjoy their rights under existing Treaties whatever may be the conditions which may in the future finally determine the relations of Russia with Manchuria, or do they mean that the foreign Powers will continue to enjoy those rights, subject, however, to any conditions which may in the future finally determine the relations of Russia and Manchuria? "

His Excellency replied that his personal view was that the first of these constructions was that which the words were intended to bear.

He felt, no doubt, that as long as the sovereignty of China was maintained, so long would the Treaty rights of the Powers remain in force; and he added that there was no question of putting an end to the sovereignty of China. But he could not, of course, say what might happen in the event of the province ever being annexed by Russia, to which I had referred as a possibility. It was enough to say that there was no question of annexation. He promised, however, that he would obtain from me an authoritative explanation of the text.

I said that I sincerely hoped that the first of the two constructions was the correct one. I added, however, that if it were accepted, and if we were to assume that there was no question of annexation, I did not quite understand the significance of the words to which I had called attention. His Excellency said that Russia was still in occupation of Manchuria, and that it was quite possible that her present relations with that province might be modified before a final settlement was come to.

I am, &c.

LANSDOWNE.

MINUTE BY KING EDWARD.

Count Benckendorff's explanation is most unsatisfactory.

E.R.

No. 277.

Sir C. MacDonald to the Marquess of Lansdowne

Tokyo, January 16, 1904.

F.O. Japan 581.   D. 9˙30 P.M.

Tel. (No. 17.) Confidential.   R. 6˙30 P.M.

Your telegram No. 12 [of January 15th repeating last paragraph of Sir C. Scott's No. 10 of January 14th].

Following is extract from Japanese Minister's telegram reporting New Year's reception interview with the Emperor of Russia. Extract commences. "During conversation His Majesty made use of such expressions as 'Russia is a big country' and 'there are limits to our patience,' but otherwise his reception was cordial.

"Empress Dowager said that war was possible and peace must be maintained. I assured Her Majesty that we were doing our best to attain a pacific settlement of present question." Extract ends.

No. 278.

The Marquess of Lansdowne to Sir C. MacDonald.

F.O. Japan 576.

(No. 17.)

Sir,   *Foreign Office, January* 16, 1904.

The Japanese Minister called at this Office to-day, and stated that information had reached his Government to the effect that M. Delcassé was contemplating the idea of an offer of mediation between Russia and Japan.

Viscount Hayashi said that the attitude of the Japanese Government with regard to this question had been in no way modified since his conversation with me on the subject on January 5, as reported in my despatch No. 6 of that date, and that they were opposed to any such offer being made. Negotiations on the subject would necessarily take time, and the Japanese Government considered that the delay which must be caused by the consideration of the proposal, in the event of its leading to no result, would only be to the advantage of Russia.

I am, &c.

LANSDOWNE.

No. 279.

The Marquess of Lansdowne to Sir C. MacDonald.

F.O. Japan 580.   *Foreign Office, January* 17, 1904.

Tel. (No. 13.)   D. 4˙45 P.M.

Sir C. Scott reports that on 15th instant Count Lamsdorff again gave an unmistakable hint of personal desire for mediation. He said he had been hoping His Majesty's Government would offer their assistance in bringing about a pacific solution, that the Emperor abhorred the idea of war, and would make any reasonable concession to avoid it.

Sir C. Scott has reason to fear Count Lamsdorff's pacific views are meeting violent opposition in very influential circles, which have lately gained upper hand, and are endeavouring to make war popular by arousing feeling against England.

The Japanese Minister here stated again yesterday that his Government were opposed to all idea of mediation.

Repeat to Peking.

No. 280.

The Marquess of Lansdowne to Sir C. Scott.

F.O. Russia 1683.   *Foreign Office, January* 19, 1904.
Tel. (No. 23.)   D. 10 P.M.

Russo-Japanese negotiations.

French Ambassador informed me yesterday, in confidence, that M. Delcassé thought Russian communication of January 8th satisfactory. He did not think Russian Government, although ready to go to great lengths in the direction of the open door in Manchuria, would be likely to give way on question of right of settlement —it was not objected to as far as European Powers were concerned, but if granted to Japanese would mean their swarming over Manchuria. Other points did not present such difficulties. Could we not bring our influence to bear on Japan.

I said that it was impossible for us to press Japanese Government to modify their demands, several of which seemed to us reasonable. As to question of settlement, I repudiated warmly the idea of our presenting to them a proposal that other Powers should have rights which would be denied to them.

There were also, I said, questions of neutral zone and territorial integrity of China in Manchuria, to both of which Japan attached greatest importance. I gathered that if settlement question were got out of the way, these two points might not present insuperable difficulties.

I was waiting for explanations for which I had asked Russian Ambassador as to ambiguous words in Russian declaration, and precise ideas of Russian Government upon settlement question.

No. 281.

Sir C. Scott to the Marquess of Lansdowne.

F.O. Russia 1678.
(No. 27.)   Secret.   *St. Petersburgh,* D. *January* 20, 1904.
My Lord,   R. *January* 25, 1904.

On the 11th instant, Mr. Kurino, the Japanese Minister, informed me that he had asked M. de Witte to accord him an interview on the subject of Russo-Japanese relations.

I have now the honour to enclose a Memorandum, embodying an account of the interview, which Mr. Kurino requested Mr. Spring-Rice to communicate to me.

For the reasons given in the Memorandum, I did not telegraph M. de Witte's views to your Lordship, which, however, appear to be of considerable interest.

Since the date of this communication the situation appears to have changed for the better, but I beg to call special attention to M. de Witte's frank pronouncement as to the utility of Treaty engagements.

                     I have, &c.
                     CHARLES S. SCOTT.

Enclosure in No. 281.

Memorandum respecting Interviews between Mr. Kurino and M. de Witte.

(Secret.)

The Japanese Minister told me that he had asked M. de Witte to accord him a private interview. M. Witte had stated that he would talk freely on one condition, viz., that Mr. Kurino should not telegraph M. Witte's observations. The Secret Cabinet was almost always able to decypher the telegrams of foreign Representatives to their Governments, and he (M. Witte) would get into trouble if it were known that he had given advice to the Japanese Legation.

Mr. Kurino gave the desired promise, and M. de Witte then made the following statement : He said that he had systematically opposed the policy pursued by the Russian Government in the Far East, and he had been throughout supported by Count Lamsdorff. Now that the two Ministers had been completely defeated, he could not hope that his advice would be listened to any more, and he played the rôle of a mere spectator. From this point of view he could say that the question was simply one of a trial of strength and endurance between the two nations. He did not attribute any real or practical value to written or spoken assurances or Treaties. Assurances of the most solemn kind had been given by Russia. Since then circumstances had altered, and with the circumstances the policy of Russia had also altered. This had been the rule, and would continue to be the rule. The question was not what Russia or any other Power was bound to do under existing engagements, but what each Power could do having regard to the force of which that Power might dispose on the spot. Now, Japan could not in the end compete with Russia, either in military, naval, or financial resources. The waiting game was in favour of Russia. Japan would be unwise to trust in Treaties or engagements which would only be binding as long as the balance of force remained equal. When Russia arrived at the point where her force was superior to that of Japan, she would proceed to look after her own interests according to her own ideas. It was not, therefore, of much advantage for Japan to establish herself in Corea under the supposed protection of Treaties. Japan should content herself with that frontier which Russia could not transgress—that is the sea. As to her commercial interests, they would be as well or as badly off as those which she possessed in Vladivostock and Siberia, where large numbers of Japanese lived and prospered.

With regard to the general question, Mr. Kurino said that he was strongly of opinion that it would be unwise for Japan to attack Russia's position in the event of the breakdown of negotiations which now appeared to be probable. In his view the wisest course for Japan to pursue would be as follows : To make one final effort to induce Russia to change her point of view; if this effort were not successful, then to issue a statement to all the Powers to the effect that out of consideration for Russia, and in the general interests of peace and the stability of trade conditions, Japan had offered to recognise formally the exceptional position occupied by Russia in certain parts of China; that Russia had refused to consider the question of her occupation of parts of China; and that in consequence Japan was obliged to take her stand on the existing situation and on the general principles of international law. According to these principles, if China had not ceded her territory to Russia, her sovereignty remained intact, and the rights of foreign nations, based on Treaties with the sovereign Power were incontestable. "This being the case, Japan declares to the Powers her intention, so far as she was concerned, of maintaining existing Treaties and the rights accruing to her and other Powers under those Treaties. In case these rights should suffer from the action of any Power or Powers, Japan reserves to herself the right to safeguard her interests in the manner which may seem best to her."

(*December* 30, 1903) *January* 12, 1904.

No. 282.

Sir C. Scott to the Marquess of Lansdowne.

F.O. Russia, 1678.

(No. 33.) Confidential. St. Petersburg, D. *January* 21, 1904.

My Lord, R. *January* 25, 1904.

The tension between Japan and Russia in the Far East has as might naturally be expected been absorbing public interest here to the exclusion of all other pending questions. . . . .

. . . . . The difficulty in regard to the " settlements " condition seems to M. Kurino likely to be got out of the way by the communication made by the United States Minister at Tokio.

The Chinese Minister here has always said that it was not the intention of his Government when opening new ports in Manchuria to grant foreign settlements with independent municipal rights to foreign States, but only the right of settlement under Consular protection to individual foreigners.

The word "sovereignty" of China in Manchuria to which Russia apparently demurred seems to have been replaced in the last Japanese note by "territorial integrity" so as to bring it into harmony with the declarations in the Anglo-Japanese and Franco-Russian agreements.

On the whole I cannot help thinking that the prospect of a satisfactory settlement between Russia and Japan, is much more hopeful than it was a few days ago, although it cannot be denied that Agreements of this kind with Russia, according to a late admission by Count Lamsdorff, lack the necessary guarantee for permanent durability inasmuch as they are limited by lapse of time and change of circumstances, and circumstances in the Far East especially, seem liable to change with almost dazzling rapidity.

I cannot help thinking that the hint given by M. Plehve to M. Kurino in regard to the danger of any reaction in case any concessions eventually made by Russia were represented as concessions wrung from her by Japan instead of concessions to the Emperor's innate love of peace and desire to scrupulously keep his promises, is one which ought to be carefully borne in mind by the public in Japan and also in England, especially now that the defeated military party are openly attempting to revenge themselves to inciting popular animosity against England as once more opposing the natural expansion of Russia.

It would I think be unjust to the Emperor to credit His Majesty with having so long lent an ear to the promptings of this party out of sympathy with its real aims. The arguments which no doubt had weight with His Majesty were those based on defensive aims; resistance to the demands of Japan was advocated as a precaution against the "Yellow Peril" which was erroneously represented as imminent if Japan secured her ends. The other argument used was the danger to the prestige of the Great White Czar in Asia, if he thought that he was demeaning himself to accept terms from Japan or even to negotiate with her on terms of equality.

Such are the arguments which one has been in the habit of hearing even from the mouths of intelligent Russians.

I have, &c.
CHARLES S. SCOTT.

MINUTES.

1 think that according to the recognised principles of International Law an engagement to respect either the *sovereignty* of China or the *territorial integrity* of China in Manchuria is equally operative and adequate for the maintenance of the Treaty rights of other Powers.

In order that those rights may be extinguished it is necessary that the State which made the contract shall disappear from the territory in question. Annexation, *i.e.*, the actual absorption of the territory into that of another State, is necessary for this purpose. Russia might exercise in Manchuria various acts of sovereignty, in virtue of agreements with China, but so long as she does so only as the representative or assignée of the Chinese Empire, she is bound by the obligations of that Empire. . . . .—T. H. S. Jan. 30, 1904.

Lord Percy.

Please see with reference to our conversation. I am not sure that Sir C. Scott's interpretation is necessarily correct.

I doubt whether the recognition of Chinese *sovereignty* would be a real protection,—but it is a pity that the word *independence* dropped out of the Jap[anese] formula. Sir C. S[cott] is incorrect in his reference to the Anglo-Jap[ane]se Agreement in which both "independence" and "integrity" are mentioned. I wish someone would guarantee the integrity of the Russian Government.—L.

Lord Lansdowne.

This is the despatch form of the telegram to which I referred. The marked passage shews that the alteration was deliberate and that Russia at all events attaches importance to it. From our point of view I imagine that the retention of Chinese sovereignty is vital. Its elimination means the substitution of a Russian pledge for Treaty rights as a guarantee of the open door. I imagine that Russia intends to assume the protectorate over and the actual administration of Manchuria, with the proviso that she will respect China's external obligations there [so long as the protectorate lasts]. When the time comes for annexation she will use the same argument for excluding foreign trade that France used when she annexed Madagascar.—P.

But annexation destroys territorial integrity quite as much as it does sovereignty. Indeed territorial integrity may remain while sovereignty is considerably impaired. Foreign rights based on Treaties with Turkey are still valid in Cyprus, except in so far as they are waived by special agreement.—T. H. S.　Jan. 30.

No. 283.

The Marquess of Lansdowne to Sir E. Monson.

F.O. France 3662.
(No. 37.)

Sir,　　　　　　　　　　　　　　　　　　　　　　　　　*Foreign Office, January* 27, 1904.

The French Ambassador spoke to me again to-day upon the subject of the Russo-Japanese negotiations, which had, he thought, taken a hopeful turn. He anticipated, however, that there would be serious difficulty in disposing of the question of the recognition of Chinese sovereignty in Manchuria. It would be extremely difficult for Russia to negotiate with Japan on this point, and he could not help thinking that it might be worth the while of the other Powers to assist in bringing about an amicable solution. I said that we had no reason to believe that either side desired mediation. M. Cambon observed that he did not suggest that there should be mediation in the accepted sense of the term, but merely good offices and sedative advice. He thought that if Great Britain, France, and the United States were to tender such advice it would probably be accepted. I said that it seemed to me at any rate necessary that we should learn the nature of the reply which Russia was about to send to the last Japanese note. We should then be better able to judge of the situation. I felt, however, convinced that Japan would require a bilateral arrangement of some kind as to Manchuria.

　　　　　　　　　　　　　　　　　　　　　　　　　　　　　　I am, &c.
　　　　　　　　　　　　　　　　　　　　　　　　　　　　　　LANSDOWNE.

No. 284.

The Marquess of Lansdowne to Sir C. MacDonald.

F.O. Japan 576.
(No. 28.)

Sir,　　　　　　　　　　　　　　　　　　　　　　　　　*Foreign Office, January* 29, 1904.

I called the attention of the Japanese Minister to-day to the fact that according to the latest Japanese proposals as reported to us, Japan was apparently demanding that Russia should enter into an engagement to respect only the "territorial integrity" of China in Manchuria. On the other hand, when it came to Corea, Japan was insisting on a mutual engagement to respect the "independence and territorial integrity" of the Corean Empire. In the Japanese proposals which had been reported to us in November 1903, Japan had asked for "a mutual engagement to respect the independence and territorial integrity of the Corean and Chinese Empires." As we were apparently approaching a moment when a good deal might depend upon the precise terms used on either side, it occurred to me to ask him whether it was to be inferred that Japan was now content to accept, in reference to Manchuria, something less than she had originally demanded. I should like, at any rate, to know whether the difference in the phraseology was intentional, and, if so, what was its significance.

Viscount Hayashi told me that he had not noticed the point to which I referred, and he doubted very much whether the difference of language was intentional. In his view, the words "territorial integrity" would probably be sufficient to secure the recognition of the sovereignty of China and to prevent the establishment of a Russian Protectorate over that province or its annexation by Russia. He would, however, make enquiries of the Japanese Government.

We afterwards had some conversation as to the negotiations. I told him that I thought I saw signs of a movement in favour—I would not say of mediation—but of an effort by the Powers to discover a solution which both Parties might accept without loss of dignity. Many people would feel, and such a feeling might manifest itself in this country, that Japan, by the success of her diplomacy, had virtually obtained all that she desired in Corea, and would observe that Russia was ready to bind herself to respect all Japanese rights in Manchuria. It might be said that, in these circumstances, the Powers owed it to themselves to make some effort to avert the calamity of war. I was anxious to know in good time what the feeling of Japan probably would be upon this point. We had hitherto refused to have anything to say to mediation, knowing that it was not desired by the Japanese Government. I asked whether Viscount Hayashi thought that, come what may, anything in the shape of a suggestion from us or from other Powers would be distasteful to the Japanese Government. I said that I asked the question because I realised that Japan, looking back at the manner in which she had been treated by the Powers in 1895 and at the subsequent conduct of Russia, might feel that there was nothing for her but to insist upon her demands to the letter even at the cost of war. It seemed to me possible that if this were so they might resent, both now and hereafter, any action on our part which might have the effect of bringing moral pressure—for there could be no question of pressure of any other kind—upon them.

Viscount Hayashi told me that in his belief nothing would content the Japanese Government but a distinct bilateral engagement on the subject of Manchuria. They had had a bitter experience of the value of Russian declarations, and they would not be put off with such declarations now. The feeling in Japan in favour of war had grown rapidly during the last few weeks. There had at one time been a peace party, and a strong one, in Japan. There was no peace party now. The Marquises Ito and Inouyé, who had at one moment been regarded as Pro-Russians and in favour of peace, had given up all hopes of it. If the other Powers could obtain an engagement from Russia with regard to the integrity of China in Manchuria, and that engagement were extended to Japan, she might be content. So long as she got the engagement herself it did not matter to her what other Powers obtained it.

Viscount Hayashi spoke with much determination, and he left me under the impression that nothing short of the complete acceptance of the Japanese proposals would avert war.

I am, &c.
LANSDOWNE.

No. 285.

The Marquess of Lansdowne to Sir C. Scott.

F.O. Russia 1683.
Tel. (No. 33.) P.   *Foreign Office, January 30, 1904.*
Russian Black Sea Fleet.

In conversation with Japanese Minister on the 27th instant I told him, in confidence, that the Cabinet had approved of the statement I had made to him on the 11th instant. I could not, I said, undertake to say what action we should take by way of response to the passage through the Dardanelles of the Russian Fleet in the event of war, but we should undoubtedly regard such a proceeding as a grave violation of the Treaty engagements which Russia had entered into with us and other Powers. There were, however, absolutely no indications that the Russian Government contemplated any such action, and we were decidedly of opinion that the contingency was not likely to arise.

Nothing is further from our intentions than to encourage Japan to proceed to extremities, or to impute perfidy to the Russian Government, and you should make this clear to Count Lamsdorff if it should come to be known at St. Petersburgh that we have been in communication with the Japanese Government on this subject. We have, on the contrary, informed the latter of our firm conviction that Russia will respect her Treaty obligations, and that she will abstain from action which is fraught with the very gravest international perils, as well as contrary to the Law of Europe.

Although we have not said as much to the Japanese, it would clearly be impossible for us to permit any ships now in the Black Sea to take part in warlike operations, and it is very desirable that this should be clearly understood by the Russian Government in time to prevent them from committing themselves, in ignorance, to a policy which must be disastrous both for Great Britain and for Russia.

You are authorised to convey this expression of our views to Count Lamsdorff should any contingency suddenly arise which would seem to render such a course necessary, but, so far as I am aware, there is no occasion to do so at present, and unless the circumstances required it, such a communication would certainly be irritating to his Excellency.

No. 286.

Sir C. Scott to the Marquess of Lansdowne.

St. Petersburgh, February 4, 1904.

F.O. Russia 1684.
Tel.　(No. 23.)　Most Confidential.
　Far East.

D. 10 A.M.
R. 12 P.M.

I have just learnt that the Emperor stated this morning that the reply would be despatched to-morrow, that its terms had been fixed after a very serious Council last night and would be found most conciliatory as he had decided to go the utmost length compatible with his honour to satisfy the claims of the Japanese Government and avert disastrous war, and that if the terms are not found acceptable at Tokyo it would simply be that Japan considered it in her interest to force an immediate appeal to arms—a contingency which His Majesty was most loath to contemplate.

No. 287.

Sir C. MacDonald to the Marquess of Lansdowne.

Tokyo, February 5, 1904.

F.O. Japan 581.
Tel.　(No. 37.)
　Russo-Japanese negotiations.

D. 8·40 P.M.
R. February 6, 9 A.M.

M.F.A. asked to see me this afternoon. He recapitulated course of above negotiations from commencement and reminded me that on January 13th and January 27th he had informed me that if the Russian reply to last Japanese proposals was unsatisfactory or unduly delayed the Japanese Government would have to consider and decide what measures they would have to take to protect their rights and interests (see my telegrams Nos. 14 and 29).

Notwithstanding that the Japanese Government has repeatedly pressed for a reply none had been received, and Japanese Minister at St. Petersburg's telegram dated February 2nd stated that no definite answer could be given for three or four days. In the meantime reinforcements were being sent out from Russia, both naval and military, and preparations were being made for sending Russian troops to the Corean frontier.

Accordingly it had been decided to break off negotiations, and instructions for the purpose would be sent this evening to Japanese Representative at St. Petersburgh.

Baron Komura said that this decision had been arrived at by an absolutely unanimous vote. He informed me in strict confidence that the Emperor, the Elder statesmen generally, more especially Ito the Prime Minister and the Minister of Marine, had been mainly instrumental in continuing the negotiations for so long, notwithstanding repeated rebuffs from Russia, in the hopes of maintaining peace, but that now they also were of the opinion that further negotiations were useless.

His Excellency further stated that Japanese Government were deeply grateful for the many marks of sympathy which they had received from British Government and people during these negotiations. They hoped that H.M. Government would recognise that it was from no lack of patience or forbearance on their part that the negotiations had fallen through.

No. 288.

The Marquess of Lansdowne to Sir M. Durand.

F.O. America 2551.
Tel. (No. 12.) Most Secret.

Foreign Office, February 5, 1904.
D. 11 P.M.

Hostilities between Russia and Japan are apparently imminent. An attempt to draw us into a movement in favour of mediation is not improbable. Such a movement may originate in France, for I hear on good authority that Delcassé has hinted at possibility of concerted action by France, United States and Great Britain.

We have announced in Parliament that mediation not being desired by Japan, we have not attempted it—our feeling is that considering nature of demands upon which Japan is insisting we should not be justified in putting even moral pressure upon her to abate them. We might, moreover, incur lasting resentment of Japan if we were to stand in her way and deprive her of an opportunity which she is apparently determined to turn to account. If she were to miss her chance now she might suffer for it hereafter.

These are our private views; there is no reason why you should volunteer a statement of them, but you should be aware of them in case the subject should be broached by the United States' Government. You might endeavour to ascertain how they regard the matter. We should be glad to find that there was no difference between their point of view and ours.

No. 289.

The Marquess of Lansdowne to Sir C. MacDonald.

F.O. Japan 576.
(No. 36.) Secret.
Sir,

Foreign Office, February 5, 1904.

The Japanese Minister informed me to-day in strict confidence that the Japanese Government would mobilise their forces to-morrow. They had been pressing the Russian Government for a reply to their last communication, but it had not yet reached them. They anticipated that it would not be satisfactory.

Viscount Hayashi again impressed upon me that the Japanese Government would not be content without an engagement amounting to a "compact" as to

[15214]
B 2

Manchuria. He repeated that whether such a compact were made between Russia and Japan or between Russia and all the Powers interested did not matter.

I told him that I had not misapprehended the views of the Japanese Government upon this point and that I had already communicated them to my colleagues.

I am, &c.
LANSDOWNE.

No. 290.

Sir C. Scott to the Marquess of Lansdowne.

St. Petersburg, February 6, 1904.

F.O. Russia 1684.
Tel. (No. 26.)

D. 3·40 P.M.
R. 4·15 P.M.

Russia and Japan.

Your telegram No. 36.

Japanese Minister has just been here to inform me that he is, by instructions, presenting note to Russian Government to-day breaking off diplomatic relations and asking for his passports to leave St. Petersburg at latest on 10th February.

Note will state fully reasons for rupture.

He is to proceed to Berlin and there await further instructions.

No. 291.

The Marquess of Lansdowne to Viscount Hayashi.

F.O. Japan 585.

Sir,

Foreign Office, February 6, 1904.

You made me this afternoon, under instructions from the Japanese Government, a statement of the reasons for which they had felt it necessary to terminate the negotiations which had lately been in progress between Japan and Russia.

With reference to your observations at the close of our conversation, His Majesty's Government recognise with satisfaction that throughout these protracted negotiations the Japanese Government have, in loyal compliance with Article V of the Agreement of 1902, been careful to keep them fully and accurately informed as to the progress of events.

The Japanese Government express the hope that any complications which may arise may be confined entirely to the two Powers concerned. His Majesty's Government share this hope, and will on their side fulfil, both in letter and spirit, their obligations under the Agreement, which imposes upon them the duty of using their efforts in order to prevent other Powers from joining in hostilities against their ally.

His Majesty's Government take note of the desire which the Japanese Government has again expressed to the effect that at the present juncture no third Power or Powers should in any way interfere between Russia and Japan.

I have, &c.
LANSDOWNE.

No. 292.

The Marquess of Lansdowne to Sir C. MacDonald.

F.O. Japan 576.
(No. 39.)
Sir,   *Foreign Office, February 6, 1904.*

Viscount Hayashi to-day communicated to me the note, of which I enclose a copy, addressed by Mr. Kurino, the Japanese Minister at St. Petersburgh, under instructions from his Government to the Russian Government, announcing the termination of the negotiations respecting Corea and Manchuria.

Viscount Hayashi was instructed, when communicating the note, to say that throughout the negotiations with Russia, the Japanese Government had been careful to keep His Majesty's Government fully and accurately informed of the progress of those negotiations, and that the Japanese Government confidently believed that His Majesty's Government, having a complete knowledge of the situation, would agree that the Imperial Government could not, with a proper sense of their own dignity, or due regard for their own welfare or for the rights and interests of Japan, longer delay breaking off the negotiations. The responsibility for the situation thus created, as well as for the consequences which might ensue, rested exclusively with Russia.

In conclusion, Viscount Hayashi said that it was the earnest desire of the Japanese Government to confine the complications entirely to Japan and Russia; that they had used their utmost efforts to secure that result; and that the Japanese Government sincerely hoped that His Majesty's Government would also use their best endeavours to prevent interference in any form, or under any "name," on the part of any third Power or Powers.

I am, &c.
LANSDOWNE.

Enclosure in No. 292.

Note addressed by Japanese Minister at St. Petersburgh to the Russian Government.

The Envoy Extraordinary and Minister Plenipotentiary of His Majesty the Emperor of Japan has the honour, in pursuance of instructions from his Government, to address to his Excellency the Minister for Foreign Affairs of His Majesty the Emperor of All the Russias the following communication :—

"The Government of His Majesty the Emperor of Japan regard the independence and territorial integrity of the Empire of Corea as essential to their own country's repose, and are consequently unable to view with indifference any action tending to render the position of Corea insecure.

"The successive rejections by the Imperial Russian Government, by means of inadmissible amendments, of Japan's proposals respecting Corea, the adoption of which the Imperial Japanese Government regarded as indispensable to assuring the independence and territorial integrity of the Corean Empire, and to safe-guarding Japan's preponderating interest in the Peninsula, coupled with the successive refusals of the Imperial Russian Government to enter into an engagement to respect China's territorial integrity in Manchuria, which is seriously menaced by their continued occupation of the province, notwithstanding their Treaty engagements with China, and their repeated assurances to other Powers possessing interests in those regions, have made it necessary for the Imperial Japanese Government seriously to consider what measures of self-defence they are called upon to take in the presence of the delay on the part of Russia in connection with the negotiation, which remains largely unexplained, and of her naval and military activities, which it is difficult to reconcile with an entirely pacific aim.

"The Imperial Japanese Government have exercised in the pending negotiation a degree of forbearance which, they believe, affords abundant proofs of their loyal desire to remove from their relations with the Imperial Russian Government every cause for future misunderstandings, but finding in their efforts no prospect of securing from the Imperial Russian Government an adhesion either to Japan's moderate and unselfish proposals, or to any other proposals likely to establish a firm and enduring peace in the Extreme East, the Imperial Japanese Government have no other alternative than to terminate the present futile negotiation.

"In adopting that course, the Imperial Japanese Government reserve to themselves the right to take such independent action as they may deem best to consolidate and defend their menaced position as well as to protect their established rights and legitimate interests. . . . .''

No. 293.

The Marquess of Lansdowne to Sir C. MacDonald.

F.O. Japan 580. *Foreign Office, February 7, 1904.*
Tel. (No. 35.) Confidential. D. 9·25 P.M.

I told Russian Ambassador this evening that I felt sure that nothing would stop Japan but Treaty engagement by Russia to respect sovereignty and integrity of China in Manchuria.

He asked whether I could suggest any form in which such an engagement might be embodied other than Treaty between Russia and Japan, to which Russia objects.

I replied that I could think of nothing but a Treaty between Russia and China, of which other Powers might be invited by both Russia and China to take note.

He asked me whether, supposing Russia were willing to agree, we would advise Japan to accept such an offer.

I said I must consult my colleagues at Cabinet to-morrow, and that I feared it might be too late, even if Russia were willing.

Ambassador's enquiry was unofficial, but I think Russia would evidently be glad to be extricated even at the last moment.

Can you tell me how matter would be regarded by Japanese Government?

Viscount Hayashi's language leads me to think they might be content with proposed solution.

No. 294.

The Marquess of Lansdowne to Sir C. MacDonald.

F.O. Japan 576.
(No. 38.)
Sir, *Foreign Office, February 7, 1904.*

The Japanese Minister called upon me this evening, and I repeated to him in confidence the substance of my latest conversation with the Russian Ambassador (see my despatch to Sir C. Scott No. 47 of the 8th February). I said that I thought it most important that before referring to the Cabinet, I should be made aware of his views. Viscount Hayashi told me that a few weeks ago—he might almost say one week ago—the Japanese Government would probably have been content to entertain a proposal upon the lines of that which I had described to Count Benckendorff. Matters had, however, now gone too far. It would not, he said, have escaped my notice that if a Treaty were to be entered into by Russia with China, with the adhesion of other Powers, a negotiation which might be lengthy would have to be commenced. The Japanese Government could not, however, tolerate further delay : they had waited three weeks for an answer; they had constantly pressed for one during the last few days, and had on each occasion been put off with a promise that the reply would be sent to-morrow. Meanwhile, Russia was daily strengthening her position. Moreover, the Chinese were so untrustworthy, that he disliked the idea of any settlement based upon an understanding with them.

The Minister told me that even if Russia were to come to Japan after hostilities had commenced with the offer of a Treaty, he doubted very much whether "the martial spirit of his countrymen could be restrained."

I begged Viscount Hayashi to understand clearly that, although I had thought it my duty to repeat to him what had been said by the Russian Ambassador, His Majesty's Government had no idea of putting pressure upon Japan. We should not have ventured to ask them to consider any proposal unless we had previously made sure that it was one which would be agreeable to them.

I am, &c.
LANSDOWNE.

No. 295.

The Marquess of Lansdowne to Sir C. Scott.

F.O. Russia 1677.
(No. 47.)
Sir, *Foreign Office, February 8, 1904.*

The Russian Ambassador asked me for an interview yesterday evening, and, under instructions from the Russian Government, made to me a statement to the following effect :—

"Acting on instructions from his Government, the Japanese Minister at the Imperial Court had presented a note, which informs the Imperial Government of the decision of Japan to break off further negotiations, and recall its Minister and the whole staff of Legation. In consequence of this, His Imperial Majesty had been pleased to order that the Russian Minister at Tokyo, with the whole staff of the Imperial Mission, should leave the capital of Japan without delay. Such an attitude on the part of the Tokyo Government, which had not even awaited the arrival of the answer of the Imperial Government (which had just been sent off) threw the whole responsibility for any consequences which might arise from a rupture of diplomatic negotiations between the two Empires on Japan."

Count Benckendorff went on to say that he had been desired by Count Lamsdorff to inform me confidentially that, in Count Lamsdorff's opinion, the differences which had arisen between Russia and Japan with regard to Corea might be easily settled, the only point presenting serious difficulty being that which had reference to the right of Japan to erect fortifications in the interior of Corea. On the other hand, the demand of Japan that Russia should recognise the sovereignty of China in Manchuria could not be admitted. The question was one which did not specially concern Japan, and, in the opinion of the Russian Government, the Sovereign Power, namely, China, and all the other Powers were as much interested in that question as Japan. Count Benckendorff was also, he said, instructed to sound me unofficially upon the following point. After an agreement with regard to Corea had been entered into between Russia and Japan, Russia would be ready to make a declaration to all the Powers, including Japan, the effect of which would be to place on record her recognition of the integrity of China in Manchuria. His Excellency asked me whether such a declaration ought not to be sufficient. I said that I felt sure that no declaration of the kind would be regarded as satisfactory by the Japanese Government. They had from the first made it clear that what they wished for was an engagement,

R 4

by Treaty or Convention, on the part of Russia. The negotiations had now lasted for more than six months, and, so far as I was aware, the Russian Government had never given the Japanese Government any indication of a readiness to meet them upon this point. It seemed to me quite impossible that we should take upon ourselves to advise them to abate their demands in this respect—demands which were, indeed, in accordance with the policy which we had ourselves proclaimed. His Excellency again pressed upon me that an official declaration was as much as could be expected. I replied that, as we were talking unofficially, I felt bound to tell his Excellency that, in a case of this kind, a mere assurance from the Russian Government could not be regarded as conclusive. It had been explained to us more than once by that Government that such assurances were given entirely with reference to the circumstances of the moment, and that if those circumstances afterwards underwent a change the Russian Government regarded the assurance as no longer binding. I cited as an instance the warning given to you by Count Lamsdorff on the 4th ultimo, in reference to the statements of the Russian Government that they had no intention of appointing Russian Agents in Afghanistan* (see your despatch No. 11 of January 7th). I felt, therefore, that the Japanese Government could scarcely be blamed if they drew a distinction between an assurance or declaration and a bilateral engagement. To my mind the situation was clear cut. The Japanese would have a bilateral engagement or go to war. Whether they alone received that engagement, or whether it was given to other Powers, did not, I believed, matter to them.

His Excellency pressed me to say whether I could not suggest some means of arriving at a general agreement such as I had described between Russia and all the Powers including Japan. I replied that such an agreement might perhaps have taken the form of a Treaty between Russia and China recognising the sovereignty of the latter in Manchuria, and to be communicated both by Russia and China to the other Powers who would in that case take note of it diplomatically.

Count Benckendorff pointed out that if this procedure were to be adopted a lengthy negotiation might ensue, but he would like to know whether, in the event of Russia being willing, we should recommend Japan to accept it. I said that I could not answer his question without referring to my colleagues, but that my own impression was that events in the Far East had gone too far, and that we should not, as matters now stood, be prepared to assume the responsibility of pressing Japan to accept this or any other solution.

His Excellency called on me again this afternoon after the meeting of the Cabinet. I told him that my colleagues entirely agreed with what I had said as to the impossibility of intervention on our part.

I pressed his Excellency, whose language had been somewhat indistinct upon this point, to tell me whether I was to regard the whole of our conversation as unofficial, or if I might take any part of his communication as having been made under instructions from the Russian Government. He informed me that he was instructed to say that, in the opinion of Count Lamsdorff, there would be no difficulty in arriving at a settlement satisfactory to Japan in regard to the Corean question.

* Count Lamsdorff then stated that the words " At present " (" pour le moment ") should have been inserted, and it would then run thus :—

" At present they had no thought of establishing a representative at Cabul, or, indeed, of sending agents of any kind to the Ameer."

He explained that the reason for inserting these two words, which appeared in the instructions to Count Benckendorff and in the Report received from Count Benckendorff of his communication to your Lordship, was simply this.

Russia could not possibly contract engagements of this kind binding for all time, circumstances might change in the course of generations, and so might the position of Afghanistan, although there was no reason to foresee at present such change in the near future.

He was convinced that most of the misunderstandings which had arisen between the two Governments on questions like these arose from our interpreting the numerous former assurances and declarations of policy and intentions which Russia had given us as engagements binding Russia for all time and under all circumstances. [L.]

The arrangement proposed by Japan in regard to Manchuria was, however, inacceptable. Russia would, nevertheless, be glad to discover a peaceful solution of that question also. I told his Excellency that all I could do was to take note of his communication. He then proceeded to tell me " à titre personnel " that Russia having from the first desired a peaceful solution of these difficulties, remaind desirous of such a solution, and that he was convinced that any endeavour which might be made by one or more Powers to discover a way out of the difficulty would be welcomed by the Russian Government. I authorised his Excellency to say that, in my opinion, the events of which we had heard during the last two or three days, were of a nature to render difficult, if not impossible, the intervention of a third Power, and that I did not see how it would be possible for His Majesty's Government under the circumstances which now confronted them to attempt such a step.

I am, &c.
LANSDOWNE.

MINUTE BY KING EDWARD.

A most admirable and clear Despatch.

E.R

No. 296.

The Marquess of Lansdowne to Sir C. Scott.

F.O. Russia 1677.
(No. 47 A.)
Sir, *Foreign Office, February 8, 1904.*

During the course of the recent negotiations between Japan and Russia it became increasingly evident that the prospect of a satisfactory conclusion turned mainly on the question whether the Russian Government would consent to enter into a binding engagement with Japan that both Powers would respect the sovereignty and integrity of China in Manchuria, Japan being on her side willing to pledge herself to respect the integrity and independence of Corea.

From the inception of the negotiations this has always been put forward as an essential portion of the Japanese demands, while, on the part of Russia, it has constantly been ignored or refused, on the ground either that it was a matter for discussion between Russia and China alone, or that it was one which equally concerned other Powers, or that the declarations and assurances already given as to the intentions and policy of the Emperor of Russia should be regarded as sufficient.

In my conversations with the Russian and French Ambassadors during the last few days the question has been tentatively and unofficially discussed whether, in the event of a satisfactory agreement being attained on the questions relating to Corea, Japan could be expected to accept as sufficient a formal declaration made by the Russian Government to all the Powers concerned (including Japan) of the intention of Russia to respect the sovereignty and territorial integrity of China in Manchuria.

I have felt bound to state my conviction that such a declaration would not be accepted by Japan as fulfilling the conditions on which she has throughout laid so much stress, and which she considers essential for the protection of Japanese interests. Its inadequacy is, in fact, the logical consequence of the construction which the Russian Government themselves have placed on such declarations and assurances, viz., that they are not to be regarded in the light of a binding compact, only capable of modification with the consent of the other Contracting Party, and obligatory as long as that other Contracting Party fulfils its own share of the contract, but that they are no more than the expression of the intentions of the Government in the existing circumstances, liable to be modified or, indeed, entirely withdrawn if, in the independent opinion of that Government, the circumstances under which they were given have materially changed.

A notable instance of the view taken by the Russian Government in this respect was afforded in the case of Batoum. The assurance on this occasion was given in the most formal manner, being embodied in Article LIX of the Treaty of Berlin of the 13th July, 1878. That Article runs as follows :—

"His Majesty the Emperor of Russia declares that it is his intention to constitute Batoum a free port, essentially commercial."

Eight years later, in July 1886, the Russian Government announced to the Signatory Powers the intention of the Emperor to terminate this arrangement, and upon objections being raised by the British Government that this constituted a violation of the Treaty of Berlin and the breach of an international engagement, M. de Giers stated distinctly in a despatch to the Russian Ambassador at this Court that in the opinion of the Russian Government "the spontaneous declaration of the intention of the Emperor to make Batoum a free port did not constitute an obligation, and that consequently the modification of that intention, which circumstances require, could not be considered as a departure from engagements which did not exist."

The same view has recently been expressed to you by Count Lamsdorff in the conversation which you had with his Excellency on the 7th ultimo (as reported in your despatch No. 11 of that date) with regard to Afghanistan.

Count Lamsdorff stated on that occasion that most of the misunderstandings which had occurred between the two Governments on such questions had arisen from our interpreting the numerous former assurances and declarations of policy and intentions which Russia had given us as engagements binding Russia for all time and under all circumstances : he referred in particular to some declarations made by Baron Jomini, who was at the time acting in the absence of the Chancellor, which he said contained the earliest declaration of Russia's intention to abstain from direct foreign relations with Afghanistan, and of her recognition that those relations were under the control of the British Government; declarations to the wording of which we had evidently given the force of a Treaty engagement binding for all time. A little thought would, he considered, be sufficient to convince any one that an independent Power like Russia could scarcely have meditated contracting a perpetual engagement on this point.

The Japanese Government cannot, in my opinion, be reasonably expected to accept declarations or assurances, the value of which has thus been authoritatively defined by the Russian Government themselves, as a sufficient security for interests to which they attach so much importance.

Nor would a more positive engagement contracted between Russia and China alone satisfy their requirements. Such an engagement could, at any time, be modified with the consent of China, or might be treated by Russia as forfeited on account of the conduct of the Chinese Government.

The Japanese Government, as I understand, have offered no objection to the engagement to respect the sovereignty and integrity of China in Manchuria being taken by Russia towards, and in company with, other Powers besides Japan, but they consider it essential that it shall be, not a mere assurance or declaration of intentions, but a distinct and formal engagement contained in a signed instrument, and bearing the character of a compact made with Japan herself.

I do not see on what grounds we could undertake to press upon her the acceptance of a less binding engagement, and I have, in my discussions with the foreign Representatives concerned, expressed that view.

I am, &c.
LANSDOWNE.

No. 297.

The Marquess of Lansdowne to Sir C. Scott.

F.O. Russia 1683.   *Foreign Office, February* 9, 1904.
Tel. (No. 38.)   D. 1 P.M.

I informed Russian Ambassador the day before yesterday that I felt sure that nothing would stop Japan but Treaty engagement by Russia to respect sovereignty and integrity of China in Manchuria.

He asked whether I could suggest any form in which such an engagement might be embodied other than a Treaty between Russia and Japan to which Russia objects.

I replied that I could think of nothing but a Treaty between Russia and China of which other Powers might be invited by both Russia and China to take note.

He asked me whether supposing Russia were willing to agree, we would advise Japan to accept such an offer.

I said I would consult my colleagues at Cabinet yesterday, and that I feared it might be too late, even if Russia were willing.

Ambassador's enquiry was unofficial.

I afterwards saw Japanese Minister, who expressed opinion that things had gone so far that even if suggested solution were now to be offered Japan could not afford to entertain it. They could not listen to any overture which might prolong negotiation.

I informed Russian Ambassador yesterday that I found my colleagues entirely agreed with what I had said as to the impossibility of intervention on our part.

In reply to enquiry whether any part of his communication had been made under instructions from Russian Government, his Excellency informed me that he was instructed to say that in the opinion of Count Lamsdorff there would be no difficulty in arriving at a settlement satisfactory to Japan in regard to the Corean question.

The arrangement proposed by Japan in regard to Manchuria was inacceptable, but Russia would be glad to discover a peaceful solution of that question also.

I told him that all I could do was to take note of this communication.

                                               L.

No. 298.

The Marquess of Lansdowne to Sir C. Scott.

F.O. Russia 1677.
(No. 48.)
Sir,   *Foreign Office, February* 9, 1904.

The Russian Ambassador called upon me this afternoon and said that he feared that a collision had actually taken place between the naval forces of Russia and Japan, and it was therefore too late to think of attempts to avert hostilities. His Excellency was anxious to know whether we should issue a Proclamation of neutrality, and, if so, when. I said that we had not done so yet, but that our Proclamation was ready, and that we should issue it as soon as war was declared or a state of war found to be in existence. I promised that I would inform him as soon as it was decided to issue the Proclamation.

His Excellency asked me what our position as the ally of Japan would be. I replied that the Anglo-Japanese Agreement was distinct in its language, and that neither side desired to read into it anything which it did not contain.

                                     I am, &c.
                                     LANSDOWNE.

No. 299.

The Marquess of Lansdowne to Sir F. Lascelles.

F.O. Germany (Prussia) 1592.
(No. 25.)

Sir, *Foreign Office, February* 10, 1904.

The German Ambassador spoke to me at Windsor to-day as to the proposal of the United States' Government that the Powers should recommend to Russia and Japan the neutralisation of China. His Excellency gave me to understand that the idea found favour with the German Government, although he did not indicate that the proposal proceeded from them. He observed that it would be necessary that the proposal should be accepted by the belligerent Powers as well as by the others, and that it did not seem to him possible that Japan would agree to it unless it were to be made clear that Manchuria was not to be included within the neutralised area.

I told his Excellency that Mr. Choate had spoken to me on this subject, and that I had raised the same point, which had, I believed, been referred by Mr. Choate to the American Government. I said that, subject to this reservation, the proposal was one which would, I believed, be acceptable to His Majesty's Government.

I am, &c.

LANSDOWNE.

[*ED. NOTE.*—Japan issued a declaration of war against Russia on the 10th February, 1904. Great Britain issued a circular to Public Offices the 10th February and a proclamation of neutrality on the 11th February, *B.F.S.P.*, XCVII, 476–84.]

CHAPTER XIV.

FRANCE, SPAIN AND MOROCCO.

No. 300.

Sir H. Drummond Wolff to the Marquess of Salisbury.

F.O. Spain 2063.
(No. 155.)   Most Confidential.   *Madrid,* D. *May* 15, 1898.
My Lord,   R. *May* 23, 1898.
    The telegram conveying the language attributed to Mr. Chamberlain advocating
the alliance of Great Britain with the United States has naturally created a great
sensation. It is supposed to imply hostility to Spain, and has increased, if possible,
the bad feeling towards England which our European friends have been stimulating
for so many years. . . . . [Reference to Press.]

I have, &c.

H. DRUMMOND WOLFF.

No. 301.

Sir H. Drummond Wolff to the Marquess of Salisbury.

F.O. Spain 2064.
(No. 176.)   Most Confidential.   *Madrid,* D. *May* 23, 1898.
My Lord,   R. *May* 28, 1898.
    It is impossible to look on the concentration of troops round Gibraltar as entirely
devoid of an intentional demonstration.   Some friends of the Government have
endeavoured in conversation to diminish the purport of the incident, much as in 1859
the despatch of troops by France to Italy was attributed to a change of regiments in
Algeria.   There is no doubt, however, that some difficulty was found in disposing
of 7,000 men prepared for service in the Philippines and not immediately required.
But the despatch of these troops to the neighbourhood of Gibraltar must be designed
partly as a demonstration against us, at all events, to the eyes of the Spanish people.
Unfortunately England is very unpopular at present in Spain, and many of the news-
papers eagerly seize every incident to our disadvantage.
    At the same time no doubt there are suspicions concerning both Ceuta and the
Canaries. The foundation of a new Russian Legation at Tangier and the departure
of the French Minister on a special Mission to Marakesh are timed to justify the
rumours of designs, including those on the Canaries by the United States, and on
Ceuta by Russia, which receives credence among a people excited by their anxieties.
. . . . [Internal affairs.]

No. 302.

Sir E. Monson to the Marquess of Salisbury.

F.O. France 3396.
(No. 401.)   Confidential.   *Paris,* D. *August* 11, 1898.
My Lord,   R. *August* 13, 1898.
    Your Lordship has been so good as to send me copies of Sir H. D. Wolff's
Despatches Nos. 251 and 254 respecting the situation in Spain, which I have read
with great interest. . . . .(¹)

(¹) [Details as to Hispano-American negotiations.]

While quite sharing the views of Her Majesty's Ambassador at Madrid as to the great increase of influence over Spain which must accrue to France by the part already taken by her, and by the decision that the final negotiations shall take place at Paris, I do not see how either the one thing or the other could have been avoided, or how any action could have been taken to prevent any such result as that which must, I think, be now contemplated as a certainty, namely, that for the future, or at any rate for a long time to come, Spain will become more or less a dependency of this country. The value of such a position as regards French interests is so evident that Europe at large could not but have anticipated that the Government of the Republic would strain every nerve and seize every opportunity to secure it. And French diplomacy has been so fortunate as to have had this chance without being obliged to compromise the existing good relations between the two Republics. In spite of the constant series of naval and military successes gained by the Americans it is clear that there is no general appetite in the United States for a continuance of the war, and France has in fact pleased both parties by contributing all the facilities in her power to the preliminary steps for its conclusion. . . . . [Internal affairs.]

With regard to the effect upon British interests, I confess that I cannot see that it need inspire apprehension. It cannot be said that we have had any reason for long past to consider ourselves as the objects of any special goodwill on the part of Spain; and the sympathy which has been unmistakably shown in Great Britain for the humanitarian grounds on which the United States declared war against her has only served to accentuate a little more than was previously the case the latent irritation caused by our retention of the command of the Straits of Gibraltar, which the recollection of all the exertions made at the commencement of the century to protect Spanish independence from foreign subjugation has never had any influence in allaying.

There is but one consideration which may modify this view, the danger, namely of a systematic co-operation of French and Spanish policy in Morocco directed to our detriment. But although such co-operation may cause inconvenience, it is, I believe, well within the power of British diplomacy and British material force to make successful opposition to such a combination so long as the latter receives no additional European support.

I have, &c.
EDMUND MONSON.

No. 303.

Sir H. Drummond Wolff to the Marquess of Salisbury.

F.O. Spain 2065.
(No. 283.) Confidential. *Madrid,* D. *August* 14, 1898.
My Lord, R. *August* 16, 1898.

The choice of Paris for the peace negotiations establishes for the moment the supremacy of French influence in Spain.

Spain, though fallen finally from her station as a Great Power and unable therefore to gratify any ambition of her own, still possesses points likely to attract the ambition of others, especially of France. Her agricultural fertility, unexplored mineral wealth, her numerous ports, and her position on the Straits will make her a valuable adjunct and appendage to her neighbour. France has deplored and reprobated the alleged ingratitude of Italy, for which, if given a free hand in the Peninsula, she may find a compensation.

The position and influence of Spain in Morocco can be utilised, while her desire for increased territory in Africa to make up for her lost Colonies may render her very susceptible to the overtures of her new ally.

I have more than once pointed out the dangers to Her Majesty's possessions if France obtained uncontrolled access to the Hinterland of Gibraltar. . . . [Details.]

No. 304.

The Marquess of Salisbury to Sir H. Drummond Wolff.

F.O. Spain 2106.
(No. 10.)
Sir,   *Foreign Office, January 11, 1899.*

 The Spanish Ambassador spoke to me this afternoon with respect to the policy which the two countries should pursue on the Moorish question. He expressed himself very earnestly in favour of the pursuit by Spain of a policy that was friendly to Great Britain. He did not mention Gibraltar, but he spoke at some length on the question of Morocco. He was anxious that, in respect of this country, Spain and Great Britain should pursue the same policy. He believed that their objects were the same. They neither of them contemplated any territorial acquisition, and would look with great regret upon any combination of events that should force the consideration of such a policy upon them. They were anxious to maintain the *status quo*, and he believed that their interests were so strongly in favour of that policy, that in combination they would be able to enforce it. Some observations were made by me with respect to the policy of France in that region; but his Excellency pointed out that, though in reference to the Valleys of Figuig and Tuat the action of the French local officers might excite suspicion, or even apprehension, it was not possible for France to make any extension of the Algerian frontier up to that coast without adopting an openly hostile attitude to Morocco, and that he thought that England and Spain together would frustrate any such attempts. I expressed the feelings of Her Majesty's Government as generally most friendly to the Government of the Queen-Regent, and most anxious to act in every matter where we could in conformity with Spanish views. I quite recognised that the policy sustaining the *status quo* was the policy which was imposed by existing conditions upon both Governments, and I expressed the hope that we should be able to co-operate heartily in maintaining it.

                  I am, &c.
                  SALISBURY.

No. 305.

Sir H. D. Wolff to the Marquess of Salisbury.

F.O. Spain 2109.   *Madrid,* D. *March* 10, 1899.
Tel. (No. 49.) Secret.   R. *March* 11, 1899.

 Señor Silvela tells me that after consultation with Minister of War and other Military Authorities Cabinet have arrived at conclusion that works near Gibraltar are useless and unnecessarily annoying to England.

He does not care for the Convention offered as he foresees difficulties in the conclusion of a Treaty. He proposes, therefore, as of his own motion to address to us a formal Note saying that since the termination of war with the United States has rendered them unnecessary, Spain without acknowledging a right will not from friendship to England construct any fortifications or emplacements that could be directed against Gibraltar. Phraseology will, of course, have to be submitted to your Lordship. Spanish Government will send us this Note unconditionally, but they would consider it a mark of friendship if in return we sent them a Note saying that England does not desire any acquisition of territory in concession and that she will undertake to prevent any hostile landing in Bay of Algeciras.

His Excellency expressed in ample terms his desire to cultivate the friendliness of England. He considered above arrangements sufficient on our part and did not wish to enter on the question of Balearic and Canary Islands.

He alluded casually to Morocco.

I should be grateful for an early answer.

No. 306.

The Marquess of Salisbury to Sir H. Drummond Wolff.

F.O. Spain 2109.   *Foreign Office, March 16, 1899.*
Tel. (No. 16.) Secret.   D. 10·30 P.M.
 Your telegram No. 56.

You may reply to Spanish note expressing the satisfaction with which Her Majesty's Government have received these friendly assurances, and their appreciation of the spirit in which they have been offered.

You may add that Her Majesty's Government wish on their part to assure the Spanish Government that they have at no time entertained the idea of making this question a ground for demanding further territorial acquisitions. They will be ready, if the occasion should arise, to give their military and naval assistance for preventing any hostile landing on the coast of the Bay of Algeciras, or any attack by sea on that coast.

[*ED. NOTE.*—Despite these friendly assurances, Señor Silvela and the Queen Regent professed to fear British designs on Ceuta and other Spanish possessions. On the 14th April, Señor Silvela expressed a wish to the German Ambassador for a secret agreement between Germany, France and Russia to strengthen Spanish hands in resisting pressure. To this Herr von Bülow replied that such a pact was unnecessary and impossible. See *G.P.* XV, pp. 115–122.]

No. 307.

The Marquess of Salisbury to Sir F. Lascelles.

F.O. Germany (Prussia) 1468.
(No. 109.)
Sir,   *Foreign Office, June 7, 1899.*

The German Ambassador spoke to me this afternoon at considerable length with respect to the desirability of concerted action between Germany and England if questions which interest them both arose.

I replied that there had never been on the part of this country any feeling other than a wish to act in concert with the German Empire wherever our interests permitted us to do so.

His Excellency then spoke especially about Morocco. I replied that I was not aware that the question of Morocco had become in any sense a burning question. Her Majesty's Government had no desire with respect to it, but that the *status quo* should be indefinitely maintained. But they felt an interest in the ownership of the Atlantic seaboard, and if by any untoward event it ceased to belong to the Empire of Morocco, Great Britain could not with indifference see it pass under any other dominion.

I asked his Excellency what the views of the German Government were with respect to Morocco, as he had raised the question. He said he did not know, but he thought it very desirable that there should be an exchange of views and ideas on the subject, whenever action should become pressing.

I am, &c.
SALISBURY.

No. 308.

The Marquess of Salisbury to Sir H. Drummond Wolff.

F.O. Spain 2106.
(No. 83.) Confidential.)
Sir, *Foreign Office, June 7, 1899.*

The Spanish Ambassador asked me what my views were with respect to Morocco, as to which his Government was becoming somewhat nervous. I said that the views of Her Majesty's Government could be very shortly stated. We were earnestly in favour of maintaining the *status quo*, and we should do all that we could to maintain that condition of things. We were aware that several countries had nourished designs with respect to the territory of Morocco. For ourselves, we have not consented to contemplate the fall of that empire, but, if it should take place, we could not see points on the Atlantic littoral pass under the dominion of any other Power. We hope they may permanently remain under the control of the Moorish Empire, but if that dominion should cease, the interest of Her Majesty's Government in the ownership of such places would become acute.

I am, &c.
SALISBURY.

No. 309.

Lord Currie to the Marquess of Salisbury.

F.O. Italy 800.
(No. 177.) Confidential. *Turin, D. August 20, 1899.*
My Lord, R. *August 23, 1899.*

I have the honour to report that I have just returned from a visit to M. Visconti-Venosta at the Certosa di Pesio. . . . .

In answer to my enquiries, M. Visconti-Venosta said that he had heard nothing recently which would lead him to apprehend any new development in regard to Morocco. So far as he was aware, the views of the French Government did not at present go beyond an extension of influence or territory in the direction of Touat, though it was not improbable that the death of the Sultan or of the Prime Minister, either of which seemed to be a likely event, might precipitate matters. He had not heard that Germany was showing any special interest in Moorish affairs.

The Italian Government was, he said, strongly in favour of the maintenance of the *status quo* in Morocco, and should anything likely to affect it come to his knowledge, he would not fail to communicate it to me for the information of Her Majesty's Government.

I have, &c.
CURRIE.

[15214] S

No. 310.

Sir H. Drummond Wolff to the Marquess of Salisbury.

F.O. Spain 2126.
(No. 89.)   Secret and Confidential.   *Madrid*, D. *June* 9, 1900.
My Lord,   R. *June* 11, 1900.

Last night I dined with a very small party at the Russian Embassy.

After dinner, M. Schevitsch, speaking to me aside, enquired, with some anxiety, whether there was a Secret Agreement between Her Majesty's Government and France respecting Morocco.

France, following the lead and advice of Russia, had abstained from any action that could embarrass England during the Boer war. But it was now plain that M. Waldeck-Rousseau, M. Delcassé, and their colleagues had adopted an English policy. The explanation which, as I gathered, he had received, was that England and France had come to an agreement whereby France would refrain from raising any question affecting Egypt if England, on her part, would assent to certain proceedings on the part of France in Morocco. The nature of these he did not state.

I replied that I had heard of nothing of the kind, and that I had no reason to believe that the report was true. According to my information, Her Majesty's Government favoured the continuance of the *status quo* in Morocco. . . . . (¹)

From the whole tone of M. Schevitsch's conversation I gather that not only he himself but his Government feel very anxious at the conduct of France as regards Morocco and generally towards England. This feeling may, perhaps, be increased by incidents elsewhere, perhaps in China, of which I have no knowledge.

He spoke with some warmth of the friendly attitude adopted by the French Government towards England, and I have little doubt that his frequent conferences with Señor Silvela are the consequence of his suspicions as to French action and that of Her Majesty's Government in Morocco.

I have, &c.
H. DRUMMOND WOLFF.

(¹)[Russian attitude to England.]

No. 311.

Sir H. Drummond Wolff to the Marquess of Salisbury.

                                                        Madrid, October 11, 1900.
F.O. Spain 2128.   D. 1·40 P.M.
Tel. (No. 63.)   Secret.   R. 2·30 P.M.

Señor Silvela implies though not directly that the partition of Morocco seems inevitable. It will however, he supposed, be postponed on account of affairs in China. He mentioned what France and Spain would wish for and said he imagined England would require Tangier. I said His Majesty's Government having always looked to the maintenance of *status quo* had not I thought yet contemplated the share they would ask.

Señor Silvela's language was vague and undecided but showed he had been considering the subject.

He was anxious to express his desire to consult the wishes of England.

No. 312.

Sir E. Monson to the Marquess of Salisbury.

F.O. France 3497.
(No. 493.) Secret.
My Lord,

Paris, D. October 12, 1900.
R. October 13, 1900.

In reply to your Lordship's despatch No. 323, Secret, of the 9th instant, transmitting translation of a letter which has been sent privately to the Queen by the Sultan of Morocco, and asking for my opinion as to the possibility and expediency of giving in any way effect to the request of the Sultan for the intervention of Her Majesty's Government for the purpose of obtaining from the French Government assurances calculated to tranquillise his anxieties, I have the honour to state that, while I think it would not be impossible to advert to the situation on the eastern frontier of Morocco without exciting suspicion in M. Delcassé's mind, it would be extremely difficult to elicit from the French Government any definite assurances of the nature desired. . . . .

I have, &c.
EDMUND MONSON.

No. 313.

Sir E. Monson to the Marquess of Salisbury.

Paris, October 17, 1900.

F.O. France 3499.
Tel. (No. 78.) Secret.

D. 8·20 P.M.
R. 11 P.M.

Your despatch No. 323 : Morocco.

I told M. Delcassé to-day that I had recently seen His Majesty's Minister at Tangier who had mentioned to me the existence of apprehension in Morocco of French designs on Eastern frontier. . . . . [Details as to frontier.]

His Excellency repeated that not only had he no intention of attacking Morocco but that he had strongly and successfully objected to excessive reinforcements being sent. If France did ever attack Morocco she would certainly do so on the North-East frontier and would never attempt hostile operations so far inland.

I think his Excellency spoke honestly. I raised the question quite incidentally and I am sure that he suspected nothing.

No. 314.

Sir M. Durand to the Marquess of Lansdowne.

Madrid, April 13, 1901.

F.O. Spain 2146.
Tel. (No. 24.) Confidential.

D. 8 P.M.
R. April 14, 9 A.M.

Your telegram No. 10.

In conversation yesterday evening with Minister for Foreign Affairs I touched upon Morocco question. He expressed his pleasure at getting an opportunity of discussing the subject and spoke very freely. He begged me to excuse any indiscretion on his part and went on to say that he had watched for some time with apprehension and surprise the steady advance of the French towards and across the old frontier. Seeing the confidence with which they acted he had come to the conclusion that they must have an understanding with England which gave them a free hand. He pressed this point rather strongly and seemed relieved at my replying that so far as I knew there was not understanding of this kind. He proceeded of his own accord to point out the interest of Spain lay in the maintenance of the *status quo* and the avoidance of any serious troubles in which Spain as the weakest party would certainly go to the wall. . . . . [Internal affairs in Morocco.]

No. 315.

The Marquess of Lansdowne to Sir M. Durand.

F.O. Spain 2146.   *Foreign Office, April* 15, 1901.
Tel. (No. 11.)   D. 7·30 P.M.
    Your telegram No. 24.
    There is no understanding between us and France which gives the latter a free hand as regards Moorish frontier. You may say so without any qualifying expression.

No. 316.

The Marquess of Lansdowne to Sir M. Durand.

F.O. Spain 2144.
(No. 32.)   Confidential.
Sir,   *Foreign Office, May* 1, 1901.
    The Spanish Ambassador reported to me to-day that he was instructed by his Government to confirm the language, which he had already used to me unofficially, with regard to the desire of the Spanish Government to maintain the *status quo* in Morocco.
    Spain would range herself on the side of any Power or group of Powers which might pursue this policy.

                                                                    I am, &c.
                                                                    LANSDOWNE.

No. 317.

Sir E. Monson to the Marquess of Lansdowne.

F.O. France 3535.
(No. 221.)   Very Secret.   *Paris,* D. *June* 14, 1901.
My Lord,   R. *June* 15, 1901.
    Your Lordship did me the honour the day before yesterday to enquire of me by telegraph as to the view which I took of the so-called "mobilisation" to be almost simultaneously made of the French Fleets and the Russian high sea squadron.
    I had no information at hand as to the movements of the latter; but as regards the concentration of the French Channel and Mediterranean Squadrons in the latter sea, I felt that the notoriety which has for months past been given to the forthcoming experiment deprived the step of all appearance of being undertaken with reference to any consideration of the existing political situation. . . . .
    I am aware that rumours are current of the possible assumption by France of the protectorate of Morocco. This rumour was discussed in my presence by the Ambassadors of Germany and Italy the day before yesterday. I took no part in that discussion, but I noticed with pleasure that Count Tornielli characterised the step as absolutely improbable. I myself cannot believe that the moment is propitious for such a new departure; but as Sir Arthur Nicolson is in England, and the presence of the Special Mission from Morocco may give His Majesty's Government exceptional

opportunities of procuring information of what is passing at Paris between the Government of the Republic and the Special Mission headed by Si Abdelkrin ben Sliman, I feel sure that the vigilance of His Majesty's Government will not neglect them. The temptation to round off the French Possessions in North Africa by repeating on a larger scale in Morocco what has been done in Tunis is evidently very great. The hints given by M. Cambon of the high value which France would attach to the permission of Great Britain to use a free hand in Morocco cannot but raise a certain suspicion. But the audacity required for springing such a surprise upon the world as that to which I have alluded, would, in my opinion, be certainly foreign to the spirit now directing the policy of the Government of the Republic.

I have, &c.
EDMUND MONSON.

No. 318.

The Marquess of Lansdowne to Sir E. Monson.

F.O. France 3532.
(No. 299.)   Extract.   *Foreign Office, July 3, 1901.*

M. Cambon assured me that the measures taken by the French Government were inevitable on account of the lawless conduct of the tribes. His Excellency, however, laid earnest stress on the fact that nothing was further from the intentions of the French Government than to raise serious questions in Morocco. They were well aware of the warlike character of the people, and an entanglement in that part of Africa—necessitating military operations on a large scale—was the last thing in the world they desired. . . . .

No. 319.

Sir E. Monson to the Marquess of Lansdowne.

F.O. France 3576.
(No. 25.)   Confidential.   *Paris, D. January 20, 1902.*
My Lord,   R. *January 25, 1902.*

I have the honour to acknowledge the receipt of your Lordship's despatch No. 19 of the 17th instant, transmitting to me copy of a letter from the Association of Chambers of Commerce respecting the proposal originally made by Mr. Thomas Barclay, who was the year before last President of the British Chamber of Commerce at Paris, for the negotiation of a general Treaty of Arbitration between the United Kingdom and the French Republic.

By the energetic exertions of Mr. Barclay, who is not a commercial man, but a lawyer practising in Paris, the Meeting of the Association of British Chambers of Commerce during the International Exhibition of 1900 in this Capital was a great success. The French Government, represented by the Minister of Commerce, treated the Representatives of the various British Chambers with excessive hospitality; and the visit was undoubtedly the occasion of an interchange of cordiality very advantageous to friendly feeling on both sides of the Channel.

So much of the credit for this was due to Mr. Barclay's personal efforts that I am not surprised that the Association has shown its recognition of his services by taking up his proposal for an Arbitration Treaty between Great Britain and France. A resolution in favour of this proposal was passed by the Chamber of Commerce here; and, fortified by this support, Mr. Barclay had very little difficulty in obtaining similar adhesions elsewhere; and if he carries on the campaign, he will no doubt be encouraged by a very general approval of his project, especially in the commercial world.

I have no knowledge of the opinion which His Majesty's Government may entertain as to the expediency or possibility of negotiating such a general treaty of Arbitration with the French Government; but I think it extremely probable that the latter would accept any overtures in that sense which might be made from London. But as I ventured to state last month at the annual dinner of the British Chamber of Commerce here, I feel that even if such a general Treaty could be negotiated, the principle of compulsory arbitration, which is what seems to be desired, could never be included in it; and as the utility of recourse to arbitration in matters of dispute of comparatively minor importance has been so often recognised by both countries in their dealings with foreign nations, I imagine that we may rest satisfied that in all differences in which the national honour is not directly concerned, there will be no hesitation on either side in consenting to their being composed by an Arbitration Court. At any rate the conclusion of any general Treaty of Arbitration appears to me to be by no means so easy a proceeding as its advocates may, in their enthusiasm, imagine; and I cannot but think that it would be for the present preferable to continue the practice of having recourse to special arrangements for arbitration in individual instances, than to run the risk of initiating a negotiation, which it might prove impossible to carry through, and the breakdown of which might to some extent discredit the reality of the friendly feeling, which I believe to exist between the two Governments, and which no one has at heart more sincerely than I have. It is because I so earnestly desire its maintenance, that I can add, that if His Majesty's Government consider that the conclusion of such a general Treaty, as I have referred to, is feasible and worth trying, I should yield to no one in my gratification that, in their more extended knowledge of the situation, they are at one with the principal elected representatives of the Commerce of Great Britain, rather than with myself. . . .

I have, &c.

EDMUND MONSON.

No. 320.

The Marquess of Lansdowne to Sir E. Monson.

F.O. France 3574.
(No. 30.)

Foreign Office, January 22, 1902.

Sir,

I had some conversation to-day with the French Ambassador in regard to Morocco.

His Excellency called my attention to the debates which had recently taken place in the French Chamber upon this question.

The French Government, he told me, was desirous of maintaining the *status quo* in Morocco, and preventing "la question Maroquine" from being raised. They had, therefore, endeavoured to come to terms with the tribes, and to lay down a boundary between their possessions and those of the Sultan, based upon tribal limits, and calculated to be for the advantage of all concerned. He earnestly hoped that the rumours which had been current in the French press, and which had been referred to in the debates of which he had spoken, rumours which pointed to the attempt on the part of Great Britain to create for herself exclusive interests in Morocco, might prove to be unfounded.

I had, his Excellency went on to say, reassured him on the question of certain commercial arrangements which the Government of Morocco had entered into at our instance at the time of Menebhi's Mission. It was now, however, stated that we had been endeavouring to obtain exclusive control of the telegraphic and postal services and in regard to railway construction. Similar designs were attributed to us in the matter of loans, although it was reported that the German Government was competing in this same direction, and was endeavouring to induce the Sultan's Government to accept a German financial adviser.

I told M. Cambon that the persons who attached importance to these rumours must be very credulous. We naturally expected to have our share in the development of new industrial enterprises, but we were not in the habit of seeking for exclusive privileges, and, so far as I was aware, no attempt had been made to obtain them.

I had heard similar rumours as to attempts to establish a French ascendency in Morocco. We had been told, for example, that there had been French intrigues against Kaid Maclean, who had earned the Sultan's confidence and had certainly not abused it, and there were plenty of people ready to warn us that the frontier arrangements made by the French authorities with the tribes were of a kind unduly favourable to France. We had not, however, questioned the good faith of these settlements, and it seemed to me desirable that neither Power should show itself unduly suspicious of the other.

His Excellency observed that such reports existed, and that he had felt bound to mention them to me.

I am, &c.
LANSDOWNE.

No. 321.

The Marquess of Lansdowne to Sir E. Monson.

F.O. France 3574.
(No. 297.) Confidential.
Sir,   *Foreign Office, July* 23, 1902.

The French Ambassador made some informal remarks to me to-day with reference to the statement which I made in the House of Lords as to the relations of His Majesty's Government with those of France and Italy.

His own opinion was, he said, that people were needlessly disposed to suspect conspiracies amongst the Powers concerned with the shores of the Mediterranean. He did not himself believe that such conspiracies existed.

I said that in my view also there was a disposition to indulge in exaggerated apprehension. As for the relations of France and Italy, I said that many people were convinced that France had designs upon Morocco. I had myself always accepted his Excellency's assurances that the French Government did not harbour any such designs and that their concern was with the tribes on their south-western frontier about which he had often spoken to me and which the French Government no doubt found it necessary to deal with.

M. Cambon replied that I was quite right and that the Franco-Italian understanding did not touch Morocco. As, however, I had mentioned Morocco, it was only right that he should tell me that he felt some uneasiness as to future developments in that country. The British Government was, he believed, perfectly sincere in its desire to maintain the *status quo*, but there were British subjects who were not equally discreet, and he was, in particular, alarmed at the position which Kaid Maclean was acquiring.

That officer had now virtually become Commander-in-Chief of the Sultan's Army, which he was organising and equipping, and which, after all, could only be intended for use against France.

I replied that the Sultan was constantly taken to task for not sufficiently restraining his own tribes and that it was therefore scarcely reasonable to object to his placing his army in a condition of greater efficiency.

My information led me to believe that Kaid Maclean's influence was not a dangerous one, and that if he interfered unduly in the politics of Morocco I felt sure that Sir Arthur Nicolson would be the first to call our attention to the fact. I did not believe myself that Kaid Maclean interfered in politics.

M. Cambon said that he could not entirely agree with me. His own idea was that it might be desirable that our two Governments should have a frank discussion

[15214]   s 4

of the situation. The attitude of the tribes had become extremely threatening of late. It was not enough that we should declare our desire to maintain the *status quo*. We must both be prepared for eventualities. He apprehended that what we really cared about was Tangier, which we could not afford to allow any other Power to possess. We might easily come to some arrangement with France under which it should be neutralised.

His Excellency went on to say that all that he had said to me represented his own opinions only, but that he proposed to ask M. Delcassé's permission to mention these subjects to me officially at some future time.

I replied that he would find me perfectly ready to discuss them with him in the frankest possible manner.

L.

No. 322.

The Marquess of Lansdowne to Sir E. Monson.

F.O. France 3575.
(No. 316A.)   Very Confidential.

Sir,   *Foreign Office, August 6, 1902.*

I had a long and interesting conversation to-day with the French Ambassador upon the subject of the relations of our two countries in Siam and Morocco.

M. Cambon told me that since our last meeting he had had an interview with M. Delcassé, whose ideas he was now authorised to explain to me. They were as follows :—

The French Government were "partisans du *statu quo* partout," and conceived that in this respect they did not differ from us. They had a colonial dominion amply sufficient not only for their present wants, but for their wants for generations to come. They had passed out of the period of expansion and had no wish to add to their responsibilities by further acquisitions. The colonial policy of France was therefore essentially conservative, and in the pursuit of such a policy M. Delcassé believed that it would be possible for them to move in accordance with us ("marcher d'accord avec vous").

This seemed to him all the easier because we were not really competitors. The French did not produce the same commodities as we did and they were therefore not rivals of ours in the markets of the world as were the United States and Germany. All that France therefore desired was to ensure the security of what she already possessed.

So far as M. Delcassé could see there were only two points at which her position was insecure, viz., Siam and Morocco.

In the case of Morocco, France had a frontier of considerable length along which she came into contact with turbulent neighbours against whom she was bound to protect herself. Nor could she allow any "influence extérieure" to establish itself in such a manner as to prevent her from doing this effectually.

In the case of Siam France was in the same position, with this difference, that England also had an extensive frontier co-terminous with that of Siam on the side of Burmah and in the Malay Peninsula. France and England had, moreover, concluded, with regard to Siam, the Agreement of 1896, under which each of us had recognised that the other possessed a sphere of influence in Siamese territory.(1)

M. Delcassé was awaiting the arrival of Phya Sri Sahadeb, who was, he understood, about to visit Paris and London for the purpose of discussing important questions with the two Governments.

M. Delcassé intended to receive him in the most conciliatory manner, and to spare no efforts in order to dispose of the somewhat trivial questions which had arisen during the last few years between the French and Siamese Governments.

(1) [Printed *B.F.S.P.*, LXXXVIII, pp. 13–4.]

I asked his Excellency whether he had not heard that Phya Sri Sahadeb was to visit Berlin.

M. Cambon replied that he believed this to be true, but that in his opinion the matters which concerned France and England in connection with Siam did not concern Germany.

The duty of the two Powers was to observe the Agreement of 1896; there was, as he had already told me, no need whatever for any rivalry between us, and it seemed to him that it was our business so far as possible to protect Siam against the intervention of Germany.

In the view of the French Government the Agreement of 1896, if carried out in accordance with its obvious intention, was sufficient, and he saw no reason for extending its scope, or for converting "the zone of influence" into "a zone of occupation." If a good understanding were maintained between our two Governments, things might well be left as they were in this respect, for the present at all events.

Returning to Morocco, his Excellency repeated what he had said to me on a previous occasion as to the alleged aspirations of some of the Englishmen who were in the employment of the Sultan. He had no doubt that designs were attributed to them which they did not really harbour, but there was a considerable risk that too energetic officers might, by the advice which they gave to the Sultan, encourage him to adopt a policy which might drive him into conflict with France, and thereby precipitate action on the part of the French Government. Their desire was, however, that the question of Morocco should not pass into the acute stage. Nevertheless, M. Delcassé thought that it would be extremely desirable that the two Governments should frankly discuss the action which they might be constrained to adopt in the event of Morocco passing "into liquidation." He did not think that there would be any difficulty in providing even for that contingency, and we should do well to come to an understanding in advance. Spain would have to be reckoned with. She occupied certain points upon the coast and would have to be given a sufficient allowance of hinterland. Tangier could not, he said, be allowed to pass into the hands of any European Power—certainly not into the hands of Great Britain or Spain, either of which Powers might then seal the western entrance of the Mediterranean. The best solution would be to make Tangier an international and open port. Beyond the Spanish line France would expect to exercise exclusive influence. Great Britain, M. Delcassé imagined, had no interests in those regions.

I told M. Cambon that I had listened to his statement with great interest, and that I was able at once to express my concurrence with some of the propositions which M. Delcassé had authorised him to advance.

I could, for example, say, without hesitation, that we, too, were in favour of maintaining the *status quo*, and that our desire was rather to consolidate our colonial possessions than to add largely to their area.

I was also inclined to agree with him in believing that the Agreement of 1896 left matters in a somewhat vague and therefore, perhaps, dangerous condition.

I had noticed that M. Cambon had spoken of that Agreement as assigning to each of the two Powers a "zone of influence." I did not think that any such expression was to be found in the Agreement. It was quite true that it established a distinction between the status of the central portion of Siam and that of those parts of the Siamese Kingdom which lay outside the Menam Valley. But we had never, so far as I was aware, given one another a free hand within the outer portions of the kingdom.

I then questioned his Excellency in some detail as to M. Delcassé's ideas of the form which French influence might be allowed to take in the proposed French sphere, and I elicited from him that what he meant was that within that sphere—

1. The French Government should have the right of taking whatever steps might be necessary for police purposes, these districts being, as he said to me, at present without any police arrangements at all.

2. France would expect to be allowed to make her own arrangements with the Siamese as to the protection of French Colonial subjects resident in Siamese territory.

3. All railway construction would naturally fall to France (I reminded his Excellency that the principal Siamese railway—that from Bangkok to Korat—had its terminus well within the French sphere).

4. France would expect priority in regard to mining and other Concessions; and

5. No questions would be raised by us as to the appointment of French officials in the French sphere.

On the other hand, the country would still remain under the Siamese Government, which would, of course, enjoy any revenues which it might produce.

Mutatis mutandis, the same arrangements would hold good as regards British influence within the British sphere, which would comprise Siamese possessions outside the Menam Valley on the western side of Siam, and the Malay Peninsula.

As to Morocco, I told his Excellency that I regarded with the greatest apprehension the idea of provoking an international controversy with regard to the future of that country; as he must be aware France and England were by no means the only Powers concerned in Morocco. Italy, Spain, and Germany had all of them at one time or another manifested an interest in its affairs. Any attempt to deal prematurely with the " liquidation " of Morocco would, in my opinion, be sure to lead to serious complications.

His Excellency did not dispute the force of this objection, but said that there could at any rate be no harm in discussing these eventualities in good time.

As to the interest of other Powers, he dwelt at some length upon the failure of Spain and of Germany to establish any hold upon the country. Germany had made a determined attempt in 1885, when M. Testa had been sent on a mission to Morocco, and had attempted to obtain the concession of a German post on the sea-board, and to bring about a combination between the Mahommedans of Morocco and those of Turkey. The attempt had failed egregiously, and Germany was at present not to the front there or elsewhere in the Mediterranean.

I noticed that his Excellency did not take up my observation as to the interest of Italy in Morocco, although I had spoken of it rather pointedly.

Before leaving the subject of Morocco, I told M. Cambon that I felt sure that the French Government did not give us sufficient credit for the absolute sincerity of our conduct with the Sultan. We had created no difficulties for the French Government in their dealings with the tribes, nor did I believe for an instant that Kaïd Maclean or any other officials in the employ of the Moorish Government indulged in intrigues against the French. As for His Majesty's Government, I could sum up the advice which we had lately tendered to the Sultan by saying that what we had most enjoined upon him was that he should not get into debt, and that he should keep his prisons cleaner.

In conclusion, I said that it was obviously impossible for me to make an official reply to so important a communication without consulting my colleagues; but I promised his Excellency that I would at once repeat to them the substance of our conversation. I added, however, that we were on the eve of the holidays, and I feared that I might not be able to say anything more to him on the subject for some weeks to come.

I am, &c.
LANSDOWNE.

No. 323.

Sir E. Monson to the Marquess of Lansdowne.

F.O. France 3579.
(No. 308.)   Secret and Confidential.   *Paris,* D. *August* 25, 1902.
My Lord,   R. *August* 28, 1902.

Your Lordship's despatch No. 316A, of the 6th instant, reached me at Paris on the 16th instant, and I have naturally read with extreme interest the record of your conversation with M. Cambon upon the subject of the relations of Great Britain and France respectively with Siam and Morocco. . . . . [Personal details.]

I confess, however, that while I am bound to believe in the accuracy of M. Cambon's presentment of his Chief's ideas, communicated to him at a special interview *ad hoc*, I should never have anticipated that M. Delcassé would have gone to the length represented by the French Ambassador of authorising the latter to propose to His Majesty's Government either the prospective liquidation of Morocco or, in Siam, an arrangement which, under the device of spheres of influence, is none the less, as it seems to me, a practical partition of the country. For such a professed adherent of the principle of the maintenance of the *status quo* as applicable to all delicate territorial questions to sanction the immediate and radical operation which the proposed solution would necessitate, is certainly a step which I should never have thought that M. Delcassé would decide upon taking; although I have not the slightest difficulty in believing that to a man of M. Cambon's temperament and ambition, such an authorisation from the French Minister for Foreign Affairs would not only be eagerly seized upon, but would lose nothing at his hands in the exposition of its scope and importance. . . . . [Details follow.]

I have, &c.
EDMUND MONSON.

No. 324.

Sir E. Monson to the Marquess of Lansdowne.

F.O. France 3580.
(No. 354.)   Most Confidential.   *Paris,* D. *October* 3, 1902.
My Lord,   R. *October* 4, 1902.

The Austrian Chargé d'Affaires, M. Dumba (who has the rank of Minister Plenipotentiary in the Diplomatic Service), called on me a few days ago, and said that his Government were in some anxiety in consequence of reports that negotiations were on foot between His Majesty's Government and that of France for arriving at an understanding over their respective interests in Siam and Morocco. He gave me to understand that as regarded Siam their own interests were chiefly concerned with the effect which such an arrangement would have commercially upon German trade, in which they participated in a secondary degree; but that with respect to Morocco their apprehensions were far more serious; for if, as he could not believe to be likely, England should ever agree to the excessive pretensions which France was known to put forward as to the future of the north-west corner of Africa, the situation in the Mediterranean would be changed in a manner extremely serious to the interests of the Austro-Hungarian Empire, as well as to those of the other Mediterranean Powers.

M. Dumba said that there did not appear to be any probability that Italy would be induced by any consideration which could be offered her to connive at an arrangement by which France could, at any moment, convert the Mediterranean, if not into a *mare clausum*, at any rate into a French preserve. Nor would it be easy to persuade Spain to renounce her prospects of territorial acquisition in Morocco. But the interest of the moment centres upon England; as any disposition on her part to enter into

French views in the direction in question would enormously impair the power of resistance on the part of the other Mediterranean Powers.

I confined myself in replying to M. Dumba to stating that both in the Far East and nearer home the policy of His Majesty's Government was always directed to the prevention of any violent territorial disturbance; nor was it at all their practice to enter into prospective engagements, the conclusions of which would inevitably tend to bring about, prematurely and unnecessarily, complications of which it would be more expedient to defer as long as possible the occurrence. As for Siam, the reports which have lately been so persistently circulated in France had been, as he would have seen, refuted by authoritative telegrams from well-informed local sources; while as regards Morocco, it is notorious that the British naval forces in the Mediterranean are at this moment far more powerful than they have ever been before, while the efficiency of the fortresses of Malta and Gibraltar occupies the constant attention of the responsible Departments. This state of things does not indicate any intention on the part of His Majesty's Government to withdraw from their traditional policy in the Mediterranean, or to allow France to indulge in speculating upon being given a free hand to work her will in Morocco. . . . . [Details of French policy in Siam.]

I have, &c.
EDMUND MONSON.

No. 325.

The Marquess of Lansdowne to Sir E. Monson.

F.O. France 3575.
(No. 405.)   Confidential.

Sir,   *Foreign Office, October* 15, 1902.

The French Ambassador called upon me to-day and spoke to me at some length upon the subject of the Agreement recently concluded between France and Siam.

He expressed the opinion that the arrangement was advantageous to Great Britain in that it diminished the, prospect of friction between France and Siam, a country in the security and tranquillity of which we were of course interested, and he said that the territory ceded to France by Siam was insignificant and that the evacuation of Chantaboum and the abolition of the 25-kilom. zone were most important concessions to Siam.

He referred to our conversation on August 6th (*vide* my despatch No. 316A of August 6th), and told me that the new Treaty, which had been carried through quicker than the French Government had expected, seemed to him to be entirely in accordance with the policy which he had then described to me.

I told His Excellency that we had scarcely had time to examine the Franco-Siamese Treaty in all its bearings, but that it contained one clause at any rate which seemed to us to involve an encroachment on our rights under the Treaty of 1855. I referred to the IVth Article in which it was stipulated that " À l'avenir, dans la partie Siamoise du bassin du Mékong, le Gouvernement Royal, s'il désire exécuter des ports, canaux, chemins de fer (notamment les chemins de fer destinés à relier la capitale à un point quelconque de ce bassin), se mettra d'accord avec le Gouvernement Français, dans le cas où ces travaux ne pourraient être exécutés exclusivement par un personnel et avec des capitaux Siamois."

M. Cambon did not dispute my contention, but replied that such an arrangement was in the spirit of the policy which he had adumbrated, and that without saying so officially, he felt no doubt that if we were to reply to the Franco-Siamese Treaty by a corresponding Anglo-Siamese arrangement in regard to other unguaranteed portions of the Siamese dominions, the French Government would readily acquiesce.

His Excellency also reminded me that it was a matter of notoriety that we had lately come to an arrangement with Siam with regard to the Malay States of Kelantan and Trengganu.

I said that I had no desire to criticise the Franco-Siamese Treaty in a pedantic spirit, and that I was quite inclined to agree with M. Delcassé in believing that these matters were capable of satisfactory adjustment between our two Governments. The Cabinet had however only just reassembled and I was not yet able to make any definite announcement to him upon this point. I observed moreover that the Treaty was not yet ratified and need not be ratified for four months, and it might I thought be better that we should not pronounce ourselves with regard to it until after its ratification.

His Excellency . . . . . said that the agitation which was proceeding against the Treaty was due to the action of a comparatively small number of Cambodians who were discontented with the new arrangements as to registration. . . . . He trusted that we should be able to arrive at an arrangement which would not only involve the recognition by each of us of the sphere of influence belonging to the other, but also enable us to make common cause against the interference of any third Power in Siamese affairs.

He repeated that the earnest desire of the French Government was that there should be no cause for misunderstanding between Great Britain and France and that the two Governments should treat one another with the fullest confidence.

I said that that was my feeling also, and that I hoped before long to place the whole of my cards upon the table. I could not do so yet, partly because the matter had not yet been fully considered by my Colleagues, and also because our arrangements as to Kelantan and Trengganu which concerned the Malay Rajahs as well as the Siamese Government were not actually concluded.

His Excellency then spoke to me again about Morocco, repeating what he had said to me on August 6th as to the desirability of an understanding with regard to that country also.

He reminded me that I had described Kaïd Maclean as a simple soldier charged with the management of the Sultan's forces. It appeared however that Kaïd Maclean had assumed the rôle of Ambassador, and had come to this country as the bearer of letters from the Sultan to the King.

I told His Excellency that one of the objects with which Kaïd Maclean had come here was to make arrangements for a Moorish loan and also for the distribution of certain railway concessions which the Sultan thought of granting. The Sultan was, I said, prepared to divide both the loan and the concessions between France, Germany, and England, and we had encouraged him in this course in order to avoid international rivalries.

M. Cambon observed that in his opinion if Kaïd Maclean were to go to Paris for the purpose of borrowing there, the French Government would endeavour to dissuade him from borrowing.

I said that I too regretted that His Majesty should wish to borrow money, but that he was bent upon executing improvements and was without resources for the purpose. I took the opportunity of saying that the Shereefian Government had attempted to provide itself with additional income by means of internal taxation applicable to foreigners and natives enjoying foreign protection, but that I understood that the French Government had hitherto refused its assent, although all the other Powers except Russia, whose interests must be quite insignificant, had notified their acceptance of the measure.

M. Cambon assured me that this was a mistake and that in his belief none of the Powers concerned had given their consent to the imposition of these taxes.

His Excellency repeated what he had said to me in August as to the respective interests of France and England in Morocco, dwelling upon the argument that we had no political concern with the interior of the country, that our concern was mainly with Tangier, and that the greater part of the seaboard was inhospitable and useless.

I refused to admit that this was a correct description, and I again said that we were not prepared to discuss a possible "liquidation" of Morocco and that so far as I could understand the terms upon which it was suggested that such a liquidation might take place, they appeared to me to be of a kind which we should have difficulty in accepting.

His Excellency assured me that the French Government had no desire to bring about a premature liquidation, but that they sought by means of an agreement as to all thorny points to diminish the chances of a liquidation becoming necessary.

I am, &c.
LANSDOWNE.

No. 326.

The Marquess of Lansdowne to Mr. Archer.

F.O. Siam 226.

(No. 93.)

Sir,   *Foreign Office, October* 17, 1902.

Phya Sri Sahadeb, the Siamese Envoy, called on me to-day in order to take leave.

He told me that he had received telegrams from Bangkok instructing him to say that the Siamese Government earnestly trusted that we would not divulge the secret Treaty of 1897.([1]) They regarded the Treaty of 1897 as more stringent than that which they had now concluded with the French Government and they felt sure that its publication would lead the French to exact further concessions.

I repeated that the conclusion of the Franco-Siamese Treaty rendered it absolutely necessary for us to show that we had taken sufficient steps to safeguard British interests in those parts of Siam with which we were specially concerned. The question of publishing the Treaty of 1897 would have to be considered by the Cabinet, and I should not fail to lay before them the objection which the Siamese Government had raised.

The Envoy then referred to his proposal that we should join with France in guaranteeing the whole of the Siamese possessions. If that were done he thought the

---

([1]) [Extract from *Memorandum respecting Siam* by Mr. L. Mallet, dated January 9, 1902 (F.O. Siam 236) :—

A secret Convention was signed on the 6th April, 1897, containing the following Articles :—

" ARTICLE I.

" His Majesty the King of Siam engages not to cede or alienate to any other Power any of his rights over any portion of the territories or islands lying to the south of Muong Bang Tapan.

" ARTICLE II.

" Her Britannic Majesty having engaged by the preceding Article to support His in resisting any attempt by a third Power to acquire dominion or to establish its influence or Protectorate in the territories or islands above mentioned.

" ARTICLE III.

" Her Britannic Majesty having engaged by the preceding Article to support His Majesty the King of Siam in resisting any attempt by any third Power to acquire dominion or to establish influence or Protectrate in any of the territories or islands above mentioned, His Majesty the King of Siam engages not to grant, cede, or let any special privilege or advantage, whether as regards land or trade, within the above specified limits either to the Government or to the subjects of a third Power without the written consent of the British Government, and Her Britannic Majesty engages to support His Majesty the King of Siam in the execution of this Article."]

Siamese Government would not object to the subsequent publication of the Treaty of 1897.

I said that there seemed to me to be considerable objections to the proposed extension of the guarantee, but that I was not prepared to give a final answer with regard to it at present. If, however, we were to arrive at any arrangement of the sort with the French Government, it was, in my opinion, impossible that we should not first take them fully into our confidence with regard to the existing agreements.

At the conclusion of our conversation, I expressed an earnest hope that the Siamese Government would respect the spirit as well as the letter of the new agreements with the Malay Rajahs, and would avoid all vexatious interference with their local affairs.

The Envoy expressed his entire concurrence.

I added that I thought that a very good effect would be produced here if the Siamese Government would release even if they did not reinstate the Rajah of Patani.

The Envoy said that the Rajah had been deported because he had disobeyed the orders of the Siamese Government.

I replied that this did not seem to me to be conclusive explanation, and that if the Siamese Government were to give the Rajahs of Kelantan and Trengganu orders inconsistent with the terms of the new agreements they must expect those orders to be disobeyed.

I am, &c.
LANSDOWNE.

No. 327.

The Marquess of Lansdowne to Sir E. Monson.

F.O. France 3575.
(No. 412.)
Sir,   *Foreign Office, October* 22, 1902.

The French Ambassador recurred to-day to the question of Siam which we had discussed on the 15th instant, and I made to him a statement which I subsequently embodied in the accompanying Memorandum, of which I sent him a copy.

His Excellency told me that I should find him perfectly ready to talk about Siamese affairs as soon as I was ready to do so.

I am, &c.
LANSDOWNE.

Enclosure in No. 327.

Memorandum.

On the 6th August overtures for an understanding with regard to Siam were made to me by M. Cambon.

M. Cambon considered that the effect of the Treaty of 1896 had been to assign to France and Great Britain respectively spheres of influence in those parts of Siam which were not included within the region guaranteed under Article I of the Treaty, and he suggested that each Power might well recognise the privileged position of the other within the zone of territory which adjoined its own possessions.

This might, he thought, be done without any attempt to convert those zones of influence into zones of actual occupation.

We were ready to examine this proposal in a friendly spirit, and to discuss with the French Government the possibility of approaching *pari passu* with them the consideration of some arrangement of the kind.

Before, however, His Majesty's Government had had an opportunity of dealing with the French proposal, the French Government came to an agreement with that of Siam as to a new Treaty.

That Treaty at certain points encroaches upon the Treaty rights of Great Britain in Siam.

Moreover, it places France in a privileged position, which will enable her to dominate by her influence the central portion of the Siamese Kingdom.

It is obvious that the situation thus created requires careful study at our hands, and that we shall have to consider whether, under existing arrangements, our interests are adequately protected.

I understand from M. Cambon that the French Government are fully alive to this view of the case, and that he has reason to believe that, should His Majesty's Government acquiesce in the new Franco-Siamese Treaty, the French Government would similarly acquiesce in and agree to respect arrangements made on our side in reference to those portions of Siam in which Great Britain is most concerned.

The principle upon which this suggestion is based seems to His Majesty's Government reasonable, and they will be prepared at the proper time to consider how it might be most usefully applied.

That time has, however, not yet arrived. The Franco-Siamese Treaty has not yet been ratified, and until it has been ratified, it would, in the opinion of His Majesty's Government, be undesirable to discuss the international arrangements which would be its complement.

This view of the case has been strongly urged by the Siamese Government, who are anxious that the Treaty should be ratified as soon as possible, and who deprecate any anouncement with regard to arrangements between Great Britain and Siam before the fate of the Treaty with France is finally assured.

For this reason His Majesty's Government do not think it would be advisable that they should lay their proposals either before Parliament or before the French Government until all uncertainty with regard to the Franco-Siamese Treaty is at an end.

I understood M. Cambon further to suggest that, while France and England might each of them agree to recognise the privileged position of the other in certain portions of Siam outside the area which was guaranteed by the Treaty of 1896, the two Powers might further agree to extend that guarantee in such a manner as to make it a matter of common interest for both to exclude any third Power from intervention within the area covered by Article I of the Treaty of 1896.

His Majesty's Government would be prepared to examine in a friendly spirit a proposal designed to effect this object, as soon as the Franco-Siamese Treaty has been ratified.

Foreign Office, October 22, 1902.

No. 328.

Memorandum for Kaïd Sir H. Maclean.

F.O. Morocco 400.
(Confidential.) *Foreign Office, October 24, 1902.*

Kaïd Sir H. Maclean has communicated to me verbally the various messages and proposals with which he was entrusted by His Shereefian Majesty the Sultan of Morocco.

These matters have received the careful attention of His Majesty's Government.

1. His Shereefian Majesty's proposal that the integrity of Morocco should be guaranteed by Great Britain, or failing that by Great Britain and Germany jointly, for a period of seven years only, and that this guarantee should lapse if before the end of the seven years the Sultan has not thoroughly reformed his Government and developed

the resources of his country, does not seem to His Majesty's Government to be well calculated to achieve the objects which his Shereefian Majesty has in view. It would for instance be easy for some interested Power to contend at the end of the seven years that the reforms had not proved effectual, and that the guarantee was therefore inoperative.

Moreover the integrity of Morocco concerns not only Great Britain, or Great Britain and Germany, but other European States also. The result of our communications with them, and particularly with France, convinces us that none of them contemplate, or are seeking to effect a disturbance of the *status quo*.

We are of course aware that the French Government desire to arrive at an arrangement which would put an end to the friction between the French and the Moorish tribes on the South-East border of the Sultan's dominions. On the other hand we have received repeated and explicit assurances from the French Government that they do not desire to raise issues involving the partition of Morocco, or to threaten the integrity of the Sultan's Empire.

As for ourselves we have always regarded, and still regard the Moorish question as one in which we have a special interest, but any attempt to interfere with the integrity and independence of Morocco would be a matter of general concern, and there is not the slightest chance of any one Power being given a free hand in that country. Great Britain will not acquiesce in any such attempt.

2. The Sultan may depend upon the personal friendship of the King and of the British Government.

3. His Majesty's Government approve of the proposal to offer the Moorish loan in England, France and Germany, and also of the plan of distributing the concessions for railways between those three countries in a manner which can be hereafter decided. This method of procedure seems well calculated both to prevent rivalry between the Powers, and also to facilitate the transactions which will be necessary. The points between which the lines of railway should be constructed, and the country to which each should be assigned, are questions which would require very careful study.

LANSDOWNE.

No. 329.

The Marquess of Lansdowne to Sir E. Monson.

F.O. France 3575.
(No. 462.) Secret.

Sir, *Foreign Office, November 19, 1902.*

I had some conversation to-day with the French Ambassador upon Siamese affairs. He evidently realised that the opposition which the recently concluded Franco-Siamese Treaty was encountering in France had become more formidable than was anticipated, but he assured me that, although M. Delcassé had been peremptorily requested by the Colonial party to withdraw the Treaty, he was not in the least likely to do so, and that he had little doubt that it would be ratified.

He told me that M. Delcassé had read with interest my Memorandum of the 22nd ultimo (see my despatch No. 412 of that date). He preferred not to treat the question officially for the present, although he was quite ready to do so whenever we thought the time had come. He remained of the opinion which he had expressed at the outset—namely, that Great Britain and France should continue to respect scrupulously the *status quo* in so far as the central portion of the Siamese kingdom was concerned, with, if possible, the addition of a stipulation which should preclude the interference of a third Power within the region thus guaranteed. As for those portions of Siam which lay outside the region in question, he recognised that, although they were not actually described as British and French spheres of influence in the Treaty of 1896, they could not, in fact, be otherwise regarded. Within these spheres, M. Delcassé considered that Great Britain and France should respectively have a privileged position; but he earnestly trusted that when we came to consider the analogous arrangements which from the language of the Memorandum we evidently contemplated in regard to the British sphere, we should not insist upon conditions largely in excess of those upon which France had insisted in the case of the Mekong Valley. There ought to be some kind of equilibrium between the arrangements made on either side of Siam, and if we were to make a new arrangement unduly favourable to British interests, the French Government would obviously find it difficult to defend its action against the criticisms of the Colonial party.

I am, &c.
LANSDOWNE.

No. 330.

The Marquess of Lansdowne to Sir E. Monson.

F.O. France 3575.
(No. 519.) Confidential.
Sir,   *Foreign Office, December* 31, 1902.

I had a prolonged conversation to-day with the French Ambassador upon the subject of the situation in Morocco.

His Excellency confirmed the statement made yesterday to your Excellency by M. Delcassé, and recorded in your telegram No. 80.

It was, in the opinion of the French Government, most important that the Powers should, at this juncture, avoid any action which might have the effect of stimulating fanaticism amongst the Moors. If we could escape a general movement directed against Europeans resident in Morocco, it did not seem to the French Government to matter much whether that country was reigned over by one Sultan or another. His Excellency told me that he was able to assure me that the French Government strongly desired that there should be no disturbance of the *status quo* in Morocco, even if the events now in progress should lead to the overthrow of the present Sultan.

In the second place, they wished to abstain, if possible, from interference with the internal affairs of the country. In the next place, it was, in their opinion, most desirable that, should intervention become inevitable, the Powers interested should take counsel together as to its nature and scope, and should agree that there should be no single-handed intervention ("intervention isolée") on the part of any one Power.

Finally, and upon this point his Excellency laid great stress, should any interference from outside become absolutely necessary, the French Government thought that action should be taken only by those Powers which have a distinct interest in Morocco, and that no others should be allowed to participate. It would be a great mistake to "internationalise such a movement overmuch."

I told his Excellency that we, too, as he was well aware, desired that the *status quo* should be maintained in Morocco. We should also be extremely reluctant to interfere in the internal affairs of the country.

Nor did I differ from him with regard to the desirability of previous consultation between the Powers concerned, should intervention unfortunately become necessary. I thought it, indeed, most important that no single Power should take advantage of the present crisis in order to play for its own hand.

Up to the present all that we had done had been to send some ships of war to Gibraltar in order that they might be in readiness if their presence was required to secure the safety of our nationals at any of the Moorish ports. We might possibly, I added, should the Sultan, for whom we had a personal regard, find himself obliged to make his escape, allow him to make use of a British ship for the purpose.

With regard to his Excellency's suggestion that should intervention become inevitable, it should be restricted to the "Puissances intéressées," I asked him for an explanation of the meaning of this expression.

He answered without hesitation that Germany was the Power which he had in his mind and which the French Government would like to exclude.

Germany had no concern with Morocco, although she had on one or two occasions unsuccesfully tried to obtain a footing there. The only Powers really interested were Great Britain, France, and Spain, and it would be most desirable that if Germany were at any moment to come forward and attempt to assume a conspicuous rôle, it should be intimated to her that she had no *locus standi*.

I told his Excellency that in my personal opinion it would, supposing international action to become inevitable, certainly be desirable to restrict as closely as possible the number of intervening Powers. The question was, however, obviously a delicate one, and I should like to examine it more closely before I expressed agreement or disagreement with the proposition which he had advanced.

I asked him whether there were any other Powers besides Germany to which his remarks might also be applied.

He said that it seemed to him not inconceivable that the United States might evince an interest in the matter. I said that I thought this not very probable, and I asked whether it would be safe to assume that Italy had no interest in Morocco.

He replied unhesitatingly that she had none, and his manner left me in no doubt that a clear understanding upon the point exists between France and Italy.

It is interesting to compare the tenour of M. Cambon's observations with that of those which he addressed to me upon the same subject on the 6th August last (see my despatch No. 316A).

At that time the French Government seemed to contemplate with equanimity, if not with satisfaction, a " liquidation " of Morocco, under which that country would be, if not partitioned, at any rate divided into spheres of influence under the control of France, England, and Spain. To-day he made no reference to any such possibilities, and represented the French Government as the leading advocate of non-intervention and of the maintenance of the *status quo*.

His Excellency informed me that the Spanish Government had been made aware of the manner in which the question was regarded by the French Government.

I am, &c.
LANSDOWNE.

No. 331.

The Marquess of Lansdowne to Sir F. Lascelles.

F.O. Germany (Prussia) 1550.
(No. 376.)
Sir, *Foreign Office, December 31, 1902.*

The German Ambassador told me to-day that in his belief all the Powers desired to maintain the *status quo* in Morocco, and wished to avoid intervention in that country.

I repeated to his Excellency the substance of Sir E. Monson's conversation with M. Delcassé, recorded in his telegram No. 80 of the 30th instant.

I am, &c.
LANSDOWNE.

No. 332.

Sir M. Durand to the Marquess of Lansdowne.

Madrid, January 3, 1903.

F.O. Spain 2177.   D. 5·45 P.M.
Tel. (No. 3.) Secret.   R. 11 P.M.

Your telegram of January 1st regarding ships of war. I saw Minister for Foreign Affairs yesterday afternoon and communicated to him the views and intentions of His Majesty's Government. He said he fully understood and personally agreed. He assured me of his desire to "act in concert" with us. He did not suggest withdrawing ship now at Tangier.

His Excellency was evidently pleased when I said His Majesty's Government recognised that Spain had an exceptional position on account of her possessions on Moorish coast. He said he hoped this meant that His Majesty's Government also recognised that Spain had a legitimate sphere of influence in Morocco. He spoke of the historical and geographical connection between the two countries and said that though Spaniards were far from wishing to embark on any policy of adventure yet they felt they had a claim to be regarded as possessing some title to influence "in a part at least" of Morocco. He pressed me as to the view taken by His Majesty's Government on this point.

I answered that as I understood your Lordship's words they were used solely with reference to existing facts and the exigencies arising from them and that I had no knowledge of the views of His Majesty's Government with regard to general question he raised.

I doubted whether such a question had been considered by His Majesty's Government, whose declared policy was the maintenance of *status quo.* He insisted and asked me to try whether I could not clear up the position in this respect and let him know how Spain really stood. He did not advance any definite claims or views, and fearing that if advanced they might prove embarrassing to His Majesty's Government I did not press him to do so.

Minister for Foreign Affairs reverted to his former assurances. He said that he had been convinced after deep study and thought that a thorough understanding with England was of vital importance to Spain, and he declared nothing would induce him to remain in office if this were not the accepted policy of Spanish Government. Speaking of a Franco-Spanish alliance, he stated in the most explicit terms that there was nothing of the kind in existence and that so long as he was in office there never would be. He even warned me against believing in apparent desire of the French for the maintenance of *status quo* in Morocco. He said that impression left on his mind by various things he had heard was that French were going against their inclinations in this respect and really hoped for something very different. I said that I had seen no signs of this and that French Foreign Office seemed as much averse as we were from any imprudent action.

I am not sure what Señor Abarzuza really expects from us, but my impression is that he wishes us to consider in time the contingency of a general break-up in Morocco or a slaughter of Europeans or other disturbing events and to think what rôle we should in such eventualities be disposed to assign to Spain with or without the assent of France. When I said that so far as I knew England claimed no exclusive or even predominant influence in Morocco but only that the country should be open to her trade and that no foreign Power should utilise Morocco to endanger her position in the Mediterranean, he suggested that in that case Spain might be of use to England in diminishing the risk of intrusion on the part of stronger Powers. I have seen it suggested that Spain should be put forward by France and England to do whatever may be necessary in Morocco, they paying expenses. Having regard to undoubted aspirations of Spaniards for an African Empire, it is conceivably possible that he wishes to suggest something of the kind. It is also possible that he wishes to suggest an alliance between Spain and England in Africa. (I should be) obliged if your Lordship would give me instructions as to my line of action in the future. So far I have tried to avoid anything which could look like a desire to work against France. Should I adhere to this attitude at the risk of discouraging possible advances or should I try to get from Señor Abarazuza a statement of his views and wishes? The two things may not be easy to combine. The sense of country is, I think, against alliances of any kind. So far as I can judge, Spain is from a military point of view in a very unfit condition for operations beyond sea.

I cannot be certain how far Señor Abarzuza represents the views of Spanish Government; it may be that he depends on a firm offer from us to enable him to carry out his policy. Personally, I believe him to be sincere and earnest, but I do not yet know him intimately and Señor Silvela might throw him over. Señor Silvela has not spoken to me about Morocco.

No. 333.

The Marquess of Lansdowne to Sir M. Durand.

F.O. Spain 2177.   *Foreign Office, January 5, 1903.*
Tel.   (No. 5.)
                                                              D. 6 P.M.
Your secret telegram of 3rd January.

We fully realise that in the event of such a catastrophe as the Minister for Foreign Affairs apparently anticipates, Spain would be entitled to a voice in any new international arrangements which might in that case be inevitable.

Minister for Foreign Affairs would find us ready at the proper time to exchange ideas with him confidentially as to these contingencies, but it does not seem to us that such a discussion would at this moment have useful results.

So far as we are able to judge, the French Government sincerely desire to avoid a disturbance of the *status quo*, and suggestions by other Powers as to arrangements consequential upon such a disturbance are therefore to be deprecated.

In these circumstances you had better not go out of your way to seek an explanation of Señor Abarzuza's ulterior objects.

No. 334.

Sir E. Monson to the Marquess of Lansdowne.

F.O. France 3618.
(No. 17.)   Confidential.
                                                   Paris, D. January 9, 1903.
My Lord,
                                                   R. January 10, 1903.
I have to acknowledge the receipt of your Lordship's despatch No. 519, Confidential, of the 31st of December last, in which you have been so good as to recount to me the conversation which you had had that day with the French Ambassador upon the situation in Morocco.

I have already, by telegraph, informed your Lordship that M. Delcassé has been too unwell to receive the members of the Diplomatic Body since New Year's Day. I have, consequently, no further information of the official views of the French Government, nor of the estimate formed on the spot by their Representative at Tangier, as to the progress of the insurrection against the Sultan. The news received, and the comments made by the Paris press, are rather optimistic than otherwise; but as yet the public in France does not appear to have excited itself upon the question.

I am very grateful to your Lordship for giving me in such detail the record of what passed between yourself and M. Cambon; and I have studied with much interest the discrepancy pointed out in your despatch between his language on the last day of the year, and that held by him on the same subject on the 6th of August last. In regard to this point, I venture, though with some hesitation, to recur to an opinion which I have before now betrayed to your Lordship as to the extent to which M. Cambon's ardent interest in the "aggressive" element, which he would undoubtedly like to characterise the foreign policy of France, leads him, not rarely, to accentuate with an interpretation, more in consonance with his own views than his chief's, the instructions which he may have received from M. Delcassé. In his conversation with your Lordship, on the 6th of August, he refers directly to M. Delcassé as having used the words "into liquidation" in speaking of a contingency in Morocco by no means so remote as to be neglected. When I subsequently adverted to this conversation during an interview with M. Delcassé, his Excellency assumed an air of innocence, and affected complete ignorance of the subject. I must add that upon two or three occasions in former years M. Delcassé, whenever I happened to mention Morocco, invariably gave me to understand that he looked upon it as a question to be by no means precipitately meddled with.

I have no reason to doubt that, at this moment, as on previous occasions, M. Delcassé realises the very formidable dimensions which the "liquidation" spoken of by M. Cambon would assume if France took any hasty or premature steps to bring it about. But it does not seem to me improbable that the echoes of M. Cambon's language have, as I ventured at the time to suggest to your Lordship, penetrated into quarters where they could not fail to inspire apprehension. I am not, therefore, surprised to find Sir Mortimer Durand confronted by reports, repeated to him by the Spanish Minister for Foreign Affairs (*vide* his telegram to your Lordship No. 3, Secret, of the 3rd instant), that the French were acting against their own wishes in declaring their desire to maintain the *status quo* in Morocco. However that may be, I am glad to believe that, from one cause or another, France is not likely under the existing Government to engage in any rash adventure; and that, happily, she is hardly in a position at this moment to take any risks. I was well satisfied to find yesterday, in the course of a long conversation with my Austro-Hungarian colleague, that he had exactly the same opinion as to the intensely pacific sentiments which animate the present Ministry, for whom, however, on matters of domestic policy and administration, he entertains the greatest antipathy.

I have, &c.
EDMUND MONSON.

No. 335.

Sir M. Durand to the Marquess of Lansdowne.

F.O. Spain 2176.
(No. 4.) Confidential. *Madrid,* D. *January* 17, 1903.
My Lord Marquess, R. *January* 24, 1903.

I have the honour to report that on receipt of your Lordship's telegram No. 5 of the 5th instant, I called upon Señor Abarzuza, and communicated to him the purport of your Lordship's answer.

He seemed pleased at your Lordship's words about the position of Spain in Morocco, and requested me to assure you most positively that, whatever proposals the French might make, Spain would refuse to do anything which would be displeasing to England. He evidently wished me to suppose that the French were inclined to make proposals for some secret Agreement, though he was somewhat indefinite in his language with regard to this point. Nothing could have been more plain and outspoken than his expressions of goodwill towards England and of his determination to maintain a thoroughly friendly understanding with us.

My belief is that Señor Silvela now sees the danger of the course he advocated eighteen months ago, and that, for the present, all likelihood of a French alliance is at an end. The feeling of the country on this subject has been shown in an unmistakable manner, and it seems to have carried conviction to his mind. . . . . [Press details.]

> I have, &c.
> H. M. DURAND.

No. 336.

Sir M. Durand to the Marquess of Lansdowne.

F.O. Spain 2177.
Tel. (No. 14.)

Madrid, February 14, 1903.
D. 1·50 P.M.
R. 8 P.M.

I saw Foreign Minister last night, and he said he had something important to tell me. He wished me to communicate it confidentially to your Lordship, and to ask for your views. He went on to say that before the fall of the Liberal Government the French Ambassador had proposed to the Spanish (Government) the division of Morocco into two zones of influence, Spain to have the coast with a strip of Hinterland, and France the rest. Fez was to fall within the Spanish zone. The French were pressing for an immediate reply when the change of Government occurred, and the matter was shelved. It has now been brought up again. Señor Abarzuza said he had (group omitted) to the French Ambassador that he was opposed to making any arrangement of the kind "without knowledge and approval of England," but no formal answer had been given to the French proposal. He further said that he was strongly in favour of maintaining the *status quo*, and avoiding the question of zones of influence until it was forced upon us. He considers particular proposal very unfavourable to Spain. He finally informed me that it would greatly strengthen his hands if he could say that British Government objected to any such arrangement. And he said that what he would really like would be a clear intimation that if any such arrangement were made we should "refuse to recognise it." Then he could put an end to the matter once for all. He said that he was greatly surprised that M. Delcassé should have put forward such a scheme. I explained your Lordship's views as stated in the accounts just received of your conversations with French Ambassador, but I promised to telegraph to your Lordship and repeat what the Foreign Minister had said. He assured me definitely that no answer would be given to French pending your Lordship's reply. He asked that the matter might be regarded as confidential. Minister for Foreign Affairs spoke in English, and the words quoted were those he used. The impression left on my mind was that he was not sure of his colleagues.

No. 337.

The Marquess of Lansdowne to Sir M. Durand.

F.O. Spain 2177.
Tel. (No. 23.)

Foreign Office, February 16, 1903.
D. 6·10 P.M.

Your telegram No. 14 of February 14th.

Convey to Minister for Foreign Affairs our thanks for confidence which he has shown in us. We regard it as of the utmost importance that Spain and Great Britain should act together in regard to Morocco. Our action in regard to the loan will have, I hope, convinced the Minister of this.

[15214]

T 4

We share his views, and I have more than once informed French Ambassador here that we deprecated attempts to bring about a virtual partition of Morocco.

We could of course recognise no such arrangement unless we were parties to it.

No. 338.

Sir M. Durand to the Marquess of Lansdowne.

F.O. Spain 2177.
Tel. (No. 17.)

Madrid, February 21, 1903.
D. 1˙30 P.M.
R. 3˙45 P.M.

Foreign Minister tells me that French Ambassador in London has persuaded M. Delcassé that England is not interested in Morocco question, and that France and Spain can safely proceed to deal with country as they please. Foreign Minister says that this view has become prevalent in Madrid. He has tried to combat it but finds this hard, as M. Cambon's assurances are positive. He declares that he is himself fully aware of great importance which Morocco must have for England on account of our position in the Mediterranean, and that nothing will induce him to agree to any partition into zones of influence without the full knowledge and co-operation of England. Sent to H[is] M[ajesty's] R[epresentative] at Tangier.

No. 339.

The Marquess of Lansdowne to Sir M. Durand.

F.O. Spain 2177.
Tel. (No. 24.)

Foreign Office, February 21, 1903.
D. 6 P.M.

You may state as strongly as possible that reports which have reached Minister for Foreign Affairs are absolutely groundless. We should certainly not tolerate an attempt to deal with Morocco without regard to British interests. Action which we are taking as to the loan question affords evidence of this.

No. 340.

The Marquess of Lansdowne to Sir E. Monson.

F.O. France 3616.
(No. 100.)
Sir,

Foreign Office, March 4, 1903.

I had a short and quite informal conversation to-day with the French Ambassador on the subject of Siam.

He volunteered the information that the Franco-Siamese Treaty was still in suspense, that the Colonial Committee had invited M. Delcassé to meet them in order to discuss the question, and that M. Delcassé had asked for a postponement of the interview on the ground that he had just commenced a fresh negotiation with the Siamese Government. M. Cambon added that he did not know what the subject of this negotiation might be. It may possibly have had reference to a proposal, mentioned to me by Phya Suriya on the 27th ultimo, to the effect that the Siamese Government should undertake to build lines of railway between certain places on the right bank of the Mekong and within the French sphere of influence.

M. Cambon told me that he had heard that our negotiations with the Siamese had been making progress.

I told him that we had for some time past been negotiating with the Siamese Government in regard to the appointment of British officers to advise the Rajahs of Kelantan and Trengganu, two Siamese Malay States which immediately adjoined our protected Malay States. I pointed out to him however that this negotiation concerned a small fraction only of the Siamese possessions and must not be regarded as being in any sense the outcome of the Franco-Siamese Treaty. I reminded His Excellency that I had always told him that whenever that Treaty was ratified we should probably have to consider with reference to it the nature of the relations existing between Great Britain and those portions of Siam which lay outside the Menam valley on the western side of the Siamese kingdom.

I am, &c.
LANSDOWNE.

No. 341.

Sir E. Monson to the Marquess of Lansdowne.

F.O. France 3619.　　　　　　　　　　　　　*Paris*, D. *March* 5, 1903.
(No. 120.)　Very Confidential.　Extract.　　　　R. *March* 7, 1903.

　. . . . I should be very glad to be able to obtain from M. Delcassé's own lips some explanation of his views on the reports sent to him by the French Ambassador in London as to the attitude of indifference which the latter ascribes to His Majesty's Government in regard to Morocco. But, after careful reflection, I have come to the conclusion not to raise the question with M. Delcassé without express instructions from your Lordship. The time may be near when you may think it advisable to make categorical declaration to the Government of the Republic in regard to British interests in Morocco; and I am of opinion that anything which I could say on my own initiative, and without your Lordship's express orders, would impair the weight of the formal communication which His Majesty's Government may eventually regard it as expedient to be made in their name. . . . .

No. 342.

Sir M. Durand to the Marquess of Lansdowne.

F.O. Spain 2176.　　　　　　　　　　　　　*Madrid*, D. *March* 15, 1903.
(No. 18.)　Extract.　　　　　　　　　　　R. *March* 21, 1903.

　The Spanish Government and press continue to show a keen interest in the affairs of Morocco. There is considerable disappointment at the failure of the Spanish loan, and this is attributed by the Spanish Foreign Office to the machinations of Germany. I am informed by Señor Abarzuza that the German Minister in Tangier and the German Ambassador here are very curious and active in all that concerns Spanish relations with the Sultan. His Excellency makes no secret of his opinion that their interference is altogether unnecessary and mischievous.

No. 343.

Sir M. Durand to the Marquess of Lansdowne.

Madrid, *March* 25, 1903.
F.O. Spain 2177.　　　　　　　　　　　　　D. 5·15 P.M.
Tel.　(No. 21.)　　　　　　　　　　　　R. *March* 26, 1·45 P.M.

　At request of Foreign Minister I called on him this morning. He says Delcassé is misled by M. Cambon regarding English interest in Morocco question. French persistently assure Spanish Government that England cares for nothing but neutralisation of Tangier. Spanish Government have steadily declined to accept this assurance or to join in any scheme of zones of influence. They want the *status quo.* Foreign Minister thinks that French may be trying to bring pressure to bear upon Spain by threatening to come to terms with Germany. He fears there is danger of their doing something rash as at Fashoda. He would like England and Spain to agree that neither should join any settlement of Morocco question without consulting the other. He thinks that this might not be palatable to France, but says that it would be a true service to France to open her eyes to the danger of assuming that she can disregard English feeling.

Repeated to Tangier.

No. 344.

The Marquess of Lansdowne to Sir M. Durand.

F.O. Spain 2177.   *Foreign Office, March 29, 1903.*
Tel. (No. 29.) Confidential.   D. 10 P.M.

Your telegram No. 21.

Pray thank Minister for Foreign Affairs for his friendly communication. We are quite willing to enter into an agreement with Spanish Government that neither will commit itself to any settlement of Moorish question without previously consulting the other. I would suggest that in order to avoid any risk of giving offence to France we should both propose to French Government to enter into a similar agreement with it.

If this should be acceptable to the Spanish Government I shall be ready to mention the matter to the French Ambassador and see how he regards the proposal.

No. 345.

Sir M. Durand to the Marquess of Lansdowne.

                                                     Madrid, March 31, 1903.
F.O. Spain 2177.   D. 2 P.M.
Tel. (No. 27.) Very Confidential.   R. 5·30 P.M.

Minister for Foreign Affairs asked me to see him last evening. He has received news that Moorish pretender is stirring up excitement among tribes adjacent to Spanish ports. Pretender himself is said to be at place fifty miles from Melilla. Minister for Foreign Affairs fears serious trouble may ensue as some of the tribes are asking for Spanish protection in case of attack and for leave to send in their women and children.

He says that it is the belief of all on the spot that the French are backing Pretender and fomenting trouble from Algeria. He believes this himself and is convinced that the French think we shall accept any situation brought about if they act boldly. Minister for Foreign Affairs seemed anxious and again referred to Fashoda. He repeated that M. Cambon was misleading M. Delcassé, and said that latter was now in a very dangerous mood. I touched upon subject of your telegram No. 29 and he seemed pleased, but said that Spanish Government had just made an important communication to French Government warning them that they were mistaken as to the real views of England pressing them not to take any steps without full knowledge of those views. He would like to await result of this communication. He spoke very strongly about the recklessness of the French and gave me the impression of being harassed and uncomfortable. . . . . [Personal details.]

No. 346.

The Marquess of Lansdowne to Sir E. Monson.

F.O. France 3616.
(No. 151.)
Sir, *Foreign Office, April 8, 1903.*

During my interview with the French Ambassador to-day, I took the opportunity of saying that our Ambassador at Madrid reported to us that the Spanish Government were seriously uneasy with regard to the outlook in Morocco. They were apparently convinced that Great Britain and France had arrived at an understanding for a partition of territory or of spheres of influence in that country, and nothing would convince them to the contrary.

I said that I had made more than one attempt to reassure them, and that I had stated emphatically that it was our policy to deal with questions concerning Morocco in concert with Spain as well as France.

M. Cambon expressed his entire agreement, and referred to the recent negotiations for loans to Morocco from France, Spain, and England as an illustration of our desire that Spain should not be left out of consideration.

His Excellency observed that these suspicions were largely due to the unfortunate telegram published some weeks ago in the "Times." All we could do, his Excellency thought, was to repeat our assurances.

I am, &c.
LANSDOWNE.

No. 347.

Sir M. Durand to the Marquess of Lansdowne.

Madrid, May 4, 1903.
F.O. Spain 2177. D. 2·50 P.M.
Tel. (No. 39.) Confidential. R. 7·30 P.M.

Your telegram No. 34.

Minister for Foreign Affairs tells me he does not regard situation as very serious. He thinks Roghi is getting on badly with Riff tribes, who want to be rid of him. He believes the rebellion has reached its highest point. He is much pleased at change in attitude of French, who now advocate *status quo.* He attributes change to plain speaking on the part of England and Spain.

No. 348.

The Marquess of Lansdowne to Sir E. Monson.

F.O. France 3616.
(No. 210.)
Sir, *Foreign Office, May 13, 1903.*

The French Ambassador told me to-day that he considered that the situation in Morocco had been seriously aggravated by the events of the last few days. A French convoy carrying provisions had been attacked and a considerable number of men had lost their lives. The attacking party belonged to a tribe which had made its submission to the French authorities at the time when the tribes on the Algerian frontier had been divided. A fraction of this particular tribe had, however, refused to come under the arrangement, and it was this fraction which had been guilty of the outrage to which his Excellency referred. It was absolutely necessary that they should be chastised and a punitive expedition would be sent against them which would, probably, destroy their villages and crops. His Excellency desired, however, to explain to me in good time that these punitive operations had no ulterior significance. He thought it would be useful for me to know this, as his Majesty's Government might be questioned upon the subject.

I thanked his Excellency for his consideration in placing me in possession of the intentions of the French Government.

I am, &c.
LANSDOWNE.

No. 349.

Sir M. Durand to the Marquess of Lansdowne.

F.O. Spain 2177.
Tel. (No. 41.)

Madrid, May 15, 1903.
D. 12˙45 P.M.
R. 5˙15 P.M.

Last evening Minister for Foreign Affairs again spoke to me about Morocco affairs, and I found him in a mood curiously different from that of the day before. He said that he had received disquieting news regarding the attitude of the French on the south-east frontier and asked whether we had any apprehension of an advance on their part. He went on to enquire whether I was quite sure that the visit of the King to Paris did not signify any change of view on the part of England in regard to *status quo.* . . . .

No. 350.

The Marquess of Lansdowne to Sir M. Durand.

F.O. Spain 2177.
Tel. (No. 39.)

Foreign Office, May 15, 1903.
D. 7˙30 P.M.

Your telegram No. 41.

Spanish Minister for Foreign Affairs may be assured that there has been no change in our policy as regards Morocco, and that we should not enter upon any fresh arrangement without knowledge of Spanish Government. . . . .

CHAPTER XV.

THE ANGLO-FRENCH TREATIES OF APRIL 8, 1904.

No. 351.

The Marquess of Dufferin and Ava to the Earl of Rosebery.(¹)

F.O. France 3121.
(No. 450.)   Confidential.
My Lord,   *Paris, November* 3, 1893.
    Your Lordship has been kept so fully informed of the proceedings connected with the Franco-Russian fêtes at Paris and at Toulon by the newspaper extracts forwarded from this Embassy that it is unnecessary for me to trouble you with a particular description of them.   There still remain, however, some interesting questions connected with their character and consequences which it may be worth while to examine.

    There can be no doubt that the exultation caused by the advent of the Russian fleet to Toulon and the visit of its officers to Paris was spontaneous, genuine and universal, for the grumblings of the anarchist press need not be taken into account.   The reason of this is not far to seek.   The people of France, like all Celtic nations, are sensitive and morbidly hungry for sympathy and admiration.   The German war and its results wounded their vanity to the quick, and though they have borne their humiliation with patience and dignity they do not the less resent it.   Nor has their twenty years isolation in the midst of Europe, aggravated as it has been by the exasperating squabbles in which they have been uninterruptedly involved with all their neighbours, proved a less fertile source of irritation.   A couple of years ago I reported from Rome that on the occasion of the visit of Admiral Hoskins to Toulon in 1890, the French officers had bitterly complained of there being no port in the Mediterranean in which they were welcome.

    Under the foregoing circumstances, it is no wonder that when the Emperor of Russia began to evince a friendly feeling towards the Republic, his advances were met with joyous alacrity.   The feelings thus engendered in the breasts of an impulsive and excitable community, which from all time has been liable to gusts of passion, were easily worked up into a condition of frenzy by those who were interested in accentuating the intimacy of these new-born relations.   Nor did the august social rank of the Emperor, and the Imperial splendour by which he is surrounded, play a small part in kindling the enthusiasm of the French democracy, who undoubtedly felt a peculiar satisfaction in possessing so " smart " a friend.

    But, however obvious may be the forces which brought about the recent Franco-Russian demonstrations, it is a more difficult task to forecast either their immediate or their ulterior effect.   One thing is certain—some effect they must have.   An event which has attracted the attention of the civilised world and has appealed to the imagination and self-love of two powerful nations can hardly remain as inconsequential as a passing dream.

    It may be argued that a good understanding between France and Russia need not necessarily prove injurious to British interests, nay, that it may tend rather to diminish than to increase the chances of a European conflict.   Evidently France dare not commence hostilities except with the consent of Russia, and it is certain that Russia will never countenance such a step unless it suits her own interests to do so, while the chances of the same identical moment being propitious for two allied nations to make war are always less than when the interests of only one have to be consulted.

    (¹) [This despatch is referred to more than once by Sir E. Monson and Sir F. Bertie as indicative of feeling in France in the time of Lord Dufferin, and is reproduced here for that reason.]

It may also be said that the personal character of the Emperor, his alleged love of peace. and the autocratic control which he exercises over the Russian administration, will both incline and enable him to damp the outbursts of French chauvinism, and prevent a mere accident, a temporary collision between France and one of her neighbours, or a wave of popular passion propagated from Paris, from setting the world in flames. On the other hand, it is certain, especially since the Emperor's last telegram, that, apart from graver issues, the diplomacy of Europe is face to face with a new situation, that as far as we are concerned we shall now find the representatives of France and Russia allied against us in respect of all the current controversies of the day in which the interests of one or other of those two Powers are concerned; and that both are likely to prove more susceptible, more exacting and peremptory than formerly.

I have already stated my belief that there is a growing dislike of war amongst the French rural population; a dislike arising, on the one hand, from the desire for ease and comfort which has expanded with the increasing wealth and prosperity of the lower classes, and, on the other, from the way in which the conscription has brought home to every family in France, and especially to the women, the fearful consequences which war would entail on their husbands, and particularly on their sons, for whom they probably care more. It is even possible that a vague expectation that the Russian alliance will render a German invasion less likely has contributed to the enthusiasm with which the former has been welcomed. But it must always be remembered that these sober tendencies are liable at any moment to be neutralised, or rather replaced by a fit of military fervour, on the first sentimental appeal which may be made to their patriotism, or rather to their love of glory, by some powerful orator or by the phantom of a popular hero such as Boulanger, while in the background and deep down in the hearts of all classes, from the highest to the lowest, sleeps a determination either to win back the conquered provinces, or to revive in some other shape the lost pre-eminence and prestige of their country. In the meantime, however, it is probable that the professions of the Government and of France's public men of a desire for peace are perfectly genuine, though from a less praiseworthy reason than that for which they would willingly be given credit. On the other hand, they doubt whether Russia will be ready to go to war for another two years or so, an opinion which is shared, I believe, by a capable diplomatist accredited to the Emperor; and they also know that their new friend will require 50 or 60 millions sterling of their money to complete his strategic railways. On the other, they suspect that they themselves are inferior to the Germans, both as regards the rifle with which their army is at present armed and in the rapidity of the fire of their artillery. In the meantime, everything in Europe, they calculate, is working so powerfully in their favour as to make it their interest to stave off the crisis for the present. The financial situation of Italy is deteriorating every day; France's efforts to injure her commerce and to depress her credit have been crowned with a considerable measure of success; and the Pope has recently accentuated his friendship for France by placing in the hands of the Republic the nomination to the Bishopric of Tunis, which hitherto had been in the gift of the Propaganda. As a result, the French anticipate that the Italian people, becoming dispirited and disgusted with the present policy of their rulers, may be led to dethrone the dynasty of Savoy, and declare a Republic in alliance with their own. At the same time they expect that Russian intrigues in Bohemia, Servia, and elsewhere, by undermining the loyalty of Austria's Slavonic populations, may create equal trouble at Prague and Vienna. Already they have noted with satisfaction that Servia has had the hardihood, through her principal Mayor, to send a message of congratulation to the French authorities on the success of the Russian fêtes, and they boast, whether rightly or not I cannot say, of similar marks of sympathy from the Bohemian Czechs. In this way they anticipate the Triple Alliance will fall to pieces of its own accord, and Germany will be left a prey to be devoured or at all events coerced by themselves and Russia at the appointed time.

But, though the immediate intentions of France may be eminently peaceful, I doubt whether the same thing can be said of Italy. In spite of his professions, I was always convinced that there was nothing Signor Crispi desired more than to bring on a European war, in view of the pickings which Italy might get in the general conflagration. There is no doubt that a little while ago there was a desperate inclination on the part of the Italians to run amuck at France at any hazard, in the expectations that neither their allies not England would allow them to be destroyed. On the other hand, the hatred of the French towards the Italians far surpasses their hatred of the Germans or of ourselves. Notwithstanding, however, these uncomfortable relations, M. Carnot took the opportunity of a recent visit paid to him by General d'Oncieux, who represented the Italian army at Marshal MacMahon's funeral, to address him in the most conciliatory and pacific language; while the attitude of the French Government in reference to the recent murders of Italian workmen has been sufficiently correct.

The foregoing slight summary of the aspect of affairs in France at this moment would not be complete unless a few words were added in reference to the light in which we ourselves are regarded. I am afraid that I can only describe the sentiments of French people of all classes towards us as that of unmitigated and bitter dislike. In part this is merely a continuation of the historical stream of tendency which has placed enmity between England and France from the days of Cressy down to those of Waterloo. Evidence of this may be gathered from the recrudescence of the admiration and worship of Joan of Arc, and from other similar indications; but its real origin in the minds of the responsible political leaders is to be referred to our attitude during the Franco-German War. Frenchmen, with their vehement impulsive natures, can never understand how anyone can remain impartial when they have a quarrel on hand with any of their neighbours. In their eyes a neutral is almost an enemy. When, therefore, we initiated the league of peace, and promoted the neutralisation of Belgium, France regarded us as really siding with her opponents. This very real and active cause of resentment has been fomented and exacerbated by the way in which our expanding commercial interests and our colonising enterprises anticipate and impede the corresponding efforts of their Government and of their merchants. They have a feeling that we are always getting the better of them all over the world, and crossing their path at the very point when it is about to open on some extraordinary advantage. Though the outward signs of their anger on this account are only visible on special occasions, and in reference to public or semi-public questions, such as Egypt, Newfoundland, Siam, &c., every mercantile house, every company that is interested in France's colonial fortunes, and each of their numerous shareholders, becomes a centre from which exaggerated complaints and false accusations against us are propagated in all directions. These causes of hatred are envenomed and intensified by the press of Paris. The press of Paris is the worst press in Europe. The people who contribute to it are very clever, and know exactly how to excite the rancour or inflame the prejudices of their readers. They have a congenital and instinctive disregard of truth, and they lie—not as an Englishman lies when he does lie, of malice prepense—but because they do not feel that a lie matters much one way or the other. They are for the most part absolutely ignorant of the history, the language, the habits, the politics, the modes of thought, and the geography of other countries, and, with a certain number of honourable exceptions, gain is their only motive, unless when it is spite or revenge. Moreover writers of this class, like angry women, find a certain excitement and relief in reviling people they dislike, even at the expense of the obvious interests of their country, and when they can have no practical end in view. On the other hand, the French newspaper-reading public requires highly seasoned and abusive articles to stimulate their attention and to feed their prejudices. Denunciations of England are therefore pretty sure to command a large and lucrative circulation. As a consequence, not a day passes that we are not taken to task for our sordid politics, our overbearing manners, our selfishness, our perfidy and our other inveterate bad qualities. It was under these circumstances that the accusations brought against this Embassy both in regard to the distribution of bribes to Members of Parliament, and in reference to the forged correspondence with the Foreign Office, received such ready credence. Nor, when once a myth of the kind is started, can it ever be eradicated. From a lie it grows into a tradition and eventually passes into history.

It is said indeed that too much importance should not be given to the utterances of the Paris press, and that its teachings do not permeate beyond Paris. In the first place this is not true, for the "Petit Journal" one of the most unscrupulous of the Paris newspapers, and peculiarly hostile to England, has an enormous circulation in the Departments. But, in any event, the Paris Press acts very powerfully not only upon the Members of both the Chambers but also upon the public opinion of the capital; and experience has over and over again exemplified the disproportionate ascendancy exercised by Paris over the rest of France.

In view, therefore, of the strong feelings of hostility towards England which prevail in this country; of its enormous armaments; of the innumerable occasions when we shall be compelled in the future to run counter to some of France's most cherished wishes and ambitions, I should not be fulfilling one of the first duties incumbent upon me as Her Majesty's Ambassador accredited to the Republic did I not call the serious attention of your Lordship to the desirability of being prepared to meet, and successfully cope with, all eventualities. I understood from Captain May, our late Naval Attaché, that both as regards the engines of her ships and her torpedo fleet, France may be considered superior to ourselves. Her navy is being continually reinforced. Colonel Talbot has more than once borne testimony to the growing improvement in her formidable army. Though, therefore, it seems to be the general opinion that France's aim is still fixed upon Alsace and Lorraine, it is possible that, with the new generation, her eagerness for the recovery of these provinces may decay, in proportion as their populations become reconciled to the domination of Germany; and the ambition of France to re-establish her pre-eminence amongst the nations of Europe may be indulged in at our expense. Only a few weeks before Austria was destroyed at Austerlitz, Napoleon was apparently intent on the conquest of England. What has happened once may happen again, and it is not therefore possible that a *volte-face* from East to West, analogous to that of Napoleon from West to East, may some day take place in this country, should some unexpected, and I must admit improbable, contingency tempt the French to try the experiment. Were Prince Bismarck in power, he would be quite capable, I imagine, of trying to bring about a diversion of the sort. At all events I believe that, if war were inevitable, a war with England would be as popular, and would be considered less dangerous, than a single-handed encounter with Germany. That such an attempt on the part of France would end in disaster, is very likely; but the danger lies, not in her accomplishing her aim, but in her fancying herself strong enough to embark upon the adventure. When living at Walmer, I have often watched the cliffs of France gleaming in the evening sun, during a succession of calm days when the smallest open boat could have safely rowed across the channel; and when I reflected that beyond them was encamped an active army of five hundred thousand men, and a force of three millions of trained soldiers in reserve, I have felt how foolish it would be if, reposing on our historical laurels, we should leave out of account the change which has been recently introduced into all the elements of warfare both by sea and land. These convictions have been only intensified by everything I have since observed in the character, in the animus, and in the warlike preparations of the French people; nor is the establishment of this close intimacy between France and Russia calculated to modify them.

I have, &c.

DUFFERIN AND AVA.

No. 352.

The Marquess of Lansdowne to Sir E. Monson.

F.O. France 3616.
(No. 228.)

Sir,   *Foreign Office, May* 19, 1903.

The French Ambassador told me yesterday that the French Government had read with interest the answer given by Mr. Balfour on the 11th instant to Mr. Beckett, M.P., as to the attitude which His Majesty's Government were likely to adopt in reference to the proposals for a permanent treaty of arbitration between Great Britain and France. The French Government had been approached as to this subject by the Governments of Holland and of Sweden and Norway. Monsieur Cambon observed that Mr. Balfour's statement was somewhat vague, and as the French Government were to be similarly questioned on an early date, he was instructed to mention the matter to me and to endeavour to ascertain how His Majesty's Government regarded it.

I said that it was notorious that we were in favour of arbitration as a mode of adjusting international disputes. We had lately in several cases given evidence of our belief in the value of such procedure. We had at the same time always maintained that there were certain questions which no self-respecting country could afford to submit to arbitration, and we were therefore not prepared to commit ourselves to the view that arbitration was a remedy of universal application. We had, however, no desire to throw cold water upon the movement, which seemed to us to be in the right direction and to be supported by persons who were entitled to our respect.

Monsieur Cambon said that there was a group of no less than 200 Deputies in favour of the project, and that the group was headed by Monsieur d'Estournelles, who was a very good friend of this country. It would therefore be, he thought, desirable that the two Governments should describe a little more distinctly the cases in which arbitration might in their opinion be resorted to.

He suggested for our consideration that both Governments might declare their readiness to accept arbitration in all cases of "divergences" as to the juridical interpretation of international conventions.

I said that this proposal seemed to me at first sight a moderate one but that it was obviously impossible for me to treat the subject officially until I had had an opportunity of discussing it with my colleagues.

I informed His Excellency to-day that I had mentioned his suggestion to the Cabinet, but that I feared that we could not, without fuller opportunities for considering so important a subject, accept a precise formula such as that which he had proposed. We should, however, certainly examine any such proposal with the utmost goodwill, and in the meanwhile, it would probably not be difficult for the French Government to reply in terms which would leave no doubt that they were not less friendly than we to the movement in favour of arbitration. We should certainly receive in good part any overtures which might be made to us in furtherance of the policy.

His Excellency asked me whether, if Monsieur Delcassé was pressed, I saw any objection to his saying that the question had been discussed by him with me. I said that I saw no objection provided it was made clear that nothing had taken place but an informal and general exchange of ideas, and that we were not committed to any specific proposal.

[I am, &c.
LANSDOWNE.]

No. 353.

Sir E. Monson to the Marquess of Lansdowne.

F.O. France 3620.
(No. 251.) Confidential.   *Paris,* D. *May* 22, 1903.
My Lord,   R. *May* 23, 1903.

I have never at any time had any conversation with M. Delcassé upon the subject of a General Treaty of Arbitration between Great Britain and France, the advisability of which was discussed by your Lordship and M. Cambon on the 18th instant. I have therefore no information as to his Excellency's personal views upon this question; but I have seen M. d'Estournelles several times within the last few months, and I know that he has been busying himself among his colleagues in the Chamber for the purpose of forming a "group" (in accordance with the French parliamentary system) with the object of pushing this propaganda.

M. d'Estournelles does not exactly pose as an "Anglophil," but he has had a considerable amount of diplomatic service in England, and has made many friendships in London. He devotes himself in the Chamber to questions of foreign policy, and has well-known ambitions in regard to the Ministry of Foreign Affairs.

The real author of the campaign in favour of the scheme of an Arbitration Treaty is Mr. T. Barclay, a former President of the British Chamber of Commerce at Paris, and by profession, but hardly by practice, a lawyer. The Foreign Office is, I believe, well aware of the character and motives of this gentleman, who has latterly devoted all his time and energy to lecturing to British Chambers of Commerce on the subject, and obtaining from them the passage of resolutions favourable to the project.

The merits of the latter are, however, in no way dependent upon the personality of its advocates, and it is quite intelligible that on both sides of the Channel an abstract proposal designed to diminish the risk of collision between two great nations must attract the support of all right-thinking people. As yet, however, I have not observed that there has been any general display of enthusiasm in regard to it on the part of the outside public, while, even on M. Cambon's own showing, the "group" in the Chamber, which M. d'Estournelles is endeavouring to form, does not contain as much as a third of the whole number of Deputies.

I have, &c.
EDMUND MONSON.

No. 354.

Sir E. Monson to the Marquess of Lansdowne.

F.O. France 3620.
(No. 263.) Confidential.   *Paris,* D. *May* 29, 1903.
My Lord,   R. *May* 30, 1903.

I mentioned to M. Delcassé the day before yesterday the conversation which your Lordship had had with M. Cambon on the 19th instant respecting the project of a general Treaty of Arbitration between Great Britain and France, as recorded in your despatch No. 228.

His Excellency at once remarked that that conversation had not been in any degree official; and that any observation made by M. Cambon in the course of it was not to be interpreted as a formal expression of the opinion of his Government.

I replied that I believed that that was entirely your Lordship's own view; and M. Delcassé went on to say that the so-called "group," of which M. D'Estournelles is the titular chief, is of no great importance. It was true that quite recently M. Waldeck-Rousseau, the Baron de Courcel, and two or three other men of distinction had accepted an honorary connection with the movement, but their adhesion was a purely "sentimental" one, and could not well be refused by men who were notoriously devoted to the cultivation of a good understanding between the two countries.

The conclusion of a general Treaty such as that advocated by Mr. Thomas Barclay would be difficult of realisation, unless the two countries were satisfied with one which bound the Contracting Parties very lightly indeed. Without in any way engaging himself, he thought that, perhaps, the suggestion that it might be confined to an agreement to accept arbitration in cases of controversy as to the "juridical" interpretation of International Conventions would be a step in the direction desired by advocates of obligatory arbitration; and would be considered by public opinion as "satisfactory progress."

His Excellency adverted to the question which was to be put to him on the subject, saying that he did not know when it would be addressed to him; and he did not wish the idea to get abroad that there had been any serious discussion between the two Governments with regard to it. His language clearly implied that he recognised the difficulties attending the practical realisation of the project and the danger of prematurely raising hopes, the disappointment of which might lead to popular misunderstanding and discouragement.

I have, &c.
EDMUND MONSON.

No. 355.

The Marquess of Lansdowne to Sir E. Monson.

F.O. France 3618.
(No. 278.)
Sir,   *Foreign Office, June* 10, 1903.

I told the French Ambassador to-day that in consequence of a communication which had been made to us by the Government of India I thought it desirable to call his attention again to the fact that the Franco-Siamese Treaty signed on October 8th last, contained provisions which encroached upon the Treaty rights of Great Britain in Siam. I had already mentioned this to his Excellency in the Memorandum with which I had furnished him on October 22nd, 1902.

The particular point to which I now wished to call his attention was this: In Article IV of the draft Treaty it was stipulated that should the Siamese Government at any time desire to construct ports, canals, or railways within the Siamese portion of the basin of the Mekong, and should be unable to execute such works with the aid of Siamese personnel or capital, the aid of the French Government should be invoked.

I pointed out to his Excellency that a portion of the upper part of the Mekong basin was included with the Menam Valley in the region within which the British and French Governments had in 1896 undertaken not to acquire any special privileges or advantages.

His Excellency replied that the Franco-Siamese Treaty was for the moment in a state of suspended animation, but he took careful note of my statement, the accuracy of which he did not challenge.

I am, &c.
LANSDOWNE.

No. 356.

The Marquess of Lansdowne to Sir E. Monson.

F.O. France 3616.
(No. 325.)   Confidential.
Sir,   *Foreign Office, July 2, 1903.*

M. Étienne called upon me at the Foreign Office to-day, and spoke to me at some length and with great freedom in regard to the political relations of France and Great Britain.

He told me that he was paying a short visit to this country in the hopes of promoting a good understanding between the two Governments.   There seemed to him to be no really serious points of divergence betwen them, and the moment appeared to be particularly propitious for such a *rapprochement* as he suggested.

He passed in view the various political questions which have lately occupied the joint attention of the British and French Foreign Offices.

He dwelt in particular on the necessity of coming to terms with regard to Morocco. The position of France in Algeria made it, in his opinion, absolutely necessary that she should have a preponderating influence in Morocco.   On the other hand, he wished me to understand clearly that he did not contemplate that that country, or any part of it, should be annexed to France.   On the contrary, he desired to maintain the Sultan's authority, and even to extend it over parts of the country in which it had up to the present been imperfectly recognised.   But it would be for France to regenerate the Sultan's Government, and to give a wise direction to his efforts. M. Étienne admitted that Great Britain had interests on the sea-board which must be taken into account, and he believed that the French Government would be found perfectly ready to neutralise Tangier and the adjoining coast.   It would, moreover, have to be arranged that the trade of Morocco should be free to all, without restrictions or preferences, so that our commercial interests should not suffer.

I told M. Étienne that we had never failed to recognise the special interests which France, as the owner of Algeria, had in that part of Morocco which adjoined her possessions, and he would, I was sure, give us credit for having maintained a friendly attitude during the recent complications which had arisen between the French authorities and the tribes in the neighbourhood of Figuig.   We had not questioned the sincerity of the assurances which had been given us by the French Government as to the object of the punitive operations lately undertaken upon that part of the frontier, and it was satisfactory to observe that not only the British Government, but the British public, had shown no tendency to be unduly alarmed at the action of France in those regions.   I added, however, that we deprecated the idea of bringing on a premature partition of Morocco.

M. Étienne observed that the Sultan's Government appeared to be on the point of falling to pieces, and that it seemed prudent to provide for the event of its complete collapse.

I said that these Eastern monarchies often managed to survive in spite of apparent decay and seemingly insurmountable difficulties.   A premature attempt to define new spheres of influence was, moreover, likely to arouse the susceptibilities of the Powers who conceived that they had an interest in Morocco.   Spain, for example, not without reason, had considerable pretensions in that country.

M. Étienne admitted that Spain had considerable interests, and that those interests would have to be taken into account, but there could be no question of assigning to Spain a predominance in any considerable part of the country. . . . .

M. Étienne then touched briefly upon the question of Newfoundland, which, he said, was capable of adjustment, although the Newfoundland Government might not be very easy to deal with.

I told M. Étienne that, like himself, I had always felt that there was room for an amicable arrangement of the Newfoundland question, and that I was sure that any proposals which the French Government might make with this object would be considered in the most friendly spirit by that of His Majesty. The present arrangements were, I thought, inconvenient both to the French fishermen and to the Colony. Cases were continually arising which illustrated this fact.

I took the opportunity of saying that I thought both Governments owed much to the tact and common sense exhibited by their naval officers, who had invariably got on well together, and disposed of minor disputes which might have had unpleasant consequences if they had been less judiciously handled.

From Newfoundland M. Étienne passed on to the New Hebrides, which he thought should be divided between the two Powers. But he recognised that the tenacity of the Australian Government might stand in the way.

M. Étienne saw no reason why there should be any differences between us as regards Siam. The arrangement of 1896 had, in fact, recognised that while the central portion of Siam was to remain independent, France on the eastern, and Great Britain on the western, side were virtually to have a predominating influence. Our action in Kelantan showed that we were acting on this assumption. He said that there was no doubt that at one time France had looked forward to the ultimate annexation of Siam. She had, however, quite given up that idea, and was prepared to treat Siam in the future as a buffer State.

After speaking briefly upon the last three points, M. Etienne dwelt at greater length and with considerable earnestness upon the necessity of a rearrangement of the frontier in the region of Sokoto.

That frontier, he said, was agreed to when neither Power was aware of the local conditions, and the arrangement had resulted in confining the French to a barren and waterless region which they were obliged to traverse, and by a circuitous route, whenever they desired to pass from their western possessions to their posts on the side of Lake Tchad. It was only equitable that we should agree to revise the boundary: France did not wish for a large accession of territory, but only to be allowed to come down to a region in which water could be obtained for the use of French convoys.

I said that I saw no reason why we should not discuss a transaction of which some such concession might form a part. The country within the Sokoto " semi-circle " was, however, ours, and we could not be expected to part with it except for a consideration.

I thought it inadvisable to express during the above conversation any definite ideas of my own as to the manner in which the different questions upon which M. Étienne had touched might be treated. I told him, however, that nothing would give me greater satisfaction than to promote a reasonable " give and take " arrangement between the two Governments, and that if the French Government would put their cards upon the table and say what they wished to obtain, and what they were prepared to concede with that object, we should be ready to meet them in a similar spirit. All our diplomatic discussions upon these questions had been perfectly amicable, and characterised by a spirit of consideration on both sides, and even if we had not as yet been able to come to terms, I thought, with him, that we had probably never been in a better position for doing so.

At the conclusion of the conversation, M. Étienne expressed his belief that the most serious menace to the peace of Europe lay in Germany, that a good understanding between France and England was the only means of holding German designs in check, and that if such an understanding could be arrived at, England would find that France would be able to exercise a salutary influence over Russia and thereby relieve us from many of our troubles with that country.

I am, &c.
LANSDOWNE

No. 357.

The Marquess of Lansdowne to Sir E. Monson.

F.O. France 3616.
(No. 336.) Very Confidential.

Sir,   *Foreign Office, July 7, 1903.*

The French Ambassador mentioned to me some days before the President's arrival that it would be agreeable to M. Delcassé to meet me during his stay in London, and to discuss with me some of the points with regard to which his Excellency and I had at various times had conversations.

M. Delcassé called upon me this morning, and we exchanged ideas at some length in regard to these questions.

After expressing the pleasure which it gave me to have this opportunity of learning his views at first hand, I said that, as he was aware, I had on several occasions discussed with M. Cambon the position of our two countries in Newfoundland, Morocco, Siam, the New Hebrides, and other parts of the world. Those discussions had, up to the present, not led to any definite results. They had, however, I thought, been useful in clearing the ground, and they certainly had led me to the conclusion that the points at issue between the two Governments were few in number, and by no means incapable of adjustment.

M. Delcassé expressed his entire agreement, and added that this view now prevailed in the French Chamber, which was inclined to take a reasonable, not to say friendly, line in regard to all such questions. As for the French Government, they had ceased to desire a wide extension of their Colonial possessions, and were intent, not upon adding to them, but upon consolidating them, and removing all sources of future trouble within them and upon their borders.

I replied that His Majesty's Government were influenced by very similar sentiments, and that I certainly thought the opportunity was in every way propitious for a frank exchange of opinions between the two Governments.

Speaking of Newfoundland, which I had mentioned first, M. Delcassé said that the question of the supply of bait, so indispensable to the French fishermen, was that which had most importance for France; the considerations which had to be taken into account by the French Government were, however, largely of a sentimental character. There was a feeling that the fish, which had of late deserted the French Shore, might some day return there, and any surrender of French rights would be resented unless it could be shown that sufficient compensation had been secured.

I replied that we also had to take into account sentimental considerations, and particularly those which had weight with our own Colonies, but that in the case of Newfoundland, it was by no means only a case of sentiment. I had had opportunities of discussing the Newfoundland question with the Colonial Office and also with Representatives of the Colonial Government, and I had found that the main obstacle to a settlement, so far as the Colonial Government was concerned, was the existence of the French system of bounties, which rendered it possible for the French fishermen, and particularly those belonging to St. Pierre and Miquelon, to compete with those of Newfoundland on terms absolutely ruinous to the latter. The Newfoundland people, on their side, were masters of the situation so far as the supply of bait was concerned, and naturally felt that this was a trump card which they were entitled to use to the best effect. I had discussed with M. Cambon the possibility of a settlement on the basis of the withdrawal of the French from the "French Shore," with compensation to the persons engaged in the fishing industry, while the French fishermen would receive facilities for obtaining a free supply of bait on the Newfoundland coast. M. Cambon had suggested that France was entitled to territorial compensation as well as to compensation in money, and although I was surprised at this demand, I had not altogether excluded the idea. I had, however, told M. Cambon distinctly that there could be no question of giving up the Gambia for which his Excellency had asked by way of territorial compensation. There might, however, be other quarters in which a concession might perhaps be made to France, but it seemed to me that it was for the French Government rather than for us to make suggestions of this kind.

M. Delcassé observed that the bounties were a matter of domestic concern to the French Government, and that it would be difficult for them to give way on this point.

I said that I admitted the difficulty, but that I thought it should not be beyond the powers of the French Government to adjust the incidence of the bounties in such a manner as to prevent their giving so great an advantage to the local fishermen. I felt sure that, unless something were done in regard to the bounties, it would be impossible for us to move the Colonial Government.

M. Delcassé here "changed the venue" by observing that the possibility of coming to an understanding as to the Newfoundland question really depended upon our attitude with regard to French interests in Morocco. If we could come to terms as to that country, all other difficulties would disappear, or become comparatively easy to deal with. He begged me to understand that the French Government had no desire to get rid of the Sultan or to annex his country. They wished, on the contrary, to maintain the Sultan's rule. Such a system was much more convenient than French administration, pute and simple. He had often wished that they had still a Dey at Algiers. Nor, again, had the French Government any desire to force the pace ("brusquer les choses").

They had shown this by their moderation in dealing with the tribes on the Algerian frontier. The conduct of these had, over and over again, been such as to afford a sufficient excuse for advancing the French frontier had the French Government desired to do so; but he had given his word that this was not to be done, and the pledge had been scrupulously respected. The Sultan had even gone the length of proposing to them that they should occupy Ujda, and that they should assist His Highness at other points; but these overtures had been persistently declined. It was, however, obvious that the authority of the Sultan was waning rapidly, and that it was insufficient to maintain order in the country, and the French Government could not regard with indifference the prevalence of chronic disorder in Morocco, or admit that it was the business of any other Power but France to undertake the task of regenerating the country. In these circumstances, what they desired was a reasonable assurance that their policy would not be obstructed by Great Britain.

I said that we had shown by our conduct during the last two years that we had no desire to call in question the right of the French Government to take measures for the pacification of the Franco-Moorish border, and we had readily accepted the assurances of the French Government that the operations in which they had lately been engaged were to be of a strictly punitive character, nor did I think it likely that this country would ever take a leading part in the pacification of the interior of Morocco, should there be a collapse of the Sultan's authority, followed by a condition of confusion and anarchy.

I added that I was glad to have this opportunity of correcting what I could not help believing to be a mistaken impression which the French Government had formed as to supposed attempts on our part to interfere in the internal affairs of Morocco. I was aware from what M. Cambon said that some suspicion had been engendered in the minds of the French Government by the Sultan's selection of Sir Harry Maclean as his Military Adviser and by the employment of a certain number of Englishmen in his service. The Sultan, no doubt alarmed by French activity on the Algerian frontier, had, not unnaturally, turned to us for assistance, and had frequently sought our advice. That which we had given to him had, I believed, been of the soundest description, and there was nothing in it to which the French Government could take exception. We had urged His Highness to keep his prisons in better order, to give reasonable facilities for trade, and to avoid extravagance, and when he had been obliged to borrow money we had recommended him to apply not to any one Power, but to the three Powers most interested in keeping him on his legs.

On the other hand, we could not be indifferent to the fate of Morocco. We were, in the first place, largely interested in its Mediterranean seaboard, and particularly in Tangier and the neighbouring coast. Besides this, I was bound to tell him that it would be impossible for us to make any arrangement affecting the balance of power in Morocco without first ascertaining how far such an arrangement would provide fairly for the interests of and be acceptable to the Spanish Government. We were on good terms with them, and had been freely consulted by them. Spain, on account of her proximity, and owing to the fact that she had possessions in several parts of Morocco, was, I said, naturally susceptible in regard to the Moorish question. In the third place, it would be impossible for us to agree to any settlement which might have an injurious effect on British commerce or British enterprise in that part of Africa, and it would, therefore, be necessary for us to show our people that we should, in any circumstances, retain equality of opportunity in those regions.

M. Delcassé said, unhesitatingly, that he felt sure of being able to satisfy us completely on these three points; he recognised that it would be impossible for us to allow another Power to establish itself at Tangier, and the neutralisation of that part of the seaboard could be provided for. With regard to Spain, it would have to be a part of the bargain that a satisfactory compromise was arranged with that country, which the French Government did not desire to ignore. It was, indeed, the policy of the French Government to remain well with Spain. As for the "open door," he undertook that there should be no difficulty whatever in regard to that.

The conversation then turned to Siam, and M. Delcassé observed that the position of France and Great Britain had virtually been determined by the Agreement of 1886, which involved the recognition of the claims of France in the valley of the Mekong, and of Great Britain in the Malay Peninsula.

I reminded M. Delcassé that Lord Salisbury had expressly guarded himself against this interpretation of the Agreement.

His Excellency said, with a laugh, that he was familiar with the passage to which I referred. There was, however, no resisting the conclusion that the two Powers, when they guaranteed the centre of Siam, had by implication admitted that they were free to deal with the external portions of the kingdom. We had, he thought, shown by our conduct in Kelantan that we considered ourselves at liberty to do what we pleased in the Peninsula.

I took the opportunity of contradicting the statement that Kelantan had been occupied by a British force; as for the valley of the Mekong, we had Treaty rights which the Franco-Siamese draft Treaty seemed to me to ignore.

M. Delcassé said that there was no desire to encroach upon our right to most-favoured nation treatment. All that the French Government had asked for was that, if railways were to be constructed in those regions, and the Siamese could not construct them themselves, France, as the adjoining Power, should have a preference.

I said that I had no reason to suppose that British capital was likely to be forthcoming for railway construction in the Mekong Valley, and that we had no desire to obstruct French railway enterprise in that part of the world. But most-favoured-nation treatment in respect of commerce was a different thing from most-favoured-nation treatment in respect of railway construction, and, so far as commerce was concerned, we should certainly expect the door to be kept open.

M. Delcassé again expressed his entire agreement.

We then spoke for a few moments of French and British interests in the New Hebrides, and I reminded M. Delcassé of the proposal for the establishment of a Commission, &c., made on the 29th October, 1901, by His Majesty's Government, which proposal had led to the French counter-proposal of the 9th April, 1902, to which we had taken exception. Since then we had not be able to advance the matter.

I asked M. Delcassé whether he would tell me what his ideas were as to the best way out of the difficulty. M. Étienne had, I observed, proposed a partition of the islands. I feared, however, that it would not be easy to give effect to this proposal, which would probably be objected to by the Australian Colonies.

M. Delcassé replied that he would gladly consider favourably any solution of the difficulty which His Majesty's Government might desire to recommend. If we could but come to terms about Morocco, the New Hebrides question could, he felt certain, be settled with the utmost ease.

With regard to Sokoto, M. Delcassé said that while he fully admitted that, according to the letter of the Convention of the 14th June, 1898, we were entitled to the territory comprised within the arc of the 100-mile circle of which Sokoto was the centre, the French Government were, in his opinion, equitably entitled to a revision of the arrangements, which had been arrived at in ignorance of the local conditions, and which compelled French convoys, when proceeding from the French possessions on the Niger to those in the neighbourhood of Lake Tchad, to follow a circuitous and waterless route.

I said that the country within the arc was now absolutely ours, and that if we agreed to a revision of the frontier or to the concession of a way-leave in this region, we should certainly expect in return a substantial concession somewhere else. I added, however, that I was personally in favour of a comprehensive settlement between the two Governments, and that possibly a concession at this point might form an element in a general settlement.

In the event of such a settlement being arrived at, we should also have to take stock of the situation in Egypt. No one, I supposed, for a moment believed that we were likely to retire from that country, and I learned with pleasure from Lord Cromer that the French representatives in Egypt were on excellent terms with ours; but I was under the impression that it might still be possible for France, if she chose, to give us trouble in matters of detail, and we should certainly have to consider this point if a general settlement were to be attempted.

M. Delcassé replied that he was entirely in favour of a comprehensive settlement, and that the Egyptian question formed part of the larger African question which could, he felt sure, be disposed of satisfactorily if only we could come to an agreement as to the position of France and Morocco.

The only other subject mentioned during the conversation which I have recorded was that of the treatment of British firms in the French Congo. I endeavoured to impress upon M. Delcassé the importance of an amicable settlement of the cases of Messrs. Holt and others, and I dwelt upon the influence of the commercial element in the British House of Commons and the mischief which was created by the constant complaints which we had received as to the treatment of these firms.

M. Delcassé replied that whenever these gentlemen had come to Paris they had apparently been well content with the explanations which they had received. I said that they had, no doubt, been treated with great courtesy by the French officials, and that what they complained of was rather the arbitrary action of the French local Tribunals, which appeared to me to have dealt them very hard measure.

M. Delcassé answered, good humouredly, that it was extremely difficult to moderate the ardour of the Colonial Courts, and that we had probably experienced similar difficulties in dealing with ours. He promised me, however, to bear in mind what I had said.

Throughout our conversation M. Delcassé spoke apparently with the utmost sincerity, and he did not attempt to disguise from me the immense importance which the French Government attached to obtaining from us a recognition of the predominance which they desired to obtain in Morocco. The impression which he evidently desired to leave upon my mind was that, in order to secure our acquiescence, they would, in regard to Morocco itself, accept the conditions upon which we should probably desire to insist, whilst they would at other points go very far indeed to comply with our requirements.

I am, &c.
LANSDOWNE.

No. 358.

The Marquess of Lansdowne to Mr. de Bunsen.

F.O. France 3616.
(No. 351.)
Sir,
Foreign Office, July 15, 1903.

The French Ambassador told me to-day that the President had been much pleased with his reception in this country, and that which he had met with on his return to Paris showed that the French people appreciated the goodwill which had been shown him in London, and approved of the friendly relations which had been created between the two nations.

We then spoke of my conversation with M. Delcassé, recorded in my despatch No. 336, Very Confidential, of July 7.

M. Cambon asked me whether I had any suggestions to make as to the manner in which the discussion might be most usefully pursued. In his view, the whole question was dominated by that of Morocco.

I said that M. Delcassé had allowed me to see that this was so, but that I did not think we could discuss the question of Morocco except in connection with other matters of interest to both Governments.

M. Cambon suggested that a summary of the French views as to Morocco might, to begin with, be prepared for my private information.

I said that I saw no objection to this, but that the discussion would inevitably extend beyond Morocco. As to Morocco, I repeated what I had said to M. Delcassé. M. Cambon observed that it would be out of the question to make any arrangement, "à l'insu de l'Espagne." He thought, however, that Spain might be rather difficult to deal with when we came to examine the details of the project.

I am, &c.
LANSDOWNE.

No. 359.

The Earl of Cromer to the Marquess of Lansdowne.

F.O. Turkey 5302.
Private.
Cairo, D. July 17, 1903.
Dear Lord Lansdowne,
R. July 27, 1903.

I hope to see you very soon, but I know how difficult it is, amidst the press of work in London, to give much time to discussion. I think, therefore, I had perhaps better put the following remarks on paper :—

I have read the despatch in which you state what passed at your recent interview with M. Delcassé. His language appears to me to be eminently satisfactory. For my own part, I may say that I did not anticipate that he would open out anything like so hopeful a prospect of settling our various outstanding differences with France. I most earnestly hope that advantage will be taken of the opportunity which is now apparently offered for settling those differences.

What it really amounts to is this : that everything depends on our attitude as regards Morocco. M. Delcassé, you say, " did not attempt to disguise from me the immense importance which the French Government attached to obtaining from us a recognition of the predominance which they desired to obtain in Morocco." I rather anticipated something of this sort, but I certainly did not expect M. Delcassé to go so far as to say that " he was entirely in favour of a comprehensive settlement, and that the Egyptian formed part of the larger African question, which could, he felt sure, be disposed of satisfactorily if only we could come to an agreement as to the position of France and Morocco." I cannot help thinking that, in making these remarks, M. Delcassé went rather further than he intended, and that it may subsequently be found that, under pressure exerted by the permanent officials at the Quai d'Orsay, and others, he will be reluctant to face the French Chamber with any Egyptian proposals which would be thoroughly satisfactory to us. However that may be, we are for the moment perfectly justified in taking him at his word.

It is to be observed that there are six outstanding questions, viz. : (1) Newfoundland; (2) Morocco; (3) Siam; (4) the New Hebrides; (5) Sokoto; and (6) Egypt. These six questions may, it would appear, be grouped thus : in Morocco, Siam, and Sokoto, the French want various things which we have it in our power to give. In Newfoundland and Egypt the situation is reversed. In these latter cases we depend to a greater extent on the goodwill of France.

The New Hebrides question does not, so far as the information contained in this despatch is concerned, fall distinctly into one or other of these two groups. I am not sufficiently well acquainted with the subject to supply the information necessary in order to classify it.

There would not appear to be any very great difficulty as regards meeting the French views in Siam.

Possibly some concession in Sokoto, where the French demands would seem to be reasonable, might be made in return for counter-concessions on their part in Newfoundland.

But the main question is manifestly Morocco.

My own opinion, which is one I have entertained for a long time, is distinctly in favour of making concessions in Morocco in return for counter-concessions in Egypt and elsewhere, but if we are to adopt this policy we ought to do so with our eyes open to what it means.

I observe that M. Étienne, in his conversation with you, stated that "the Sultan of Morocco's Government appeared to be on the point of falling to pieces," to which you replied that "these Eastern Monarchies often managed to survive in spite of apparent decay and seemingly unsurmountable difficulties." This is perfectly true, but the reason is also obvious. It is that the agony of these decadent Oriental States, such as Turkey and Persia, is prolonged owing to the dissensions and rivalries amongst the possible heirs to the succession. I think it would be found, in practice, that if once the French succession were secured, the agony of Morocco would not be of long duration. Some opportunity would speedily occur for putting an end to it. Hence, in spite of M. Delcassé's statement, of which I do not doubt the sincerity, that the French Government has no desire to "brusquer les choses," I have very little doubt that, when once the French are assured that they can make good their rights to the succession, without any risk of serious interference on our part, Morocco will, to all intents and purposes, become before long a French province.

The question, therefore, to my mind is this : have we any objection to Morocco becoming a French province? Personally, I see none, provided always (1) that we get an adequate *quid pro quo* in Egypt and elsewhere; and (2) that the French comply with your three conditions as regards Morocco. These, if I understand rightly, are (1) the seaboard is to be neutralised; (2) a proper regard is to be shown to Spanish interests and susceptibilities; and (3) a guarantee is to be obtained that British trade and enterprise will not be placed at any legal disadvantage in Morocco.

I base my opinion on the following considerations :—(1) that there appears to be no particular reason why we should endeavour to prolong the existence of a bad native Government in Morocco; (2) that that country is manifestly destined to fall within the sphere of influence of some European Power; (3) that, under these circumstances, it is necessary, and under present circumstances, desirable to decide which of the European Powers should exercise a predominating influence; (4) that we certainly do not wish to be burthened with the government of the interior of Morocco; (5) that M. Étienne is right in saying that the Spaniards are quite incapable of dealing with the question; and (6) that therefore the French had better be allowed a free hand in the matter.

To speak now of Egyptian affairs. I understand you to approve of a suggestion I made, to the effect that Sir Eldon Gorst should go to Paris in the autumn, with a view to sounding the French as regards their attitude in respect to the Conversion of the Egyptian Debt, and the abolition of the Caisse de la Dette.

After reading your account of M. Delcassé's language, I am confirmed in the opinion which I had previously entertained, namely, that if Sir Eldon Gorst attempts to negotiate about Egyptian affairs in Paris without some idea as to the attitude of His Majesty's Government as regards Morocco, his mission is foredoomed to failure; but that if some indication is given that we should be prepared to consider favourably the French proposals in that quarter, there would be a fair chance of success. What, therefore, I now venture to suggest is this—that, before Sir Eldon Gorst goes to Paris, the Government should come to some decision as to the general lines of their policy in respect to Morocco.

I have one further observation to make. It relates to our engagements towards Spain.

That any arrangement which we may make with France as regards Morocco will be distasteful to the Spanish Government is more than probable. I do not, however, conceive that we are in any way pledged to go so far as to sacrifice our own interests to those of Spain. On the other hand, it is essential that there should not even be any appearance of a breach of faith. Manifestly, after all that has passed, we cannot make any arrangement with France in connection with Morocco without previous consultation with Spain. As you said to M. Delcassé, we are bound to " ascertain how far such an arrangement would provide fairly for the interests of, and be acceptable to, the Spanish Government."

On the other hand, M. Delcassé said : " With regard to Spain, it would have to be a part of the bargain that a satisfactory compromise was arranged with that country, which the French Government did not desire to ignore." Somewhat similar, although less precise, language was used by M. Étienne.

In all diplomatic negotiations there is always a danger of moving either too fast or too slow. In the present case possibly the danger lies rather on the side of moving too slow. Personally, I should be inclined not to delay too long, but to take advantage of the present phase of Anglo-French tendencies and relations. It is conceivable that it may not last. I would suggest that—unless, as I trust may not be the case, the Government decides to reject altogether the idea of French predominance in the interior of Morocco—the first preliminary step in the negotiation should be to enquire more precisely into the nature of the " satisfactory compromise," to which M. Delcassé alluded in his conversation.

On the assumption that we are to negotiate on the general lines which, as you will see, commend themselves to me, there remains to be considered the nature of the concessions which should be demanded in return for our acquiescence in French aspirations as regards Morocco. I have not sufficient knowledge of the situation in Newfoundland, the New Hebrides, &c., to discuss with any advantage the attitude we should adopt in respect to those issues. Neither do I propose at present to enter into any discussion on the Egyptian question. It seems to me that the first point which has to be decided is whether or not any radical objection in principle exists as regards acquiescence in the French view of the Morocco question. Supposing this question to be answered in the sense which commends itself to me, the counter-concessions which we should demand in Egypt will require very careful consideration. I will at present only say that I think that they should be of a substantial nature. I rather doubt whether mere acquiescence in the financial proposals recently under discussion would suffice. I should be inclined, in the first instance at all events, to negotiate on the basis of an explicit, or, in any case, implicit recognition by the French that Egypt falls within our sphere of influence, as Morocco would fall within theirs.

I trust that you will excuse me if, in expressing my opinions thus frankly, I have almost of necessity been driven to discuss matters which strictly speaking lie outside my proper and immediate sphere of action.

Very sincerely yours,
CROMER.

MINUTE BY KING EDWARD.

A most able and interesting letter and I entirely agree with the views expressed in it excepting Siam.

E.R.

No. 360.

The Marquess of Lansdowne to Sir E. Monson.

F.O. France **3616.**

(No. 369.)

Sir, *Foreign Office, July* 21, 1903.

The French Ambassador asked me to receive him this morning for the purpose of speaking to me privately with regard to the visit of Baron d'Estournelles and other members of the French Chamber to this country, in connection with the movement now in progress for the settlement by arbitration of differences between the French and British Governments.

M. Cambon told me that the French members would certainly approach M. Delcassé on their return to Paris, and that he would particularly like to know what His Majesty's Government thought of the movement before deciding what reply he should make to such an overture.

His Excellency left with me, for my confidential information, a copy of a draft Agreement which had been submitted unofficially to M. Delcassé by M. Anatole Leroy-Beaulieu, President of the Committee formed for promoting a good understanding between France and England. A copy of the draft is enclosed.

I promised M. Cambon that I would consult my colleagues, who were to meet immediately, upon the subject, and, after the question had been discussed by the Cabinet, I wrote his Excellency a private letter, of which a copy is also attached to this despatch.

I am, &c.
LANSDOWNE.

Enclosure 1 in No. 360.

Annexes.

(No. 1.)

Draft Agreement.

Les Hautes Parties Contractantes conviennent que s'il se produisait entre elles des différends tombant sous l'application de l'Article XVI de la Convention pour le règlement pacifique des conflits internationaux conclue à La Haye le 29 Juillet, 1899, c'est-à-dire des différends d'ordre juridique ou relatifs à des difficultés d'interprétation ou d'appréciation des Conventions existantes, et à la condition, cependant, qu'ils ne touchent ni aux intérêts vitaux ni à l'honneur des dites Parties Contractantes, et que, d'autre part, ils ne puissent être résolus par la voie diplomatique, c'est à la Cour Permanente d'Arbitrage qu'il appartiendra d'en connaître, conformément aux dispositions de la Convention susmentionnée.

Enclosure 2 in No. 360.

(No. 2.)

The Marquess of Lansdowne to M. Cambon.

F.O. France 3640.
Confidential.

Sir,   *Foreign Office, July* 21, 1903.

I informed my colleagues this morning that you had questioned me as to the attitude of His Majesty's Government towards the movement which Baron d'Estournelles and his friends are promoting for the settlement of our international differences by arbitration.

I found the Cabinet extremely well disposed towards the project, and ready to examine in the most friendly spirit any proposals which may be made to us with this object.

I showed them, in confidence, the draft Agreement which M. Anatole Leroy-Beaulieu had submitted to M. Delcassé. They would be quite ready to accept such a draft as a basis for discussion, although the actual wording would no doubt require careful examination by both Governments.

I understood from you that M. Delcassé wished to know what we thought of the draft. Pray, therefore, if you think fit, repeat to him what I have said. It will, I trust, be sufficient for his purpose.

I have, &c.
LANSDOWNE.

No. 361.

Sir E. Monson to the Marquess of Lansdowne.

F.O. France 3622.

(No. 394.) Confidential.   *Paris,* D. *July* 24, 1903.

My Lord,   R. *July* 25, 1903.

When I called upon M. Delcassé at his weekly reception the day before yesterday I found him still full of the impressions produced by his visit to London.

His appreciation of all the details was given in very much the same terms as those which I have reported (in my despatch No. 388 of the 22nd instant) as employed by M. Loubet in his conversation with me of the 20th instant; but I was particularly struck by the contrast which he drew between the universality of English sentiment, and the extent to which internal political differences prevented entire unanimity in France.

His Excellency explained that he could not but admire the manner in which British politicians sank their political differences when they met in society. He had found that they personally all seemed the best of friends; and that in his own case many members of the Government had seemed quite as anxious to introduce him to prominent members of the Opposition as to their own partisans. It was this social element that gave to the reception of the President the absolutely *national* character which, under present circumstances, it would be impossible to reproduce in France in the case of any demonstration whatever.

M. Delcassé further observed that he had been greatly charmed with the extreme geniality and "empressement" of everyone with whom he had come in contact during his stay in England; and that it was impossible to have any doubt as to the genuineness of the friendly feelings entertained alike by society and by the public at large, as well as by the official world, towards the French Nation and the Executive Chief.

I said that I was glad to know that he had had the opportunity of finding that there was, behind all the public demonstration, a very real desire on the part of His Majesty's Government to meet with readiness the official assurances which he had made to your Lordship and to the Prime Minister, of the honest disposition of the Government of the Republic to come to a satisfactory settlement of all outstanding questions between the two countries. I had always been anxious that his Excellency should have this opportunity of discussing such questions with your Lordship, and I had learned with much pleasure that the recent occasion had been utilised with such success.

M. Delcassé said that it had been of course impossible to enter into a minute discussion upon every point; but that he had been able to convince himself thoroughly that a general and satisfactory understanding was well within reach; and that he had greatly appreciated your Lordship's frankness and conciliatory attitude; and he added that he had not failed to express the hope that you would be tempted by the success of the exchange of views already made, to visit Paris at no distant date, and develop the intimacy of the personal relations which had been now established between you.

I have, &c.
EDMUND MONSON.

No. 362.

Sir E. Monson to the Marquess of Lansdowne.

F.O. France 3622.
(No. 395.) Confidential.   *Paris,* D. *July* 24, 1903.
My Lord,   R. *July* 25, 1903.

M. Delcassé referred the day before yesterday to the activity recently displayed by the advocates of a General Arbitration Treaty between France and Great Britain, and the campaign undertaken by them with the various Chambers of Commerce on both sides of the Channel; and asked me what I thought would be the effect of the visit of the French Deputies belonging to the Arbitration Group, now in progress in London; saying that with all the stir which is being made he supposed that it would be necessary to take some practical step.

I could only reply that I agreed with him that, in view of all the talk upon the subject, the public would probably expect that an attempt would be made to conclude a Convention; but that I still remained of the opinion that any International Agreement of the kind would of necessity be of such a nature as to be little more than a formal concession to a very praiseworthy but unpractical sentiment. In that direction it might be advisable to attempt to do something; although there would always be the risk of negotiations for the conclusion of a Treaty being wrecked by the inherent difficulties of the transaction, which, as I believed, many people who had given calm consideration to the question had not failed to recognise. There were, however, so many high authorities who had pronounced in favour of a General Treaty that I felt that I was rather a " killjoy " (" trouble-fête ") when I argued against it.

In answer to my enquiry M. Delcassé said that he had not mentioned the subject to your Lordship; and I am very sorry that he did not, for I know that it is one on which he feels some embarrassment: all the more, perhaps, that his personal sentiments towards the leader of the party now visiting London are not of a very cordial character.

I have, &c.
EDMUND MONSON.

No. 362.

The Marquess of Lansdowne to Sir E. Monson.

F.O. France 3616.
(No. 382.)   Very Confidential.

Sir,   *Foreign Office, July 29, 1903.*

The French Ambassador called on me to-day on his return from Paris. His Excellency told me that he had discussed at some length with M. Delcassé the possibility of an understanding betwen our two countries in regard to Morocco and other questions which I had discussed with the Minister for Foreign Affairs when he was in London. It seemed to M. Delcassé that we were virtually in agreement, and M. Cambon was authorised to place me in possession of M. Delcassé's views, which were as follows :—

As to Morocco, M. Delcassé thought that the two Governments might agree that the existing constitution of that country, "au point de vue politique," as well as "au point de vue territorial," should be maintained.

The British Government might, on the other hand, accord full recognition to the fact that France, having a frontier of vast extent coterminous with that of Morocco, has a peculiar interest in maintaining peace within that country, and in assisting the Moorish Government to bring about the administrative, economical, and financial improvements of which Morocco stands so much in need.

The French Republic would, however, declare expressly that these improvements should be carried out in such a fashion that the principle of commercial liberty would be absolutely respected, and that there would result from them no inequality either in the matter of the customs duties levied in the Moorish ports or as regards the rates charged for the transport of goods by rail. His Excellency explained to me that the reservation as to railway rates was suggested in deference to an observation which Mr. Balfour had made to M. Delcassé upon this subject.

M. Delcassé considered that the two Governments, holding as they did that the free passage of the Straits of Gibraltar should be secured, might undertake to act together with the object of preventing the erection of any fortifications on the Moorish coast of the Straits. I observed to his Excellency that it would scarcely be correct to represent Great Britain as being interested only in that part of the Morocco coast-line which abutted on the Straits of Gibraltar. There were other parts of the Moorish littoral to which we could not afford to be indifferent. His Excellency observed that he saw no difficulty in meeting my objection. France was, indeed, interested in preventing any Power from establishing itself, not only in the neighbourhood of the Straits, but at other points on the Moorish coast which could be used with effect for strategical purposes.

As to Spain, M. Delcassé thought that the two Governments, recognising the interests which accrued to her as the result of her possession of the "Présides," might agree that a direct understanding should be come to between the French and the Spanish Governments. Such an understanding would have to be consistent with the arrangement come to between France and Great Britain at other points, and its terms would be communicated by the French to the British Government.

I asked M. Cambon, in reference to what he had said as to an arrangement between France and Spain, whether the Spanish Government had yet been approached. He replied that this was the case, and that proposals had been made to Señor Sagasta's Government last autumn. No answer had, however, been received; . . . . .

Passing to Siam, M. Delcassé's ideas might be summed up as follows : The Convention of 1896 ought to be maintained in regard to the basin of the River Menam. British influence would be recognised on the western and French influence on the eastern sides of the basin of Menam. Although the British sphere would under such a division be less extensive than the French, the former would be distinctly more valuable in respect of the richness of its soil, its mineral wealth, and the strategic positions which it affords.

In regard to Newfoundland, M. Delcassé had told me that the French would consent to surrender their Treaty rights in return (1) for an indemnity paid to those engaged in the prosecution of the fishing industry upon the French shore; (2) for a guaranteed right to catch or buy bait; (3) for a territorial compensation.

I interrupted his Excellency at this point by calling his attention to the fact that the question of the bounties granted by France to her fishermen would certainly be raised by the Newfoundland Government, and we must endeavour to discover some way of dealing with it.

Finally, in regard to the New Hebrides, M. Delcassé observed that Great Britain interested herself in those islands on account of her connection with Australia, that France interested herself in them on account of her connection with New Caledonia, and because a considerable part of the private property in the New Hebrides is in French hands. In these circumstances, a division seemed to M. Delcassé the most obvious solution, and it would only be, in the event of our attempts to arrive at such a division proving fruitless, that some other solution might have to be looked for.

When his Excellency had completed his statement, of which he allowed me to take a note, I called his attention to the fact that he had made no mention of one country in which both France and England had interests, and which it would be impossible to exclude from consideration if a comprehensive settlement were to be attempted. I referred to Egypt. I was sure M. Delcassé would bear me out when I said that I had particularly mentioned the question of Egypt to him. M. Delcassé had said to me in reply that Egypt, like Morocco, formed part of the "African question," and that, if we could come to terms as to Morocco, there would probably be no great difficulty in coming to terms as to Egypt also.

M. Cambon said that my recollection was not in fault, but that I had said nothing particular about Egypt to him, and that he had no instructions on the subject from M. Delcassé. Would it not, M. Cambon asked, be possible for us to deal with the other points which he had enumerated, and to leave Egypt alone for the present?

I replied that it was, to my mind, out of the question that we should leave Egypt out of consideration. It was quite true that our Representatives in Egypt at this moment were on excellent terms, but I could well conceive that difficulties might some day present themselves to us in that country.

M. Cambon said that there was one difficulty which would certainly have to be faced in the near future—he referred to the conversion of the Egyptian Debt. His own idea, however, was that an arrangement might be come to as to Egypt upon the basis of a recognition of existing institutions. He cited particularly the interest of France in Egyptian archæological researches, which she had done so much to promote. She would expect to retain her museums and other scientific institutions.

I told M. Cambon that I should have much pleasure in repeating his observations to my colleagues. They seemed to be useful as a basis for further discussion, but there were many points which I felt sure we should require to examine very carefully before we could proceed further.

No reference was made by M. Cambon to the question of Sokoto, and I inferred that the territorial compensation, which was asked for in return for the abandonment of French rights in Newfoundland, would probably be looked for in that direction.

I am, &c.
LANSDOWNE.

No. 364.

The Marquess of Lansdowne to Sir E. Monson.

F.O. France 3617.
(No. 390A.)
Sir, *Foreign Office, August 5, 1903.*

The French Ambassador to-day returned to the subject of Morocco, which we had discussed on the 29th ultimo. He had, he told me, since that date, been in communication with M. Delcassé, who had confirmed the statement made to me by his Excellency on the occasion in question. M. Delcassé remained of opinion that, so far as Morocco was concerned, there was no difference of opinion between us.

I replied that, in my estimation, our difficulties would commence when we got to close quarters in matters of detail. The proposals which M. Delcassé had made as to commercial freedom in that country, the neutralisation of a part of the coast, and the recognition of Spanish interests, had been merely outlined, and we should have to fill in the description with the utmost care. Moreover, he must not forget that I had consented to deal with the question of Morocco only upon the condition that it was discussed as forming part of a general settlement which was to comprehend other points in which both Governments were interested. I said that since our last meeting I had submitted to the Cabinet a report of the conversation which had taken place between us. I had found my colleagues unanimous as to the necessity of including Egypt in any arrangement which might be made, and I was convinced that they would not entertain any proposals which did not include one for the regularisation of our position in that country. M. Cambon said that M. Delcassé had understood me to refer merely to the necessity of removing certain financial restrictions which we found inconvenient, and that a formal recognition by France of our position in that country was a much more serious matter. I could have no idea of the extent to which "l'esprit Français" was moved by the Egyptian question. France had missed her opportunity in Egypt; we had seized ours; but we had announced that our occupation was not to be permanent. The French nation clung to this idea, and held us in theory to that engagement, although, perhaps, with no very definite expectation that we should fulfil it. Any French Government which proposed to recognise the permanency of our hold upon the country would require an immense amount of nerve ("d'estomac"); but M. Delcassé was not deficient in courage and was prepared to face the attempt. We must, however, clearly understand that, if it was to be made, and if France was to be so obliging as to extract this "big thorn from the foot of Great Britain," she would look for "une grosse compensation." It might take the shape of greater liberty of action in Morocco— something less remote and conjectural ("moins hypothétique") than she had yet asked for. We should, moreover, remember that the Egyptian question concerned not France alone, but other Powers, with whom we should have to reckon. If, however, we wanted concessions in Egypt, M. Delcassé thought we should formulate our requirements.

I said that I was prepared to do so, and that I had, indeed, always contemplated the necessity of putting in a statement of the concessions which we should require in return for those which France hoped to obtain at our hands, and I begged his Excellency to remember that, if we were to give France what she desired in Morocco, we, too, should require the same kind of nerve when we came to justify our proposals to the people of this country.

We then spoke of Spain. His Excellency told me that in August 1902, and again during the last few months, the French Government had approached the Spanish Government with regard to the Moorish question. The overture had been favourably received, both by Señor Sagasta's Government and by that of Señor Silvela, although the matter had not been at all advanced by either. I gathered from what his Excellency told me that the proposal made had been to the effect that, if ever a liquidation of Morocco should become inevitable, but not otherwise, Spain would receive a considerable slice of the Moorish coast line in the neighbourhood of her existing possesions, with a certain amount of adjoining hinterland, and that it was contemplated that, under such an arrangement, Tangier would fall to the lot of Spain. That country would, however, be bound not to erect fortifications within the territory thus assigned to it, nor to dispose of that territory to another Power. A full and complete neutralisation of any part of the coasts seemed, M. Cambon said, impossible, as it would involve the adhesion of other Powers, but for our purposes it would be enough if Great Britain, France, and Spain were to agree that none of them were to erect fortifications within limits to be agreed upon, or allow other Powers to do so.

I asked M. Cambon what he thought Germany would say to such an arrangement. He said that Germany had at one time certainly wished for a coaling station near the mouth of the Muluya River, but that nothing had recently been heard of German designs in Morocco.

I said that I should no doubt be questioned by the Spanish Government as to our policy towards that country. They were, of course, aware of M. Delcassé's interview with me, and it would be obvious to them that no interchange of ideas was likely to have taken place without some reference to Morocco. I proposed, therefore, to tell the Spanish Government that His Majesty's Government had determined tô do nothing behind their back, and that although we considered that it might be simpler and more convenient that Spain should be directly approached by France, we should make it our business to ascertain that she was fully consulted, and that her interests were adequately provided for. M. Cambon agreed, saying that although he thought it might be inconvenient that we should bind ourselves to keep the Spanish Government informed of everything that passed between us, he thought we might safely tell the Spanish Government that we both held that it was above all necessary that Spain should be satisfied ("que l'Espagne, avant tout, doit avoir satisfaction").

I told his Excellency that I would do my best during the next few weeks to prepare a full description of the terms upon which His Majesty's Government would be prepared to enter into an arrangement of the kind which we had been discussing. The members of the Government would, however, separate for the holidays next week, and it would, therefore, not be easy for me for some little time to supply him with a final statement upon the subject.

I am, &c.
LANSDOWNE.

No. 365.

Memorandum by the Earl of Cromer.

F.O. Turkey 5302.   *August* 7, 1903.

I assume that we do not wish to go as far as to annex Egypt, but that our main objects are (1) to acquire a political *status* which will be recognised by the French Government; and (2) to obtain as much freedom of action as possible in the administration of the country.

It must be börne in mind that complete freedom of action, such as would enable the Capitulations to be abolished, cannot, save by annexation, be obtained without the consent of all the Powers of Europe.

I should be inclined, in the present negotiations, to limit ourselves to what may be obtained by an understanding with France alone.

I.—The first and essential point is that the French Government should recognise the occupation—in other words, that our pledge to withdraw the British garrison should be cancelled with the explicit, or at all events the implied assent of the French Government. I suggest the following formula :—

"The Government of the French Republic recognises that the British occupation of Egypt, which was originally intended to be temporary, has, under the force of circumstances, acquired a character of permanency, and they are willing that the period of its duration should be left to the discretion of His Britannic Majesty's Government."

II.—The second point is to obtain complete liberty of action in financial matters.

If the French assent to this general proposition, and if, at the same time, the British Law Officers confirm the opinion expressed by the Egyptian Law Officers to the effect that the Egyptian Government has a right to convert the debt, I think we may proceed without consultation with any other Powers. I suggest the following formula :—

"The Government of the French Republic recognises that, under the altered condition of affairs, the existence of the Caisse de la Dette and of the Railway Administration, as at present constituted, is no longer necessary.

"They will, therefore, offer no opposition to the conversion of the Egyptian Debt (Guaranteed, Preference, and Unified), under such conditions as may be arranged between His Britannic Majesty's Government and the Egyptian Government. Neither, as an incident of the conversion, will they oppose the abolition of the Caisse de la Dette, or the reorganisation of the Railway Administration, in such a manner as may be arranged between His Britannic Majesty's Government and the Egyptian Government."

III.—The other points where the international system—commonly known under the name of the Capitulations—infringes on the internal rights of sovereignty of the Egyptian Government are :—

1. No legislation applicable to all the inhabitants of Egypt, foreign and native, can be undertaken without the consent of all the Powers.
2. Civil jurisdiction in all cases between Europeans and natives is exercised by the Mixed Courts.
3. Criminal jurisdiction over Europeans is exercised by the Consular Courts.

I should be inclined to leave these matters alone for the present.

My reasons are as follows :—

In the first place, even if we had a comparatively free hand, it would be impossible at present to put forward any thorough solutions for any of these questions, all of which present difficulties of no common order.

In the second place, the most trifling change of detail would require the consent of all the Powers.

In the third place, my belief is that, if once financial liberty of action is acquired, and the permanency of the British occupation is recognised, time will eventually bring about a solution of all other points.

It is, however, worthy of consideration whether we should not stipulate for some such clause as the following, to be inserted in a Convention or in an exchange of notes :—

"His Britannic Majesty's Government has no present intention of proposing any changes in the method under which alone legislation binding on foreigners can now be undertaken in Egypt. Neither do they at present propose any fundamental changes in the systems under which civil and criminal jurisdiction are exercised over foreigners. They consider, however, that in respect to these points the existing methods and systems are open to many serious objections.

" They reserve to themselves the right of proposing at some future time such alterations as may eventually be deemed necessary. The Government of the French Republic, on their side, recognise that the Capitulations in Egypt must eventually be abolished, and will offer no objection to any proposals eventually made by His Britannic Majesty's Government tending, so far as local circumstances permit, to assimilate the Egyptian legislative and judicial systems to those in force in other civilised countries.

IV.—One further point remains to be considered.

A time must, I think, come when the position of the British Consul-General will have to be defined. Possibly it may be necessary to provide that he should attend the meetings of the Council of Ministers, and that no Khedival Decree should be issued without his sanction.

Also, I am inclined to think that, amongst Anglo-Egyptian officials, the Financial Adviser occupies too predominant a position, and that other English Heads of Departments should have seats at the Council. The Council of Ministers is at present little more than a body which gives formal assent to measures which have been arranged by others. I am inclined to think that it should be turned into a real governing body.

On the whole, however, I think we had better assume that these matters can be arranged without any reference to other Powers. Under this assumption, the matter need not be mentioned in the course of the present negotiation.

C.

August 7, 1903.

No. 366.

The Marquess of Lansdowne to Sir M. Durand.

F.O. Spain 2176.

(No. 89.)   Very Confidential.

Sir,   *Foreign Office, August* 11, 1903.

I have from time to time made you aware of the purport of the discussions which have taken place between myself and the French Ambassador at this Court in regard to various questions in which the territorial and other interests of Great Britain and France are concerned, and I forwarded to you with my No. 77, Secret, of July 17th a copy of my despatch No. 336 to Sir E. Monson,([1]) containing an account of my conversation with M. Delcassé on the occasion of his recent visit to this country. . . . .

You will have observed that throughout those communications I have never failed to impress upon the French Government the fact that we desired to discourage all proposals for a partition of Morocco, and that, should such a partition become inevitable, it would be essential that the interests of Spain should receive adequate recognition.

I desire to call your particular attention to the fact that the French Government have given explicit assurances that they have no desire to annex Morocco or to bring about the removal of the Sultan. They contend, however, that the proximity of His Highness' possessions to the Algerian possessions of France, with which they are coterminous along a frontier of several hundred miles, gives to France an interest in the interior of Morocco which no other foreign Power can reasonably claim, and they argue that, in these circumstances, the Sultan, who is not likely to hold his own for long without European assistance and advice, must necessarily turn for guidance and for assistance in improving the administration of his country to France, which would, as a logical consequence, thereby acquire a predominant position at the Moorish Court. . . . . .([2])

([1]) [*V. supra*, No 357, pp. 294–7.]

([2]) [Reference to enclosure not reproduced.]

[15214]   x 3

You are authorised to make a communication in the sense of this despatch to the Spanish Minister for Foreign Affairs. You should point out that up to the present our communications with the French Government have been of the most general character, and that we have not yet approached the discussion of details. It will, however, be in dealing with these that the most formidable difficulties will present themselves, and our task will be greatly facilitated by a full knowledge of the views of the Spanish Government.

You can, if you think proper, take this opportunity of reassuring the Spanish Government with regard to the idle rumours which have from time to time attributed to this country aggressive designs upon Spanish possessions in various quarters. His Majesty's Government have at no time harboured any such designs. They have, on the contrary, recognised, and still recognise, the value of the friendship which has so long subsisted between the two countries, and they have never contemplated any action inconsistent with these valuable traditions, which they desire to maintain and, if possible, to strengthen.

I am, &c.
LANSDOWNE.

No. 367.

Sir E. Monson to the Marquess of Lansdowne.

F.O. France 3622.
(No. 457.)   *Paris,* D. *August* 23, 1903.
My Lord,   R. *August* 25, 1903.

In view of the long duration of my official relations with the Marquess of Salisbury, as well as of the position of seniority which I enjoy in His Majesty's Diplomatic Service, I think that your Lordship will not find it surprising that I should be desirous of addressing to the Foreign Office a few words to express the sorrow with which the news of his death must be received by all those who have had the honour of serving in responsible posts under his immediate superintendence.

I have, of course, no authority to speak for any of my Colleagues, but my own experience inspires me with the conviction that none of us can have failed to be impressed by his profound sagacity, tact and dexterity, in the conduct of the Foreign Affairs of the Empire at periods of no small difficulty and complication. And I am sure that all those who have been at critical moments his agents in the execution of his orders must have felt, as I have done, that his policy and his instructions were ever the result of very exceptional mastery of details, as well as of the highest instinct of statecraft.

I have had at this moment of writing no opportunity of hearing the verdict passed upon his statesmanship by Frenchmen of authority now that he has left the scene of his labours; but of recent years, since I have been in Paris, I have been repeatedly struck by the genuine appreciation on the part of such persons, of his great and admirable qualities; and I have noted that at moments of extreme tension, when public men in England, whether members of the Government or the Opposition, have been the objects of attack in France, there has never failed to be much greater moderation, and a conspicuous absence of bitterness, in the treatment of, and the comments on, Lord Salisbury. Even before the occasion of their meeting in Paris, M. Hanotaux, certainly no Anglophil more than once in conversation with me, spoke of Lord Salisbury as the "*tête dominante*" of Europe. Since that meeting he never failed, in mentioning it, to say how deep had been the impression made upon him by Lord Salisbury's personality and conversation.

At the various posts at which I have represented Great Britain, I have found but one opinion as to the eminence of Lord Salisbury's statesmanship; and especially was this the case at Vienna during Count Kalnoky's tenure of office. That great Foreign Minister, like one of his most distinguished predecessors, Count Andrassy, always spoke of Lord Salisbury as a "pillar of strength" in the Continental system; and was ever ready to express his admiration of, and respect for, the Chief of the British Foreign Office. . . . . [Personal details.]

No. 368.

The Marquess of Lansdowne to Sir E. Monson.(¹)

(No. 472.) Confidential.

Sir, *Foreign Office, September* 23, 1903.

The French Minister told me to-day that the French Government were prepared to sign the draft Treaty with regard to Arbitration in case of differences between Great Britain and France, of which I had given him a copy on the 16th instant.

M. Cambon would probably suggest some slight verbal amendments in the text.

I am, &c.
LANSDOWNE.

(¹) Original not traced. The Text is taken from the Confidential Print.

No. 369.

The Marquess of Lansdowne to M. Cambon.

F.O. France 3640.

Personal and Confidential.

My dear Ambassador, *Foreign Office, October* 1, 1903.

I have on several occasions had the advantage of discussing with you the possibility of an understanding between the French and British Governments in regard to certain questions in which both are interested; and upon the occasion of M. Delcassé's visit to this country I had the honour of an important conversation with him upon the same subject. You were good enough on the 29th July to unfold to me, more fully than he had been able to do, his views as to the possibility and character of such a settlement as had been proposed, and I promised you that I would lay before my colleagues an account of the opinions which you had expressed on his behalf.

I have done this, and I am now able to place before you, unofficially and confidentially, a statement of the conditions upon which we should be disposed to accede to such an arrangement as the French Government contemplated.

Morocco.

Throughout my discussions with your Excellency you have assigned the first place to the question of Morocco, and M. Delcassé did not conceal from me the importance which he attached to a satisfactory solution of that question. The suggestion of the French Government is, I understand, that we should agree that the existing constitution, and the Government of His Highness the Sultan should, if possible, be maintained, and that we should alike endeavour to avoid either territorial or constitutional changes in that country. But the French Government contend that, considering the proximity of Morocco to the possessions of France in Algeria, and the length of the frontier along which those possessions are coterminous with Moorish territory, France has an altogether peculiar interest in maintaining peace and order within that territory, and that the task of assisting the Sultan's Government in bringing about the administrative, economical, and financial improvements of which Morocco stands so much in need should therefore be recognised as belonging to France rather than to any other Power.

The French Government are, however, ready to declare that in the performance of this task, and in exercising the preponderance which they would thus acquire, they intend to observe certain conditions in accordance with the suggestions of His Majesty's Government.

The first of these has reference to the facilities which would be enjoyed by the commerce of other countries in Morocco. As to this the French Government would declare expressly that the principle of commercial liberty would be absolutely respected, and that there would in no circumstances result from the preponderance of French influence any inequality as between one Power and another in the matter of customs duties levied in the Moorish ports, or as regards the rates charged for the transport of goods by rail.

His Majesty's Government regard this reservation as absolutely indispensable. The trade of Great Britain with Morocco largely exceeds that of any other country. The British imports to Morocco, taking the average of the years 1899–1901, was 44·7 of the whole, as compared with 22·1 representing French and 11·6 representing German imports during the same years. It is, moreover, obvious that—given improved methods of administration, a reform of the currency, and cheaper land transport—foreign trade with Morocco would be largely increased—an increase in which this country would certainly look to have its share.

It will be observed that the rights and privileges of Great Britain in Morocco in respect of commercial affairs are regulated by the Convention of Commerce and Navigation concluded between the two countries in December 1856, and that the rights of British subjects to reside or travel in the dominions of the Sultan are provided for in the General Treaty of the same year between the same two countries.

The Convention entitles British subjects to trade freely in the Sultan's dominions on the same terms as natives or subjects of the most-favoured nation, and stipulates that their right to buy and sell is not to be restrained or prejudiced by any monopoly, contract, or exclusive privilege, save as regards a limited number of imported articles, which are specifically mentioned.

The Treaty gives to British subjects the right of residing or travelling in the dominions of the Sultan, and further entitles the British Government to appoint Consular officers at the cities and ports in Morocco, and establishes Consular jurisdiction over British subjects, besides providing for the usual privileges in respect of the right of British subjects to hire dwellings and warehouses, and to acquire and dispose of property, for exemption from military service and forced loans, for the security of persons and property, and for the inviolability of residences, &c.

The whole of these rights would, of course, remain intact.

Your Excellency will readily understand that, in these circumstances, His Majesty's Government will be expected to obtain absolute security that, whatever may be the future of Morocco, the avenues of trade will in any eventuality remain completely open to British enterprise.

A second condition which His Majesty's Government regard as essential is, we understand, also readily accepted by the French Government. It has reference to the greater portion of the Moorish littoral, upon which both Governments desire that no Power should be allowed to establish itself or to erect fortifications or strategical works of any kind. That portion ought, in the view of His Majesty's Government, to comprise the whole seaboard now in the possession of Morocco, from the Algerian frontier to Mazaghan, including that seaport.

It would be agreed that, neither now nor hereafter, should either of the two Powers themselves create any military or naval works within the area thus described, or permit other Powers to do so.

A third condition has reference to Spain.

An adequate and satisfactory recognition of Spanish interests, political and territorial, has been from the first, in the view of His Majesty's Government, an essential element in any settlement of the Morocco question.

Spain has posessions of some importance on the Moorish coast, and the close proximity of the two countries has, not unnaturally, led to a reasonable expectation on the part of the Spanish Government and people that Spanish interests would receive special consideration in any arrangement affecting the future of Morocco.

M. Delcassé suggested that an understanding with regard to the recognition of Spanish interests in Morocco might be most conveniently brought about by means of direct communications between the French and Spanish Governments. He admitted, however, that such an understanding would have to be consistent with the arrangement come to as to Moorish affairs generally between Great Britain and France, and he agreed that its terms should be communicated by the French to the British Government.

His Majesty's Government are glad to believe that, so far as the principle involved is concerned, the two Governments are in entire accord, and that it is the object of the French, as it is that of the British Government, to deprive Spain of any reason for alleging either that she has been treated with insufficient consideration, so far as questions of form are concerned, or that her material interests have been inadequately taken into account.

The course suggested by M. Delcassé appears to us, *primâ facie*, reasonable. It will be simpler, and probably more convenient, to both parties that the terms of any arrangement which might be come to for the purpose of safeguarding Spanish interests, either at the present time or in the event of a future division of Morocco into spheres subject to foreign influence, should be discussed, in the first instance at all events, between the French and Spanish Governments. His Majesty's Government desire, however, to state at this stage that it would probably be advisable that a certain amount of territory immediately adjoining the Spanish possessions at Ceuta, Melilla, and other points, should be recognised as destined to fall under Spanish influence; and further, that in the event of a complete collapse of the Sultan's authority, Spain should be entrusted with the duty of administering the seaboard now in the possession of Morocco from the Algerian frontier as far as Mazaghan.

It would, however, have to be stipulated that Spain would be precluded from fortifying this portion of the coast, and also from alienating it or her existing possessions in Morocco to another Power.

Egypt.

If, in the eyes of the French Government, an understanding as to their position in Morocco is essential, in the view of His Majesty's Government an understanding with regard to the position of Great Britain in Egypt would form an equally essential element in any general settlement. It would be the natural and obvious counterpoise of any such admission of French predominance in the western part of North Africa as the French Government desire.

The manner in which the Egyptian question might be dealt with can be described in a very few words.

His Majesty's Government have no desire to alter the political status of Egypt, or, so far as Powers other than France are concerned, to raise at this moment questions affecting the international position of Great Britain in that country. They desire, however, that the Government of the French Republic should recognise that the British occupation of Egypt, which was originally intended to be temporary, has, under the force of circumstances, acquired a character of permanency. It would therefore, as between Great Britain and France, be understood that the period of its duration should be left entirely to the discretion of His Majesty's Government.

They also desire that the French Government should recognise that, under the condition of affairs which has arisen, the existence of the Caisse de la Dette and the railway administration, as at present constituted, is no longer necessary. The

French Government would, therefore, undertake to offer no opposition to the conversion of the Egyptian Debt (Guaranteed, Preference, and Unified) under such conditions as might be arranged between His Britannic Majesty's Government and the Egyptian Government.

Neither, as an incident of the conversion, will they oppose the abolition of the Caisse de la Dette or the reorganisation of the railway administration in such a manner as may be arranged between His Britannic Majesty's Government and the Egyptian Government.

His Britannic Majesty's Government have no present intention of proposing any changes in the method under which alone legislation binding on foreigners can now be undertaken in Egypt, neither do they at present propose any fundamental changes in the system under which civil and criminal jurisdiction are exercised over foreigners. They consider, however, that in respect to these points the existing methods and systems are open to many serious objections.

They accordingly reserve to themselves the right of proposing at a future time such alterations as may eventually be deemed necessary. The Government of the French Republic, on their side, would recognise that the Capitulations in Egypt must eventually be abolished, and would place it on record that they are prepared to examine, in consultation with His Britannic Majesty's Government, proposals tending, so far as local circumstances permit, to assimilate the Egyptian legislative and judicial systems to those in force in other civilised countries. His Majesty's Government would, on their side, be ready to examine, in consultation with the Government of the French Republic, similar proposals with regard to Morocco, if at any future period France should acquire so predominant a position in Morocco as to become outwardly responsible for the good government of the country.

Newfoundland.

My discussions with your Excellency have left no room for doubt in regard to the object which the two Governments have in view in desiring to arrive at an agreement with regard to the Newfoundland fisheries.

The French Government desire to secure for their fishermen a constant supply of the bait which is so essential to them for the prosecution of their industry.

The British Government desire to put an end to a practice by which the French fishermen exercise their preferential rights of fishing, and the right of drying fish upon the Treaty Shore under conditions which constantly lead them to commit infractions of the law, and which have the effect of retarding and obstructing the development of the Colony within the regions by which that shore is adjoined. The French Government have, in these circumstances, expressed their readiness to surrender the Treaty rights of France in return—

1. For an indemnity paid to those engaged in the prosecution of the fishing industry upon the French Shore;
2. For a territorial compensation; and
3. For a guaranteed right to catch or buy bait.

In regard to (1), His Majesty's Government would be prepared to agree that the amount of compensation should be fixed either by mutual agreement or by The Hague Tribunal.

In regard to (2), they do not desire to exclude the idea of territorial compensation in the event of a satisfactory arrangement being arrived at in regard to the other points at issue. They call attention, however, to the fact that of late years the yield of these fisheries has been insignificant, and that the rights of the French fishermen cannot accordingly be treated as an asset of much practical value. While, therefore, His Majesty's Government are prepared to discuss in a friendly spirit the proposals which the French Government may think well to make to them in regard to compensation of this kind, they feel bound to express their expectation that these proposals will be based upon the assumption that it is claimed in respect of the surrender of rights which have a sentimental rather than a substantial importance.

A serious difficulty, however, as you are aware, presents itself in regard to (3), which, in the opinion of His Majesty's Government and the Government of Newfound-land, could not be satisfactorily adjusted except in connection with a modification of the system under which the French Government now grants bounties to French fishermen frequenting the shores of Newfoundland. We are informed by the Colonial Government that the bounty received by the fishermen of St. Pierre and Miquelon is from 12 fr. to 20 fr. per quintal, an amount which renders it absolutely impossible for the Newfoundland fishermen to compete, upon reasonable terms, with those of St. Pierre and Miquelon in the foreign market.

While, therefore, His Majesty's Government recognise that it might be difficult for the French Government to modify the bounty system so far as it affects French fishermen belonging to the Metropolitan fleet, it is, in our opinion, reasonable to request that the fishery conducted from the above-named islands should be excluded from participation in these bounties.

Siam.

Our conversations with regard to Siam and the Malay States have, I am glad to say, left me under the impression that there is little or no divergence between the views of the two Governments. His Majesty's Government concur with M. Delcassé in his opinion that the Convention of 1896 should be maintained in regard to the basin of the River Menam.

Outside of this area British influence would be recognised on the western and French influence on the eastern side, all Siamese possessions lying to the east and south-east of the guaranteed area falling within the French, and all Siamese possessions lying to the west of it and of the Gulf of Siam, including those in the Malay Peninsula and the adjacent islands, within the British sphere. The Declaration of 1896 would accordingly be supplemented by a further Declaration to the effect that, while both Parties disclaim all idea of annexing Siamese territory, or encroaching in any respect upon existing Treaty rights, the action of France will, as far as Great Britain is concerned, be unfettered within the sphere of French influence, and that within the sphere of British influence the action of Great Britain will, so far as France is concerned, be equally unfettered.

New Hebrides.

Of the questions which we have at different times discussed there remain those of the New Hebrides and of the Nigerian frontier in the region of Sokoto.

In regard to the former of these, the French Government have suggested, as a possible solution of the difficulty, a partition of the islands between the two Powers.

This proposal is not one to which His Majesty's Government could consent. Any such arrangement would, from the point of view of the Australian and New Zealand Governments, present insurmountable difficulties. There should, however, be no difficulty in arriving at an arrangement which would put an end to the difficulties at present arising from the absence of jurisdiction over the natives of the group.

Nigeria.

As for Nigeria, you have more than once called my attention to the dissatisfaction of the French Government with the boundary of Sokoto, as laid down by the Convention signed at Paris on the 14th June, 1898, and expressed the desire that His Majesty's Government should consent to a revision of that boundary, which, in their opinion, had been arrived at in ignorance of the local conditions, and which compelled the French convoys, when passing from the French possessions on the Niger to those in the neighbourhood of Lake Chad, to follow a circuitous and waterless route.

Although His Majesty's Government do not desire to reopen the questions settled in 1898, they would be prepared, in order to meet the views of the French Government, to consent to a readjustment of the boundary as part of a general settlement of the kind we are discussing, and in return for equivalent concessions at other points.

Such an equivalent might be found in the surrender of the French rights on the Treaty Shore of Newfoundland, to which subject I have already referred in this Memorandum.

Advantage might be taken of this opportunity in order to reconsider and revise the arrangement made in 1898, under which two small pieces of land were leased to the French Government on the Niger. These enclaves are not believed to be of great value to the French Government, and would no longer be required when the French railway from Dahomey reaches the Niger. They have not, we understand, been used at all for commercial purposes, but only for the transhipment and storage of goods on the occasions, occurring about twice a year, when a flotilla is sent up the river with Government stores.

On the other hand, the existence of these enclaves might at any moment lead to friction, and we believe that it would be possible for us to offer facilities which would enable French trade to pass up the Niger without any inconvenience.

Zanzibar.

As your Excellency is aware, two questions in connection with the Sultanate of Zanzibar are still outstanding between Great Britain and France, namely, the exercise of French jurisdiction and the existence of a French post-office. With regard to the former, His Majesty's Government would be willing to accept the terms mentioned in the draft communicated by M. Daeschner on the 29th June last, subject to one or two modifications.

With regard to the French post-office, His Majesty's Government desire that it should now be definitely closed in accordance with the repeated engagements to that effect on the part of the French Government.

It would be understood that this arrangement should apply not only to the islands of Zanzibar and Pemba, but to the mainland dominions of the Sultan as well.

Madagascar.

A summary of the questions outstanding between the two countries could not be complete without some reference to Madagascar. Your Excellency is no doubt aware of the protests which my predecessor thought it his duty to address to the French Government in 1896 and 1897 on the subject of the withdrawal of the privileges and immunities secured to British subjects by Treaty in that island in consequence of its annexation by France, and in disregard of the assurances which had previously been given by the French Government on the first establishment of a French Protectorate, and during subsequent military operations.

Those protests were renewed in a further despatch which was communicated to M. Delcassé on his Excellency's assumption of the office of Minister of Foreign Affairs in July 1898.

They have never received any satisfactory reply, and although His Majesty's Government have refrained from further correspondence, the matter remains according to their view, one in which engagements entered into by the French Government have been set aside without any attempt at compensation on the grounds of convenience. Nor can it be said that the grievance is one of sentiment alone, for there can be no doubt that British trade with the island has suffered severely from the substitution of a Tariff differentiating in favour of French products, and imposing on British imports duties largely in excess of the *ad valorem* limit laid down in the Treaty of 1865 between Great Britain and Madagascar.

His Majesty's Government would be content, as part of a general settlement of pending questions, to withdraw their claims and protests on this account.

Believe me, &c.

LANSDOWNE.

No. 370.

The Marquess of Lansdowne to Sir E. Monson.

F.O. France 3617.

(No. 503. Secret.)

Sir,

Foreign Office, October 7, 1903.

The French Ambassador, who has just returned to London, called upon me this afternoon, and at once proceeded to discuss the Personal and Confidential letter which I addressed to him on the 1st instant with regard to the possibility of an understanding between the French and British Governments upon certain questions in which both are interested.

M. Cambon told me that he had seen M. Delcassé on his way through Paris, and that, in the short time at his disposal, the Minister for Foreign Affairs, who had received a copy of my letter, had evidently studied it with close attention. A considerable part of the letter dealt, in M. Delcassé's opinion, with affairs of comparatively secondary importance, which might be settled without difficulty at any moment, although our suggestion as to the bounties given to the French fishermen frequenting the coast of Newfoundland would, he feared, occasion considerable difficulties. These bounties were given under the French law, which applied to the Colonies as well as the mother country, and M. Delcassé thought it would be impossible to deprive the fishermen of St. Pierre and Miquelon of the privilege which they now enjoyed.

The two questions, however, which really signified were those that concerned Morocco and Egypt.

M. Delcassé had not understood from my conversation with him that I intended to raise the whole Egyptian question, and our proposals seemed to him to be very far-reaching. I said that, in my short discussion with M. Delcassé, it had obviously been impossible for me to put forward in full detail our proposals with regard to Egypt, and that when I had introduced the subject, M. Delcassé had at once met me with the observation that the Egyptian and Moorish questions alike formed part of the African question' and that he had no objection to examine them simultaneously.

M. Cambon then said that, according to our proposals, France would not receive in Morocco a sufficient equivalent for the immense concessions which she was asked to make in Egypt. In return for such concessions, the French Chamber would naturally look for immediate and concrete advantages. All we gave her was "a hope," the realisation of which might be remote—for I must bear in mind that she was to be precluded from annexing the country and bound to maintain the Sultan's authority. We, on the contrary, would obtain immediate advantages in Egypt.

I replied that it seemed to me a mistake to argue that France would not receive immediate advantages in Morocco. We had, as his Excellency was aware, hitherto taken a close interest in the affairs of that country, and I reminded him that he had himself, on more than one occasion, complained to me of the presence of British officers in it and of alleged attempts to keep the Sultan in British tutelage. We were ready to meet the views of the French Government at this point, and as to Egypt, I begged him to remember that we were there already, and that there was not the slightest prospect of our withdrawing. We were, in reality, only asking the French Government to recognise the facts as they exist.

M. Cambon said that, so far as the finances of Egypt were concerned, France was established in the country just as securely as we were, and we were asking her to abdicate in our favour.

He added that there was this further difference between the two cases, viz., that, after we had made way for France in Morocco, she would still have other Powers to deal with. Spain, to begin with, would present considerable difficulties, and I had no doubt noticed that the Spanish Government had become extremely suspicious as to our proceedings; but that was not all—Germany, too, was watching them with jealous attention, and France might have to reckon with the pretensions of that Power. In these circumstances, M. Delcassé was obliged to scrutinise our proposals very carefully, and he would require a little time for this purpose. M. Cambon suggested, as his own idea, that our programme, so far as it affected Egypt and Morocco, might be carried out gradually. I had, he thought, admitted this principle in my letter, when I proposed that, should the Capitulations eventually be abolished and the Egyptian system be assimilated to that in force in other countries, the two Governments should discuss the possibility of applying similar proposals to Morocco, in the event of France at any future period acquiring a predominant position in that country. Why might we not, he said, proceed gradually in our dealings with the Egyptian Debt and the control, on the understanding that these changes should be introduced *pari passu* with correlative changes in Morocco. I said that I saw considerable difficulties in the attempt to proceed throughout *pari passu*, and we certainly could not agree to an indefinite postponement of the recognition of the permanent character of our occupation. That, at any rate, was a request for which we should expect an immediate " Yes " or " No." I also pointed out that we should have other Powers to reckon with in Egypt, just as France might have other Powers to reckon with in Morocco.

M. Cambon expressed general agreement with regard to our proposals as to Spain, but told me that we had assigned to that country far too extensive a proportion of the Moorish coast-line. Should the " liquidation " of Morocco ever take place, it would never do for France to find herself enveloped by a strip of Spanish territory reaching from Mazaghan to the Algerian frontier.

I said that I should be prepared to discuss the geographical question with him whenever he was ready to do it, but that there seemed to me to be great advantages in neutralising as much of the Moorish seaboard as possible. Moreover, there were scarcely any important ports between the points named.

At the close of our conversation, I said that while I quite understood M. Delcassé's desire to consider our proposals at leisure, I earnestly trusted that he would make me aware of his conclusions at the earliest possible date. The public was beginning to get wind of the negotiations, and if they were prolonged until the meeting of Parliament, we should certainly have some troublesome questions with regard to them.

I am, &c.
LANSDOWNE.

No. 371.

The Marquess of Lansdowne to Sir E. Monson.

F.O. France 3617.
(No. 513. Secret.)
Sir, *Foreign Office, October* 14, 1903.

The French Ambassador called upon me this morning for the purpose of signing the Treaty of Arbitration concluded between Great Britain and France.([1])

([1]) [An arbitration treaty on the lines of the Anglo-French treaty was signed with Italy on the 1st February, 1904.]

He told me that he was leaving for Paris this afternoon, and would, during his stay there, again discuss with M. Delcassé the Personal and Confidential letter which I had addressed to him on the 1st of October.

I repeated that it seemed to me of the utmost importance that we should arrive at a decision upon the points at issue with as little delay as possible.

His Excellency said that he quite agreed with me, and that he knew that M. Delcassé had the same feeling, but our Egyptian proposals were of a very serious kind.

I am, &c.
LANSDOWNE.

No. 372.

Sir E. Monson to the Marquess of Lansdowne.

F.O. France 3623.
(No. 554.) Confidential.   *Paris,* D. *October* 22, 1903.
My Lord,   R. *October* 24, 1903.

Having gone yesterday to the Élysée to speak to the President upon the subject of the short-horned cattle which the King is going to send him from the Royal Farm at Windsor, I had an opportunity of conversing with M. Loubet at some length respecting the recent visit of the King and Queen of Italy.

The President said that Their Majesties entirely realised the description which he had had of them from King Edward. He had been greatly impressed by the frank, straightforward character of the King, his intelligence, his knowledge, and his powers of observation; while it would be impossible to over-estimate the charm of manner, the graciousness, and the dignity of the Queen.

He was convinced that this visit, which had really excited considerable enthusiasm in Paris, had put the finishing touch to the *rapprochement* between France and Italy, and that the past bitterness was completely buried (to employ the very words which the King himself had used in conversation with him).

M. Loubet went on to say that he was delighted that the publication of the Arbitration Agreement between Great Britain and France had synchronised with the arrival of Their Italian Majesties; and he added that the Government of the Republic had been most anxious that this Agreement should be the first of a series which are in process of negotiation with several other countries. He explained that some of these were already so far advanced that it would have been quite possible to have announced them, but that he and his Ministers had felt that priority was due to the Anglo-French Agreement, and was at the same time politic in regard to its influence.

M. Loubet, before leaving the subject, observed very earnestly that he trusted that this Agreement would be followed by another of greater importance and more extensive and varied scope. He could assure me that he and M. Delcassé had this deeply at heart, and that, though the questions to be solved are difficult, and even intricate, he could not but believe that a settlement would be found practicable.

I replied that the reception given by your Lordship in July last to M. Delcassé's original overtures must have convinced the French Government that that of His Majesty is animated by a desire for a satisfactory settlement quite as sincere and thoroughgoing as that entertained in France, and that I knew that your Lordship, while fully recognising the difficulties on both sides, was most anxious to expedite the negotiation—any premature publicity about which, it was, I hoped, felt as much in Paris as in London, would not accelerate the progress of the confidential discussion now being carried on.

I have, &c.
EDMUND MONSON.

No. 373.

M. Cambon to the Marquess of Lansdowne.

F.O. France 3640.

Personnelle et Confidentielle.   *Ambassade de France,* D. *le 26 Octobre* 1903.

Cher Lord Lansdowne,   R. *October* 27, 1903.

A la suite de votre conversation avec M. Delcassé lors de son passage à Londres vous avez bien voulu, par votre lettre du 1ᵉʳ courant, me faire connaître officiusement et confidentiellement les vues de vos collègues du Cabinet et les vôtres sur la possibilité d'un règlement de certaines questions intéressant nos deux Gouvernements.

J'ai soumis votre lettre à M. Delcassé, qui m'a communiqué à son tour et m'a autorisé à vous faire connaître sa manière de voir sur la conclusion d'un accord de ce genre.

M. Delcassé désire très sincèrement mettre fin à la plupart des difficultés pendantes depuis trop longtemps entre la France et l'Angleterre, mais il estime que, pour être équitable et donner satisfaction à l'opinion publique dans les deux pays, un arrangement doit comporter des avantages réciproques et une corrélation aussi exacte que possible entre nos mutuelles concessions.

C'est en s'inspirant de ces vues qu'il a examiné les questions posées par votre Seigneurie et qu'il s'est déclaré prêt à les régler de la façon suivante :

Maroc.

Le Gouvernement de Sa Majesté Britannique reconnaîtra l'intérêt exclusif qu'a la France, comme Puissance limitrophe du Maroc sur une vaste étendue, de veiller à la tranquillité de ce pays et de lui prêter son assistance pour les réformes administratives, économiques, financières, et militaires dont il a besoin.

Le Gouvernement de la République déclarera que ces réformes seront réalisées de telle sorte que le principe de la liberté commerciale sera absolument respecté et qu'il n'en résultera aucune inégalité, pas plus dans l'établissement des droits de douane dans les ports que dans l'établissement des tarifs de transport par chemin de fer.

La France respectera les dispositions inscrites tant dans le Traité Général Anglo-Marocain du 9 Décembre 1856, que dans la Convention de Commerce du même jour, visés dans la lettre personnelle de votre Seigneurie du 1ᵉʳ Octobre, sauf les clauses du présent arrangement.

Afin de garantir la liberté du Détroit de Gibraltar, les deux Gouvernements s'engageront à ne pas établir et à ne permettre à aucune autre Puissance d'établir des fortifications militaires ou maritimes sur la partie du littoral Marocain comprise entre Melilla sur la Méditerranée et les hauteurs qui dominent la rive droite du Sébou. Les deux Gouvernements s'engageront en outre à maintenir, sauf les conséquences du présent accord, le *statu quo* territorial dans un rayon de 500 milles autour du dit Détroit.

Les deux Gouvernements sont d'accord pour admettre que la reconnaissance des intérêts politiques et territoriaux de l'Espagne résultant de sa situation même et de ses possessions territoriales sur les côtes du Maroc, est un élément essentiel dans le règlement de la question Marocaine. Ils reconnaissent que certaines parties du territoire Marocain adjacentes aux possessions Espagnoles au Maroc doivent tomber dans la sphère d'influence de l'Espagne. A celle-ci reviendrait notamment, la garde et l'administration des territoires bordant la mer depuis Melilla jusqu'aux hauteurs qui dominent la rive droite du Sébou. Une entente directe interviendra à ce sujet entre la France et l'Espagne, lesquelles conviendront aussi que les territoires faisant partie de l'Empire Marocain compris dans leur sphère d'influence ne pourront pas être cédés à une Puissance tierce. Les termes de cette entente seront portés à la connaissance du Gouvernement Britannique.

L'Espagne devrait accepter, comme la France et l'Angleterre, les dispositions relatives à la liberté du Détroit de Gibraltar et, pour les territoires situés dans sa sphère d'influence, les dispositions relatives à la liberté commerciale.

Egypte.

Le Gouvernement du Roi ayant reconnu la tâche qui incombe à la France au Maroc et pour laquelle pleine liberté d'action lui est laissée, le Gouvernement de la République se déclarera disposé à ne point entraver l'action de l'Angleterre en Égypte et à ne pas demander qu'un terme soit fixé à l'occupation Britannique.

Désireux de donner tout de suite au Gouvernement Britannique une preuve de son bon vouloir, il se déclarera prêt, dès que l'entente générale sera conclue entre les deux Gouvernements, à ne pas faire d'objection à l'emploi du fonds d'économies des conversions de 1890, à la seule condition que ce fonds soit employé dans l'intérêt de l'Égypte comme, par exemple, à l'amélioration du réseau des chemins de fer ou à d'autres grands travaux publics.

Le Gouvernement Britannique, bien qu'il n'ait pas l'intention de proposer, quant à présent, des modifications au régime des Capitulations et à l'organisation judiciaire en Égypte, estime cependant que le système actuel présente certains inconvénients. Votre Seigneurie suggère, en conséquence, que le Gouvernement Français promette d'examiner les propositions qui lui seraient éventuellement adressées en vue d'introduire en Égypte, en ce qui concerne les étrangers, un système conforme aux règles suivies dans les autres pays civilisés. De son côté le Gouvernement Britannique s'engagerait à examiner les propositions qui lui seraient adressées éventuellement dans le même ordre d'idées par le Gouvernement de la République pour le Maroc, le jour où la France serait en mesure d'assumer la responsabilité de l'administration de ce pays, vis-à-vis des Puissances étrangères.

M. Delcassé accepte volontiers la corrélation ainsi posée par le Gouvernement Britannique entre la renonciation éventuelle au bénéfice des Capitulations par la France en Égypte et par l'Angleterre au Maroc. C'est même, dans sa pensée, conformément à ce principe, que devraient être résolues les autres questions soulevées à propos de l'Égypte par le Gouvernement Britannique.

L'administration des finances est particulièrement défectueuse au Maroc et c'est sans doute par elle que devront commencer les réformes permettant à ce pays d'entrer dans la voie de la civilisation. Dès que sa prépondérance financière sera établie au Maroc, au moyen d'un contrôle effectif, le Gouvernement de la République sera prêt à renoncer à sa part dans le contrôle financier de l'Égypte ainsi qu'au droit qui lui appartient de faire obstacle à la conversion des dettes Égyptiennes.

Une entente analogue pourrait intervenir en ce qui concerne la participation de la France à l'administration des chemins de fer Égyptiens, le jour où le Gouvernement de la République aurait établi son contrôle sur les travaux publics au Maroc.

On conviendrait aussi que le Gouvernement Britannique ne pourrait pas établir en Égypte des droits différentiels et devrait y maintenir le principe de la liberté commerciale.

Enfin les deux Gouvernements, mus par les mêmes considérations d'intérêt général qui ont inspiré les dispositions prises pour assurer la liberté du transit au Détroit de Gibraltar, conviendraient que le libre usage en tout temps du Canal de Suez sera aussi garanti conformément aux principes inscrits au Traité du 29 Octobre, 1888.

Terre-Neuve.

Sur la question de Terre-Neuve votre Seigneurie rappelle que le Gouvernement Français a subordonné son assentiment à l'abandon du "French Shore" à trois conditions :

1. Une indemnité financière.
2. Une compensation territoriale.
3. La liberté du commerce de la boëtte.

Sur la première condition, nous admettons volontiers avec l'Angleterre que le Tribunal de La Haye soit chargé de fixer le montant de l'indemnité à attribuer aux établissements Français intéressés, ainsi qu'aux armateurs et aux pêcheurs qui fréquentent le " French Shore."

Sur la deuxième condition, le Gouvernement de la République croit devoir faire observer que ses droits n'ont pas seulement le caractère sentimental que paraît leur attribuer le Gouvernement Britannique, par le motif qu'ils sont fondés sur un Traité solennel et qu'ils ont été confirmés ultérieurement par plusieurs autres Conventions. D'autre part, dans l'appréciation de la valeur réelle du " French Shore," doit entrer en ligne de compte non pas seulement son utilité actuelle, mais celle qu'il a eue et qu'il ne manquerait pas de recouvrer, si les morues qui fréquentaient naguère les parages de Terre-Neuve et qui les ont désertés, y revenaient de nouveau, comme il a déjà été constaté cette année qu'elles tendaient à y revenir.

Le Gouvernement de la République pense que la Colonie Anglaise de la Gambie, enveloppée de possessions Françaises et dont il est bien permis de dire que la possession a surtout une valeur sentimentale pour la Grande-Bretagne, semblerait répondre aux conditions de convenance réciproques et d'équité requises dans un échange de cette nature.

Quant à la troisième condition, le Gouvernement Britannique désire subordonner la liberté du commerce de la boëtte à la suppression de la prime dont jouissent actuellement les pêcheurs Français de Saint-Pierre et Miquelon. Il admettrait seulement que la prime fût allouée aux pêcheurs Français de France. Cette distinction, contraire à la loi même qui a institué les primes, est contraire aussi à l'esprit de la législation Française, ainsi qu'à la tendance nouvelle qui, en France comme d'ailleurs en Angleterre, pousse la Métropole à assurer aux Colonies une situation privilégiée. M. Delcassé espère que le Gouvernement de Sa Majesté Britannique n'insistera pas.

Siam.

Notre Ministre des Affaires Étrangères constate avec satisfaction qu'en ce qui concerne les affaires du Siam, le Gouvernement Britannique partage la manière de voir qu'il a exposée lui-même le 7 Juillet dernier à votre Seigneurie. Il serait convenu que la Convention Franco-Anglaise de 1896 serait complétée par une Déclaration aux termes de laquelle—les deux parties écartant l'idée de s'annexer des territoires Siamois et de porter atteinte aux Traités existants—l'action de la France serait libre dans la sphère d'influence Française, c'est-à-dire à l'est du bassin de la Meinam, et l'action de l'Angleterre libre dans la sphère d'influence Anglaise, c'est-à-dire à l'ouest du bassin de la Meinam et dans la presqu'île Malaise.

Nouvelles-Hébrides.

M. Delcassé regrette vivement que le Gouvernement de Sa Majesté Britannique ne croie pas pouvoir entrer dans ses vues en ce qui concerne le partage des Nouvelles-Hébrides. Cette solution, qui eût été la seule vraiment équitable, ne pouvant être réalisée, le Gouvernement de la République n'a pas d'objections à rechercher avec celui de Sa Majesté Britannique les moyens de parer aux difficultés résultant de l'absence de juridiction sur les indigènes—sans que le *statu quo* soit modifié.

Niger.

L'Angleterre désire introduire des modifications aux dispositions de la Convention du 14 Juin, 1898, concernant les deux Enclaves réservées à la France sur le Niger. Le Gouvernement de la République ne refusera pas d'examiner les propositions du Gouvernement Britannique à cet égard lorsque le chemin de fer Français du Dahomey atteindra le Niger.

Zanzibar.

Quant à Zanzibar, le Gouvernement de la République s'est déjà déclaré prêt à renoncer à la juridiction Consulaire et à son Bureau de Poste, sauf certaines dispositions à prendre en ce qui concerne nos protégés. Il dépend du Gouvernement Britannique de hâter la solution de cette question, qui ne saurait être l'occasion d'une difficulté réelle.

Madagascar.

Votre Seigneurie rappelle, en terminant, les réclamations de son Gouvernement contre le Tarif Douanier établi à Madagascar après l'annexion de cette île à la France. Au point de vue de droit, cette annexion a eu pour conséquence, conformément à une règle universellement admise, de faire tomber les Traités liant l'ancien Gouvernement Malgache aux autres Gouvernements. Il n'eût pu en être autrement en ce qui concerne le Traité Anglo-Malgache de 1865 que si le Gouvernement de la République avait promis que, même en cas d'annexion, il respecterait cet acte. Or, il avait seulement déclaré que l'établissement du Protectorat n'affecterait aucun des droits ou immunités dont jouissaient les Anglais dans la Grande Ile.

Lorsque plus tard l'attitude des Hovas a rendu cette annexion indispensable, le Gouvernement de la République s'y est résolu dans sa pleine liberté d'action.

D'autre part, en ce qui concerne l'importance des intérêts Britanniques engagés dans la question, il n'est pas inutile de rappeler que tout le monde en Angleterre ne partage pas l'opinion de votre Seigneurie, car en 1896 Lord Salisbury, causant avec l'Ambassadeur d'Italie à Londres, s'exprimait dans les termes suivants : '' Je dis que nos intérêts en Madagascar n'étaient pas en eux-mêmes très considérables et que par suite notre sollicitude était plutôt excitée par la crainte de laisser s'établir un principe pernicieux que par la perspective immédiate de perte matérielle.'' (Blue Book, Africa, No. 8, p. 36, 1897.)

Le Gouvernement de la République ne rend pas moins hommage au sentiment qui a inspiré à votre Seigneurie l'idée de profiter de l'arrangement général en préparation pour retirer les réclamations que le Foreign Office avait cru devoir formuler après l'annexion de Madagascar à la France.

Telles sont les vues de M. Delcassé sur tous les points visés dans la lettre de votre Seigneurie du 1ᵉʳ Octobre.

Croyez, &c.
PAUL CAMBON.

No. 374.

Earl of Cromer to the Marquess of Lansdowne.

F.O. Turkey 5303.
Tel. (No. 34.) Secret. Extract. *Cairo, October* 30, 1903.

(¹) . . . . Do you think you could go so far as to make the general arrangement with the French on Morocco, and other points dependent on satisfactory settlement of Egyptian questions with or without the consent of other Powers?

I repeat I would not be in too great a hurry to make any detailed proposals to the French before the bases of negotiation are more definitely settled.

As regards M. Cambon's statement that two-thirds of the debt are held in France, this is, certainly, a great exaggeration.

It is impossible to speak confidently about the distribution of debt, as it is certain that a large number of the coupons paid in Paris are sent from London to avoid payment of income tax. But even on the French showing, as stated in their '' Official Journal '' of 25th September, 1902, they only hold 39,000,000 fr. out of a total of 103,000,000 fr.

(¹) [Details as to Morocco and Egypt.]

No. 375.

Sir E. Monson to the Marquess of Lansdowne.

F.O. France 3623.

(No. 568.)   *Paris,* D. *October* 30, 1903.

My Lord,   R. *October* 31, 1903.

A large party of the Representatives of the commercial world of London arrived in Paris the day before yesterday in response to an invitation addressed to them by the Republican Committee of Commerce and Industry presided over by M. Mascuraud. . . . . [Personal details.]

There is no doubt that the hospitality shown has been most bountiful and the reciprocal enthusiasm most genuine. The Nationalist Opposition has made fun of the whole thing, and even a serious journal like the " Journal des Débats " has pointed out that the Municipality has rather had its hands forced by an association of second-class tradesmen and mercenary politicians, who had no right to speak and act in the name of the City of Paris. But the manner in which the members of the Government finally associated themselves with the demonstration, and the excellent grace with which the Municipal Body, with but few exceptions, followed suite, have secured a most successful issue for an undertaking which may very likely have originated in the interested motives of a somewhat obscure clique.

At any rate, such demonstrations contribute to the energy of the current of goodwill which has been established between the two nations, and which is now flowing with a steadiness almost incredible to those who have studied the situation in France for the last few years. . . . . .

I have, &c.
EDMUND MONSON.

No. 376.

The Marquess of Lansdowne to M. Cambon.

F.O. France 3640.

Private and Confidential.

My dear Ambassador,   *Foreign Office, November* 19, 1903.

I have had an opportunity of discussing with some of my colleagues the proposals embodied in your Confidential letter of the 26th October, and I am able to give you a general idea of the manner in which they are regarded.

I will preface my observations by saying that we entirely recognise the reasonableness of M. Delcassé's stipulation that any general arrangement entered into between the two Governments should be based upon reciprocal advantages and mutual concessions, which should be, as nearly as possible, equivalent.

Morocco.

I do not think there should be much difficulty in reconciling M. Delcassé's views upon the subject of Morocco with those which are expressed in my letter of the 1st October. There is only one point at which, as I understand your letter, any important modification of our proposals upon this subject is suggested. It was suggested by me that no Power should be allowed to establish itself or to erect fortresses or strategical works of any kind upon the Moorish seaboard from the Algerian frontier to Mazagan. M. Delcassé proposes that this restriction should apply only to the Moorish littoral between Melilla and the heights which command the right bank of the River Sebou.

In order to meet M. Delcassé's wishes, we are prepared to consent to a modification of our original proposal and to agree that the portion of the Atlantic coast thus neutralised shall extend from Melilla as far as Rabat, including the port of that name, which is about 20 miles south of the Sebou River.

We are unable to understand the proposal that the two Governments should agree to maintain the *status quo* within a radius of "500 milles" from the Straits of Gibraltar. This definition would extend beyond the boundaries of Morocco and would include a part of Algeria.

It should be understood that the absolute commercial equality which the French Government engage to maintain would include freedom of the coasting trade granted in 1901, equality of opportunity in regard to mining concessions and tenders for the construction of railways, docks, and other public works, and all other advantages now enjoyed by British subjects and Companies in connection with trade and navigation.

Egypt.

Passing to Egypt, we understand that M. Delcassé is prepared to give an undertaking that France will not obstruct the action of Great Britain in Egypt, and will recognise the permanency of our occupation of that country. He is also ready to agree that the economies resulting from the conversion of 1890, which are now under the control of the "Caisse," *shall be used in Egyptian interests, as, for instance, in the construction of railways or other large public works.*(¹) He readily accepts the principle of reciprocity in regard to modifications in the régime of the Capitulations in Egypt and Morocco respectively.(²)

He is not, however, prepared to undertake that France shall at present withdraw from her part in the financial control, *from the right claimed by the French Government to oppose the conversion*(³) of the Egyptian debts, or from the administration of the Egyptian railways. M. Delcassé's suggestion is that the French Government might agree to make these concessions as soon as the Government of the Republic have established an effective control over the financial system and the Public Works Department of Morocco.

His Majesty's Government are unable to agree to this proposal, or to negotiate on the basis of an arrangement under which the abandonment of financial control by France in Egypt would proceed only *pari passu* with the acquisition of financial control by France in Morocco.

In order, however, to meet the objections of the French Government, the following proposal is offered :—

1. That the "Caisse de la Dette" should be maintained, but that its function should be strictly limited to receiving *the sum necessary*(⁴) for the service of the debt, with a right to sue the Egyptian Government in the Law Courts should that sum not be punctually paid.

   An essential part of the arrangement would be that the railways, telegraphs, and port of Alexandria should cease to be governed by a Mixed Administration.(⁵)

2. That the French Government should agree to join with us in addressing the other Powers for the purpose of securing their assent to these proposals, and it would be understood that, should the consent of the other Powers be refused, France will not oppose any steps which His Majesty's Government may hereafter find it expedient to take for the purpose of *giving' effect to*

(¹) [Substituted by Lord Cromer, telegram No. 38, Secret, of the 13th November, for (Lansdowne, telegram No. 32, of the 11th November) " placed at the disposal of the Egyptian Government to be used in that country on works of public utility."]

(²) [Added by Lord Cromer *ib.*]

(³) [Substituted by Lord Cromer *ib.* for " from her right to oppose conversion."]

(⁴) [Substituted by Lord Cromer *ib.* for " pledged revenues not exceeding the sum annually due."]

(⁵) [Altered by Lord Cromer *ib.*]

the agreement which the French and British Governments will have arrived at.([6])

3. That the French Government should not object to the Egyptian Government exercising its right to convert the Egyptian debts *whenever an opportune moment for effecting this operation may occur.*([7])

As part of a general settlement in which the other questions referred to in this correspondence were dealt with to their satisfaction, His Majesty's Government would be ready to give an assurance that differential duties should not be imposed in Egypt, and that the principle of commercial liberty should be maintained there, and they would guarantee the free passage of the Suez Canal in accordance with the principles embodied in the Treaty of the 29th October, 1888, *but without specific observance of Article VIII of that Convention, which is incompatible with the necessary consequences of the British occupation.*([8])

Newfoundland.

The Newfoundland problem presents considerable difficulties.

M. Delcassé suggests that the British Colony of the Gambia would form a suitable equivalent for the surrender of the French rights on the Treaty Shore.

A proposal of this kind was fully considered by His Majesty's Government in the summer of 1901, when it was informally put forward by your Excellency. I then informed you, after referring the point to my colleagues, that it was impossible for us to entertain the proposal. Our objections to it are insuperable, and, if territorial compensation should be found inevitable, we must look for it elsewhere. I venture to recall to your Excellency's attention the suggestion contained in my last letter, that a readjustment of the boundary of the British possessions in Nigeria would in that case afford an equitable solution of the difficulty. Your Excellency has repeatedly called my attention to the inconvenience of the present boundary, and we should probably be able to meet the views of the French Government at this point.

A not less formidable difficulty presents itself in the refusal of the French Government to take into consideration the propriety of abolishing the bounties received by the French fishermen at St. Pierre and Miquelon.

Having regard to M. Delcassé's decided language upon this point, His Majesty's Government do not desire to press it further, but they are obliged to observe that the consent of the Colonial Government is not likely to be given to any arrangement under which French vessels would acquire a right to obtain supplies of bait on the shores of Newfoundland, if this practice, so unfair in its operation as regards the colonial fishermen, is allowed to survive.

If, therefore, we are to assume that M. Delcassé's refusal to deal with the question of bounties is final, it must, I fear, be also assumed that we shall be unable to concede the right to the free purchase of bait in the bays of the south coast of Newfoundland lying outside the Treaty Shore, and it becomes necessary to consider whether any modified arrangement is possible under which we might get rid of the main source of the existing trouble—viz., the obstacle presented to the development and utilisation of the coast and the adjacent country by the French rights of drying their fish on the shore. With this object we are willing to confer with the Newfoundland Government

([6]) [Substituted by Lord Cromer *ib.* for " of relieving Egypt from the excessive and embarrassing restrictions to which at present her Financial Administration is subjected." Lord Cromer suggested that the latter wording " might frighten the French and make them think that a pretext for annexation is being sought."]

([7]) [Substituted by Lord Cromer *ib.* for " for five years." The immediately following clause in the Lansdowne draft " His Majesty's Government to agree to the acquisition by France of complete financial control in Morocco as soon as (but not before) an understanding has been arrived at with all the Powers concerned upon this point," was struck out at suggestion of Lord Cromer.]

([8]) [Added at suggestion of Lord Cromer.]

as to the possibility of an arrangement, confined to the Treaty Coast, of the following kind :—

The right of the French to fish for any kind of fish, whether bait-fish or others, or to purchase bait on the Treaty Coast might be continued, but they would give up their right of using the shore for the purpose of drying fish. If such an arrangement were come to, we should be prepared to compensate the owners of existing French establishments, but in that case no claim for territorial compensation could be admitted.

The above observations have reference to the more important questions raised by your letter. The remaining points do not seem likely to give rise to any difficulty.

New Hebrides.

I should, however, add, with regard to the New Hebrides, that His Majesty's Government consider it most important that an arrangement should be come to for disposing of questions raised between the two Governments as to land titles as well as questions concerning jurisdiction over natives.

Madagascar.

I also desire to observe, with reference to the claims of His Majesty's Government in regard to Madagascar, that it is impossible for us to admit that the French Government could be considered as liberated from its specific engagements to respect British Treaty rights by the simple conversion of the French Protectorate into an annexation. Nor can they agree that the loss which British commerce has suffered is immaterial. In 1896, when Lord Salisbury made the observation quoted by your Excellency, the French General Customs Tariff had not yet been applied to the island. That measure was adopted in July 1897, and the subjoined Table(1) shows how serious has been the effect on British trade.

The grievance, therefore, which His Majesty's Government are offering to waive, should a full settlement of other questions be arrived at, appears to them to be a very substantial one, both in principle and substance.

I am led by a consideration of the case of Madagascar to offer a further observation. It was contended by the French Government that, when the island was annexed by France, the French Government were, *ipso facto*, relieved from their existing engagements in regard to it. As I have just stated, His Majesty's Government have from the first contested this view. We are therefore anxious to leave no room in any settlement which may now be come to as to Egypt and Morocco for an eventual conflict of opinion, however remote, upon a similar issue.

M. Delcassé was good enough to assure me, on the occasion of our interview on the 7th July last, that the French Government had no desire to annex Morocco. His Majesty's Government have, on their side, no desire to annex Egypt. It would, nevertheless, be desirable that we should place it on record that, should either Power at any future time find itself compelled, by the force of circumstances, to modify its policy in this respect, any engagements into which that Power had entered as to commercial equality shall remain intact, and that if either side should in any way depart from those engagements, the other side will be at liberty to do the same.

Believe me, &c.
LANSDOWNE.

(1) Not reproduced.

No. 377.

The Marquess of Lansdowne to Sir E. Monson.

F.O. France 3617.
(No. 586.) Confidential.

Sir, *Foreign Office, November 20, 1903.*

The French Ambassador told me to-day that he had forwarded my letter of the 19th to M. Delcassé.

He said that it would be premature to discuss it with me at this stage, but he, nevertheless, proceeded to make one or two interesting comments upon it. He thought that we might as well not have insisted on neutralising the Moorish coast-line beyond the mouth of the Sebou River. Rabat was, he said, of little use as a port, and might safely be left outside the limits of the neutralised area.

He admitted that there must be a mistake in the French stipulation that the *status quo* should be maintained within a radius of "500 milles" from the Straits of Gibraltar.

As to Egypt, he thought we could scarcely expect the French Government to join with us in pressing our proposals upon the other Powers. To accept them was one thing; to support them in a controversy was another. Russia, he thought, was not likely to give trouble if France was satisfied, but there were other Powers to reckon with.

He again deplored our refusal to give up the Gambia, and said that no concessions in Nigeria were worth considering as a counterpoise to those for which we asked in Newfoundland.

I pointed out that, as we were standing firm in regard to the Gambia, and as the French apparently also wished to stand firm in regard to the bounty question, we should, I presumed, have to fall back on my alternative proposal, under which the case for territorial compensation would not arise.

I told His Excellency that, to the best of my belief, the Cabinet would have separated for the Christmas holidays by the middle of December. I therefore earnestly trusted that we should be favoured with M. Delcassé's views before that date.

His Excellency said he would do his best, but I was not giving him much time.

My observation led him, however, to say a few words as to the part which Spain might play in the negotiations.

The French Government had undertaken to consult the Spanish Government, but Spanish Ministers were notoriously dilatory, and it would be intolerable if, when the French and British Governments had come to terms, the whole transaction were to be hung up because Spain did not answer the communications which might be made to her.

I said that, as his Excellency was aware, we attached the greatest importance to obtaining the concurrence of the Spanish Government. The matter was, however, of such importance that I should certainly object to any action on the part of the Spanish Government which might have the effect of needlessly delaying the conclusion of an arrangement to which Great Britain and France were ready to agree. In the event supposed we should have to take counsel together as to the course to be pursued.

Although the conversation which I have recorded was desultory and quite informal, I noticed with satisfaction that M. Cambon's tone was by no means severely critical; indeed, he went so far as to say that there seemed to him to be the materials for a compromise in the proposals which I had laid before him.

I am, &c.

LANSDOWNE.

No. 378.

The Marquess of Lansdowne to Sir E. Monson.

F.O. France 3617.
(No. 617A.)   Secret.
Sir,   *Foreign Office, December 9, 1903.*

The French Ambassador called upon me to-day, and informed me that since our last meeting he had had two conversations with M. Delcassé with reference to the communication which I had made to him on the 19th ultimo. His Excellency said that he had brought with him some "stenographic" notes of M. Delcassé's observations, and, reading from these notes, he made a statement which I shall reproduce in this despatch. For this purpose his Excellency was good enough to let me have for my private use a Memorandum embodying the substance of the notes, and it is upon this Memorandum that I have relied for the account which I now proceed to give of his Excellency's language.

M. Cambon said that M. Delcassé was pleased to see that I shared his views as to the necessity of basing a general arrangement between the two Governments on reciprocal and, as far as possible, equivalent advantages or concessions. It was, indeed, on this basis, and this basis only, that the arrangement would be favourably received by public opinion.

As regards Morocco, M. Delcassé had noted that I accepted Melilla as the point of departure on the Mediterranean for that portion of the Moorish littoral on which no fortifications were to be erected, and that I substituted Rabat for Mazagan as the point on the ocean at which the neutral strip of littoral was to terminate.

M. Delcassé saw serious objections to extending the neutral strip beyond the heights bordering the mouth of the Sebu on its right bank. The difference in point of extent was not great; but Rabat was a port where it was of importance that French action should have a free hand, being the outlet of a plain which would probably be crossed later on by a railway. Rabat must, therefore, remain open to French influence.

As regards the maintenance of the *status quo* within a certain radius around Gibraltar, M. Delcassé had extended this radius in order to meet certain apprehensions, and to place the Straits and the approaches to them beyond the reach of all dangerous enterprises. The radius could, however, be modified on the Algerian side.

As regards freedom of commerce, his Excellency stated that M. Delcassé would have no hesitation in declaring that it should be complete, and that there should be no inequality either in the customs duties imposed at the ports, in the railway transport tariffs, or in freedom to take part in the coasting trade between the Moorish ports. M. Delcassé, however, called attention to the fact that the State was too directly interested in the railways and ports to allow of their construction and administration not being under direct Government control. It was, no doubt, for this reason that I had in my letter made analogous demands proving the importance attached by England to complete control over Egyptian railways and the port of Alexandria. M. Delcassé had, however, no idea whatsoever of excluding foreign capital from the more important undertakings in Morocco. Subject to the above reservation, it would be admitted on the same terms as French capital.

As regards Egypt, M. Delcassé again expressed his readiness to engage not to hamper our action in that country, or to ask us to fix a date for evacuation. These engagements would be the counterpart of the French liberty of action which England would recognise in Morocco. The principle of reciprocity would be accepted on both sides as regards the eventual suppression of the Capitulations in Egypt and Morocco. But this principle, his Excellency added, which had been put forward by me as governing the whole negotiations, did not seem to be observed in dealing with the financial questions in regard to which I had in my letter stated my inability to proceed *pari passu*. It was proposed that France should give her consent at once, without receiving any compensation, to the important concessions which she was invited to make with regard to the Caisse de la Dette. The survival of the Caisse was, indeed, conceded with a view to meeting French objections. Its functions were, however, according to my proposal, to be strictly limited to receiving the sums necessary for the service of the Debt with the right of suing the Egyptian Government before the Tribunals in case of non-payment. In addition to this, the French Government were to abandon their right to oppose any conversion of the Egyptian Debts.

On this subject M. Delcassé had made the following observations :—

The conversion of the Egyptian Debts is a matter of considerable importance to the French Government. The French creditors, who are the most numerous, had already suffered a very serious loss at the time when the rate of interest was reduced from 7 to 4 per cent. The debtor State having provided for a system of amortisation, they had the right to expect that their shares should no longer be liable to repayment or conversion, it being a fundamental rule that a debt subject to amortisation can neither be converted nor repaid at the pleasure of the debtor. Besides this, the powers of the Commission de la Dette afforded a special security for the protection of the creditors. M. Delcassé admitted that the right which would be left to the Commission to sue the Egyptian Government would have its value, but it could only be exercised in the event of the Government being already in a very bad financial position and administrative powers had been granted to the Commission precisely with a view to protect the Government from their own imprudence and to prevent them from falling into such a situation. M. Delcassé did not deny that, in the actual state of the Egyptian finances, these powers did not appear to be indispensable, but he considered them to be valuable as guarantees against bad times. The Egyptian Administration might be wanting in prudence, involve the Government in expensive undertakings, and compromise the resources pledged to the creditors, and the prospect of an action before the Egyptian Tribunals did not constitute sufficient security for the bondholders against these risks.

M. Cambon had informed M. Delcassé that at his last interview with me I had told him that means could be found to give the creditors the most ample guarantees. M. Delcassé had replied that he was quite ready to try to agree with me on some arrangement which would secure to the creditors, if they must suffer a fresh loss of interest, a security equivalent to what they would lose if the Commission de la Dette were no longer in a position adequately to defend their interests.

M. Delcassé was also of opinion that if conversion was decided upon, it would be necessary to fix a time during which the bondholders would no longer be exposed to having their bonds again paid off or converted.

The same remarks applied to my request for the abolition of the mixed Administration of the railways. This Administration had been organised to secure the service of the Privileged Debt. The French holders of this Debt, who were very numerous, had suffered heavy reductions of interest. To inflict a fresh reduction on them, and to deprive them at the same time of the security given to them by the presence of one of their countrymen on the Council of the Administration, would appear to them an abandonment of their rights, and the French Government could not sacrifice their interests so far.

With regard to my proposal that the French Government should join with us in asking other Powers to assent to the agreement that might be arrived at on the subject of the Debt, M. Delcassé could only leave His Majesty's Government to take the initiative in the matter ; it was, of course, understood that the Government of the Republic would place no obstacle in the way.

As regards French commerce in Egypt, the British Government would engage to give the same assurances as those which the French Government would engage to give as regards British commerce in Morocco. There would thus be no inequality of treatment either in regard to customs or transport tariffs. I had given assurances that His Majesty's Government had no more desire to annex Egypt than the French Government had to annex Morocco, but I had wished that it should be stipulated that if either of the two Governments found themselves one day obliged by force of circumstances to modify their policy in this respect the engagements in regard to commercial equality should remain intact, and that, if either of the Contracting Parties should depart from that course, the other should be free to do so too.

M. Delcassé willingly agreed to this proposal. He thought, however, that the mutual obligations of the two countries would be strengthened if, instead of endowing them with a character of permanency, regardless of time and circumstances, they were assigned a definite duration of, say, fifteen or twenty years, with the option of renewing the agreement at the end of that time.

M. Delcassé had begged M. Cambon to call my attention to the case of the French officials in the service of the Egyptian Government, some of whom held office under formal contracts, which would, of course, be respected, and some without contracts. With regard to the latter, he asked that those who services were satisfactory should be retained in their posts.

Passing to the Suez Canal, M. Cambon said that M. Delcassé had taken note with pleasure of my statement that the British Government would undertake to guarantee the free use of the Canal in accordance with the principles of the Treaty of the 29th October, 1888. I had made, however, a reservation as to Article VIII of this Treaty, which appeared to me hardly compatible with the British occupation of Egypt, and M. Cambon said he would be obliged if I could tell him wherein lay this incompatibility, which was not apparent at first sight. He remarked that in this matter France, no less than Great Britain, had obligations towards the Signatory Powers of the Convention of 1888.

The third question treated in my letter was that of Newfoundland. I had admitted that it was impossible for the French Government to distinguish between French fishermen from France and those from St. Pierre and Miquelon in the matter of bounties, and I had proposed the following compromise ("combinaison"): that the French should have the right for fishing for any kind of fish, including bait, on the Treaty Shore; that they could also buy bait on the Treaty Shore; but that they should not have the right of drying their fish there. That Frenchmen, proprietors of establishments on the Treaty Shore, should be indemnified, but that no territorial compensation should be given to the Government of the Republic.

M. Delcassé recognised that this proposal would assure to French fishermen the maintenance of the right to fish in the waters of the Treaty Shore, but it, none the less, entailed for France the loss of the rights embodied in the Treaties: "those rights of user by future generations of which the French State is the depository"— to use M. Delcassé's words. On each occasion that the question of Newfoundland had been discussed, it had always been understood that it could only be settled on three conditions: indemnity for those affected, free purchase of bait, and territorial compensation.

M. Cambon said that I had subsequently raised the question of the bounties, but he supposed that it was my intention that the limitation that I had proposed for the trade in bait was to serve as compensation for the bounties.

The question of territorial compensation remained untouched. I had asked the French Government to formulate a demand; he had spoken to me of the Gambia, which was an "enclave" in their possessions, and of which the trade was in their hands and of no advantage to us whatever. I had begged them to ask for something else; they had found nothing, and he had himself begged me to make an offer.

They could discover no reasons which compelled us to refuse the cession of the Gambia, except our possible interest in retaining our establishment of St. Mary Bathurst, at the mouth of the river. If that was our only interest—and it was impossible to imagine any other—M. Delcassé proposed a compromise which might give us satisfaction. We might give up the Gambia, retaining the island and town of St. Mary Bathurst, but we ought then to offer them also some advantage in regard to the delimitation of their possessions on the Niger.

Territorial compensation seemed to M. Delcassé indispensable.

The argument that in the last few years fish seemed to have deserted the Treaty Shore appeared to him to be of little or no value. It was true that four years ago the fishing season was very bad, but since that time the fish had been returning, and it was probable that in a few years from now the shore fisheries would become as profitable as in former times.

Although during the above statement his Excellency closely followed his notes, he made a digression of some length upon the subject of alleged German designs upon Morocco. He explained that it was with reference to these designs that M. Delcassé had suggested that the two Powers should agree to maintain the *status quo* within a radius of 500 miles from the Straits of Gibraltar. These designs, M. Cambon said, were of long standing, and recent events indicated that they had not been abandoned. They would, moreover, not improbably be encouraged by Spain. The French Government had reason to know that the Queen of Spain during her recent visit to the Continent had been in communication with the German Emperor upon the subject of Morocco. The King of Spain was, moreover, about to visit Lisbon, and the question was not unlikely to be discussed by His Majesty with the King of Portugal. His Excellency added that, so long ago as 1887, Señor Moret had proposed that a European Conference should be held at Madrid for the discussion of the Moorish question. This proposal, which had been somewhat prematurely announced in the Speech from the Throne on the occasion of the opening of the Cortes on the 1st December, 1887, had fallen through, mainly because the British Government had thrown cold water upon it. It was quite likely that some such proposal might now be revived. It was in view of these circumstances that the French Government had proposed the maintenance of the *status quo* within a radius of 500 miles from the Straits—a radius which would include the Balearic Islands, in which Germany might perhaps desire to obtain a footing.

In regard to Egypt, his Excellency said distinctly that, if we came to terms, the French Government would not only not oppose us in our dealings with the other Powers in the matter of the Caisse, but that they would assist us in the attempt. The expression that he used was "nous vous seconderons."

With regard to his Excellency's renewed demand for territorial compensation on account of the withdrawal of the French from the Treaty Shore of Newfoundland, I told him that I saw no prospect of obtaining the approval of His Majesty's Government for M. Delcassé's proposal that Great Britain should retain the Island of St. Mary Bathurst, at the mouth of the Gambia, whilst surrendering the rest of the Colony to France. I said that we attached great importance to the harbour, and that the mere retention of the island, which could no doubt be commanded from the mainland, would, in my opinion, be quite insufficient for the purpose.

I have only to add that throughout our conversation his Excellency seemed to desire earnestly that we should come to terms.

I promised him that his proposals should be carefully examined, and as soon as possible.

I am, &c.
LANSDOWNE.

No. 379.

The Earl of Cromer to the Marquess of Lansdowne.

Cairo, December 11, 1903.

F.O. Turkey 5303.   D. 3·45 P.M.
Tel. (No. 44.) Secret.   R. 5·45 P.M.

Your telegram No. 38. I think the French answer is very satisfactory.

I would suggest that the negotiations on details should now be continued by Sir E. Gorst in Paris.

Judging from what the French Consul-General says to me I gather that the two points to which they attach importance are firstly, that the Caisse de la Dette should still preserve such funds as not to "render them ridiculous," and secondly, the railways. The first point is fairly well met by our detailed proposals, and I hope that we may deal with second by removing the railways from pledged revenues.

We can afford to be very generous as regards French employés.

I wish to draw your attention to the point that the French proposal as regards last paragraph of your letter of November 19th will probably lead to the extinction of British trade with Morocco after the expiration of the "definite period."

As regards the Suez Canal, I think that we may yield, save on one point. I do not like permanent presence of an Ottoman Commissioner here. He is liable to become a centre of local intrigue, and, moreover, in view of general situation in Turkey, he may at any moment become a rallying point for Mahommedan fanatics and pro-Turkish proclivities. This special provision appears to have been inserted in the course of the negotiations. It is absent in the draft given on page 39, Egypt No. 1, 1888. It might be difficult to get Sultan to agree to entire omission of the clause. Neither do I much mind so long as Mouktar Pasha stays. But might it not be arranged that when, for whatever reason, he retires he should not be replaced by anyone from Constantinople, but that the "Khedivial Commissioner" should preside at the meetings and represent Turkish interests? The French would probably raise no objection to this course.

No. 380.

The Marquess of Lansdowne to Sir E. Monson.

F.O. France 3617.
(No. 626A.) Secret.
Sir,   *Foreign Office, December* 11, 1903.

The French Ambassador called on me to-day after the meeting of the Cabinet, and I gave him a general account of the manner in which my colleagues regarded the proposals which he had made to me on the 9th instant.

I told his Excellency that we disliked the idea of excluding the Port of Rabat from that portion of the Moorish littoral which was to be neutralised under the proposed Agreement. If the French required a "débouché" for a line of railway on that part of the coast, we could not see why such a "débouché" should not be found within the neutralised area.

M. Cambon objected to this that, should "a liquidation" of Morocco ever become inevitable, the neutralised area would probably fall to Spain, and it would be most inconvenient that a French line should have its terminus in Spanish territory. I said that we regarded with apprehension the idea of an arrangement which would leave it open to France to fortify Rabat or to establish there a torpedo-boat station.

M. Cambon replied that France certainly had no idea of fortifying Rabat.

I said that we could not accept the proposal under which the two Powers were to undertake the maintenance of the *status quo* within a radius of 500 miles of Gibraltar. This area would include the greater part of Spain and part of the Sahara Desert, as well as the Balearic Islands. Such an arrangement seemed to us altogether outside the scope of the proposed Agreement, which was intended to be limited to questions at issue, or likely to be at issue, between Great Britain and France. I trusted that the proposal would not be pressed.

I said that we had no objection to concede to the French Government the right of constructing and administering railways and ports, it being understood that whatever privileges were given in this respect to France in Morocco would be given to us in Egypt.

With regard to the latter country, I said that we were prepared to make further proposals for the purpose of absolutely securing the position of the French bondholders. I was not able to describe these precisely at the present moment, but I might say that we contemplated an arrangement whereby a reserve fund would be provided, to which, in the event of default by the Egyptian Government, the Caisse might have recourse.

The Caisse might also be given the right to call on certain specified revenues until the deficit was made good. It should, moreover, also I thought, be possible to provide that, if the debt were converted, the bondholders should be protected against another conversion following closely upon the first; it might, indeed, prehaps, be better to defer the conversion for a few years, in order to meet this point.

I said that I had noticed with satisfaction his Excellency's statement that, in the event of our approaching the other Powers after we had come to terms with the French Government, the latter would be prepared to " second " our efforts. We should certainly expect them to do this.

As to the duration of the arrangement for securing commercial equality in Egypt and Morocco, we saw no objection to fixing a term for the duration, and we proposed fifty years, upon the understanding that the Agreement should remain in force after the expiration of the term, if neither side denounced it. His Excellency's only observation on this was that fifty years was a very long time.

As to French employés in the service of the Egyptian Government, I said that the French Government might rely on our treating them in the most considerate manner. His Excellency said that some of these persons were employed under contract, and that precautions should be taken to prevent their arbitrary dismissal. The French Government took a particular interest in some of their " fonctionnaires," who were employed in museums. I promised that I would consider the case of these gentlemen, with every desire to do them justice. It might perhaps be agreed that, if their offices were abolished, they should receive compensation in accordance with the practice in our own service.

I said that we remained of opinion that Article VIII of the Suez Canal Convention should be got rid of; it seemed to us to bring in, in a shape which might prove very inconvenient, the intervention of the other Powers. We had no desire to have yearly meetings of their Representatives under the presidency of an Ottoman Commissioner.

His Excellency said that the Article formed part of the Convention, and that it would probably be a mistake to denounce it. The Convention could not be modified without the concurrence of the other Powers. He could not see that its retention would cause us any practical inconvenience. We had, moreover, always contended that the whole Convention was inoperative so long as the British occupation continued.

As to Newfoundland, I said we did not desire to exclude absolutely the idea of territorial compensation, but we held strongly that French rights on the Treaty Shore were of very slight value; they would have less value still if it had not been for the considerate manner in which we had dealt with the question. If the fishing interest were to become more important, we should no doubt have to enforce our rights more strictly than we had been in the habit of doing. The Cabinet had, as I anticipated, finally refused to part with the Gambia even upon the conditions which M. Delcassé had suggested. If there was to be any territorial compensation, it might be found, but on a modest scale, in the neighbourhood of Sokoto, and I had already indicated our ideas on this subject. If, however, the boundary was to be revised, we should expect the French Government to give up the Niger enclaves.

His Excellency deplored our refusal to give up the Gambia, but did not suggest that it was fatal. He told me that he would communicate the substance of what I had said to M. Delcassé, and that he would as soon as possible send me a written answer to the letter which I had addressed to him on the 19th ultimo.

I am, &c.
LANSDOWNE.

No. 381.

Memorandum communicated to M. Cambon, December 24, 1903.([1])

F.O. France 3765.

With reference to M. Delcassé's observations on the Egyptian proposals put forward in my letter of the 19th November, His Majesty's Government are prepared to do their utmost to meet M. Delcassé's wishes in respect to the situation of the bondholders.

In the first place, M. Delcassé considers that the right of the Caisse de la Dette to sue the Egyptian Government in the Law Courts in case of default is not, by itself, a sufficient guarantee for the bondholders. With a view to meeting this objection, His Majesty's Government would be prepared to agree to an arrangement whereby in the event of the Egyptian Government failing to pay the sum necessary for the service of the Debt at the stipulated time, the Caisse could have recourse to a reserve fund which would be specially established for this purpose and would remain in its possession. The Caisse might further be given the right to call upon the receivers of certain specified revenues to pay them directly to it, until the deficit was made good.

The security offered by this arrangement would seem to be in no way inferior to that enjoyed under the present system.

In the second place, M. Delcassé appears to apprehend that the position of the preference bondholders will be rendered less secure by the proposal to abolish the Board which administers the railways, telegraphs, and Port of Alexandria.

The arrangement described above would seem, however, equally to meet this objection, it being of course understood that the preference bondholders would still have a prior claim over the holders of Unified Stock on all moneys in the hands of the Caisse. It may further be mentioned that the revenues which the Caisse might eventually retain in the event of default would consist of land tax, and not the present assigned revenues. The assignment for such purpose of the land tax in a certain number of provinces, in place of the existing pledged revenues, would be a more satisfactory arrangement for the creditors, inasmuch as that tax is the most certain branch of the Egyptian revenue, and one of which the tendency is constantly to increase.

In the third place, M. Delcassé urges that some special steps should be taken in order to secure the bondholders against the loss which they might incur owing to the suggested conversion of the Egyptian Debt. His Majesty's Government cannot agree that the bondholders, whose security has so largely increased in value during the last twenty years, have any moral claim to exceptional treatment. Nevertheless, His Majesty's Government, being desirous of meeting M. Delcassé's views in every possible way, and in order to manifest the conciliatory spirit in which they have undertaken these negotiations, are prepared to consent to a postponement of the conversion of the Egyptian Debt for a further period of five years on the distinct understanding that, after its expiration, no objection will be raised to the Egyptian Debts being paid off at par.

As a consequence of the above proposals, the economies from the former conversion would cease to exist, and the present Economies Fund, as well as the General Reserve Fund, would revert to the Egyptian Government.

Further, in the event of an agreement being come to between the two Governments on the above points, I would suggest that, in order to avoid the possibility of future misunderstandings, a Khedivial Decree be issued embodying the new arrangements and cancelling all past Decrees relating to the Egyptian Debt and the Caisse de la Dette. The draft of this Decree would be submitted to the Government of the Republic, and should form an annex to any agreement at which the two Governments may arrive.

December 24, 1903.   LANSDOWNE.

([1]) [This Memorandum was drawn up by Sir E. Gorst.]

No. 382.

M. Cambon to the Marquess of Lansdowne.

F.O. France 3640.   *Paris, D. le* 27 *Décembre*, 1903.
Cher Lord Lansdowne,   R. *December* 28, 1903.

Je me suis entretenu avec M. Delcassé de la compensation territoriale qui pourrait nous être accordée dans le réglement de la question de Terre-Neuve.

Il regrette vivement que vous n'ayez pas cru pouvoir abandonner la Gambie, et en cherchant sur quel point nous pourrions trouver une satisfaction suffisante il a pensé à une rectification de notre frontière sur le Niger.

Lors des négociations de 1898 nous avions réclamé un accès au Niger au-dessous des Rapides; il ne nous avait pas été accordé, et pour en tenir lieu vous nous aviez concédé les deux enclaves de Badjibo et de Forcados. Si vous nous abandonniez la rive droite du Niger jusqu'à la Rivière Moussa, dont l'embouchure est à peu près en face de Badjibo, nous laisserions nos enclaves, et M. Delcassé pense qu'il pourrait faire accepter cette compensation par notre Gouvernement et par les Chambres; l'affaire de Terre-Neuve se trouverait ainsi réglée.

M. Delcassé est très absorbé en ce moment par la discussion de notre Budget. Après le 1ᵉʳ Janvier il compte s'absenter pendant une semaine; il aura vu Sir E. Gorst avant de partir et lui aura demandé des éclaircissements pour causer avec ses collègues du Cabinet. Je serai moi-même de retour à Londres Lundi ou Mardi prochain. Je vous verrai le Mercredi, 5 Janvier, et j'espère que nous pourrons entrevoir une solution.

P. CAMBON.

No. 383.

Memorandum communicated to M. Cambon, January 5, 1904.

F.O. France 3640.

The proposal embodied in M. Cambon's private letter of the 27th December has been carefully examined. It is to the effect that, by way of territorial compensation for the abandonment of French rights on the Treaty Shore of Newfoundland, Great Britain should cede to France a large tract on the right bank of the River Niger, in the hinterland of Lagos. The tract in question comprises no less than 10,000 square miles of valuable territory, and contains several places, notably Illo and Boussa, to which, as shown by the negotiations of 1898, His Majesty's Government attach great importance. By the Convention of the 14th June of that year, this territory was, after prolonged discussion, finally assigned to Great Britain. The boundaries have since then been marked out, the administration of the country has been organised, and the native inhabitants have been given assurances that they are to continue under British rule.

It would be quite impossible for His Majesty's Government to defend in Parliament the cession of so valuable an area by way of an equivalent for the concession made by France in Newfoundland. As Lord Lansdowne has more than once ventured to point out, the rights of the French Government on the Treaty Shore are of a strictly limited kind, and have for some time past been declining steadily in value. The number of men engaged in the fishery in 1902 was 322, a number which had fallen to 258 in the following year. The gross value of the product of the fisheries, including the lobster fishery and that of the " petits pêcheurs," is estimated at about £14,000, against which must be set a considerable expenditure on account of bounties, and the cost of the cruisers employed by the French Government. It can hardly be contended, in the face of these figures, that the industry is a profitable one. It is, moreover, only by the indulgence of the British authorities in allowing French citizens to exercise privileges in regard to their buildings, &c., in excess of their Treaty rights, that the French fishermen are able to carry on their profession at all. The restriction of these privileges within the precise limits sanctioned by the Treaties would probably lead to the total extinction of the coast fishery. These facts are well known in this country, and His Majesty's Government would certainly be attacked if, in the face of them, they were not only to compensate private interests, but also to make an extensive cession of British territory by way of national compensation.

In the opinion of His Majesty's Government, considering the fact that the French are not asked to give up the substantive right of participating in the Newfoundland fisheries, the case is not one in which, strictly speaking, any claim for territorial compensation should have been made. If such a claim is to be admitted at all, it must be moderate in point of extent, and should not affect any territory in which British administration has been definitely established.

The objections indicated would not apply, at all events in the same degree, to a revision of the boundary between the British and French West African possessions, where it is formed by the arc of a circle drawn with a radius of 100 miles from Sokoto, so as to give a practicable route in French territory between the Niger and Zinder. An arrangement of this kind was mentioned during the course of Lord Lansdowne's conversation with M. Delcassé on the 7th July, 1903, and Lord Lansdowne was under the impression that M. Delcassé regarded it favourably.

Foreign Office, January 5, 1904.

No. 384.

The Marquess of Lansdowne to Sir E. Monson.

F.O. France 3662.
(No. 15.)   Secret.
Sir,   *Foreign Office, January 13, 1904.*

The French Ambassador, who has been detained in Paris by a somewhat severe indisposition, called upon me to-day.

He told me that he had communicated to M. Delcassé the substance of the Memorandum which I forwarded to him on the 5th instant, explaining the reasons for which we were unable to agree to the proposal that a large area on the right bank of the River Niger should be ceded to France by way of " territorial compensation " for the abandonment of her rights on the Treaty Shore of Newfoundland.

M. Delcassé had, he said, received this intimation with great regret. He had throughout regarded it as indispensable that France should receive territorial compensation of a substantial kind for the surrender of these rights. He had suggested the " Gambia," and we had put our foot down. Now he had suggested a slice of territory in Western Africa, which could scarcely be regarded as of the first importance, and he was again met with a blank refusal. His Excellency said that M. Delcassé could not accept my statement that the French rights on the Treaty Shore would be of little value but for the forbearance shown by the British Government. If French rights were limited, so were the British rights, and forbearance had been necessary on both sides.

There was a strong feeling in France on the subject of Newfoundland, and his Excellency was convinced that no French Minister could afford to announce the retirement of France unless he could show that he had obtained a *quid pro quo* elsewhere.

I said that, in deference to the views of the French Government, the Cabinet had authorised me to entertain the idea of territorial compensation, although we were quite unable to admit either the first or the second French proposal. I begged his Excellency to remember that we, too, should have to defend and justify any arrangement to which we might agree. I felt, no doubt, that, as it was, we should be told that we were giving too much and receiving too little. Comparisons would inevitably be made between the concessions which we were making and those which we were receiving. Our position in Egypt was practically unassailable, although we should be glad to regularise it. In Morocco, on the other hand, France had no position corresponding to ours in Egypt, and we should certainly be told that we were retreating ignominiously from that country.

Again, we were giving France a free hand in a large region lying to the east of Siam, and receiving in exchange freedom of action which we virtually possessed already in the Malay Peninsula. If in return for the withdrawal of the French fishermen from the Treaty Shore, where they were pursuing a comparatively valueless and moribund industry, we were to pay not only compensation in money, but also national compensation in the shape of a cession of valuable territory, we should find ourselves in a position which it would be impossible to defend.

His Excellency said that these arguments were specious, but he could not admit them to be conclusive. France, for instance, would still have to negotiate with Spain, and perhaps with other Powers, about Morocco, and she could, if she chose, make herself very inconvenient to us in Egypt.

His Excellency thought that it would be a grievous misfortune if our negotiations, which had proceeded so satisfactorily, should break down upon the point which we were now discussing. He regarded the Egyptian part of the question as virtually settled, although he thought that Sir E. Gorst and Lord Cromer had taken a somewhat over-sanguine view of the result of the former's conversation with M. Delcassé and the officials of the French Foreign Office. He admitted, however, that with a few slight modifications, the terms which Sir E. Gorst had proposed in Paris might be accepted as the basis of a settlement. If we did not give them the tract on the right bank of the Niger, was there nothing else we could offer? I said that I could think of nothing, except the rectification of the frontier to the north of Sokoto.

His Excellency replied that this could not be regarded as territorial compensation of a substantial kind. The region in question consisted of what Lord Salisbury had once spoken of as " light land," and had no known value. Its importance from the French point of view had, moreover, been much diminished by the discovery of water on the French side of the line, and wells had now been dug along the whole course of the route from Say to Zinder. I asked whether these wells would not require a good deal of watching, and I pointed out that it must be of some importance to the French Government to avoid the long détour which their convoys now had to make in order to remain on their own side of the line.

After some further conversation, I summed up what I had to say by telling his Excellency that my refusal of the tract on the right bank of the Niger was the result of a discussion with my colleagues, who had considered the question in all its bearings, and I was obliged to add that in my belief it was useless to renew the request.

M. Cambon again asked me whether I could think of nothing else which might be offered, and I said it seemed to me useless for me to make offers of the kind, and I had no authority to make them.

His Excellency said that he would repeat the substance of my observations to M. Delcassé. I added that I thought it better not to enter into the discussion of other outstanding points until this had been disposed of, but I let fall the remark that my colleagues were much opposed to the exclusion of Rabat from the neutral portion of the Moorish coast-line, and that, in my opinion, no concession at that point could be looked for unless the question of territorial compensation were settled to our satisfaction.

I am, &c.

LANSDOWNE.

No. 385.

The Marquess of Lansdowne to Sir E. Monson.

F.O. France 3662.
(No. 16.)   Secret.

Sir,   *Foreign Office, January* 13, 1904.

During the course of my conversation with the French Ambassador to-day, I asked him whether he had considered the shape which, in the event of our coming to an Agreement about the different questions which we had discussed, that Agreement might take.

He told me that he thought there would first have to be an exchange of notes citing generally the outline of the Agreement, and that after that "on devra régler chaque question par soi," in the manner appropriate to each. Thus, the Egyptian part of the Agreement would have to be embodied in a Khedivial Decree, and the terms as to Morocco in notes to be exchanged between the two Governments, while Newfoundland would have to be dealt with in a Treaty.

I am, &c.
LANSDOWNE.

No. 386.

The Marquess of Lansdowne to Sir E. Monson.

F.O. France 3662.
(No. 26.)

Sir,   *Foreign Office, January* 18, 1904.

The French Ambassador asked me to receive him this afternoon.

He told me that he had now received M. Delcassé's instructions with regard to the communication which I had made to him on the 13th instant.

M. Delcassé found it absolutely impossible to accept my suggestion that the French Government should be content with a rectification of the frontier to the north of Sokoto by way of territorial compensation for their retirement from the Treaty Shore of Newfoundland. That retirement would certainly be regarded in France as involving the surrender of extremely important rights, and the concession of a tract of comparatively valueless country in the region of Sokoto would not be considered a reasonable equivalent.

I expressed my great regret at M. Delcassé's decision, which seemed to me to bring our negotiations to a deadlock. All I could for the present say was that I would report the matter to the Cabinet, which was to recommence its meetings this week, but, as I had already told his Excellency, I did not think there was much chance of my colleagues changing their mind as to the territory on the right bank of the Niger.

I am, &c.
LANSDOWNE.

No. 387.

The Earl of Cromer to the Marquess of Lansdowne.

F.O. Turkey 5368.
Tel. (No. 9.)   Secret.

Cairo, January 21, 1904.
D. 1 P.M.
R. 4 P.M.

My immediately preceding telegram.

I have little doubt from what I hear on the spot that the danger of a breakdown of the negotiations is serious. I venture to urge most strongly the necessity either of making concessions which will enable Newfoundland question to be settled or of dealing with Morocco and Egypt separately. The former is by far the best solution but the latter is preferable to doing nothing. To allow negotiations to break down now would in my opinion be little short of a calamity, whether from the general or the local Egyptian point of view. Also I cannot but think that it would be severely criticised by the public who already know more or less what is going on.

It has to be borne in mind that the French concessions to us in Egypt are in reality far more valuable than those we are making to them in Morocco and moreover than they can hamper us greatly here whereas if they choose they can carry out their Morocco policy without our help. They are perfectly well aware of this.

Further, the recognition of the occupation removes what must otherwise always remain a source of danger to peace. I cannot but think that this point, which appears to me of the utmost importance, would be understood in England and would serve as an adequate justification for some concessions elsewhere.

No. 388.

The Marquess of Lansdowne to Sir E. Monson.

F.O. France 3662.
(No. 32.) Secret.
Sir,
                                                    Foreign Office, January 23, 1904.

I told the French Ambassador to-day that I had again brought before the Cabinet the question of the "territorial compensation" which France might receive for her abandonment of the Treaty Shore of Newfoundland. I had told my colleagues that, in M. Delcassé's opinion, the proposed cession of British territory in the neighbourhood of Sokoto was wholly insufficient, and that the French Government still pressed for the cession either of the Gambia or of the triangle on the right bank of the Niger, of which the River Moussa formed the base. I had found, as I anticipated, that my colleagues were strongly opposed to both of these proposals. In regard to the Gambia, we had come to the conclusion that it would be impossible to defend the abandonment of an old British Colony, which had been British long before the French had occupied the surrounding country. It was, moreover, remarkable that on two previous occasions—once in 1869–70, when Mr. Gladstone was Prime Minister; and again in 1876, when Mr. Disraeli was Prime Minister—proposals to cede the Gambia had been made, and had encountered violent opposition. On the former occasion, Mr. Gladstone had been compelled to assure the House of Commons that there had never been any intention of parting with the Colony without an appeal to Parliament. In 1876, when the negotiations were renewed, an arrangement was suggested under which, in return for the cession of the Gambia to France, Great Britain was to have received an engagement on the part of the French Government not to interfere with any portion of the coast from a point north of Sierra Leone to the Equator. This proposal, very advantageous as compared with that which we were now discussing, was again so strongly opposed in Parliament that the negotiations had to be abandoned. It was, moreover, necessary to remember that, upon that occasion, the cession of the Gambia was proposed in the interests of the West African Colonies, whereas, we were now asked to let it go for the benefit of a Colony on the other side of the world. I had already explained to his Excellency that, for equally strong reasons, the cession of the territory on the right bank of the Niger was, in our view, impossible.

While, however, I had found the Cabinet quite decided upon these points, they had shown their readiness to accept any reasonable arrangements which might be proposed for the purpose of giving easier access or greater facilities for French trade, whether upon the Niger or upon the Gambia River. We discussed this question at some length, but his Excellency did not regard my suggestion as a very hopeful one, although I said that I believed the Cabinet would grant such facilities in addition to the rectification of the frontier to the north of Sokoto and at the point where it strikes

Lake Chad. As to facilities on the Gambia, I pointed out that the frontier was apparently so drawn as to bar the French from access to the river below the rapids. I thought we should probably be ready to agree to a readjustment of the line so as to give them access to the navigable part of the river. His Excellency, although evidently dissatisfied with my reply, said emphatically that he hoped we should not allow the negotiation to fall through at this stage.

I took the opportunity of asking his Excellency whether he had had any further communications with the Spanish Government with regard to the negotiations. He replied that there had been so many changes of administration in Spain that it was extremely difficult to do business with the Spanish Government. The situation had, however, been thoroughly explained to them as long ago as the autumn of 1902, when M. Delcassé had spoken fully to the Spanish Ambassador at Paris upon the subject. M. Delcassé had, on that occasion, given M. Castillo a full account of what was contemplated by the French Government, and had explained to him that any arrangement to be arrived at between Great Britain and France would have to be based upon the assumption that the *status quo* would, so far as the form of Government was concerned, be maintained, that Spain would be entitled to a sphere of influence in northern Morocco, that the Straits were to be neutralised, and that Spain had been fully satisfied. M. Castillo had raised no difficulties, but although the question had been subsequently referred to more than once, the Spanish Government had never made any reply to the French communication.

I said that I thought it most important that the Spanish Government, which naturally watched the progress of events in Morocco with an anxious eye, should not be taken by surprise.

I am, &c.
LANSDOWNE.

No. 389.

The Marquess of Lansdowne to M. Cambon.

F.O. France 3686.
Private and Confidential.
My dear Ambassador,   *Foreign Office, February 5, 1904.*

You were good enough to suggest on the 27th ultimo that I should supply you, for M. Delcassé's information, with a more precise statement of the proposals which I had made to you as to the territorial compensation which France might receive for the abandonment of the right of using the Treaty Shore of Newfoundland for the purpose of drying fish. Our conversation had reference to five points :—

1. The question of facilities for navigation on the Gambia;
2. The question of similar facilities on the River Niger;
3. The rectification of the frontier in the neighbourhood of Sokoto;
4. The rectification of the frontier where it impinges upon Lake Chad; and
5. The Isles de Los.

I have now to offer the following observations upon these points :—

1. The Gambia River is, I find, navigable up to and beyond the Anglo-French boundary by vessels of light draught, and vessels of 10 feet draught can pass up it to a point about 1 mile above Yarbutenda, even during the dry season. We should be ready to readjust the frontier so as to include the town of Yarbutenda in French territory. You mentioned to me that you had been told that the river was not navigable above the Isle des Biches (Deer Island). You must, I think, have been misinformed upon this point. We could not at any rate entertain a proposal to draw the frontier-line so low down the river as the last named island.

2. With reference to the navigation of the Niger, you mentioned to me that under Article 8 of the Agreement of 1898 France was already entitled to a passage for goods in transit across British territory from a point on the Anglo-French frontier to the French enclave on the right bank of the river. This is no doubt the case. The proposal which we were prepared to make, had, however, reference not to this right of passage, but to facilities for landing goods at certain places on the river above the enclave, and for their transport by land round the rocks and rapids which impede the navigation of the river.

The facilities which we are prepared to offer would be of the following kind :—

(*a*.) To make Jebba—about 17 miles below the enclave—a " port of entry "; to place a warehouse there (or let the French establish a private bonded warehouse there), and allow them to bond and tranship there.

(*b*.) To allow cases of goods, sealed in accordance with the Regulations, to be transhipped from boat to boat *en route*.

(*c*.) To allow the officers in charge of convoys to land the goods at certain specified places (*i.e.*, at the rapids), and carry them overland for specified distances round the rapids which impede the transit of laden boats or barges.

(*d*.) To help the French to get any native labour necessary to complete the " portages."

The French Government have repeatedly had to apply for permission to transport stores in this manner. The permission has, however, only been granted in the specific cases in which application for facilities has been made, and will not necessarily be granted in future. We are prepared to secure it to French convoys by a permanent Agreement.

3. You explained to me that the French Government desired that the new frontier should leave the Niger at Gomba and follow the course of the river shown as running north and north-east from Gomba and then passing to the north of Sokoto, and that the line should be carried out so as to give Maradi to France You also explained that, if this line were adopted, it would be necessary that France should obtain the small triangle on the opposite, or right, bank of the Niger, including Gomba and Ilo

This proposal has been carefully examined and has, I regret to say, proved quite inadmissible The region between the Sokoto River and the Anglo-French frontier contains districts which have been for some years under British administration, and the inhabitants of them have been assured that they are to remain British subjects. During our negotiations with the French Government in 1898 the French Government more than once insisted upon the difficulty of parting with districts in which the French had established themselves, and it was for this reason that the frontier was drawn so as to leave Nikki to France. There are, moreover, I am afraid, other reasons for which it is impossible for us to accept the Sokoto River as a boundary. Rivers are not, as a rule, convenient international limits, but in this case the objection is intensified by the fact that the river passes close to the town of Sokoto, and the existing frontier, which now forms the arc of a circle with a radius of 100 miles from Sokoto, was drawn in this manner because in 1898 it was fully admitted by M. Hanotaux in the Niger negotiations that a certain amount of territory round Sokoto was for us a necessity.

If there is to be a rectification of the frontier, all we can offer is that it should leave the existing line at a point on the arc 15 kilom. due north of Mataankari, and that it should be drawn thence in a direct line to a point 20 kilom. due north of Konni, thence in a direct line to a point of 15 kilom. due south of Maradi, and thence direct to the point of intersection of the parallel of 13° 20′ north latitude with the meridian through a point of 70 miles east of the second intersection of the 14th degree of north latitude and the Sokoto arc. Such a rectification would afford the French a practicable route to Zinder, and about 9,750 square miles of territory, some of which is of considerable value.

4. You suggested that the boundary where it approaches Lake Chad should be so drawn as to cut off the rectangular excrescence shown in the neighbourhood of Barrua.

We are not unwilling to entertain this proposal if we are able to come to terms at other points. I have, however, to observe that if the boundary near Lake Chad were altered as you suggested, we should lose control of the important trade route running through Kabi, Buddam, and Maini Zumber, and that we should also lose part of a very valuable salt district from which we expect to obtain revenue derived by Excise duties, and which attracts a large trade from the south and west. In any case we should have to stipulate that the new line, after following the parallel of 13° 20' north latitude up to the point where it reaches the Koinadugu Waube, should follow that stream to the shore of the lake. Even with this modification the proposed concession involves a further surrender of no less than 7,000 square miles of territory, making altogether with the Sokoto concession between 16,000 and 17,000 square miles.

His Majesty's Government consider that the concessions which I have enumerated in the preceding paragraphs are of very material importance, and afford amply sufficient compensation for the surrender of the French rights of using the Treaty Shore, which are not, strictly speaking, territorial rights at all.

5. You mentioned to me, however, the desire of the French Government to obtain possession of the group of islands known as the Isles de Los, opposite to Conakry. These islands, lying at the door of French Guinea, and distant about 5 miles from the capital of that colony, must obviously be of considerable value to France. The Admiralty point out that any State holding these islands would have a convenient deep-water port considerably nearer to Sierra Leone than any now possessed by an European nation. They are admirably adapted for a coaling station, and whenever the question of their cession has been discussed it has been deprecated. We are not prepared to throw in these islands as a makeweight unless the French Government on its side will add something on our side of the scale. We suggest that in order to balance the transaction, the French Government should agree that, instead of the existing arrangement in regard to the New Hebrides under which France and England are pledged not to prefer any claim to territorial rights, the French Government should agree to offer no objection to the establishment of British protection over the group, subject to an arrangement being made for a Tribunal to settle promptly the question of land titles.

I am, &c.
LANSDOWNE.

No. 390.

M. Cambon to the Marquess of Lansdowne.

F.O. France 3686.
(Privée et Confidentielle.)
Cher Lord Lansdowne,

Ambassade de France, Londres,
D. *le 18 Février,* 1904.
R. *February* 19, 1904.

J'ai communiqué à M. Delcassé votre lettre privée et confidentielle du 5 courant relative à la compensation territoriale qui pourrait être accordée à la France en échange de ses droits à Terre-Neuve.

Sur les différents points traités dans cette lettre, M. Delcassé m'a chargé de vous présenter les observations suivantes :

1. En ce qui concerne la navigabilité de la Rivière Gambie. Les "Instructions Nautiques," publiées en 1896 sous le No. 777 par le service hydrographique de la Marine Française, placent à l'Ile des Biches (Deer Islands) le terminus de la véritable navigation de la rivière. Au delà, son cours ne serait accessible qu'à des côtes

z 4

indigènes, qui d'ailleurs devraient s'arrêter une soixantaine de kilomètres plus haut, à l'Ile Macarthy, distante encore elle-même de 200 kilom. de Yarboutenda.

Ces indications sont en contradiction avec celles qui ont été fournies à votre Seigneurie et d'après lesquelles les navires ayant 10 pieds de tirant d'eau pourraient remonter la rivière même pendant la saison sèche à un mille en amont de Yarboutenda.

Il semble à M. Delcassé que de nouvelles explications pourraient s'échanger pour éclaircir cette question de la navigabilité du fleuve.

2. En ce qui concerne la question d'accès au Niger, votre Seigneurie reconnaît que l'Article VIII de la Convention de 1898 confère déjà à la France un droit de passage à travers le territoire Britannique entre l'enclave sur la rive gauche et un point à déterminer sur la frontière Française. Vous proposez seulement de nous accorder de nouvelles facilités pour le transbordement de nos marchandises, leur débarquement et leur transport par terre le long des rapides—facilités déjà réclamées par nous à plusieurs reprises, qui, d'après votre Seigneurie, nous ont été accordées à titre occasionnel et qui pourraient nous être concédées à titre permanent.

M. Delcassé estime que cette concession permanente ne saurait constituer un avantage nouveau, car, en vertu de l'Article XXIX de l'Acte de Berlin de 1885, nous y avons déjà droit. J'ai d'ailleurs exposé moi-même à votre Seigneurie les vues de mon Gouvernement à ce sujet par une note en date du 26 Octobre, 1903.

Si le Gouvernement Britannique était disposé à nous abandonner les territoires de la rive droite du Niger entre Ilo et la Rivière Moussa, l'accès au Niger navigable nous serait naturellement assuré sans le concours de l'Administration Anglaise. Mais si ces territoires ne nous sont pas concédés, nous considérons cette Administration comme tenue de nous procurer des facilités qui ne peuvent pas entrer en ligne de compte dans la discussion actuelle.

3. En ce qui concerne les rectifications de frontière dans le voisinage de Sokoto et du Lac Tchad, votre Seigneurie déclare impossible de nous céder les territoires de Gomba et d'Ilo, de façon à nous donner comme limite la Rivière de Sokoto ou la Rivière Goulbi, par la raison que sur une partie de ces territoires l'Administration Anglaise est déjà installée, que les rivières constituent une mauvaise frontière, et, enfin, que la Rivière Goulbi est trop voisine de la ville de Sokoto. Mais M. Delcassé fait observer que les propositions de votre Seigneurie réduisent singulièrement le tracé que nous avions envisagé, et que les territoires qui nous sont offerts n'ont en eux-mêmes aucune valeur réelle. Ce n'est pas, à proprement parler, une compensation territoriale qui nous est proposée, mais seulement une route, et pour que cette route soit " praticable," suivant l'expression même de votre Seigneurie, il importe qu'elle permette d'assurer le ravitaillement régulier et normal des établissements à desservir. On peut se demander si le passage à travers de larges étendues sablonneuses répond à cette nécessité, et en se bornant à la question de ravitaillement, il est utile que la route soit établie à travers des régions offrant quelques ressources.

Au double point de vue de la compensation territoriale et des communications avec Zinder, l'offre de votre Seigneurie ne semble donc répondre aucunement à ce que nous pouvons espérer.

Dans la région à l'est de Zinder du côté du Lac Tchad, M. Delcassé n'a pas été en mesure, même avec les cartes publiées l'an dernier par le War Office, d'identifier la route indiquée dans la lettre de votre Seigneurie comme passant par Kabi, Buddam, et Maini Zumber, non plus que le " Salt District," dont il y est fait également mention.

Quoiqu'il en soit, M. Delcassé pense que si nous acceptions pour frontière le 13° 20′ de latitude nord jusqu'au Komadougou, puis le cours de cette rivière jusqu'au Lac Tchad, nous nous trouverions acquérir ainsi une voie de communication entre Zinder et le lac; les cartes ne fournissent à cet égard aucun renseignement, et il importe que l'établissement de cette voie de communication soit bien précise.

De ce côté M. Delcassé déclare ne rechercher aucun accroissement de territoire ; les voies de communication peuvent seules être pour nous de quelqu'intérêt, et encore ne faut-il pas en exagérer l'importance.

Sur ces différents points M. Delcassé ne croit pas que pratiquement les divergences soient essentielles, et il espère qu'après s'être livré à un nouvel examen, votre Seigneurie voudra bien formuler une offre permettant de considérer l'abandon d'une portion des territoires du Sokoto comme un sérieux élément de compensation territoriale.

4. En ce qui concerne les Iles de Los, M. Delcassé ne peut dissimuler qu'il est surpris de la réponse que je lui ai transmise. Il craint que dans certaines branches de l'Administration Anglaise on ne soit pas suffisamment animé de l'esprit de cordiale entente qui lui a permis d'accepter la conversation sur Terre-Neuve.

On a invoqué des raisons de sentiment pour nous refuser la Gambie. Si nous envisagions au même point de vue la question du " French Shore," il pourrait devenir malaisé de poursuivre l'entretien.

Mais pour les Iles de Los on ne peut supposer une difficulté de ce genre. C'est le résidu de négociations aujourd'hui closes et de prétentions territoriales abandonnées. L'Angleterre n'en fait rien, et ne peut les exploiter.

M. Delcassé ne veut pas s'arrêter aux raisonnements de l'Amirauté, mais je me permettrai de faire remarquer à votre Seigneurie l'étrangeté d'une résistance qui n'a d'autre but que de réserver à l'Administration Navale Britannique la faculté fort éventuelle de créer en face de la côte Française un établissement maritime destiné à annuler notre port de Konakri.

Au moment où nous cherchons de la meilleure foi du monde et dans l'esprit le plus amical à supprimer autant que possible les sources de conflit entre les deux pays et à effacer les points de friction, l'Amirauté semble vouloir conserver les Iles de Los comme un clou d'attente où s'accrochera plus tard quelque difficulté.

Je ne crois pas cette manière de voir conforme aux vues générales des deux Gouvernements.

La possession des îles de la côte de notre Nouvelle-Guinée ne répond plus pour l'Angleterre à aucun intérêt véritable.

Aujourd'hui qu'à l'ancien éparpillement des comptoirs Européens sur la côte occidentale d'Afrique se sont substitués des groupements homogènes la fissure que fait la Gambie dans nos possessions est déjà anormale, mais pour les Iles de Los il y aurait vraiment quelque chose d'excessif à nous les refuser.

M. Delcassé ne considère pas leur valeur en elle-même comme bien importante. Pratiquement, leur intérêt est presque nul, mais il y a là un élément moral, une manifestation tangible des dispositions actuelles des deux Gouvernements, et c'est à ce titre que M. Delcassé insiste sur cette cession.

Quant aux Nouvelles-Hébrides, il ne peut admettre qu'à ce propos il en soit question.

L'immigration Française dans cet archipel, l'importance de ses établissements y dépassent tellement les autres entreprises étrangères qu'en se plaçant seulement au point de vue des intérêts engagés, ce serait la France qui pourrait réclamer les Nouvelles-Hébrides.

Je prends la liberté de soumettre toutes ces observations à votre Seigneurie. Nos demandes sont aussi modérées qu'équitables, et j'espère qu'un nouvel examen nous permettra d'arriver à une entente dont mon Gouvernement désire très vivement la réalisation.

Votre bien sincèrement dévoué,

PAUL CAMBON.

No. 391.

The Marquess of Lansdowne to Sir E. Monson.

F.O. France 3662.
(No. 97.)   Secret.
Sir,   *Foreign Office, February 25, 1904.*

I told the French Ambassador to-day that I had laid his letter of the 18th instant before the Cabinet, and that I had obtained their consent to offer him the terms described in my letter of the 5th, including the cession of the Isles de Los, but without insisting upon our demand for the establishment of a British Protectorate over the New Hebrides. His Excellency asked me whether His Majesty's Government could not be induced to modify, in favour of the French Government, the line which we had proposed to the north of Sokoto. I said that now that we had given up the Isles de Los this demand seemed to me to be inadmissible. We agreed that the question of the navigation of the Gambia should be further considered as soon as we were able to decide with certainty at what point the river ceased to be navigable.

His Excellency agreed to meet me at this Office on Saturday at 4 o'clock, when I promised that a Representative of the Colonial Office would attend with maps showing exactly where the boundary lines, which we proposed, should run.

I reminded his Excellency of what I had said to him on the 23rd ultimo as to the necessity of taking Spain into our confidence. We were, I said, particularly anxious that Spain should not be able to say that we had entered into an arrangement, which she would regard as vitally affecting her interests, behind her back. I had told the Spanish Ambassador in general terms that we had been discussing the question of Morocco with the French Government, and that both the French and the British Governments recognised that they had to reckon with Spain and that it was essential that the claims of that Power should be taken into consideration.

M. Cambon said that he felt the force of my observations, and suggested that, as soon as we had come to terms, the nature of the arrangement contemplated might be made known to Spain. We could not well, he thought, consult her at any earlier stage.

I am, &c.
LANSDOWNE.

No. 392.

The Marquess of Lansdowne to Sir E. Egerton.

F.O. Spain 2193.
(No. 25.)
Sir,   *Foreign Office, February 27, 1904.*

I told the Spanish Ambassador to-day that, in consequence of the observations which he had made to me on the 17th instant in reference to rumours of an Agreement between France and Great Britain as to their interests in Morocco, I had again spoken to the French Ambassador upon the subject. I had found his Excellency quite as much disposed as I was to admit that, in any arrangement which might be made between us, due consideration should be given to the special interests of Spain. Both France and England desired that the *status quo* should be disturbed as little as possible, and that the authority of the Sultan should be preserved. We were also of one mind as to the necessity of maintaining the open door in regard to international commerce, and as to the desirability of neutralising a great part of the Moorish coast-line. We also recognised that Spain had considerable territorial rights in Morocco—rights which must in any case be respected, and which gave her a further and indirect interest in that part of the Sultan's possessions which adjoined her own. I added that, should we see our way to a settlement with France affecting the status of Morocco, Spain would certai ly be taken into our confidence.

I am, &c.
LANSDOWNE.

No. 393.

The Marquess of Lansdowne to Sir E. Monson.

F.O. France 3662.
(No. 108.) Secret.
Sir,   <i>Foreign Office, March 1, 1904.</i>

I informed the French Ambassador to-day that I had laid before the Cabinet the substance of our recent discussions with regard to the definition of the areas which we were prepared to cede to France to the north of Sokoto and in the neighbourhood of Lake Chad. In regard to the former, my colleagues were willing to agree that the line running westwards from Konni to the Sokoto arc should be drawn further to the south. As for the line in the neighbourhood of Lake Chad, we proposed that, in order to provide for the inclusion of the trade route within the area to be ceded, the frontier should be described as follows :—

"Thence it follows the parallel of 13° 20′ north-eastward until it strikes the left bank of the River Waube (Ouobé), which bank it then follows to the shore of Lake Chad. If, however, before meeting this river it attains a distance of 5 kilom. from the caravan route from Zinder to Yo through Sua Kololua (Soua Kololoua), Adeber, and Kabi, the boundary shall then be traced at a distance of 5 kilom. from and to the south of this route until it strikes the left bank of the River Waube (Ouobé), which bank it then follows to the shore of Lake Chad as before."

I added that if these two extensions of territory were agreed to, on our part we should expect the French Government to offer no objection to the proposal which we intended to make, to the effect that a British Consul should be appointed at St. Pierre. The French Government already had an Agent at St. John's, Newfoundland, whom however, we did not recognise as Consul. The most reasonable arrangement would be that this official's position should be regularised, and that a British Consul should be appointed to St. Pierre. It was most desirable that there should be a British Consul at the latter place, owing to the extent to which it is used as a basis for smuggling operations.

M. Cambon said that he expected M. Delcassé's reply to-morrow, and would make me aware of its contents as soon as possible.

I am, &c.
LANSDOWNE.

No. 394.

The Marquess of Lansdowne to Sir E. Monson.

F.O. France 3662.
(No. 109.) Secret.
Sir,   <i>Foreign Office, March 2, 1904.</i>

The French Ambassador told me to-day that he had not yet received M. Delcassé's instructions upon the proposals which we had discussed on the 1st instant. He had, however, received some enquiries from the Minister which he thought he had better pass on to me. It appeared that M. Delcassé had not, up to the present time, taken the Colonial Minister into his confidence. This, M. Cambon explained to me, was due to M. Delcassé's extreme anxiety that the secrecy of the negotiations should be maintained. The Colonial Minister has now made suggestions to M. Delcassé in regard to certain points of detail. These were to the following effect :—

1. In 1899–1900, the French Government had made Treaties with various Sultans ruling in the region adjoining the frontier. Amongst these Treaties were one with the Sultan of Tessawa and Maradi, a second with the Sultan of Zinder, and a third with the Sultan of Gummel. The latter place proving to be entirely within British territory, the Treaty had not been ratified. The other two Treaties had, however, been ratified by the President. The French Government, in these circumstances, were extremely anxious that, under the arrangement which we were about to conclude, the whole of the territory belonging to the Sultan of Tessawa-Maradi should remain on the French side of the line. His Excellency was under the impression that the line, as we proposed to draw it, would have this effect, but there should be no doubt about it. Similarly the Sultan of Zinder was believed to rule over a small extent of territory to the south of the degree of latitude which was to form the frontier at this point. The French Government would therefore like the line to be deflected so as to throw the whole of Zinder on the French side.

2. Passing to Lake Chad, his Excellency pointed out that the eastern boundary of Bornu had, in the map which accompanied the Convention of 1898, been drawn so as apparently to intersect the middle of Lake Chad, the idea presumably being that the French should be given facilities for crossing by water from their possessions to the north of Lake Chad to their possessions lying south and east of the Lake. It had now been discovered that a great part of what was shown as water belonging to the Lake—in Justus Perthes' Map of 1892, annexed to the Convention—was, in reality, marsh and sandbank, and, therefore, not navigable. In these circumstances it was suggested that the line should be drawn in such a manner as to give the French access across the Lake from their northern to their southern possessions.

I told his Excellency that, considering the difficulty I had had in inducing my colleagues to agree to the modifications which he had already accepted, it was very embarrassing for me to apply to them for still further concessions. I added that, if these concessions were to be made on the ground that it was inconvenient to divide tribal territory, we should certainly have to insist that the same principle should be applied throughout the whole extent of the line, in which case we might have to modify it at other points to the disadvantage of the French.

His Excellency expressed a doubt whether corresponding circumstances would be found to exist at other points, but evidently felt the force of my objection.

His Excellency then referred to the question of the Gambia, and explained that what the French Government desired was that they should be given access to the river at a point where it becomes navigable for sea-going craft. They had no establishments at the mouth of the river, and it was therefore necessary that their goods should be conveyed up the river in the vessels which carried them across the sea. What they wanted was "la navigation maritime," not "la navigation fluviale." I said that we had reason to believe that vessels of considerable draft were able to go up the river as far as Yarbutenda, and that gun-boats, which certainly were sea-going craft, had reached points far above the Isles des Biches. His Excellency explained that the facts as to the navigation would require to be verified, and that the French Government assumed that, if the river prove not to be navigable as far as Yarbutenda, and if we adhere to our refusal to give up territory lying to the west of that place, we should, at any rate, be prepared to give them reasonable access to the river up to the point, wherever it might be, at which the river proved to be indisputably navigable.

I promised to refer these suggestions to the Colonial Office, and I dwelt again upon the inconvenience of opening up these new questions at the last moment. His Excellency did not deny that it was unfortunate; but urged the great importance of enabling M. Delcassé to keep his Colonial colleague in good humour.

At the close of our conversation, I asked his Excellency whether he could not obtain an answer for me in regard to my demands for permission to appoint a British Consul at St. Pierre. He said that he would take upon himself to say that no objection would be made to this proposal.

I am, &c.
LANSDOWNE.

No. 395.

The Marquess of Lansdowne to M. Cambon.

F.O. France 3686.
Dear M. Cambon, *Foreign Office, March* 3, 1904.

I have mentioned to the Colonial Office your suggestion that it might be arranged that the boundary-line in the region of Sokoto and Lake Chad should be drawn so as to give you the whole of the possessions of the Sultan of Tessawa Maradi, as well as everything belonging to the Sultan of Zinder.

I find that we have no information whatever as to the territorial limits of either of these Sultanates nor should we be likely to obtain any until we have received the report of the Delimitation Commission now at work. We cannot, however, expect that report for some time to come, and in the meanwhile I am afraid it would be impossible for us to discuss in complete ignorance of the local conditions these suggestions for the alteration of the boundary upon ethnological or other grounds.

My own inclination would, therefore, be to adhere to the line as originally settled. If, however, M. Delcassé really cares very much about the point, we might, I think, agree to a formula which would provide that the line, as originally settled, should hereafter be subject to modification with the consent of both parties in order to make it accord so far as possible with tribal or other acknowledged divisions.

We might in the same way agree that the line where it intersects Lake Chad from north to south should be so drawn as to give the French access by water from their possessions on the north to their possessions on the south of the Lake.

Should you be disposed to call on me at my house to-morrow morning, I shall be delighted to see you at any hour before one—say at 12·30.

I have, &c.
LANSDOWNE.

No. 396.

M. Cambon to the Marquess of Lansdowne.

F.O. France 3686.
(Privée et Confidentielle.) *Ambassade de France, Londres, le* 4 *Mars,* 1904.
Cher Lord Lansdowne, R. *March* 5.

J'ai communiqué à M. Delcassé votre lettre privée d'hier, relative à la délimitation de nos possessions entre le Niger et le Tchad. Je ne sais ce qu'il en pensera, mais à titre tout personnel, il me semble utile de vous faire part de mes réflexions et de chercher une formule susceptible d'être adoptée.

Cette délimitation, telle que nous la concevons, est l'un des éléments essentiels du réglement de la question de Terre-Neuve.

Une compensation territoriale a été stipulée entre nous pour l'abandon de nos droits. Celle qui paraissait de nature à donner à l'opinion Française une sérieuse satisfaction était, aux yeux de M. Delcassé, l'abandon de la Gambie.

Il voyait là un moyen d'assurer tous ses effets à l'œuvre d'apaisement et d'entente que nous poursuivons, et ce réglement lui semblait plus conforme que tout autre à la situation résultant du système territorial actuel de la Côte Occidentale d'Afrique.

Je sais que M. Delcassé regrette vivement qu'il n'ait pas paru possible au Gouvernement Britannique d'adopter cette solution. Il a dû en chercher une autre. Il vous a demandé l'Archipel de Los, qui en lui-même n'a d'importance ni pour vous ni pour nous, mais qui, situé sur nos côtes de la Nouvelle-Guinée, pouvait constituer dans l'avenir une source de difficultés entre nos deux pays. Vous avez bien voulu accéder à son désir sur ce point, et il a été heureux de prendre acte de votre adhésion.

Mais les îlots de Los ne pouvaient être considérés comme une suffisante compensation, et M. Delcassé vous a demandé sur le Niger et dans la région située entre ce fleuve et le Lac Tchad des territoires destinés à nous assurer des moyens de communication qui nous manquent et à compléter, d'une façon normale, des possessions dont ni les uns ni les autres ne connaissions la nature au moment où fut conclue la Convention du 14 Juin, 1898.

Vous avez écarté nos demandes de territoires sur le Niger par la raison que l'Administration Anglaise avait déjà pris possession de régions qui s'étendent entre Ilo et la Rivière Moussa, et pour atténuer ce refus dans une certaine mesure, vous avez bien voulu nous proposer un accès à la partie navigable de la Rivière Gambie. Sur ce point l'accord paraît possible si nous sommes mis en possession de Yarbutenda, et si, dans le cas où la navigation maritime ne pourrait s'exercer jusque-là, nous sommes assurés d'un accès en aval.

Il reste à régler la question de délimitation entre la région du Niger et celle du Lac Tchad. Le tracé établi en 1898 sur le papier, sans aucune reconnaissance préalable, n'est qu'un tracé théorique, qui ne doit devenir définitif qu'après une revision opérée par une Commission Franco-Anglaise; c'est une indication, une figure géométrique, et rien de plus.

On s'est aperçu depuis cette époque que s'il était définitif, nous n'aurions aucun moyen de communication entre nos possessions de la Nigeria et celles du Lac Tchad. Or, la pensée des auteurs de l'Arrangement de 1898 était certainement d'assurer aux deux pays la jouissance paisible de leurs possessions et d'écarter les malentendus et les conflits qui résultent toujours d'incursions sur le territoire du voisin. C'est là le principe et la raison d'être de la Convention de 1898, et vous savez aussi bien que moi, par les demandes réitérées de passage que je vous ai adressées pour nos convois de ravitaillement, qu'il est indispensable de modifier le tracé de cette Convention, afin de nous mettre en possession d'une route praticable.

Convaincu comme nous de cette nécessité, le Gouvernement Britannique a consenti, sur votre proposition, à adopter dans la région du Sokoto et dans celle qui avoisine le Lac Tchad un tracé qui nous donne la libre disposition des routes suivies par les caravanes. Mais entre ces deux régions la délimitation de 1898 a été fixée au parallèle 13° 20′, afin de nous laisser la possession de Zinder et de Tessaoua.

Seulement on ignorait alors que le Sultanat de Zinder s'étend quelque peu au sud du parallèle 13° 20′; et qu'il comprend le pays dénommé par les indigènes Damaguerrem; on ne savait pas davantage que le Sultan de Tessaoua couvre de son autorité la région de Maradi.

Si on l'avait su, il est évident qu'on aurait stipulé que le tracé engloberait dans la zone Française la totalité des territoires relevant de Zinder et de Tessaoua.

Pour ce dernier point le tracé que vous avez bien voulu proposer en dernier lieu à M. Delcassé, afin d'assurer nos communications entre la Nigeria Française et Zinder, laisse Maradi au nord et coincide à peu près avec les limites du Sultanat de Tessaoua. S'il y a une rectification à faire, elle est de peu d'importance, et la Commission Franco-Anglaise de Délimitation s'acquittera facilement de cette mission. Il n'en est pas de même du pays de Damaguerrem, ou Sultanat de Zinder. Ses limites sont assez faciles à fixer, car il est borné au sud par le petit Sultanat de Goumel et au sud-est par le

Bornou. Nos explorateurs ont passé un Traité avec le Chef de Goumel, mais comme ce territoire est tout entier dans votre zone, mon Gouvernement ne l'a pas ratifié; quant à Bornou, il est à vous.

Il s'agit donc tout simplement aujourd'hui de donner à la Commission de Délimitation l'instruction de suivre un tracé qui laisserait le Damaguerrem, c'est-à-dire, l'intégralité du Sultanat de Zinder, dans la zone Française.

C'est là le désir de M. Delcassé, et il est obligé d'insister pour sa réalisation, parce que la question de Terre-Neuve sera réglée par un Traité; que ce Traité devra être ratifié par notre Parlement, et que la ratification serait refusée à un arrangement qui ne contiendrait pas des stipulations précises et fermes.

Dans votre lettre d'hier, 3 Mars, vous exprimez l'avis que le tracé de 1898 devrait être maintenu, mais que la Commission de Délimitation pourrait être autorisée à la modifier, avec le consentement des deux Gouvernements, de façon à respecter autant que possible les divisions des tribus ou les autres frontières qui seraient reconnues.

Cette formule est à peu près conforme à la demande de M. Delcassé, mais elle a l'inconvénient d'être vague et de laisser planer le doute sur le sort futur de la partie sud du Sultanat de Zinder. Vous avez bien voulu me dire ce matin que vous teniez à laisser autant que possible à cette affaire un caractère de simple délimitation, et je vous ai promis de chercher une formule pouvant concilier votre point de vue avec celui de M. Delcassé.

Il me semble que nous pourrions dire ceci—

"Comme il résulte de certaines informations, dont il a été jusqu'à ce jour impossible de vérifier l'exactitude, que certaines localités faisant partie des Sultanats de Tessaoua-Maradi et de Zinder seraient situées au sud du tracé actuel, les Commissaires chargés respectivement de la délimitation devraient, le cas échéant, établir la ligne frontière de façon à comprendre ces localités dans la zone Française."

J'ignore si cette formule sera du goût de M. Delcassé, mais si elle était du vôtre il est probable qu'elle recevrait un bon accueil à Paris et qu'on l'examinerait avec un sincère esprit de conciliation.

Je vous serai très reconnaissant de me dire ce que vous en pensez, car je compte me rendre à Paris Dimanche et je verrai M. Delcassé Lundi.

Votre bien dévoué,

PAUL CAMBON.

No. 397.

The Marquess of Lansdowne to M. Cambon.([1])

Private and Confidential.

Dear M. Cambon, *Foreign Office, March 5, 1904.*

I am much obliged for your letter of yesterday. I will not attempt to follow you in your review of the negotiations which have led us up to the point at which we have now arrived. Each side will probably remain of opinion that the other is driving too hard a bargain. We have, however, each of us to think of the effect which will be produced upon the public mind by the concessions which we may make; and I fully realise that, just as we have to reckon with our Parliament, so you have to take into account the criticisms to which you will be exposed in your Chambers.

So far as we are at this moment concerned, the only outstanding point appears to be that which concerns the boundary where it follows the parallel 13° 20′ between the Sokoto section and that which adjoins Lake Tchad. No question concerning this portion of the frontier was raised by you until Wednesday last, although we have been discussing these matters for some time past. During the later stage of our

([1]) [No original has been found of this letter. The text is taken from the *Confidential Print.*]

negotiations I have had to make several successive appeals to my colleagues for a reconsideration of the instructions which they had given to me, and you will, I am sure, understand that I should be reluctant to go back to them again in reference to an entirely new point. I do not, however, see why we should not arrive at an understanding which will substantially effect what M. Delcassé requires.

You have explained to me that a portion of the Sultanate of Zinder lies to the south of 13° 20′, and that possibly a portion of the Sultanate of Tessaoua lies to the south of the line which we have accepted in the neighbourhood of Maradi. The latter case could, you feel sure, be provided for by a quite unimportant modification of the line, but you go on to say that " il n'en est pas de même " in regard to the former case.

We may, therefore, infer that, in your opinion, a considerable part of the Sultanate of Zinder lies to the south of 13° 20′. Now, I find that we are absolutely without information as to the details of the geography of this region, and it therefore, not unnaturally, seems to us impossible that we should accept, for better or for worse, a frontier founded upon tribal limits of the situation of which we are entirely unaware.

It must moreover be borne in mind that these tribal limits are of the most elastic and uncertain description. A tribe belongs to one petty ruler at one moment, and to another petty ruler at another. We cannot, therefore, attribute to such boundaries the sanctity of well-established limits. There is, moreover, this consideration of which we cannot lose sight—that if the line is to be corrected at one point in order to prevent the division of a French-protected tribe, we shall have to insist upon analogous deflections for the purpose of preserving the integrity of tribes enjoying our protection.

Primâ facie, therefore, any arrangement for the correction of the frontier must be of a bilateral character. I should have no objection to admit, as a qualification of this principle, that, in the case of those portions of the frontier which are to be drawn so as to bring certain trade routes within the French sphere, the trade route, and not the tribal limit, must be the dominant consideration. But in regard to other portions of the line we could not accept a wording which would in effect imply that no modification should be made except in favour of France.

Holding these views, I do not think we can say more than this—that when the Commissioners now engaged in delimiting the conventional frontier return in the course of this spring and can be consulted, the two Governments will, except as to those regions where the position of the frontier is governed by that of the trade routes, be prepared to consider any diversions of the conventional line which may seem desirable in order to avoid inconvenience to either party by interference with well recognised and established tribal limits.

I trust that you will consider that this formula sufficiently provides for the case of the Sultanate of Zinder.

I am, &c.
LANSDOWNE.

No. 398.

The Marquess of Lansdowne to Sir E. Monson.

F.O. France 3662.
(No. 127.) Secret.
Sir,   *Foreign Office, March* 11, 1904.

The French Ambassador, who returned last night from Paris, called on me this morning. He told me that, subject to the adjustment of one or two points of detail, M. Delcassé saw no reason why the negotiations which we have been conducting during the last few months should not now be satisfactorily concluded.

It seemed to him inevitable that the question of Newfoundland should be dealt with by a Convention; as for the rest, there might be an exchange of written statements embodying the views of the two Governments, and it would be necessary to agree as to the terms of any declarations which might be made in Parliament.

The case of Egypt would have to be provided for by a Khedivial Decree.

M. Delcassé thought it most important that no time should be lost in concluding matters, and his Excellency suggested that Sir Eldon Gorst should start at once for Paris with this object.

The French Government would probably make a declaration to Germany (which Power had at different times exhibited an interest in the Moorish question) with regard to the arrangement as to Morocco, but it did not seem necessary that, either in this declaration or in the statements to be made to Parliament, we should explain what was intended to take place in the event of the present régime in Morocco breaking down altogether.

I reminded his Excellency that it would be necessary to take Spain also into our confidence. It would, I presumed, be intimated to her that it was intended to maintain the open door, to avoid, so far as possible, any disturbance of the territorial *status quo*, and to provide for the neutralisation of a considerable part of the Moorish sea-board.

His Excellency agreed as to this.

M. Cambon reminded me that we had not yet settled whether the neutralised area was to include Rabat, or to stop at the heights on the right bank of the River Sebou.

I said that this point seemed to have dropped somewhat out of sight, and that I wished to refer to my papers before expressing a final opinion with regard to it.

We then had some discussion as to the line which might be followed by the boundary in the northern part of Nigeria, and his Excellency suggested, with reference to the suggestion made by me to him on the 5th instant (see my despatch No. 121 of the 10th instant), that the following formula should be adopted :—

"Il est convenu que dans la portion du tracé où la frontière n'est pas déterminée par les routes commerciales, il sera tenu compte autant que possible des divisions politiques actuelles des territoires, les tribus relevant des Sultanats de Tessaoura, Maradi, et Zinder devant être laissées à la France et celles relevant des Sultanats de la zone Anglaise au sud du parallèle 13° 20' devant rester à la Grande-Bretagne."

His Excellency called upon me again later in the day, and I read to him the preceding parts of this despatch in order that I might be sure that I had correctly understood the views which he had expressed. He admitted that I had done so. I then proposed to his Excellency, as an alternative to the formula which he had left with me in the morning, the following :—

" Afin d'éviter les inconvénients qui pourraient résulter, de part et d'autre, d'un tracé qui s'écarterait des frontières reconnues et bien constatées, il est convenu que dans la portion du tracé où la frontière n'est pas déterminée par les routes commerciales, il sera tenu compte des divisions politiques actuelles des territoires de façon à ce que les tribus relevant des Sultanats de Tessaoua, Maradi, et Zinder soient autant que possible laissées à la France et celles relevant des Sultanats de la zone Anglaise soient laissées à la Grande-Bretagne."

His Excellency said that he would refer this formula to M. Delcassé, adding, at the same time, that it seemed to him unobjectionable.

I told his Excellency that after considering what he had said to me this morning I had come to the conclusion that it was necessary that we should embody in a formal Agreement, to be presented to Parliament, the terms of the understandings at which we proposed to arrive with regard to Morocco, Egypt, and Siam. I saw, however, no objection to recording our Agreement as to the arrangements which might be made in the event of the "liquidation" of Morocco in a separate and secret document. The arrangements with regard to Newfoundland, the Gambia, the Niger, the Isles de Los, and the Nigerian frontier would be embodied in a Treaty which would, of course, be laid before Parliament.

I told his Excellency that we had come to the conclusion that it was not necessary for us to insist upon neutralising the coast of Morocco as far as Rabat, and that we would agree that the line should be drawn so that the neutralised portion of the coast line should extend up to the heights on the right bank of the Sebou River.

I again impressed upon his Excellency the necessity of fully informing Spain of our intentions, and I said that I proposed to speak to the Spanish Ambassador upon the subject next week. I expressed a strong hope that a similar course would be pursued by M. Delcassé.

I am, &c.
LANSDOWNE.

No. 399.

The Marquess of Lansdowne to Sir E. Monson.

F.O. France 3662.
(No. 128.)   Secret.
Sir,   *Foreign Office, March 13, 1904.*

The French Ambassador asked me to see him this evening. He told me that he had heard from M. Delcassé, who accepted my amendments in the formula which his Excellency had proposed to me for the description of the Nigerian frontier. M. Delcassé also took note, with pleasure, of my statement that the neutralised portion of the Morocco coast-line need not extend beyond the heights on the right bank of the River Sebou.

M. Delcassé would now await the result of the discussions which were to take place this week between Sir Eldon Gorst and the Representatives of the French Ministry for Foreign Affairs, and hoped they would enable us to come to terms. His Excellency said that M. Delcassé was most anxious that we should sign something before the Chamber separated for the Easter holidays. He thought, however, that there might be considerable difficulty in drafting a statement for Parliamentary purposes, and that it might be desirable to postpone this.

I said that if we were in a position to sign we should, in my opinion, also be in a position to present the papers to Parliament. There might be one or two points which we should have to deal with in secret notes, but the greater part of the arrangement would have to be embodied in papers which it would be impossible for us to withhold from our Parliament. The explanations to be given in Parliament were another matter, and as to these each side must have a reasonable amount of freedom.

M. Cambon said that he agreed with me as to this.

Finally, M. Delcassé wished me to know that he thought it most inadvisable that anything should be said to Spain until it was quite clear that we had come to terms.

I am, &c.
LANSDOWNE.

No. 400.

The Earl of Cromer to the Marquess of Lansdowne.

Cairo, March 14, 1904.
D. 11·30 A.M.
R. 1·30 P.M.

F.O. Turkey 5368.
Tel. (No. 22.)   Secret.   P.
French negotiations.

The most important point of all in the Egyptian Arrangement seems to me to make it quite clear that French Government agree to give us a completely free hand to act as occasion may require in the event of its being impossible to obtain consent of the other Powers. I would therefore insist strongly on the third article of Convention as drafted by Gorst, especially the latter part of it.

We are almost sure to have much difficulty with Germany.

No. 401.

The Marquess of Lansdowne to Sir E. Monson.

F.O. France 3662.
(No. 140.)   Secret.
Sir,   *Foreign Office, March 21, 1904.*

The French Ambassador left with me to-day the enclosed drafts of a Convention dealing with the Newfoundland Fishery question, and of two Declarations recording Agreements between the two Governments respecting Egypt, Morocco, Siam, and the New Hebrides.(¹)

His Excellency told me that he did not regard the proposals embodied in these documents as differing ''fundamentally'' from those which I had put forward. I agreed to examine the French drafts carefully, and to discuss them with his Excellency when I had done so.

He mentioned to me with regard to our proposals as to the application of the North Sea Convention to the Newfoundland coast, that the Convention of 1889 in regard to the sale of liquor to fishing vessels had never been ratified by the French Parliament. The Convention of 1882 in regard to Police had been ratified, but had occasioned a good deal of friction. For this reason, the clause referring to these two questions had been omitted in the French drafts. His Excellency added, however, that he did not think that the French objections were insurmountable, and he himself believed that in the case of the Newfoundland fisheries it would be desirable to adopt some measure of an analogous character.

M. Cambon added that M. Delcassé did not like our proposal that Article VIII of the Suez Canal Convention of 1888 should not be brought into operation. This Article provided—

1. For meetings of the Commission upon special occasions when the neutrality of the Canal might appear to be menaced, and
2. For an annual meeting of the Commission under the presidency of a Representative of the Sultan.

M. Delcassé attached great importance to the retention of the first of these provisions, but was quite ready to give up the second.

I am, &c.
LANSDOWNE.

(¹) [*V. infra*, pp. 374–398.]

No. 402.

The Marquess of Lansdowne to the Earl of Cromer.

F.O. Turkey 5368.
Tel. (No. 17.)   Secret.   *Foreign Office, March 25, 1904.*

Your telegram No. 25.

We have constantly kept in view desirability of obtaining from the French Government an engagement that they will assist us in bringing about execution of Decree, and I am insisting on retention of clause to this effect.

I have also said that it must form part of the published Agreement. From your telegram I infer that you wish to go much further and that you would like to include in published part of Agreement an Article in which French Government would undertake that should other Powers refuse their consent, and should we thereupon take the law into our own hands and proceed as if that consent had been given, French Government will not oppose us.

There would in my belief be no prospect of obtaining consent of French Government to such a clause, and I do not see how we can expect them to proclaim their intention of encouraging us to violate Treaty engagements to which both they and we are parties. From our point of view objection to this course would be not less strong. We have always professed respect for international obligations and denounced the conduct of those who ignored them. We may at any moment be confronted with questions raising this principle, *e.g.*, that of egress of Russian Black Sea Fleet.

An open announcement that we had gone over to the side of the international law-breakers would strike a fatal blow at our reputation.

Finally, it seems obvious that public announcement of our intention to over-ride opposition of other Powers would scarcely fail to increase our difficulties in dealing with them.

I doubt, however, whether you really intend this, and although I gathered from your letters that you contemplated something like a financial *coup d'État*, I did not suppose that you wished to make the French Government bind themselves by a public engagement to acquiesce in it.

What I am asking for is that France should publicly agree—

(1.) To support us in procuring adhesion of other Powers.

(2.) In the meanwhile, not to thwart or oppose us in our conduct of Egyptian business. As to this, I think we could probably get private promise that French representative would always act with ours on Caisse and on Railway Board.

No. 403.

The Earl of Cromer to the Marquess of Lansdowne.

Cairo, March 27, 1904.

F.O. Turkey 5368.

Tel. (No. 28.) Secret.

D. 8·50 P.M.
R. 10 P.M.

Your telegrams Nos. 17 and 19.

Objections to publicity are certainly very strong.

I was just about to propose to you a secret Agreement in the sense of that which you have adopted. I hope that you will insist on it, as otherwise we shall be wholly at the mercy not only of the other Powers but also of the French. Their help to get Decree accepted will presumably be rather half-hearted.

You will, of course, understand that, inasmuch as right to convert is contested, this plan does not obviate altogether the risk of finding ourselves faced by alternatives of either taking law into our own hands or yielding, but my hope and belief is that other Powers will get an inkling of secret Agreement, and if they once feel that we are fully determined to carry the thing through with or without their consent, they will probably come to terms.

No. 404.

The Marquess of Lansdowne to Sir E. Monson.

F.O. France 3662.
(No. 159.) Secret.

Sir,   *Foreign Office, March* 30, 1904.

I had lengthy discussions with the French Ambassador yesterday and to-day upon the subject of the draft Declaration dealing with French and British interests in Egypt and Morocco. I attach to this despatch a copy of the revised draft handed to me by his Excellency and of the amendments which I have suggested thereon.(¹)

With reference to Article IX, in which the French Government undertakes that it will give us its diplomatic support in obtaining the execution of the Declaration, I told his Excellency that considering the language of this Article, as well as that of the first Article, in which the French Government undertakes not to impede our action in Egypt, we should certainly expect that the French Representatives on the Caisse and on the Railway Administration would from the time of the signature of the Convention co-operate loyally with our Representatives at all points. It would not in our view be enough that they should maintain an attitude of neutrality; we should expect their active support. His Excellency expressed entire agreement, and said that considering the general tenour of the Agreement, it was inevitable that the cordial support of their Representatives should be forthcoming whenever it was needed.

In reference to Secret Article IV, in which it is provided that should the other Powers not give their adhesion to the Khedivial Decree, the French Government will offer no objection to the conversion of the Privileged Debt in the year 1910, his Excellency said that I might interpret this Article as meaning that the French Government, whose influence over the French bondholders was, as I was aware, considerable, would make it their business to facilitate the operation, should the Egyptian Government determine to proceed to conversion in the year 1910. There was, his Excellency said, some doubt whether there was a legal right to convert, and unless the bondholders were favourably disposed, difficulties would certainly arise. His Excellency said, however, that he had consulted French financiers in Paris, and had found them fully disposed to admit that if it were accepted that conversion was to be put off from 1905 till 1910, every facility would be given so far as the French market was concerned.

I am, &c.
LANSDOWNE.

(¹) [*V. infra*, pp. 374–398.]

No. 405.

Sir E. Monson to the Marquess of Lansdowne.

Paris, March 30, 1904.

F.O. France 3693.   D. 7·40 P.M.
Tel. (No. 13.) Secret.   R. ·10 P.M.

Minister for Foreign Affairs in a hurried interview this afternoon said that he expected to hear to-morrow morning result of your discussion yesterday with French Ambassador, but that he did not see how he could give way over the "bait," Article III in his draft, on account of feeling which the want of such a provision would excite in France.

No. 406.

The Marquess of Lansdowne to Sir E. Monson.

F.O. France 3693. *Foreign Office, March* 30, 1904.
Tel. (No. 39.)   D. Midnight.
Your No. 13 of to-day.

I am quite unable to understand Minister for Foreign Affairs' attitude. We made it perfectly clear from the first that we could not entertain a proposal which would give French fishermen unrestricted right of procuring bait on whole coast of New-foundland unless French Government was willing to deal with question of bounties.

As they refused to touch bounties we fell back on an arrangement under which right of French fishermen to procure bait was restricted to Treaty Shore. This was clearly explained in my letter of November 19th to M. Cambon, and his reply of December 10th shows that he clearly understood the point, which he presumably explained to Minister for Foreign Affairs.

The negotiation has since proceeded on this basis, which has been accepted by the Cabinet and by the Colonial Government in whose eyes the bait question is of vital importance.

The French Government now reinsert a clause giving them right of obtaining bait throughout whole coast.

We shall certainly break off the negotiation if this demand is pressed.

Do you think M. Delcassé really knows the history of the case or understands the utter unreasonableness of making this demand at the eleventh hour after concessions on each side have been carefully balanced?

He may also not realise that, under clauses which we have accepted, French fishermen will be allowed right of procuring bait throughout Treaty shore.

French Ambassador tells me that Minister for Foreign Affairs is about to receive a deputation from St. Malo, and reserves his reply until he has heard their statement.

I leave it to your judgment whether to attempt an explanation.

No. 407.

The Earl of Cromer to the Marquess of Lansdowne.

Cairo, March 31, 1904.
F.O. Turkey 5368.   D. 1·10 P.M.
Tel. (No. 32.) Secret.   R. 3·30 P.M.
I have received French Draft Convention.

Article I. Phrase that we had no intention to change status of Egypt may and probably will be interpreted by other Powers as pledging us to maintain capitulations intact.[1] It is far more disadvantageous to us than the proposed secret article is to the French about Morocco, but the other Powers are not concerned in the Morocco article.

I should be inclined to make the public recognition of permanency of our occupation a *sine quâ non* condition of acceptance. It is the only certain advantage we obtain.[2] Rest depends on acceptance of other Powers.

Without going quite so far as regards article dealing with capitulations, I would insist very strongly on the adoption of our text without any serious modifications, and on its publication.[3]

[1] But if it were omitted, we should at once be supposed to be about to annex. We can easily explain that this is not so, and also that we have come to an understanding with the French as to the capitulations which Lord Cromer does not desire to touch at present.
[2] We have got an engagement not to demand " qu'un terme soit fixé."
[3] I don't think the text has been modified. The question of publishing was carefully considered and the French objection which was apparently insuperable was admitted.

Unless these two points are carried we shall have very little to show to the public.

Whole of the details of article I had certainly better be relegated to the decree.([4]) We can however, Sir E. Gorst says perfectly well omit any allusion to the conversion from the convention.

I hope marginal note (B)([5]) will not be inserted in article I and that that article will close at the words "arrangement." I understand objections to any public hint that we intend to take the law into our own hands, but between this and public and formal engagement given in the marginal note there is a very wide difference. Moreover if, as I understand is the case, you intend to insist on the first portion of the old article 3([6]) being in the published convention, phrase is superfluous as the necessity of referring to Powers will be indicated with sufficient fairness in the published convention. This phrase would take away from us all power of bluffing, and it is this rather than any serious intention to take the law into our own hands that I have always contemplated.([7])

I hope you will obtain article about firman.([8]) Its importance consists in the fact that the impossibility of altering the firman without the consent of France and England is recognised.

I do not think similar rights have ever been recognised as regards other Powers. French Ambassador appears to have misunderstood this point.

As regards the Suez Canal, though I prefer your text, I think that we might accept the French proposal if some concession is necessary. It is of course quite clear both from the text of Canal Convention and from Freycinet's letter to the French Ambassador of the 8th June, 1886, that executive action rests entirely with the Egyptian Government. Recent events have shown that this is absolutely necessary.

([4]) This has been done.
([5]) It means that the Powers are to be told that, if they accept the decree, it cannot be altered subsequently without their consent. Would they be likely to accept on any other conditions?
([6]) This is the article about diplomatic support. We have got it in different wording.
([7]) Lord Cromer has misunderstood. We promise not to alter the Decree *if it is accepted.* We give no assurance as to what we may do if it is *not* accepted.
([8]) Covered by new Article IX.

[*ED. NOTE.*—The annotations to this document are by Lord Lansdowne.]

No. 408.

The Marquess of Lansdowne to Sir E. Monson.

F.O. France 3662.
(No. 160.) Secret.
Sir,   *Foreign Office, March 31, 1904.*

The French Ambassador called upon me late last evening by appointment. He had hoped to have received M. Delcassé's instructions with regard to the outstanding points in the draft dealing with Newfoundland and the question of "territorial compensation."

His Excellency, however, informed me with evident signs of discomfiture that he had received no instructions from the Minister for Foreign Affairs, but that M. Delcassé was to receive to-day a deputation from contractors at St. Malo and others interested in the Newfoundland fisheries, who intended to press upon him the extreme importance of procuring for the French fishing fleet frequenting the Newfoundland banks the right of procuring bait throughout the whole coast of Newfoundland. M. Delcassé was much alarmed at the prospect of opposition from these fishing interests, which were powerful in Britany and Normandy, and capable of causing serious Parliamentary trouble. I told his Excellency that I had received, with feelings of consternation, the proposal that this question should be reopened. I again reminded him of the explicit statement contained in my letter to him of November 19th upon this subject, and of his reply, dated December 10th, which showed that my meaning had not been misunderstood. I had then made it absolutely clear that the unrestricted right of buying bait would only be conceded as part of an arrangement under which the French Government would undertake to modify their system of bounties which operated so unfairly upon the British fishing industry. M. Delcassé had refused to touch the bounties, and we had thereupon intimated that any concession in regard to fisheries and the supply of bait, &c., must be limited to the Treaty Shore. The whole negotiation had been conducted upon this basis, and it was upon this understanding that I had obtained the consent of my colleagues to the proposals which I had been able to accept. It was upon the same assumption that we had obtained the concurrence of the Newfoundland Government, to which the bait question was one of vital importance. I told his Excellency plainly that if this demand were persisted in I should be obliged to break off the negotiation altogether, and in this event the whole arrangement, including those parts of it which had reference to Morocco, Egypt, and Siam, would have to be abandoned.

His Excellency did not deny that the matter had been clearly explained by me in the autumn of last year. He seemed, however, to doubt whether M. Delcassé had really understood the situation.

His Excellency called upon me again this morning, and said that since he had seen me he had received a telegram as well as a note from M. Delcassé, and that he gathered that, in view of the strong objections which I had urged, M. Delcassé would probably not press for the retention of the French bait clause. His Excellency was, however, instructed to ask me whether I would not consent to a compromise under which some point outside of the Treaty Shore and nearer to the Newfoundland banks might be selected as a depôt at which the French fishermen would be allowed to obtain bait without having to go all the way to the Treaty Shore for the purpose. I said that this concession was, in my opinion, out of the question, and I could not undertake to refer it to my colleagues. It was in effect an abandonment of the position which we had taken up, and, for reasons which I had already given to his Excellency, I considered myself bound not to retreat from that position.

His Excellency then made a further attempt to induce me to reconsider my decision in regard to the use of the word " exclusivement " in Article 2 of the Declaration respecting Egypt and Morocco. I said that I had obtained the consent of the Cabinet to the clause as it now stood without the word in question, and that I could not give way upon the point. His Excellency said that he should leave for Paris to-day, and would communicate what I had said to M. Delcassé. He appeared to be hopeful that we might yet succeed in coming to terms.

I am, &c.
LANSDOWNE.

No. 409.

Sir E. Monson to the Marquess of Lansdowne.

Paris, March 31, 1904.
D. 6·30 P.M.
R. 8 P.M.

F.O. France 3669.
Tel. (No. 16.)
    Anglo-French negotiations.
    Your telegram No. 39.
    I have been able to see M.F.A. before his reception of St. Malo deputation, and I gave him a French paraphrase of first 4 paragraphs of your telegram No. 39.

    He said that he was being asked to do a very hard thing, and it seemed to me that he had never realised his exact position under the correspondence between you and French Ambassador, to which I referred him.

I carefully abstained from any suggestion of rupture of negotiations, but I hinted that it was impossible for you to give way on this point, and that his own authority in Parliament is so great that he would be able to get over this difficulty.

He finally said that he would do his best with the delegates he was about to see, and begged me to tell Y.L. that he would telegraph to French Ambassador afterwards the result, and that he on his side must couple with his concession on the "bait" question your acceptance of formula which he has now communicated through the French Ambassador of the first Article of the Declaration about Egypt, stating that French Government "n'entravera d'aucune façon, &c."

He considers that this formula covers everything that H.M. Government can ask.

French Ambassador should receive news of result of deputation meeting at 7 this evening.

On my return to Embassy, I received your telegram which reached me too late to prevent my interview with M.F.A.

No. 410.

M. Cambon to the Marquess of Lansdowne.

F.O. France 3686.   *Ambassade de France à Londres,*
Privée.   D. *le 31 Mars,* 1904.
Cher Lord Lansdowne,   R. *April* 1, 1904.

J'ai reçu, après votre départ, une communication de M. Delcassé en réponse à l'envoi de votre projet de Déclaration relative à l'Égypte et au Maroc et des premières indications que je lui ai fait parvenir sur le projet de Convention de Terre-Neuve.

Pour la Déclaration, M. Delcassé pense que le commencement du § 2 de l'Article I pourrait être rédigé de la façon suivante :—

"De son côté, le Gouvernement de la République déclare qu'il n'entravera *d'aucune façon* l'action de l'Angleterre dans ce pays, et qu'il donne son adhésion," &c.

Cette expression "d'aucune façon" s'applique à tous vos moyens d'action, à votre occupation militaire comme au reste, et M. Delcassé est d'avis qu'elle est de nature à vous donner entière satisfaction sur le fond comme sur la forme.

Dans l'Article II M. Delcassé consent à supprimer le mot "exclusivement," mais il préfère ne le remplacer par aucune autre expression. La phrase serait donc ainsi rédigée : "De son côté, le Gouvernement Britannique reconnaît qu'il appartient à la France," &c. . . . .

No. 411.

The Marquess of Lansdowne to M. Cambon.

F.O. France 3686.
My dear Ambassador,   *Foreign Office, April* 1, 1904.

I have just received your notes of the 31st March and of to-day, and I have scarcely time to examine with the care which they deserve, before the post leaves, the suggestions which M. Delcassé has instructed you to make. As to one of them, however, I am able to give you an immediate reply. We cannot accept the proposal to omit from Article I the words "ne demandera pas qu'un terme soit fixé à l'occupation Britannique." Those words are already weaker than those which had seemed to us necessary. But, such as they are, we cannot do without them. We cannot go to

Parliament without *at least* an admission to this extent that the French Government recognises the permanency of our occupation of Egypt. It will not be regarded as an equivalent that you should announce your intention "de n'entraver en aucune façon l'action de l'Angleterre." The formula which you desire to omit, and which we desire to retain, was that used in your letter of October 26th, 1903. Your words were, "le Gouvernement de la République se déclarera disposé à ne point entraver l'action de l'Angleterre en Égypte, *et* à ne pas demander qu'un terme soit fixé à l'occupation Britannique." I am convinced that the Cabinet would not give up these words, which we regard as essential to our Parliamentary case.

I therefore most earnestly beg you to explain to M. Delcassé that, anxious as I am to meet his wishes, I am precluded from doing so at this point.

The omission of "spécialement" in Article II might probably be agreed to if other questions could be satisfactorily disposed of.

The remaining points I must, I fear, reserve, or I shall miss the post.

I have, &c.
LANSDOWNE.

[Substance sent as telegram No. 40 to Sir E. Monson, the 2nd April: France 3669.]

No. 412.

The Marquess of Lansdowne to the Earl of Cromer.

F.O. Turkey 5368.   *Foreign Office, April 2, 1904.*
Tel. (No. 24.) Secret.   D. 5·20 P.M.

Your telegram No. 32. French negotiations.

Copies of amended drafts were sent to you last night with explanations by Gorst. They meet most of the points raised by you.

Article 1. Phrase regarding political status of Egypt desirable in order to reassure other Powers that we are not intending to annex Egypt or place it under a formal protectorate. If necessary we can easily explain that it does not refer to Capitulations. The secret article on this point makes our position quite clear so far as French Government are concerned.

As regards recognition of occupation we propose to insist on an engagement from the French not to ask for a limit to its duration. This gives practically what we want.

The financial details taken from Draft Decree have now been omitted. You have misunderstood clause about no altering decree without assent of Powers. This only applies to the case of decree being accepted. We give no assurance as to what we may do if decree is not accepted.

Article about Sultan's firman is covered by a new article, replacing article 3, under which each country promises the other diplomatic support to secure execution of agreement.

Lastly, as regards article about Capitulations, text adopted binds the French to examine our proposals when we are ready to bring them forward, and omits any stipulation that they shall be dependent on simultaneous consideration of similar reforms in Morocco. Question of publication of this article was carefully considered, and French objection, which was apparently insuperable, was admitted.

No. 413.

The Marquess of Lansdowne to Sir E. Monson.

F.O. France 3662.
(No. 171.) Confidential.

Sir,   *Foreign Office, April* 6, 1904.

I had further interviews to-day with the French Ambassador upon the subject of the negotiations in which we have lately been engaged. The following were the most important points :—

In Article I of the Declaration as to Egypt and Morocco his Excellency proposed that the beginning of the second paragraph should run as follows :—

"De son côté le Gouvernement de la République déclare qu'il n'entravera pas l'action de l'Angleterre dans ce pays en prenant l'initiative de demander qu'un terme soit fixé à l'occupation Britannique," &c.

I took strong exception to the insertion of the words "en prenant l'initiative," and his Excellency, after some discussion, agreed that they might be omitted. . . . . [Details.]

We had protracted discussion with regard to the possibility of an understanding as to the New Hebrides, but we were unable to come to an agreement upon this point, his Excellency insisting upon words which would bind the Commission to accept registration of title at Fiji or Noumea as of itself sufficient evidence of ownership. I pointed out to his Excellency that registration by the officials of the High Commission for the Western Pacific is a purely Ministerial act, and amounts to no more than a record of the fact that a claim has been made. No investigation of title takes place prior to registration, and it was therefore impossible for us to accept registration as conclusive evidence.

We finally decided that as there was no prospect of an agreement upon this point, it would be better merely to place it upon record that the two Governments were agreed on preparing an Arrangement which, without modifying the political *status quo*, would put an end to the difficulties arising from the absence of jurisdiction over natives, and that they would appoint a Commission for the settlement of disputes as to landed property, the competency and procedure of which should form the subject of a preliminary Agreement between them.

I am, &c.
LANSDOWNE.

No. 414.

The Marquess of Lansdowne to Sir E. Monson.

F.O. France 3662.
(No. 172.) Confidential.

Sir,   *Foreign Office, April* 6, 1904.

The French Ambassador called my attention to-day to the fact that His Majesty's Government had, on the 13th March, 1895, entered into a Treaty with the Sultan of Morocco, under which His Highness was bound not to alienate to any other Power, without the concurrence of His Majesty's Government, certain portions of Moorish territory in the neighbourhood of Cape Juby. This Treaty had never been communicated to the French Government, which was not, therefore, officially aware of its existence. It might, however, his Excellency thought, occasion serious inconvenience in certain eventualities which might arise in consequence of the Agreement about to be entered into between the French and British Governments as to the affairs of Morocco. His Excellency suggested that, in the circumstances, the French Government should receive a formal assurance by letter that we would not take advantage of the existence of this Treaty in order to create difficulties for France in any arrangement which she might desire to make with the Spanish Government in reference to those parts of Morocco to which the Treaty applied. I promised that I would endeavour to find some means of meeting the wish which his Excellency had expressed.

I am, &c.
LANSDOWNE.

No. 415.

The Earl of Cromer to the Marquess of Lansdowne.

Cairo, April 7, 1904.

F.O. Turkey 5368.   D. 1·20 P.M.
Tel. (No. 39.) Secret.   R. 3·30 P.M.

French negotiations.

I gather from letters received last night that M. Delcassé objects strongly to stating that French Government will not ask for any limit of time to be asked for the occupation.

My view is that we must insist on something which will virtually cancel the pledges to withdraw which were undoubtedly given by successive British Ministers. I think that this is the only Egyptian point on which, unless we can obtain what we want, it would be justifiable to break off negotiations. I do not much care about the phraseology so long as we get the substance.

I put forward following suggestion for your consideration. We might as a "pis aller," though I do not like it, turn the matter round, and instead of asking the French to make a declaration, make a declaration ourselves in the following sense :—

"His Majesty's Government declare that although British occupation of Egypt was originally intended to be temporary, circumstances have arisen which render it impossible to assign any limit to its duration. Government of the French Republic takes note of this declaration."

This might be easier for them to accept than the present formula. You will understand the idea. Possibly wording admits of improvement.

No. 416.

The Marquess of Lansdowne to Sir E. Monson.

F.O. France 3765.([1])
(No. 173 A.)
Sir,   *Foreign Office, April 8, 1904.*

I have from time to time kept your Excellency fully informed of the progress of my negotiations with the French Ambassador for the complete settlement of a series of important questions in which the interests of Great Britain and France are involved. These negotiations commenced in the spring of last year, and have been continued with but slight interruptions up to the present time.

Such a settlement was notoriously desired on both sides of the Channel, and the movement in its favour received a powerful impulse from the visit paid to France by His Majesty King Edward VII in May last and by the return visit of President Loubet to this country. Upon the latter occasion, the President was accompanied by the distinguished Statesman who has so long presided over the French Ministry of Foreign Affairs. It is a matter for congratulation that his presence afforded to

([1]) [There is a rough draft only in this volume. The text is taken from the *Confidential Print.* The despatch was published in 1904, *Accounts and Papers,* 1904 (*Cd.* 1952), CX, pp. 315–22.]

His Majesty's Government the great advantage of a full and frank exchange of ideas. It left us in no doubt that a settlement of the kind which both Governments desired, and one which would be mutually advantageous to both countries, was within our reach.

The details of the questions at issue have since been examined in confidential discussions with the French Ambassador, to whose personal knowledge of many of the points involved and wide diplomatic experience it is largely due that I am now able to announce to you the Agreement which has been arrived at. I enclose copies of the Convention and Declarations which were signed to-day by his Excellency and myself.([2])

Among the questions which it has been our duty to examine, that of the position of Great Britain in Egypt and of France in Morocco have necessarily occupied a foremost place.

From a British point of view there is no more remarkable episode in recent history than that which concerns the establishment and the gradual development of British influence in Egypt. Our occupation of that country, at first regarded as temporary, has by the force of circumstances become firmly established. Under the guidance of the eminent public Servant who has for the last twenty years represented His Majesty's Government in that country, Egypt has advanced by rapid strides along the path of financial and material prosperity. The destruction of the power of the Mahdi and the annexation of the Soudan have increased that influence and added to the stability of our occupation.

But while these developments have, in fact, rapidly modified the international situation in Egypt, the financial and administrative system which prevails is a survival of an order of things which no longer exists, and is not only out of date but full of inconvenience to all concerned. It is based on the very elaborate and intricate provisions of the Law of Liquidation of 1880, and the London Convention of 1885. With the financial and material improvement of Egypt, these provisions have become a hindrance instead of an aid to the development of the resources of the country. The friction, inconvenience, and actual loss to the Egyptian Treasury which it has occasioned have been pointed out by Lord Cromer on many occasions in his annual Reports. It is well described in the following passage which occurs in Lord Milner's standard work on Egypt :—

" The spectacle of Egypt, with her Treasury full of money, yet not allowed to use that money for an object which, on a moderate calculation, should add 20 per cent. to the wealth of the country, is as distressing as it is ludicrous. Every year that passes illustrates more forcibly the injustice of maintaining, in these days of insured solvency, the restrictions imposed upon the financial freedom of the Egyptian Government at a time of bankruptcy—restrictions justifiable then, but wholly unjustifiable now. No one would object to the continuance of the arrangement by which certain revenues are paid in the first instance to the Caisse de la Dette. But as long as these revenues suffice to cover the interest on the Debt and to provide any sinking fund which the Powers may deem adequate, the balance ought simply to be handed over the Egyptian Government to deal with as it pleases, and the antiquated distinction of 'authorised' and 'unauthorised' expenditure should be swept away. No reform is more necessary than this, if the country is to derive the greatest possible benefit from the improved condition of its finances which has been attained by such severe privations."

The functions of the Caisse, originally limited to receiving certain assigned revenues on behalf of the bondholders, have in practice become much more extensive.

([2]) [Convention respecting Newfoundland; Declaration respecting Morocco and Egypt; Declaration respecting Siam, Madagascar, and the New Hebrides.]

Its members have claimed to control, on behalf of the Powers of Europe, the due execution by the Egyptian Government of all the complicated international Agreements regarding the finances of the country. Their assent is necessary before any new loan can be issued. No portion of the General Reserve Fund can be used without their sanction; and all assigned revenues are paid directly to them by the collecting Departments without passing through the Ministry of Finance. In the same way, the receipts of the railways, telegraphs, and port of Alexandria, administered by a Board consisting of three members—an Englishman, a Frenchman, and an Egyptian—are paid, after deduction of the expenses, into the Caisse.

The inconvenience of the arrangements which I have described has not been contested by the French Government, and they have shown themselves fully disposed to concert with us the means of bringing the system of financial administration into more close accord with the facts as they now present themselves.

The case of Morocco presents different features. The condition of that country has for a long time been unsatisfactory and fraught with danger. The authority of the Sultan over a large portion of his dominions is that of a titular Chief rather than of a Ruler. Life and property are unsafe, the natural resources of the country are undeveloped, and trade, though increasing, is hampered by the political situation.

In these respects the contrast between Morocco and Egypt is marked. In spite of well-meant efforts to assist the Sultan, but little progress has been effected, and at this moment the prospect is probably as little hopeful as it has ever been. Without the intervention of a strong and civilised Power there appears to be no probability of a real improvement in the condition of the country.

It seems not unnatural that, in these circumstances, France should regard it as falling to her lot to assume the task of attempting the regeneration of the country. Her Algerian possessions adjoin those of the Sultan throughout the length of a frontier of several hundred miles. She has been compelled from time to time to undertake military operations of considerable difficulty, and at much cost, in order to put an end to the disturbances which continually arise amongst tribes adjoining the Algerian frontier—tribes which, although nominally the subjects of the Sultan, are, in fact, almost entirely beyond his control. The trade of France with Morocco is again—if that across the Algerian frontier be included—of considerable importance, and compares not unfavourably with our own. In these circumstances, France, although in no wise desiring to annex the Sultan's dominions or to subvert his authority, seeks to extend her influence in Morocco, and is ready to submit to sacrifices and to incur responsibilities with the object of putting an end to the condition of anarchy which prevails upon the borders of Algeria.

His Majesty's Government are not prepared to assume such responsibilities, or to make such sacrifices, and they have therefore readily admitted that if any European Power is to have a predominant influence in Morocco, that Power is France. They have, on the other hand, not lost sight of the fact that Great Britain also has interests in Morocco which must be safeguarded in any arrangement to be arrived at between France and Great Britain. The first of these has reference to the facilities to be afforded to our commerce, as well as to that of other countries, in Morocco. Our imports to that country amount to a considerable percentage of the whole; and it is obvious that, given improved methods of administration, a reform of the currency, and cheaper land transport, foreign trade with Morocco should be largely increased—an increase in which British merchants would certainly look to have their share.

The rights and privileges of Great Britain in Morocco in respect of commercial affairs are regulated by the Convention of Commerce and Navigation concluded between the two countries in December 1856, and the rights of British subjects to reside or travel in the dominions of the Sultan are provided for in the general Treaty between the two countries of the same year.

The Convention entitles British subjects to trade freely in the Sultan's dominions on the same terms as natives or subjects of the most favoured nation, and stipulates that their right to buy and sell is not to be restrained or prejudiced by any monopoly, contract, or exclusive privilege, save as regards a limited number of imported articles, which are specifically mentioned.

The Treaty gives to British subjects the right of residing or travelling in the dominions of the Sultan, and further entitles the British Government to appoint Consular officers at the cities and ports in Morocco, and establishes Consular jurisdiction over British subjects, besides providing for the usual privileges in respect of the right of British subjects to hire dwellings and warehouses, and to acquire and dispose of property, for their exemption from military service and forced loans, and for the security of their persons and property.

It would have been impossible for His Majesty's Government to consent to any arrangement which did not leave these rights intact and the avenues of trade completely open to British enterprise.

A second condition which His Majesty's Government regard as essential is also readily accepted by the French Government. It has reference to certain portions of the Moorish littoral, upon which both Governments desire that no Power shall be allowed to establish itself or to erect fortifications or strategical works of any kind.

A third condition has reference to Spain. An adequate and satisfactory recognition of Spanish interests, political and territorial, has been from the first, in the view of His Majesty's Government, an essential element in any settlement of the Morocco question.

Spain has possessions on the Moorish coast, and the close proximity of the two countries has led to a reasonable expectation on the part of the Spanish Government and people that Spanish interests would receive special consideration in any arrangement affecting the future of Morocco.

His Majesty's Government have observed with satisfaction that, so far as the principle involved is concerned, the two Governments are in entire accord, and that it is the object of the French, as it is that of the British Government, to ensure that the special consideration, which both agree is due to Spain, shall be shown in respect of questions of form no less than in respect of her material interests.

The Declaration, of which a copy is attached to this despatch, embodies the terms upon which the two Governments propose to deal with the cases of Egypt and Morocco respectively.

The first, and from the point of view of Great Britain the most important, part of the Agreement which has been concluded in respect of Egypt is the recognition by the French Government of the predominant position of Great Britain in that country. They fully admit that the fulfilment of the task upon which we entered in 1883 must not be impeded by any suggestion on their part that our interest in Egypt is of a temporary character, and they undertake that, so far as they are concerned, we shall not be impeded in the performance of that task. This undertaking will enable us to pursue our work in Egypt without, so far as France is concerned, arousing international susceptibilities. It is true that the other Great Powers of Europe also enjoy, in virtue of existing arrangements, a privileged position in Egypt; but the interests of France—historical, political, and financial—so far outweigh those of the other Powers, with the exception of Great Britain, that so long as we work in harmony with France, there seems no reason to anticipate difficulty at the hands of the other Powers.

The importance of this engagement cannot be overrated. Although the attitude of the French Government in regard to Egyptian questions has been considerably modified of late years—in great measure owing to the harmonious relations which have recently prevailed between the Representatives of the two countries in Cairo—the possibility of French opposition has had, nevertheless, constantly to be taken into account; its disappearance will be an unqualified benefit to both Governments, and will greatly facilitate the progress of the task which we have undertaken in Egypt.

It has long been clear that, in the interests of all parties, it was desirable to introduce very considerable modifications in the international arrangements established in Egypt for the protection of foreign bondholders. The new Khedivial Decree annexed to the Declaration and accepted by the French Government will, if it be accepted by the other Powers concerned, have the effect of giving to the Egyptian Government a free hand in the disposal of its own resources so long as the punctual payment of interest on the Debt is assured. The Caisse de la Dette will still remain, but its functions will be strictly limited to receiving certain assigned revenues on behalf of the bondholders, and ensuring the due payment of the coupon. The Caisse will, as soon as the Decree has come into operation, have no right and no opportunity of interfering in the general administration of the country. The branches of revenue assigned to the service of the Debt have also been changed, and the land tax has been substituted for the customs duties and railway receipts. This arrangement will give the bondholders the advantage of having their rights secured on the most stable and certain branch of the Egyptian revenue, and one which shows a constant tendency to increase. On the other hand, the Egyptian Government will no longer be hampered in the administration of the customs and railways, and as a corollary, the mixed administration which has hitherto controlled the railways, telegraphs, and port of Alexandria, will disappear.

The fund derived from the economies of the conversion of 1890, which since that date has been uselessly accumulated in the coffers of the Caisse, and which now amounts to £5,500,000, will be handed over to the Egyptian Government, who will be free to employ it in whatever way most conduces to the welfare of the people.

Though we still maintain our view as to the right of the Egyptian Government to pay off the whole of their debt at any time after 1905, the French Government have strongly urged the claims of the bondholders to special consideration in view of the past history of the Egyptian Debt. In order to meet their wishes in this matter the present arrangement provides that the conversion of the Guaranteed and Privileged Debt shall be postponed till 1910 and the conversion of the Unified Debt till 1912—a postponement which confers a very material advantage on the existing bondholders, and should remove all grounds of complaint whenever the conversion is carried through.

The Decree abolishes various other provisions of the old Law which experience has shown to be unnecessary and inconvenient. It will be sufficient to mention the two most important of these. In the first place, the consent of the Caisse will no longer be necessary in the event of the Egyptian Government desiring to raise further loans for productive expenditure or for other reasons. In the second place, the plan devised in the London Convention of fixing a limit to the administrative expenditure of the Egyptian Government has been swept away. The manifold inconvenience, and even loss, to which this system has given rise in a country which is in the process of development, and where, consequently, new administrative needs are constantly making themselves felt, have been frequently pointed out by Lord Cromer.

Your Excellency will not fail to observe that the Khedivial Decree in which these measures are embodied will require the consent of Austria, Germany, Italy, and Russia before it can be promulgated by the Egyptian Government. The amount of the Egyptian Debt held in these countries is, however, quite insignificant. France and Great Britain, indeed, between them hold nearly the whole of the Debt, with the exception of the small proportion which is held in Egypt itself. In these circumstances it is reasonable to hope that no serious difficulties will be encountered in other quarters regarding proposals which are considered by the two Governments as giving entire satisfaction to the legitimate interests of the bondholders, and which those two Governments are formally pledged to support. Should, however, unexpected obstacles present themselves, we shall, in virtue of our Agreement with France, be able to count upon the support of French diplomacy in our endeavours to overcome them.

It is necessary that I should add a few words as to the other points in which the internal rights of sovereignty of the Egyptian Government are subject to international interference. These are the consequences of the system known as that of the

Capitulations. It comprises the jurisdiction of the Consular Courts and of the Mixed Tribunals, the latter applying a legislation which requires the consent of all the European Powers, and some extra-European Powers, before it can be modified. In Lord Cromer's opinion the time is not ripe for any organic changes in this direction, and His Majesty's Government have not, therefore, on the present occasion, proposed any alterations in this respect. At the same time, whenever Egypt is ready for the introduction of a legislative and judicial system similar to that which exists in other civilised countries, we have sufficient grounds for counting upon French co-operation in effecting the necessary changes.

It will be observed that an Article has been inserted in the Agreement declaring the adhesion of His Majesty's Government to the Treaty of the 29th October, 1888, providing for the neutrality of the Suez Canal in time of war. In consequence of the reservation made by Lord Salisbury at the time respecting the special situation of this country during the occupation of Egypt, some doubt existed as to the extent to which Great Britain considered herself bound by the stipulations of the Convention. It appears desirable to dissipate any possible misunderstanding by specifically declaring the adhesion of His Majesty's Government. It is, however, provided that certain executive stipulations which are incompatible with Lord Salisbury's reservation should remain in abeyance during the continuance of the occupation.

In regard to Morocco, your Excellency will find that the Convention contains the following stipulations on the part of the two Powers : the Government of the French Republic places upon record a Declaration that it has no intention of disturbing the political status of Morocco; that the rights which Great Britain enjoys in virtue of Treaties and Conventions and usage are to be respected; and that British commerce, including goods in transit through French territory and destined for the Moorish market, is to be treated on a footing of absolute equality with that of France. His Majesty's Government, on the other hand, recognises that it belongs to France to maintain order in Morocco, and to assist the Moorish Government in improving the administrative, economic, financial, and military conditions of that country.

The two Governments undertake a mutual obligation to construct no fortifications themselves, and to allow no other Power to construct fortifications on the more important portions of the Moorish sea-board.

Finally, with regard to Spain, both Governments place on record their admission that that country has exceptional interests in certain portions of Morocco, and that those interests are to be respected by both Powers alike. The French Government has undertaken to come to an understanding with that of Spain as to the mode in which effect can best be given to this stipulation, and to communicate to the Government of His Majesty the terms of the Arrangement which may be made with this object.

Your Excellency is familiar with the circumstances which confront us in the Colony of Newfoundland.

The Treaty of Utrecht (1713) by Article XIII recognised that the Island of Newfoundland should thenceforth belong wholly to Great Britain, but it gave to the French "the right to catch fish and to dry them on land on that part of the coast which stretches from Cape Bonavista to the northern point of the island, and from thence running down by the western side to Point Riche." They were not to erect any buildings there besides stages made of boards and huts necessary and usual for drying fish, or to resort to the island beyond the time necessary for fishing and drying of fish. This right was renewed and confirmed by Article V of the Treaty of Paris, 1763.

By the Treaty of Versailles, 1783, the French renounced their right of fishing from Cape Bonavista to Cape St. John on the east coast, and acquired the right to fish from Cape St. John on the east coast to Cape Ray on the west, passing by the north. This change was made in order to prevent the frequent quarrels which took place between the fishermen of the two nations. With the same object Great Britain undertook, in the Declaration of the 30th September, 1783, appended to the Treaty, that measures should be taken to prevent British subjects from interrupting in any manner, by their competition, the fishery of the French during the temporary exercise of it granted to them by the Treaties, and that fixed settlements by the British on the portion of the coast above described should be removed.

Great diversities of opinion have arisen between the two Governments as to the interpretation of these stipulations. To summarise the chief heads of the dispute, the French have contended that the Treaties give them an exclusive right of fishery on the coast mentioned, and that all British fixed settlements, of whatever nature, on the coast are contrary to the Treaties. On the other hand, the British contention has been that British subjects have the right to fish concurrently with the French, provided that they do not interrupt them, and that the fixed settlements referred to in the British Declaration of 1783 are fixed fishing settlements only, and that other fixed settlements are not contrary to the Declaration.

Periodical attempts have been made since 1844 to dispose of the various questions arising out of these differences. Negotiations for the purpose were undertaken successively in 1857, 1860, 1874, 1881, and 1885, but without success. On two occasions—in 1857 and 1885—Conventions were actually signed limiting the area within which the French rights were to be exercised, and, in return, acknowledging those rights and conceding some further privileges. These arrangements were, however, viewed with such strong disapproval by the Colonial Legislature that they were in both cases abandoned and were never ratified.

On each occasion the failure of the arrangement was succeeded by a renewed assertion of the French rights in their extremest form, and instructions were issued to the French cruisers stationed off the coast which threatened to lead to a serious rupture.

The Bait Act, which was passed by the Newfoundland Legislature in 1886, and enforced in 1887, and by which the sale of bait to French fishing vessels on all parts of the shore not affected by the Treaties was prohibited, was a fresh source of irritation, and gave rise to fresh controversies.

The French, restricted in their supply of this essential material for the pursuit of the cod-fishery, resorted in considerable numbers to the establishment of lobster fisheries on the portion of the coast reserved to them, and contested the legality of the British lobster factories which had long been established there. The British Government, on the other hand, contended, on behalf of the Colony, that the taking and preserving of lobsters were not included in the privileges conceded to French fishermen by the Treaties.

The negotiations which ensued on this question resulted in the establishment in 1890 of a *modus vivendi*, under which both parties were allowed to take part in the lobster fishery, under certain restrictions. These, however, have proved inconvenient in their practical working, and do not afford means for the necessary protection of the fishery from deterioration by excessive destruction of the lobsters.

In 1891 an Agreement was arrived at between the two Governments for referring to arbitration the questions in dispute with regard to the lobster fishery. This, again, has never been acted upon, in consequence of the refusal of the Colonial Government and Legislature to comply with the condition made by the French Government that the necessary legislation for carrying the award into effect should first be passed.

In 1901 a fresh attempt was made to effect a settlement, but the negotiation was again unsuccessful, as the Colony declined to make concessions in regard to the sale of bait unless the French system of bounties on the sale of fish by their citizens were abandoned or at least modified in important particulars.

The summary which I have given is sufficient to show how constant a source of risk and anxiety this question has been.

It was obviously our duty to find some means of terminating the condition of things which I have described. It has been fraught with inconvenience to all concerned. It has involved a constant risk of collisions between the two Governments, in consequence of disputes as to the rights of persons engaged in the fishing industry, both on shore and at sea. Such collisions have, in fact, been averted only by the tact, moderation, and good temper exhibited by the naval officers of both Powers, to whose cognisance these local disputes have in the first instance been brought.

As for the shore, no land has, up to the present time, been leased or granted on the Treaty Shore except in terms which require the lessee or grantee to comply with the stipulations of the Treaties, and with any orders by the Crown for their enforcement; so long, therefore, as any possible doubts remained as to the security of tenure on the parts of the coast affected, capitalists could not embark freely on the development of its resources. Indeed, if the French view were correct, and had been strictly enforced, it would have been impossible to develop them at all.

It is, therefore, no exaggeration to say that to the Colony the existence of these French rights throughout an extent representing some two-fifths of the whole coast-line of the island have meant the obstruction of all useful local developments as well as of mining and other industrial enterprises.

Under the Convention which has been concluded it is provided that the French rights of landing on the Treaty Shore conferred by Article XIII of the Treaty of Utrecht shall be once and for all abandoned.

For this abandonment His Majesty's Government recognise that compensation is due both to the persons actually engaged in the fishing industry and to the French nation.

The former will be obliged to remove their property from the Treaty Shore, and to give up the premises which they have there erected. For the loss thus inflicted on them, and for any loss clearly due to the compulsory abandonment of their business, compensation will be paid to individuals. A simple and expeditious form of procedure has been adopted for determining the amount of these indemnities. But irrespectively of this question of personal compensation, the French Government claim with reason that they are required to renounce on behalf of the nation a privilege which cannot be estimated merely at its present pecuniary value. On grounds, therefore, of sentiment, as well as of interest, they cannot be expected to surrender it unless they are able to show that they have secured an adequate equivalent elsewhere.

To meet this legitimate view we have offered to France at various points concessions of importance to her, but which can in our opinion be granted without detriment to British interests.

These are :—

(a.) A rectification of the Eastern frontier of the Colony of the Gambia, which will give to France an access to the navigable portion of that river.

(b.) The cession of a small group of islands known as the Iles de Los, situated opposite to Konakry. These islands are of small extent and of no intrinsic value. Their geographical position, however, connects them closely with French Guinea, and their possession by any Power other than France might become a serious menace to that Colony.

(c.) A modification of the boundary fixed between the French and British possessions in Nigeria by the Convention of the 14th June, 1898. The line then laid down has had the effect of compelling French convoys, when proceeding from the French possessions on the Niger to those in the neighbourhood of Lake Chad, to follow a circuitous and waterless route, so inconvenient that they have been obliged to obtain permission to pass by a shorter and less inconvenient way through British territory. The new boundary will bring to France an accession of territory, the importance of which is due mainly to the fact that it gives her the use of a direct route between the points which I have mentioned.

An Agreement has also been come to with the French Government in regard to the interests of the two Powers in the neighbourhood of Siam. It will be in your Excellency's recollection that by an Agreement arrived at in 1896, France and Great Britain undertook to refrain from any armed intervention, or the acquisition of special

2 B 2

privileges, in the Siamese possessions which were included within the basin of the Menam River. It was explained by my predecessor that the restriction of the undertaking thus given did not imply any doubts as to the validity of the Siamese title to those portions of her possessions which lay outside the Menam Valley. To this view His Majesty's Government adhere. The Agreement of 1896 has none the less been regarded as implying that the relations of the two Powers to Siam and to one another in respect to the regions lying to the east and to the west of the guaranteed area differed from their relations to her and to one another in respect of the central portion of the kingdom. In point of fact, British influence has for some time past prevailed in the western, and French influence in the eastern, portions of the Siamese dominions. The Agreements which have been entered into with Siam by His Majesty's Government as to the Malay Peninsula, and by the French Government as to the Mekong Valley, show that the two Powers have each on its side considered themselves at liberty to acquire a preponderating influence in those parts of the Siamese Empire.

The exercise of such influence is compatible with the absence of all idea of annexing Siamese territory, and in order that this may be made abundantly clear, both parties to the Convention have placed in on record that neither of them desire to take for themselves any portion of the possessions of the King of Siam, and that they are determined to maintain the obligations which they have incurred under existing Treaties.

These Treaties, as your Excellency is aware, entitle Great Britain to most-favoured-nation treatment in all parts of the Siamese dominions.

Advantage has been taken of this opportunity to further regularise the position of Great Britain in Zanzibar and of France in Madagascar, and the two Powers have intimated their intention of endeavouring to arrive at an arrangement for putting an end to the difficulties which have arisen in the New Hebrides in consequence of the absence of any effectual mode of settling disputes as to land titles in those islands.

In the preceding observations I have endeavoured to give some account of the reasons for which, in the opinion of His Majesty's Government, the Agreements which have been concluded are, if considered by themselves and on their intrinsic merits, believed to be desirable.

It is, however, important to regard them not merely as a series of separate transactions, but as forming part of a comprehensive scheme for the improvement of the international relations of two great countries.

From this point of view their cumulative effect can scarcely fail to be advantageous in a very high degree. They remove the sources of long-standing differences, the existence of which has been a chronic addition to our diplomatic embarrassments and a standing menace to an international friendship which we have been at much pains to cultivate, and which, we rejoice to think, has completely overshadowed the antipathies and suspicions of the past.

There is this further reason for mutual congratulation. Each of the parties has been able, without any material sacrifice of its own national interests, to make to the other concessions regarded, and rightly regarded, by the recipient as of the highest importance.

The French privilege of drying fish on the Treaty Shore of Newfoundland has, for example, been lately of but little value to the persons engaged in the industry; but the existence of that privilege may be said to have, so far as our Newfoundland colonists are concerned, sterilised a great part of the littoral of the Colony.

Similarly, in Egypt the rights accruing to the French Government under the laws of 1879, 1880, and subsequent years, have not really conferred any practical benefits either upon the French nation or upon the French holders of Egyptian securities, but the existence of those rights has been a constant hindrance in the way of Egyptian administration, and has seriously retarded the progress of the country. .

In Morocco His Majesty's Government have been able to gratify the natural aspirations of France, and have willingly conceded to her a privileged position, which, owing to her geographical situation, she is specially competent to occupy; but they have done this upon conditions which secure for our commerce an absolute equality of opportunity, which guarantee the neutrality of the most important portions of its sea-board, and which provide for the due recognition of Spanish requirements, which they have from the first desired to see treated with due respect.

In Siam, again, they have admitted the preponderance of France within an area over which she has, in fact, of late years, exercised a preponderating influence, and with which they have neither the desire nor the opportunity to interfere. They have, on the other hand, obtained the recognition of a corresponding British preponderance at points where they could not have tolerated the interference of another Power, and where the influence of this country has in fact already been established with the best results.

For these reasons it is fair to say that, as between Great Britain and France, the arrangement, taken as a whole, will be to the advantage of both parties.

Nor will it, we believe, be found less advantageous if it be regarded from the point of view of the relations of the two Powers with the Governments of Egypt, Morocco, and Siam. In each of these countries it is obviously desirable to put an end to a system under which the Ruler has had to shape his course in deference to the divided counsels of two great European Powers. Such a system, leading, as it must, to intrigue, to attempts to play one Power off against the other, and to undignified competition, can scarcely fail to sow the seeds of international discord, and to bring about a state of things disadvantageous and demoralising alike to the tutelary Powers, and to the weaker State which forms the object of their solicitude. Something will have been gained if the understanding happily arrived at between Great Britain and France should have the effect of bringing this condition of things to an end in regions where the interests of those two Powers are specially involved. And it may, perhaps, be permitted to them to hope that, in thus basing the composition of longstanding differences upon mutual concessions, and in the frank recognition of each other's legitimate wants and aspirations, they may have afforded a precedent which will contribute something to the maintenance of international goodwill and the preservation of the general peace.

I am, &c.
LANSDOWNE.

[*ED. NOTE.*—The English text of the Conventions concerning Newfoundland, and Egypt and Morocco, respectively, signed at London, the 8th April, 1904, is given in *B.F.S.P.*, XCVII, pp. 31–36 and in *Accounts and Papers*, 1904 (*Cd.* 1952), CX, 313. The text of supplementary assurances contained in an exchange of notes was published in February 1905, *Accounts and Papers*, 1905 (*Cd.* 2384, pp. 18–9), CIII, 265.]

No. 417.

[The texts of the Convention and Declarations of the 8th April, 1904, were drafted, after the preliminary negotiations, in the following way :—

1. The British Foreign Office (in consultation with Lord Cromer and Sir Eldon Gorst) prepared a series of drafts in December–February 1904. These were reprinted in the form shown here on the 14th–16th March.
2. M. Cambon presented the French drafts to Lord Lansdowne on the 21st March. Lord Lansdowne made a number of suggestions for amendments.
3. M. Cambon presented revised drafts on the 29th–30th March, embodying some of Lord Lansdowne's amendments. Other suggestions for amendments were then discussed.
4. The final text was agreed on the 6th April, and the treaties signed on the 8th April.]

[*ED. NOTE.*—The use of italics in the drafts indicates wording identical with that of the final text.]

Convention between the United Kingdom and France respecting Newfoundland, and West and Central Africa. Signed at London, April 8, 1904.([1a])

[Ratifications exchanged at London, December 8, 1904.]

BRITISH DRAFT OF MARCH 16, 1904.	FRENCH DRAFT OF MARCH 21, 1904.	FINAL TEXT.
	Le Président de la République Française et Sa Majesté le Roi	His Majesty the King of the United Kingdom of Great Britain and Ireland and of the British Dominions beyond the Seas, Emperor of India, and the President of the French Republic, having resolved to put an end, by a friendly Arrangement, to the difficulties which have arisen in Newfoundland, have decided to conclude a Convention to that effect, and have named as their respective Plenipotentiaries:
	ayant résolu de mettre fin par un Arrangement amiable aux difficultés survenues à Terre-Neuve *du fait que les dispositions des anciens Traités y confèrent aux Français un Privilège qui rend impossible la mise en valeur d'une partie des côtes de l'île, dont la population depuis le Traité d'Utrecht est passée de 5,000 à 210,000 habitants,* ([1]) *ont nommé pour leurs Plénipotentiaires:*	
		His Majesty the King of the United Kingdom of Great Britain and Ireland and of the British Dominions beyond the Seas, Emperor of India, the Most Honourable Henry Charles Keith Petty - Fitzmaurice, Marquess of Lansdowne, His Majesty's Principal Secretary of State for Foreign Affairs; and The President of the French Republic, His Excellency Monsieur Paul Cambon, Ambassador of the French Republic at the Court of His Majesty the King of the United Kingdom of Great Britain and Ireland and of the British Dominions beyond the Seas, Emperor of India; Who, after having communicated to each other

([1a]) [Presented to both Houses of Parliament in February 1905, *Accounts and Papers*, 1905 (*Cd.* 2383), CIII, 241.]

([1]) [The French version of the 30th March was identical with that of the 21st March, except that the section marked * . . . . * was omitted.]

BRITISH DRAFT OF MARCH 16, 1904.	FRENCH DRAFT OF MARCH 21, 1904.	FINAL TEXT.

their full powers, found in good and due form, have agreed as follows, subject to the approval of their respective Parliaments :—

Article I.

The liberty accorded to French citizens by Article XIII of the Treaty of Utrecht to take fish in common with British subjects on the coast of Newfoundland from Cape St. John by the north to Cape Ray, during the usual fishery season ending on the 20th October of each year, shall remain undisturbed ; but in the exercise of their fishery, British subjects and French citizens shall be subject alike to the laws and regulations now in force, or which may hereafter be passed for the establishment of a close time in regard to any particular kind of fish or for the preservation or improvement of the fisheries. Notice of any fresh laws or regulations for this purpose shall be given to the French Government three months before they come into operation.

Article II.

The joint fishery on this proportion of the coast shall be regulated and policed in the manner provided in Articles XIV to XXXVIII of the North Sea Fisheries Convention of 1882, and the provisions of the Convention of 1887 respecting the Liquor Traffic in the North Sea shall also apply to the said fishery.

Article Ier.

La France renonce au privilège de faire sécher le poisson sur la partie de la côte de Terre-Neuve comprise entre le Cap Saint-Jean et le Cap Raye.(²)

Article I.

France renounces the privileges established to her advantage by Article XIII of the Treaty of Utrecht, and confirmed or modified by subsequent provisions.

(²) [In the French draft of the 30th March, the text of this clause is identical with the final text up to the word " Utrecht." The rest of the clause was added by Lord Lansdowne.]

BRITISH DRAFT OF MARCH 16, 1904.	FRENCH DRAFT OF MARCH 21, 1904.	FINAL TEXT.
Article III.	**Article II.**	**Article II.**

Article III.

French citizens shall not hereafter have any right to land at any part of the aforesaid coast for the purpose of drying their fish or for other purposes. *They may,* however, *enter any port or harbour on the said coast* for the purpose of purchasing *supplies* or for *shelter, subject* always *to the local laws* and *regulations* affecting such port or harbour.

They shall be free to *fish at the mouths of rivers* on the aforesaid coast up to a straight line drawn between the two opposite headlands where the river enters the sea, but no further.

They shall not make use of stake-nets or fixed nets for the purpose of fishery.

Article II.

La France conserve(³)

le *droit de péche dans les eaux territoriales* du rivage ainsi déterminé.

Les Français pourront donc y pécher toute espèce de poisson, y compris la boëtte, ainsi que les crustacés. Ils pourront entrer dans tout port ou havre de cette côte pour *s'y procurer des approvisionnements,* ou pour *s'y abriter, en restant soumis aux Règlements locaux en vigueur. Ils pourront aussi pécher à l'embouchure des rivières, sans toutefois pouvoir dépasser une ligne droite qui serait tirée de l'un à l'autre des points extrémes du rivage entre lesquels* la (³) *rivière se jette dans la mer.*

Article II.

France retains for her citizens, on a footing of equality with British subjects, the right of fishing in the territorial waters on that portion of the coast of Newfoundland comprised between Cape St. John and Cape Ray, passing by the north*; this right shall be exercised during the usual fishing season closing for all persons on the 20th October of each year.

The French may therefore fish there for every kind of fish, including bait and also shell fish. They may enter any port or harbour on the said coast and may there obtain supplies or bait and shelter* on the same conditions as the inhabitants of Newfoundland, but they will remain subject to the local Regulations in force; they may also fish at the mouths of the rivers, but without going beyond a straight line drawn between the two extremities of the banks, where the river enters the sea.

They shall not make use* of stake-nets or fixed engines without permission of the local authorities.

On the above-mentioned portion of the coast, British subjects and French citizens shall be subject alike to the laws and Regulations now in force, or which may hereafter be passed for the establishment of a close time in regard to any par-

(³) [The French draft of the 30th March has here " pour ses ressortissants, sur le pied d'égalité avec les sujets Anglais," as in the final text. This draft is identical with the final text throughout this article, except that it lacks the phrase " en passant par le nord " in the first paragraph indicated by *; has " ou pour s'y abriter " in the second paragraph after " Terre-Neuve " (instead of " et pour s'y abriter " in the final position); has " de ' seines ' et " before " d'engins fixes à terre " in the third paragraph.]

BRITISH DRAFT OF MARCH 16, 1904.	FRENCH DRAFT OF MARCH 21, 1904.	FINAL TEXT.
		ticular kind of fish, or for the improvement of the fisheries. Notice of any fresh laws or Regulations shall be given to the Government of the French Republic three months before they come into operation.
		The policing of the fishing on the above-mentioned portion of the coast, and for prevention of illicit liquor traffic and smuggling of spirits, shall form the subject of Regulations drawn up in agreement by the two Governments.

Article III.

| [No such clause.] | Les Français pourront achêter la boëtte dans toute l'Ile de Terre-Neuve dans les mêmes conditions que les indigènes.([4]) | [No such clause.] |

Article IV.	**Article IV.**	**Article III.**
From and after the of the French citizens now engaged in the fishery on the Treaty Coast shall surrender all their buildings and appurtenances other than boats, nets, or other movable fishing gear or stores for their own use or for use in the fishery, and His Majesty's Government shall pay to the Government of France, for payment to the owners of such establishments, the value of such buildings and appurtenances so surrendered as assessed	*Une indemnité pécuniaire sera allouée*([5]) aux pêcheurs Français *qui seront obligés de renoncer à leur industrie* ou de la modifier par suite des dispositions de la présente Convention.	A pecuniary indemnity shall be awarded by His Britannic Majesty's Government to the French citizens engaged in fishing or the preparation of fish on the "Treaty Shore," who are obliged, either to abandon the establishments they possess there, or to give up their occupation, in consequence of the modification introduced by the present Convention into the existing state of affairs.
		This indemnity cannot be claimed by the parties in-

([4]) [This appeared again in the French version of the 30th March, but was marked by Lord Lansdowne for omission. *V.* Lansdowne to Monson, No. 160, Secret, of the 31st March, 1904, *supra* p. 359.]

([5]) [The French version of the 30th March is virtually identical with the final text in the first paragraph (the term " French Shore " is used instead of " Treaty Shore ").

The second paragraph ran : " Cette indemnité s'étendra aux marins et employés à un titre quelconque à bord des navires ou dans les établissements de pêche ou homarderies susvisés." The final text was proposed by Lord Lansdowne on the 31st March.

The third paragraph ran : " La Cour de La Haye statuera tant sur la recevabilité des demandes que sur le montant desdites indemnités; les détails réglant la constitution du Tribunal et les conditions des enquêtes à ouvrir pour mettre les demandes en état feront l'objet d'un arrangement spécial entre les deux Gouvernements."]

BRITISH DRAFT OF MARCH 16, 1904.	FRENCH DRAFT OF MARCH 21, 1904.	FINAL TEXT.

by the British and French naval officers commanding on the Newfoundland Fisheries Station.

If the said naval officers should be unable to agree upon the amount of compensation to be awarded in any case, the question shall be referred to the two Governments, and submitted by them, if necessary, to The Hague Tribunal.

terested unless they have been engaged in their business prior to the closing of the fishing season of 1903.

Claims for indemnity shall be submitted to an Arbitral Tribunal, composed of an officer of each nation, and, in the event of disagreement, of an Umpire appointed in accordance with the procedure laid down by Article XXXII of The Hague Convention. The details regulating the constitution of the Tribunal and the conditions of the enquiries to be instituted for the purpose of substantiating the claims, shall form the subject of a special Agreement between the two Governments.

Article V.

The British Government shall have the right of appointing a Consul to reside at St. Pierre, and the French Government shall reciprocally have the right of appointing a Consular Officer to reside at St. John's, Newfoundland.([6])

[No such clause.]

[No such clause.]

[No such clause.]

Article V.

Article IV.

Le Gouvernement Britannique, reconnaissant qu'en outre de l'indemnité dont il est parlé à l'Article précédent, une compensation territoriale est due à la France pour l'abandon de son privilège sur la partie de l'Île de Terre-Neuve visée à l'Article I, convient avec le Gouvernement de la République des dispositions qui font l'objet des Articles suivants([7]):—

His Britannic Majesty's Government, recognising that, in addition to the indemnity referred to in the preceding Article, some territorial compensation is due to France in return for the surrender of her privilege in that part of the Island of Newfoundland referred to in Article II, agree with the Government of the French Republic to the provisions embodied in the following Articles:—

([6]) [N.B.—Notes were exchanged on the 8th April, 1904, agreeing to the Mutual Appointment of Consuls at St. John's, Newfoundland, and St. Pierre, on the Signature of the Convention and Declaration of the 8th April, 1904. The text is in *B.F.S.P.*, XCIX, 962–3.]

([7]) [The French version of the 30th March is identical with that of the 21st March.]

379

BRITISH DRAFT OF MARCH 16, 1904.	FRENCH DRAFT OF MARCH 21, 1904.	FINAL TEXT.
Article VII.	**Article VI.**	**Article V.**

Article VII.

Subject to the assent of the British Parliament, the boundary between the British and French possessions on the Gambia, as laid down in the arrangement of the 10th August, 1889, shall be readjusted so as to include Yarbutenda in French territory.

Article VI.

La frontière existant entre la Sénégambie et la Colonie Anglaise de la Gambie sera modifiée de manière à assurer à la France la possession de Yarboutenda et de ses abords et dépendances.

Au cas où la navigation maritime ne pourrait s'exercer jusque-là, un accès sera assuré en aval au Gouvernement Français sur un point de la Rivière Gambie qui sera reconnu d'un commun accord comme étant accessible en toute saison aux bâtiments de haute mer.

Les conditions dans lesquelles seront réglés le transit sur la Rivière Gambie et ses affluents, ainsi que le mode d'accès au point qui viendrait à être réservé à la France, en exécution du paragraphe précédent, feront l'objet d'arrangements à concerter entre les deux Gouvernements.

Il est, dans tous les cas, entendu que ces conditions seront au moins aussi favorables que celle du régime institué dans la partie Anglaise du Bassin du Niger et notamment par application de l'Acte Général de la Conférence Africaine du 26 Février, 1885, et de la Convention Franco-Anglaise du 14 Juin, 1898. ([8])

Article V.

The present frontier between Senegambia and the English Colony of the Gambia shall be modified so as to give to France Yarbutenda and the lands and landing-places belonging to that locality.

In the event of the river not being open to maritime navigation up to that point, access shall be assured to the French Government at a point lower down on the River Gambia, which shall be recognised by mutual agreement as being accessible to merchant ships engaged in maritime navigation.

The conditions which shall govern transit on the River Gambia and its tributaries, as well as the method of access to the point that may be reserved to France in accordance with the preceding paragraph, shall form the subject of future agreement between the two Governments.

In any case, it is understood that these conditions shall be at least as favourable as those of the system instituted by application of the General Act of the African Conference of the 26th February, 1885, and of the Anglo-French Convention of the 14th June, 1898. to the English portion of the basin of the Niger.

([8]) [The French version of the 30th March is identical with that of the 21st March, with the following modification :—

The second paragraph ended with the words " accessible aux bâtiments marchands de haute mer." The final phrase was suggested by Lord Lansdowne on the 30th–31st March.

The fourth paragraph had the following phrase (instead of " dans la partie Anglaise du Bassin du Niger ") " ou à instituer dans la partie Anglaise du Bassin du Niger, et notamment." It was marked for omission by Lord Lansdowne, and the final phrase of the paragraph added.

In his annotation of the 31st March, Lord Lansdowne proposed to preface the Article by the words " Sous réserve de l'approbation du Parlement Britannique." This was not adopted.]

BRITISH DRAFT OF MARCH 16, 1904.	FRENCH DRAFT OF MARCH 21, 1904.	FINAL TEXT.
Article VI.	**Article VII.**	**Article VI.**
Subject to the assent of the British Parliament, the Isle de Los shall be assigned to France.	*Le groupe désigné sous le nom d'Iles de Los, et situé en face de Konakry, est cédé par le Gouvernement Britannique à la France* (⁹).	The group known as the Iles de Los, and situated opposite Konakry, is ceded by His Britannic Majesty to France.
Article IX.		**Article VII.**
The French Government will allow to all persons natives of the British territories ceded to France by Articles VI and VII of this Convention the right of opting for British nationality by means of a declaration made by themselves, and, in the case of children under age, by their parents or guardians, which must be sent in before the	[No such clause (¹⁰).]	Persons born in the territories ceded to France by Articles V and VI of the present Convention may retain British nationality by means of an individual declaration to that effect, to be made before the proper authorities by themselves, or, in the case of children under age, by their parents or guardians.
All persons natives of the British territories thus ceded, and their children born before the date of the signature of the present Agreement, are free from the obligation of service in the military and naval forces of France.		The period within which the declaration of option referred to in the preceding paragraph must be made shall be one year, dating from the day on which French authority shall be established over the territory in which the persons in question have been born.
Native laws and customs now existing will, as far as possible, remain undisturbed.		Native laws and customs now existing will, as far as possible, remain undisturbed.
The French Government binds itself not to increase the Customs Tariff at present in force in the territories thus ceded until the		In the Iles de Los, for a period of thirty years from the date of exchange of the ratifications of the present Convention, British fishermen shall enjoy the same rights as French fishermen with regard to anchorage in all weathers, to taking in provisions and water, to
All rights of property which private persons or existing Corporations have acquired in the ceded terri-		

(⁹) [The French version of the 30th March is identical with that of the 21st March. Lord Lansdowne proposed to add at the beginning " sous réserve de l'approbation du Parlement Britannique."]

(¹⁰) [In the French version of the 30th March this Article appears in a form virtually identical with the final text.

In the first and second paragraphs " domiciliées " is used instead of " nées."

After " tuteurs " at the end of the first paragraph there was added the following sentence marked for omission by Lord Lansdowne : " Mais, dans ce cas, le Gouvernement Français se réserve la faculté d'exiger qu'elles transportent leur résidence hors du territoire Français."]

BRITISH DRAFT OF MARCH 16, 1904.	FRENCH DRAFT OF MARCH 21, 1904.	FINAL TEXT.

tories in connection with the British Government are maintained ; obligations resulting from them are transferred to the French Republic.

The rights of British fishermen with regard to *anchorage in all weathers, to taking in provisions and water, to making repairs, to transhipment of goods, to the sale of fish and to the landing and drying of nets* remain undisturbed.

making repairs, to transhipment of goods, to the sale of fish, and to the landing and drying of nets, provided always that they observe the conditions laid down in the French Laws and Regulations which may be in force there.

Article VIII.

To the east of the Niger the frontier separating the British and French possessions shall follow the line laid down in Article IV of the Convention of the 14th June, 1898, until, on the circumference of the circle drawn with a radius of 100 miles from the centre of the town of Sokoto, it reaches a point 5 kilom. to the southward of the intersection of the road from Maiatikwara through Doguncluchi to Matamkari with the circumference of the same circle.

Article VIII.

A l'est du Niger, et sous réserve des modifications que pourront y comporter les stipulations insérées au dernier paragraphe du présent Article, le tracé suivant sera substitué à la délimitation établie entre les possessions Françaises et Anglaises par la Convention du 14 Juin, 1898 :

Partant du point sur la rive gauche du Niger indiqué à l'Article III de la Convention du 14 Juin, 1898, c'est-à-dire, la ligne médiane du Dallul-Maouri, la frontière suivra cette ligne médiane jusqu'à sa rencontre avec la circonférence d'un cercle décrit du centre de la ville de Sokoto avec un rayon de 160,932 mètres (100 milles). De ce point, elle suivra l'arc septentrional de ce cercle jusqu'à un point situé à 5 kilomètres au sud du point d'intersection avec ledit arc de cercle de la route de Dosso à Matankari par Maouérédé.

Article VIII.

To the east of the Niger the following line shall be substituted for the boundary fixed between the French and British possessions by the Convention of the 14th June, 1898, subject to the modifications which may result from the stipulations introduced in the sixth and seventh paragraphs of the present Article.

Starting from the point on the left bank of the Niger laid down in Article III of the Convention of the 14th June, 1898, that is to say, the median line of the Dallul Mauri, the frontier shall be drawn along this median line until it meets the circumference of a circle drawn from the town of Sokoto as a centre, with a radius of 160,932 mètres (100 miles). Thence it shall follow the northern arc of this circle to a point situated 5 kilomètres south of the point of intersection of the above-mentioned arc of the circle with the route from Dosso to Matankari viâ Maourédé.

From this point the frontier *shall be drawn in a direct line to a point 20 kilom. due north of Kouni,*

Elle gagnera de là, en ligne droite, un point situé à 20 kilomètres au nord de Birni-Kouni, puis un point situé à

Thence it shall be drawn in a direct line to a point 20 kilomètres north of Konni (Birni-N'Kouni), and

BRITISH DRAFT OF MARCH 16, 1904.	FRENCH DRAFT OF MARCH 21, 1904.	FINAL TEXT.
thence *in a direct line to a point 15 kilom.* due *south of Maradi, and thence in a direct* line to the point where the *meridian passing 70 miles to the east of the second intersection of* the arc of the above-mentioned circle with *the 14th parallel of north latitude* intersects the parallel of 13° 20' north latitude. Thence it shall follow *the parallel 13° 20' north latitude until it strikes the left bank of the River Waubé (Ouobé)*, which bank *it will then follow to the shore of Lake Chad ; but, if before meeting this river, it attains a distance of 5 kilom. from the caravan route from Zinder to Yo, through Sua Kololua (Soua Kololoua), Abeber, and Kabi, the boundary shall then be traced at a distance of 5 kilom. from,* and *to the south of, this route until it strikes the left bank of the River Waubé* (Ouobé), which bank it shall then follow to the shore of Lake Chad as before.	*15 kilomètres au sud de Maradi, et rejoindra ensuite directement* le point *d'intersection du parallèle 13° 20' de latitude nord avec un méridien passant à 70 milles à l'est de* l'intersection *du 14e degré de latitude nord avec l'arc septentrional du cercle précité.* *De là, la frontière suivra, vers l'est, le parallèle 13° 20' de latitude nord jusqu'à* un point situé à 5 kilomètres en deçà de l'intersection de ce parallèle avec la route venant de Zinder et passant par Adeber et Kabi. Du point susdit, la frontière rejoindra le thalweg de la Rivière Komadougou, en se tenant à une distance de 5 kilomètres en deçà de la route précitée et de la périphérie des localités habitées.	then in a direct line to a 15 kilomètres south of Maradi, and thence shall be continued in a direct line to the point of intersection of the parallel 13ᶜ 20' north latitude with a meridian passing 70 miles to the east of the second intersection of the 14th degree of north latitude and the northern arc of the above-mentioned circle. Thence the frontier shall follow in an easterly direction the parallel of 13° 20' north latitude until it strikes the left bank of the River Komadugu Waubé (Komadougou Ouobé), the thalweg of which it will then follow to Lake Chad. But, if before meeting this river the frontier attains a distance of 5 kilometres from the caravan route from Zinder to Yo, through Sua Kolulua (Soua Kololoua), Adeber, and Kabi, the boundary shall then be traced at a distance of 5 kilometres to the south of this route until it strikes the left bank of the River Komadugu Waubé (Komadougou Ouobé), it being nevertheless understood that, if the boundary thus drawn should happen to pass through a village, this village, with its lands, shall be assigned to the Government to which would fall the larger portion of the village and its lands. The boundary will then, as before, follow the thalweg of the said river to Lake Chad.
From the point where it meets the shore of the lake the boundary shall be drawn due east as far as its *intersection with the meridian* passing *35' east of the centre of the town of Kuka,* and then along this meridian	Elle suivra ensuite le thalweg de la Rivière Komadougou jusqu'à Lac Tchad, et enfin *le degré de latitude passant par le thalweg de l'embouchure de la dite rivière jusqu'à son intersection avec le méridien pas-*	Thence it will follow the degree of latitude passing through the thalweg of the mouth of the said river up to its intersection with the meridian running 35' east of the centre of the town of Kouka, and will then follow

BRITISH DRAFT OF MARCH 16, 1904.	FRENCH DRAFT OF MARCH 21, 1904.	FINAL TEXT.
until it intersects the southern shore of the lake.	*sant à 35' est du centre de la ville de Kouka, puis ce méridien vers le sud jusqu'à son intersection sur la rive sud du Lac Tchad.*	this meridian southwards until it intersects the southern shore of Lake Chad.
It is agreed, however, that, when the Commissioners of the two Governments at present engaged in delimiting the line laid down in Article IV of the Convention of the 14th June, 1898, return home and can be consulted, the two Governments will be prepared to consider any diversions of the frontier line now agreed upon which may seem desirable for the purpose of delineating the line of demarcation with greater accuracy. In order to avoid the inconvenience to either party by interference with well-recognised and established tribal limits, it is agreed that in those portions of the line where the frontier is not determined by the trade routes, regard shall be had to the actual political divisions of the territories so that the tribes belonging to the Sultanates of Tessaoua–Maradi and Zinder shall, as far as possible, be left to France, and those belonging to the Sultanates of the British zone shall be left to Great Britain.	*Afin d'éviter les inconvénients qui pourraient résulter de part et d'autre d'un tracé qui s'écarterait des frontières reconnues et bien constatées, il est convenu que, dans la partie du tracé où la frontière n'est pas déterminée par les routes commerciales, il sera tenu compte des divisions politiques actuelles des territoires, de façon à ce que les tribus relevant des territoires de Tessaoua–Maradi et Zinder soient, autant que possible, laissées à la France, et celles relevant des Sultanats de la zone Anglaise soient, autant que possible, laissées à l'Angleterre.*	It is agreed, however, that, when the Commissioners of the two Governments at present engaged in delimiting the line laid down in Article IV of the Convention of the 14th June, 1898, return home and can be consulted, the two Governments will be prepared to consider any modifications of the above frontier line which may seem desirable for the purpose of determining the line of demarcation with greater accuracy. In order to avoid the inconvenience to either party which might result from the adoption of a line deviating from recognised and well-established frontiers, it is agreed that in those portions of the projected line where the frontier is not determined by the trade routes, regard shall be had to the present political divisions of the territories so that the tribes belonging to the territories of Tessaoua–Maradi and Zinder shall, as far as possible, be left to France, and those belonging to the territories of the British zone shall, as far as possible, be left to Great Britain.
The two Governments will also be prepared to consider any alteration of the frontier lines in Lake Chad which may be required in order to give the French access by water from their possessions on the north to their possessions on the south of the Lake.	*Il est en outre entendu que, sur le Tchad, la limite sera, s'il est besoin, modifiée de manière à assurer à la France, par eau libre entre les parties inférieure et supérieure du Lac, une communication tout au moins proportionnelle à la répartition de la nappe d'eau tracée sur la carte formant l'Annexe No. de la Convention du 14 Juin, 1898.*[11]	It is further agreed that, on Lake Chad, the frontier line shall, if necessary, be modified so as to assure to France a communication through open water at all seasons between her possessions on the north-west and those on the south-east of the Lake, and a portion of the surface of the open waters of the Lake at least

[11] [The French version of the Article in the draft of the 30th March is identical with the final text, except that in the fourth paragraph the phrase " et de la périphérie des localités habitées situées sur la dite route " appeared in the same position as in the draft of the 21st March. Also at the end of the fifth paragraph the word " sultanats " is used instead of " territoires."]

BRITISH DRAFT OF MARCH 16, 1904.	FRENCH DRAFT OF MARCH 21, 1904.	FINAL TEXT.

proportionate to that assigned to her by the map forming Annex 2 of the Convention of the 14th June, 1898.

In that portion of the River Komadugu which is common to both parties, the populations on the banks shall have equal rights of fishing.

Article IX.

La présente Convention sera ratifiée et les ratifications seront échangées à dans le délai de six mois,([12]) *et plutôt si faire se peut.*

Article IX.

The present Convention shall be ratified, and the ratifications shall be exchanged, at London, within eight months, or earlier if possible.

In witness whereof his Excellency the Ambassador of the French Republic at the Court of His Majesty the King of the United Kingdom of Great Britain and Ireland and of the British Dominions beyond the Seas, Emperor of India, and His Majesty's Principal Secretary of State for Foreign Affairs duly authorised for that purpose, have signed the present Convention and have affixed thereto their seals.

Fait à , en double exemplaire, *ie*

Done at London, in duplicate, the 8th day of April, 1904.

(L.S.) LANSDOWNE. (L.S.) PAUL CAMBON.([12a])

([12]) [The French version of the 30th March has " six mois " also.]

([12a]) [In the original Treaty, preserved at London, the English and French texts are placed in parallel columns, the English on the left and the French on the right. Lord Lansdowne's signature is beneath the former, and M. Cambon's beneath the latter.

The French text is given on pp. 402–7.]

Declaration between the United Kingdom and France respecting Egypt and Morocco. Signed at London, April 8, 1904.([13])

BRITISH DRAFT OF MARCH 14, 1904.	FRENCH DRAFT OF MARCH 21, 1904.	FINAL TEXT.
Article I (Egypt).	**Article I.**	**Article I.**

The Government of the French Republic undertake *not to obstruct the action of Great Britain in* Egypt, and recognise that the British occupation of Egypt, which was originally intended to be temporary, has under the force of circumstances acquired a character of permanency, and they are willing that the period of its duration should be left entirely to the discretion of His Majesty's Government.

Le Gouvernement Britannique *déclare qu'il n'a pas l'intention de changer l'état politique de l'Égypte.*

De son côté, le Gouvernement Français *déclare qu'il n'entravera pas l'action de Angleterre dans ce pays*([14]) *et qu'il donne son adhésion aux dispositions du projet de Décret Khédivial annexé au présent Arrangement,* sous les conditions suivantes qu'exige la sauvegarde de ses droits et de ses intérêts :

(a.) . . . [details follow] . . .

His Britannic Majesty's Government declare that they have no intention of altering the political status of Egypt.

The Government of the French Republic, for their part, declare that they will not obstruct the action of Great Britain in that country by asking that a limit of time be fixed for the British occupation or in any other manner, and that they give their assent to the draft Khedivial Decree annexed to the present Arrangement, containing the guarantees considered necessary for the protection of the interests of the Egyptian bondholders, on the condition that, after its promulgation, it cannot be modified in any way without the consent of the Powers Signatory of the Convention of London of 1885.

Article II (Egypt).

The Government of the French Republic further recognise that, under the altered condition of affairs, the arrangements made for the *protection of the Egyptian bondholders* require modification, and they agree to the proposals embodied in the draft Khedivial Decree annexed to the present Convention.

(b.) See pp. 389–90.

([13]) [This Declaration was published in *Accounts and Papers*, 1904 (*Cd.* 1952), CX, pp. 323–4, but the Secret Articles were only presented to both Houses of Parliament in November 1911, *Accounts and Papers*, 1911 (*Cd.* 5969), CIII, pp. 353–60. The annexes published in *Cd.* 1952 allude to the Khedivial Decree.]

([14]) [The French draft of the 29th March added here " par la demande de fixer un terme à l'occupation Britannique." This Lord Lansdowne marked " to be omitted," adding instead above, after the word " déclare," the following sentence " qu'il ne demandera pas qu'un terme soit fixé à l'occupation Britannique."

The rest of the draft of 29th March was identical with the final text except that it lacked the closing phrase " Signataires de la Convention de Londres." This was added by Lord Lansdowne.]

2 c

BRITISH DRAFT OF MARCH 14, 1904.	FRENCH DRAFT OF MARCH 21, 1904.	FINAL TEXT.
	(c.) *Il est convenu que la Direction Générale des Antiquités en Égypte continuera d'être confiée à un savant Français,*([15]) *choisi par le Gouvernement Égyptien, d'accord avec le Gouvernement de la République.*	It is agreed that the post of Director-General of Antiquities in Egypt shall continue, as in the past, to be entrusted to a French *savant.*
	(d.) *Les écoles Françaises en Égypte* ([16]) *jouiront, comme par le passé, d'une entière liberté et ne seront l'objet d'aucune mesure qui serait de nature à entraver leur fonctionnement normal.*	The French schools in Egypt shall continue to enjoy the same liberty as in the past.

Article X (Egypt).

The Government of the French Republic will support His Majesty's Government in endeavouring to obtain from the Sultan a modification of the existing Firmans in the sense of removing the Sultan's right of veto on the borrowing powers of the Egyptian Government.([17])

[No such clause.]

[No such clause.]

Article I (Morocco).	Article II.	Article II.
	Le Gouvernement de la République déclare qu'il n'a pas l'intention de changer l'état politique du Maroc.	The Government of the French Republic declare that they have no intention of altering the political status of Morocco.
The Government of His Britannic Majesty recognises that France, as having a frontier of great extent coterminous with that of Morocco, has a special interest in maintaining	*De son côté, le Gouvernement Britannique reconnaît qu'il appartient,* exclusivement([18]) *à la France, notamment, comme Puissance limitrophe du Maroc, sur une vaste étendue, de* main-	His Britannic Majesty's Government, for their part, recognise that it appertains to France, more particularly as a Power whose dominions are conterminous for a great distance with those of

([15]) [Lord Lansdowne suggested on the 22nd March omission of rest of paragraph; and this was adopted in French draft of the 29th March.]

([16]) [Lord Lansdowne suggested on the 22nd March emendation to final form; adopted in French draft of the 29th March.]

([17]) [No corresponding article appeared in M. Cambon's draft of the 21st March. Lord Lansdowne proposed that it should be added to it, as Section I A. It was not however embodied in the French version of the 29th March, *cf.* Cromer's telegram of the 31st March (*v. supra* p. 358).]

([18]) [Lord Lansdowne proposed on the 22nd March the omission of " exclusivement." It was retained in the French draft of the 29th March. Lord Lansdowne then proposed to substitute " spécialement."]

BRITISH DRAFT OF MARCH 14, 1904.	FRENCH DRAFT OF MARCH 21, 1904.	FINAL TEXT.
peace within that country and in assisting to bring about the *administrative, economical, financial and military reforms* of which it stands in need.	tenir (*veiller à*) *la tranquillité dans ce pays, et de lui prêter son assistance pour toutes les réformes administratives, économiques, financières, et militaires dont il a besoin.*	Morocco, to preserve order in that country, and to provide assistance for the purpose of all administrative, economic, financial, and military reforms which it may require.
It engages *not to obstruct* or oppose *the action* which may be *taken by* the French Government for these objects within the limits and subject to the conditions specified in the present Agreement.	*Il déclare qu'il n'entravera pas l'action de la France à cet effet, sous la réserve que cette action laissera* (19) *intactes les* dispositions du Traité Anglo-Marocain du 9 Septembre 1856, de la Convention Commerciale du même jour, et ne gênera point l'exercice du *droit de cabotage entre les ports Marocains dont* jouissent *les navires Anglais depuis 1901.*	They declare that they will not obstruct the action taken by France for this purpose, provided that such action shall leave intact the rights which Great Britain, in virtue of Treaties, Conventions, and usage, enjoys in Morocco, including the right of coasting trade between the ports of Morocco, enjoyed by British vessels since 1901.

	Article III.	**Article III.**
[See end of Article II (Morocco), p. 388.]	*Le Gouvernement Britannique, de son côté, respectera les droits dont, en vertu des Traités, Conventions, et usages* (20), *la France jouit en Égypte, y compris le droit de cabotage accordé aux navires Français entre les ports Égyptiens.*	His Britannic Majesty's Government, for their part, will respect the rights which France, in virtue of Treaties, Conventions, and usage, enjoys in Egypt. including the right of coasting trade between Egyptian ports accorded to French vessels.

Article VIII (Egypt).	**Article IV.**	**Article IV.**
His Majesty's Government undertake that differential duties shall not be imposed in Egypt, and that the principle of commercial liberty shall be maintained there.	*Les deux Gouvernements, également attachés au principe de la liberté commerciale tant en Égypte qu'au Maroc, déclarent qu'ils ne s'y prêteront à aucune inégalité, pas plus dans l'établissement des droits de douanes, dans les ports,* (21) *que dans l'éta-*	The two Governments, being equally attached to the principle of commercial liberty both in Egypt and Morocco, declare that they will not, in those countries, countenance any inequality either in the imposition of customs duties or other

(19) [From this point the French draft of the 29th March is identical with the final text.]

(20) [On the 22nd March Lord Lansdowne commented "we should require further explanation as to the usages referred to." The clause was retained unaltered in the draft of the 29th March.]

(21) [On the 22nd March Lord Lansdowne proposed to add " et. sur les frontières." This was not added in the draft of the 29th March, which was identical with that of the 21st March, except that " dans les ports " was omitted. On the 29th March Lord Lansdowne proposed adding after " douanes " " ou autres taxes." This was accepted.]

2 c 2

BRITISH DRAFT
OF MARCH 14, 1904.

FRENCH DRAFT
OF MARCH 21, 1904.

FINAL TEXT.

blissement des tarifs de transport par chemin de fer.([22])

taxes, or of railway transport charges.

Article II (Morocco).

The French Government engages that these reforms shall be carried out in such manner that the principle of commercial liberty shall be absolutely respected, that there shall result from them no inequality either in the customs duties, port dues, or other charges at the ports, or in the rates charged for the transport of goods by road or rail, and that merchandize, the produce or manufacture of any part of the British Empire, imported into Morocco in transit through Algeria or Senegambia shall receive in these respects equal treatment with French merchandize similarly imported. Merchandize exported from Morocco in transit through French territory to any part of the British Empire shall, in like manner, receive equal treatment with merchandize similarly exported to France.

The same absolute commercial equality shall be maintained as regards the freedom of the coasting trade granted in 1901, and in general all advantages at present enjoyed by British subjects and companies in connection with trade and navigation.

The French Government further engages to respect the provisions of the General Treaty between Great Britain and Morocco of the 9th December, 1856, as well

The trade of both nations with Morocco and with Egypt shall enjoy the same treatment in transit through the French and British possessions in Africa. An Agreement between the two Governments shall settle the conditions of such transit and shall determine the points of entry.

([22]) [On the 29th March Lord Lansdowne proposed to add a paragraph as follows :—

" Le commerce Britannique avec le Maroc transitant par les possessions Françaises en Afrique, jouira du même traitement que celui appliqué au commerce Français."

The corresponding paragraph of the final text was proposed by M. Cambon on the 6th April and accepted by Lord Lansdowne.]

BRITISH DRAFT
OF MARCH 14, 1904.

FRENCH DRAFT
OF MARCH 21, 1904.

FINAL TEXT.

as those of the Treaty of Commerce of the same date, except in so far as they may be affected by the present arrangements.

Article IX (Egypt).

Should either of the two Governments at any future time find themselves compelled by the force of circumstances to modify their policy in respect to Egypt or Morocco, the engagements entered into in Articles   , as regards commercial equality, shall remain intact for a period of fifty years from the date of the present Convention, and shall continue in force after the expiration of that term, unless denounced by one side or the other.

Cet engagement réciproque est valable pour une période de trente ans. Faute de dénonciation expresse faite une année au moins à l'avance, cette période pourra être prolongée de cinq ans en cinq ans.

This mutual engagement shall be binding for a period of thirty years. Unless this stipulation is expressly denounced at least one year in advance, the period shall be extended for five years at a time.

Toutefois, le Gouvernement Français au Maroc et le Gouvernement Britannique en Égypte se réservent de veiller à ce que les concessions de routes, chemins de fer, ports, &c., soient données dans des conditions telles que l'autorité de l'État sur ces grandes entreprises d'intérêt général demeure entière.([23])

Nevertheless, the Government of the French Republic reserve to themselves in Morocco, and His Britannic Majesty's Government reserve to themselves in Egypt, the right to see that the concessions for roads, railways, ports, &c., are only granted on such conditions as will maintain intact the authority of the State over these great undertakings of public interest.

Article VI (Egypt).

As regards the situation of the French officials in the service of the Egyptian Government, His Majesty's Government are prepared to give an assurance, on behalf of that Government, that those whose services

Article I (b).

Le Gouvernement Britannique déclare qu'il usera de son influence pour que les fonctionnaires Français actuellement au service Égyptien([24]) soient placés, en ce qui concerne les appointements, l'avancement, et les retraites,

Article V.

His Britannic Majesty's Government declare that they will use their influence in order that the French officials now in the Egyptian service may not be placed under conditions less advantageous than those applying

([23]) [These two paragraphs remained unaltered in version of the 29th March.]
([24]) [Lord Lansdowne proposed on the 22nd March to substitute " ne soient pas mis dans une position d'infériorité vis-à-vis des fonctionnaires Anglais au même service." He added a note : " This will be combined with Article II of the secret portion and appear as Article IV (a). The revision was accepted in the draft of the 29th March. Lord Lansdowne then proposed a further amendment to " ne soient pas mis dans des conditions de service inférieures à celles appliquées aux."]

[15214]

2 c 3

BRITISH DRAFT OF MARCH 14, 1904.	FRENCH DRAFT OF MARCH 21, 1904.	FINAL TEXT.
are satisfactory shall not be arbitrarily discussed.	dans les mêmes conditions que les fonctionnaires Anglais.	to the British officials in the same service.

Secret Article II.

The French Government are prepared to give an assurance that their influence shall, if necessary, be exercised to obtain similar favourable treatment of British subjects in the employment of the Sultan of Morocco.	*Le Gouvernement de la République, déclare qu'il usera de son influence pour que les fonctionnaires Anglais actuellement au service Marocain soient placés, en ce qui concerne les appointements, l'avancement, et la retraite, dans les mêmes conditions que les fonctionnaires Français.*[25]	The Government of the French Republic, for their part, would make no objection to the application of analogous conditions to British officials now in the Moorish service.

Article VII (Egypt).	Article V.	Article VI.
His Majesty's Government guarantee the free passage of the Suez Canal in accordance with the principles embodied in the Treaty of the 29th October, 1888. Nevertheless, the measures prescribed in Article VIII for the execution of the Treaty will remain in abeyance during the continuance of the British occupation of Egypt.	*Afin d'assurer le libre passage du Canal de Suez, le Gouvernement Britannique déclare adhérer aux stipulations du Traité conclu le 29 Octobre, 1888, et accepter qu'elles soient mises immédiatement en vigueur.* *Le libre passage du Canal étant ainsi garanti,*[26] le Gouvernement Français ne réclamera pas l'exécution du *paragraphe 2 de l'Article VIII de ce Traité.*	In order to insure the free passage of the Suez Canal, His Britannic Majesty's Government declare that they adhere to the stipulations of the Treaty of the 29th October, 1888, and that they agree to their being put in force. The free passage of the Canal being thus guaranteed, the execution of the last sentence of paragraph 1 as well as of paragraph 2 of Article VIII of that Treaty will remain in abeyance.

Article III (Morocco).	Article VI.	Article VII.
With a view to securing the free passage of the Straits of Gibraltar *the two Governments agree not* to erect, or *permit* any other Power to erect, *any* military or naval *fortifications on that portion of the* Moorish sea-board which is *comprised between Melilla,* on the Medi-	*Afin d'assurer le libre passage du Détroit de Gibraltar, les deux Gouvernements conviennent de ne pas élever, et de ne laisser aucune autre Puissance élever, des fortifications ou des ouvrages stratégiques quelconques sur la partie de la côte Marocaine comprise*	In order to secure the free passage of the Straits of Gibraltar, the two Governments agree not to permit the erection of any fortifications or strategic works on that portion of the coast of Morocco comprised between, but not including, Melilla and the heights which com-

[25] [This paragraph appeared in the draft of the 29th March in its final form.]

[26] [On the 23rd March Lord Lansdowne wished to substitute " le Gouvernement Britannique garantit le libre passage du Canal de Suez conformément aux principes inscrits au Traité du 29 Octobre, 1888, mais " adding to the end " ni de la dernière phrase du paragraphe 1." M. Cambon " could not see the force " of the change, and Lord Lansdowne agreed to reconsider it. The draft of the 29th March repeated the original wording, and it was accepted in principle by Lord Lansdowne. He suggested amending " et accepter qu'elles soient mises immédiatement en vigueur " to " et à leur mise en vigueur." He also suggested the amending of the last phrase to its final form.]

BRITISH DRAFT OF MARCH 14, 1904.	FRENCH DRAFT OF MARCH 21, 1904.	FINAL TEXT.

terranean, *and the heights* on *the right bank of the Sebou.*

entre Melilla et les hauteurs qui dominent la rive droite du Sebou exclusivement.

Toutefois, cette disposition ne s'applique pas aux points actuellement occupés par l'Espagne sur la rive Marocaine de la Méditerranée.(27)

mand the right bank of the River Sebou.

This condition does not, however, apply to the places at present in the occupation of Spain on the Moorish coast of the Mediterranean.

Article IV (Morocco).

The two Governments recognize as an essential element in the settlement of the Moorish question, the political and territorial interests which accrue to Spain in view of her geographical position and her territorial possessions on the coast of Morocco.

A direct understanding on this subject will be arrived at *between France and Spain*, the terms of which *shall be communicated to His Britannic Majesty's Government.*

Spain, in the same manner as France and Great Britain, shall agree to the arrangements relative to the free passage of the Straits of Gibraltar, and those respecting commercial liberty in so far as regards any territories which may come under her influence.

Article VII.

Les deux Gouvernements prennent en particulière considération les intérêts que l'Espagne tient de sa position géographique et de ses possessions territoriales sur la côte Marocaine de la Méditerranée.(28)

Communication sera faite au Gouvernement de Sa Majesté Britannique de l'accord qui pourra intervenir à ce sujet entre la France et l'Espagne.

Article VIII.

The two Governments, inspired by their feeling of sincere friendship for Spain, take into special consideration the interests which that country derives from her geographical position and from her territorial possessions on the Moorish coast of the Mediterranean. In regard to these interests the French Government will come to an understanding with the Spanish Government.

The agreement which may be come to on the subject between France and Spain shall be communicated to His Britannic Majesty's Government.

Article V (Morocco).

In all other respects not provided for in the preceding articles, the two Governments will agree to maintain, so far as lies in their power, the territorial *status quo* on the coast of Morocco and the adjacent islands.

[No such clause.]

[No such clause.]

---

(27) [The French version of the 29th March was identical with that of the 21st March.]

(28) Lord Lansdowne commented on the 22nd March "A paragraph should be inserted to the effect that the French Government will endeavour to arrive at a direct understanding with Spain on this subject." M. Cambon agreed. In the draft of the 29th March the paragraph was worded in its final form as far as "la côte Marocaine de la Méditerranée." There then followed a further sentence "et son désir d'en assurer le développement légitime." This was omitted at Lord Lansdowne's instance. He proposed adding a sentence "La France concertera avec l'Espagne pour trouver une solution de nature à satisfaire ces intérêts." The final wording was agreed on the 6th April.]

BRITISH DRAFT OF MARCH 14, 1904.	FRENCH DRAFT OF MARCH 21, 1904.	FINAL TEXT.
They will invite the Government of Spain to join with them in an Agreement to this effect.		

Article IX.

| [See p. 394.] | [No such clause.](^{29}) | The two Governments agree to afford to one another their diplomatic support, in order to obtain the execution of the clauses of the present Declaration regarding Egypt and Morocco. |

In witness whereof his Excellency the Ambassador of the French Republic at the Court of His Majesty the King of the United Kingdom of Great Britain and Ireland and of the British Dominions beyond the Seas, Emperor of India, and His Majesty's Principal Secretary of State for Foreign Affairs, duly authorized for that purpose, have signed the present Declaration and have affixed thereto their seals.

Done at London, in duplicate, the 8th day of April, 1904.

(L.S.) LANSDOWNE. (L.S.) PAUL CAMBON.(^{29a})

	Secret Article I.	Secret Article I.
[No such clause.]	Pas, plus que l'Angleterre ne désire annexer l'Égypte, la France ne désire annexer le Maroc. Toutefois,(^{30}) *Dans le cas où l'un des deux Gouvernements se verrait contraint, par la force des circonstances, de modifier sur ce point sa politique, les engagements qu'ils ont contractés l'un envers l'autre par l'article IV de la Déclaration de ce jour demeureraient intacts.*	In the event of either Government finding themselves constrained, by the force of circumstances, to modify their policy in respect to Egypt and Morocco, the engagements which they have undertaken towards each other by Articles IV, VI and VII of the Declaration of to-day's date would remain intact.

(^{29}) [In the French version of the 29th March a paragraph identical with the final paragraph of the final text appeared here.]

(^{29a}) [See Note (^{12a}) on p. 384. The French text is given below, pp. 404–5.]

(^{30}) [The draft of the 29th March began here.]

BRITISH DRAFT OF MARCH 14, 1904.	FRENCH DRAFT OF MARCH 21, 1904.	FINAL TEXT.
Article V (Egypt).	**Secret Article III.([31])**	**Secret Article II.**

BRITISH DRAFT OF MARCH 14, 1904.

Article V (Egypt).

Though His Majesty's Government have no present intention of proposing any changes in the system known as the Capitulations or in the methods under which civil and criminal jurisdiction is exercised over foreigners in Egypt, they nevertheless consider that the existing system is open to many serious objections, and they accordingly reserve to themselves the right of proposing at any future time such alterations as may eventually be deemed necessary. The Government of the French Republic, on their side, recognise that the Capitulations in Egypt must eventually be abolished, and are prepared to examine, in consultation with His Majesty's Government, proposals which may be submitted to it for the purpose of assimilating the Egyptian legislative and judicial systems in regard to foreigners to those in force in other civilised countries.

His Majesty's Government will, on their side, be ready to examine, in consultation with the Government of the French Republic, similar proposals with regard to Morocco.

FRENCH DRAFT OF MARCH 21, 1904.

Secret Article III.([31])

Le Gouvernement Britannique n'a pas l'intention de proposer, quant à présent, aux Puissances de modifications au régime des Capitulations et à l'organisation judiciaire en Égypte.

Dans le cas où il serait amené à envisager l'opportunité d'introduire à cet égard en Égypte des réformes tendant à assimiler la législation Egyptienne à celle des autres pays civilisés, la France *ne refuserait pas d'examiner ces propositions, mais à la condition que le Gouvernement Britannique* fût prêt à *examiner* en même temps *les suggestions* qu'elle *pourrait avoir à lui adresser pour introduire au Maroc des réformes du même genre.*

FINAL TEXT.

Secret Article II.

His Britannic Majesty's Government have no present intention of proposing to the Powers any changes in the system of the Capitulations, or in the judicial organisation of Egypt.

In the event of their considering it desirable to introduce in Egypt reforms tending to assimilate the Egyptian legislative system to that in force in other civilised countries, the Government of the French Republic will not refuse to entertain any such proposals, on the understanding that His Britannic Majesty's Government will agree to entertain the suggestions that the Government of the French Republic may have to make to them with a view of introducing similar reforms in Morocco.

Separate Article (Morocco).	**Secret Article IV II.**	**Secret Article III.**

Separate Article (Morocco).

The two Governments agree that certain portions of Moorish territory adjoining the Spanish possessions in Morocco should fall

Secret Article IV II.

Les deux Gouvernements conviennent qu'une certaine quantité de territoire Marocain adjacente à Melilla, Ceuta et autres Présides doit,

Secret Article III.

The two Governments agree that a certain extent of Moorish territory adjacent to Melilla, Ceuta and other *Présides* should, when-

---

([31]) [This clause was transposed to the secret part of the Treaty because M. Cambon "objected to introducing the subject of the Capitulations into the part of the Declaration which it was intended to publish" (Lansdowne to Monson, No. 144, of the 22nd March). It appeared as secret Article II of the draft of the 29th March in a form identical with that of the 21st March. The alteration of "fût prêt à" to "accepterait à" and the omission of "en même temps" were suggested by Lord Lansdowne.]

BRITISH DRAFT OF MARCH 14, 1904.	FRENCH DRAFT OF MARCH 21, 1904.	FINAL TEXT.
within the sphere of influence of Spain if the Sultan's authority over them should at any time cease, and that in particular Spain should, in such an eventuality, be entrusted with the duty of administering the seaboard from Melilla to the right bank of the Sebu.	*le jour où le Sultan cesserait d'exercer sur elle son autorité, tomber dans la sphère d'influence Espagnole et que l'administration de la côte depuis Melilla jusqu'aux hauteurs de la rive droite du Sébou exclusivement sera confiée à l'Espagne*	ever the Sultan ceases to exercise authority over it, come within the sphere of influence of Spain, and that the administration of the coast from Melilla as far as, but not including, the heights on the right bank of the Sebou shall be intrusted to Spain.
The Agreement which shall be come to on this point between the Governments of France and Spain shall contain the further stipulation that neither Power will alienate any portion of the territories now forming part of the Moorish Empire which may fall under its authority or within its sphere of influence.	*Toutefois, l'Espagne devra au préalable donner son adhésion formelle aux dispositions des Articles IV et VI de la Déclaration de ce jour, et s'engager à les exécuter.* *Elle s'engagera en outre à ne point aliéner,* à une Puissance tierce, ([32]) *tout ou partie des territoires placés sous son autorité ou dans sa sphère d'influence.*	Nevertheless, Spain would previously have to give her formal assent to the provisions of Articles IV and VII of the Declaration of to-day's date, and undertake to carry them out. She would also have to undertake not to alienate the whole or a part of the territories placed under her authority or in her sphere of influence.

Secret Article IV.

| | *Si l'Espagne, invitée à adhérer aux dispositions,* du présent *Article, croyait devoir s'abstenir, l'Arrangement entre la France et* l'Angleterre, *tel qu'il résulte de la Déclaration de ce jour, n'en* subsisterait *pas moins, et serait immédiatement applicable.* ([33]) | If Spain, when invited to assent to the provisions of the preceding article, should think proper to decline, the Arrangement between France and Great Britain, as embodied in the Declaration of to-day's date, would be none the less applicable. |

Article III (Egypt).

The Government of the French Republic will support His Majesty's Government in endeavouring to obtain the assent of the other Powers signatory of the London Convention to the draft Decree mentioned in the preceding Article; and should the consent of any of those Powers be

[No such clause.]

[No such clause.]

([32]) [Lord Lansdowne proposed the omission of the words "à une Puissance tierce." M. Cambon agreed, and the article appeared in its final form in the version of the 29th March.]

([33]) [In the French version of the 29th March the text was identical with that of the 21st March. The alteration of "subsisterait pas moins et serait" to "serait pas moins" was made by Lord Lansdowne.]

BRITISH DRAFT
OF MARCH 14, 1904.

FRENCH DRAFT
OF MARCH 21, 1904.

FINAL TEXT.

withheld, the Government of the French Republic will not oppose any step which His Majesty's Government may hereafter find it expedient to take for the purpose of giving effect to the aforesaid proposals.([34])

BRITISH DRAFT
OF MARCH 16, 1904.

Article IV (Egypt).

The Government of the French Republic having urged the claims of the Egyptian bondholders to exceptional treatment in consideration of what has happened in the past, His Majesty's Government, though unable to consider such claims as justified, agree to advise the Egyptian Government to postpone the execution of their right to convert the Guaranteed, Privileged and Unified Debts up to the 15th of July, 1910, on the distinct understanding that, after the above-mentioned date, no objection will be raised to the Egyptian Debt being paid off at par.

[No such clause.]([35])

Secret Article V.

Should the consent of the other Powers to the draft Decree mentioned in Article I of the Declaration of to-day's date not be obtained, the Government of the French Republic will not oppose the repayment at par of the Guaranteed, Privileged and Unified Debts after the 15th July, 1910.

Done at London, in duplicate, the 8th day of April, 1904.

(L.S.) LANSDOWNE. (L.S.) PAUL CAMBON.([35a])

([34]) [At the interview with Lord Lansdowne on the 21st March, M. Cambon said that he "thought that this article was either superfluous or dangerous. It would be superfluous if it merely meant that France was to regard our action with a friendly eye; it would be dangerous if we intended that France should support us in ignoring our Treaty obligations with other Powers." Lord Lansdowne proposed its transference to its present position, but it was not embodied in the revised French draft of the 29th March.]

([35]) [The clause finally inserted as Secret Article V was proposed by Lord Lansdowne on the 30th March and accepted by M. Cambon on the 6th April. M. Cambon proposed to substitute "15th July, 1912" for "15th July, 1910," but the original date was retained.]

([35a]) [See Note ([12a]) on p. 384. The French text is given below, p. 406.]

Declaration between the United Kingdom and France concerning Siam, Madagascar, and the New Hebrides.—Signed at London, April 8, 1904.([36])

BRITISH DRAFT OF MARCH 14, 1904.	FRENCH DRAFT OF MARCH 21, 1904.	FINAL TEXT.
Siam.	**I.—Siam.**	**I.—Siam.**
THE two Governments confirm the stipulations of the Anglo-French Declaration of the 15th January, 1896, in regard to the territories specified in Article 1 of that Declaration.	*Le Gouvernement de* la Grande-Bretagne *et le Gouvernement de la République Française maintiennent les Articles 1 et 2 de la Déclaration signée à Londres le 15 Janvier, 1896, par* Lord Salisbury, *Principal Secrétaire d'État pour les Affaires Étrangères, et le Baron de Courcel, Ambassadeur* de France.	THE Government of His Britannic Majesty and the Government of the French Republic confirm Articles 1 and 2 of the Declaration signed in London on the 15th January, 1896, by the Marquess of Salisbury, then Her Britannic Majesty's Principal Secretary of State for Foreign Affairs, and Baron de Courcel, then Ambassador of the French Republic at the Court of Her Britannic Majesty.
	Toutefois, en vue de compléter ces dispositions, ils déclarent d'un commun accord que l'influence de la Grande-Bretagne sera reconnue par la France sur les territoires situés à l'ouest du bassin de la Meinam, et celle de la France sera reconnue par la Grande-Bretagne sur les territoires situés à l'est de la même région, toutes les possessions Siamoises à l'est et au sud-est de la zone susvisée relevant ainsi désormais de l'influence Française et, d'autre part, toutes les possessions Siamoises à l'ouest de cette zone et du Golfe de Siam, y compris la Péninsule Malaise et les îles adjacentes, relevant de l'influence Anglaise.	In order, however, to complete these arrangements, they declare by mutual agreement that the influence of Great Britain shall be recognized by France in the territories situated to the west of the basin of the River Menam, and that the influence of France shall be recognized by Great Britain in the territories situated to the east of the same region, all the Siamese possessions on the east and south-east of the zone above described and the adjacent islands coming thus henceforth under French influence, and, on the other hand, all Siamese possessions on the west of this zone and of the Gulf of Siam, including the Malay Peninsula and the adjacent islands, coming under English influence.
The two Governments, while *disclaiming all idea of annexing Siamese territory,* or encroaching in any respect upon, *existing Treaty* rights, further *agree that* Great Britain will not oppose or obstruct the	*Les deux Parties Contractantes, écartant d'ailleurs toute idée d'annexion d'aucun territoire Siamois, et résolues à s'abstenir de tout acte qui irait à l'encontre des dispositions des Traités existants, conviennent que sous cette*	The two Contracting Parties, disclaiming all idea of annexing any Siamese territory, and determined to abstain from any act which might contravene the provisions of existing Treaties, agree that, with this reser-

([36]) [This Declaration was published in *Accounts and Papers*, 1904 (*Cd.* 1952). CX, pp. 340–1.]

BRITISH DRAFT OF MARCH 14, 1904.	FRENCH DRAFT OF MARCH 21, 1904.	FINAL TEXT.
action of France within the Siamese territories lying to the east and south-east of the area above specified, and that France will not oppose or obstruct the action of Great Britain within the territories lying to the west and south-west of the said area, including the Malay Peninsula and the adjacent islands.	*réserve et en regard de l'un et de l'autre, l'action respective des deux Gouvernements s'exercera librement sur chacune des sphères d'influence ainsi définies.*	vation, and so far as either of them is concerned, the two Governments shall each have respectively liberty of action in their spheres of influence as above defined.

	II.—Madagascar.	**II.—Madagascar.**
[No such clause.]	*Le Gouvernement Britannique renonce à la réclamation qu'il avait formulée contre l'introduction du tarif douanier établi à Madagascar après l'annexion de cette île à la France. Le Gouvernement de la République prend acte de cette déclaration.*	In view of the agreement now in negotiation on the questions of Jurisdiction and the postal service in Zanzibar, and on the adjacent coast, His Britannic Majesty's Government withdraw the protest which they had raised against the introduction of the Customs tariff established at Madagascar after the annexation of that island to France. The Government of the French Republic take note of this Declaration.

New Hebrides.	**III.—Nouvelles-Hébrides.**	**III.—New Hebrides.**
The two Governments agree to concert with a view to arriving at *an arrangement* which *shall put an end to the difficulties arising from the absence of jurisdiction over the natives* of the islands, without modifying the *status quo.*	*Les deux Gouvernements conviennent de préparer de concert un Arrangement qui, sans impliquer aucune modification dans le* statu quo, mettra *fin aux difficultés résultant de l'absence de juridiction sur les indigènes des Nouvelles-Hébrides.*	The two Governments agree to draw up in concert an Arrangement which, without involving any modification of the political *status quo*, shall put an end to the difficulties arising from the absence of jurisdiction over the natives of the New Hebrides.
They further *agree to* the appointment, within three months of the signature of this Declaration, of a Judicial *Commission* to inquire into and settle the claims to land of their respective nationals. This Commission will consist of three members, of whom each of the High Contracting Parties shall nominate one, and the third shall be	*Ils conviennent* aussi de *nommer,* dans les trois mois de la signature de la présente déclaration, *une Commission* chargée de régler les *différends fonciers de leurs ressortissants respectifs dans lesdites îles. Cette Commission* sera composée de trois membres ; chacune des Parties Contractantes en désignera un. Le troisième	They agree to appoint a Commission to settle the disputes of their respective nationals in the said islands with regard to landed property. The competency of this Commission and its rules of procedure shall form the subject of a preliminary Agreement between the two Governments.

BRITISH DRAFT OF MARCH 14, 1904.	FRENCH DRAFT OF MARCH 21, 1904.	FINAL TEXT.

nominated by them jointly, or if they should be unable to agree on the choice by

sera désigné par les deux premiers, et au cas où ceux-ci ne pourraient se mettre d'accord, par

In witness whereof His Britannic Majesty's Principal Secretary of State for Foreign Affairs and His Excellency the Ambassador of the French Republic at the Court of His Majesty the King of the United Kingdom of Great Britain and Ireland and of the British Dominions beyond the Seas, Emperor of India, duly authorised for that purpose, have signed the present Declaration and have affixed thereto their seals.

Done at London in duplicate, the 8th day of April, 1904.

(L.S.) LANSDOWNE. (L.S.) PAUL CAMBON.(¹)

(¹) [See Note (¹²ᵃ) on p. 384. The French text is given below, pp. 406–7.)

[ED. NOTE.—The exchange of notes connected with the above was also published in *Accounts and Papers*, 1904 (*Cd.* 2095), CX, 343, and the Arbitration Treaty with France signed 14th October, 1903, in *Accounts and Papers*, 1904 (*Cd.* 1837), CX, 351.

A number of agreements dealing with the commercial relations of the two Powers in their colonies were ratified or completed in 1904 or 1905. The list is in *Accounts and Papers*, 1905, CIV, Index. The most important of these are two agreements with reference to Newfoundland, *ib.* 1906, CXXXVI, pp. 203–270. The Convention on the frontier East of the Niger, signed 29th May, 1906, exchange of ratifications, 29th August, *ib.* 1906, CXXXVI, pp. 223–236, and the New Hebrides Convention of 27th February, 1906, *ib.* pp. 237–270.]

No. 418.

Sir E. Monson to the Marquess of Lansdowne.

F.O. France 3665.

(No. 219.)   *Paris*, D. *April* 12, 1904.

My Lord,   R. *April* 14, 1904.

The comments of the French Press on the Anglo-French arrangement of the 8th instant have been made up, to the present, with a certain reserve, and though their tone has been on the whole distinctly favourable, there has been a disposition to await the publication of the full text before pronouncing a definite judgment.

Yesterday morning the leading papers of the Capital were enabled to satisfy their readers in this respect, the Convention and the two Declarations, together with the draft Khedivial Decree, being published with the omission, of course, of certain Articles.

It is too soon yet to gauge the full effect upon public opinion of this important disclosure. I may say, however, that apart from the Extreme Nationalist Press, and from a few reserves in the "Figaro" in respect of the failure of France to obtain the right to fortify the coast of Morocco, nothing has been said to disturb the first impression produced in France by the Agreement, which is certainly one of considerable self-congratulation at having obtained a recognition of the priority of French influence in Morocco and a solution of many troublesome questions at a sacrifice which, though involving such substantial concessions to England, will not inflict any serious loss on this country.

There is also an inclination to regard the Agreement as the possible precursor of a similar understanding with Russia, and this feeling has been stimulated by the report in yesterday's "Temps," as transmitted herewith, of an interview with M. Nelidow, Russian Ambassador in Paris, who appears to have expressed unreservedly the satisfaction with which he states that the arrangement is regarded in Russia, and to have hinted at a disposition on the part of his Government to regard as their friends the friends of their ally. . . . .

[I am, &c.
E. MONSON.]

No. 419.

Sir E. Monson to the Marquess of Lansdowne.

F.O. France 3665.
(No. 222.)   Extract.   *Paris,* D. *April* 15, 1904.
My Lord,   R. *April* 16, 1904.

. . . . . It may be regarded as presumptuous on my part to express an opinion on the manner in which the respective negotiators have acquitted themselves of their task : nevertheless, in offering to His Majesty's Government my respectful congratulations on the result I cannot refrain from asking your Lordship to accept my assurances of the admiration with which I have watched your Lordship's firm, judicious and dexterous maintenance of the interests committed to your charge; an admiration rendered all the more keen by the knowledge that in encountering the advocate of French interests you have found a disputant of the highest capacity and resource.

I am bound to say that from the very earliest moment after the return of M. Delcassé from London in the month of July last, the French Minister of Foreign Affairs himself professed the conviction that, in spite of all the inherent difficulties of the situation, the greatness of which he never disguises from himself, the future attainment of a satisfactory settlement would be assured by the frankness, the straightforwardness, and the conciliatory spirit of which he saw such complete evidence in your Lordship during his interview with you in England. I hope that your Lordship will forgive my laying stress, in this connection, upon the great qualities shown by M. Delcassé in his own conduct of these negotiations, for there can be no doubt that he courageously took upon himself a responsibility which he shared with no one, except, indeed, his able Representative in London, and that, as he himself confessed to me not many days ago, it was only the fact that he had had several years apprenticeship to the treatment of Colonial questions, acquired during his former experience as Minister of the Colonies, which enabled him to undertake with comparative confidence the consideration of the details connected with the Colonial compensations which he was anxious to secure for France. . . . .

[I am, &c.
E. MONSON.]

No. 420.

Sir E. Monson to the Marquess of Lansdowne.

F.O. France 3665.

(No. 235.)   Confidential.   Paris, D. April 22, 1904.

My Lord,   R. April 23, 1904.

At an interview which I had yesterday with the President of the Republic, M. Loubet said that nothing in the course of events since he had been installed as Chief of the State had given him more pleasure than the conclusion of the Anglo-French Agreement.

He considered it not only as an international act tending to the mutual advantage of the two countries parties to it, but as the setting of an example of world-wide importance calculated to exercise an influence of far reaching effect upon all civilised Powers.

He could not be sufficiently emphatic in stating his gratification that this happy understanding had been arrived at during his Presidency. It would certainly be one of the most pleasing recollections which he would carry with him into retirement when his official functions terminated. . . . .

[I am, &c.
E. MONSON.]

[*NOTE.*—KING EDWARD AND THE FORMATION OF THE *ENTENTE.*

The King minuted Lord Cromer's letter of the 17th July, 1903 (*v.* No. 359, p. 208) as follows :—

"*A most able and interesting letter, and I entirely agree with the views expressed in it excepting Siam.*

E.R."

The letter dealt mainly with Morocco and Egypt. As to Siam, Lord Cromer wrote " There would not appear to be any very great difficulty as regards meeting the French views in Siam."

The King made two suggestions in the Draft Letter (F.O. France 3666) to the French Ambassador from Lord Lansdowne of the 21st September, 1903; the final draft of which was adopted on the 1st October (*v.* No. 369, p. 311) :—

Lansdowne Draft.	*Corrections in the King's own hand.*
" His Majesty's Government have no desire to annex Egypt."	Underlined words struck out.

Lord Lansdowne ultimately substituted for this " no desire to alter the political status of Egypt."

| As regard the preservation of equality of trade and commercial status in Morocco—Lansdowne wrote " His Majesty's Government attach much importance to this reservation." | King Edward struck out this underlined passage—and substituted—
" *regard as absolutely essential.*" |

Lord Lansdowne ultimately altered the phrase to " regard as absolutely indispensable." On the conclusion of the *Entente* on the 8th April, 1904, its reception in Paris was described by Sir E. Monson in a despatch No. 222—April 15, 1904 (F.O. France 3665) (*v. supra.* No. 418, pp. 398–9). King Edward wrote on the back of this despatch in blue pencil—

" *An excellent despatch.*

E.R."

[The following despatch, which was much altered in draft by Lord Lansdowne, throws some light on the situation of the *Entente* Agreements.]

The Marquess of Lansdowne to Sir E. Monson.

F.O. France 3663.   *Foreign Office, April* 29, 1904.

          Circulated to :—
               The King.
               Prince of Wales.
               The Cabinet.
               Embassies.
               Peking.
               Tokyo.
               Admiralty. Secret. Intelligence Department.

Sir,
    The French Ambassador said a few words to me to-day upon the subject of the relations of Great Britain with Russia. He told me that His Majesty the King had expressed to him his earnest desire that those relations should be improved, *that, if possible, an agreement *should be arrived at for the settlement of †*some of* the questions which had occasioned friction and misunderstanding between the two Governments in the past. His Excellency cordially approved of the idea, but recognised the immense difficulties of giving effect to it, particularly at the present time.
    I expressed my agreement *and added* an expression of satisfaction that public feeling in both countries had during the last few weeks apparently ‡*become much calmer.* I said that we desired to avoid all possible causes of misunderstanding at the present time, and should spare no efforts to do so. There seemed to me, indeed, to be only one point which might, although I did not think this was likely, give rise to §*really* serious trouble. I referred to the possibility of an attempt on the part of the Russian Government to send their Black Sea Fleet through the Dardanelles. It would be quite impossible for us to acquiesce in such a step, and, if it were taken, we should be driven to meet it by adequate measures, §*which might render a collision inevitable.* We had always insisted upon the view that the passage of the Straits must be denied to Ships of War, and we had on several occasions protested against minor infractions of these Treaty obligations. The passage of the Straits by a Russian Squadron (*Ships of War* erased by Lord L.) for the purpose of attacking our Ally in the Far East ‖could not ¶*therefore* be tolerated by this country. I rejoiced, however, to say that, so far as I was aware, there were no signs of any such intention on the part of the Russian Government and I was indeed under the impression that for many reasons they would be unlikely to send their Ships out of the Black Sea at the present time.

                                                             L.

  * Added by Lord Lansdowne.
  † Erased by Lord Lansdowne.
  ‡ Substituted by Lord Lansdowne for " with what we had said."
  ‡ Substituted by Lord Lansdowne for " undergone a marked improvement."
  § Added by Lord Lansdowne.
  ‖ Substituted for " would " by Lord L.
  ¶ Added by Lord L.

APPENDIX.

[The French text of the Convention and Declarations is given here for purposes of reference.]

Convention . . . respecting Newfoundland, and West and Central Africa, signed at London, April 8, 1904.

Sa Majesté le Roi du Royaume-Uni de la Grande-Bretagne et d'Irlande et des Territoires Britanniques au delà des Mers, Empereur des Indes, et le Président de la République Française, ayant résolu de mettre fin, par un arrangement amiable, aux difficultés survenues à Terre-Neuve, ont décidé de conclure une Convention à cet effet, et ont nommé pour leurs Plénipotentiaires respectifs :

Sa Majesté le Roi du Royaume-Uni de la Grande-Bretagne et d'Irlande et des Territoires Britanniques au delà des Mers, Empereur des Indes, le Très Honorable Henry Charles Keith Petty-Fitzmaurice, Marquis de Lansdowne, Principal Secrétaire d'État de Sa Majesté au Département des Affaires Étrangères; et

Le Président de la République Française, son Excellence Monsieur Paul Cambon, Ambassadeur de la République Française près Sa Majesté le Roi du Royaume-Uni de la Grande-Bretagne et d'Irlande et des Territoires Britanniques au delà des Mers, Empereur des Indes;

Lesquels, après s'être communiqué leurs pleins pouvoirs, trouvés en bonne et due forme, sont convenus de ce qui suit, sous réserve de l'approbation de leurs Parlements respectifs :—

ARTICLE I.

La France renonce aux privilèges établis à son profit par l'Article XIII du Traité d'Utrecht, et confirmés ou modifiés par des dispositions postérieures.

ARTICLE II.

La France conserve pour ses ressortissants, sur le pied d'égalité avec les sujets Britanniques, le droit de pêche dans les eaux territoriales sur la partie de la côte de Terre-Neuve comprise entre le Cap Saint-Jean et le Cap Raye en passant par le nord; ce droit s'exercera pendant la saison habituelle de pêche finissant pour tout le monde le 20 octobre de chaque année.

Les Français pourront donc y pêcher toute espèce de poisson, y compris la boëtte, ainsi que les crustacés. Ils pourront entrer dans tout port ou havre de cette côte et s'y procurer des approvisionnements ou de la boëtte et s'y abriter dans les mêmes conditions que les habitants de Terre-Neuve, en restant soumis aux Règlements locaux en vigueur; ils pourront aussi pêcher à l'embouchure des rivières, sans toutefois pouvoir dépasser une ligne droite qui serait tirée de l'un à l'autre des points extrêmes du rivage entre lesquels la rivière se jette dans la mer.

Ils devront s'abstenir de faire usage d'engins de pêche fixes (" stake-nets and fixed engines ") sans la permission des autorités locales.

Sur la partie de la côte mentionnée ci-dessus, les Anglais et les Français seront soumis sur le pied d'égalité aux Lois et Règlements actuellement en vigueur ou qui seraient édictés, dans la suite, pour la prohibition, pendant un temps déterminé, de la pêche de certains poissons ou pour l'amélioration des pêcheries. Il sera donné connaissance au Gouvernement de la République Française des Lois et Règlements nouveaux, trois mois avant l'époque où ceux-ci devront être appliqués.

La police de la pêche sur la partie de la côte susmentionnée, ainsi que celle du trafic illicite des liqueurs et de la contrebande des alcools, feront l'objet d'un Règlement établi d'accord entre les deux Gouvernements.

ARTICLE III.

Une indemnité pécuniaire sera allouée par le Gouvernement de Sa Majesté Britannique aux citoyens Français se livrant à la pêche ou à la préparation du poisson sur le " Treaty Shore," qui seront obligés soit d'abandonner les établissements qu'ils y possèdent, soit de renoncer à leur industrie, par suite de la modification apportée par la présente Convention à l'état de choses actuel.

Cette indemnité ne pourra être réclamée par les intéressés que s'ils ont exercé leur profession antérieurement à la clôture de la saison de pêche de 1903.

Les demandes d'indemnité seront soumises à un Tribunal Arbitral composé d'un officier de chaque nation, et en cas de désaccord d'un sur-arbitre désigné suivant la procédure instituée par l'Article XXXII de la Convention de La Haye. Les détails réglant la constitution du Tribunal et les conditions des enquêtes à ouvrir pour mettre les demandes en état feront l'objet d'un Arrangement spécial entre les deux Gouvernements.

ARTICLE IV.

Le Gouvernement de Sa Majesté Britannique, reconnaissant qu'en outre de l'indemnité mentionnée dans l'Article précédent, une compensation territoriale est due à la France pour l'abandon de son privilège sur la partie de l'Ile de Terre-Neuve visée à l'Article II, convient avec le Gouvernement de la République Française des dispositions qui font l'objet des Articles suivants :—

ARTICLE V.

La frontière existant entre la Sénégambie et la Colonie Anglaise de la Gambie sera modifiée de manière à assurer à la France la possession de Yarboutenda et des terrains et points d'atterrissage appartenant à cette localité.

Au cas où la navigation maritime ne pourrait s'exercer jusque-là, un accès sera assuré en aval au Gouvernement Français sur un point de la Rivière Gambie qui sera reconnu d'un commun accord comme étant accessible aux bâtiments marchands se livrant à la navigation maritime.

Les conditions dans lesquelles seront réglés le transit sur la Rivière Gambie et ses affluents, ainsi que le mode d'accès au point qui viendrait à être réservé à la France, en exécution du paragraphe précédent, feront l'objet d'arrangements à concerter entre les deux Gouvernements.

Il est, dans tous les cas, entendu que ces conditions seront au moins aussi favorables que celles du régime institué par application de l'Acte Général de la Conférence Africaine du 26 Février, 1885, et de la Convention Franco-Anglaise du 14 Juin, 1898, dans la partie Anglaise du bassin du Niger.

ARTICLE VI.

Le groupe désigné sous le nom d'Iles de Los, et situé en face de Konakry, est cédé par Sa Majesté Britannique à la France.

ARTICLE VII.

Les personnes nées sur les territoires cédés à la France par les Articles V et VI de la présente Convention pourront conserver la nationalité Britannique moyennant une déclaration individuelle faite à cet effet devant l'autorité compétente par elles-mêmes, ou, dans le cas d'enfants mineurs, par leurs parents ou tuteurs.

Le délai dans lequel devra se faire la déclaration d'option prévue au paragraphe précédent sera d'un an à dater du jour de l'installation de l'autorité Française sur le territoire où seront nées les dites personnes.

Les lois et coutumes indigènes actuellement en vigueur seront respectées autant que possible.

Aux Iles de Los, et pendant une période de trente années à partir de l'échange des ratifications de la présente Convention, les pêcheurs Anglais bénéficieront en ce qui concerne le droit d'ancrage par tous les temps, d'approvisionnement et d'aiguade, de réparation, de transbordement de marchandises, de vente de poisson, de descente à terre et de séchage des filets, du même régime que les pêcheurs Français, sous réserve, toutefois, par eux de l'observation des prescriptions édictées dans les Lois et Règlements Français qui y seront en vigueur.

ARTICLE VIII.

A l'est du Niger, et sous réserve des modifications que pourront y comporter les stipulations insérées au dernier paragraphe du présent Article, le tracé suivant sera substitué à la délimitation établie entre les possessions Françaises et Anglaises par la Convention du 14 Juin, 1898 :—

Partant du point sur la rive gauche du Niger indiqué à l'Article III de la Convention du 14 Juin, 1898, c'est-à-dire, la ligne médiane du Dallul-Maouri, la frontière suivra cette ligne médiane jusqu'à sa rencontre avec la circonférence d'un cercle décrit du centre de la ville de Sokoto avec un rayon de 160,932 mètres (100 milles). De ce point, elle suivra l'arc septentrional de ce cercle jusqu'à un point situé à 5 kilomètres au sud du point d'intersection avec le dit arc de cercle de la route de Dosso à Matankari par Maourédé.

Elle gagnera de là, en ligne droite, un point situé à 20 kilomètres au nord de Konni (Birni-N'Kouni), puis de là, également en ligne droite, un point situé à 15 kilomètres au sud de Maradi, et rejoindra ensuite directement l'intersection du parallèle 13° 20' de latitude nord avec un méridien passant à 70 milles à l'est de la seconde intersection du 14e degré de latitude nord avec l'arc septentrional du cercle précité.

De là, la frontière suivra, vers l'est, le parallèle 13° 20' de latitude nord jusqu'à sa rencontre avec la rive gauche de la Rivière Komadougou Ouobé (Komadugu Waube), dont elle suivra le thalweg jusqu'au Lac Tchad. Mais si, avant de rencontrer cette rivière, la frontière arrive à une distance de 5 kilomètres de la route de caravane de Zinder à Yo, par Soua Kololoua (Sua Kololua), Adeber, et Kabi, la frontière sera tracée à une distance de 5 kilomètres au sud de cette route jusqu'à sa rencontre avec la rive gauche de la Rivière Komadougou Ouobé (Komadugu Waube), étant toutefois entendu que si la frontière ainsi tracée venait à traverser un village, ce village, avec ses terrains, serait attribué au Gouvernement auquel se rattacherait la partie majeure

2 D 2

du village et de ses terrains. Elle suivra ensuite, comme ci-dessus, le thalweg de la dite rivière jusqu'au Lac Tchad.

De là elle suivra le degré de latitude passant par le thalweg de l'embouchure de la dite rivière jusqu'à son intersection avec le méridien passant à 35′ est du centre de la ville de Kouka, puis ce méridien vers le sud jusqu'à son intersection avec la rive sud du Lac Tchad.

Il est convenu, cependant, que lorsque les Commissaires des deux Gouvernements qui procèdent en ce moment à la délimitation de la ligne établie dans l'Article IV de la Convention du 14 Juin, 1898, seront revenus et pourront être consultés, les deux Gouvernements prendront en considération toute modification à la ligne-frontière ci-dessus qui semblerait désirable pour déterminer la ligne de démarcation avec plus de précision. Afin d'éviter les inconvénients qui pourraient résulter de part et d'autre d'un tracé qui s'écarterait des frontières reconnues et bien constatées, il est convenu que, dans la partie du tracé où la frontière n'est pas déterminée par les routes commerciales, il sera tenu compte des divisions politiques actuelles des territoires, de façon à ce que les tribus relevant des territoires de Tessaoua–Maradi et Zinder soient, autant que possible, laissées à la France, et celles relevant des territoires de la zone Anglaise soient, autant que possible, laissées à la Grande-Bretagne.

Il est en outre entendu que, sur le Tchad, la limite sera, s'il est besoin, modifiée de façon à assurer à la France une communication en eau libre en toute saison entre ses possessions du nord-ouest et du sud-est du Lac, et une partie de la superficie des eaux libres du Lac au moins proportionnelle à celle qui lui était attribuée par la carte formant l'Annexe No. 2 de la Convention du 14 Juin, 1898.

Dans la partie commune de la Rivière Komadougou, les populations riveraines auront égalité de droits pour la pêche.

Article IX.

La présente Convention sera ratifiée, et les ratifications en seront échangées, à Londres, dans le délai de huit mois, ou plus tôt si faire se peut.

En foi de quoi son Excellence l'Ambassadeur de la République Française près Sa Majesté le Roi du Royaume-Uni de la Grande-Bretagne et d'Irlande et des Territoires Britanniques au delà des Mers, Empereur des Indes, et le Principal Secrétaire d'État pour les Affaires Étrangères de Sa Majesté Britannique, dûment autorisés à cet effet, ont signé la présente Convention et y ont apposé leurs cachets.

Fait à Londres, en double expédition, le 8 Avril, 1904.

Declaration . . . respecting Egypt and Morocco.

Article I.

Le Gouvernement de Sa Majesté Britannique déclare qu'il n'a pas l'intention de changer l'état politique de l'Égypte.

De son côté, le Gouvernement de la République Française déclare qu'il n'entravera pas l'action de l'Angleterre dans ce pays en demandant qu'un terme soit fixé à l'occupation Britannique ou de toute autre manière, et qu'il donne son adhésion au projet de Décret Khédivial qui est annexé au présent Arrangement, et qui contient les garanties jugées nécessaires pour la sauvegarde des intérêts des porteurs de la Dette Égyptienne, mais à la condition qu'après sa mise en vigueur aucune modification n'y pourra être introduite sans l'assentiment des Puissances Signataires de la Convention de Londres de 1885.

Il est convenu que la Direction-Générale des Antiquités en Égypte continuera d'être, comme par le passé, confiée à un savant Français.

Les écoles Françaises en Égypte continueront à jouir de la même liberté que par le passé.

Article II.

Le Gouvernement de la République Française déclare qu'il n'a pas l'intention de changer l'état politique du Maroc.

De son côté, le Gouvernement de Sa Majesté Britannique reconnaît qu'il appartient à la France, notamment comme Puissance limitrophe du Maroc sur une vaste étendue, de veiller à la tranquillité dans ce pays, et de lui prêter son assistance pour toutes les réformes administratives, économiques, financières, et militaires dont il a besoin.

Il déclare qu'il n'entravera pas l'action de la France à cet effet, sous réserve que cette action laissera intacts les droits dont, en vertu des Traités, Conventions, et usages, la Grande-Bretagne jouit au Maroc, y compris le droit de cabotage entre les ports Marocains dont bénéficient les navires Anglais depuis 1901.

Article III.

Le Gouvernement de Sa Majesté Britannique, de son côté, respectera les droits dont, en vertu des Traités, Conventions, et usages, la France jouit en Égypte, y compris le droit de cabotage accordé aux navires Français entre les ports Égyptiens.

Article IV.

Les deux Gouvernements, également attachés au principe de la liberté commerciale tant en Égypte qu'au Maroc, déclarent qu'ils ne s'y prêteront à aucune inégalité, pas plus dans l'établissement des droits de douanes ou autres taxes que dans l'établissement des tarifs de transport par chemin de fer.

Le commerce de l'une et l'autre nation avec le Maroc et avec l'Égypte jouira du même traitement pour le transit par les possessions Françaises et Britanniques en Afrique. Un accord entre les deux Gouvernements réglera les conditions de ce transit et déterminera les points de pénétration.

Cet engagement réciproque est valable pour une période de trente ans. Faute de dénonciation expresse faite une année au moins à l'avance, cette période sera prolongée de cinq ans.

Toutefois, le Gouvernement de la République Française au Maroc et le Gouvernement de Sa Majesté Britannique en Égypte se réservent de veiller à ce que les concessions de routes, chemins de fer, ports, &c., soient données dans des conditions telles que l'autorité de l'État sur ces grandes entreprises d'intérêt général demeure entière.

Article V.

Le Gouvernement de Sa Majesté Britannique déclare qu'il usera de son influence pour que les fonctionnaires Français actuellement au service Égyptien ne soient pas mis dans des conditions moins avantageuses que celles appliquées aux fonctionnaires Anglais du même service.

Le Gouvernement de la République Française, de son côté, n'aurait pas d'objection à ce que des conditions analogues fussent consenties aux fonctionnaires Britanniques actuellement au service Marocain.

Article VI.

Afin d'assurer le libre passage du Canal de Suez, le Gouvernement de Sa Majesté Britannique déclare adhérer aux stipulations du Traité conclu le 29 Octobre, 1888, et à leur mise en vigueur. Le libre passage du Canal étant ainsi garanti, l'exécution de la dernière phrase du paragraphe 1 et celle du paragraphe 2 de l'Article VIII de ce Traité resteront suspendues.

Article VII.

Afin d'assurer le libre passage du Détroit de Gibraltar, les deux Gouvernements conviennent de ne pas laisser élever des fortifications ou des ouvrages stratégiques quelconques sur la partie de la côte Marocaine comprise entre Melilla et les hauteurs qui dominent la rive droite du Sébou exclusivement.

Toutefois, cette disposition ne s'applique pas aux points actuellement occupés par l'Espagne sur la rive Marocaine de la Méditerranée.

Article VIII.

Les deux Gouvernements, s'inspirant de leurs sentiments sincèrement amicaux pour l'Espagne, prennent en particulière considération les intérêts qu'elle tient de sa position géographique et de ses possessions territoriales sur la côte Marocaine de la Méditerranée; et au sujet desquels le Gouvernement Français se concertera avec le Gouvernement Espagnol.

Communication sera faite au Gouvernement de Sa Majesté Britannique de l'accord qui pourra intervenir à ce sujet entre la France et l'Espagne.

Article IX.

Les deux Gouvernements conviennent de se prêter l'appui de leur diplomatie pour l'exécution des clauses de la présente Déclaration relative à l'Égypte et au Maroc.

En foi de quoi son Excellence l'Ambassadeur de la République Française près Sa Majesté le Roi du Royaume-Uni de la Grande-Bretagne et d'Irlande et des Territoires Britanniques au delà des Mers, Empereur des Indes, et le Principal Secrétaire d'État pour les Affaires Étrangères de Sa Majesté Britannique, dûment autorisés à cet effet, ont signé la présente Convention et y ont apposé leurs cachets.

Fait à Londres, en double expédition, le 8 Avril, 1904.

2 D 3

Articles Secrets.

ARTICLE I.

Dans le cas où l'un des deux Gouvernements se verrait contraint, par la force des circonstances, de modifier sa politique vis-à-vis de l'Égypte ou du Maroc, les engagements qu'ils ont contractés l'un envers l'autre par les Articles IV, VI, et VII de la Déclaration de ce jour demeureraient intacts.

ARTICLE II.

Le Gouvernement de Sa Majesté Britannique n'a pas l'intention de proposer, quant à présent, aux Puissances de modification au régime des Capitulations et à l'organisation judiciaire en Égypte.

Dans le cas où il serait amené à envisager l'opportunité d'introduire à cet égard en Égypte des réformes tendant à assimiler la législation Égyptienne à celle des autres pays civilisés, le Gouvernement de la République Française ne refuserait pas d'examiner ces propositions, mais à la condition que le Gouvernement de Sa Majesté Britannique accepterait d'examiner les suggestions que le Gouvernement de la République Française pourrait avoir à lui adresser pour introduire au Maroc des réformes du même genre.

ARTICLE III.

Les deux Gouvernements conviennent qu'une certaine quantité de territoire Marocain adjacente à Melilla, Ceuta et autres Présides doit, le jour où le Sultan cesserait d'exercer sur elle son autorité, tomber dans la sphère d'influence Espagnole et que l'administration de la côte depuis Melilla jusqu'aux hauteurs de la rive droite du Sébou exclusivement sera confiée à l'Espagne.

Toutefois, l'Espagne devra au préalable donner son adhésion formelle aux dispositions des Articles IV et VII de la Déclaration de ce jour, et s'engager à les exécuter.

Elle s'engagera en outre à ne point aliéner tout ou partie des territoires placés sous son autorité ou dans sa sphère d'influence.

ARTICLE IV.

Si l'Espagne, invitée à adhérer aux dispositions de l'Article précédent, croyait devoir s'abstenir, l'Arrangement entre la France et la Grande-Bretagne, tel qu'il résulte de la Déclaration de ce jour, n'en serait pas moins immédiatement applicable.

ARTICLE V.

Dans le cas où l'adhésion des autres Puissances ne serait pas obtenue au projet de Décret mentionné à l'Article I de la Déclaration de ce jour, le Gouvernement de la République Française ne s'opposera pas au remboursement au pair, à partir du 15 Juillet, 1910, des Dettes Garantie, Privilégiée, et Unifiée.

Fait à Londres, en double expédition, le 8 Avril, 1904.

Declaration concerning Siam, Madagascar, and the New Hebrides.

I.—SIAM.

Le Gouvernement de Sa Majesté Britannique et le Gouvernement de la République Française maintiennent les Articles 1 et 2 de la Déclaration signée à Londres le 15 Janvier, 1896, par le Marquis de Salisbury, Principal Secrétaire d'État pour les Affaires Étrangères de Sa Majesté Britannique à cette époque, et le Baron de Courcel, Ambassadeur de la République Française près Sa Majesté Britannique à cette époque.

Toutefois, en vue de compléter ces dispositions, ils déclarent d'un commun accord que l'influence de la Grande-Bretagne sera reconnue par la France sur les territoires situés à l'ouest du bassin de la Meinam, et celle de la France sera reconnue par la Grande-Bretagne sur les territoires situés à l'est de la même région, toutes les possessions Siamoises à l'est et au sud-est de la zone susvisée et les îles adjacentes relevant ainsi désormais de l'influence Française, et, d'autre part, toutes les possessions Siamoises à l'ouest de cette zone et du Golfe de Siam, y compris la Péninsule Malaise et les îles adjacentes, relevant de l'influence Anglaise.

Les deux Parties Contractantes, écartant d'ailleurs toute idée d'annexion d'aucun territoire Siamois, et résolues à s'abstenir de tout acte qui irait à l'encontre des dispositions des Traités existants, conviennent que, sous cette réserve et en regard de l'un et de l'autre, l'action respective des deux Gouvernements s'exercera librement sur chacune des deux sphères d'influence ainsi définies.

II.—Madagascar.

En vue de l'Accord en préparation sur les questions de juridiction et du service postal à Zanzibar, et sur la côte adjacente, le Gouvernement de Sa Majesté Britannique renonce à la réclamation qu'il avait formulée contre l'introduction du Tarif Douanier établi à Madagascar après l'annexion de cette île à la France. Le Gouvernement de la République Française prend acte de cette Déclaration.

III.—Nouvelles-Hébrides.

Les deux Gouvernements conviennent de préparer de concert un Arrangement qui, sans impliquer aucune modification dans le *statu quo* politique, mette fin aux difficultés résultant de l'absence de juridiction sur les indigènes des Nouvelles-Hébrides.

Ils conviennent de nommer une Commission pour le règlement des différends fonciers de leurs ressortissants respectifs dans les dites îles. La compétence de cette Commission et les règles de sa procédure feront l'objet d'un Accord préliminaire entre les deux Gouvernements.

En foi de quoi le Principal Secrétaire d'État pour les Affaires Étrangères de Sa Majesté Britannique et son Excellence l'Ambassadeur de la République Française près Sa Majesté le Roi du Royaume-Uni de la Grande-Bretagne, et d'Irlande et des Territoires Britanniques au delà des Mers, Empereur des Indes, dûment autorisés à cet effet, ont signé la présente Déclaration, et y ont apposé leurs cachets.

Fait à Londres, en double expédition, le 8 Avril, 1904.

INDEX OF PERSONS.

SHOWING WRITERS OF DESPATCHES, &C., AND OFFICIAL POSITIONS OF THE PRINCIPAL PERSONS MENTIONED IN THE TEXT.

Subject Index.

ALLIANCE—*(continued)*.
Specific Alliances—*(continued)*.
Anglo-Japanese—*(continued)*.
Viscount Katsura on, 106–7 (No. 118, *encl.*).
M. Komura and, 98 (No. 106), 100 (No. 112).
Manchuria and, 125 (No. 132), 126 (No. 135), *v. sub* Manchuria.
Publication of, 100 (No. 111), 102 (No. 115), 120 (No. 126), 122 (No. 127), 123 (No. 129), 137 (No. 148).
Russia and, 124 (No. 130), 125 (No. 134), 130 (No. 140), 131 (No. 141), 131 (No. 142), 131 (No. 143), 132 (No. 144), 135–6 (No. 146).
Sir T. H. Sanderson on, 137 (No. 140).
Sir E. Satow on, 125 (No. 135, *note*).
Signature of, 113 (No. 124), 121 (No. 127).
Text of, 115–20 (No. 125).
United States and, 109–10 (No. 120), 125 (No. 133).
Dual (Franco-Russian),
Attitude to Anglo-Japanese Alliance, 135–6 (No. 146).
King Edward on, 136 (No. 146, *min.*).
Franco-Russian agreement *re* Far East, 135 (No. 145), 136–7 (No. 147, *encl.*).
French attitude to, 44 (No. 56).
No information of new arrangement (March 1901), 44 (No. 56).
Reported offers to Japan (1902), 137 (No. 148).
Franco-Spanish, denial of, by Spain, 276 (No. 332), 279 (No. 335).
Triple,
Adherence to, by Great Britain, proposed, 65 (No. 82, *encl.*), 78 (No. 92), 80–2 (No. 94), 83 (No. 95).
Count Bülow on, 73 (No. 90).
European influence of, 129 (No. 139).

AUSTRALIA.
Attitude to partition of New Hebrides, 293 (No. 356), 296 (No. 357), 305 (No. 363), 315 (No. 369).
Interests in Indian and Pacific Oceans, 75 (No. 91).
Tariff of,
German Emperor on, 9 (No. 7).

AUSTRIA-HUNGARY.
V. sub Germany, Italy, Morocco, Russia, Treaties (Anglo-German Agreement).

BAGDAD RAILWAY.
Agreements *re*, 174–6 (No. 202), 182 (No. 210), 194 (No. 223).
Anatolian Railway Company,
Convention with Turkish Government, 174 (*note*), 190 (No. 219).
Formation of, 174 (*note*).
Anglo-German negotiations *re*, 177–8 (No. 204).

BAGDAD RAILWAY—*(continued)*.
Bagdad Railway Company, concession to, 174 (*note*).
Berlin Convention and, 177 (No. 203).
France and, 176–7 (No. 203), 178 (No. 205). 194–5 (No. 223).
Great Britain and, 174–6 (No. 202), 176–7 (No. 203), 178 (No. 205), 181 (No. 208), 182–3 (No. 210), 183–5 (No. 212), 186–7 (No. 215), 189–90 (No. 218), 190–1 (No. 219), 191 (No. 220), 194–5 (No. 223).
British financiers and,
Assurance to, by His Majesty's Government, 185 (No. 213), 185–6 (No. 214).
Public outcry and, 196 (No. 224, *min.*).
Desirability of co-operation,
French wish for, 194–5 (No. 223).
Lord Lansdowne on, 178–9 (No. 205, *min.*), 179–80 (No. 206), 185–6 (No. 214), 187–8 (No. 216), 196 (No. 224, *min.*).
Sir N. O'Conor on, 177 (No. 203), 191–3 (No. 221).
Question in Parliament, 186–7 (No. 215), 190–1 (No. 219).
Russia and, 176–7 (No. 203), 182 (No. 209), 188–9 (No. 217).
Turkish guarantee for, 175 (No. 202), 177 (No. 203), 178 (No. 204), 178 (No. 205), 189 (No. 218).

BELGIAN CONGO.
German designs on, 74 (No. 91).

BERLIN ACT (1885), 344 (No. 390).

BERLIN, Treaty of (1878), 250 (No. 296).

BLOCKADES, pacific, *v. sub* Venezuela.
By Great Britain against,
New Granada (1837), 157 (No. 174).
St. Juan and Nicaragua (1842 and 1844), 157 (No. 174).
Rio (1882), 157 (No. 174).
By Great Britain and France against,
Argentine (1845 and 1847), 157 (No. 174).
By France against,
Formosa (1884), 157 (No. 174), 158 (No. 175).

BOXER REVOLT.
1 (No. 1 and *note*), 3 (No. 2, *note*), 58–9 (*note*).

CANADA.
Tariff of,
German Emperor on, 9 (No. 7).

CANARY ISLANDS, 253 (No. 301).

CARIBBEAN SEA.
German designs in, 164 (No. 184).

CEUTA.
British designs on, 256 (*note*).
Russian designs on, 253 (No. 301).

2 E 4

Errata for Volume II.

Addition to Volume II, p. 53.

[ED. NOTE.—The phrase " unmitigated noodles ", applied by the Emperor William II to the British Ministers, was quoted from a telegram of Sir Frank Lascelles of 10th April, 1901 (v. Gooch & Temperley, Vol. I, p. 332). This telegram was not further quoted because the interview, to which it refers, was more fully given in his despatch No. 94 of 11th April, printed in Vol. II, pp. 53–5. As some interest has been expressed in the phrase " unmitigated noodles " by readers, we reproduce here the full text of the telegram in so far as it relates to this description :

Sir F. Lascelles to the Marquess of Lansdowne.

Berlin, April 10, 1901.
D. 1·20 P.M.
R. 3·20 P.M.

F.O. Germany (Prussia) 1524.
Tel. (No. 24.)

I had an official audience of the Emperor last night to present my new credentials. His Majesty was personally most gracious and amiable and much pleased at the composition of the special Mission, but he criticized severely the action of His Majesty's Government whom, with his usual exaggeration, he described as a set of " unmitigated noodles." He was distressed that His Majesty's Gov[ernmen]t should have missed the opportunity afforded by the question of Manchurian Agreement to assert the position of England in the East, and her consequent loss of prestige . . . .

The rest of the telegram is omitted as being already more fully reproduced in the despatch we have previously published.

A repetition of the phrase " noodles " seems to have been made to Colonel Waters by the German Emperor early in 1902, on the communication of the Anglo-Japanese Treaty. v. Brigadier-General W. H. Waters : *Private and Personal* (1928), p. 189.]

British Documents on the Origins of the War

1898–1914

Vol. II
1927

XV. 2. 14/2